IN/FORMAL Marketplaces
Experiments with Urban Reconfiguration

nai010 publishers
Peter Mörtenböck and Helge Mooshammer

Table of Contents

Acknowledgements

This book is part of a multi-sited research project carried out over the past two decades, which has investigated the complex worlds of informal marketplaces. It is a follow-up publication to the two-volume set *Informal Market Worlds*,[1] which brought together case studies of 72 informal marketplaces around the world as well as texts by important voices in debates about urban informality, such as Keith Hart, Saskia Sassen, Ananya Roy, Gayatri Chakravorty Spivak, AbdouMaliq Simone, Vyjayanthi Rao, Teddy Cruz and Fonna Forman. A key aim of this worldwide survey of informal marketplaces was to demonstrate the global dimension and relevance of informal trade. Our goal was to expose the different ways in which the informal economy is a vital part of today's globalised world and how it is intertwined with everyday life everywhere. In the *Informal Market Worlds Atlas*, we grouped the extensive array of case studies into nine categories, ranging from 'notorious markets' and 'post-conflict markets' to 'people's markets' and 'hipster markets'. This broad spectrum not only illustrates the structural variety and operational diversity of these markets, but also points to crucial differences in how these spaces are perceived, evaluated, and valued, a theme which serves as one of the guiding threads of this new publication.

In keeping with the fact that one of the most powerful characteristics of informal markets is their constant state of flux, the focus of this book is on processes of transformation, not only in terms of physical changes to existing marketplaces but also with regard to the growing interaction between the formal and informal spheres. While formal-informal linkages and hybrid economic governance are commonly perceived as buzzwords that characterise contemporary processes of urban reconfiguration, it cannot be overlooked that incorporating informality into the workings of the formal economy is just as conflict-laden as efforts to regulate informal markets. Both directions of integration have transformative effects that leave neither end untouched. The book aims to investigate these tensions by systematically examining the transformations underway at twelve marketplaces selected from our initial global survey. With a particular focus on the correlation between on-site spatial transformation and cross-sectoral development policies, the book maps and analyses the spectrum of spatial interventions in the setting and operation of distinct informal markets. In doing so, it seeks to yield new insights into the changing relationship between the formal and informal sectors in terms of participants and operational methods, as well as emergent strategies of resistance.

In collaboration with a range of onsite research partners, we have focused on selected sites that were already part of our original informal market survey in order to delineate the scope, intersections and tensions of ongoing processes of 'incorporating informality' in as much detail as possible. We hope that the findings of these studies will provide a timely assessment of the ongoing and accelerating hybridisation of formal and informal economic practices and their speculative deployment in the pursuit of new market opportunities. Since such developments are designed not least to incorporate the economic power of informal productivity, a precise diagnosis is needed as to how the fabric of finely tuned collaborations and mutual arrangements that sustain informal marketplaces is impacted by far more influential economic actors. Our main proposition here is that attempts at integrating the economic potential of informal marketplaces differ widely, ranging from market closures and relocations, to structural upgrades and the transformation of informal markets into closely regulated shopping environments, regardless of their role as a crucial lifeline for millions of people at the bottom of the economic pyramid. Building on existing models of investigating the implications of formal-informal linkages through typologies of governance transformation, such as 'replacement – undermining – support – competition'[2] and 'complementary – accommodating – substitutive – competing',[3] we have developed a multi-dimensional mapping matrix that aims to extend these analytical frameworks by adding four distinctive *spatial* parameters, which are mirrored in the

1   Peter Mörtenböck and Helge Mooshammer, eds., *Informal Markets Worlds – Atlas* (Rotterdam: nai010 publishers, 2015); Peter Mörtenböck, Helge Mooshammer, Teddy Cruz and Fonna Forman, eds., *Informal Markets Worlds – Reader* (Rotterdam: nai010 publishers, 2015).
2   Gretchen Helmke and Steven Levitsky, 'Informal Institutions and Comparative Politics: A Research Agenda,' *Perspectives on Politics* 2, no. 4 (2004): 725–40.
3   Anna Grzymala-Busse, 'The Best Laid Plans: The Impact of Informal Rules on Formal Institutions in Transitional Regimes,' *Studies in Comparative International Development* 45, no. 3 (2010): 311–33.

structure of this book: Forced closure / Relocation / Improvement / Appropriation.

Exemplifying rather than representing the diversity of informal marketplaces currently being transformed into hubs of formal economic activity, each type has been investigated in three different locations in order to trace particular patterns of economic incorporation across sites that can be distinguished from other types of intervention. Acknowledging both the multi-facetted economic, social, political and cultural aspects of each site and the complexity of its spatial and logistical arrangements, the book includes a range of forms of graphic representation – maps, tables, diagrams and other formats – in order to highlight different kinds of 'integration' as well as corresponding spatial policies. Making visible the patterns of spatial intervention and their correlation with a network of state and non-state actors, communities of interests, economic powers, conflicts and negotiations on a local, regional and global level, these visualisations bring into focus different degrees of economic incorporation as well as policy trends, regional tendencies, and other demographic, social and cultural dynamics. By producing novel insights into these developments, we hope to advance our understanding of how formal and informal economic practices converge into new kinds of hybrid urban governance. We also hope to contribute to current debates around the form and direction of how economic informality should intersect with local environments, national policies and supranational actors, and especially to discussions about how these linkages, incorporations and reconfigurations can contribute to envisioning more equitable urban environments.

The making of this publication has been intertwined with a series of international research forums conducted in collaboration with distinguished universities and initiatives. We would like to extend our gratitude to Chulalongkorn University's International Program in Design and Architecture (INDA) for hosting the Informal Market Worlds International Research Forum III held in Bangkok in January 2023, and to Vineet Diwadkar, Pitchapa Jular and Christo Meyer for their invaluable support. Our sincere thanks also go to Mauricio Corbalan and the m7red collective for their active involvement in hosting the Informal Market Worlds International Research Forum IV in Buenos Aires in October 2023. These international research meetings were preceded by two similar forums in San Diego and Shanghai, which were instrumental in shaping the two-volume publication *Informal Market Worlds* in 2015. The first forum, Informal Market Worlds International Research Forum I, took place in February 2012 and was hosted by Teddy Cruz and Fonna Forman, directors of the Center for Urban Ecologies and the Center on Global Justice respectively at the University of California San Diego. The second forum, Informal Market Worlds International Research Forum II, was held in November 2012 at Hong Kong University's Shanghai Study Centre under the academic directorship of Pascal Berger and facilitated by Jonathan D Solomon, who as Dean of HKU's School of Architecture initiated the first steps that led to this gathering. We are truly grateful to all of our hosts for recognising the shared interest in exploring informal market worlds and embarking on this endeavour together with us.

The organisation of this series of international research forums, as well as the fieldwork for and the production of this book, would not have been possible without the generous financial support provided by the Austrian Science Fund (P 22809, P 30232), for which we express our sincere gratitude. Many of the authors represented in this publication have already participated in the long-term exchange of ideas, approaches and outcomes guiding this work, and we would like to take this opportunity to thank all of our contributors for their ongoing encouragement and commitment. We would also like to thank Storefront for Art and Architecture, California College of the Arts, UCLA CityLab and Architekturzentrum Wien for generously hosting presentations of our initial survey study and outcomes of this research.

Furthermore, we are indebted to numerous colleagues and friends for engaging with the issues raised in this book and advancing our understanding of them by hosting or contributing to talks, seminars, exhibitions and conferences, inviting submissions of and commenting on related journal articles and book contributions, and sharing critical observations and fruitful conversations. Among many others, we wish to thank Neera Adarkar, Emanuel Admassu, Jorella Andrews, Juan Manuel Arbona, Friederike Bahl, Gulsen Bal, Anette Baldauf, Andrew Ballantyne, Niko Besnier, Mabe Bethônico, Adrian Blackwell, Adam Bobbette, Brigitta Busch, Wellington Cançado, Raul Cardenas, Georgia Cardosi, Giacomo Castagnola, Rosa Cerarols Ramirez, Wan Chantavilajwong, Andrew Charman, Marty Chen, Steven Chen, Annie Chéneau-Loquay, Steven Chodoriwsky, Chatpong Chuenrudeemo, Gracia Clark, Cognate Collective, Kari Conte, Dana Cuff, Julián D'Angiolillo, Jonathan Darling, Desheng Xue, Misael Diaz, Adrian Doron, Eveline Dürr, Alejandro Echeverri, Rika Febriyani, Jennifer Finnegan, Arpine Galfayan, Emiliano Gandolfi, Maria Beatriz Garcia, Maria Fernanda Garcia Rincon, Cordula Gdaniec, Gengzhi Huang, Marcelo della Giustina, Gustavo Gomez-Mejia, Iris C. Gonzales, Thiresh Govender, Nora Guan, Laurent Gutierrez, Joachim Hackl, Simon Harvey, Alfonso Hernández, Daniel Hirata, Hou Hanru, Caroline Humphrey, Marcel Jäggi, Jacob Jansen, Jiang Jun, Anisha Jogani, Evelyne Jouanno, Asel Kadyrbaeva, Stephanie Kappacher, Jongwoong Kim, Sunhyung Steffen Kim, Andreas Kofler, Gergely Kovács, Andres Lepik, Jolyon Leslie, Lawrence Liang, Wibke Liebhart, Denis Linehan, Anastasia Loukaitou-Sideris, Rick Lowe, Renata Marquez, Claudia Martinez Mansell, Lydia Matthews, Andrea Maurer, Rahul Mehrotra, Milan Mijalkovic, Natalia Mirimanova, Mobile Kultur Byrd, Klaus Molterer, Alfonso Morales, Juliane Müller, Gerald F. Murray, Bert de Muynck, Robert Neuwirth, Farid Noufaily, Mick O'Kelly, Irene Nierhaus, Ademola Omoegun, Kyong Park, Daniele Pario Perra, Leif Petersen, Doina Petrescu, Alessandro Petti, Edgar Pieterse, Olivier Pliez, Tadej Pogačar, Valerie Portefaix, Marjetica Potrč, Fernando Rabossi, Sylvain Racaud, Morshedur Rahman, Jennifer Renteria, Oliver Ressler, Lee Rodney, Daan Roggeveen, Irit Rogoff, Lorenzo Romito, Amy Sanchez, Caroline Schmitt, Andrea Seidling, Richard Sennett, the late Werner Sewing, AbdouMaliq Simone, Soranart Sinuraibhan, Vera Skvirskaja, Chris Smith, Brechtje Spreeuwers, Stealth.ultd, Griet Steel, Julián Suárez, Robert Sumrell, Yann Philippe Tastevin, Ade Tinamei, Hakan Topal, Glenda Torrado, Pio Torroja, Jilly Traganou, Renata Tyszczuk, Katharina Urbanek, Ignacio Valero, Kazys Varnelis, Jean-Philippe Vassal, Felipe Vera, Matias Viegener, Asta Vonderau, Joanna Warsza, Aleksandra Wasilkowska, Richard Weston, Helen Wilson, Emrah Yildiz, Geovanni Zamudio, and Maite Zubiaurre. Their generous invitations, comments and reviews have been indispensable to the process of researching, writing, designing and editing this publication. Many students in seminar and studio courses have further contributed with their work to delineating the global contours of informal market worlds.

The compilation of visual material in the book has been a collaborative effort and we are particularly indebted to Bilal Alame, Lovro Koncar-Gamulin and Joanna Zabielska, who have developed intricate visualisations that illuminate the complex reconfigurations of in/formal market environments and open them up to public reflection. Batu Dündar helped to edit the huge range of photographic material used in these visualisation processes. We also owe a debt of gratitude to Carmen Lael Hines for her invaluable facilitation of communication with our contributors, editing chapter drafts, and preparing the manuscript for production. We would also like to thank Mark Hamilton and Joe O'Donnell for their meticulous copy-editing of the texts.

It has been an absolute pleasure to work with Koehorst in 't Veld, who judiciously and skilfully developed the right graphic design for this project. As always, Eelco van Welie, director of nai010 publishers, deserves special mention for enthusiastically embracing and supporting this book.

Peter Mörtenböck and
Helge Mooshammer, July 2023

INCORPORATING INFORMALITY
Peter Mörtenböck and Helge Mooshammer

In recent years, open-air marketplaces have enjoyed a steady growth in popularity unequalled by almost any other type of urban facility. Community markets, organic produce stands, seasonal handicraft bazaars, eye-catching container structures, colourful street food vans and customised pop-up stalls are all now part of the repertoire of nearly every urban renewal programme. This boom in markets in the urban space has been accompanied by changing perceptions of the unfinished, improvised, recycled and handmade. In times of uncertainty and multiple intersecting crises, the 'old', 'uncompromised' and 'authentic' has gained significant currency. Along with new lifestyles, changing patterns of consumption, deregulated urban development, resentment towards industrial mass-production, and the desire for meaningful experiences and instant gratification, marketplaces have become the expression of an avant-garde culture of urban entrepreneurship, entertainment and excitement. They epitomise the forms of cultural capital deemed most appropriate in the neoliberal restyling of urban space.

While many features of such marketplaces evoke a sense of informality and spontaneity, the way in which they furnish the urban space is shaped by a finely calibrated aesthetic. As a facilitator of curated retail environments, elevated customer experiences and meticulously controlled design, informality refers in this context to a particular style rather than a structural condition. As part of a precisely detailed aesthetic staging, this informal appeal defines a space for those who are committed to the new culture of entrepreneurial urban upgrading. For them, the marketplace, charged with nostalgic attributes, social media moments and urban pioneer spirit, is simultaneously an identity-forming moment and a professional stage – an amenity of live-work-play-scapes designed for the new urban culture class. A closer look, however, reveals that beyond its informal *appeal* informality also has a *structural* aspect: precarious employment, opaque supply chains and contracts, selective governance of market participation, strategically curated diversity, and variegated levels of accessibility all mark the emergence of logics of informality outside the confines of the so-called 'informal sector'.

Yet while we are seeing a mushrooming of strategically erected new marketplaces meant to exude a sense of authenticity and immediacy, large numbers of longstanding 'informal' markets that have hitherto escaped regulatory attention are increasingly coming under threat. Some are being shut down, some evicted and relocated, while others are being transformed in such a way that not just their appearance but their entire anatomy and mode of operation is affected, as evidenced by significant changes in the composition of vendors, consumers and offerings. The variation in the degrees and forms of transformation is mirrored in the array of political motifs, policy instruments, architectural typologies and actors involved: providing for basic needs is overshadowed by the promotion of consumer satisfaction; well-coordinated processes that enable low-key, equal access are supplanted by visions of the city as playground; the duty of care for public space is transformed into entrepreneurial opportunity. Together, these dynamics illustrate an expanding array of actions aimed at, on the one hand, formalising informality (by integrating informal activities into hegemonic flows of power) and, on the other, informalising selected protocols of urban economic conduct (by ostensibly transferring agency to target subjects). While each of these developments merits closer inspection, as a whole they seem to signify a shift in urban cooperation that entails a repositioning, reformatting, and reconfiguring of social and economic agencies. Important here is not so much the conflicting views and interests involved but the convergence of trajectories of the incorporation of informality.

Contextualising the forces driving these evolving amalgamations of market environments highlights not just the fact that struggles around defining informality are still not over but that they are intrinsically tied to changing combinations of structural and aesthetic concerns. What constitutes the confines of the formal and informal is thus often a matter of perception and interpretation, and is prone to misinterpretation and confusion depending on one's role, position, and where and how one relates to a particular site. In a meeting at a prestigious US university during the course of this research, one of the foremost thinkers on urban informality shared an anecdote about a research team from another highly regarded academic institution that had set out to study an informal settlement in the Global South. The team had already spent an entire week on site, meticulously recording every detail of the neighbourhood, producing drawings and maps, and taking pictures of every nook and cranny, when they suddenly realised that the site they were studying was not an informal settlement at all, but a government-supported housing scheme that merely looked 'informal'.

The message here, of course, is not to confuse appearance with substance and that aesthetic appeal should not be mistaken for the structural makeup of an environment, in particular when a sophisticated understanding of the interplay between informal aesthetics and the political economy of informality is required. Far from merely providing flavour or enhancing appearance, aesthetics seems to have emerged as a potent catalyst for driving structural change, not least through its cloaking capacities. The attraction of informally styled new marketplaces in neighbourhoods facing intense gentrification pressure, for instance, obscures the increasing informalisation that has become a hallmark of structural

Top: Patpong Night Market, Bangkok, 2023
Bottom: Roadside market, Salton City, California, 2022

changes in labour, production and trade. In such markets, informality presents itself as an aesthetic spectacle not *despite* but *because of* commonly exercised structural informalisation. This spectacle disguises the outsourcing of responsibilities to individual vendors, the precarious employment of support staff, and the lack of quality control of merchandise.

This uncritical celebration of 'informally' styled marketplaces highlights a parasitic relationship between structure and aesthetics in the different pathways of spatialised capital accumulation. From custom branded wall murals and monumental follies used as visual markers to hand-painted signage, out-of-place objects and specially curated programmes of urban greening – the immediacy of captivating aesthetic interventions in the urban landscape that have emerged at the nexus of global capital and neoliberal modes of expression often serves to mask unresolved issues of excessive privatisation, displacement, underpayment, social cleansing, inequality and exclusion. It also obfuscates the way in which cities themselves are becoming primary business actors rather than mere locations for business operations. Turning marketplaces into arenas in which these dynamics are played out and formal-informal linkages are crafted between different urban actors has become a favoured approach in contemporary city-making. This pattern is not confined to the well-known cities associated with neoliberal urban economic development, such as London, New York, Paris and Tokyo, but is evident worldwide in cities as diverse as Ahmedabad, Bangkok, Barcelona and Dubai, as they strive to attract 'impatient capital'.[1]

Urban economic development practices

Paralleling the conflict-ridden surge of marketplaces that mobilise new conditions of informality are thousands upon thousands of existing markets around the world whose long tradition as a crossroads of formal and informal economic trajectories has also come under pressure in recent years. These marketplaces can be found in diverse settings, ranging from cross-border trading hubs and the underground economies of popular markets to clandestine workshops and unregulated online trade channels. Over the years, these sites have shown enormous persistence and creativity as they navigate the challenges of persecution, expulsion, restructuring and incorporation. Strategically complying with and subverting laws to assert themselves in the face of adversity, they often intersect with the realms of defectors, warlords, smugglers, middlemen, speculators, profiteers, migrant workers, self- entrepreneurs and petty dealers of all kinds. It is this crowded intersection of otherwise

1   Rahul Mehrotra, 'Between Equity and Impatient Capital: Making Indian Cities,' *Journal of International Affairs* 65, no. 2 (2012): 133–37.

disjointed sets of experiences that enables informal marketplaces and their actors to inconspicuously redefine the boundaries of assigned identities and assume multiple roles. One of the most important, yet sometimes overlooked roles these sites play in the political and ideological framework of neoliberalism is their trailblazing function in the reconfiguration of the city. Whether as a mechanism for urban renewal efforts and subsequent gentrification or as an alleged nuisance whose elimination promises better things, wherever there is financial pressure on 'improvable' urban space, markets are loaded with potential.

Due to their visible presence in the urban fabric, informal marketplaces are the spatially most tangible part of the informal economy, an economy that serves to secure the livelihood of half the world's population. More than five decades have passed since the anthropologist Keith Hart first coined the term *informal economy* in an attempt to give a name to unrecognised income-generating activities that he had studied in Ghana and to 'insert a vision of irregular economic activity into the debates of development professionals'.[2] His point of departure was the widespread lack of openness he saw in academic and professional circles towards the plurality of forms of social and economic conduct that exist in different parts of the world. Significantly, Hart's conceptualisation of the informal drew on an understanding of form as a mental construct. However, in the following years he also saw the idea of the informal economy operationalised in institutional efforts to organise society along formal lines imbued with power. Revisiting his earlier take on the informal economy in the *Informal Market Worlds Reader* forty years later, Hart pointed out that within the money/power nexus of neoliberalism 'the informal economy seems to have taken over the world while cloaking itself in the rhetoric of free markets.'[3] In view of the increasingly complex interlinkages and entanglements between formal and informal aspects of economic operations, he concluded that it has become a matter of urgency to develop a more dynamic understanding of the informal economy and to expose the principles that organise formal-informal linkages today.

Given this change in the political, economic and cultural parameters impacting the linkages between the formal and informal, it is worth considering whether we are currently encountering a comparable discursive ignorance, at a moment when studies of informality have become well established across a wide range of academic disciplines and policy-making is prioritising the incorporation of informal energies into the workings of the formal sector. Are we once again being confronted with a prevailing perception that remains oblivious to the uncharted ways in which formal-informal

2   Keith Hart, 'How the Informal Economy Took Over the World,' in *Informal Market Worlds: The Architecture of Economic Pressure – Reader,* eds. Peter Mörtenböck and Helge Mooshammer (Rotterdam: nai010 publishers, 2015), 35.
3   Hart, 'How the Informal Economy Took Over the World,' 33.

linkages are currently unfolding in cities around the world? Are we relying on a hegemonic vocabulary and institutionalised thinking that primarily serve 'to organise a segment of the academic and policy-making bureaucracy'?[4] And are we as a consequence unable to articulate the subtle yet nonetheless significant changes in the morphogenesis, role and dynamics of informality?

Blurring boundaries

Over the past decades, several areas of concern have arisen that problematise the prevailing framing of informality as tied to income-generating activities operating outside the regulatory framework of the state. One pertains to the fact that with the exposure of urban populations to the forces of globalisation and neoliberalisation, income generating activities have become far more complex and diverse and are now often embedded in contexts that blur the difference between formal and informal aspects of economic operations. This changing landscape of income generation, social development and political participation has necessitated acknowledgement of the intricate interconnections between formal and informal elements of economic activity. Another factor contributing to the debates around formal-informal linkages is the rise of new urban realities that have emerged in the wake of technological developments, economic crises and new forms of labour. For many people today, working hours – as related to income generation – are no longer confined to a designated workplace but have become just one of multiple parallel strands in their daily routines. This shift not only makes it difficult to define what constitutes work and remuneration – for instance, for purposes of taxation or legal protection – but also blurs the boundaries between spheres, such as the private and the public domains. Recalibrated modes of exchange and cooperation across distinct segments of urban populations, new forms of urban mobilisation and new cultures of social entrepreneurship have dramatically changed the assumptions and organisational contexts underpinning the relationship between formal and informal economies. In light of these changes, we are currently seeing increased interest across the political and institutional spectrum in accessing the potential of the informal economy by integrating its entrepreneurial energies, assets and networks into wider economic circuits.[5]

Attesting to this growing interest, the development of many informal marketplaces around the world has been characterised by a variety of attempts at integration. Besides juridical (trade licences,

Incorporating Informality

14

4   Hart, 'How the Informal Economy Took Over the World,' 35.
5   See, for instance, International Labour Office, *Women and Men in the Informal Economy: A Statistical Picture*, third edition (Geneva: International Labour Organisation (ILO), 2018); Rina Agarwala, 'Incorporating Informal Workers into Twenty-first Century Social Contracts,' UNRISD Working Paper No. 2018-13 (Geneva: United Nations Research Institute for Social Development (UNRISD), 2018); Martha Chen and Francoise Carré, eds., *The Informal Economy Revisited: Examining the Past, Envisioning the Future* (London and New York: Routledge, 2020); Franziska Ohnsorge and Shu Yu, eds., *The Long Shadow of Informality: Challenges and Policies* (Washington, DC: World Bank Group Publications, 2022).

rights of use, etc.), financial (access to credit, poverty alleviation, etc.), infrastructural and organisational measures (access to piped water, electricity supply, agreements with informal workers' unions, etc.) such attempts often revolve around spatial organisation and range from the forced removal and relocation of informal markets to urban fringes or the dispersal of market activities into other neighbourhoods to the demarcation of dedicated areas that do not interfere with formal business and the allocation of trading space in permanent market halls, where maintenance and services are provided on a fee-for-service basis. Street vendors, even though they are the ones most affected by the regulation and management of informal trade, rarely feature in these decision-making processes. Despite the vast networks of actors involved in creating distinct spatio-economic contexts for these developments – policy-makers, planning officers, architects, property owners, developers, legal representatives, vendors' associations, political activists, NGOs, and other stakeholders – many 'integration' projects are thus still governed by an authoritarian, paternalistic concept of realigning the workings of informal economic activities and making them fully compliant with the requirements of formalised settings based on exclusionary principles and standards.[6]

Old Baltic Station Market, Tallinn, 2017

6   Chen and Carré, *The Informal Economy Revisited.*

What spatial interventions into informal marketplaces thus bring to the fore is the absence of intrinsic boundaries between 'formal' and 'informal' economic conduct. Both terms reflect particular roles assigned within a continuous economic fabric. Although often characterised by uneven power relations, the distinction between 'formal' and 'informal' is not necessarily synonymous with the disparity between the wealthy and the poor. There is 'informality from above', just as there is 'informality from below'[7]; there is 'elite informality', just as there is 'subaltern informality'.[8] And there are degrees of planning, order, deliberations, and protocols relating to informal markets, just as there are to formal markets. It is partly due to these porosities and overlaps, then, that the term 'integration' masks a range of extra-market processes, ideologically biased goals and purpose-driven interventions that are central to the ongoing creation of a global market and economic standardisation. For these reasons, it is important to acknowledge that beyond direct and overt strategies of transforming informal markets there are also political and social undercurrents linked with the struggle to control these sites and to benefit from their economic informality.

This wider field of influences on urban market environments is reflected in two different developments, both of which are linked to the increasing dominance of neoliberal forms of economic urban restructuring. Firstly, there is a revised understanding of the informal economy as an alternative, multi-faceted mode of economic governance outside state regulation.[9] This mode of governance is characterised by dynamic interactions encompassing spatio-economic integration, transnational capital flows, institutional processes and bottom-up restructuring. It is within these interactions that links are forged between the current integration of informal vendors into urban/global value chains and the restructuring of formal-informal linkages into new techniques of governance. Employing terms such as 'bricolage', 'synergy', 'composition' and 'hybrid governance', the language often used to describe these endeavours suggests a parity of relations in the urban realm. But what these accounts of incorporation of informal economic practices tend to overlook are the distinctive needs of entrepreneurial and survivalist informal actors, the developmental impact of hybrid governance arrangements and the different ways of integrating informal vendors into economic growth and civic participation.

Secondly, the changing relationship between the informal and formal sector is also reflected in the recent rise of self-employment and increasing state support for start-ups, micro-businesses, social entrepreneurship, and peer-to-peer industries (micro-lending,

7   Gustavo Lins Ribeiro, 'Economic Globalization from Below,' *Etnográfica* 10, no. 2 (2006): 233–46.
8   Ananya Roy, 'Urban Informality: Toward an Epistemology of Planning,' *Journal of the American Planning Association* 71, no. 2 (2005): 147–58.
9   Kate Meagher, 'Unlocking the Informal Economy: A Literature Review on Linkages between Formal and Informal Economies in Developing Countries,' WIEGO Working Paper No. 27 (April 2013).

crowdfunding, and platform services, to name just a few) in countries of the Global North as well as the Global South. Sanctioned by the state, this surge in new forms of income generation, which for growing numbers of workers means long working hours, poor pay and no protection by state laws, situates the transformation of informal marketplaces within historical trajectories of strategic urban transformation, colonial exploitation and political resistance. Key shifts in global economic conduct and their impact on the current transformation of informal marketplaces are thus informed by two different aspects of neoliberal economic urban governance. On the one hand, expansive capital interests increasingly target economies of poverty as frontiers of investment and accumulation.[10] On the other, novel entrepreneurial cultures such as those instigated by peer-to-peer marketplaces, social entrepreneurship and the gig economy animate a changing climate of development policies both in contemporary urban economies in the Global North and in top-tier emerging economies in the Global South. Both aspects converge in marketplaces that are at the forefront of urban reconfiguration and have become the site of experiments with the incorporation of informality in cities around the world.

The architecture of formal-informal linkages

The ongoing spatial transformation of informal markets is not only indicative of these macro-economic changes. It is also playing an instrumental role in the generation of new economic climates. In some cases, it signifies generative activity through alternative knowledge and use of city services, land, and livelihood strategies. In others, it represents an expansion of the market economy's reach into new territories, particularly within the framework of markets run by the poor in developing countries. What emerges from these dynamics are distinct incorporations of informality, both in the sense of absorbing the economic capacities of informal activities and in the sense of adopting informal methods in the conduct of the formal economy. This highlights the need for urgent discussions about how and by whom this process is to be managed and controlled. In this respect, informal markets need to be addressed as important sites of negotiation where new forms of interaction and new kinds of entanglement involving a variety of urban as well as global actors are explored.

From Bangkok to New York and from Amsterdam to Buenos Aires, in/formal marketplaces demonstrate how the growing interaction between informal and formal spheres has a transformative effect on both – leading to a formalisation of the informal sector and an 'informalisation' of the formal economy. The phrase 'incorporating informality' thus seems to beg the question as to *what* precisely

10   Ananya Roy, *Poverty Capital: Microfinance and the Making of Development* (London and New York: Routledge, 2010).

Top: IJ-Hallen Flea Market, Amsterdam, 2022
Bottom: Smorgasburg Los Angeles, 2023

is incorporated into *what*. What are the contours of the socio-economic sphere into which something is incorporated and what is the nature of the incorporated information? Instead of directing our analysis at the supposedly immutable identity and enduring stability of a receptive body that goes by a particular name, we propose focusing on the mutually transformative effect of processes of incorporation. The incorporated entity alters the incorporating body as much as it is absorbed, processed and transformed by it. Incorporation cannot take place without such interaction, influence, and mutual impact.

Placing an emphasis on the *relationships* between economic informality and other domains, as well as current *practices* of in/formalisation,[11] shifts the focus of such debates from measuring the size and properties of the informal sector to developing an analytical matrix that captures the dynamics of strategic interventions in the informal economy. These dynamics include not only the different degrees of integration involved and the policies pursued in the incorporation of informality into mainstream economic activity, but also the mutual effects of these processes, as well as the impact of actions from below on forms of governmental organisation. Rahul Mehrotra has located these dynamics in the mutual arrangements between what he has termed 'static' and 'kinetic' cities. The Kinetic City and its dependency on 'mutual integration without the obsession of formalised structures', he notes, 'is where the intersection of need (often at the level of survival) and of the unexploited potentials of existing infrastructure engenders innovative services.'[12] Supporting and blurring the formal and informal, this urban fabric is sustained by volatile, piecemeal linkages between different worlds whose separate identities collapse in moments of incorporation.

Architecture is what gives material shape to these linkages. Its physical and symbolic operations temporarily solidify the fugitive qualities of incorporations into more comprehensible forms. Holding in place situations that are in flux, architecture creates a forum through which differing aspirations, values and capacities can momentarily become compatible with each other. Rather than merely expressing such linkages, architecture actively regulates processes of incorporation and transition in the built environment. In this role as an organising device, the function of architecture is not so much to accommodate the social and economic practices that connect different urban actors, but to engage in creating, maintaining and propelling a variety of linkages between the formal and informal. Always generating new possibilities, volatile mixtures and short-lived situations, formal-informal linkages are less hard-wired ties than the constant creation of compatibilities. As both site

11   Colin McFarlane, 'Rethinking Informality: Politics, Crisis, and the City,' *Planning Theory & Practice* 13, no. 1 (2012): 89–108.
12   Rahul Mehrotra, *The Kinetic City & Other Essays* (Berlin: ArchiTangle, 2021), 186.

Street trade alongside Feria do Antiguedados y Libreros, La Merced, Valparaíso, 2017

and practice of mediation, they provide a stage for simultaneously bringing together and keeping apart different market actors.

Embedding conditions of improvisation, impermanence and transience into the built environment, architecture often emulates the dynamic qualities of incorporation. It does so by signalling, both structurally and aesthetically, the ephemeral character of sites dedicated to commerce and trade. Pop-up tents, folding tables, bag chairs, collapsible canopies, inflatable decorations, rolling carts and container market stalls: a vast and increasingly complex array of flexible strategies has emerged to manifest the volatile and transient character of open-air marketplaces, even if these markets have achieved a sustained presence in the urban fabric over a longer period of time. Suggesting a sense of mobility has become a kind of lifeline for the precarious yet increasingly endorsed existence of trade situated, intentionally or unintentionally, at the intersection of formal and informal economic operations. Notwithstanding the many difficulties that might be associated with their concrete form of occupying space and time, one of the greatest, albeit still not always recognised, assets and achievements of such strategies is the collective creation of new market environments – sites of trade and commerce – that offer opportunities for economic growth.

If the predominant goal thus no longer seems to be to overcome or eradicate informality as such, then the different configurations of informal-formal linkages take on a new importance. A central question here is how particular aspects of the formal and informal can become, or be made, compatible. Since there is a variety of different perspectives, experiences and assumptions involved in the practices that affect informal marketplaces, it is important to consider the different qualities of compatibility and incorporation that are made possible through the emergence and management of a particular set of interfaces. This uneven field of experimentation with urban reconfiguration constitutes the current terrain of critical engagement with formal/informal linkages, particularly as dominant approaches to the integration of the economic potential of informality differ significantly, ranging from market closures and relocations to structural upgrades and the transformation of informal markets into closely regulated shopping environments.

Tracing the ways in which architecture is employed in these attempts opens up a range of new questions. How do forms of spatial integration (or disintegration) relate to contemporary shifts in socio-economic frameworks and policy-making? How can these relations be understood in ways that go beyond simple dichotomies (e.g. enabling vehicle vs. Trojan horse) and pseudo-causal linear processes (e.g. economic integration follows spatial integration)? What kinds of dynamics have evolved in response to the problem of making formal and informal economies compatible? Who benefits most from the values created with the compatibilities and incorporations they engender? How do such interfaces come into being, what governs their operations, and what are the consequences associated with their variations?

*From clamping down on informal trade to appropriating
urban environments*

Simultaneously geared towards inclusion and exclusion, the assiduous reshuffling of urban economic opportunities and the tension it implies has become one of the main concerns of our long-term research into informal markets specifically and urban informality in general.[13] The apparent struggle between bottom-up initiatives and top-down manipulation, between recognition and disavowal of the values generated by informal traders and its reflection in the implementation of contrasting spatio-economic policies has led us to further investigate emergent and diverging forms of *incorporating informality*.[14] It is precisely the constantly fluctuating character not just of the varied interventions in informal marketplaces but of the informal sector itself that makes attempts at categorisation seem

13   See for instance the two-volume publication *Informal Market Worlds – Atlas & Reader,* which brings together more than 70 case studies of informal marketplaces from around the world and highlights the global dimension of informal trade in the twenty-first century, and which concluded the five-year research project Other Markets: Peter Mörtenböck and Helge Mooshammer, eds. *Informal Market Worlds: The Architecture of Economic Pressure - Atlas* (Rotterdam: nai010 publishers, 2015) and Peter Mörtenböck, Helge Mooshammer, Teddy Cruz, and Fonna Forman, eds. *Informal Market Worlds: The Architecture of Economic Pressure - Reader* (Rotterdam: nai010 publishers, 2015).
14   Between 2018 and 2023 researchers and activists from around the world, including Vyjayanthi Rao, Allan Cain, Paul Chu, Vineet Diwadkar, Melisa Vargas, Samar Halloum, Mauricio Corbalan, Pio Torroja, Trude Renwick and Anton Nikolotov, amongst others, joined us once again in a global forum to explore the formal-informal linkages that shape the relationships between informal trade, neoliberal governance, and urban development.

initially futile and meaningless. However, what can be contended is that there exists a spectrum of transformative political interventions ranging from the eviction of informal traders and their expulsion from urban public space to the simulation of informal market cultures as a means of breathing urban vitality into 'emergent' neighbourhoods. In contrast to a methodology of categorisation that separates different entities, and thus disconnects them, the framing of this vast theatre of action as a spectrum allows us to focus our attention on the forces and vectors shaping the continuous re-assemblage of this field – whether they collide, merge, intersect or overlap, emerge from within, enter from outside or escape altogether. These dynamics produce a chain of four distinct force fields, ranging from *forced closure* and *relocation* to *improvement* and *appropriation*. One end of this spectrum is dominated by the wholesale denial and eviction of informal trade in the form of market closures. This is followed by the relocation of marketplaces, which partially recognises their economic prowess and social function but seeks to avoid direct contact and visibility. If informal markets are allowed to remain where they are, they are often forced to undergo substantial processes of realignment readily framed as improvements. Lastly, the other end of the spectrum is characterised by a kind of informalisation of the formal economy, in which the set-up, atmosphere and allure of informal marketplaces are emulated at purpose-built or chosen sites in order to capture some of their entrepreneurial energy.

The closure of long-running informal markets such as the vast Cherkizovsky Market in Moscow, the Saphan Lek street market in Bangkok, and the open-air La Salada market in Buenos Aires, one of the largest sites of trade in counterfeits in Latin America, can be seen as the most radical way of intervening in the vitality and productive functions of such global nodes of informal trade. Markets of this size require a complex management of contacts between different elements, a 'heterogeneity of articulations that requires rethinking the ways in which value is produced, the subsumption of that productive diversity to the power of capitalist rule, and ways of inhibiting, counteracting, and even resisting that subsumption.'[15] Clamping down on these markets undermines the ambiguities that help to sustain the logistical and territorial framework of their operations and dismisses the values generated in a web of informal activities, collaborative capacities and entrepreneurial dynamics in favour of simple narratives of good and evil. In many cases, disputes regarding the spatial conditions of these marketplaces – unbearable overcrowding, lack of sanitation, and fire hazards – have been strategically linked with ideological attitudes, such as anti-immigrant sentiments, nationalistic sympathies and pro-liberal market biases.

15   Verónica Gago, *Neoliberalism from Below* (Durham, NC: Duke University Press, 2017), 38.

Top: Moskva Mall, Moscow, 2022
Bottom: La Salada Fair, Buenos Aires, 2022

Saphan Lek Market (demolished), Bangkok, 2012

Moscow's Cherkizovsky Market was the largest of several such key distribution nodes for 'grey' imports from China and Eurasia into Eastern Europe that have been shut down in recent years. These markets served armies of 'shuttle traders', who ferried bulk goods to far-away villages and towns. Often constructed out of stacked shipping containers, they offered precarious habitats for many thousands of undocumented migrants. In the case of Cherkizovsky Market, racially motivated arson attacks and the discreditation of non-Russian oligarchs not only fuelled political polarisations surrounding the market's closure in 2009 and the subsequent economic fall-out, but also helped to legitimise the incorporation into new economic ventures of profitable networks and business relationships that were the market's existential foundation. Positioning informal markets as extra-legal spaces that need to be reined in may

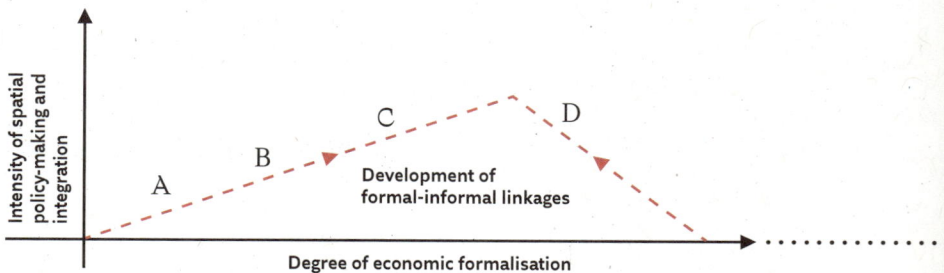

Forms of incorporation
A: market closure   B: relocation   C: onsite improvement   D: entrepreneurial appropriation

lead to a suspension of trade but can leave enough continuity in place for some market actors to reorient the formal-informal linkages created during the markets' operations towards other modes of capital accumulation. The flexibility, contingency and volatility of these linkages are often manifested in the pursuit of other kinds of arrangements, styles of operation and modes of trade.

The eviction of vendors from and demolition of such informal markets frequently leads to a fragmentation of value chains and a displacement of activities to other neighbourhoods. Many traders try to make the most of the situation and negotiate provisional arrangements elsewhere, before they are once again forced to move on. This continuous dispersal of trade keeps transactions on the move, exploits the differentials of mobility, and perpetuates the experimental character of activities rather than consolidating them in a particular location and fostering community-based growth. In the aftermath of recurring closures of territorially based informal markets, an explosive growth of online trade platforms, such as Mercado Libre in Buenos Aires and the darknet platforms Hydra, OMG, Kraken, Blacksprut and Mega in Russia, has increasingly absorbed substantial portions of these economic circuits. The shutdown of trade thus selectively disrupts particular formal-informal linkages and thwarts precisely coordinated local arrangements, while at the same time widening the geography of informal trade beyond the limits of site-specific accumulation and leverage.

More often than not, international intervention is one of the factors that lead to the forced closure of informal marketplaces once they attain a significant scale. As a way of securing favourable trade agreements and attracting global finance, authorities often strive to shore up a city's reputation as a global business hub. As a result, international economic pressure is brought to bear on local spatial development policies and a range of measures are taken that demonstrate efforts to tackle the trade in counterfeits. For instance, local and regional authorities in Thailand have a long tradition of targeting selected marketplaces as priority areas of anti-counterfeit enforcement. Bangkok's 'Red Zones' are regularly listed in the

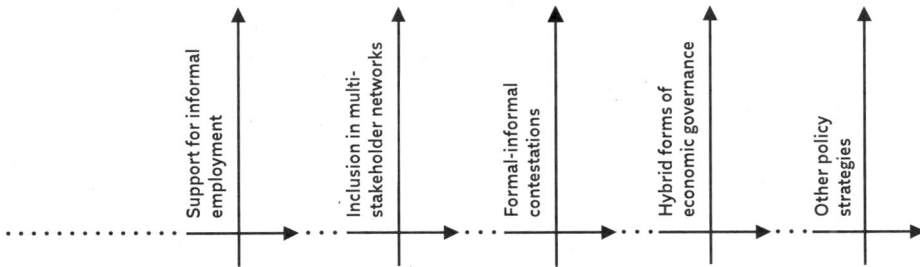

Support for informal employment

Inclusion in multi-stakeholder networks

Formal-informal contestations

Hybrid forms of economic governance

Other policy strategies

Further parameters of incorporation

United State Trade Representative's annual Special 301 Report on countries' compliance with US copyright policies and in its annual Review of Notorious Markets for Counterfeiting and Piracy (Notorious Markets List)[16]. Street vendors operating in market areas included in this expansive documentation of alleged violations of intellectual property rights, such as Saphan Lek, Siam Square and Khlong Thom, have been evicted and whole markets demolished due to mounting international pressure. However, there have been no suitable contingency plans provided for evicted vendors. Although this course of action conflicts with other municipal programmes that seek to recognise informal trade as an integral part of urban development, it follows the long colonial tradition of "indirect rule", in which power takes on an insubstantial and vicarious character, functioning through deputising governmental projects rather than direct foreign intervention. Today, with the intensification of struggles over immaterial property, such conflicts over the ownership, use, and dissemination of intangibles are becoming ever more relevant. The closure of informal marketplaces is now employed as a means of leveraging policy-making, legislation, and enforcement efforts in countries around the world.

Relocation of informal markets: from displacement to displaceability

While efforts to shut down informal markets focus on incorporating informality by redirecting the nominal volume of informal economic operations, relocation programmes seek to utilise informal traders as helpful facilitators of this trade flow, albeit under highly altered and much more controlled circumstances. In such attempts at more 'peripheral' incorporation, legal and policy instruments tend to converge with particular spatial typologies that suggest a more orderly and defined form of trade. Often it is rising land prices in central city locations or the attempt to make unique areas in a city 'more presentable', to bring them into line with the visual appearance of global, that is to say investable, cities, that trigger the impulse to relocate informal markets to areas on the urban fringes that are out of the way of global business operations. Be it spatial interventions within the framework of international development programmes as in the case of the Dajabón binational border market, national restructuring efforts as in the case of Luanda's once bustling Roque Santeiro market, or the local appeasement of global capital as in the case of Ahmedabad's Gujari Bazaar, the displacement of vendors from inner city locations to places external to and distant from the city has become a systemic condition.

Oren Yiftachel has suggested interpreting these processes less as spatio-political acts than as governmental techniques, as giving shape to conditions of 'displaceability'. Other than the term

16   For the most recent issues of both publications see: Office of the United States Trade Representative, *https://ustr.gov/*

Binational Market, Dajabón, Dominican Republic, 2012

'displacement' (the factual fulfilment of the intention to displace vendors), displaceability denotes the 'susceptibility of people, groups and developments to be removed, expelled or prevented from exercising their right to the city.'[17] It is linked to control exercised through an omnipresent threat of displacement and the complex struggle over future urban continuities and ruptures. These conditions are at the heart of the precarious character of urban citizenship negotiated in the imposed restructuring of spatial settings that organise trade. The relocation of the Dajabón binational market on the Haitian-Dominican border, for instance, formed part of a major EU-funded development programme that involved the erection of a two-storey market building next to the diverted and also new-built main border crossing. Initially located in the streets in central Dajabón, this binational market is enabled by temporary relaxations of border restrictions, allowing Haitian intermediary traders, predominantly women, to cross into the Dominican Republic on selected days. This intertwinement of the market's spatial development with the volatile geopolitical position of the Caribbean island of Hispaniola is emblematic of different registers of incorporation at play in creating linkages between different economic agents.

Displaceability is also a mechanism that reaches far into the future and requires flexible adaptation to uncertainties yet to come caused

17   Oren Yiftachel, 'Displaceability - A Southeastern Perspective,' The Displacement Research and Action Network Blog (2018), http://mitdisplacement.org/symposium-oren-yiftachel; Oren Yiftachel, 'From Displacement to Displaceability,' City 24, no. 1-2 (2020): 151–65.

Top: Roque Santeiro, Luanda, 2005
Bottom: Gujari Bazaar, Ahmedabad, 2022

by the subjugating requirements of ever new places. Faced with long periods of political instability, the market of Roque Santeiro, situated on a former waste dump next to Luanda's port, played a central role in Angola's informal economy. With the onset of peace after 2002, the Angolan government announced a programme to restructure the local trade of 20,000 vendors, which involved relocating their operations from Roque Santeiro to purpose-built structures at a new market on the outskirts of the city. Development policies providing strict frameworks of economic cooperation have shaped the new market's spatial arrangement and vendors have either adapted to these measures of commercial re-organisation or have developed alternative lines of business, such as operating from their homes, renting small shops or reverting to street trade. While the market was able to survive as such, the relocation has led to a huge drop in sales because the originally more than 100,000 daily market customers do not travel to the outskirts to purchase goods and are thus no longer part of the formal-informal linkages that made the market thrive.

Inducing similar conditions of displaceability, the self-governed Gujari Bazaar on Ahmedabad's Sabarmati River has been under threat by plans for a transformational riverfront development and the replacement of the existing bazaar with a new marketplace aimed at higher income groups and foreign visitors. Gujari Bazaar has formed part of the riverbanks' centuries-old use as a commons, accommodating up to 1,000 additional ad-hoc traders who set up around adjacent dry channels in the riverbed. A significant part of Ahmedabad's living cultural heritage and the backbone of the city's informal economy, Gujari Bazaar has long been a vital site for the intersection of many urban communities and the establishment of relations across social class divides. The eviction of traders from their original location has been guided by entrepreneurial forms of urban governance and the repurposing of narratives of the market. While the dreamy visions of a Dubai-style riverfront have only partly been realised and the only half-completed redesign of public spaces now seems stuck in limbo, the uprooting of the old market has negatively impacted informal livelihoods and community networks to a significant extent. And yet despite the non-human scale of the riverfront redevelopment and the violence that engendered it, some segments of informal trade have managed to co-exist with fragmented spatial interventions and take up space in niches that have been preserved or newly created amid environmental regulation.

Promises and pitfalls of on-site infrastructural improvement

While in the case of market relocations resistance often arises from breaking with a tradition of places and milieus deemed worth preserving, development policies that aim at improving existing marketplaces represent a subtler but sometimes equally contested way of intervening in linkages between the formal and informal. Again and again, urban development policies promise substantial improvements in the infrastructures of everyday life, including sites for all kinds of social and economic interaction such as squares, parks and marketplaces. Such policies suggest a win-win situation in which increased hygiene, order and tidiness will result in safer and more attractive neighbourhoods benefitting both vendors and visitors as well as the city and its economy as a whole. Typically, there is a whole range of spatial elements involved in implementing these measures: standardised market stalls and awnings, area markings, drainage systems, storage areas, roller shutters, transport aids, regulated opening times, and other elements that facilitate market activities. Such upgrades of the existing infrastructure of informal marketplaces are often associated with significant interventions in the complex processes, arrangements and liaisons that make up the tightly woven fabric of a market. This is equally relevant for the top-down restructuring of transnational trading hubs, private-public partnerships set up to absorb the informal vibe of a location, and the high-profile redesign of long-established marketplaces.

The most elementary form of improvement applied across multiple locations is the provision of a clearly regulated market environment for street vendors. The nature and direction of these regulations is set out in improvement policies, which usually go hand in hand with the reorganisation of administrative and policing powers, as well as with shifting regional and international economic alliances. As can be seen in markets as diverse as São Paulo's Feirinha da Madrugada, one of the largest distribution centres in Latin America for cheap goods imported mainly from Asia, Hong Kong's dawn markets and Dubai's long-standing Karama market, this shift of commerce from street vending to consolidated enterprises often involves periodic closures of the market and the standardisation of market facilities as well as an extension of policing powers to confiscate goods, all of which tends to push street trade into the surrounding areas. The redistribution of market access excludes those vendors for whom remaining in the market would no longer provide the necessary returns, whether because they can no longer afford the rent, because they are losing their particular role in the cooperative network, or because their old customers are no longer interested in visiting the new market.

Such forms of incorporation of informality critically intervene in the niches carved out by informal markets in big cities, be it interstitial spaces, underused infrastructures, or zones of transition. While providing some kind of spatial improvement, these interventions also replace particular operational milieus and exclude traders that are not compatible with the new environments. Rather than

Top: Karama Market, Dubai, 2023
Bottom: Skylight Market, Tin Shui Wai, Hong Kong, 2022

Els Encants, Barcelona, 2022

trying to avoid the congestion of daytime traffic as in the case of the big wholesale fairs in São Paulo, traders at Hong Kong's dawn markets, for instance, seek to operate outside the working hours of hawker-control teams. Catering to the city's elderly poor, vendors operate on a day-to-day basis, offering salvaged houseware, second-hand clothes and home-grown produce. Hong Kong's administration has launched initiatives to 're-site eligible hawkers into new public markets', the operational requirements of which exceed the resources of most dawn-market vendors. The spatial logics of these new public markets and their programmed community activities are also more in tune with the streamlining spirit of prevalent urban development schemes than with the actual lives of street vendors operating at the margins of the city. Such vendors' individual and collective capacities are less receptive to being integrated into proposed urban improvement schemes than to the proliferation of opportunities to make their own way in urban life.

Proliferation pertains to the coming together of different kinds of 'economic practices, demeanours, behavioural tactics, forms of social organisation, territory, and mobility' that generate new values and possibilities for what AbdouMaliq Simone and Vyjayanthi Rao identify as 'urban majorities', the practices and configurations that make 'the multitude of individual and collective lives of the poor, the working class, and the lower-middle class intersect with each

Arizona Market, Brčko, 2022

other, form intricate webs of interdependency and reciprocity.'[18] Such modes of mobilisation and collaboration are put under enormous pressure by recent tendencies to absorb the styles, energies and vulnerabilities of informal marketplaces into grand architectural gestures with which cities compete with each other for attention in the global competition of investment flows. The new design of Barcelona's centuries-old Encants Vells flea market, for instance, has been awarded numerous international prizes. Situated just across from its previous site, the new structure is part of a string of spectacular architectures lining one of the city's prime development axes and is embedded in the wider transformation of the surrounding working-class neighbourhood into a global investment destination. From Encants Vells' acclaimed new design in Barcelona to contested sites such as Dubai's Karama market and the transformation of its unassuming environment into a colourfully painted tourism hotspot, the far-reaching effects of architectural interventions in informal marketplaces are evident in a multitude of projects in which infrastructural and aesthetic improvement ties in with the spatial redevelopment of neighbourhoods through government-enticed real estate investment. In most such cases the replacement of existing housing stock with much pricier new homes and condominiums impacts not only the character of trade but also the formal-informal linkages and arrangements between the different actors who have collectively shaped a location with their activities.

18   AbdouMaliq Simone and Vyjayanthi Rao, 'Counting the Uncountable: Revisiting Urban Majorities,' *Public Culture* 33, no. 2 (2021): 152.

Top: Brooklyn Flea, Dumbo, New York, 2023
Bottom: Talad Rot Fai, Bangkok, 2023

One of the lessons to be learned from incorporations of informality is that improvement cuts both ways. Just as improvements in infrastructure, facilities and appearance are meant to 'upgrade' the operations of informal markets, so the formal economy is improved by incorporating the informal. Tainted assets and illicit transactions may not be part of this process of incorporation but other aspects of informality are readily appropriated: the availability of social ties, the creative energy of self-entrepreneurialism, the authentic appearance of informal aesthetics, and the lived experience of decentralised, malleable collaborations between different market actors. The measures used to appropriate the entrepreneurial potential of informal markets typically range from the wholesale privatisation of informal markets and their transformation into corporately managed shopping malls, as seen in the case of Arizona Market in post-war Bosnia and Herzegovina, to cultivating the emerging phenomenon of hipster markets, where a young urban crowd engages in more or less informal peer-to-peer exchange. With regard to the latter there have been numerous attempts to build trendy brands for 'informal' markets, such as Brooklyn Flea (New York) and Talad Rot Fai (Bangkok). In recent years such brands have gained increasing value as assets in the global competition for economic growth and future market share.

A pioneering example of the emergent wave of branded festival-like markets, the Brooklyn Flea in New York temporarily occupies former warehouses and empty lots. Many of the enterprises in this bohemian-style environment emerged in the wake of the 2008 financial crisis. We are now seeing a consolidation phase, in which businesses have begun to open up further branches or to distribute their wares via other channels. This brand-building deploys specific market aesthetics that allude to authenticity and community experience – locally sourced, home-baked, self-made – processes that illustrate the incorporation of 'informal' flavours as a strategic tool. While the management of these markets may be formalised in legal terms, there is far less certainty about the in/formality of outsourced operations and the working conditions of vendors.

Some of the hipster markets currently mushrooming in Bangkok point to a new development in this global battle over the exploitation of formal-informal linkages. Talad Rod Fai is a growing network of weekend night markets popular with Bangkok's urban young and retails easy-to-consume entertainment in a retro-styled setting. The cultivation of this market environment, which has long been geared towards informal start-ups producing personalised goods and trendy street food, fosters a new kind of exchange economy, a lifestyle community shared by both vendors and buyers in which business activities and enjoyment become seemingly

interchangeable. There is an emergent global cultural vocabulary
of informality, manifested in both the physical expression and
the economic conduct of this new type of market environment. It
includes highly evocative arrangements of colourful tents nestled
inside industrial structures, well-staged workshops that ooze an
atmosphere of Old World craftsmanship, and super-sized displays
of out-of-place artefacts, collectibles and ephemera. The purpose of
these installations is not to satisfy any kind of functional need but
to act as markers of improvisation, mobility and a good life. The
deceitful furnishing of these spaces enacts both a sense of belonging and displacement, depending on one's context and capacity for
keeping up with the adaptive processes of urban transformation. It
assigns distinct roles to different actors in a frontier culture fuelled
by an eclectic mix of financial speculation, logistical coordination,
and urban mood-board design.

Reconfiguring the urban

Cities and their accelerating engagement of capital, technologies
and human creativity are the central sites determining the global
economic and political order of the twenty-first century. They offer
a platform for a diversity of people to take advantage of some of the
opportunities emerging in changing urban contexts. Providing the
framework for likely and unlikely encounters, informal markets
have always played an important role in these processes of urban
collaboration and exchange. Significantly, though, conflicts around
the use of urban space by informal markets often serve as a primary pretext for spatial policy interventions that aim to regulate these
kinds of transactions. Although such encroachments on self-regula-
tion usually serve as governmental means of control, these interventions can also provide arenas of negotiation where different actor constellations and new forms of civic participation can emerge.

In the face of today's multiple crises, informality is seen by many
as a lifeline, whether as a means of relieving hardship and securing
one's livelihood or as a way of identifying and tapping into unexploited economic potential and fuelling even more urban speculation. In both cases, the formal and the informal blur into new
configurations of the urban: amalgamations of neoliberal urban
renewal and informal market activity, online trading and urban
infrastructure, street food culture and urban food production, platform labour and the gig economy produce complex geographies in
which experiments with deep entanglements between the formal
and informal constitute critical sites of city-making. This laboratory of the city yet to come is defined by the affinities, intersections,
struggles and tensions between formal and informal urban practices that feed off one another while at the same time undermining
each other's presence. These ambiguous dynamics open up the question of urban development to changing patterns of formal-informal

linkages and the government policies and socio-economic realities that inform them.

Linking fluctuating formal-informal ties to the broader dynamics of a neoliberalisation from below, authors such as Verónica Gago, in her depiction of an emerging 'assemblage economy', have stressed the inscription of 'fractual accumulation' into the market space,[19] – the way people adapt to the mindset of neoliberal ideals and incorporate corresponding patterns of economic conduct into their daily lives. Different types of capture and enclosure pave the way for connecting these processes to experiments with reconfiguring the urban. The construction of market halls, designated stalls, regulated operating hours and administrative structures, for instance, guarantee a level of continuity and integration for market vendors, but such enclosures also enable the siphoning off of time, creativity and potential via organised access to atomised productivity. This kind of reconfiguration is reflected not least in the current rise of e-commerce platforms and the way in which the COVID-19 pandemic has expanded in/formal market operations of all kinds into the digital realm. Blurring the boundaries between social media activities, urban engagement and online trade, the actuation of more dynamic and hybrid formal-informal economic arrangements brings to the fore new possibilities as well as forms of exploitation arising from this amalgamated top-down/bottom-up urban landscape.[20]

Whatever agency one has in such environments, in/formal markets play a critical role in reconfigurations of the urban by acting as infrastructural nodes, both in a material and immaterial sense, providing access to goods, services, know-how, networks and all the things that different actors need to make a life worth living. From both a neoliberal perspective and that of many formal sector actors, the most attractive achievement of informal marketplaces is thus the creation of new market environments – places for trade and commerce that offer opportunities for economic empowerment and growth. The spatial and architectural presence of the market is what links informal trade to urban speculation. The marketplace itself constitutes the most critical linkage between small-scale entrepreneurial activity and global real estate operations. For many investors and developers, their attention and speculative interest is not so much focused on the concrete workings of a market per se, but on its potential value for attracting global capital to a particular neighbourhood, city or region. By transforming the potential of marketplaces into an asset class, individual ways of being in the city and engaging with the future through urban citizenship are thus inevitably tied up with urban speculation and global capital flows.

37

19   Gago, *Neoliberalism from Below*, 122.
20   Teddy Cruz and Fonna Forman, *Socializing Architecture: Top Down/Bottom Up* (Berlin: Hatje Cantz, 2023).

One of the ensuing problems is that today in/formal marketplaces are not only experiencing increasing pressure from state and corporate actors, but the orientation of this pressure is changing as well. Informality is being changed from a deficiency that needs to be fixed into a question of management, not only in terms of managing informality but also in terms of informality becoming a way of managing social and economic relations. This is reflected in a shift in debates on informality, with the focus now less on the political economy of informality than on opportunities to informally manage the relations between different civic and economic actors. Epitomised by the on-demand labour model of the platform economy and corresponding forms of urban government by experiment, this shift devalues the political potential inherent in informality and turns it into a vehicle for opening up new markets. Along with the rampant privatisation of urban space, the political space of informality is being fragmented and transformed into easily controllable and manageable environments of informal domesticity.

Digital technologies and data analysis are gradually being utilised to harness and exploit the unruly nature of informality for uneven growth and profit-making. However, it is uncertain whether the many leakages, spills, and incidents that emerge within the social ecologies of informality can be fully controlled and contained by agreements solely focused on exploiting their inherent potential. This uncertainty is apparent not only in the struggles of informal workers as they fight for their rights to the city but also in the ceaseless appropriation and transformation of top-down implemented infrastructures into environments that can accommodate the urban realities of highly agonistic relationships permeated by formal-informal hybridities. Urban majorities are both used to and dependent on inhabiting such kinds of relationships. In contrast to the objective of making informality quantifiable, predictable and available, both activist urban practice and academic analysis should thus strive not to make informality more productive and profitable but to strengthen our understanding of the complexity of its dynamics and the reciprocity of influences and possibilities inherent in formal-informal linkages. Understanding urban reconfiguration in this way means acknowledging that the tension between formal and informal spaces is not a marginal issue affecting only urban peripheries, but a fundamental dynamic that applies to any urban setting.

REFERENCES

Agarwala, Rina. 'Incorporating Informal Workers into Twenty-first Century Social Contracts,' UNRISD Working Paper No. 2018-13. Geneva: United Nations Research Institute for Social Development (UNRISD), 2018.

Chen, Martha, and Francoise Carré, eds. *The Informal Economy Revisited: Examining the Past, Envisioning the Future*. London and New York: Routledge, 2020.

Cruz, Teddy, and Fonna Forman. *Socializing Architecture: Top Down/ Bottom Up*. Berlin: Hatje Cantz, 2023.

Gago, Verónica, *Neoliberalism from Below*. Durham, NC: Duke University Press.

Grzymala-Busse, Anna. 'The Best Laid Plans: The Impact of Informal Rules on Formal Institutions in Transitional Regimes.' *Studies in Comparative International Development* 45, no. 3 (2010): 311–33.

Hart, Keith. 'How the Informal Economy Took Over the World.' In *Informal Market Worlds: The Architecture of Economic Pressure – Reader*, edited by Peter Mörtenböck and Helge Mooshammer, 33–44. Rotterdam, nai010 publishers, 2015.

Helmke, Gretchen, and Steven Levitsky. 'Informal Institutions and Comparative Politics: A Research Agenda.' *Perspectives on Politics* 2, no. 4 (2004): 725–40.

International Labour Office. *Women and Men in the Informal Economy: A Statistical Picture* (third edition). Geneva: International Labour Organisation (ILO), 2018.

McFarlane, Colin. 'Rethinking Informality: Politics, Crisis, and the City.' *Planning Theory & Practice* 13, no. 1 (2012): 89–108.

Meagher, Kate. 'Unlocking the Informal Economy: A Literature Review on Linkages between Formal and Informal Economies in Developing Countries.' WIEGO Working Paper No. 27, April 2013.

Mehrotra, Rahul. 'Between Equity and Impatient Capital: Making Indian Cities.' *Journal of International Affairs* 65, no. 2 (2012): 133–37.

Mehrotra, Rahul. *The Kinetic City & Other Essays*. Berlin: ArchiTangle, 2021.

Mörtenböck, Peter, and Helge Mooshammer, eds. *Informal Market Worlds: The Architecture of Economic Pressure – Atlas*. Rotterdam: nai010 publishers, 2015.

Mörtenböck, Peter, Helge Mooshammer, Teddy Cruz, and Fonna Forman, eds. *Informal Market Worlds: The Architecture of Economic Pressure – Reader*. Rotterdam: nai010 publishers, 2015.

Office of the United States Trade Representative. 'Review of Notorious Markets for Counterfeiting and Piracy,' yearly editions. *https://ustr.gov/*

Office of the United States Trade Representative. 'Special 301 Report,' yearly editions. *https://ustr.gov/issue-areas/intellectual-property/special-301*

Ohnsorge, Franziska, and Shu Yu, eds. *The Long Shadow of Informality: Challenges and Policies*. Washington, DC: World Bank Group Publications, 2022.

Ribeiro, Gustavo Lins. 'Economic Globalization from Below.' *Etnográfica* 10, no. 2 (2006): 233–46.

Roy, Ananya, 'Urban Informality: Toward an Epistemology of Planning.' *Journal of the American Planning Association* 71, no. 2 (2005): 147–58.

Roy, Ananya. *Poverty Capital: Microfinance and the Making of Development*. London and New York: Routledge, 2010.

Simone, AbdouMaliq, and Vyjayanthi Rao. 'Counting the Uncountable: Revisiting Urban Majorities.' *Public Culture* 33, no. 2 (2021): 151–60.

Yiftachel, Oren. 'From Displacement to Displaceability.' City 24, no. 1-2 (2020): 151–65.

A FORCED CLOSURE

A1	Cherkizovsky Market	*Moscow*
A2	Saphan Lek Market	*Bangkok*
A3	La Salada Fair	*Buenos Aires*

B RELOCATION

B1	Dajabón Binational Market	*Dajabón*
B2	Roque Santeiro	*Luanda*
B3	Gujari Bazaar	*Ahmedabad*

D2

C

B1

A3

C IMPROVEMENT

C1	Karama Market	*Dubai*
C2	Tin Shui Wai Dawn Market	*Hong Kong*
C3	Encants Vells	*Barcelona*

D APPROPRIATION

D1	Arizona Market	*Brčko*
D2	Brooklyn Flea	*New York*
D3	Talad Rot Fai	*Bangkok*

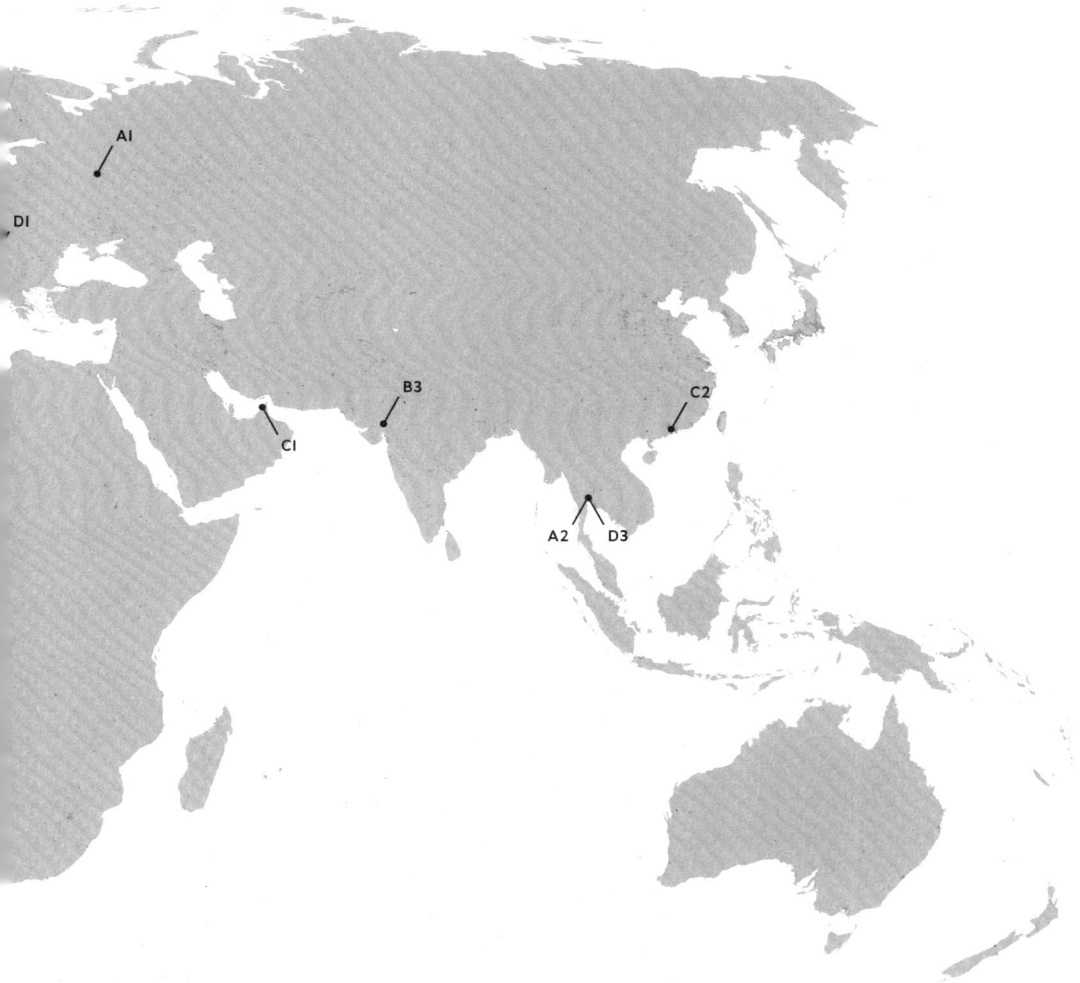

A1

D1

CI

B3

C2

A2   D3

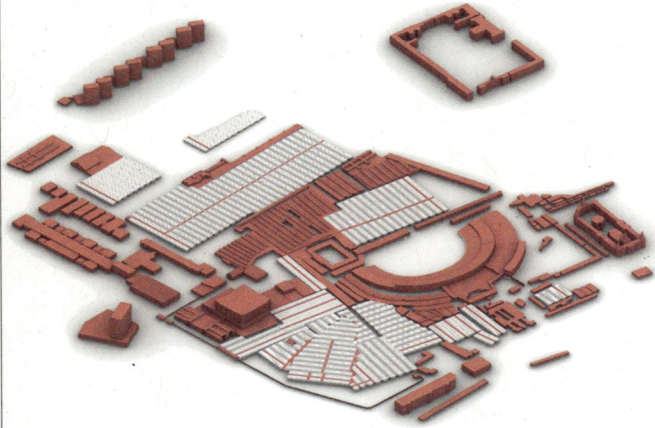

AI Cherkizovsky Market

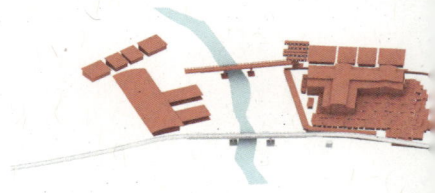

BI Dajabón Binational Market

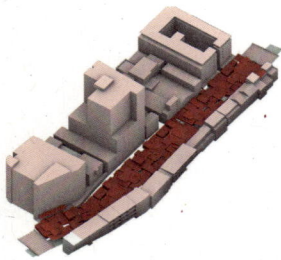

A2 Saphan Lek Market

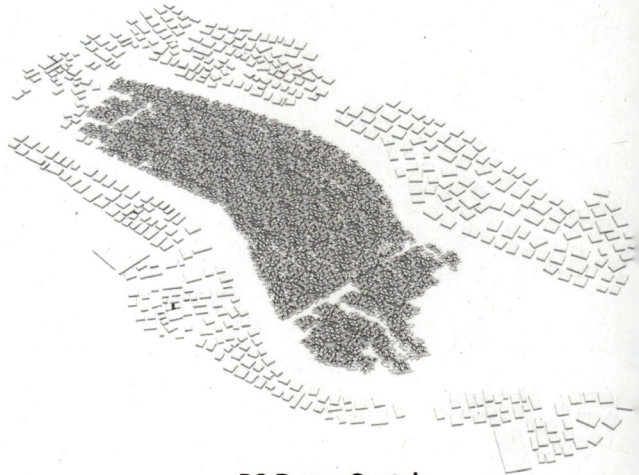

B2 Roque Santeiro

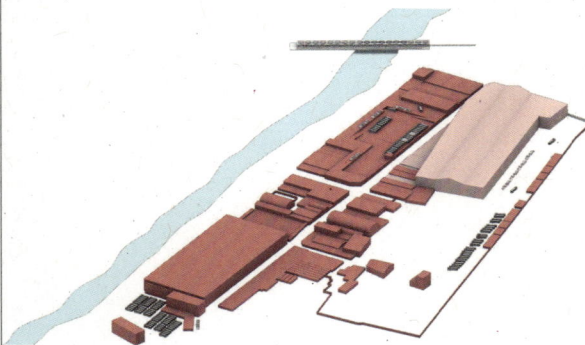

A3 La Salada Fair

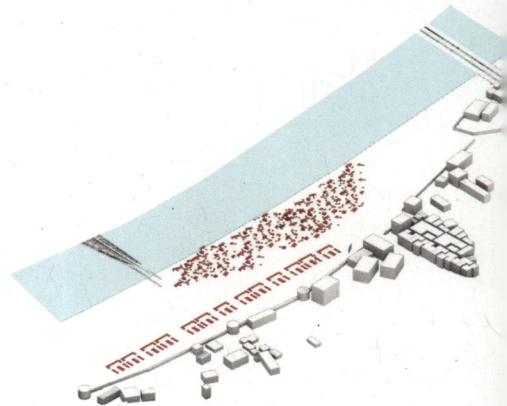

B3 Gujari Bazaar

Spatial contexts and morphologies of twelve different in/formal marketplaces

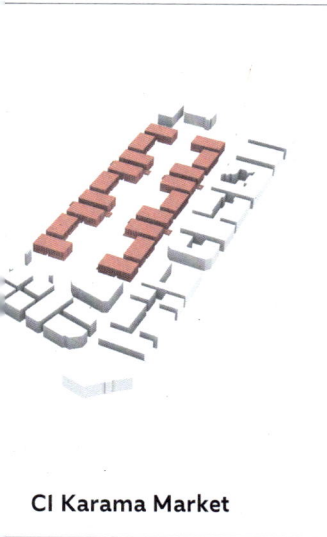

C1 Karama Market

D1 Arizona Market

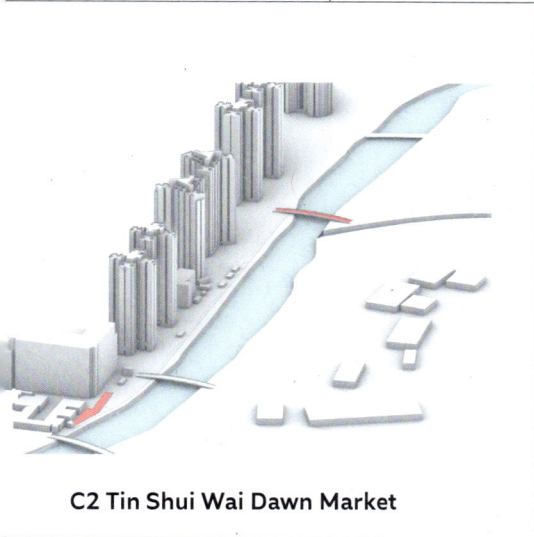

C2 Tin Shui Wai Dawn Market

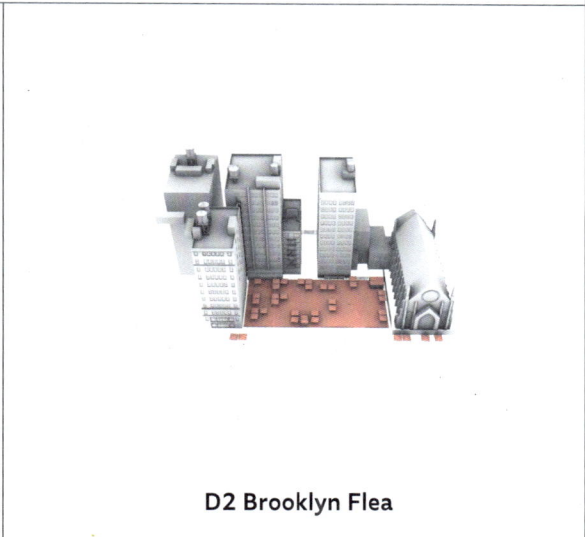

D2 Brooklyn Flea

C3 Encants Vells

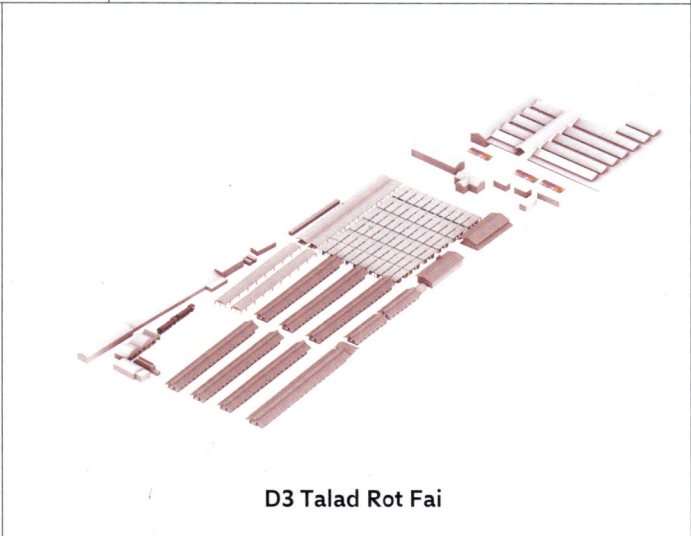

D3 Talad Rot Fai

A — Forced closure   B — Relocation   C — Improvement   D — Appropriation

Incorporating Informality

44

2007

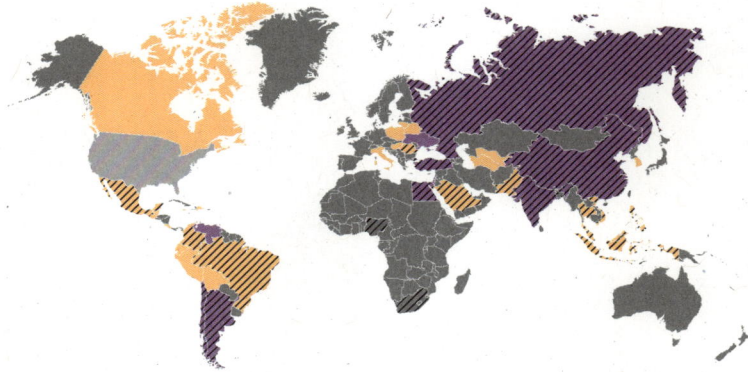

PRIORITY WATCH LIST:	Argentina, Chile, China, Egypt, India, Israel, Lebanon, Russia, Thailand, Turkey, Ukraine, Venezuela
WATCH LIST:	Belarus, Belize, Bolivia, Brazil, Canada, Colombia, Costa Rica, Dominican Republic, Ecuador, Guatemala, Hungary, Indonesia, Italy, Jamaica, Kuwait, Lithuania, Malaysia, Mexico, Pakistan, Peru, Philippines, Poland, Republic of Korea, Romania, Saudi Arabia, Taiwan, Tajikistan, Turkmenistan, Uzbekistan, Vietnam

2010

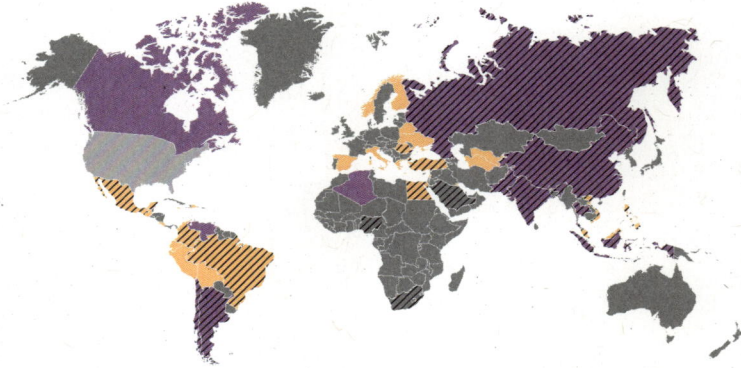

PRIORITY WATCH LIST:	Algeria, Argentina, Canada, Chile, China, India, Indonesia, Pakistan, Russia, Thailand, Venezuela
WATCH LIST:	Belarus, Bolivia, Brazil, Brunei, Colombia, Costa Rica, Dominican Republic, Ecuador, Egypt, Finland, Greece, Guatemala, Italy, Jamaica, Kuwait, Lebanon, Malaysia, Mexico, Norway, Peru, Philippines, Romania, Spain, Tajikistan, Turkey, Turkmenistan, Ukraine, Uzbekistan, Vietnam

2013

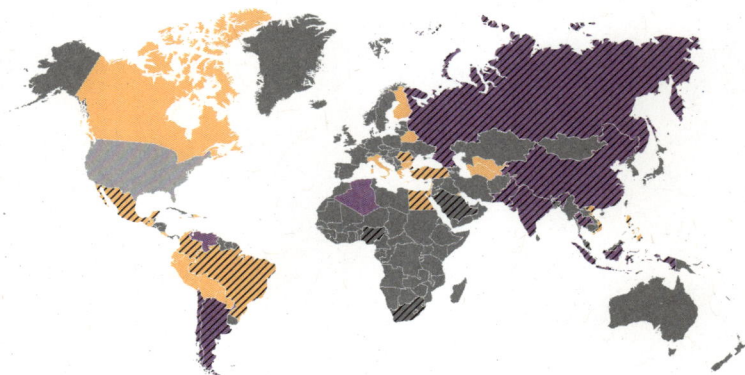

PRIORITY WATCH LIST:	Algeria, Argentina, Chile, China, India, Indonesia, Pakistan, Russia, Thailand, Venezuela
WATCH LIST:	Barbados, Belarus, Bolivia, Brazil, Bulgaria, Canada, Colombia, Costa Rica, Dominican Republic, Ecuador, Egypt, Finland, Greece, Guatemala, Israel, Italy, Jamaica, Kuwait, Lebanon, Mexico, Paraguay, Peru, Philippines, Romania, Tajikistan, Trinidad and Tobago, Turkey, Turkmenistan, Uzbekistan, Vietnam

Economies targeted by the United States Trade Representative's 301 Special Reports on Intellectual Property Rights, 2007-2022

2016

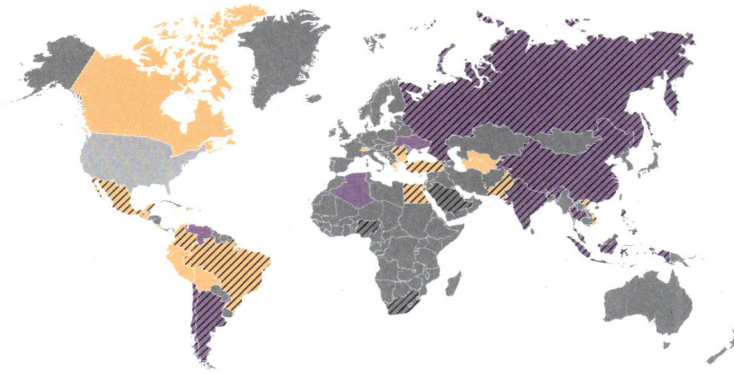

PRIORITY WATCH LIST: Algeria, Argentina, Chile, China, India, Indonesia, Kuwait, Russia, Thailand, Ukraine, Venezuela
WATCH LIST: Barbados, Bolivia, Brazil, Bulgaria, Canada, Colombia, Costa Rica, Dominican Republic, Ecuador, Egypt, Greece, Guatemala, Jamaica, Lebanon, Mexico, Pakistan, Peru, Romania, Switzerland, Turkey, Turkmenistan, Uzbekistan, Vietnam

2019

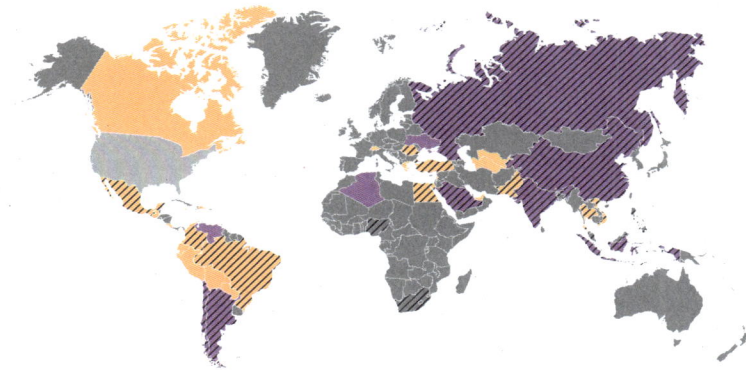

PRIORITY WATCH LIST: Algeria, Argentina, Chile, China, India, Indonesia, Kuwait, Russia, Saudi Arabia, Ukraine, Venezuela
WATCH LIST: Barbados, Bolivia, Brazil, Canada, Colombia, Costa Rica, Dominican Republic, Ecuador, Egypt, Greece, Guatemala, Jamaica, Lebanon, Mexico, Pakistan, Paraguay, Peru, Romania, Switzerland, Thailand, Turkey, Turkmenistan, UAE, Uzbekistan, Vietnam

2022

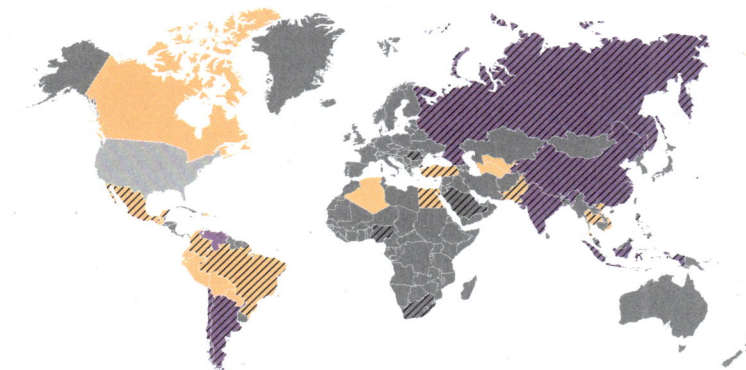

PRIORITY WATCH LIST: Argentina, Chile, China, India, Indonesia, Russia, Venezuela
WATCH LIST: Algeria, Barbados, Bolivia, Brazil, Canada, Colombia, Dominican Republic, Ecuador, Egypt, Guatemala, Mexico, Pakistan, Paraguay, Peru, Thailand, Trinidad and Tobago, Turkey, Turkmenistan, Uzbekistan, Vietnam

▨ **Emerging economies**
(Source: Emerging Markets Institute, Cornell University)

🟧 **Special 301 Report – Watch List**
(Source: USTR)

🟪 **Special 301 Report – Priority Watch List**
(Source: USTR)

A – FORCED CLOSURE

1990 1991 1992 1993 1994 1995 1996 1997 1998 1999 2000 2001 2002 2003

A1 Cherkizovsky Market   1   2   3

A2 Saphan Lek Market   11   12

A3 La Salada Fair   18

B – RELOCATION

1990 1991 1992 1993 1994 1995 1996 1997 1998 1999 2000 2001 2002 2003

B1 Dajabón Binational Market   22   23

B2 Roque Santeiro   27

B3 Gujari Bazaar

C – IMPROVEMENT

1990 1991 1992 1993 1994 1995 1996 1997 1998 1999 2000 2001 2002 2003

C1 Karama Market   40   41   42   43

C2 Tin Shui Wai Dawn Market   47

C3 Encants Vells   52

D – APPROPRIATION

1990 1991 1992 1993 1994 1995 1996 1997 1998 1999 2000 2001 2002 2003

D1 Arizona Market   55   56   57

D2 Brooklyn Flea   61   62

D3 Talad Rot Fai   11   12

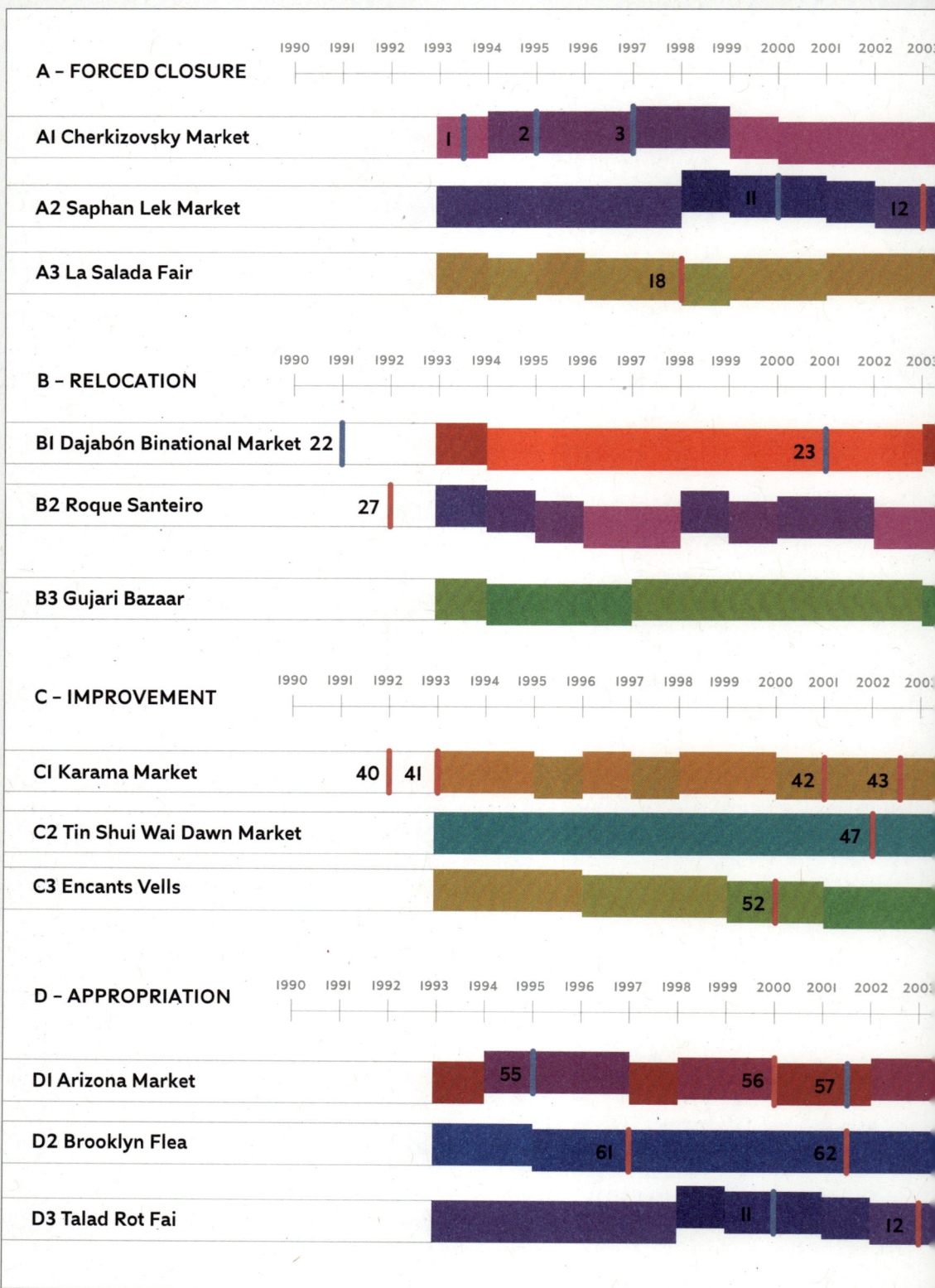

Interventions into informal marketplaces: timelines of policies targeting informal trade and the changing size of the informal economy

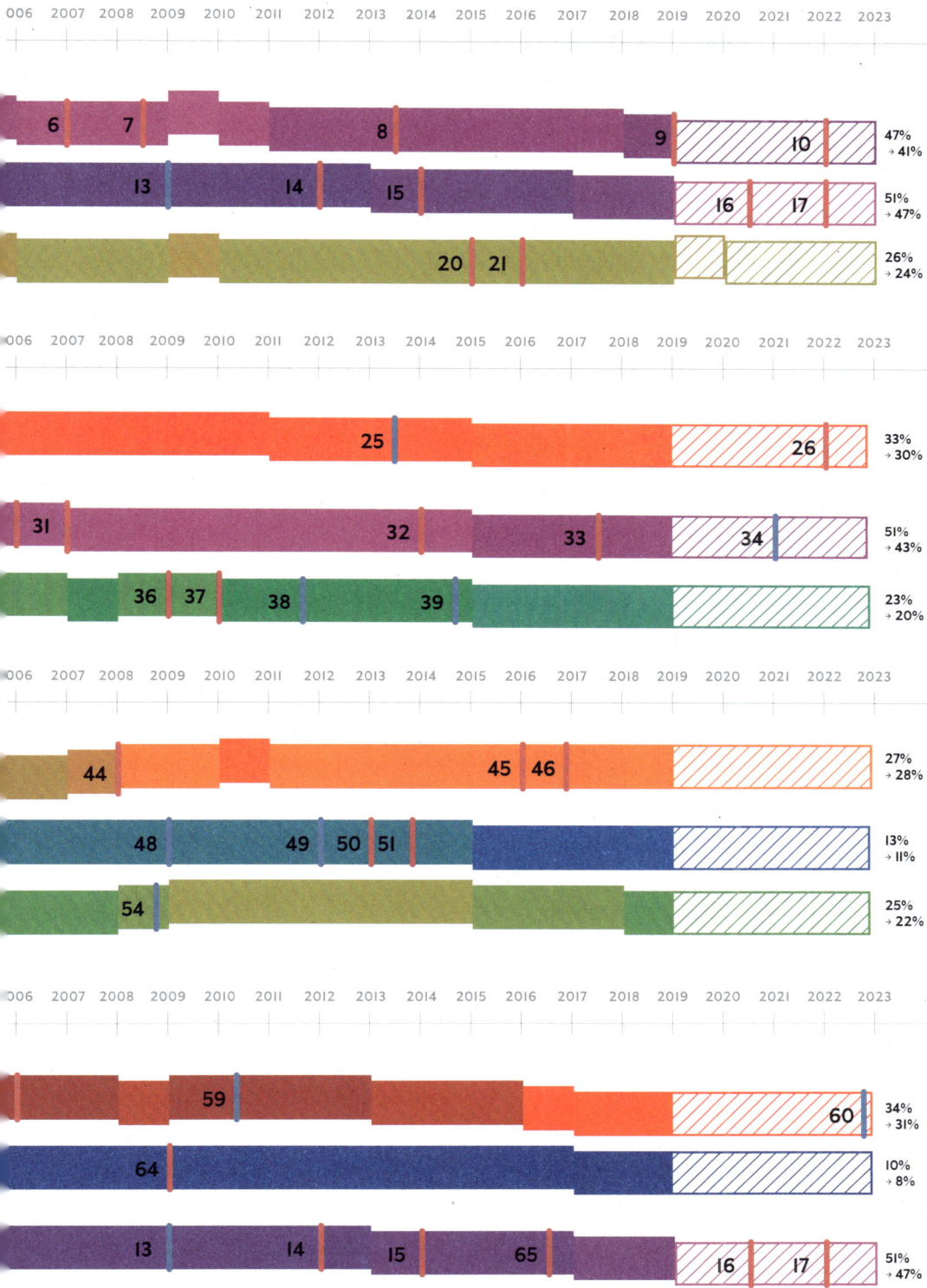

Estimates of informal output
(percentage of total GDP, 1993-2018; source: World Bank)

8% ▬ 54%

■ Restricting policies towards informal markets   ■ Accommodating policies towards informal markets

A FORCED CLOSURE

1 Cherkizovsky Market vendors start importing their goods using the 'grey customs clearance'.
2 Law (de)regulating street trade and markets passed
3 Approval of plans to expand the Cherkizovsky Market
4 State-led investigation of the Cherkizovsky Market
5 Crackdown on informal markets
6 Vladimir Putin approves plans to ban foreigners from trading at open-air markets.
7 Policies introduced to ban all open-air markets
8 Beginning of investigations and raids to reduce criminality at the Sadovod Shopping Complex
9 Raids in Sadovod, Lyublino and Food City targeting foreign workers
10 Russia plans to increase taxes for e-commerce.
11 Governor Sundaravej authorises the establishment of 353 new designated areas, accommodating 11,438 vendors. Additionally, restrictions on designated no-vending days are removed.
12 Governor Kasayodhin initiates a comprehensive city-wide clean-up campaign aimed at restoring order to street vending. The campaign includes targeted enforcement actions against street vendors in markets lacking proper regulation, such as Bo Bae and Khlong Thom markets.
13 Governor Paribatra introduces a series of policies that demonstrate strong support for street vendors. These include a proposal to authorise an additional 275 designated vending areas to accommodate 6,749 vendors. The 'Street Vending as the City's Charm' project and a soft loans policy for licensed vendors are implemented.
14 Under the administration of Governor Sukhum-bhand, a shift towards more stringent regulation on street vending occurs. Each district's administration is instructed to restrict and control the number of available vending spots.
15 Public space cleanup programme lead by the BMA comes into effect following the military coup.
16 The Khlong Ong Ang Walking Street project estimated at a cost of 275 million baht is completed.
17 BMA begins with another round of street clean-ups.
18 A severe economic crisis in Argentine leads to high unemployment and increase in informal economic activities.
19 Stalls added along the river in 2001 are evicted in the midst of violent clashes resulting in one vendor's death.
20 The new government increases attempts to reduce the size of the informal sector.
21 The increasing criminalisation of La Salada Fair reflects a change in attitude towards the 'popular economy'.

B RELOCATION

22 Opening of borders between Haiti and the Dominican Republic (DR) as part of efforts to promote cross-border trade
23 Law 28-01: Special Border Development Zone Law passed to promote economic development and social integration in the border region
24 European Union agrees to financially support the building of a new market hall for the Binational Market in Dajabòn.
25 Opening of the new market building in Dajabòn
26 Start of a 160 km-long 'intelligent' border fence project
27 The first land law (Lei de Terras) confers the state with authority over agricultural land and paves the path for the involvement of private investors.
28 A new land law (Law no. 09/04) mandates landowners to undergo an official registration process for their land before the designated deadline in 2010. Failure to comply would result in the transfer of ownership of any unregistered land in Angola to the state.
29 The government implements a strategy aimed at regaining control over urban space and eradicating the musseques.
30 The Angolan government initiates PRESILD (Programme of Structuring the System of Logistics and Distribution of Essential Products to the Population) which seeks to formalise and restructure the commercial supply network.
31 The implementation of the Law of Housing Development introduces a provision enabling the state to demolish constructions deemed 'inappropriate'.
32 The government announces a regime of heavy fines targeting not only informal vendors but also their customers.
33 Measures against informality culminate in 'Operation Resgate' with arrests and heavy fines against informal vendors.
34 The government embraces a transformative approach, known as the Informal Economy Transition Programme (PREI), which marks a departure from the 'Operation Resgate' strategy, which aimed to eliminate the informal economy but proved ineffective.
35 The Ahmedabad Municipal Corporation (AMC) launches the Sabarmati Riverfront Development Project, envisioning the transformation of the riverfront as an opportunity to attract global investment.
36 Sabarmati Riverfront Development Corporation demolishes most of the informal settlements along the riverbanks.
37 An eviction notice is served to the Gujari Bazaar vendors.
38 Public Interest Litigation filed by Navdeep Mathur, a professor at Ahmedabad's Indian Institute of Management, argues for the inclusion of Gujari Bazaar in the Sabarmati Riverfront Development Project.
39 Gujari Bazaar officially relocates to its new premises within the Sabarmati riverfront redevelopment.

C IMPROVEMENT

40 The Dubai government establishes the Dubai Economic Department (DED) as the regulatory body responsible for enforcing intellectual property rights and combating counterfeit trade.

41 Introduction of the first federal trademark law (Law no. 37/1992) in the UAE

42 DED announces that shops in Karama Market have two weeks to sell any remaining illicit stock before the imposition of heavy fines and unannounced raids.

43 Amendment of the federal trademark law to meet international standards and criteria

44 Sheikh Mohammed bin Rashid Al Maktoum issues Law no. 25/2008 giving the DED the responsibility for planning and regulating the overall economic performance of Dubai, supervise its functions and enhance economic development.

45 Introduction of the Anti-Commercial Fraud Law (Law no. 19/2016) increases the fines for counterfeiting and introduces prison sentences.

46 DED introduces measures against online counterfeiting.

47 A programme lasting for five years is introduced, urging itinerant hawkers to willingly give up their licenses. In return, they are offered various incentives, including a single, one-time ex gratia payment, the option to rent an empty stall in public markets under favourable terms, or the opportunity to become a fixed pitch hawker selling non-cooked food. As a result of this initiative, there is a significant reduction in the number of licensed hawkers.

48 A batch of new licenses is issued after a review of the hawker licensing policy was implemented.

49 The Tung Wah Group of Hospitals (TWGH), a non-profit local Non-Government Organisation (NGO), puts forward a proposal to the government to establish a market that would offer affordable rental stalls for street traders and TSW residents. This initiative would enable them to earn a livelihood by selling daily food, groceries, and other goods. The primary goals of this plan are described as increasing shopping options for the community, generating employment opportunities for disadvantaged groups, providing street traders with legitimate and proper stalls for conducting business, and ultimately replacing the informal 'dawn' markets.

50 The government offers lump sums of 120,000 HK dollars to hawkers who are willing to surrender their licenses. More than 310 licenses are forfeited in one year.

51 The Hong Kong Government implements an assistance scheme in 43 fixed-pitch hawker areas starting June 2013 to reduce the fire risks and enhance the operating environment of the hawker areas.

52 Inception of 22@ – a smart city government initiative introduced with the intention to make Barcelona a hub for innovative technology companies. 22@ uses the adjacent neighbourhood of Poblenou as a testbed for design-led economic growth.

53 The first Universal Forum of Cultures takes place and is hosted in buildings that started a wave of high-profile architectures along Avenida Diagonal such as the Forum Building by Herzog & de Meuron, the Parc dels Auditoris by Foreign Office Architects (FOA) and the Torre Agbar by Jean Nouvel.

54 Barcelona City Council announces a European competition for the construction of a market complex that should become the new permanent home of Encants Vells.

D APPROPRIATION

55 Informal roadside vendors cluster next to a checkpoint on Arizona Route; tolerated by the international community (OHR, OSCE, UNMIBH, SFOR) these operations soon expand into adjacent fields with fixed stalls forming the first Arizona Market.

56 The international community's Office of the High Representative raises concerns about the steep rise in illicit activities and commits to ridding the market of these problems.

57 The Supervisor of the Brčko Distric invites tenders from private enterprises for building and operating a new and improved Arizona Market.

58 Introduction of new tax rates for the Brčko District and the Arizona Market in accordance with the rest of BiH (prior to this, the district was granted favourable taxation)

59 The Brčko District Assembly claims negligence in the running and development of the market by Italproject and awards its sole management to another enterprise, Santovac.

60 Initially planned beginning of the expansion of Arizona Market

61 A special type of zoning called 'Mixed-use District Zoning' is introduced to attract investment and enhance the vitality of existing neighbourhoods in NYC.

62 The Bloomberg Administration introduces a major zoning initiative known as the New York City Zoning Resolution of 2002.

63 Rezoning: Williamsburg transitions to mixed-use district zoning.

64 Rezoning: Dumbo transitions to mixed-use district zoning.

65 The eviction of street vendors from Bangkok's city centre contributes to making private and temporary market ventures more profitable than ever.

Jodd Fairs, Bangkok, 2023

Forced Closure

Porters at Moskva Mall, Moscow, 2022

Anton Nikolotov

Popular Markets in Moscow and Their Border Spectacles

Map data: Google, imagery date: 10/3/21-newer, Maxar Technologies

A street vendor sells fruit and vegetables on the pavement near one of Moscow's large markets. We can call her Ferusa.[1] I heard this story from a relative in autumn 2022 as the mobilisation in Russia was gathering pace. Ferusa came from Uzbekistan in the early 1990s and is now a pensioner. After many years, she and her family acquired Russian citizenship. Her son used to work on a construction site and as a cook, but he was mobilised after Russia's invasion of Ukraine and sent to a training camp near Belgorod and the Ukrainian border. Ferusa received messages from her son telling her he had nothing to eat. Problems with drinking water and food supplies forced her son to fetch water from a river. Ferusa wanted to send him money so he could buy food in a local shop. He would not only be purchasing food for himself, she reportedly insisted, but would also share it with other conscripts. Ferusa planned to visit and cook for him and others in his camp.

I   The names of interlocutors are pseudonyms and some details of their biographies and places were changed by the author.

The old Izmailovo stadium, which became completely engulfed by the Cherkizovsky Market, was built during the 1930s. It is a fragment of the envisaged 'Central Stadium of the Soviet Union' planned under Stalin to accommodate 120,000 spectators.

Bunker Museum, operated by the Central Museum of the Armed Forces since 1999.

Cherkizovsky Market emerged in the early 1990s in the Izmailovo district of Moscow near several major highways. The market covered an area of fifty hectares and leased much of the land from the Russian State University of Physical Education, Sport, Youth and Tourism. It accommodated a labour force of 100,000 small businessmen and women, vendors, porters, and cleaners.

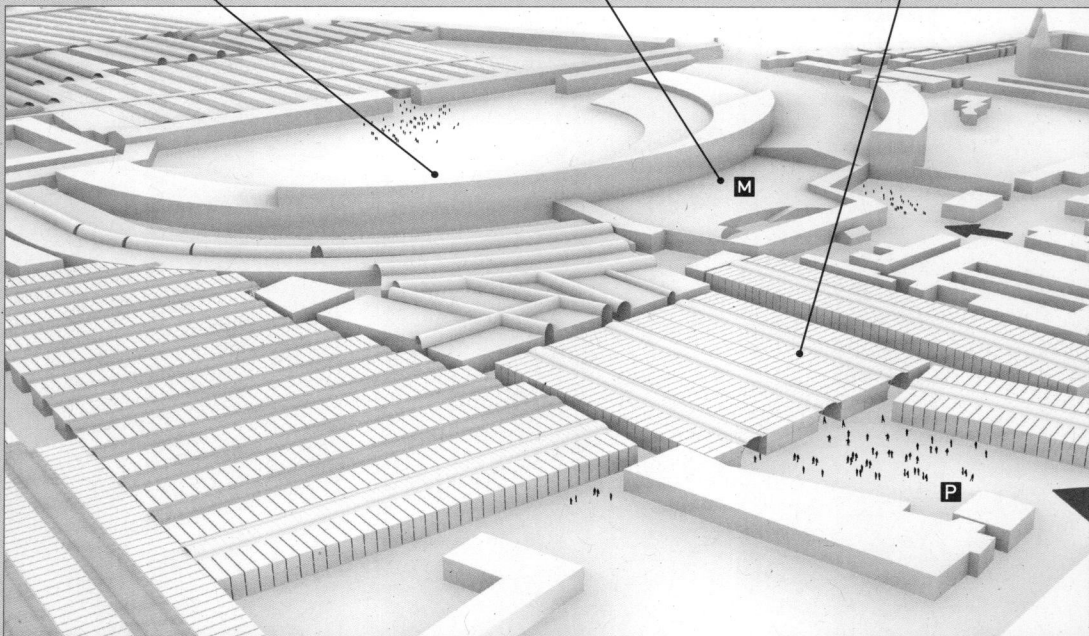

Shipping containers were repurposed and transformed into individual retail units. The containers were stacked and arranged in a grid-like pattern to create rows and alleys for vendors to set up their shops. Lower containers were used for display and direct sales, while upper containers were used for storage.

When the market was closed in 2009, container rows were dismantled with confiscated stock locked up in underground warehouses. Some new housing has been built on the eastern fringes of the site though most of the land has since sat empty.

She explained that it was hard for her son at first, but once he was reunited with his old school friend, they could take care of one another – 'everything was good now,' she said. Ferusa's labour at the market to send money to her son demonstrates how the Russian state's necropower[2] has expanded its reach to the workers in Moscow's informal economies rather than just in its low-income peripheries. As of spring 2023, the state's borders fluctuate depending on its military successes and failures, making them operate much more like mobile frontiers.

These fluctuating borders inform and shape both the history and present of Russian patronal capitalism. Moscow's popular markets are sights where the state projects these politics of control inwards onto urban environments, and everyday social relations. This chapter will show how the state's frontiers and borders appropriate and re-signify the informal market space and the workers that inhabit it.

Scholars have examined contexts where geopolitical borders, signifying fixed boundaries, and frontiers, which function as zones and open spaces of imperial expansion, dissolve or intertwine.[3] An extension and loose interpretation of Nicolas De Genova's influential concept of 'border spectacles' and Clifford Geertz's 'theatre state' can help to analytically frame the connections between the bordering and frontiering practices of the state on the one hand and patronal politics and the redevelopment of popular markets in Moscow on the other.[4] Importantly, the concept of 'border spectacle' links the simultaneous exclusions and inclusions of migrant labour to various public technologies of discourse and representation. A border spectacle, De Genova writes, 'sets a scene – an ostensible scene exclusion' that is 'accompanied by its shadowy, publicly unacknowledged or disavowed, obscene complement: the large-

scale recruitment of criminalised migrants as legally vulnerable, precarious, and thus controllable and exploitable labour.'[5] The state relies on the public mediation of its raids, mass document checks, detentions, and deportations of migrant workers to naturalise the hierarchical and racialised labour market. However, focusing exclusively on the violent aspects of frontiers and bordering rather limits our understanding of the relationship between borders and spectacular enchantment. Meanwhile, scholarship on post-Soviet Eurasian cities has explored how spectacle functions as a powerful technology of legitimation, nation-building, and urban future-making, rather than merely as a technology of disciplinary governance.[6]

The following sections will situate Ferusa's story of her family's capture by the new necropolitical frontier in a broader context of the socio-material and symbolic transformations of a crucial popular market in Russia. The chapter will show how the market and its workers inhabit different kinds of spectacle. This condition, I argue, reflects what Sandro Mezzadra and Brett Neilson call the global 'multiplication of borders,' but also, crucially, the local political economy of patronage between Russian commercial and ruling elites.[7] These spectacles include 1) border reinforcement as the technology of disciplining the business elites; 2) celebratory aspects of urban redevelopment and the emergence of new spaces for both prestigious consumption and affordable class distinction; 3) symbolic and commemorative spectacles of the Second World War linked to state promoted patriotism.

The spaces of popular markets provide critical stages or 'scenes' for these different spectacles for different audiences, and invariably function as echo chambers and conduits for geopolitical tensions, flows of experience, information, conflict, and affective encounters,

2   Achille Mbembe, 'Necropolitics,' *Public Culture* 15, no. 1 (Winter 2003): 11–40.
3   See: Chiara Brambilla et al., *Borderscaping: Imaginations and Practices of Border Making* (Oxford: Routledge, 2016); Sandro Mezzadra and Brett Neilson, *Border as Method, or, the Multiplication of Labor* (Durham: Duke University Press, 2013); Prem Kumar Rajaram and Carl Grundy-Warr, *Borderscapes: Hidden Geographies and Politics at Territory's Edge* (Minneapolis: University of Minnesota Press, 2007).
4   Nicholas De Genova, 'Spectacles of Migrant "Illegality": The Scene of Exclusion, the Obscene of Inclusion,' *Ethnic and Racial Studies* 36, no. 7 (2013): 1180–98. On the concept of the 'theatre state' and the use of spectacle as a political technology of governance see: Clifford Geertz, *Negara: The Theatre State in 19th Century Bali* (Princeton: Princeton University Press, 1980).
5   De Genova, 'Spectacles of Migrant "Illegality",' 1181.
6   See: Laura Adams, *The Spectacular State: Culture and National Identity in Uzbekistan* (Durham: Duke University Press, 2010); Natalie Koch, *The Geopolitics of Spectacle: Space, Synecdoche, and the New Capitals of Asia* (Ithaca: Cornell University Press, 2018).
7   Mezzadra and Neilson, *Border as Method*; See: Iván Szelényi and Pter Mihlyi, *Rent-Seekers, Profits, Wages and Inequality: The Top 20%* (London: Springer International Publishing, 2018); Eleanor Townsley et al., *Making Capitalism Without Capitalists: Class Formation and Elite Struggles in Post-Communist Central Europe* (London: Verso, 1998); Ruslan Dzarasov, *The Conundrum of Russian Capitalism: The Post-Soviet Economy in the World System* (London: Pluto Press, 2014).

Typical infrastructural components, Cherkizovsky Market, Moscow

such as those between Ferusa and my aunt. Focusing on one of the largest markets in Moscow, Sadovod, I will show the emerging social differentiations, symbolic connections, and detachments of the market space from state narratives, as well as the recurring conflicts. I conducted my fieldwork in Sadovod from 2014 to 2015 and have continued to visit almost every year until September 2022. My partial perspective here emphasises Sadovod as a border zone that produces a social interface between regions, cores and peripheries, customers, sellers, and heterogeneous borders and boundaries. The aim of the drawing *Street Traders with Sons Sent to War* (opposite page, top) is to illustrate and make visible the relationships between the stories and lives of the vendors, and the effects of the state's borders and boundaries, which might otherwise remain invisible. In the following sections, I will first provide a background to some of the changes in the patron-client relationships among the owners of the Moscow markets and their deeper integration into the upper inner-circle of the ruling class in Russia in the 2010s. I will then describe some of the most significant ongoing transformations in the spaces of the Sadovod, before returning to Ferusa.

SPECTACLES OF PATRONAL CAPITALISM

Over the past twenty years, the relationship between the state and Moscow's informal markets has undergone several changes. Initially, the markets replaced Gosplan as the main distribution centres and were seen as symbols of emerging capitalism. The 1992 decree On Freedom of Trade legalised the trading of almost anything, anywhere, transforming former 'speculators' into respectable and aspirational figures of *kommersant* and entrepreneurialism.[8] Soon, however, the commercial markets in Moscow and elsewhere began to acquire significant characteristics that both integrated them into the social fabric of the cities and the racial divisions of labour and circulation, as well as orientalised and stigmatised them.[9] With the rapid increase of labour migration from Central Asia sparked by economic growth and the construction boom in the 2000s, state-controlled media and anti-migrant nationalist discourse promoted by opposition parties started to link the markets, and their migrant market traders, with illegality, shady deals and crime. Both portrayed migration and the large Moscow markets as threats to the state's control of financial flows, public health, and national security.[10]

The famous Cherkizovsky Market, nicknamed 'Cherkizon,' has become one of the symbols of untamed post-Soviet capitalism or the 'wild nineties,' the narrative of contrast and legitimation with the supposed 'order' of Putin's regime and its 'power vertical.'[11] Its closure and demolition is probably one of the most well-known border spectacles that claimed to consolidate the control over informal flows of mobile labour, commodities, and commercial capital. Cherkizovsky Market emerged in the early 1990s in the eastern part of Moscow in the Izmailovo district, near several major highways. The market covered an area of fifty hectares and leased much of the land from the Russian State University of Physical Education, Sport, Youth and Tourism. Parts of the sports stadium used by the university were originally constructed in the 1930s as part of Joseph Stalin's vision to stage spectacular sports events that would compete with Nazi Germany's Olympics and its stadiums.[12] The Central Stadium of the Soviet Union was never completed, but it was reconstructed and later served as one of the stadiums for the Soviet Olympic Games in the 1980s. Cherkizovsky's improvisational commercial urbanism and its massive labour force of 100,000 small businessmen and women, vendors, porters, and cleaners from all over the former USSR and beyond squatted this key site of the state's political technology of governance, mass spectacle, and international superpower symbolism.

8   Decree of the President of Russia, No. 65, On Freedom of Trade, 29 January 1992, *http://www.kremlin.ru/acts/bank/1526/print*
9   Viktor Diatlov et al., Базар и Город: Люди, Пространства, Образы [Bazaar and the City: People, Spaces, and Images] (Irkutsk: Irkutsk State University, 2019).
10 Stephen Hutchings et al., *Ethnicity and Race on Russian Television: Mediating Post-Soviet Difference* (Oxford: Taylor & Francis, 2015); Vera Tolz and Sue-Ann Harding, 'From "Compatriots" to "Aliens": The Changing Coverage of Migration on Russian Television,' *The Russian Review* 74, no. 3 (2015): 452–77.
11 Olga Malinova, 'Framing the Collective Memory of the 1990s as a Legitimation Tool for Putin's Regime,' *Problems of Post-Communism* 68, no. 5 (September 2021): 429–41.
12 Peter Mörtenböck and Helge Mooshammer, *Networked Cultures: Parallel Architectures and the Politics of Space* (Rotterdam: nai010 publishers, 2008), 149–51; 'Cherkizovsky Market,' Other Markets (research blog), *http://www.othermarkets.org/index.php?tdid=8*

Top: *Street Traders with Sons Sent to War*, drawing by author, 2022
Bottom: Izmailovo Kremlin under construction, Moscow, 2008

Cherkizovsky Market, Moscow, 2006

One of the main owners of the Cherkizon territory was the eccentric businessman Telman Ismailov and his company AST. Many former market workers ironically claim that AST stands for 'Allah save the Tajiks' because of the surreal and often highly exploitative conditions in which they found themselves. Other parts of the market were owned by Zahar Iliev and God Nisanov and we will come back to them later. Ismailov became an icon of the commercial oligarchs of the 1990s. Flaunting his wealth left and right, Ismailov opened luxurious hotels in Antalya. He hosted lavish parties with invited Hollywood celebrities, pop stars, and influential political figures, including the former Mayor of Moscow Yuri Luzhkov. In 2006 Luzhkov appeared in a video at one of Ismailov's opulent birthday parties. 'Telman, you are our friend!' Luzhkov is seen exclaiming and raising a toast. 'You are our friend forever! Telman, we are with you! We are going through life with you [...] Live forever! Be always healthy!' Luzhkov's opponents and political rivals used the photos and videos of the hedonistic parties to undermine his image and derail his political ambitions.

After another lavish hotel opening and celebration in 2009, Vladimir Putin, then acting as prime minister, reprimanded officials in charge of cracking down on untaxed income and called for arrests. Cherkizon was closed shortly thereafter, and its buildings bulldozed, despite the protests of Chinese and Kyrgyz diplomats in support of the interests of a large number of Chinese and Kyrgyz merchants. A year later, Dmitry Medvedev, who was president at the time, fired Luzhkov for 'loss of trust.' Soon Ismailov lost his position of power as well, as the courts eventually confiscated all of his Russian assets, and he had to flee the country, fearing arrest on several criminal charges.[13]

Media coverage largely portrayed the closure of Cherkizovsky as bringing 'order' to the city and evidence of the crackdown on financial flows out of a country, illegal migration, and the reining in of unchecked oligarchs.[14] Meanwhile, in 2009, thousands of traders had their stock confiscated and locked up in Cherkizovsky's underground warehouses, where some claim it still remains. Most of

13 'Медведев Рассказал, Почему Уволил Лужкова [Medvedev Explained Why He Fired Luzhkov],' *RIA Novosti,* 29 September 2010, https://ria.ru/20100928/280106282.html

14 See for instance the state media report: 'Cherkizovsky Market Closed to Restore Order,' *Vesti,* 26 June 2009, https://www.vesti.ru/article/2207259

these traders and market workers eventually relocated to the Sadovod and Moskva Markets, which are now controlled by a group of Ismailov's former business associates. Got Nisanov, Zahar Iliev, and Ilgam Ragimov have emerged as the new 'kings' of commercial informality, expanding their business empire far beyond the clothing and vegetable markets. The trio founded a joint-stock company, Kievskaya Ploshchad, which is now the largest real estate developer in Moscow and often wins government redevelopment contracts.[15] Forbes has ranked Kievskaya Ploshchad as the number one real estate developer for several consecutive years, estimating its profits at 1,565 million US dollars in 2019 alone.[16]

If Luzhkov and Ismailov represented the era of kickbacks and informal backdoor deals, Nisanov, Ragimov, and Sobyanin are now reflections of what Svetlana Barsukova has called the centralised, patronage-based state redistributive economy.[17] Arguably this new patronage alliance resulted in a new urban development strategy aimed at appeasing the emergent middle classes in Moscow.[18] Shortly after becoming the mayor of Moscow in 2010, Sobyanin launched a campaign to 'civilise trade' and eliminate the urban informality of kiosks, markets, and small street shops.[19] Proclaiming to have as its primary aim the creation of a 'comfortable city,' the Moscow government developed several programmes aimed at what it called *blagoustroistvo*.[20] The term *blagoustroistvo* combines the word *blago* (good) with *ustroistvo* (establishment or designing, ordering, constructing). It has a long history of use in the Tsarist and later Bolshevik radical urban redevelopment in the 1920s. However, whereas the Bolshevik project aimed to re-engineer urban space comprehensively, Sobyanin's *blagoustroistvo*

of 'low-investment/high-effect upgrading of public spaces' targets selected areas for partial infrastructural improvements that cater to the tastes and expectations of comfort of the Westernised middle classes.[21] This has also been reflected in the government policy towards commercial structures whereby makeshift trading formats became marginalised. By 2013, dozens of markets were closed across Moscow, as required by the updated Federal Law on Retail Markets to conduct trade in 'capital structures' (*kapital'nye stroeniya*).[22] The government gave street kiosks and markets selling perishable goods a little more time to adapt and comply. In February 2016, to the shock of their owners, government workers bulldozed kiosks and shops overnight. Since 2017, a part of these modernisation campaigns of *blagoustroistvo* has entailed a housing construction and renovation programme.[23] The programme aims to build housing on an unprecedented scale to replace the Soviet-era public housing, known as *Khrushchevkas*, which were first built in the 1950s.[24] It seems symbolic that where the previously mighty and famous Cherkizovsky market once supplied the city and much of the country with low-cost goods, there are now new high-rises and an empty field.

In contrast to earlier strategies of outright destruction and demolition, however, the government strategy of the late 2010s aimed at moulding different trade formats, displacing the markets to the urban peripheries and centralising their ownership under its control. The question in late 2023 in Russia is whether the state has enough sovereign power to continue remaking and reformatting popular commercial spaces according to this doctrine. Here it is necessary to examine urban spectacles not as instruments of intimidation and

15 Maria Zhalobova, Roman Badanin, and Andrej Zaharov, 'Год Азербайджана в России. Портрет Года Нисанова, человека, Умеющего Дружить и Торговать [The Year of Azerbaijan in Russia. Portrait of God Nisanov, a Man Who Knows How to Make Friends and Trade],' *Project Media*, 16 December 2020, *https://www.proekt.media/portrait/god-nisanov/*

16 Maria Abakumova et al., 'Короли Российской Недвижимости - 2019. Рейтинг Форбс [The Kings of Russian Real Estate - 2019. Forbes Ranking],' *Forbes*, 25 January 2019, *https://www.forbes.ru/biznes-photogallery/371499-koroli-rossiyskoy-nedvizhimosti-2019-reyting-forbes*

17 Svetlana Barsukova, 'Informal Practices of Big Business in the Post-Soviet Period: From Oligarchs To "Kings of State Orders",' *Demokratizatsiya: The Journal of Post-Soviet Democratization* 27, no. 1 (2019): 31–49; Simon Kordonsky, *Socio-Economic Foundations of the Russian Post-Soviet Regime: The Resource-Based Economy and Estate-Based Social Structure of Contemporary Russia* (New York: Columbia University Press, 2016).

18 Mirjam Büdenbender and Daniela Zupan, 'The Evolution of Neoliberal Urbanism in Moscow: 1992–2015,' *Antipode* 49, no. 2 (2017): 294–313.

19 A typical state news article of the time ends with 'Sobyanin will have to break this system. Otherwise, Moscow will never become a civilized city.' See: 'Оптовые Рынки Попадут под Прицел Собянина [Soyanin Will Take Aim at the Wholesale Markets],' *Vesti*, 13 November 2010, *https://www.vesti.ru/article/2127091*

20 The official website of the Mayor of Moscow, *https://www.mos.ru/city/projects/blagoustroistvo/*

21 Büdenbender and Zupan, 'The Evolution of Neoliberal Urbanism in Moscow,' 306; see also: Elena Trubina, 'Sidewalk Fix, Elite Maneuvering and Improvement Sensibilities: The Urban Improvement Campaign in Moscow,' *Journal of Transport Geography* 83 (2020); Markus Lähteenmäki and Michał Murawski, 'Blagoustroistvo: Infrastructure, Determinism, (Re-)Coloniality and Social Engineering in Moscow, 1917–2022,' *Comparative Studies in Society and History* 65, no. 3 (2023): 1–29; Maria Gunko et al., 'From Policy Mobility to Top-down Policy Transfer: "Comfortization" of Russian Cities beyond Neoliberal Rationality,' *Environment and Planning* 40, no. 6 (2022): 1382–400.

22 The State Duma of the Russian Federation, 'Federal Law on Retail Markets and Changes to the Labor Code of the Russian Federation,' Federal Law No. 271, 12 December 2006.

23 Moscow Renovation Programme, Government of Moscow, 2017, *https://stroi.mos.ru/novaia-proghramma-rienovatsii-piatietazhiek*

24 '5 лет Реновации: Сколько Расселили, Построили, Как Подорожали Пятиэтажки [5 Years of Renovation: How Many Were Resettled, How Much Was Built and How Expensive the Housing Got],' *RBC*, 1 July 2022, *https://realty.rbc.ru/news/62be89af9a794755a480bf3b*

Fashion Street, Sadovod Shopping Complex, Moscow, 2022

the disciplining of the oligarchs but also as mise-en-scènes of fantasy and symbolism of national unification, comfort, growing uncertainty, antagonisms, discontent, and fragmentation. In the case of Moscow, we need to look at the programme of *blagoustroistvo* that has facilitated and normalised spectacularised consumption and the broad availability of prestige in times of repeated socioeconomic crises.

NEW SPACES AND SPECTACLE'S PRESTIGE

The implementation of *blagoustroistvo* in urban policy and redevelopment practice began in earnest with Putin's presidential decree in May 2018. Several initiatives supported the decree's implementation, including the 'National Priority Project: Formation of a Comfortable Urban Environment,' issued a year earlier in 2017.[25] More detailed blueprints for what particular state agencies claimed to implement and what their clients among the business elite would need to adapt to can be found in the federal trade development strategies. Arguably, the strategies present urban development policy that different spectacles accompany and facilitate. Analysing the two programmes of 2011 and 2019 helps discern essential shifts in the state's aspirational visions of *blagoustroistvo*. Whereas the 2011 strategic plan for the development of commerce focused on creating 'modern commercial formats' such as supermarket chains, the 2019 strategic plan speaks the contemporary language of neoliberal development, aiming at the 'development [...] of a pleasant habitat.'[26] The strategy sets out to promote 'traditional trade formats' such as markets and fairs, seeing them as stimulators of effective demand and facilitators of competition. In contrast to the earlier rhetoric directed at Cherkizovsky, the 2019 strategy proclaims all trade formats to be 'civilised' and aims to develop 'multi-format trade' across Russia.[27] With the onset of Western sanctions, spiralling inflation and a slowing economy, the government appears to

be beginning to openly promote regulated and licensed street trading, standardised kiosks, and open-air markets.[28] Sadovod Market has reflected the impact of these policies and more.

Sadovod is the largest wholesale and retail market in Moscow and a direct successor of Cherkizon. Located in relative proximity to other markets owned by Kievskaya Ploschad, Sadovod (9,500 trading spaces), along with Moskva Market (6,000 spaces) and Yuzhnye Vorota (3,000 spaces) form a network for commercial logistics, warehousing, financial exchange and credit. Of the three, Sadovod is the largest, most diverse and most spectacularly renovated commercial centre.[29] While there are no public figures on the number of vendors and other workers in Sadovod, I estimate the number to be at least 25,000 since each *torgovoe mesto* (trading space) is typically run by at least two people (a trader and an employed seller). However, many solo traders rent small areas and tiny spaces in the narrow corridors of the market. This figure could be a gross underestimation or an exaggeration. One of my interviewees, for example, estimated that there were as many as 100,000 vendors and workers of various kinds. Since the market is an opaque entity to the gaze of state statistics, the numbers remain unmeasurable. Sadovod, like Moskva and Yuzhnye Vorota, is located on the border between the capital and its peripheral regional towns, right on the city's outskirts and next to the MKAD (Moscow Ring Road). This frontier location makes it both a factor in the congestion of the surrounding area and a catalyst for government road expansion projects and redevelopment. The recent widening of the MKAD has relieved the heavy traffic generated by the interregional trucks and buses that bring goods in and out of the capital. The incessant flow of trucks delivers goods to the smaller markets across the European parts of Russia and beyond to the North Caucasus and even the Far East. Additionally, the introduction of a free public bus service

25   Gunko et.al., 'From Policy Mobility to Top-down Policy Transfer,' 1387–88.
26   Ministry of Industry and Trade of the Russian Federation, 'Стратегии Развития Торговли в Российской Федерации на 2011–2015 годы и период до 2020 [Strategy for the Development of Trade in the Russian Federation for 2011–2015 and up to 2020]'; 'Стратегия: Развития Торговли в Российской Федерации до 2025 [Strategy: Development of Trade in the Russian Federation until 2025],' 2019, 1–5.
27   Ministry of Industry and Trade of the Russian Federation, 'Strategy: Development of Trade in the Russian Federation until 2025,' 2019, 4–5.
28   Evgenija Perzeva and Anna Kaledina, 'Срок Выгодности: в России Возрождают Оптово-Розничные Рынки [The Term of Profitability: Russia is Reviving Wholesale and Retail Markets],' *Izvestiya*, 24 May 2022, https://iz.ru/1338669/evgeniia-pertceva-anna-kaledina/srok-vygodnosti-v-rossii-vozrozhdaiut-optovo-roznichnye-rynki
29   Although no exact figures are available, Sadovod's website mentions a daily flow of 250,000 visitors and 9,500 'trading places' (*torgovye mesta*). See the Sadovod official website: *https://sadovodtk.ru/about/*

in 2018 made it easier for customers to reach Sadovod from the local subway stations. Despite its peripheral location, Sadovod arguably consolidates Moscow's position of dominance and socio-economic centrality over the regions. At the same time, Sadovod and other interconnected markets form an alternative socio-economic nexus to the city's historical centre. They accumulate, circulate, and redistribute commercial goods and services, information, and socio-symbolic capital across the country and sometimes beyond.[30] In this broader perspective, Sadovod and other popular markets in Moscow function as vital logistical hubs for capital concentration and regional socio-economic differentiation. The markets distribute goods delivered from China, now usually via Kazakhstan, and create numerous socioeconomic links and dependencies between the country's capital and its many peripheries. The internal spatial transformations in Sadovod, or its economic practices, may also provide examples for other regional governments, commercial elites, and also ordinary traders to imitate and replicate elsewhere across Russia.

By 2022, Sadovod's administration carried out renovations and added several new buildings. In 2020, a new mall-like building named Block B opened that Sadovod's official press release calls a 'turning point in the development of wholesale and retail trade standards' and 'modern retail formats.'[31] Shiny and spotless white on the outside, minimalist and functionalist on the inside, Block B houses cafés and restaurants on the first floor and dedicated lines for online wholesale and retail shops on the second. Unlike the retro-futuristic constructions of the recently built Zaryadye Park near Red Square, which aim to make infrastructure invisible by turning architecture into an ocular spectacle, Sadovod's new space does not hide wiring, pipes and cables.[32] Following the trend of white, minimalist shopping malls, Block B, with its shiny floors, self-contained lighting, supporting columns, and ventilation pipes, seems to reflect Sadovod's industrial surroundings, such as Moscow's oil refinery. Here, the visitor's mind

will juxtapose the semi-transparent walls and smooth surfaces of the mall with the aged box-like warehouses and rows of modified shipping containers from the open-air market, while the pyramid-shaped concrete pipes of the nearby refinery rise like giant concrete volcanoes somewhere on the horizon. This socio-material concentration reflects not only the proverbial uneven capitalist development but also a more evolutionary and gradual approach by the state in projecting its power to modernise, 'civilise,' and make 'comfortable' these commercial spaces. In contrast to the erasure of Cherkizon and the levelling of the kiosks, the case of Sadovod shows how patron-client relations between the ruling and commercial elites in Moscow can result in the remaking of the market into a multi-layered and multi-formatted commercial centre. This remaking of popular informal markets, and the renovations and infrastructural improvements that normalise them, also create new forms of social stratification and spectacles of enchanted, prestigious consumption and veracity.

Sadovod's renovation became much more visibly spectacular by the end of 2022. For example, the so-called 'Fashion Street' or 'Loft Fashion' in passageways number five and fourteen in the clothes section as well as the 'Fashionable Street' in Block B feature renovated and expanded pavilions, expensive pavements, artificial trees, high-quality wooden benches, and unusual mannequins. The radio announcements and YouTube advertisements for the opened brands and lines claim a particularly luxurious quality to the shirts, coats, and shoes sold there. The garments themselves, while usually much more expensive, are not necessarily much different from those sold elsewhere in Sadovod. However, the market is now able to emphasise, advertise, and claim the conspicuous consumption, glamour, and privilege associated with high-end boutiques for itself.

Nevertheless, because these shoes, bags, coats and suits are usually just high-quality copies of existing Western brands, they

30 For the early discussion on Moscow development into a global capitalist city before the imposition of Western sanctions as well as the context of Moscow developing into a polycentric megaregion, see: Robert Argenbright, 'Moscow on the Rise: From Primate City to Megaregion,' *Geographical Review* 103, no. 1 (2013): 20–36; Vladimir Kolossov and John O'Loughlin, 'How Moscow is Becoming a Capitalist Mega-City,' *International Social Science Journal* 56, no. 181 (2004): 413–27.

31 'Новый 'Садовод': Как Открытие Нового ТЦ Изменит Формат и Культуру Торговли [New 'Sadovod': How the Opening of the New Mall Will Change the Format and Culture of Trade],' Sadovod website, https://oaosadovod.ru/news/novosti/novyy-sadovod-kak-otkrytie-novogo-tts-izmenit-format-i-kulturu-torgovli-/

32 Michał Murawski, 'Falshfasad,' *American Ethnologist* 49, no. 4 (2022): 461–77.

Moskva Mall, Moscow, 2022

remain relatively affordable. Sadovod's high-end retail lines perform prestige and status by rewiring Russian consumption habits into 'low-end globalisation.'[33] When I was casually talking with traders and vendors in 2022, some mentioned jokingly that the goods sold on Fashion Street are all 'fake' just like every-where else. The vendors on Fashion Street usually speak good Russian and proudly claim to work in boutiques, rather than in 'containers' or 'pavilions.' In that sense, they may look condescendingly at their neighbours from other lines who offer cheaper copies in comparison to selling superior goods that are *fabrichnoe proizvodstvo* (factory-made). Sellers circulate between different parts of the markets, changing employers. They form different networks and connections with each other, which leads them to maintain a degree of solidarity despite working in these different environments. More research needs to be done to understand the emergence of new signs of class distinctions in the markets and how the workers inhabit and use them. The luxury spaces such as Fashion Street and Fashion Loft are just some of many mark-ers of the emerging class divide in popular

markets such as Sadovod. The growing digital divide between those merchants who are in-tegrated into e-commerce and those without a popular online presence is another. Alongside these and many other lines and processes of fragmentation, the market has also produced sites that attempt to unify and centralise the spatial experience or produce a convenient cover that enables many other events and socioeconomic relations to take place.

COMMEMORATIVE SPECTACLES AND SYMBOLIC INTEGRATION

Recent renovations of Sadovod have created a space with a central focal point that effec-tively transforms the continuous flows of movement and dispersed stopping points into a much more unified and symbolically cen-tralised space. For example, Sadovod's main street, renovated around 2017–2018 includes a fountain and a public sculpture consisting of three-dimensional letters and a heart that reads 'I love Sadovod.' Wooden benches surround the fountain, while an exhibition of photography or reproductions of paintings surround the benches from the outside. In

67

September 2022, the booths celebrated 'City Day' and displayed large photographs and informational posters about Moscow's architectural landmarks. These included Stalin's Baroque high-rises and the recently opened Zaryadye Park.

From the perspective of casual retail customers and visiting wholesalers, both Cherkizovsky and, until recently, Sadovod were relatively functional spaces. They had minimal recreational infrastructure, little atmospheric decoration, and mall-style lighting. Except for the tourist markets in the Izmailovo Kremlin, which also currently functions as a children's entertainment centre, and possibly Slavyanskij Mir, most popular markets in Moscow have seldomly performed strong socio-symbolic connections to Russian historical imaginaries, the architectural centre of Moscow, or the regional neighbourhoods. Usually, the vernacular and highly mediatised expression referred to the markets of the 1990s and early 2000s as self-enclosed entities or *states within states* as depicted in the television series: *Cherkizona. One-off People*. Several waves of urban renovation have changed this. They have integrated the markets of Moscow, and Sadovod in particular, in partial but seemingly effective ways. Sadovod's fountain square and the regular exhibitions around it now symbolically link the market to Moscow's urban core, producing signifiers that evoke Soviet-era ideals of *kulturnost* (cultured-ness), which now intermixes with neoliberal symbols and aesthetics of prestige.[34] Sadovod's central speakers play a mix of Russian chanson and pop songs, presumably intended to appeal to the average consumer from Russia's peripheries or Moscow's working class. The ambient musical soundscapes, as well as the exhibition displays near the fountain, are signs that aim to anchor the heterogeneous market flows in a national cultural core. Sound takes over the diversity of signs and affects them, re-signifying and delimiting them as a Russian national space. The Sadovod administration has also organised exhibitions of children's drawings, chess competitions, and celebrations of the

Jewish holidays Yom Kippur and Hanukkah in the market's synagogue, and hosted numerous delegations of foreign garment manufacturers and state officials.[35]

The market also attempts to normalise its presence as a social and public space integrated into the neighbouring communities and the capital city as a whole. The most important of these public relations campaigns is probably Sadovod's participation in the celebrations of 9 May. This day commemorates the victory of the USSR over Nazi Germany in the Second World War and has become the hallmark of Russian nationalism.[36] The Kremlin has almost completely appropriated the representation of the memory of World War II, instrumentalising it as a justification for its neo-imperial ambitions and war frontiers. Since 2014, Sadovod has been holding annual celebrations of the events with invited veterans, parades of men and women in 1950s military uniforms, and exhibitions of old cars and even replicas of weapons and tanks. The focus on retro re-enactments and aesthetics, glorifying past military victories and replaying Soviet nostalgia, has integrated the state's ideological imaginary as part of the market's social space. A variety of commemorative events took place all over the city before their cancellation in 2023, ostensibly due to security reasons. From 2014 to 2019, colourful celebratory leaflets and flowers with the Sadovod logo appeared regularly in the central parks and squares of Moscow. Specially hired young men and women distributed various gifts to pedestrians and random car drivers. Meanwhile, a concert stage was set up in Sadovod and singers and bands performed during the commemorative festivals. Sadovod also organises other festivities on its premises throughout the year. For instance, the management organised highly visible celebrations of the New Year and City Day until the COVID-19 lockdowns. Contrastingly, the Islamic celebrations of Kurban Bayram (Eid al-Adha) and Uraza Bayram (Eid al-Fitr) remain largely inconspicuous or completely invisible to the general public and Sadovod's surrounding neighbourhoods. Until 2019, the

34 Catriona Kelly and Vadim Volkov, 'Directed Desires: Kul'turnost' and Consumption,' in *Constructing Russian Culture in the Age of Revolution: 1881–1940*, eds. Catriona Kelly and David Shepherd (Oxford: Oxford University Press, 1988), 291–313; Sheila Fitzpatrick, *The Cultural Front: Power and Culture in Revolutionary Russia* (Ithaca: Cornell University Press, 2018).
35 As reported by Sadovod Trade Complex, 2023, https://sadovodtk.ru/news/
36 Helge Blakkisrud, *Russia Before and After Crimea: Nationalism and Identity, 2010–17* (Edinburgh: Edinburgh University Press, 2017); Zeffry Alkatiri and Reynaldo De Archellie, 'National Patriotic Day Parade: The Politics of Historical Memory and Reconstruction of the Russian Identity during Putin Era,' *Cogent Arts & Humanities* 8, no. 1 (2021); Gulnaz Sharafutdinova, *The Red Mirror: Putin's Leadership and Russia's Insecure Identity* (Oxford: Oxford University Press, 2020).

Market tents outside Moskva Mall, Moscow, 2022

celebratory collective prayer Salat al-Eid was usually held in a parking lot at the neighbouring Yuzhnye Vorota Market, rather than in Sadovod itself.

The staging and performing of Russian national celebrations such as the New Year, Victory Day (9 May), or Defender of the Fatherland Day (23 February), and others synchronise or intertwine the heterogeneous temporalities of market flows with the state national calendar and its focus on the construction of a collective national memory based on post-Soviet reinterpretations of the sacrifices of the Second World War. The 9 May celebrations in Moscow are spectacles that valorise the pride of military victory and sacralise the ideas of sacrifice and territorial defence against the invaders, now understood as the hostile, collective West. Interestingly, however, the 9 May celebrations in 2022 in Sadovod seemed rather low-key and inconspicuous. They paled in comparison to the playful and spectacular re-enactments and celebrations of previous years. In 2023, the official celebrations were cancelled in many cities in Russia, and barely occurred in Sadovod. It seems that the symbolic temporal connection between federal state power and market spaces like Sadovod is weakening, and the market reacquires a degree of symbolic distance and autonomy.

How do market workers experience this spatial fragmentation, growing social stratification, and intense presence of state power as *blagoustroistvo*, police raids, or everyday presence in patriotic songs played on the Sadovod's speakers? The narrative of a dream had by one of my interlocutors during COVID-19 lockdowns in 2020 seems to capture the state's intense yet incredibly ambiguous and frightening presence. Azim, one of my long-time interlocutors, was working in Sadovod at the time as a broker and vendor and recorded the following dream of meeting the Russian President.

'I dreamt that I saw President Vladimir Vladimirovich Putin, and he turned out to be our relative. He came to our house. We had a long sofa and a table, and he sat with us and talked to my grandmother and grandfather. All fifteen people were sitting there, and he was so serious. I wanted to take a selfie with him, but he said no. I got mad at him and I walked out and he left too, but not with me. I walked out of the house and down the street. There was a black Porsche. In the Porsche was a security guard, Ivan, dressed in black. He got out of the car and said, "Come here." I said, "What do you want?" He said, "Here, this is my business card; take it!" I thought he was trying to distract me so he could force me into his car because I felt like he had a taser in his hands. So, I kind of ran away from him and that was the end of the dream.'

Azim's dream demonstrates the close relationship between fragmentation, splintering, Russian state power, and deportable migrant market workers. The kinship between Azim, his extended family, and the Russian head of state underscores the intimate familiarity that many Central Asian market workers feel with Russian sovereign and biopolitical power. The domestic space of the dream minimises and domesticates state power, which usually communicates through television, legislation documents, and police officers. At the same time, this power is withdrawn, cold and distant, as when Putin refused to take a selfie with Azim. The withdrawal of the Russian state, which turns into a deadly threat, is revealed in what seems to be the obscene double of power – the security guard Ivan. Dressed 'in black' and standing next to an expensive sports car, Ivan represents aspirational prestige, status, and an uncanny resemblance to Putin himself, who is often depicted in memes wearing a black suit and dark glasses. Is this, therefore, another manifestation of unified power and its other face as a subordinated guard or an independent power representing the state's unruly multiplicity? This double of power lures Azim with a 'business card,' but maybe he is actually planning to taser him, shove him into the back of his sports car, and kidnap him. During the lockdowns and the daily restrictions on workers' mobility, this split, double-faced power seems to have become especially palpable. Azim's narrative appears to represent state power as a unified force linked through the similitude of their dress and relations of subordination.

However, in his pre-war oneiric experience of the state, the very presence of the potentially threatening security guard may arguably point to the anticipation of emergent sources of violence both alongside and independent of the state. Something that has become a pertinent force in 2023 with the visibility of private armies and the figure of Prigozhin. The launch of the Kremlin's so-called 'special military operation' is likely to intensify for many Azim's contradictory and ambiguous experiences of the state power's simultaneous proximity, distance, threat and fragmentation. Especially for those market workers who, like Ferusa, have acquired Russian citizenship, the threatening figure of the bodyguard and the unknown dangers of the streets in Azim's dream may overshadow the social imagination of kinship with the Russian state. The deportability is here replaced or enhanced with the deportability into new frontiers and their war fronts. Meanwhile, the materialisation of both *blagoustroistvo* and Russian national state ideology, with its military retro aesthetics of pseudo-Soviet nostalgia, appears in a much more weakened and mono-semiotic form vulnerable to avoidance and appropriation.

INHABITING THE MARKET'S BORDERSCAPES

Ferusa, the street vendor whose son was conscripted to the army, as well as other traders, porters and panhandlers in Sadovod, increasingly find themselves living in spaces prescribed by ideological spectacles of national military memory and newly emerging stratified environments. The latter continues to perform the sterile whiteness and modernity that may continue to be relatively affordable for the popular masses, yet coded and spatialised as luxury and prestigious consumption. These newly constructed spaces overlap with the logistical aesthetics and functionalism of the era of shipping container markets and their early modifications. The commodification of the markets does not so much erase earlier formats as it creates a layered, uneven development and more centralised, categorised, and ritualised forms of movement and orientation.

Earlier, the chapter analysed the spectacles reaffirming the social imagination of closed national borders as well as the hierarchical patronage of the state over business elites. Using the example of the closure of the Cherkizovsky market and other police raids on Sadovod aimed at cracking down on undocumented migration, labour conflicts, or illegal cash banks, this brief examination reveals the disciplinary side of the urban spectacle as it plays out in Sadovod. The spectacle of capitalist enchantment and disciplinary intimidation do not exhaust the borderscapes of the market and the spaces where informal improvisation and exteriority interconnect with state power. Therefore, the last section outlined the existence of the symbolic and commemorative spectacle. The retro aesthetics and parades of the 9 May celebrations turn Sadovod and other similar markets into event spaces that reproduce the social imagination of a collective multinational state. Arguably, the decline of these spectacles and celebrations since 2022 speaks of the state's symbolic failure to impose its military frontiers as cultural hegemony and produce popular border spectacles in spaces of popular consumption. Instead, the typically mundane encounter and casual conversation between a street vendor and a customer, such as my aunt, produced an 'obscene supplement' of rumour and narrative.

These publicly invisible representations and expressions, feelings, grievances, and narratives, in this particular case, linked the experiences of Ferusa's son, his friend, and the military border zones with the Russian customer and then with myself. Encounters like these circulate among relatives, media, and online platforms, often with open-ended effects: they can naturalise the presence of the war fronts and their imposition of the deportability of citizens (and occasionally non-citizens) to the frontlines, or they can generate indignation, resistance, resilience, and solidarity. Customers, vendors, and their families spread rumours, speculate, argue, debate, and judge the morality of each other's actions, talk about their fortunes and misfortunes in the everyday conversations that circulate in kitchens and on social media. They condemn or support governments, take sides, and ponder the future or next steps. Thus, the market emerges as an interface

Gorbushka Market, Moscow, 2006

of interactions between different kinds of borders, market workers and their customers, and multiple forms of spectacles. Without being spectacular, such market encounters remain both disruptive and complementary to the state frontier and border spectacles. They link the informal spaces of popular economies of survival and resilience to the formalising and mobilising power of the state and potentially to its failures.

As we have already seen with Azim, inhabiting such interfaces and intersections and being exposed to the longer histories and legacies of Soviet and Russian state power manifests itself as an ambiguous relationship. It is the relationship to the double of the state as a relative in the kitchen and a potential kidnapper on the street. The urban spectacles of comfort, the Kremlin's nationalist ideology of remembrance, and the current deportation and frontier regimes may often turn markets into events of such doubling. At the same time, the markets continue to be much more than that. The revival of markets like Sadovod intensifies the flow and circulation of low-cost goods that must be constantly assembled and reassembled, broken into smaller or larger units, taped, sealed, marked, repaired, packaged,

and repackaged in order to be shipped across the country and beyond. The merchants and vendors use these goods, packages and boxes as an anti-spectacular architecture that steals the voids of new and old commercial spaces, snatching the possibilities of existing spatial configurations to create temporary furniture, sofas, and walls or curtains out of commercial circulation, at the temporal border between the realisation of the commodity's value and its consumption. This is to say that while the regulated projects of blagoustroistvo multiply and create new socio-economic borders, and generate demarcations that compartmentalise movement with dominant centres, they also generate and reproduce outsides and voids that the workers fill and appropriate. The large packages on which the vendors often sit, lie, or sleep create interstices of comfort and pleasure that exist as another kind of standard and value of urban habitation to the projects of patronal neoliberal comfort. These anti-spectacular architectures create practices of another type of blagoustroistvo where the workers assemble and reassemble commodities into temporary environments for dreaming and relaxing, where the power of different kinds of border spectacle opens up possibilities for imagining it becoming an ambiguous double, emergent force, or something entirely different. As the market workers subjectify and improvise around these newly constructed spaces, their constellation of practices and dreams heralds a new spatiality of popular resilience and imagination.

REFERENCES

Abakumova, M., et al. 'Короли Российской Недвижимости – 2019. Рейтинг Форбс [The Kings of Russian Real Estate–2019. Forbes Ranking].' *Forbes,* 25 January 2019. https://www.forbes.ru/biznes-photogallery/371499-koroli-rossiyskoy-nedvizhimosti-2019-reyting-forbes

Adams, L. *The Spectacular State: Culture and National Identity in Uzbekistan.* Durham: Duke University Press, 2010.

Alkatiri, Z., and R. De Archellie. 'National Patriotic Day Parade: The Politics of Historical Memory and Reconstruction of the Russian Identity during the Putin Era.' *Cogent Arts & Humanities* 8, no. 1 (2021).

Argenbright, R. 'Moscow on the Rise: From Primate City to Megaregion.' *Geographical Review* 103, no. 1 (2013): 20–36.

Barsukova, S. 'Informal Practices of Big Business in the Post-Soviet Period: From Oligarchs To "Kings of State Orders."' *Demokratizatsiya: The Journal of Post-Soviet Democratization*, 27, no. 1 (2019): 31–49.

Blakkisrud, H. *Russia Before and After Crimea: Nationalism and Identity, 2010–17.* Edinburgh: Edinburgh University Press, 2017.

'Cherkizovsky Market.' Other Markets (research blog). http://www.othermarkets.org/index.php?tdid=8&part=1&txt=1&poststart=0

Brambilla, C., et al. *Borderscaping: Imaginations and Practices of Border Making.* Oxford: Routledge, 2016.

Büdenbender, M & Zupan, D. 'The Evolution of Neoliberal Urbanism in Moscow: 1992-2015.' *Antipode* 49, no. 2 (2017): 294–313.

De Genova, N. 'Spectacles of Migrant "Illegality": The Scene of Exclusion, the Obscene of Inclusion.' *Ethnic and Racial Studies* 36, no. 7 (2013): 1180–98.

Diatlov, V., et al. *Базар и Город: Люди, Пространства, Образы* [Bazar and the City: People, Spaces, and Images]. Irkutsk: Irkutsk State University, 2019.

Dzarasov, R. *The Conundrum of Russian Capitalism: The Post-Soviet Economy in the World System.* London: Pluto Press, 2014.

Fitzpatrick, S. *The Cultural Front: Power and Culture in Revolutionary Russia.* Ithaca: Cornell University Press, 2018.

Geertz C. *Negara: The Theatre State in 19th Century Bali.* Princeton: Princeton University Press, 1980.

Gunko, M., et al. 'From Policy Mobility to Top-down Policy Transfer: "Comfortization" of Russian Cities beyond Neoliberal Rationality.' *Environment and Planning* 40, no. 6 (2022): 1382–400.

Hutchings, S., et al. *Ethnicity and Race on Russian Television: Mediating Post-Soviet Difference.* Oxford: Taylor & Francis, 2015.

Kelly, C. and V. Volkov. 'Directed Desires: Kul'turnost' and Consumption.' In *Constructing Russian Culture in the Age of Revolution, 1881–1940*, edited by C. Kelly and D. Shepherd, 291–313. Oxford: Oxford University Press, 1988.

Koch, N. *The Geopolitics of Spectacle: Space, Synecdoche, and the New Capitals of Asia.* Ithaca: Cornell University Press, n.d.

Kolossov, V., and J. O'Loughlin. 'How Moscow is Becoming a Capitalist Mega-City.' *International Social Science Journal* 56, no. 181 (2004): 413–27.

Kordonsky, S. *Socio-Economic Foundations of the Russian Post-Soviet Regime: The Resource-Based Economy and Estate-Based Social Structure of Contemporary Russia.* New York: Columbia University Press, 2016.

Kumar Rajaram, P., and C. Grundy-Warr. *Borderscapes: Hidden Geographies and Politics at Territory's Edge.* Minneapolis: University of Minnesota Press, 2007.

Lähteenmäki, M., and M. Murawski. 'Blagoustroistvo: Infrastructure, Determinism, (Re-)Coloniality, and Social Engineering in Moscow, 1917–2022.' *Comparative Studies in Society and History* 65, no. 3 (April 2023): 1–29.

Malinova, O. 'Framing the Collective Memory of the 1990s as a Legitimation Tool for Putin's Regime.' *Problems of Post-Communism* 68, no. 5 (September 2021): 429–41.

Matthews, G. *Ghetto at the Center of the World: Chungking Mansions, Hong Kong.* Chicago: University of Chicago Press, 2011.

Mbembe, A. 'Necropolitics.' *Public Culture* 15, no. 1 (Winter 2003): 11–40.

Mezzadra, S., and B. Neilson. *Border as Method, or, the Multiplication of Labor.* Durham: Duke University Press, 2013.

Mörtenböck, P., and H. Mooshammer. *Networked Cultures: Parallel Architectures and the Politics of Space.* Rotterdam: nai010 publishers, 2008.

Murawski, M. 'Falshfasad.' *American Ethnologist* 49, no. 4 (2022): 461–77.

Sharafutdinova, G. *The Red Mirror: Putin's Leadership and Russia's Insecure Identity.* Oxford: Oxford University Press, 2020.

Szelényi, I. and Mihlyi, P. *Rent-Seekers, Profits, Wages and Inequality: The Top 20%.* London: Springer International Publishing, 2018.

Tolz, V., and S. Harding. 'From "Compatriots" to "Aliens": The Changing Coverage of Migration on Russian Television.' *The Russian Review* 74, no. 3 (2015): 452–77.

Townsley, E., et al. *Making Capitalism Without Capitalists: Class Formation and Elite Struggles in Post-communist Central Europe.* London: Verso, 1998.

Trubina, E. 'Sidewalk Fix, Elite Maneuvering and Improvement Sensibilities: The Urban Improvement Campaign in Moscow.' *Journal of Transport Geography* 83 (2020).

Zhalobova, M., R. Badanin, and A. Zaharov. 'Год Азербайджана в России. Портрет Года Нисанова, человека, Умеющего Дружить и Торговать [The Year of Azerbaijan in Russia. Portrait of God Nisanov, a Man who Knows how to Make friends and Trade].' *Project Media,* 16 December 2020. https://www.proekt.media/portrait/god-nisanov/

1990-1995
1 Collapse of the USSR
2 Transition to a market-based economy
3 Cherkizovsky Market's opening, Sadovod Market's inception
4 Cherkizovsky Market vendors start importing their goods using the 'grey customs clearance'.

1995-2000
5 Law (de)regulating street trade and markets passed
6 Opening of Stalin's bunker museum
7 Synagogue opened at Cherkizovsky Market
8 Approvement of plans to expand Cherkizovsky Market
9 Beginning of campaign to attract foreign workers

2000-2005
10 Fire at the Cherkizovsky Market
11 Sadovod Market's modernisation
12 Powerful fire causes Cherkizovsky Market roof to collapse.

2005-2010
13 State-led investigation of Cherkizovsky Market
14 Crackdown on informal markets
15 Informal banking network 'Hawala' appears at Cherkizovsky Market.
16 Racially motivated bomb blast at Cherkizovsky Market kills fourteen and injures many visitors at the market.
17 Vladimir Putin approves plans to ban foreigners from trading at open-air markets.
18 Confiscation of 6,000 containers of smuggled goods intended for sale at Cherkizovsky Market
19 Policies introduced to ban all open-air markets
20 Official closure of Cherkizovsky Market
21 Beginning of a severe displacement of foreign traders due to the market's closure
22 Demolition of Cherkizovsky Market

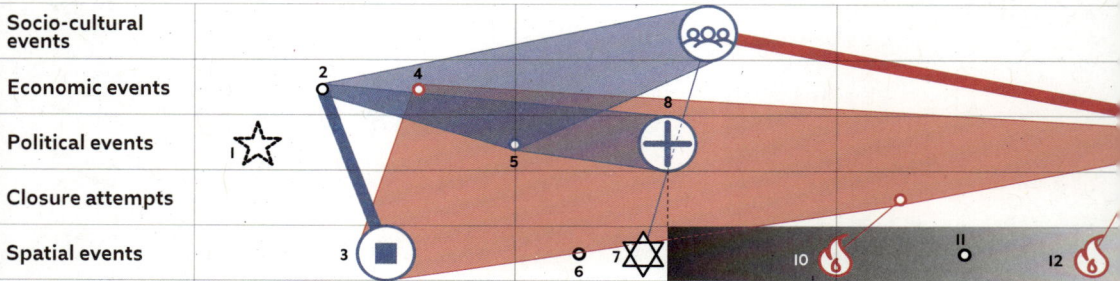

Socio-cultural events

Economic events

Political events

Closure attempts

Spatial events

Spatial expansion of Cherkizovsky Ma

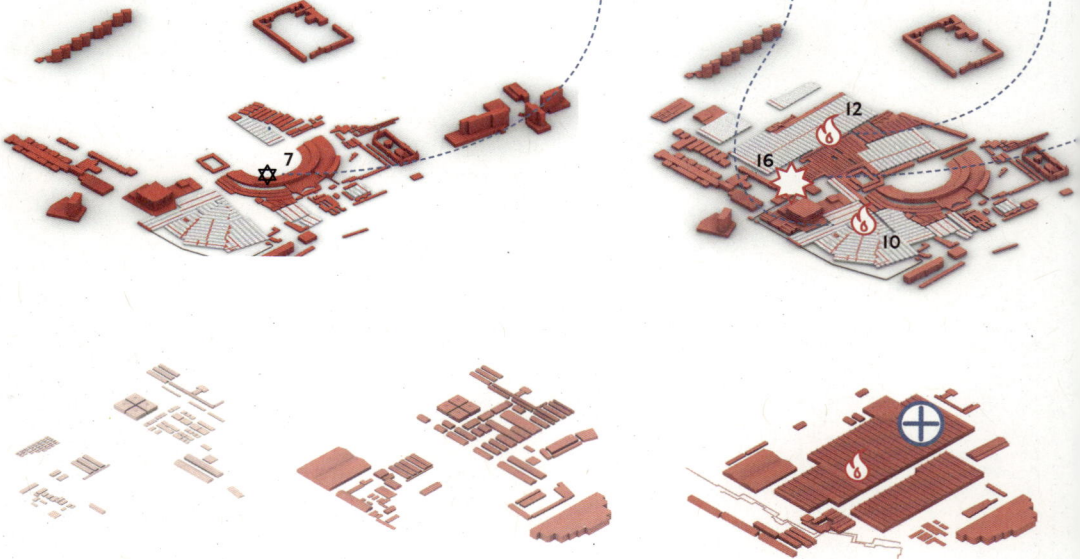

1990 1991 1992 1993 1994 1995 1996 1997 1998 1999 2000 2001 2002 2003 2004

Timeline of key events shaping the transformation of Moscow's informal markets

74

2010-2015

23 Fire at Sadovod Market
24 Increase in the migrant workforce at Sadovod Market
25 Rebranded Sadovod Shopping Complex undergoes major renovation and expansion.
26 Migrant workers found in illegal underground sweatshops at the site of the former Cherkizovsky Market
27 Beginning of investigations and raids to reduce criminality at the Sadovod Shopping Complex

2015-2023

28 More than 20,000m² added to the already existing 40,000m² of the Sadovod Shopping Complex
29 Market workers' protests at the Sadovod Shopping Complex
30 Reports on the use of cryptocurrency in Moscow's informal markets as an informal money transfer system
31 Demolition of informal kiosks and shops in Moscow
32 Market workers' riots at the Sadovod Shopping Complex
33 Completion of Sadovod's expansion.
34 Raids in Sadovod, Lyublino and Food City targeting foreign workers
35 Money laundering using cryptocurrency as well as fire safety named as key reasons for the raids

36 Public demonstrations at the Sadovod Shopping Complex
37 Sadovod24 online platform launches in response to restrictions due to the COVID-19 pandemic.
38 Russia plans to increase taxes for e-commerce.
39 Fire at the Sadovod Shopping Complex
40 Public demonstrations at the Sadovod Shopping Complex

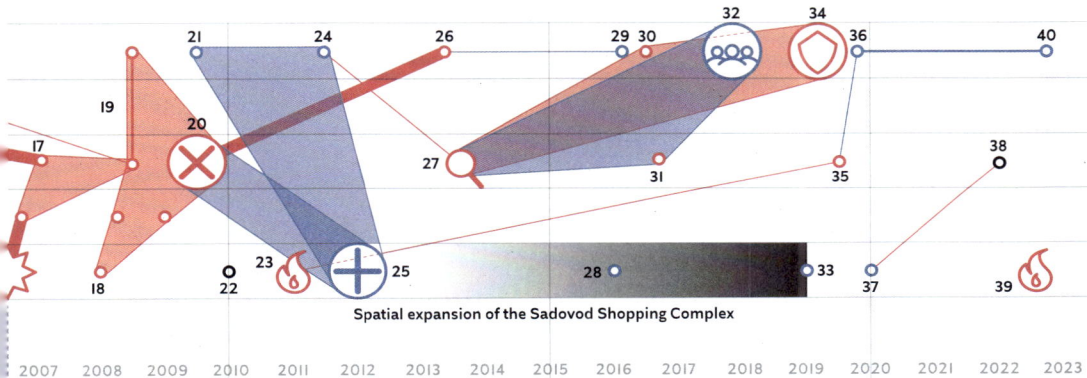

Spatial expansion of the Sadovod Shopping Complex

2007 2008 2009 2010 2011 2012 2013 2014 2015 2016 2017 2018 2019 2020 2021 2022 2023

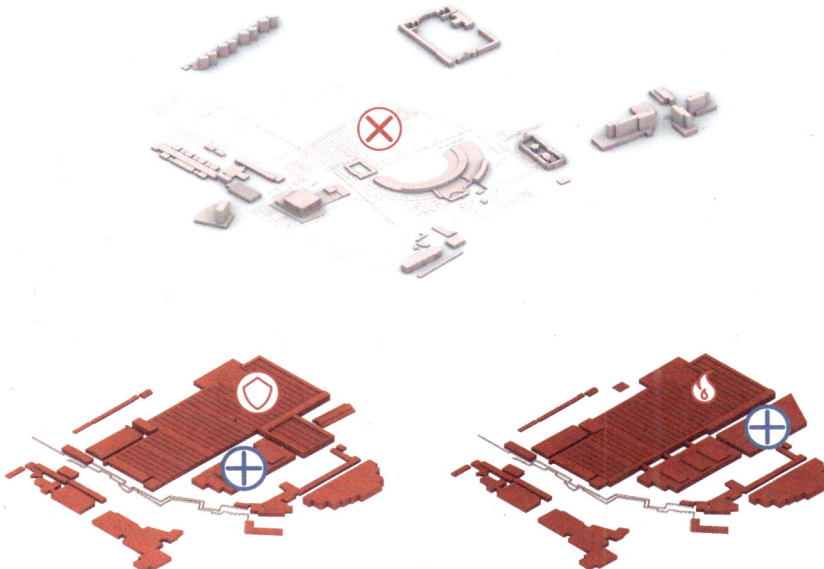

■ Spatial, social, economic and political interventions into in/formal markets
■ Informality as a survival method and means of adapting to changing socio-economic and political circumstances

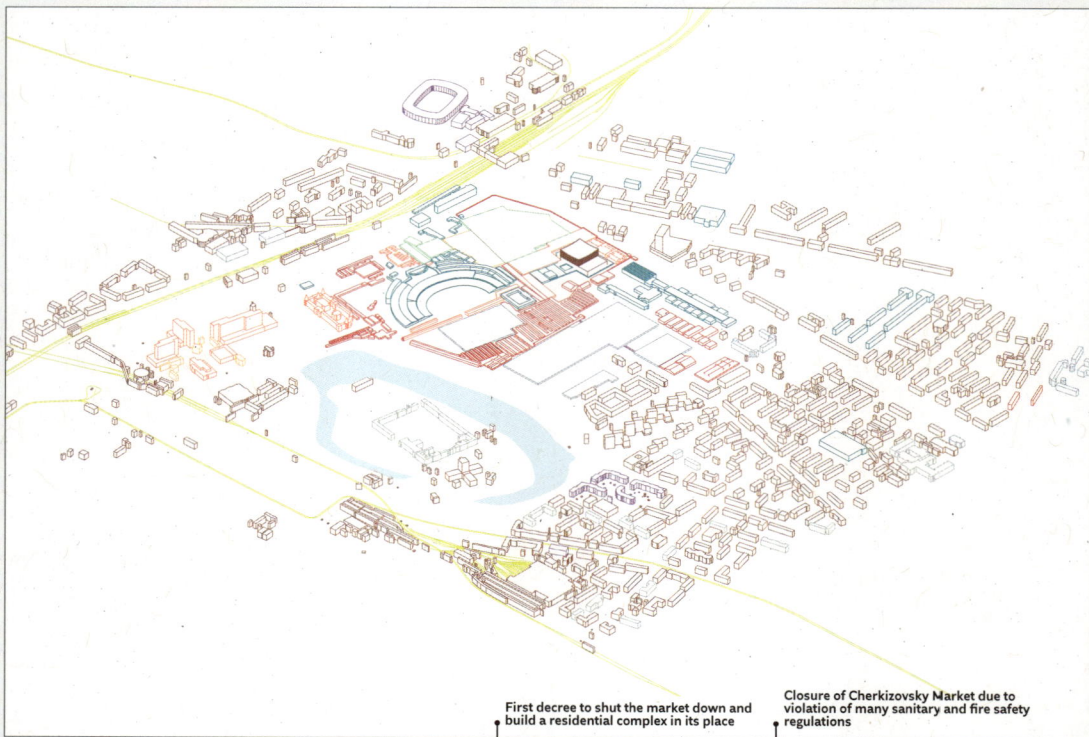

First decree to shut the market down and build a residential complex in its place

Closure of Cherkizovsky Market due to violation of many sanitary and fire safety regulations

■ 1671　■ 1953　■ 1989　■ 1996　■ 1998　■ 2001　■ 2003　■ 2007　■ 2009

Construction of Izmaylovo Estate

Opening of Cherkizovsky Market on an area of 234 hectares

Second attempt to close the market; proposal to reconstruct sections of the market as a shopping centre

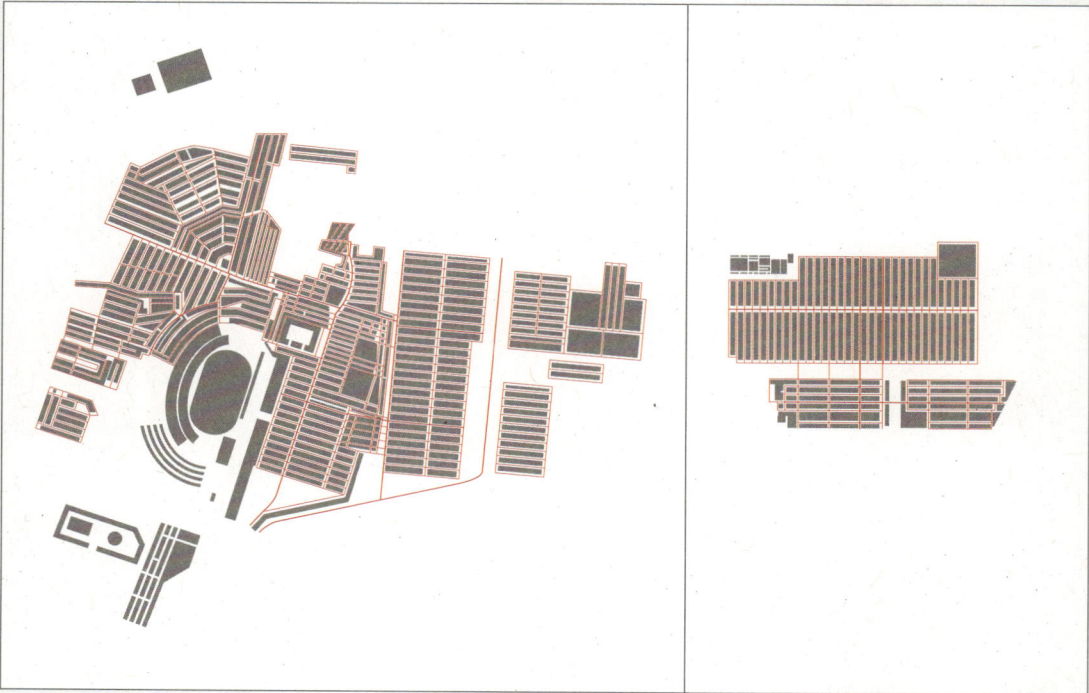

0m　100　200　400　800m

Top:　　Cherkizovsky Market neighbourhood: key phases of spatial development
Bottom:　Comparison of footprints of Cherkizovsky Market (left) and Sadovod Shopping Complex (right)

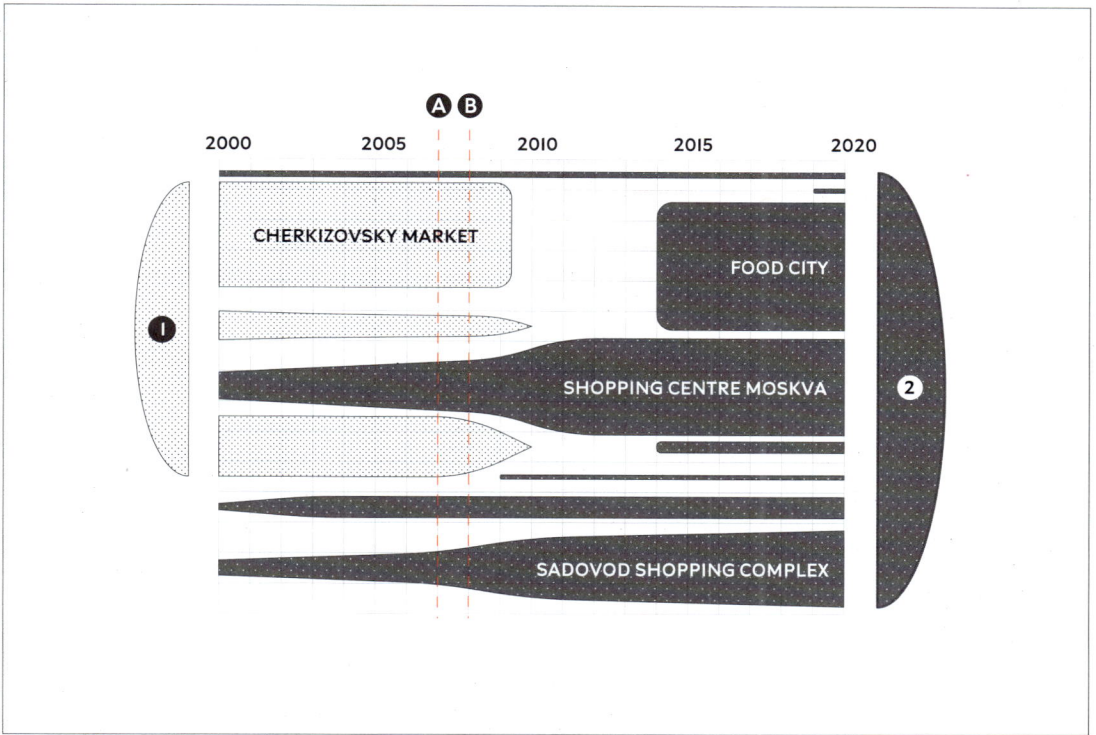

Changes in footprint of different marketplaces in Moscow between 2000 and 2020

I footprint in 2000: 1,235,000 m²
2 footprint in 2020: 2,300,000 m²

A Ban on foreign workers in outdoor markets (2007)
B Introduction of policies which aimed to close all outdoor markets (2008)

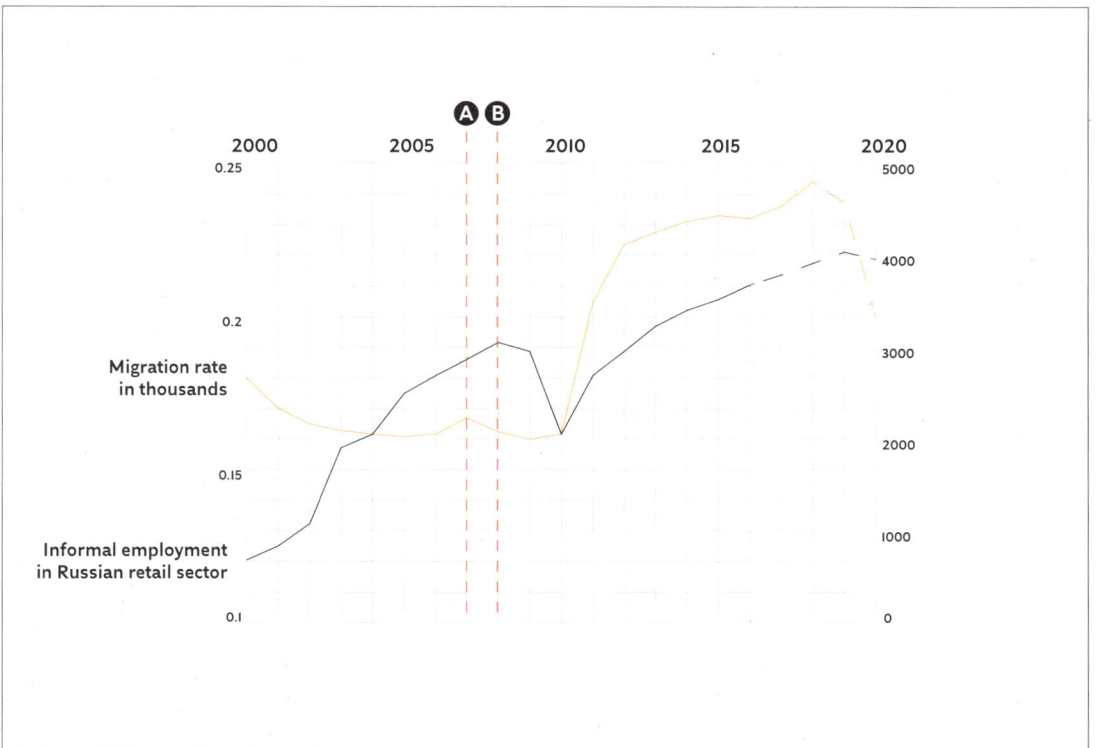

Changes in migration rate and informal employment in the retail sector in Russia between 2000 and 2020

Typical infrastructural components, Cherkizovsky Market, Moscow

Improvised canopy facilitated
for market trade under all
weather conditions

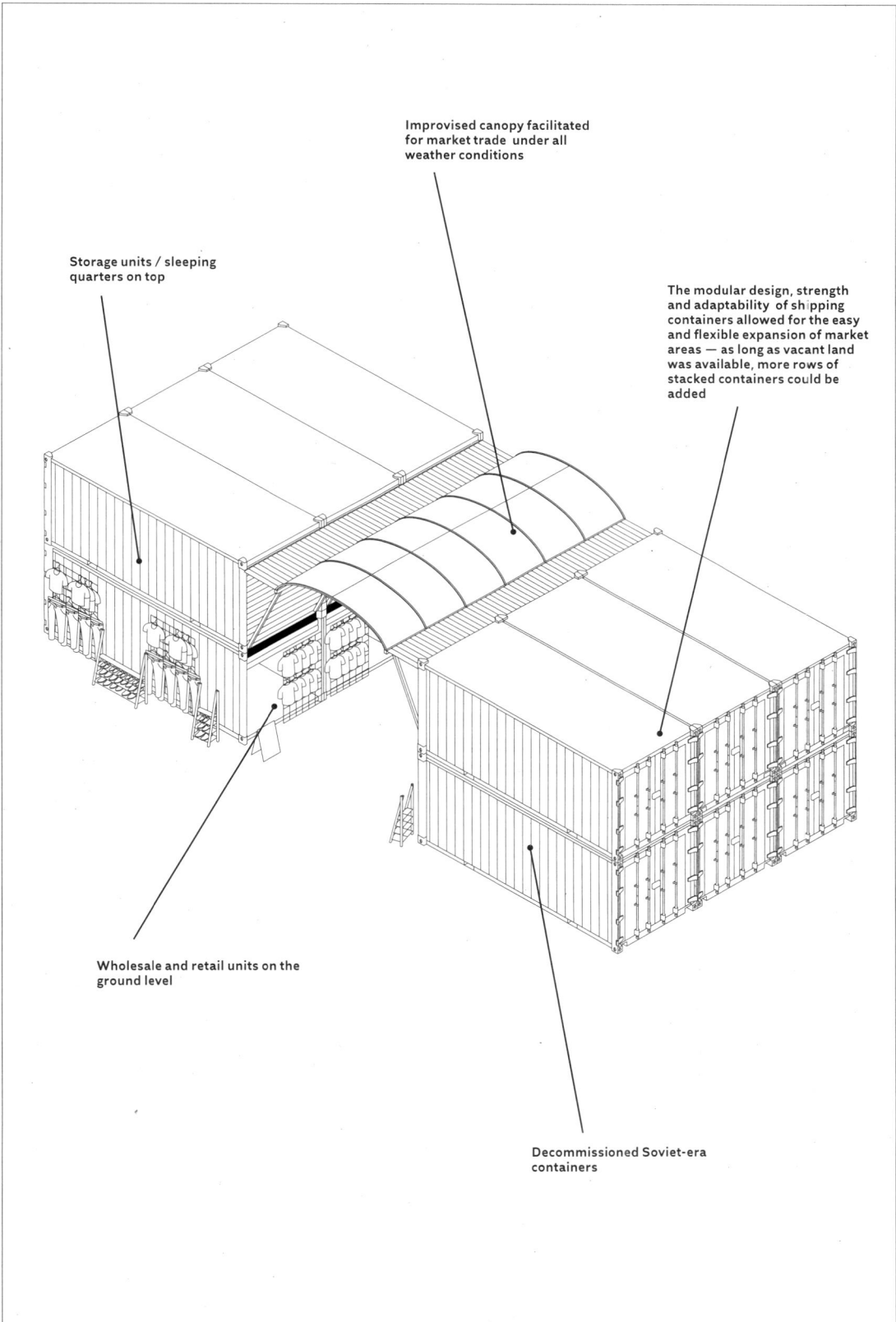

Storage units / sleeping
quarters on top

The modular design, strength
and adaptability of shipping
containers allowed for the easy
and flexible expansion of market
areas — as long as vacant land
was available, more rows of
stacked containers could be
added

Wholesale and retail units on the
ground level

Decommissioned Soviet-era
containers

Decommissioned containers served as primary building blocks for large parts of Cherkizovsky Market, Moscow.

0   2,5   5m

The vendor's family

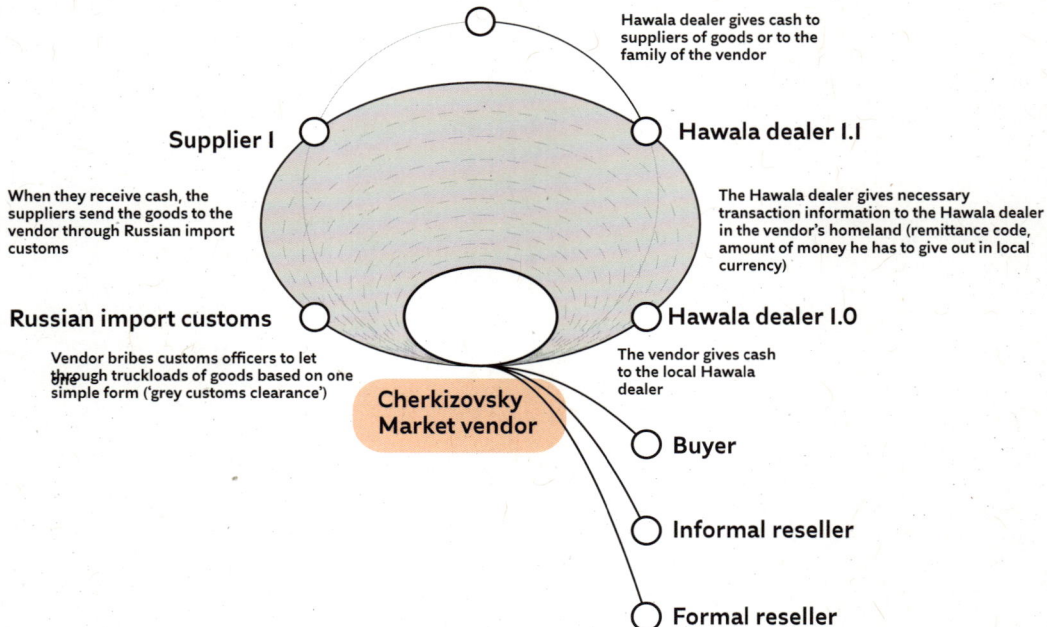

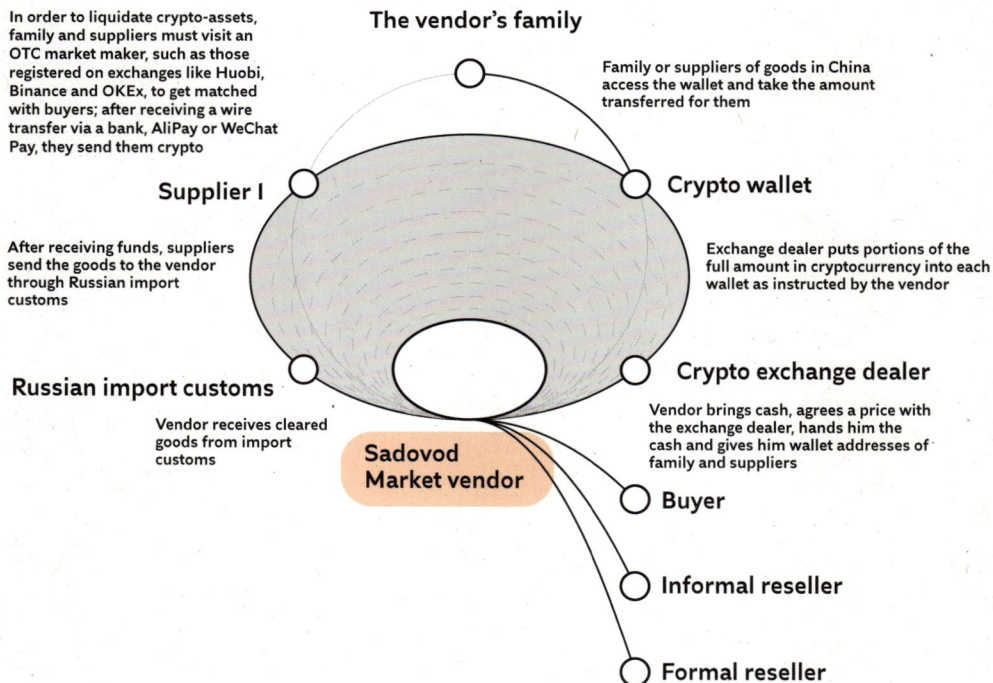

Supplier I

When they receive cash, the suppliers send the goods to the vendor through Russian import customs

Russian import customs

Vendor bribes customs officers to let through truckloads of goods based on one simple form ('grey customs clearance')

Cherkizovsky Market vendor

Hawala dealer gives cash to suppliers of goods or to the family of the vendor

Hawala dealer I.1

The Hawala dealer gives necessary transaction information to the Hawala dealer in the vendor's homeland (remittance code, amount of money he has to give out in local currency)

Hawala dealer I.0

The vendor gives cash to the local Hawala dealer

Buyer

Informal reseller

Formal reseller

In order to liquidate crypto-assets, family and suppliers must visit an OTC market maker, such as those registered on exchanges like Huobi, Binance and OKEx, to get matched with buyers; after receiving a wire transfer via a bank, AliPay or WeChat Pay, they send them crypto

The vendor's family

Family or suppliers of goods in China access the wallet and take the amount transferred for them

Supplier I

After receiving funds, suppliers send the goods to the vendor through Russian import customs

Crypto wallet

Exchange dealer puts portions of the full amount in cryptocurrency into each wallet as instructed by the vendor

Russian import customs

Vendor receives cleared goods from import customs

Crypto exchange dealer

Vendor brings cash, agrees a price with the exchange dealer, hands him the cash and gives him wallet addresses of family and suppliers

Sadovod Market vendor

Buyer

Informal reseller

Formal reseller

Comparison of market operations: Cherkizovsky Market (top) and Sadovod Shopping Complex (bottom)

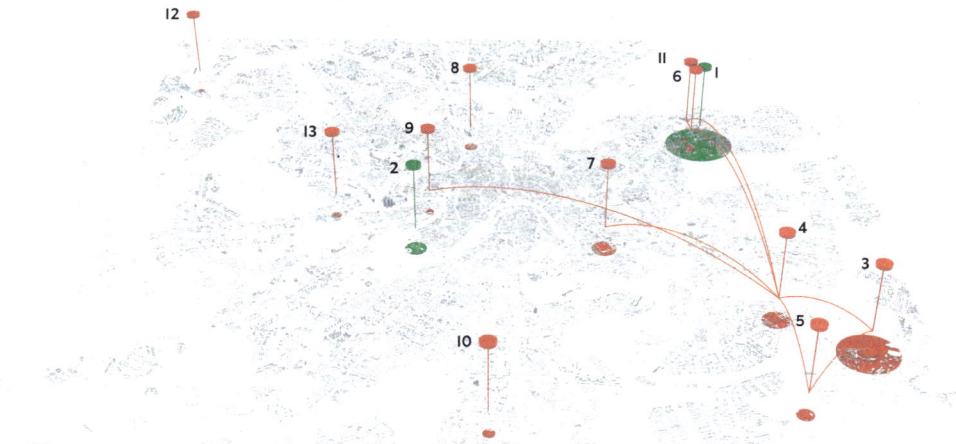

Retail areas of post-Soviet informal markets and contemporary informal markets:

1 Cherkizovsky market area
   50 hectares

2 Luzhniki market area
   15 hectares

65 hectares

Post-Soviet informal
markets total area

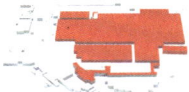

3 Sadovod market area
   40 hectares

4 Moskva mall area
   17,5 hectares

5 Juzhnye Vorota mall area
   11 hectares

6 Izmailovsky Kremlin area
   3,5 hectares

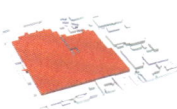

7 Dubrovka market area
   16,5 hectares

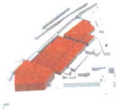

8 Savelovsky mall area
   5 hectares

9 Evropeysky mall area
   18 hectares

10 Electronics Paradise +
   El Dorado mall area
   1.5 hectares

11 Novocherkizovsky market area
   1 hectare

12 Mitinsky mall area
   >1 hectare

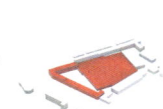

13 Gorbushka market area
   6 hectares

121 hectares

Contemporary informal
markets total area

Spatial footprints of major marketplaces in Moscow: post-Soviet (green) and contemporary markets (red)

1   Old ACT Market
2   Ilyev Market
3   Rosklas Market
4   Izmailovsky Market
5   Produce market
6   Entrance to Bunker Museum
7   Synagogue

8   Stadium
9   'Fora Bank' ATM
10   Storage
11   Izmailovsky Kremlin
12   Arson attack on 26 March 2005
13   Russian Court / Business Centre
14   Vernisazh crafts market

15   Long distance buses
16   Chinese restaurants
17   Uzbek restaurants
18   Chinese food market
19   Vietnamese food market
20   Bomb blast on 21 August 2006
21   Eurasia Market

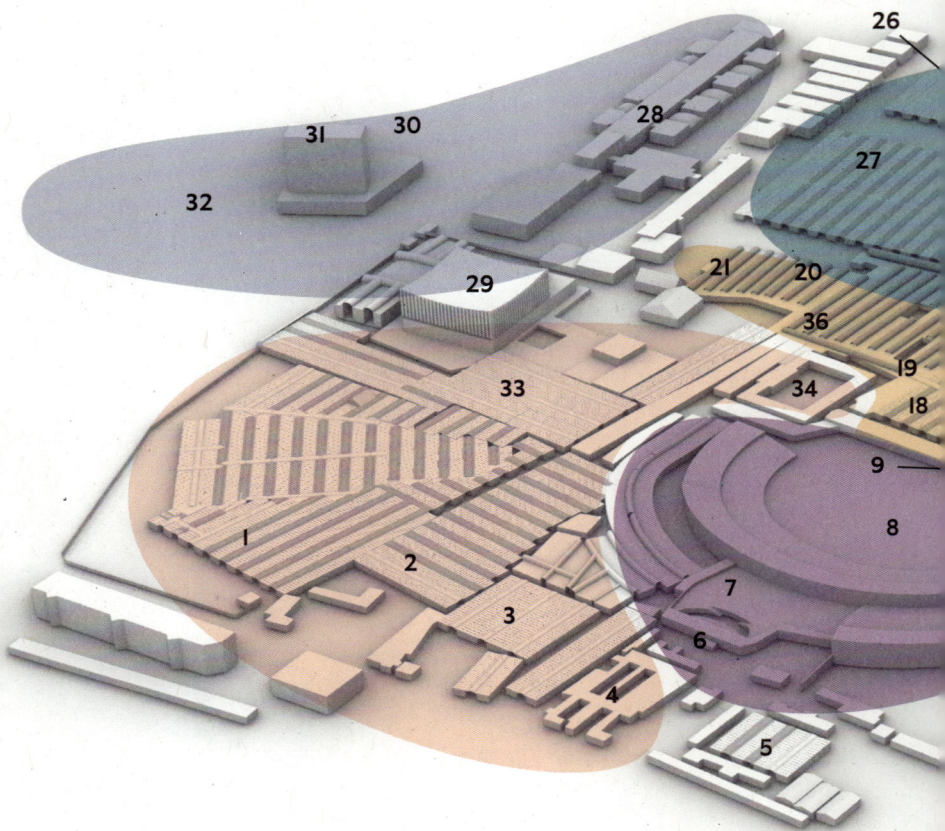

Main sections of Cherkizovsky Market, Moscow and locations of key sites and events

22 Long-distance buses
23 Warehouses
24 Taxi, minibuses
25 Fair ground
26 Souvenir market
27 ACT Market
28 Russian State University of
    Physical Education (RGUFK)

29 RGUFK Sports Complex
30 Clothing and leather goods
31 Consulate of Tajikistan
32 Cherkizovskaya metro station
33 New Eurasia Market
34 Yellow House
35 Golden ("Seagull") Market

36 Lilac Market
37 AST Mall

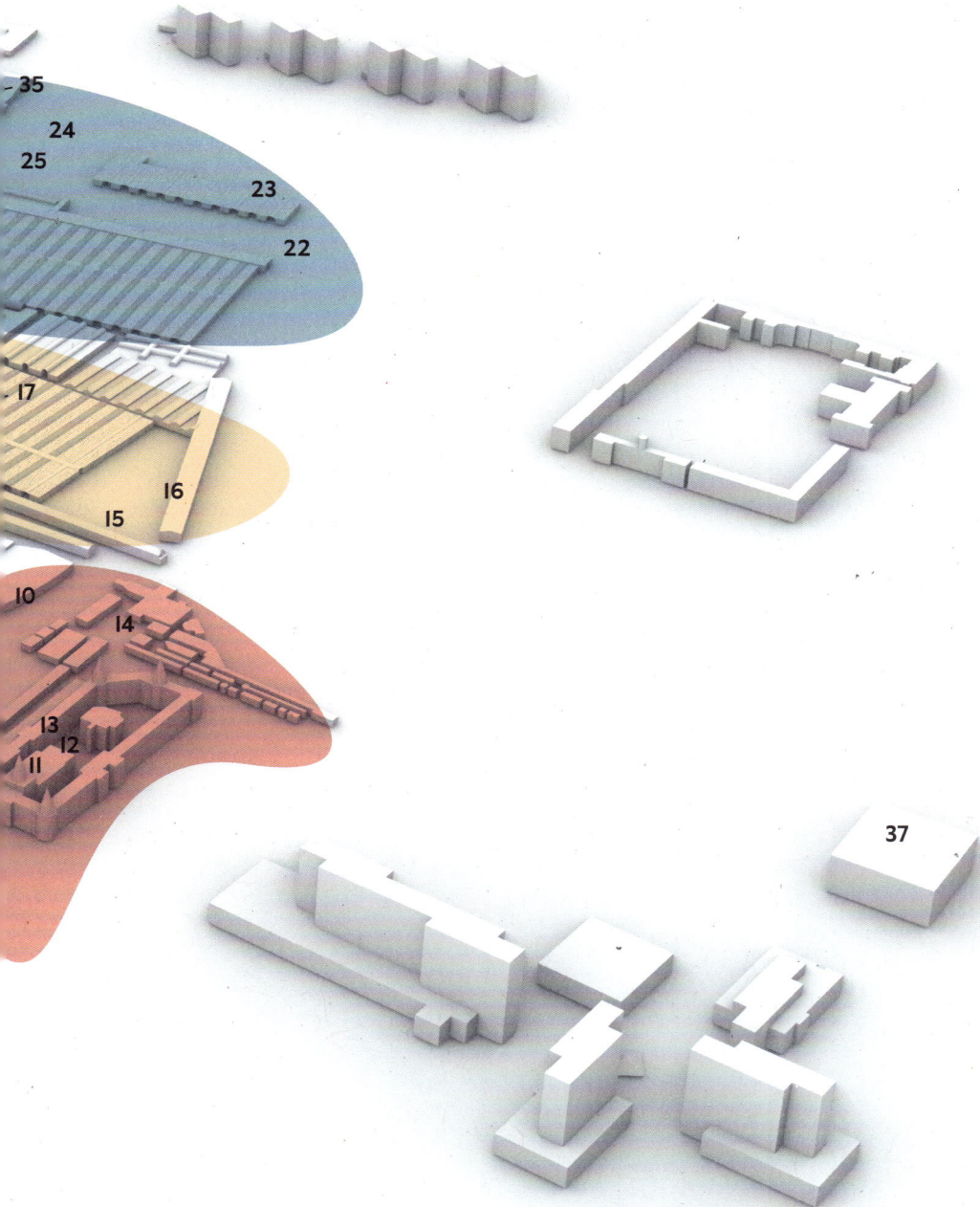

35

24

25

23

22

17

16

15

10

14

13

12

11

37

■ Eurasia market   ■ ACT market   ■ Old ACT Market   ■ Tourist market   ■ State educational facility   ■ Stadium

СОМРНО

Cherkizovsky Market

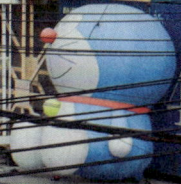

Always One Plaza, adjacent to Saphan Lek Market (demolished), Bangkok, 2023

Trude Laura Renwick

Waterways, Heritage, and the Politics of 'Good' Commerce in Bangkok

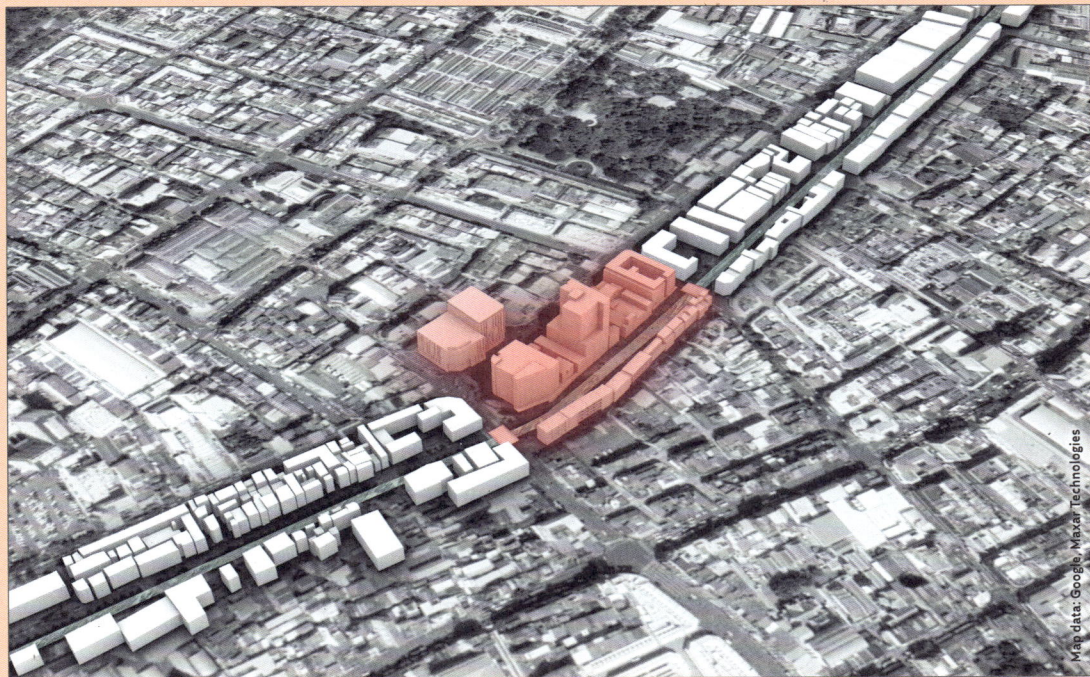

Map data: Google, Maxar Technologies

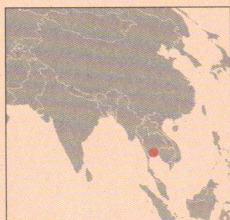

In March 2021, it was announced that Thailand would receive an award from the UN-Habitat Regional Office for Asia and the Pacific for its renovation project of Klong Ong Ang or the Ong Ang Canal in Bangkok. Until 2015, Klong Ong Ang, one of the oldest centres for trade in Bangkok, was the location of the Saphan Lek Market. This market was built atop the canal on concrete pylons and consisted of densely packed shops where vendors sold counterfeit goods and toys. As a 'red zone,' police regularly raided shops and confiscated counterfeit and pirated products from the Saphan Lek Market.[1] After persisting for decades in this neighbourhood despite eviction warnings, the market was dismantled in October 2015 by the municipal government of Bangkok. Vendors were given only two weeks of notice before the eviction.

87

1 Peter Mörtenböck and Helge Mooshammer, 'Bangkok's Red Zones,' in *Informal Market Worlds: The Architecture of Economic Pressure - Atlas* eds. Peter Mörtenböck and Helge Mooshammer (Rottterdam: nai010 publishers, 2015), 28–35.

Erected on top of the covered-up Ong Ang Canal, Saphan Lek Market was a dense labyrinth of stalls that specialised in consumer electronics and toys.

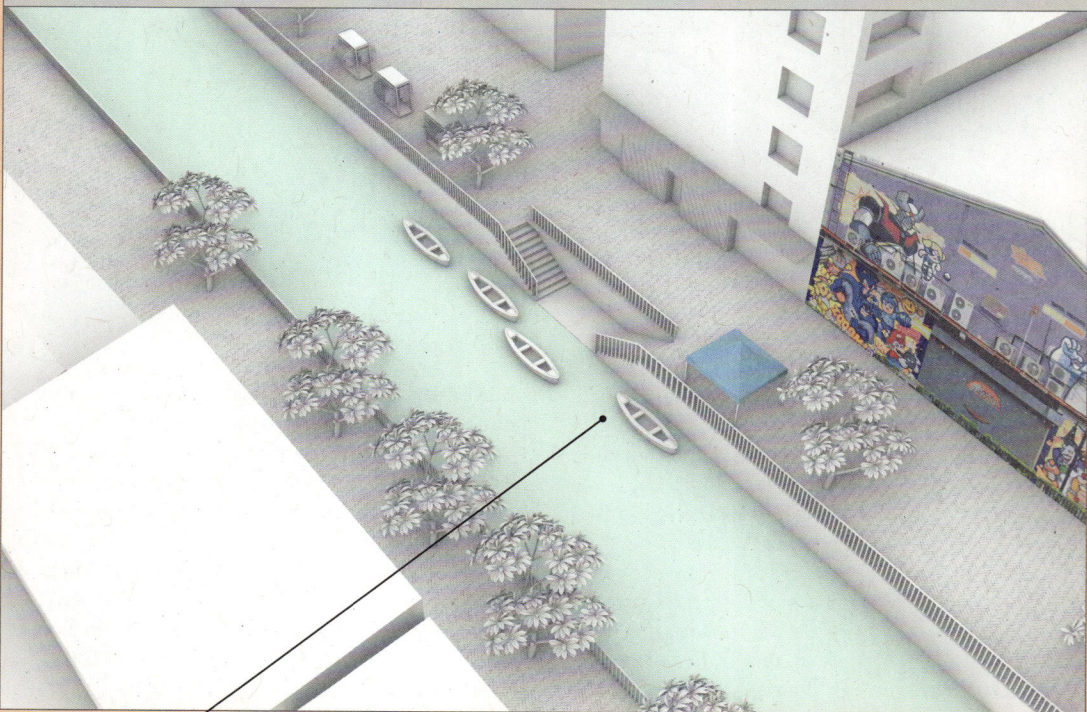

After the demolition of Saphan Lek Market in 2015, the banks of the canal were converted into the Khlong Ong Ang Walking Street. Street markets are organised on weekends and free kayaking is offered to tourists and locals in order to promote the area.

Several years after its demolition, the 2020 UN Asian Townscape Awards celebrated the transformation of this once bustling market into a walking street (pedestrian precinct), enforced by the Bangkok Metropolitan Administration (BMA).[2] Where a dense labyrinth of shops once covered the canal, a wide, mostly empty brick sidewalk with large murals now defines the banks of Klong Ong Ang. Walking along the newly renovated canal market, open only in the evenings Friday through Sunday, one encounters a number of vendors scattered along its banks. While some of these vendors include individuals who previously sold in the Saphan Lek Market, most evicted vendors now trade in a mall just a block from the canal.

At first glance, this forced closure of the Saphan Lek Market and the canal's reopening as the Khlong Ong Ang Walking Street could be considered a token example of urban renovation and/or gentrification. However, if one visits this site or discusses the new market with the vendors who currently and previously sold along the canal, the story is not so black and white. Many of the Saphan Lek Market vendors managed to survive total eviction from this district. Their survival, however, owes no thanks to the municipal government's award-winning canal revitalisation project. Drawing on interviews and fieldwork with street vendors, their advocates, and government officials from the past decade, this analysis gives context to the eviction of the Saphan Lek Market vendors and the street vending restrictions in Thailand that began in 2014 and accelerated in 2016. The forced closure of the Saphan Lek Market and the reopening of the canal reflects the unique position of street markets relative to nation-building in Thailand.[3]

HISTORY OF THE ONG ANG CANAL – STREET MARKETS, NATION-BUILDING, AND MINORITY IDENTITY IN BANGKOK

Throughout Thailand's modern history, nation-building and street vending have existed in a push and pull relationship. Street vending has always been a predominantly minority practice grounded in the Chinese community as they were neither required nor obligated to undertake corvée labour for the king in the city's earliest years. During times of economic crisis laws and restrictions on street vending are often relaxed. However, during periods of military rule and political unrest, urban problems are often blamed on street vendors who are framed as outsiders infringing upon the rights of Bangkok's rightful urban citizens. As one of Bangkok's oldest commercial areas, established in 1783, the Ong Ang community has been a part of this push and pull relationship between nation-building and street vending since its beginnings.

Ong Ang is adjacent to Yaowarat or Chinatown and the Phahurat neighbourhood. While Yaowarat is well known for its street food, Phahurat is defined by its large Indian population and textile shops. When the capital of Thailand was moved from Ayutthaya to Bangkok in the eighteenth century along the Chao Phraya River, Bangkok was a Chinese trading village. The ethnic Chinese population living on the proposed site of the grand palace was relocated just south of Rattanakosin Island when the complex was constructed in the 1780s by Rama I, the first king of the Chakri Dynasty. Two canals were constructed to create the mandala-inspired layout of the capital. Canals in Bangkok served as transportation routes as well as sites of commerce in the city's early decades as the capital. Ong Ang is the second outer canal. Its name meaning pottery canal, is a nod to the pottery market first located on this site.

Dubbed 'the Venice of the East,' early images and postcards of Bangkok feature the canal's

2   In the case of the Asian Townscape Awards, the winners are selected on the basis that they meet five criteria including: 'Harmonious coexistence with regional environment; safety, convenience and sustainability; respect for regional culture and history; high artistic quality; and contributions to local development, capabilities of becoming models for other cities.' Municipal governments, developers, and architects apply for these awards rather than being nominated by a third party. '2022 Asian Townscape Awards: Call for Applications,' UN-Habitat Regional Office for Asia and the Pacific (Fukuoka), *https://fukuoka.unhabitat.org/en/information/4092/*

3   Trude Renwick, 'Jay Fai and the Anomaly of the "Good" Street Vendor,' *Food, Culture & Society* 24, no. 1 (January 2021): 127–41.

iconic bridges (Saphan) that have since been reconstructed in different styles. Saphan Han, or swivel bridge, has been referred to as Bangkok's Rialto Bridge. As Bangkok's roadways were developed in the late nineteenth and early twentieth century, markets and vending activities moved to the city's new roads. In 1962 bridges in this neighbourhood would be replaced with reinforced concrete structures to support the growing number of cars in the city. Although this new infrastructure was inserted into the urban fabric, the Ong Ang neighbourhood would remain defined by its narrow alleys, markets and the descendants of predominantly Teochew immigrants. The bridges traversing the Ong Ang Canal are painted white, creating an austere, neoclassical flare to their otherwise minimalist designs. Yet the memory of the early history of Saphan Han and its swivel bridge remains central to the area's identity. Murals have been installed along the canal, depicting early life in this neighbourhood as revolving around the wooden bridge and the waters below. Many postcards and pictures of early Bangkok also feature canal scenes of Ong Ang and similar neighbourhoods.

However, these idyllic images represting early city life in Bangkok fail to capture the tense relationship between the state and Chinese minorities beginning in the nineteenth century. Chinese communities were widely discriminated against throughout the history of Bangkok as capital, especially as economic alliances were formed with European colonial powers over more regionally based powers. Perhaps one of the most famous instances of this discrimination is an article produced by Rama VI or King Vajiravudh in 1914. In his book *The Crown and the Capitalists*, Wasana Wongsurawat describes how in 'The Jews of the East' the king, writing under the pen name Atsawaphhu, stated that:

> 'The Chinese did not come to settle down in [any foreign] land and refuse to become true citizens of other countries. They always feel like speakers of a foreign language. Although some try to assimilate, the secret society leaders

do not allow them to do so. It cannot be denied that they generate wealth from the land, but it should not be forgotten that they also transport that wealth out of the country. As for the part that they must spend in their host country, they try their best to spend as little as possible. The food and utensils they consume daily are also imported from China. Since this is the case, the Chinese must be considered as those who siphon the wealth of their host nation [to their country of origin]. They are like vampires that suck human blood.'[4]

The incendiary and sinophobic language behind this op-ed was partially directed at the Chinese community in Ong and nearby Yaowarat. The Chinese secret societies noted by Vajiravudh were located in these neighbourhoods. Mainly aimed at rich colonial subjects and poor political activists, these comments were meant to challenge Chinese business people to prove their loyalty by donating money to the Crown.[5] However, this language that criticises the consumption of Chinese goods and the community itself has salience to this day.

Although Vajiravudh's diatribes were not always followed with direct action against the Chinese community, Phibun Songkram, the military leader who took over the government after the fall of the absolute monarchy in 1932, built on this anti-Chinese sentiment established in the decades prior to institute discriminatory policies against Chinese minorities. Members of the Chinese community were forced to attend Thai schools, noodle stalls were banned in certain parts of the city, and Chinese publishers were widely censored.[6] Songkram and his government appropriated activities like street vending into a symbol of Thai national identity and heritage. He established markets in every village and city, including Bangkok, where it was located in Sanam Luang or the royal field directly in front of the grand palace. This market would eventually be moved north to Chatuchak District in 1989, where it remains to this day (discussed further in the Train Market

4   Wasana Wongsurawat, *The Crown and the Capitalists: The Ethnic Chinese and the Founding of the Thai Nation* (University of Washington Press, 2019). Translation from Wongsurawat, 68.
5   Wongsurawat, *The Crown and the Capitalists*, 71–73.
6   Wongsurawat, *The Crown and the Capitalists*, 74.

Saphan Lek Market (demolished in 2015), Bangkok, 2012 (top and bottom)

สะพาน 7

Saphan Lek

Saphan Lek Market (demolished in 2015), Bangkok, 2012

Case Study). Under Songkram's rule in the mid-twentieth century, pad Thai was also created by appropriating traditional Chinese noodles into Thai nationalism calling the dish pan-fried 'Thai.'[7] These policies and strategies appropriated Chinese activities into Thai national identity set the groundwork for how street vending and minority groups are dealt with to this day in Thailand. Street vending is to be celebrated as inherently Thai, yet the state must closely regulate it.

Contemporary restrictions on street vending since the last decade of the twentieth century tend to focus on migrant workers from Thailand's peripheries who come to Bangkok seeking income above that of agricultural work. This was partially born out of the 1997 economic crisis. In the years preceding the crisis, Thailand had the fastest-growing economy globally, peaking at 13.3 percent in 1988, according to the World Bank.[8] As the economy grew, so did Bangkok's urban population, with many citizens from agricultural communities moving to the nation's capital to expand their job prospects. However, when the 1997 Asian financial crisis hit, blame focused on the greed of these upwardly mobile populations. Rhetoric produced by the municipal and national government surrounding street vending along the city's sidewalks since the crisis maintains a sinophobic tone established against the Chinese community in the early decades of the twentieth century. Street vendors are considered outsiders infringing upon the rights of Bangkok's citizenry.

'RETURNING THE PAVEMENT TO CITIZENS'

The Saphan Lek Market was shut down amidst restrictions on street vending that began in 2014 and accelerated in 2016 throughout Bangkok. The military-led government, known as the National Council for Peace and Order (NCPO) that came to power after the ousting of populist Prime Minister Yingluck Shinawatra, drove these nationwide restrictions.[9] In Bangkok, this policy was named 'the return of pavements to the citizens.'[10]

Historically the capital's municipal government and Thailand's national government agendas have not always aligned, however, with the appointment of Asawin Kwanmuang as governor in 2016 by the military government, these two major administrative bodies were suddenly working in tandem. Together the municipal and national governments enacted some of the most severe restrictions and largest-scale evictions that the city had seen in decades. District by district, the city government posted notices that vendors would no longer be allowed to operate in these areas and that previous vending permits were void.

In the case of Saphan Lek, the vendors received several eviction warnings in 1997 and 2004, however it was in October 2015 that a fifteen-day notice, permitted under a 1959 martial law, was posted. This was exceptionally short notice compared to other markets that were shut down during this period in Bangkok. This law, established by dictator Gen. Sarit Dhanarajata, permits the clearing of public heritage space. In announcements distributed to the community, the government cited that the market clogged the canal that also constituted a historical site. Requests for a delay in the eviction were denied and the vendors had to remove all of their goods prior to demolition on 19 October. Ultimately 2,700 vendors were displaced after the closure of the Saphan Lek Market. The 750-metre section between Saphan Lek and Osathanon bridge would remain vacant until repairs were made to the canal in 2018.[11]

Other markets to be demolished after Saphan Lek during this period included the Banglamphu Market, Phra Arthit Pier and Chang Pier Markets along the Chao Phraya River. This closure of markets in some of Bangkok's oldest neighbourhoods along the river, served as a precedent for the closure of street markets in Bangkok's modern commercial districts. However, not all of these vendors were treated similarly by authorities. Pak Khlong Dtalat, one of the city's oldest and largest flower and vegetable markets, located a stone's throw away from the Saphan

7   'Finding Pad Thai / Alexandra Greeley,' *Gastronomica* (blog), 10 February 2009, *https://gastronomica.org/2009/02/10/finding-pad-thai/*
8   'GDP growth (annual %) – Thailand,' World Bank Data, https://data.worldbank.org/indicator/NY.GDP.MKTP.KD.ZG?end=1996&locations=TH&start=1985
9   After the 1997 economic crisis, politician and telecommunications tycoon Thaksin Shinawatra came to power. Mainly backed by Thailand's rural populations, Thaksin would be forced out in 2006 and his sister Yingluck Shinawatra would serve as prime minister (2011–2014) until she was ousted by the military.
10 'Giving the Pavement Back to Pedestrians,' *The Nation*, 26 November 2014, *https://www.nationthailand.com/perspective/30248642*
11 Sasiwan Mokkhasen, 'This Is What Saphan Lek Looks Like Now (video),' *Khaosod English* (blog), 14 July 2016, *https://www.khaosodenglish.com/news/bangkok/2016/07/14/saphan-lek-looks-like-now-video/*

Shop at Saphan Lek Market (demolished in 2015), Bangkok, 2012

Lek Market, was also closed in early 2016. Although both these markets were historically located in this portion of the city, their evictions played out very differently. As a red zone, like many markets in Bangkok's more modern commercial districts, Saphan Lek's vendors were less likely to be protected. Red zones are areas closely monitored by Thai authorities due to high levels of piracy and counterfeiting activities. In interviews with authorities and even other vendors and vendor advocates, these markets where the products sold are predominantly 'made in China' are typically considered less worthy of protection. Leaders also see red zones as a global problem. In late July of 2016, the Ministry of Commerce announced that they were aiming to eliminate pirated goods in twenty-seven areas in 2016. In this announcement, the head of the Department of Intellectual Property (DIP) stated that 'if the Thai government could achieve the roadmap, the country's image should improve among foreign investors, and that would draw more investment to the country in the long run.'[12] To control these spaces, the Defence Ministry, the Internal

Security Operations Command, the Royal Thai Police, and the Department of Special Investigation joined forces with the DIP. In contrast, Pak Khlong Dtalat was relocated to several large, public and private sites not far from its previous location. One of these complexes housing Pak Khlong Dtalat's flower vendors is the Yodpiman Riverwalk, a newly developed shopping mall along the river. This mall, designed in a neoclassical colonial style, holds a range of commercial spaces, including a Starbucks and other tourist and flower shops.[13] Not only do these vendors merit the government's support by selling heaps of flowers and vegetables used at shrines and restaurants all over the city, but they also reproduce a well-established nostalgic image of early life in Bangkok that can be sold to an international audience.

THE KHLONG ONG ANG WALKING STREET

After the opening of the Sam Yot MRT subway station in 2019, Saphan Lek and Khlong Ong Ang are now easily accessible from

12   'Sale of Pirate Goods in 27 "Red Zones" to Be Targeted,' *The Nation*, 31 July 2016, *https://www.nationthailand.com/business/econ/30291818*
13   See the chapter 'Precedent or Problem: An Ecology of Thailand's Private Markets' for more details on this heritage mall.

neighbourhoods across the city. Taking the escalators up from the subway, images of the station's revival-style architecture and historical images of tramlines that ran through this neighbourhood until the early twentieth century are featured in its entryways and waiting areas. The entrance to the new canal-side market from the train station is not clearly marked, and the market itself is cut off by Charoen Krung Road, which forces pedestrians to jaywalk across this busy street in order to access the southern portion of the market that flows towards the river. Before the opening of the train station, a long bus ride or boat trip were the main methods of public transportation available to get to the market. Although the market was a walkable distance from some of Bangkok's most prominent tourist hot spots, the heat and inconvenience of walking in this portion of the city made this market an unlikely site for customers to stumble upon.

Visible along the canal, which was once hidden by a maze of shops built on stilts above its polluted waters, are references to government projects focused on environmental improvement throughout the city. The rationale for the evictions of riverside and canal side communities is often connected to large-scale flooding that occurred in the city in 2011.[14] Today signs posted by the BMA throughout the market announce 'together for sustainability.' This rhetoric is also present in articles written about the UN Asian Townscape Awards. In one article written by the tourism authority of Thailand, the text reads as follows:

> 'More recently, a restoration and beautification project by city authorities saw the area transformed from a crowded enclave of hawker stalls and a polluted waterway into the recreational oasis of today that is the Khlong Ong Ang Walking Street. The canal water was cleaned, the canal banks paved with concrete and the historical bridges renovated.'[15]

A small boat launch run by the park service provides free kayaking for tourists and visitors who come to the market. This service echoes the sustainability rhetoric visible in nearby murals and posters produced by the municipal government. When I stopped to chat with those operating the kayaking along the canal, the manager pointed out that they also manage boat services in Lumpini Park, the large, 'central park' of Bangkok.

Large murals painted along the waterway also feature government workers sweeping the sidewalks, historical images of the canal, and children biking. Some of these murals are painted in a brown hue similar to historical images in the newly constructed MRT station.[16] In the southern sections of the walking street intersected by bridges, shops open up onto the carefully laid brick sidewalk. However, one cannot help but notice that many of these murals cover vacant shops. The Khlong Ong Ang Walking Street is also not far from Bangkok's first creative district just south of Saphan Lek and Yaowarat, where numerous bars and Michelin-rated restaurants are opening along the riverside's small streets.[17] Promotional materials for the creative district celebrate the Khlong Ong Ang project, and the murals and art commissioned along the canal are highlighted. These murals include work by Alex Face, Bigdel, Pakorn and Asin, Bonus Tmc, Mauy & MSV, Alaii, Joker EB and artists from Happening Group.

Tesagit, or Bangkok municipal police officers are posted throughout the market. Although it is free to sell in the allotted plots along the canal-side, there remain many empty stretches of designated selling spaces. Vendors sit in small plots that are numbered. There is little room to set up anything larger than a small card table to sell food or goods. Street vendors and shop owners who I interviewed within and around the market did not feel that businesses were doing well along Khlong Ong Ang. Some vendors located along the canal used to sell in the market prior to the eviction.

14 Tunya Sukpanich, 'Living over Troubled Waters,' *Bangkok Post*, 1 January 2012, https://www.bangkokpost.com/thailand/special-reports/273298/living-over-troubled-waters
15 'Award-Winning Khlong Ong Ang Walking Street Isn't Your Average Walking Street,' *TAT Newsroom* (blog), 16 March 2021, https://www.tatnews.org/2021/03/award-winning-khlong-ong-ang-walking-street-isnt-your-average-walking-street/; 'The Changing Nature of Klong Ong Ang,' Thailand NOW, 31 December 2020, https://www.thailandnow.in.th/life-society/the-changing-nature-of-klong-ong-ang/
16 In 2015 the municipal government was also promoting a riverside boulevard project that evicted numerous riverside settlements. This project was eventually put on hold due to resistance from hotel developers along the river.
17 The Thailand Creative Design Center was moved to the Charoen Krung neighbourhood after it was originally established in central Bangkok along Sukhumvit Road atop a luxury mall. This move to Bangkok's riverside was part of a larger nation-building campaign by the military government that emphasised returning to the city's roots through the construction of monumental urban interventions along the Chao Praya River.

One man who was selling antique cards featuring historic sites in Thailand stated that he decided to partially retire after the market closed. He comes to the canal on the weekend to sell a bit as the rent is free, but is now trying to get rid of his stock primarily through online sales. Like many vendors, he doubts that he will return once the government starts charging rent to sell along the canal.

Like other street market areas where evictions occurred, vendors were offered an alternative location quite far from Saphan Lek on the western side of the city. The risk of losing its customer base and a move far away from this neighbourhood where many vendors live was too high. As a result, many decided to sell from a nearby mall: Mega Plaza Saphan Lek, previously known as the Merry King department store. Since 2015, Mega Plaza Saphan Lek was taken over by the Bawornpong company, headed by Vallop Komolwisit, the son of a controversial Thai-Chinese politician Chuwit Komolwisit who grew up in Yaowarat.

Walking through Mega Plaza Saphan Lek, the mall is full of shop owners who once sold in the Saphan Lek Market, creating a similar visual effect. Goods are piled up throughout the mall. In its back corners, boxes of goods are stacked high, and one moves through dizzying aisles of anime figurines and toys. Although Mega Plaza Saphan Lek is a far cry from Bangkok's most famous luxury malls, after paying little or no rent at Saphan Lek, rent at Mega Plaza is a whopping 10,000–12,000 THB per month (290–350 US dollars per month).

When I asked vendors why they choose not to sell in the Khlong Ong Ang Walking Street, they pointed out that the new market space is 'quiet,' making it exceptionally difficult to make ends meet when they can only sell a few days a week along its banks. However, they do return to the canal to sell on holidays like Loi Gratong and the New Year.[18] In addition, returning to sell along the canal banks was made more difficult as the government took three years to launch the new market, forcing vendors to find a new location to sell their goods.

Journalists documenting the transformation of Khlong Ong Ang note that shop owners near the canal state that business has improved to a certain degree and that there are fewer problems related to sewage backup since the government evicted the Saphan Lek vendors. However, some residents complain that the canal area has become quite hot during the day as there are no longer any covered walkways protecting pedestrians. This lack of shade also dissuades potential customers from returning to the neighbourhood and visiting the walking street after the BMA intervention. The municipal government has not responded to requests to carry out additional improvements to the canal side according to some articles.

RED ZONE HERITAGE

Over the past decade, gentrification is a term that has become ubiquitous in debates surrounding the displacement of poorer residents in cities the world over. In contexts like New York, literature on this type of displacement focuses on racial inequality that has led to many minorities being pushed out of once affordable neighbourhoods.[19] Intellectual discourse around gentrification has also expanded globally in tandem to design trends promoting the creative industries, a movement documented by figures like Richard Florida.[20] On the surface level, the eviction of the Saphan Lek vendors can be read as a case of what Lees et al describe as 'planetary gentrification,' where the Thai government is displacing long-standing groups of vendors in the name of environmentalism and the promotion of the creative industries.[21] However, building on the work of Ghertner as well as Thai studies scholarship on displacement more generally, I argue that the term gentrification does not quite capture the complex processes of development and displacement

18   Loi Gratong meaning 'floating lamp/vessel' is a festival found in many Southeast Asian countries in which people create Krathong, small floating containers from leaves and flowers, that are typically set afloat in waterways.
19   Sharon Zukin, 'Gentrification in Three Paradoxes,' City and Community 15, no. 3 (September 2016): 202–07.
20   Richard Florida, Rise of the Creative Class (Tandem Library, 2003); 'Richard Florida Is Sorry,' Suburban Alliance (blog), https://www.suburbanalliance.com.au/single-post/2017/08/21/Richard-Florida-is-sorry
21   Lees et al. argue that a 'state of planetary gentrification' is emerging where cities all over the world are 'leading to institutionalized apartheid, creating new spaces of exclusion justified as progress and even framed as helping the poor.' See: Loretta Lees, Hyun Bang Shin, and Ernesto López-Morales, Planetary Gentrification (Cambridge: Polity Press, 2016).

Inside Mega Plaza, Bangkok, 2022

Top: Ong Ang Canal (just north of the former site of Saphan Lek Market), Bangkok, 2023
Bottom: Market day (Fridays to Sundays) at the new 'Walking Street' along Ong Ang Canal, Bangkok, 2022

playing out in Khlong Ong Ang, as well as in many other Bangkok neighbourhoods.[22]

Ghertner argues that a planetary or global approach to examining gentrification still remains grounded in the North Atlantic and fails to illuminate the complex dynamics surrounding mechanisms of displacement beyond this post-industrial core.[23] While acknowledging that gentrification does occur at a global scale, Ghertner points out that there are 'risks associated with extending this theory into contexts that have strong traditions of public land ownership, socialist land policies, or diverse non-ownership-based tenure regimes.'[24] Labelling displacement in such contexts as gentrification not only simplifies complex histories of displacement playing out within them but also ignores the distinct context from which the term emerged.

In the case of Saphan Lek and the Khlong Ong Ang neighbourhood, the pre-existing commercial ecosystem has been shifted rather than eliminated or totally gentrified in the wake of vendor eviction. The illicit activities that the government has deemed so problematic continue to play out just a block away from where the market once was in Mega Plaza Saphan Lek. Many of the individuals selling along the canal banks during the walking street market are from the neighbourhood. The canal space has also not been turned over to a private developer. Mega Plaza Saphan Lek, where many previous vendors presently sell, is run by a family of Chinese-Thai descent with roots in this portion of the city. Although vendors are now selling in a mall at a much higher rate of rent (from little or no rent to 10,000–12,000 THB per month), it is important to note that this mall was located in the neighbourhood for decades prior to the eviction of the Khlong Ong Ang vendors.

The eviction of vendors from Khlong Ong Ang is also distinct from other types of displacement and 'participatory dispossession' examined by Thai studies scholars. The work of

Hayden Shelby and Eli Elinoff shows well-established community planning programmes are used to move 'informal settlements' to other locations within and outside of Bangkok. Through organisations like the Four Regions Slum Network and the Community Organizations Development Institute (CODI), residents are often voluntarily moved into housing projects that are in some cases, *common-ed* private land.[25] Many street vendors throughout Bangkok, especially those in red zones, however, are not consulted or incorporated into eviction and urban beautification processes.[26] In the case of Saphan Lek, many of the vendors had sold in the market for decades, making alternative sites in the city's peripheries untenable.

The elimination and 'revitalisation' of Saphan Lek Market and other street vendors in 2016 speaks to larger issues related to minority identity, the right to commercial space, and nation-making in Thailand, where certain types of commercial practices are deemed 'good' and 'bad.' Rather than gentrification driven by the politics of land value alone, I argue that karmic politics also play an important role in reshaping Khlong Ong Ang, where success and right to rule are all tied to good deeds done in one's previous life. Wasana Wongsurawat describes how in the early twentieth-century ethnic Chinese populations were divided into 'good' and 'bad' groups along class lines. Wealthy, royalist, Thai-Chinese businessmen were considered 'good' by the Thai state and the poorer communities that were predominantly located within and around Yaowarat were considered revolutionary and 'bad.'[27] In contemporary Bangkok, the 'low' karmic status of street vendors is deemed by many individuals in positions of power to be a fault of their own. As a result, many vendors, considered lacking in wisdom or *panya*, are not incorporated into the planning process by the BMA. Under karmic logic, as a minority group that was previously warned about their red zone status and as space that was seen as causing flooding and

22   See: Asher D. Ghertner, 'Why Gentrification Theory Fails in "Much of the World."' *City* 19, no. 4 (2015): 552 –63.
23   Asher D. Ghertner, 'India's Urban Revolution: Geographies of Displacement beyond Gentrification,' (2014) *Environment and Planning A* 46 (7): 1554–71.
24   Ghertner, 'Why Gentrification Theory Fails,' 1555.
25   See: Eli Elinoff, *Citizen Designs: City-Making and Democracy in Northeastern Thailand* (University of Hawaii Press, 2021); Michael Herzfeld, *Siege of the Spirits: Community and Polity in Bangkok* (Chicago: University of Chicago Press, 2016); Hayden Shelby. *Never Settled: Community, Land, and the Politics of the Urban Commons in Bangkok*. Doctoral Dissertation, University of California Berkeley, 2019.
26   In the case of Saphan Lek, many of the vendors had sold in the market for decades, making alternative sites in the city's peripheries untenable.
27   In her article, 'Rule by Good People,' Daena Funahashi describes how health workers see themselves as 'good people' with *panya* who have taken responsibility for governing in the wake of the military government's rule. With their 'mental immunity' to economic interests and party politics, they can guarantee good governance See: Daena Funahashi, 'Rule by Good People: Health Governance and the Violence of Moral Authority in Thailand,' *Cultural Anthropology* 31, no. 1 (February 2016): 108.

Typical infrastructural components of the new 'Walking Street' along Ong Ang Canal, Bangkok

pollution, from the perspective of officials, the Saphan Lek vendors forewent their right to shape the future of this market. In contrast, the revitalisation of the nearby mall, Mega Plaza Saphan Lek, by the controversial Komolwisit family is considered a 'good' alternative retail space that is not questioned by the municipal government. The family possesses the economic and political power necessary to legitimise their success in the wake of the market's demolition.

According to karmic logic, the historic location and the red zone status of this market made the Saphan Lek market especially problematic. Not only do vendors selling in red zones lack social status, but they sell goods that do not fit the heritage-infused image that governments have so carefully crafted over the past century. This attitude is echoed in interviews I conducted with government figures responsible for these vending restrictions and evictions, as well as vendor advocates. When other red zone vendors in the central commercial district of Pathumwan were evicted, Vallop Suwandee informed me in an interview that 'they are not the good guys' and argued that in fact, vendors in Bangkok's central commercial districts were greedy, opportunistic, and taking advantage of mall developers, property owners, and tourists. In vendor advocacy meetings I attended between 2016 and 2018, this sentiment was echoed when street vendors from red zones like Siam Square (located in the central commercial district of Pathumwan) and Saphan Lek were often framed as 'bad' by other vendors and their advocates.[28] These critics would distinguish their own businesses from those groups by pointing out that the products sold in Siam Square and Saphan Lek were not supporting the Thai economy as they were 'made in China.'

In 2016, the height of the street vending restrictions, many academics, chefs, media outlets, and non-governmental organisations expressed their criticism of these government restrictions. However, municipal government officials pushed back against this criticism. They often pointed out that they were not banning street vending but regulating and supporting it in areas like Chinatown. It is the historic context of Khlong Ong Ang that distinguished the Saphan Lek Market from other red zones and presented a challenge to municipal authorities.[29] How could they eliminate vendors who had been selling in this market for generations while also 'preserving' street vending as a part of national heritage? Applying to the UNESCO award was one way that the Bangkok municipal government could promote ts contentious policies to a global audience and pacify its critics.[30] As a *red zone* located in a *heritage* neighbourhood, Saphan Lek was the perfect market to shut down and reopen as a walking street. The government would not only make an example of vendors in a red zone, but they could also use the walking street to demonstrate their own 'good' governance. The resulting signs thanking vendors for giving back the sidewalk to the public, BMA murals showing government workers cleaning the sidewalk, the environmental rhetoric focused on canal pollution, and the emphasis on creative rather than red zone products reflect this karmic narrative of vendors as 'bad' and the government as 'good.' Drawing on the global discourse surrounding the creative industries, heritage, environmental planning, and intellectual property, the Bangkok government used the Khlong Ong Ang Walking Street and its international recognition to demonstrate its wisdom and right to shape Bangkok's commercial landscape.

The neighbourhood's transformation demonstrates how Saphan Lek Market and its vendors were not just framed as a 'matter out of place' by authorities but also as lacking the capacity or wisdom to consider the nation's greater good.[31] A project like this would not be possible in a neighbourhood lacking such history or where government officials would have to battle developers over the sidewalk.

28   Renwick, 'Jay Fai and the Anomaly of the "Good" Street Vendor,' 127–141.

29   In fact, the Asian Townscape Award is given to a project on the basis that it 'stands in harmony with local history and culture' and 'that it is accepted by local people, and having contributed to local development.' '2022 Asian Townscape Awards: Call for Applications' UN-Habitat Regional Office for Asia and the Pacific (Fukuoka), *https://fukuoka.unhabitat.org/en/information/4092/*

30   In Michael Herzfeld's work, he argues that the heritage language used against certain communities was appropriated by the communities themselves. A process which he calls 'subversive archaism.'
       See: Michael Herzfeld, *Siege of the Spirits: Community and Polity in Bangkok* (Chicago: University of Chicago Press, 2016); Michael Herzfeld, *Subversive Archaism: Troubling Traditionalists and the Politics of National Heritage*, The Lewis Henry Morgan Lectures (Durham, NC: Duke University Press, 2022).

31   Mary Douglas, *Purity and Danger: An Analysis of the Concepts of Pollution and Taboo* (Routledge and Kegan Paul, 1966).

It is the newest iteration of what began in the mid-twentieth century when the weekend market was placed in the royal field, and magazines emphasised this market as an example of 'authentic' Thai culture. The historical context along a polluted Bangkok canal in which this market was set gives the vendors a right to sell on this land and grounds for the government to reclaim it. For those living and selling in this historic neighbourhood, this canal revitalisation project is not new. It is the latest iteration of nation-building projects that appropriate and discipline minority commercial space in Bangkok to sell it to a global audience.

REFERENCES

'2022 Asian Townscape Awards: Call for Applications.' UN-Habitat Regional Office for Asia and the Pacific (Fukuoka). *https://fukuoka.unhabitat.org/en/information/4092/*

'Award-Winning Khlong Ong Ang Walking Street Isn't Your Average Walking Street.' TAT Newsroom (blog), 16 March 2021. *https://www.tatnews.org/2021/03/award-winning-khlong-ong-ang-walking-street-isnt-your-average-walking-street/*

Douglas, M. *Purity and Danger: An Analysis of the Concepts of Pollution and Taboo.* London: Routledge and Kegan Paul, 1966.

Elinoff, E. *Citizen Designs: City-Making and Democracy in Northeastern Thailand.* Honolulu: University of Hawaii Press, 2021.

'Finding Pad Thai / Alexandra Greeley.' *Gastronomica* (blog). 10 February 2009. *https://gastronomica.org/2009/02/10/finding-pad-thai/*

Florida, R. *The Rise of the Creative Class.* New York: Basic Books, 2002.

Funahashi, D. 'Rule by Good People: Health Governance and the Violence of Moral Authority in Thailand.' *Cultural Anthropology* 31, no. 1 (February 2016): 107–30.

'GDP growth (annual %) – Thailand.' World Bank Data. *https://data.worldbank.org/indicator/NY.GDP.MKTP. KD.ZG?end=1996&locations=TH&start=1985*

Ghertner, A. 'India's Urban Revolution: Geographies of Displacement beyond Gentrification.' *Environment and Planning A* 46, no. 7 (2014): 1554–71.

Ghertner, A. 'Why Gentrification Theory Fails in "Much of the World."' *City* 19, no. 4 (2015): 552–63.

'Giving the Pavement Back to Pedestrians.' *The Nation.* 26 November 2014. *https://www.nationthailand.com/perspective/30248642*

Hayden, S. *Never Settled: Community, Land, and the Politics of the Urban Commons in Bangkok.* Doctoral Dissertation. Berkeley: University of California Berkeley, 2019.

Herzfeld, M. *Siege of the Spirits: Community and Polity in Bangkok.* Chicago: University of Chicago Press, 2016.

Herzfeld, M. *Subversive Archaism: Troubling Traditionalists and the Politics of National Heritage.* The Lewis Henry Morgan Lectures. Durham, NC: Duke University Press, 2022.

Lees, L., et al. *Planetary Gentrification.* Cambridge: Polity Press, 2016.

Mörtenböck, P., and H. Mooshammer. 'Bangkok's Red Zones.' In *Informal Market Worlds: The Architecture of Informal Pressure - Atlas,* edited by P. Mörtenböck and H. Mooshammer, 28–35. Rotterdam: nai010 publishers, 2015.

Mokkhasen, S. 'This Is What Saphan Lek Looks Like Now (video).' *Khaosod English* (blog), 14 July 2016. *https://www.khaosodenglish.com/news/bangkok/2016/07/14/saphan-lek-looks-like-now-video/*

Renwick, T. 'Jay Fai and the Anomaly of the "Good' Street Vendor."' *Food, Culture & Society* 24, no. 1 (January 2021): 127–41.

'Richard Florida Is Sorry.' Suburban Alliance (blog). *https://www.suburbanalliance.com.au/single-post/2017/08/21/Richard-Florida-is-sorry*

'Sale of Pirate Goods in 27 "Red Zones" to Be Targeted.' *The Nation,* 31 July 2016. *https://www.nationthailand.com/business/econ/30291818*

Sukpanich, T. 'Living over Troubled Waters.' *Bangkok Post,* 1 January 2012. *https://www.bangkokpost.com/thailand/special-reports/273298/living-over-troubled-waters*

'The Changing Nature of Klong Ong Ang.' Thailand NOW, 31 December 2020. *https://www.thailandnow.in.th/life-society/the-changing-nature-of-klong-ong-ang/*

Wongsurawat, W. *The Crown and the Capitalists: The Ethnic Chinese and the Founding of the Thai Nation.* University of Washington Press, 2019.

Zukin, S. 'Gentrification in Three Paradoxes.' *City and Community* 15, no. 3 (September 2016): 202–07.

1976-2000

1 Saphan Lek starts to operate on the Ong Ang Canal.
2 Governor Rattakul implements strict measures to regulate street vending, resulting in the persecution of both street vendors and their customers.
3 The Thai baht is devalued after the removal of its peg to the US dollar, triggering the Asian financial crisis.
4 Thailand's economy experiences a severe recession, with GDP contracting by approximately 10% alongside a sharp increase in unemployment.

2000-2010

5 Governor Sundaravej authorises the establishment of 353 new designated areas, accommodating 11,438 vendors. Additionally, restrictions on designated no-vending days are removed.
6 Governor Kasayodhin initiates a comprehensive city-wide clean-up campaign aimed at restoring order to street vending. The campaign includes targeted enforcement actions against street vendors in markets lacking proper regulation, such as Bo Bae and Khlong Thom markets.
7 Thai coup d'état

2010-2015

8 Major political protests and demonstrations erupt in Bangkok.
9 Governor Paribatra introduces a series of policies that demonstrate strong support for street vendors. These include a proposal to authorise an additional 275 designated vending areas to accommodate 6,749 vendors. The 'Street Vending as the City's Charm' project and a soft loans policy for licensed vendors are implemented.
10 A reported six million products are seized in Bangkok's illegal markets.

Socio-cultural events									
Economic events				3 4					
Political events									
Vending policies	2					5			
Spatial events	1								

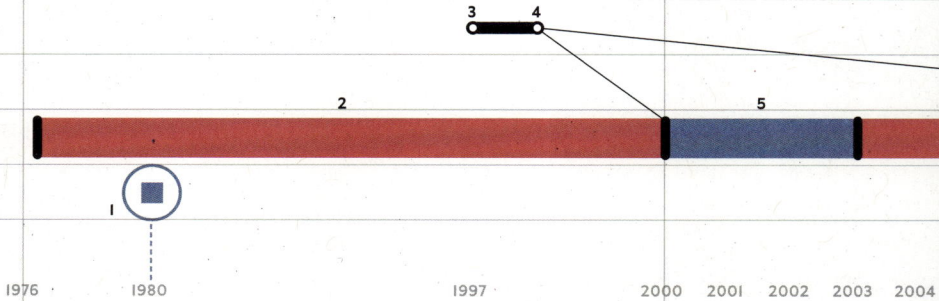

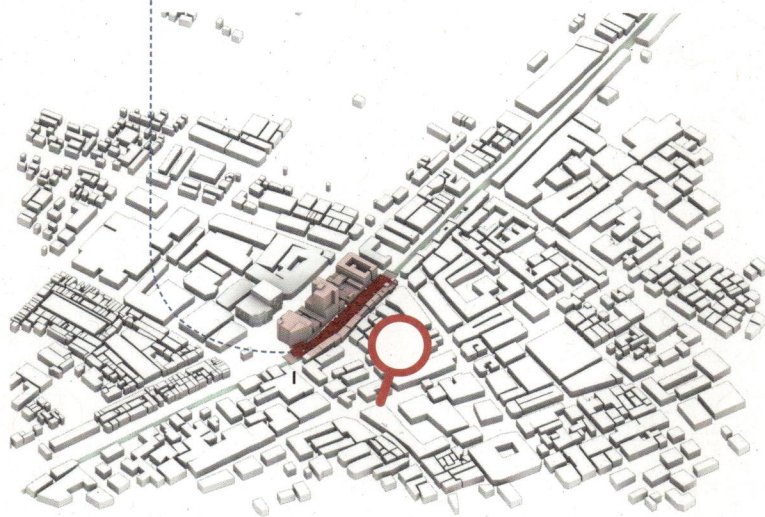

1976   1980   1997   2000 2001 2002 2003 2004

Timeline of key events shaping the transformation of Saphan Lek Market, Bangkok

11 Under the administration of Governor Sukhum-bhand, there is a shift towards more stringent regulation on street vending. Each district administration is instructed to restrict and control the number of available vending spots.
12 Thai coup d'état
13 Demolition of Saphan Lek Market and displacement of 2,700 vendors

2015-2023

14 Saphan Lek vendors relocate to the nearby Mega Plaza Saphan Lek shopping mall.
15 Public space cleanup programme led by the BMA comes into effect following the military coup.
16 The opening of the Sam Yot MRT subway station in 2019 makes the Ong Ang Canal and the Saphan Lek area more accessible.
17 Art installations and graffiti start off the BMA's redevelopment of the canal into a walking street.

18 Approximately 40 traditional communities are affected by the canal's redevelopment and gentrification.
19 The Khlong Ong Ang Walking Street project estimated at a cost of 275 million baht is completed.
20 Thailand announced as a recipient of a 2020 Asian Townscape Award from the UN-Habitat Regional Office for Asia and the Pacific for its renovation project of the Ong Ang Canal in Bangkok
21 BMA begins with another round of street clean-ups.

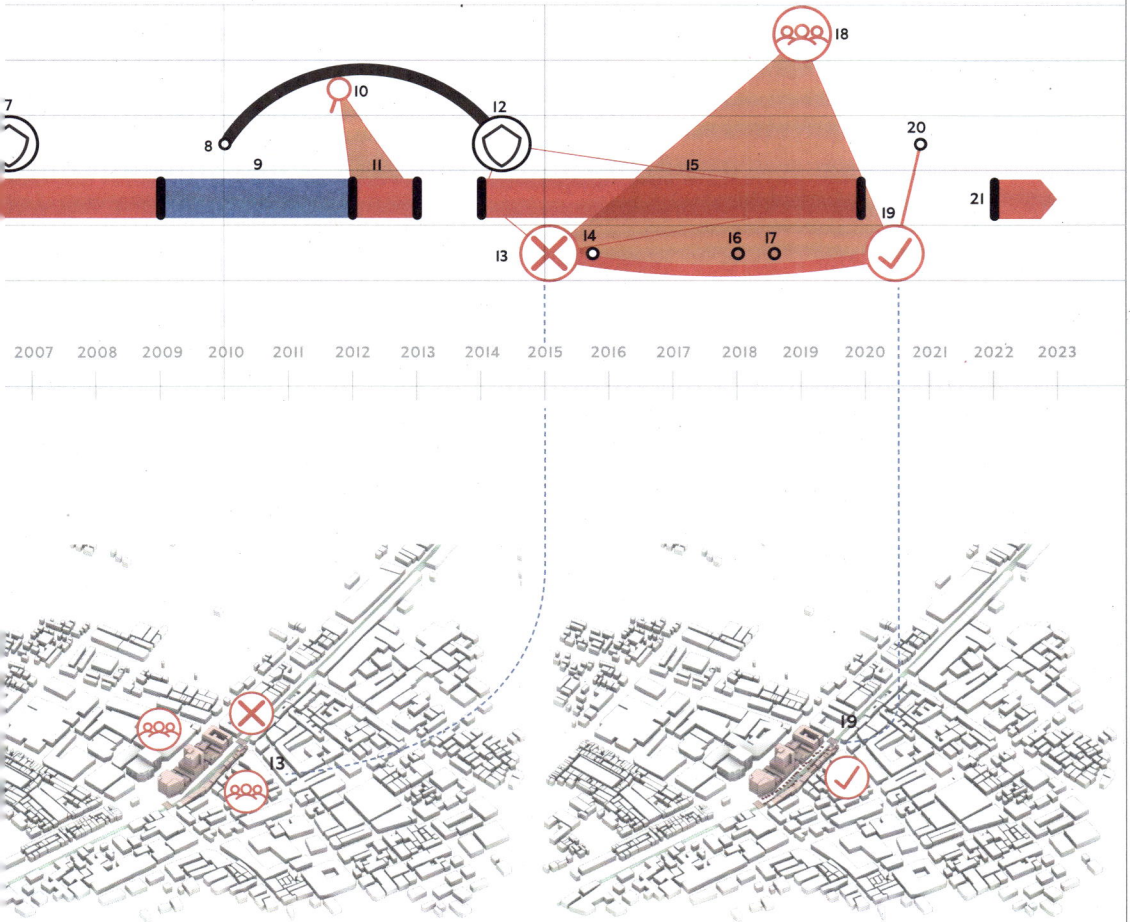

2007 2008 2009 2010 2011 2012 2013 2014 2015 2016 2017 2018 2019 2020 2021 2022 2023

■ Spatial, social, economic and political interventions into in/formal markets
■ Informality as a survival method and means of adapting to changing socio-economic and political circumstances

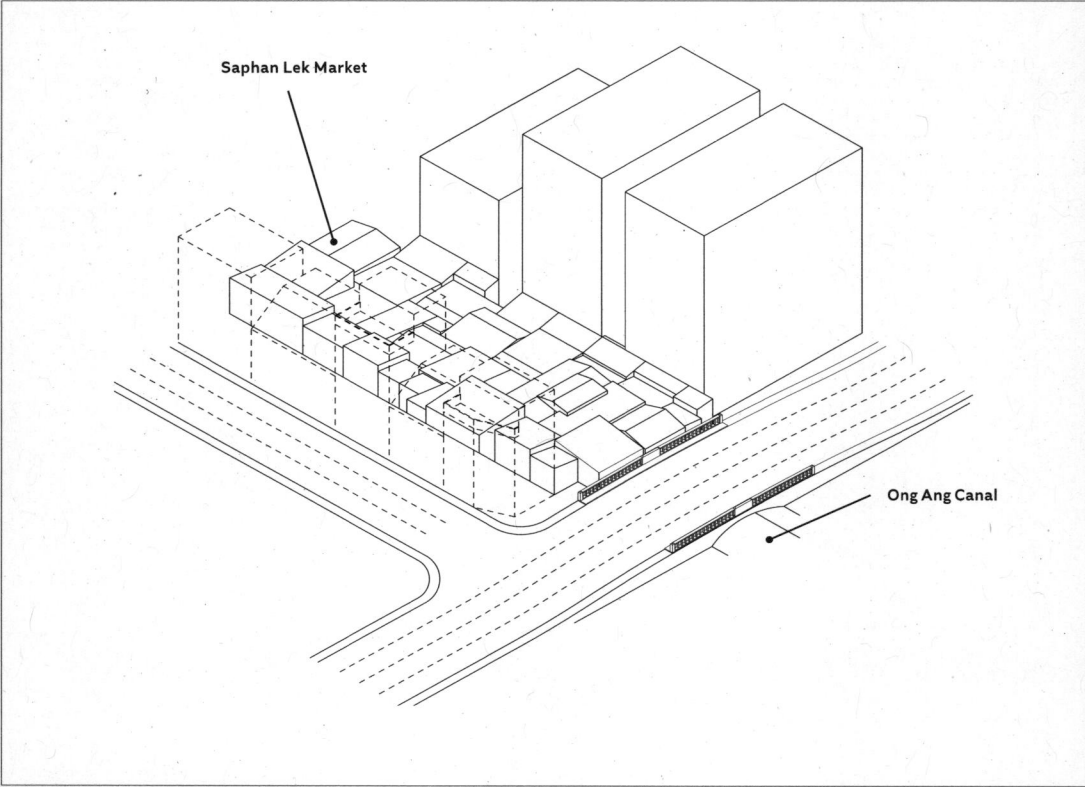

Saphan Lek Market

Ong Ang Canal

Saphan Lek Market (1980s – 2015)

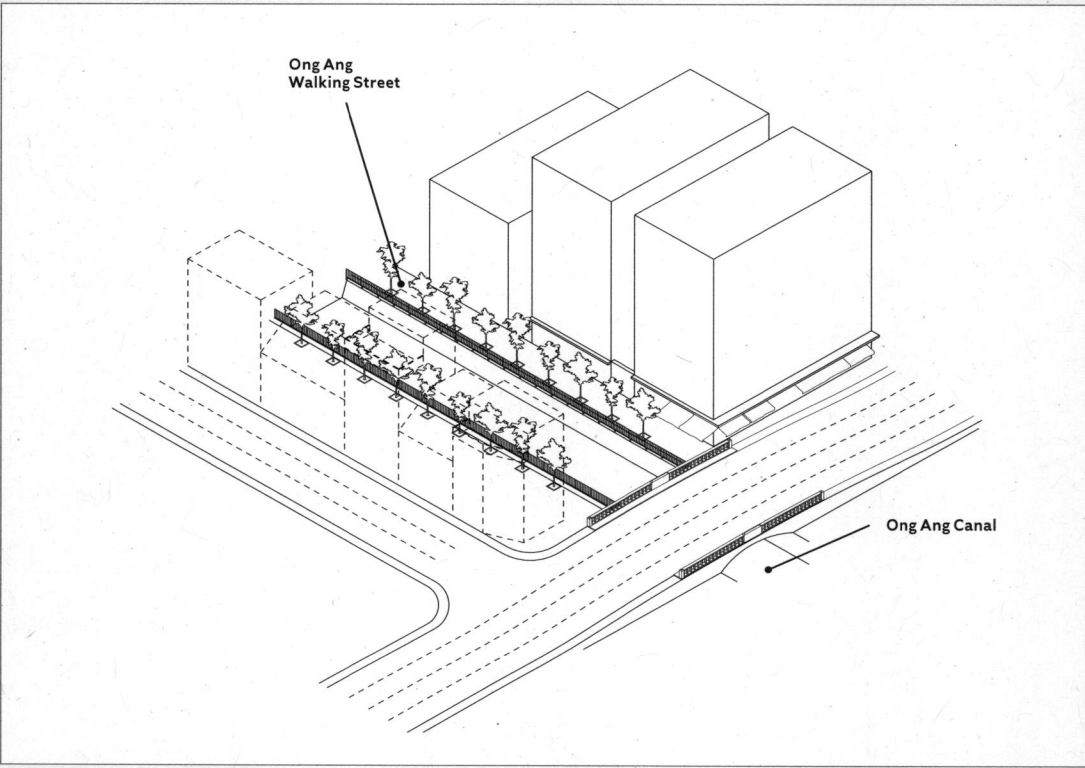

Ong Ang
Walking Street

Ong Ang Canal

Khlong Ong Ang Walking Street (since 2020)

Saphan Lek ('Iron Bridge') in 2012 (top) and 2023 (bottom)

1976 - 2015

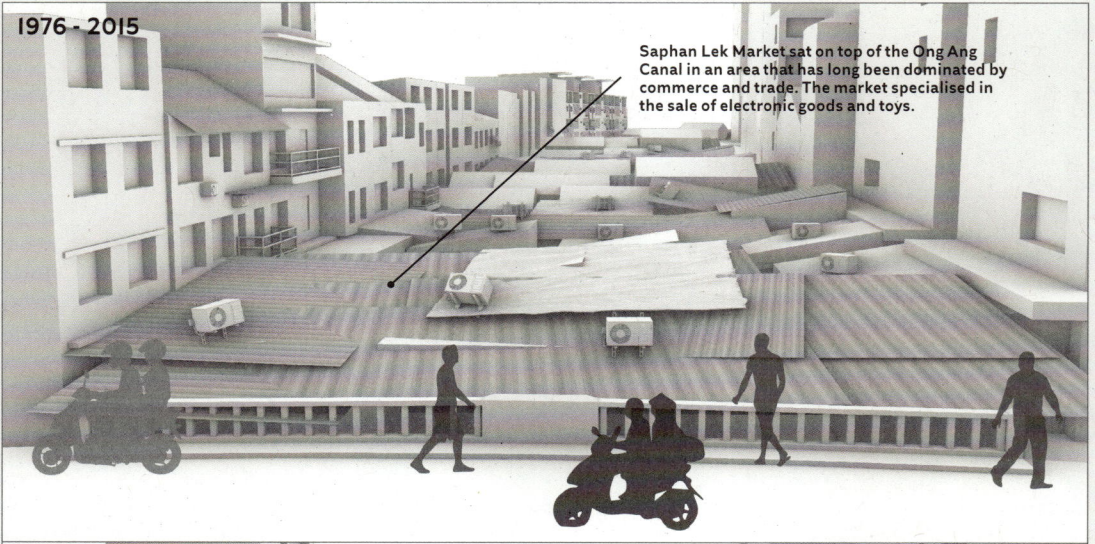

Saphan Lek Market sat on top of the Ong Ang Canal in an area that has long been dominated by commerce and trade. The market specialised in the sale of electronic goods and toys.

2015 - 2016

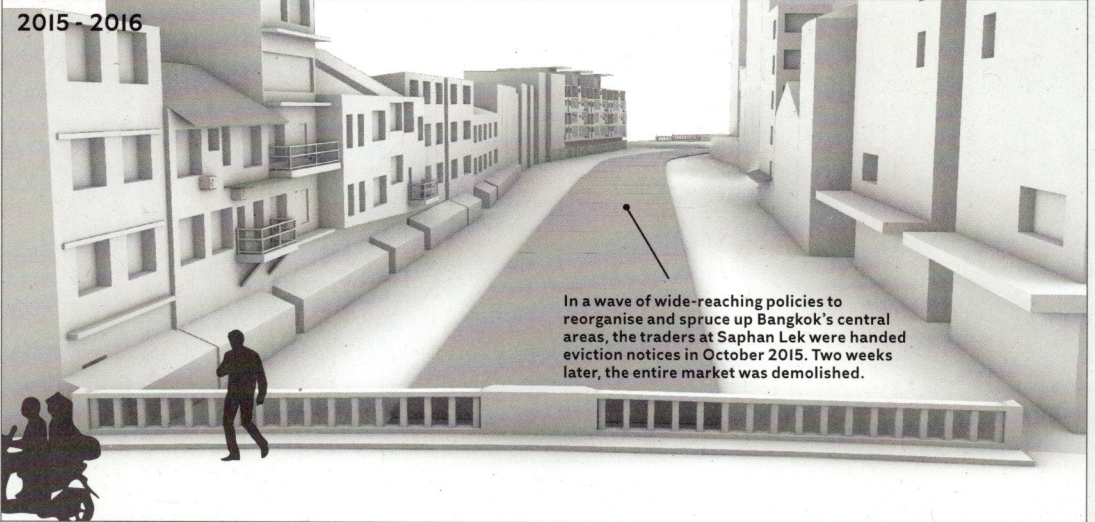

In a wave of wide-reaching policies to reorganise and spruce up Bangkok's central areas, the traders at Saphan Lek were handed eviction notices in October 2015. Two weeks later, the entire market was demolished.

2017

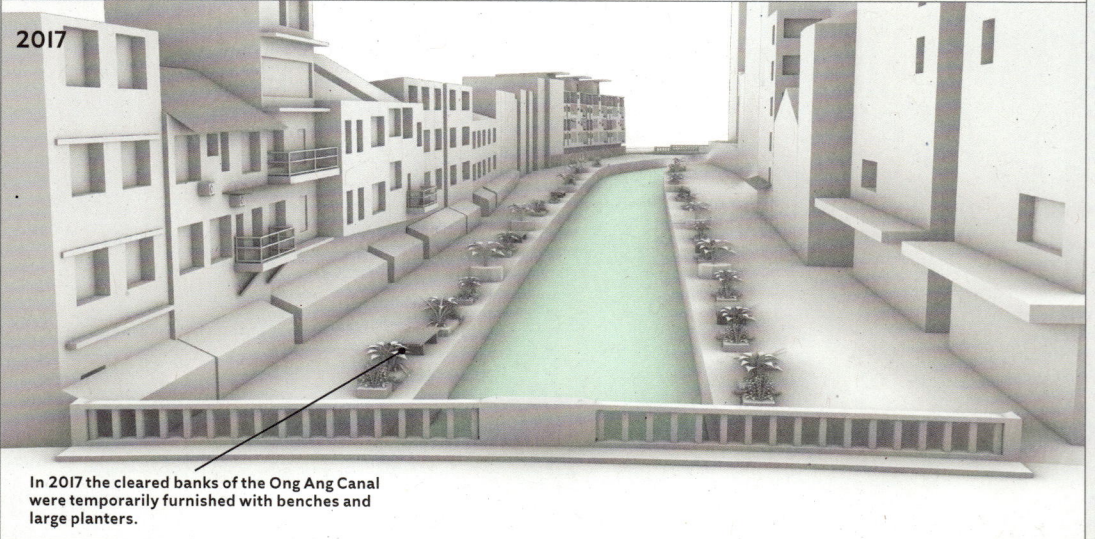

In 2017 the cleared banks of the Ong Ang Canal were temporarily furnished with benches and large planters.

2018

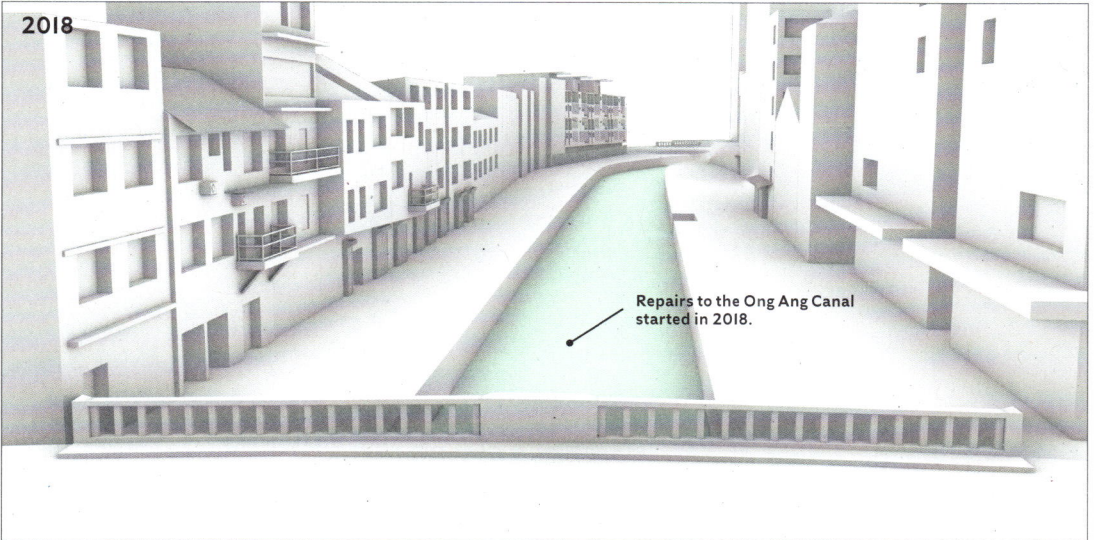

Repairs to the Ong Ang Canal started in 2018.

Since 2021 (non-market days)

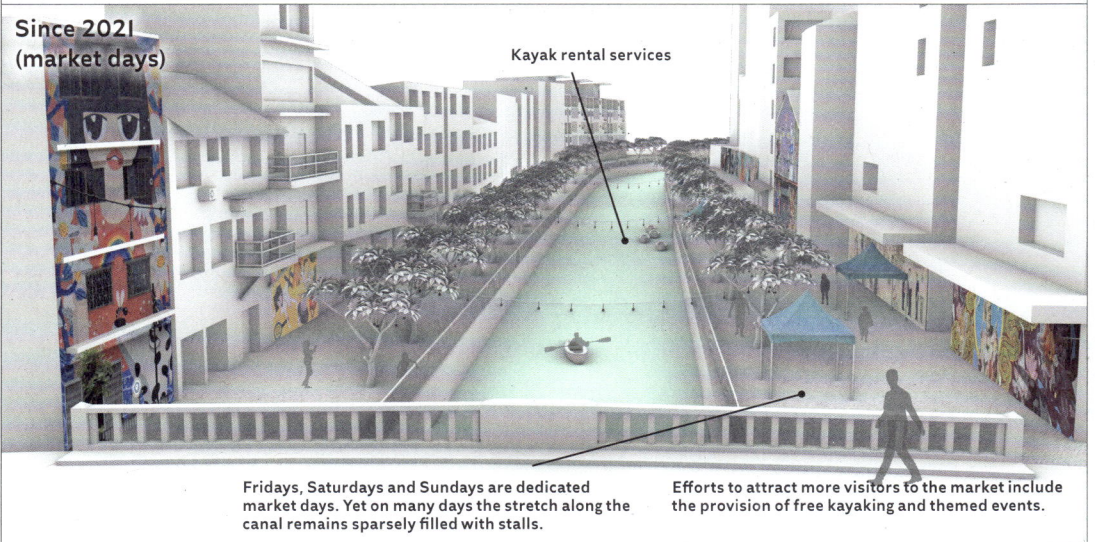

The Klong Ong Ang Walking Street is now completed with BMA murals and signifiers that identify it as a 'creative zone', such as holiday lights and colourful signage.

Since 2021 (market days)

Kayak rental services

Fridays, Saturdays and Sundays are dedicated market days. Yet on many days the stretch along the canal remains sparsely filled with stalls.

Efforts to attract more visitors to the market include the provision of free kayaking and themed events.

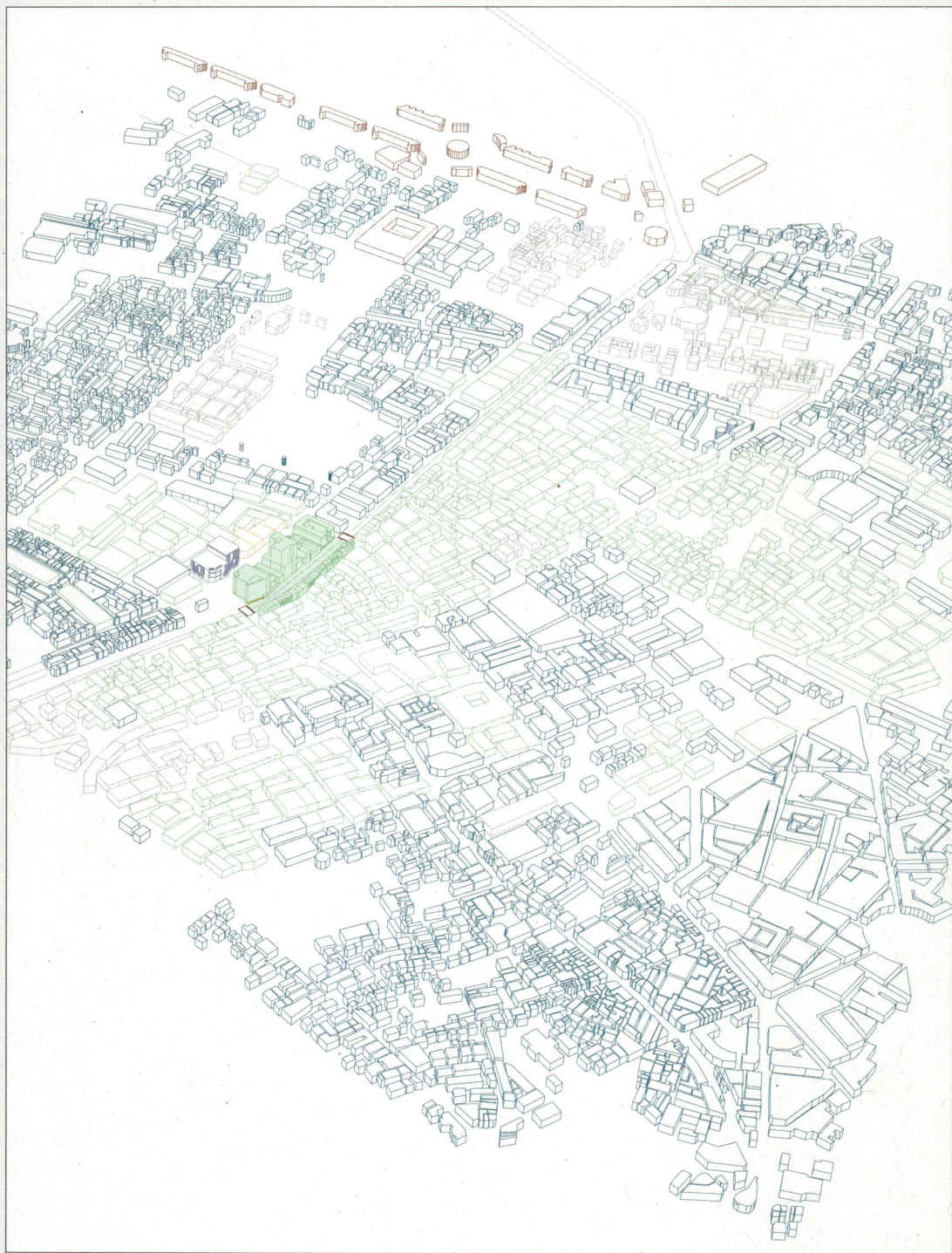

| ■ 1793 | ■ 1940 | ■ 1960 | ■ 1980 | ■ 2001 | ■ 2004 | ■ 2009 | ■ 2015 | ■ 2022 |

Ong Ang neighbourhood: key phases of spatial development

Top: Khlong Ong Ang Walking Street
Bottom: Unrenovated stretch of the Ong Ang Canal north of Khlong Ong Ang Walking Street

Market stalls
(now demolished)

Steel platform over the canal

Trees and
new railings

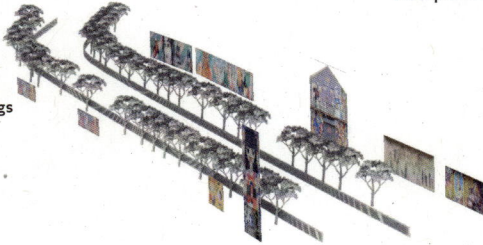

Commissioned murals

Mega Plaza accommodates the majority of
vendors who previously operated in the Saphan
Lek Market. Spread across seven oors, the mall
houses over 600 stalls, offering products
ranging from toys and computer games to
cameras, remote controls and BB guns.

Walking street continues
and connects with Saphan
Han, Sampeng Market and
Chinatown.

Phanuphan bridge

Kayak launch
station

Damrong Sathit Bridge

Impassable section of the canal

Transformation of the Ong Ang Canal from Saphan Lek Market to Khlong Ong Ang Walking Street

Floors

7   Office / Sale Office
6   Mega Food Center / Showcase /
    Model
5   RC / Camera / Card Game / Toys
4   Showcase / Model / Toys / Lego
3   Lego / Showcase / BB Gun / Toys
2   Game / Lego / BB Gun / Toys
1   Game / Lego / Toys

Retail levels of Mega Plaza mall, Ong Ang neighbourhood, Bangkok

WINNIE SERVIC
รับซ่อมเครื่องเกมส์
ซ่อมจอยเกมส์
แปลงระบบ อัปเกรดเครื่

Electronics stall at Mega Plaza, Bangkok, 2022

La Salada, Buenos Aires, aerial view, 2022

Paraformality in Buenos Aires, 2001–2023

Map data, Google imagery date, 9/24/2

The *La Salada* phenomenon can be understood on three interconnected scales formed through specific historical moments and a culturally situated political matrix. The fair is at the crossroads of these three scales. The first is the 'micro,' which comprises extended family units of the popular classes that are consolidated in times of economic crisis and who work by combining the 'subsistence' or 'reproduction' economy with small-scale commercial enterprises.

The second is an intermediate scale that implies the insertion of the fair in the human and non-human ecosystem of the Matanza-Riachuelo River basin, one of the most polluted in the world, now in the process of environmental recomposition, as well as the economic, social and political fabric of the Buenos Aires Metropolitan Area (AMBA, for its initials in Spanish). The third is the macro, which relates to Latin America's population and geography. On this scale, the fair's organisers are articulated with the formal commercial networks, the local political agreements, and a regional scale where the commercial network of the fair extends to numerous

Food stands and market stalls cluster along the tracks

Matanza-Riachuelo River

Unused railway bridge serves as a footbridge to parking on the other side of the Río Matanza Riachuelo

Long-distance buses

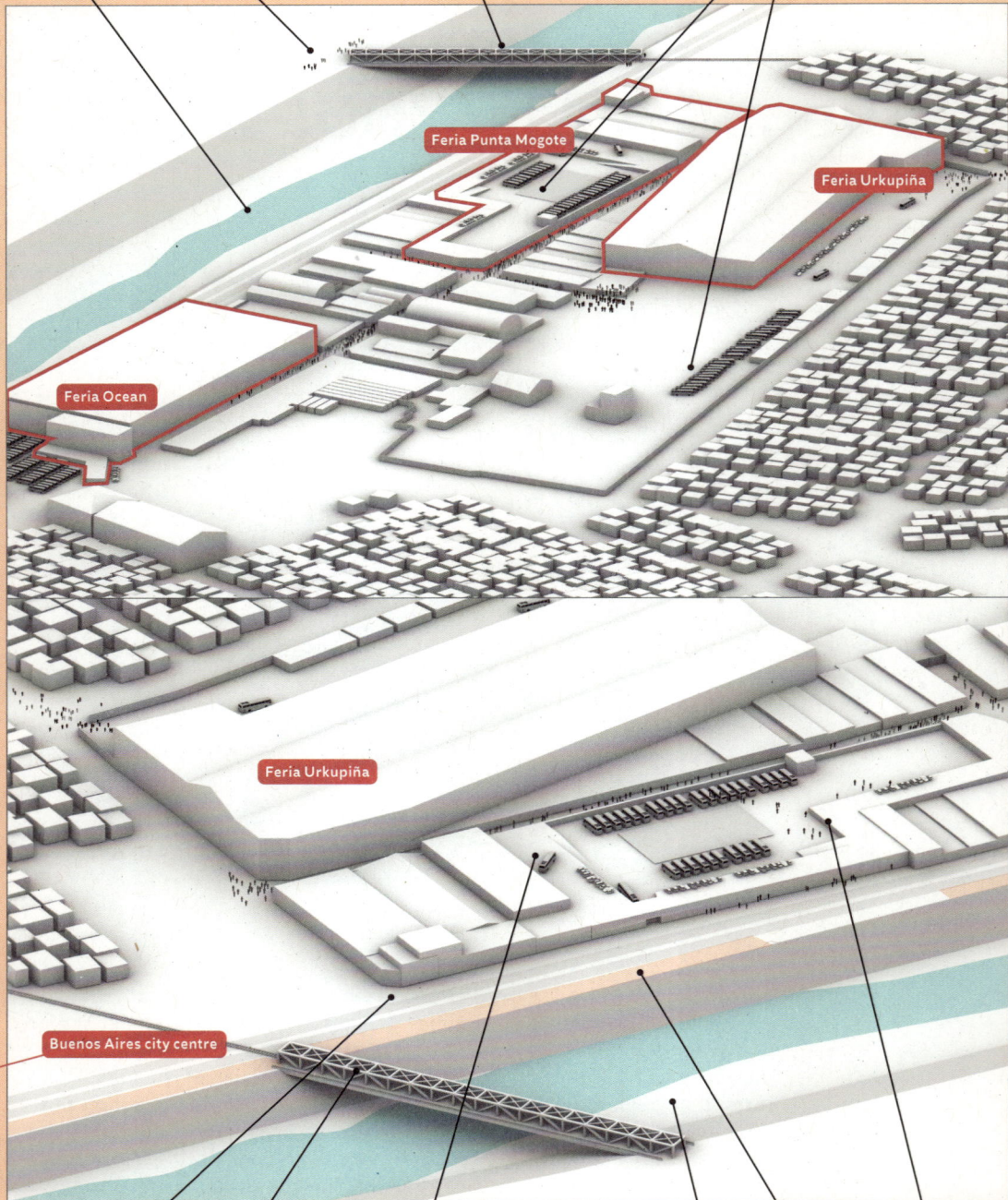

Feria Punta Mogote

Feria Urkupiña

Feria Ocean

Feria Urkupiña

Buenos Aires city centre

Minibus drop-off point

The La Ribera section occupied the banks along the Matanza-Riachuelo River. At its height, it comprised around 10,000 stalls, many of which were built on stilts. Responding to concerns about the market's impact on the river ecology, La Ribera was shut down and bulldozed in January 2012.

Long-distance buses

The distribution centre of MercadoLibre, the largest e-commerce platform in Latin America, is located a mere 300 metres from La Salada across the Riachuelo River.

Eat / gamble / socialise

La Ribera Fair (relocated July 2020)

The Matanza-Riachuelo River Basin, one of the most polluted in the world, is now undergoing a process of environmental recomposition to restore the eco-system.

provinces of Argentina and some neighbouring countries' cities.

The rise of the fair is a response by marginalised sectors to global capitalism's integration process. But the experiment of forming an overseas commercial circuit between La Salada and Luanda, Angola, is interesting as an indication of a scale change: a local network of informal urban sectors can trade directly on a global scale. La Salada was born during the peak of Argentina's neoliberal integration into the world which only grew in strength despite the progressive decline of that model. The 2001 financial crisis was economic, political, but above all systemic in that it provided the conditions for developing paraformal economic networks.[1]

These processes of *paraformality* develop within the particular Argentine cultural matrix, which shares a common root with the Hispanic culture of Ibero-America (language, customs, and religion) and also its idiosyncrasies. This is due to a heterogeneous social composition stemming from more than four centuries of intermingling between populations of Indigenous and/or Spanish descent that continues with the European migration of the late nineteenth century, integrated through the 'full employment' policies during the twentieth century. This created moments of significant social mobility alongside cyclical crises that generated abrupt inequality.

First, it is essential to consider whether formal and informal categories are mutually exclusive. If the informal is an accident, an 'exception' within the formality, or both are poles of a single process, of a single economy, the process goes from one pole to the other and creates interconnected networks. In the La Salada ecosystem, we see that 'family economies' are connected with formal and semi-formal raw material and marketing circuits. This intertwining between economies of reproduction and production makes it possible to ameliorate the pressure of cyclical 'adjustment' shocks and economic disadvantages while maintaining certain standards of

living. This hybridisation process may have to do with the high degree of urbanisation and rural industrialisation of the country that began in the 1990s with the introduction of genetically modified organism technology, the consequence of which was the agro-export complex successfully integrating into global value chains, but at the high cost of expelling rural inhabitants into urban centres, especially to the Buenos Aires Metropolitan Area. This situation created conditions for interaction on the margins for those highly informal sectors that had not yet been integrated, as were the waves of immigration in the previous century.

To understand this, it is essential to refer to the formation of cities in Argentina at the end of the nineteenth century, during which the state promoted a policy of reception and integration for overseas immigrants. Each group's arrival supposes, in the Argentine case, the emergence of a phase of informality or little adaptation, the creation of community ties and then a progressive socio-economic integration. *Slums* ('villas miseria,' now also called 'emergency neighbourhoods') and informal settlements proliferated within this hybrid system, forming an urbanism of reproduction that is organically generated and that is inserted in the interstices or the margins of the *formal* city's grid, outside urbanisation, law and regulations. These groups and dynamics are installed in the grid of the Hispanic city and its diffuse edges, forming a support that sustains this heterogeneous system's coexistence in a reticulated process, but one that is open and constantly evolving.

These self-generated spaces are initially segregated at the spatial and infrastructure level. Still, they are intertwined in economic status through production and capital systems: urban recycling, textile workshops, construction industry labour, and domestic services. However, these 'formless' neighbourhoods are highly permeable to urbanisation processes. The organic and irregular grid, isolated, is articulated and transformed in part with the existing grid. There is another

---

1   *Paraformality* is a concept developed by m7red from 2008–2012. It tries to capture precisely those processes of creation, generation or invention of ecosystems in a state of gestation. Processes configured beyond regulations or regularities cannot be identified either as informal (since they are full of configurational seeds, and stabilisation experiments) or formal (since neither the parts nor the wholes are stabilised; they are a process of transformation in progress). This concept tries to envelop changing environmental conditions, both the processes of metropolitan degradation and the incipient state programmes for environmental reconstitution, and the socio-economic conditions in the process of reconfiguration at the same time. See Gris Público Americano, m7red, *Paraformal: Urban ecologies*, Apuntes CCEBA 2011 Collections (Buenos Aires: Bisman Editions, 2011).

form of socio-spatial integration, which is not a spontaneous process but a collective strategy, which occurs in informal and illegal land grabs, which re-distribute the space of lots and streets continuously and articulate with the Hispanic grid, which is the official urban system.

This paradoxical proliferation of segregated spaces outside the traditional grid's formalisation system also happens in society's most integrated and formalised sectors. This is made evident in the phenomenon of closed and private neighbourhoods promoting an inverse process: the uncoupling of urban centres' spatial and infrastructural continuity to generate relative self-sufficiency on land without services – this dialectic process between the formal, the informal, and ambiguous information is typical of Argentina. La Salada, a cultural phenomenon and popular production ecosystem, was consolidated during the 2001 crisis. It was criminalised in 2017 and finally closed during the COVID-19 pandemic. Although the quarantine closures seemed definitive under these hostile conditions, the markets found new ways of production and of strengthening the *paraformal* economy, which made the La Salada Fair case not only a resilient phenomenon but also a benchmark for dynamic employment generation models emerging from the crisis.

2001–2010: LA SALADA'S BOOM AFTER THE FINANCIAL CRISIS OF 2001

In the 1940s, on the land occupied by La Salada, beach resorts with saltwater pools arose, which had been discovered in the area during the rectification process of the Matanza-Riachuelo basin. Food and clothing were sold, mainly coming from clandestine workshops located in the area. During the crisis of hyperinflation in 1989 and prior to the creation of the fair, there were 'manteros' fairs (street vendors who sell wares from a small blanket on the ground, hence their name) in the Buenos Aires suburbs, which were itinerant and persecuted by the police.

In 1991 the fairs and textile workshops' organisation founded by the Bolivian community that participated in these exchanges purchased one of the old disused beach resorts,

La Noria, which was part of the complex popularly known as *La Salada*. The first of the fairs was launched there, Urkupiña, named after the Bolivian Virgin of Urkupiña. The low to no conversion rates of the Argentine peso during those years facilitated the sale of products from neighbouring countries, via the networks of these Bolivian and Paraguayan migrant communities. In 1994 the Ocean Fair was created, made up mainly of Argentinian and Korean sellers, unlike Urkupiña, where the Bolivian community predominated. At that time, the Urkupiña Fair operated on Mondays, and the Ocean Fair on Thursdays. As the fairs experienced exponential growth during the 2001 crisis, the poverty rate in Argentina shot up to 54 percent, while unemployment remained at 20 percent.

Besides the fair, people exchanged products at barter clubs, from the 'family's basic basket' (a set of basic products that, when compiled, are used as an economic index in Argentina) on neighbourhood and regional scales. Alongside this, the presence of the state was sparse, which led to a lack of controls on the margins of the metropolitan area of Buenos Aires, already located on an edge where several jurisdictional boundaries converged. A key piece of information in financial crises is added here: some stallholders' advantage of possessing informal capital in dollars accumulated outside the banking circuit, which wouldn't suffer from government restrictions when a withdrawals cap was placed on banks (known as *El Corralito*), was the trigger for the debt default that precipitated the political crisis that followed the financial one.

In 2001, the main administrators of the Urkupiña Fair were arrested. Later, the area known as *La Ribera* was added, with outposts on the south bank of the Riachuelo, in some cases, built on land reclaimed from the river. These stalls were evicted in September 2004 in the midst of clashes in which one vendor died. The consuls of Bolivia and Peru participated in negotiations with the then mayor of Lomas de Zamora, Jorge Rossi, with the aim that the illegal street stalls would be incorporated into the Urkupiña Fair. However, the illegal outposts were set up again after a few days.

La Salada, Buenos Aires, 2011 (top and bottom)

La Salada, Buenos Aires, 2011

This sector, in which hooligans from different football clubs participated, sparked clashes between gangs, resulting in fatalities. In 2012, another eviction was carried out in the same sector, on that occasion requested by the Matanza Riachuelo Basin Authority (ACUMAR), the body responsible for the water course parallel to the land where the fair is situated, to enable the construction of the 'Camino de Sirga' (a towpath).

By 2003, it was estimated that 50,000–60,000 people per day passed through the fair, and 400–500 buses arrived daily from inside the country and from neighbouring countries, including Perú. In 2006 a small logistics network that developed through long-distance buses modified to carry passengers and cargo connected La Salada with several Argentine provinces, and also began to make trips to Paraguay. There were also charter services from the centre of Buenos Aires to the fair. The difficult territory of the suburbs, through which the fair's merchandise and capital entered and departed, had been targeted for robberies regularly. This was relatively 'pacified' by the provincial police as the fair complex was gaining importance.

2010–2012: LA SALADA BECOMES A MODEL FOR GLOBALISATION IN THE GLOBAL SOUTH

An analysis by *The Economist* magazine in 2011 found that in 2010, six of the world's ten fastest-growing economies were in sub-Saharan Africa. One of them was Angola. Angola, a member of OPEC since 2007, is Africa's second-largest oil exporter. This activity constitutes 85 percent of GDP and, between 2004 and 2008, generated annual growth of more than 15 percent. Although Angola suffered a civil war from 1975 to 2002, recovery was possible. The oil rent allowed them to create a food reserve. During the first wave of globalisation, South-to-South cooperation was a goal that was always declared but never achieved.

Between October 2004 and August 2005, Argentina conducted two commercial missions to Angola. In 2012 the Secretary of Commerce, Guillermo Moreno, organised yet another trade mission to the country. A delegation of 250 business people accompanied the secretary in a round of meetings held in Luanda during the first days of March. This mission was considering a geopolitical vision for the South Atlantic basin, based on the historical relationship between Brazil and Africa, which dates to the times of the Portuguese and the slave trade. Brazil was the first country to recognise Angola's independence in 1975 and developed a policy of close diplomatic relations with the Portuguese-speaking countries of Africa. Over the last thirty years, Brazil has defined its African policy as *strategic*, understanding that its African links would be very useful in the establishment of itself as a global power, and replacing Portugal in that area of the world. Brazil is a permanent spokesperson for the Luso-African countries in the G20, and they support Brazil's candidacy to join the United Nations Security Council.

For Petrobras, the Brazilian state-owned oil firm with a presence in Angola since 1979, the West Coast of Africa is one of the strategic regions for its activities outside Brazil due to the geological similarities with its own coast. As Argentina and Brazil are strategic partners in the South American continent thanks to MERCOSUR (Southern Common Market), a shared space and economic block were a possible multilateral trade circuit that the then politically aligned governments of Argentina and Brazil would have desired to develop. Jorge Castillo, one of the La Salada representatives (perhaps the most charismatic, and a businessman with a high profile in local media) and administrator of the Punta Mogotes complex, not only expanded his La Salada business to the interior of the country through the 'Saladitas,' but also tried his luck in Africa. More precisely in Angola, a country to which he gained entrée thanks to the Secretary of Commerce, Guillermo Moreno, who included him in the delegation headed by Cristina Kirchner, former president of Argentina. At that time, the merchants prepared to export. Four of the largest textile producers from the largest illegal fair in the country focused on manufacturing jeans, jackets, T-shirts and sweaters, went on the mission as SME producers. At that time in 2012, La Salada textile products were lower in price than Chinese ones. 'The secretary of commerce [Guillermo Moreno] invited us, and we thought it was a good opportunity.

Although some discriminate against us, we are in a position to export what we manufacture in Argentina,' confirmed Castillo himself.[2] The fair administrator's goal was to recreate his business model in the African country, which would mean millions in profits for the nation state.

However, Castillo later stated that no investment was made in Angola because 'there was no legal certainty.' At this point, the Brazilian experience would have been taken into account. Brazilian commercial policy in Angola is supported by Brazilian financing and export insurance, through which a good part of the businesses are managed by Brazil, which collects on them from the Angolan State through the oil supply. This is fundamental because if State-to-State agreement is not formalised, eventual Argentine suppliers or investors would not have had any mechanism for charging for their products or contracts. Although the La Salada suppliers came back 'with the dollars' of an eventual deal, the La Salada model could not be replicated in Angola mainly due to the informal trade system of the country at that time.[3]

2015 – 2017: CRIMINALISATION OF THE FAIR AND NEOLIBERAL GOVERNMENT RHETORIC

The La Salada ecosystem was criminalised between 2016 and 2018. The attack on the fair was promoting a change in attitude towards what academics call the 'popular economy.' By this term, institutions from government and academia understand a political actor that the state intends to integrate into the fabric (although not in the general economy) through the constitution of various types of social plans, and support for the creation of cooperatives and other kinds of collective organisations that must make concessions in exchange for public subsidies. This phenomenon echoed the change in government: in 2015, Mauricio Macri took office as President of Argentina, a benchmark for a coalition of traditional centre parties and new liberal-leaning parties.

2   'El día que el kirchnerismo llevó La Salada a Angola,' *Perfil*, 21 June 2017, *https://www.perfil.com/noticias/politica/el-dia-que-el-kirchnerismo-llevo-la-salada-a-angola.phtml*

3   Patricio Eleisegui, 'La Salada "for export": detalles del mega emprendimiento que se levantará en Angola, para alegría de Moreno,' *IProfesional*, 10 July 2012, *https://www.iprofesional.com/negocios/140090-la-salada-for-export-detalles-del-mega-emprendimiento-que-se-levantara-en-angola-para-alegria-de-moreno*

This puts the popular economy constantly at risk of being perceived as delinked from the general economy. Still, at the same time, the popular economy is an actor that has had to adapt to constant modernisation, with the ultimate goal of converting many of these plans and aid into training systems for future jobs in the formal sector. This was the point of contingency where neoliberal governments and left-progressive ones converged: the complete faith that full employment was lost forever and that precarity is the general framework to develop new segmentation techniques to manage the economy. Paradoxically, the neoliberal government during those years skyrocketed spending on subsidies to the organisations of the popular economy, due to their high negotiating strength and capacity for political pressure. This scheme brought a mostly stable social peace throughout the four years of neoliberal experimentation. Still, it was plunged into crisis when the pandemic hit, and public spending snowballed into the highest inflation of the last thirty years.

In this context, the attack on La Salada had, on the one hand, a symbolic angle, which showed a government that presented itself as a government of CEOs, efficient and meritocratic, and indicating that popular economy games no longer have to be informal or semi-formal. Fake legality and compliance were weaponised against the legitimacy of the fair, built upon several years of operation and evident by the number of producers that made a living there and the continuous flow of consumers looking for affordable options. This was the idea of the 'shadow' economy that had to be exposed into open daylight. The fair and its environment were branded as mob-like activities because they wanted to send a broad message to society, discouraging a growing and dynamic, but not formalisable, economic model: this small-scale model was not fit to reach the globalisation scale. This had already been disproved a couple of years previously when the fair was admitted to Angola's trade mission.

On 22 June 2017, in a highly visible media-orchestrated operation that included fifty-five raids, Jorge Castillo was arrested in his mansion at an exclusive country club in an investigation concerning criminal association, along with thirty other suspects. They also dismantled stalls in La Salada. Because of the scale of media coverage, this attack managed to fulfil its destabilising intentions and eclipsed the fair's unprecedented boom for a year or two. Then the pandemic hit.

2019–2022: PANDEMIC AND POST-PANDEMIC

'The economic problem is not the lockdowns, but the pandemic.'

- Alberto Fernández, President of Argentina

The IFE (Ingreso Familiar de Emergencia or Emergency Family Income, economic aid distributed to family groups during the pandemic)[4] was implemented for the self-employed and informal workers of the economy during the first three months of the lockdowns. It was money printed by the government to help those in the informal sector that did not have a regular income. It was later extended to those inhabiting areas that, until October 2020, were kept under strict lockdowns, like the Buenos Aires Metropolitan Area, where 17 million people, almost one-third of the national population live.

While the government projection was 3.6 million people, the IFE was requested by 13.4 million, of which 8.9 million met the requirements. The high rate of eligibility had a significant impact with respect to the visibility of the economically active population, heterogeneous in its composition and not recognised as such in official statistics, putting in crisis how state systems monitor this sector, generally defined as 'informal.' This definition of 'informal' is one of the main difficulties when quantifying this demographic, as it takes as a starting point the legal forms of coupling with the labour market, thus reducing a broad and complex diversity of labour relations, production and reproduction of life.

---

4   The Emergency Family Income (IFE) was created on March 23 by decree 310/2020, and implemented rapidly by April, given the urgency of responding to those sectors that had been left without income. As a non-contributory monetary benefit, the programme has represented an exceptional payment equivalent to 10,000 pesos a month, intended for 'workers affected by precarious job placements (low-category "monotributistas," workers in private homes, informal employees and the unemployed).'

La Salada, Buenos Aires, 2011

The informal sector's exponential growth during lockdowns was motivated by the flow of printed money that mainly went on daily spending, but that was also intended to boost consumption in urban middle classes. The following reboot of the economy also created a boom in construction, fuelled mainly by the savings of the upper middle classes to improve housing first and to develop new neighbourhoods on the outskirts of the city for those that escaped lockdowns in search of cheap land to 'go back to nature.' But the picture afterwards had an impact on public spending, and now the country has an incredibly high rate of inflation. However, with low unemployment and high poverty levels, a contradictory situation questions political, sociological and economic analyses. La Salada Fair is a highly symbolic resource disputed in these narratives about the crisis.

In Argentina, the textile industry is a key sector to measure the economic present: in times of crisis, it is one of the first to collapse, and in times of improvement, it is one of the first to get down to business. For this reason, the cessation of imports after the crisis of

2001, and the reactivation of activity under progressive governments, led to the resurgence of local production, exemplified in the case of La Salada. Because of this, during the first phases of the pandemic, the mainstream media went to La Salada to measure the level of activity and the impact of lockdowns on the sectors that represent the fragile link between those surviving on a daily basis and the self-employed. The narrative of the urban informal sector's territories was shaped by the testimonies of those hardly hit by the closure of La Salada.

'The confinement and immediate discovery of the "tied with wire" numbers thanks to that shocking image of the informal economy changed the map of reality forever.'
- Lorena Alvarez, textile entrepreneur and journalist[5]

For most of the population, the economic problem was the lockdown, not the pandemic; you can find some testimonies regarding the pandemic after the lockdown. 'Most of my neighbours work independently or in the shadow economy. Lockdowns were terrible

125

La Salada, Buenos Aires, closed during the COVID-19 pandemic, 2021 (top and bottom)

for them because they don't have a monthly salary; they're masons or seamstresses or janitors at private homes, and now with the lockdown, what's happening is they can't go to work or claim a salary since they work in informality. Most IFEs were rejected; my daughter applied but didn't qualify. Some have AUHI5;[6] some have nothing. Many don't because they've been working independently or in informality, so they don't give you permission to apply, or simply don't have time to fill in the application.'

'I don't have a formal job; I work every day in the informal economy by sewing clothes. I have to take a long trip to go to work [...] Most people I know are sewing, but they do it where they live, in their informal settlements and slums; they're small workshops, not legal. Most of my fellow Bolivian citizens work only on that. My husband's a bricklayer in construction, but in the shadow economy, his national ID is being processed; he has only a precarious one. Some worked by the hour in family homes, others were coffee sellers in carts on the street, and others went out to collect cardboard or do odd jobs for a day. These jobs can no longer be done now because of the lockdown. Others worked from home, prepared food and went out to sell it outside. Those jobs are also not enough.'

- Liliana,
social leader of the New House,
Villa Playón de Chacarita,
another 'emergency neighbourhood.'[7]

THE EMERGENCE OF THE 'BARRANI ECONOMY'

'If the state is not going to help me, then don't break my balls.'

- Anonymous

Locked at home, many people had to develop a way to earn a living. Some became entrepreneurs by opening virtual shops selling what they could produce or exchange; others became the weak link of the logistical delivery systems that escalated during lockdowns.

The exponential printing of money to supply the IFE and other subsidies for low-income families created a new economy called 'barrani,' a clandestine economy that people saw as a legitimate way to overcome the onerous restrictions imposed by lockdowns. This was a legitimation of what was known before in the bureaucratic and academic world as 'the informal sector.' Across social media networks this legitimation was popularly known as 'barrani.' The 'barrani' revolution can be attributed first to gastronomy, driven by a group of establishment owners who preferred to work behind closed doors during the lockdowns and off the books to preserve the little profit they had left. Carlos Maslatón, a representative of the libertarian party, can be pointed out as *the creature's father*. His statements on the matter were as follows: 'Barrani is the name of an Egyptian town also known as Sidi Barrani. The term is attributed to Sephardic Turks who use it as a synonym for 'black' and is used to mention what is an illegal, clandestine forester, and as a type of gastronomy it's related to street food in the Middle East, absent from any state regulation.'[8]

Lorena Álvarez, a self-employed entrepreneur who sells her textile designs in fairs all over Buenos Aires was very aware of this and in fact, wrote consistently on social media about her impressions of what was going on with those who made their daily bread in the informal urban sectors. The landscape she noted emerging after the lockdowns was very different from that portrayed by the media:

'In 2023, entrepreneurship and independent work are on the rise in Argentina. This helps to maintain moderate unemployment levels. This is evident in places like the Once neighbourhood, where the employment situation has changed significantly, thinking back to 2003/2015. Just compare photos of the past to remember: from prosperous locals with several employees to an impressive number of street vendors. Clothing turned from the wholesale axis and is today focused in Avellaneda street, for the middle classes, or La Salada Fair, the main suppliers of affordable clothing.'[9]

127

6   A national government subsidy meant to cover part of child rearing costs, in exchange for their continued education and vaccination.
7   Mariela Paula Díaz et.all, 'Hábitat popular y prácticas de subsistencia en villas del AMBA (Argentina) en contexto de pandemia,' *Revistainvi*, 37, no. 104 (2022): 230–52.
8   'Qué significa "barrani" la moda de la gastronomía clandestina.' *Perfil*, 28 August 2020, https://www.perfil.com/noticias/economia/que-significa-barrani-la-moda-de-la-gatronomia-clandestina.phtml
9   Álvarez, 'El amor después del Amor.'

After the explosion of the 'Saladitas' (smaller fairs copying the La Salada model, more than 600 were located in Buenos Aires back in 2017), another retail area located in the southwest of the city gained momentum because of the economic crisis and growing inflation left by the pandemic. During 2022 Avellaneda Avenue became an option for the impoverished middle classes of Buenos Aires. Because of the lockdowns, the famous shopping tours, long-distance buses coming from provinces and sometimes beyond national borders, and small buses for those coming from metropolitan areas could not reach the city. This had a huge impact not only on La Salada, but also on Avellaneda Avenue.

The blow the lockdowns imposed was huge. Of 7000 stalls established in Avellaneda, 1800 were closed and never returned after its reopening in 2021. But the subsequent reboot of the economy during 2022 and the growing loss of purchasing power due to rampant inflation created the opportunity for the impoverished middle classes to discover this urban retail area where Koreans own half of the stalls, and the other half by Argentines. We can say that after the lockdown, a specialisation emerged: La Salada now works mostly as a place for retail reselling. The aforementioned shopping tours and Avellaneda work as an 'open shopping mall' for Buenos Aires, a direct purchasing experience that differs from the standards of online selling like Mercado Libre.

MercadoLibre is the number one e-commerce platform in Latin America. It was founded in Buenos Aires in 2000, and is owned by the business mogul Marcos Galperín. The impact of online selling for new entrepreneurs during the lockdown and the availability of several payment methods embedded in this platform created a phenomenon that was impossible to achieve before the rapid financialisation of vast sectors of the informal economy.

MercadoLibre developed MercadoPago, a massive payment-processing platform that connects to all banks and functions as a banking account in and of itself, having even a MasterCard and investment fund options. These apps create territorial fluidity by capturing money fluxes from the informal sector to create synergies across the whole

MercadoLibre online ecosystem. In 2010, La Salada Fair was far more significant in selling volume than MercadoLibre and developed its own online platform, La Salada Online. Ten years later, what remains of La Salada Online is a virtual shop embedded into the MercadoLibre platform. Avellaneda Avenue has an app of its own but it does not offer e-commerce options, only the visualisation of available products, prices and the location of their storefronts.

The main MercadoLibre logistic warehouse, a huge automatised depot that serves the whole country, is close to La Salada Fair, just 300 metres across the Matanza-Riachuelo River. Along with the Mercado Central de Buenos Aires (Buenos Aires Central Market), which is the main node of distribution of vegetables and fresh produce for the whole Buenos Aires Metropolitan Area, these nodes generate density in a strategic area with a big local workforce. They are easily connected to the AMBA main roads. So, the historic and strategic location of La Salada Fair, close in terms of logistics to the city of Buenos Aires but outside its legal and regulatory jurisdiction, proved that the ecosystem of Mercado Central/MercadoLibre/Feria La Salada, far from being a national logistics pole on its own terms, is a fragment of urban ecology where many dimensions and scales are articulated.

INTERVIEW WITH GUILLERMO MORENO, ARGENTINA'S SECRETARY OF COMMERCE BETWEEN 2006 AND 2013

These are segments from an interview with Guillermo Moreno, economist, former Argentine Secretary of Commerce in the period 2006–2013, and former Secretary of Communication in the period 2003–2006; Moreno was a promoter of the expansion of the economic and social model of the La Salada Fair, understanding it as an organic part of the entire economy and not as a separate sector. He argues that in the Argentine case, the formal and informal sectors are intertwined, and there are passages from one to the other. Moreno is a representative of the Peronist ideology, which presents itself as an alternative option to the left and the right, and sympathises with sectors of the left, Catholics, agro-industrialists, and the national business community.

La Salada, Buenos Aires, aerial views, 2021 (top) and 2022 (bottom)

Typical infrastructural components, La Salada, Buenos Aires

La Salada, Buenos Aires, aerial view, 2022

He has founded a party, Principles and Values, and participates in the 2023 electoral bid on the Peronist ticket.[10]

Q: How did you come to think that the La Salada Fair was an exportable model, and how could it relate to other places in the world?

A: During globalisation, in its beginnings, 1989 and 1990, with the fall of the [Berlin] Wall, structural adjustments took place. This conceptually implies the hegemony on a global scale of the Austrian model; globalisation is the evolution of that cluster of ideas with its two political tools: neoliberal or social democratic proposals. At that time, globalisation permeated all disciplines. Structural adjustments were on the rise, so an incipient phenomenon in the South American region was the urban informal sector, which is beginning to be studied with financing from multilateral credit organisations and the World Bank. There are beginning to be resources for professionals to study this subject. The arrival of Trump ends all that. Approaching [the subject] from the urban informal sector in the region, there are two diametrically opposed models: The model of the Pacific, Peru and Ecuador, and the Argentine model. They differ in the conceptualisation of the articulation between the formal and informal economy and the degrees of that articulation. Those who stand out are the Peruvians; it's a very vital moment in Peruvian politics because it's the emergence of the political organisation Sendero Luminoso (Shining Path, 1980–1990), which operated through the imposition of ideas through violent acts. But these were very characteristic violent acts because they had to do with sowing terror, linked even with the Cambodian sectors of the Khmer Rouge, which are further connected to the division between urban and rural because Cambodians are the first to stop recognising cities as a sphere of belonging to the population. Shining Path has something to do with it.

Hernando de Soto writes 'The Other Path,' and this analysis has an impact, because it's the urban informal sector seen from [the point of view of] the system, seen from globalisation. As a reaction, academics appear to try to articulate those families that 'rummaged' their income in informal urban areas. The general consensus until the recent crisis of President Castillo, which led to his deposal in 2023, is that there are two parallel economies, which touch each other very little. There is a formal economy and an informal one, the high [upper] one [formal employment, companies etc] and the low [lower] one [informal, street markets]. This study method, the formal and informal differentiation, tries to be replicated in other countries to make a general outline of the region. Still, in Argentina, the reality is different.

Here the urban informal sector is part of a single economy. In Argentina, there aren't two surpluses like in Peru, where the economy of the poor generates its surplus and its distribution. In Argentina, the urban informal sector increases the profit rate of the formal sector. Recycled cardboard ends up in toilet paper consumed by the ABC1 sectors. Recyclables come out of carts pushed by urban informal recyclers. A sound economic policy, understanding these specificities, will try to increase the bargaining power of the urban informal sector for a more significant application of that surplus. And that's why businessmen and merchants from La Salada travel to Angola. Because their suppliers are from the formal sector, the surplus comes from the formal sector, and therefore, despite being informal, they can export. And indeed, they did. Even within a relatively informal marketing system such as that of Angola they came back with dollars. The textile industry of La Salada, in those years of the Trade Mission to Angola which occurred in 2012, was cheaper than that of the Chinese.

La Salada Fair is an interface between the formal and the informal because the raw material is formal, and the machinery is also formal. It's transformed into an informal urban sector not because of tax issues but because of the characteristics of capital accumulation where the income of the company and that of the family are in the same accounting, which is carried by the owner of the enterprise, who is the head of the family at the same time. This is what typifies the Argentine urban informal sector. What happened in the previous government (2015–2019) was an attempt to shrink that sector, of that marketing space, with the argument of legalisation and with

unverifiable accusations of illicit associations against the directors of the fairs; I don't care about that. It's a legitimate and interesting source of work and produces textile garments that are more than affordable for the popular sectors. When we were in government, we had to take care of generating employment, La Salada and other similar environments are a source of employment where you had to provide the conditions for the informal to become formal. But the core is not its relationship with taxes but its relationship with the division of accounting between the family and the business, with a process that isn't forced. That's the characteristic of the urban informal sector in Argentina.

There are no separate accounts in the Argentine 'informal' economy, and labour relations are flexible. They have a family base, and the employees are not just employees but collaborators; they are integrated into the family group. And there develops a modus vivendi where you urbanists enter: how they travel, how and where they live, etc.

Q: This difference that you make between 'two types of formality' is interesting.

A: Those who are studying these things from the outside do not understand them. They think that they are third-world things or underdevelopment things because the approach is from capital, not from work. Entrepreneurial capitalism, entrepreneurship in general is the World Bank's vision, it's what tried to encourage globalisation. That's why they directly pivoted to the microcredits proposed by the Nobel Prize winner in Economics, Amartya Sen.

Q: In the early years of the La Salada phenomenon, from the point of view of urban planners, La Salada was a problem: they did not know how to approach it, they did not understand the scale, if it was a phenomenon that had to be studied or not. From your position in the government, how did you see that network in those years?

A: Like another part of the economy. They generated employment, period. For me as Secretary of Commerce, the economy was and is one. You have to create the conditions for them to appropriate more of the social

La Salada, Buenos Aires, aerial view, 2022

surplus. The economy is one. The government cannot deal with two economies, it has to integrate them into one.

Q: And how do you see these characteristics of the particular informality of the Argentine economy, now that it has dragged on for more than ten years of uninterrupted crisis?

A: It remains the same; what happens is that the concentration of income in the upper deciles creates a more unfair society. And what's disturbing is the accumulation of capital in those concentrated sectors. You have to generate a macroeconomic model to discuss the surplus of the informal sectors or the base of the pyramid. If you go towards a concentrator model you have these levels of poverty.

Q: Ten years ago there was a moment where the phenomenon of La Salada began to be read under the paradigm of entrepreneurship.

A: That was the World Bank's vision, that is how they tried to encourage globalisation. We encouraged families to accumulate capital, not from entrepreneurship but from sewing together. I think that we accompanied the La Salada phenomenon, it wasn't something that bothered us, that's why I took them to export to Angola. At that time, the textile products of La Salada were cheaper than the Chinese ones.

Q: You spoke in another report about this vision of the crossroads between Brazil and South Africa, Argentina and Angola in the definition of a commercial space in the South Atlantic ...

A: That's more geopolitical, but that was why we went to Angola. What happens is that later you have to make commercial relations, which were the reason for those first trips in 2004/5.

Q: And looking to the future, how do you see the La Salada process?

A: To the extent that you reindustrialise the country and part of the surplus flows to the popular sectors, their standard of living ostensibly improves. In La Salada those who traded there came to have a middle-class standard of living. Private schools, cars, etc. They continued to be part of the urban informal sector due to their characteristics, but in social terms, they had a middle-class standard of living.

Q: What do you think of the term 'barrani' that has been circulating lately in the media to describe the current situation of the Argentine economy? Is it a way of naming an articulation between the formal and the informal? Is it another way of saying that there is only one economy?

A: In Argentina, of course, yes. Not in other economies in the region. In Peru and Ecuador, they are still disparate. In Colombia, informality had another merchandise. In Venezuela, they have a problem of capital accumulation. In Brazil, I would say that the urban informal sector is part of the hard core of poverty, and it doesn't come out from there; they have a very low accumulation rate. In Argentina, there's a scheme, but the activity of collecting recyclables in the streets has increased enormously, with cardboard, and plastics. All of the urban recyclers' activity ends up in large manufacturing companies that transform them. In incipient industrialisation, these urban informal sectors are integrated from their own activity or leave the activity. Industrialisation formalises through work.

REFERENCES

Alvarez, L. 'El amor después del Amor.' *Revista Panamá*, Buenos Aires, May 2023.
https://panamarevista.com/el-amor-despues-del-amor/

Díaz, M., et al. 'Hábitat popular y prácticas de subsistencia en villas del AMBA (Argentina) en contexto de pandemia.' *Revistainvi* 37, no. 104 (2022): 230–52.

'El día que el kirchnerismo llevó La Salada a Angola.' *Perfil*, 21 June 2017.
https://www.perfil.com/noticias/politica/el-dia-que-el-kirchnerismo-llevo-la-salada-a-angola.phtml

Eleisegui, P. 'La Salada "for export": detalles del mega emprendimiento que se levantará en Angola, para alegría de Moreno.' *Profesional*, 10 July 2012.
https://www.iprofesional.com/negocios/140090-la-salada-for-export-detalles-del-mega-emprendimiento-que-se-levantara-en-angola-para-alegria-de-moreno

Gris Público Americano, m7red. *Paraformal: Urban ecologies.* Apuntes CCEBA 2011 Collections (Buenos Aires: Bisman Editions, 2011).

'Qué significa "barrani" la moda de la gastronomía clandestine.' *Perfil*, 28 August 2020.
https://www.perfil.com/noticias/economia/que-significa-barrani-la-moda-de-la-gatronomia-clandestina.phtml

1940s–2000

1 In the 1940s, on the land today occupied by the fair, beach resorts were established around salt water pools discovered in the area during the rectification of the Matanza- Riachuelo basin.
2 During the hyperinflationary crisis of 1989 and prior to the creation of the La Salada Fair, there were 'manteros' fairs.
3 The fairs and textile workshops' organisation run by the Bolivian group of traders purchases one of the old disused beach resorts which was part of the complex popularly known as 'La Salada', marking the inception of the fair.

4 The first fair that appears in La Salada is 'Urkupiña' fair.
5 The inception of La Salada's Ocean fair
6 Severe economic crisis in Argentina leading to high unemployment and rise in informal activities
7 Inception of the 'MercadoLibre', an informal e-commerce platform in Buenos Aires

2000–2005

8 The experiment in forming an overseas commercial circuit between La Salada and Luanda, Angola, is interesting as an indication of a scale change: a local network of informal urban sectors can trade globally.
9 La Salada as a cultural phenomenon and popular production ecosystem gains traction during the financial crisis.
10 Expanding spatially, La Salada attracts an immense amount of both new vendors and visitors.
11 Political crisis in Argentina.
12 The main administrators of the Urkupiña Fair are arrested; the area known as La Ribera is added, with posts placed on the south bank of the Riachuelo, in some cases, built on land reclaimed from the river.

Timeline of key events shaping the transformation of La Salada, Buenos Aires

Socio-cultural events

Economic events

Political events

E-commerce

Spatial events

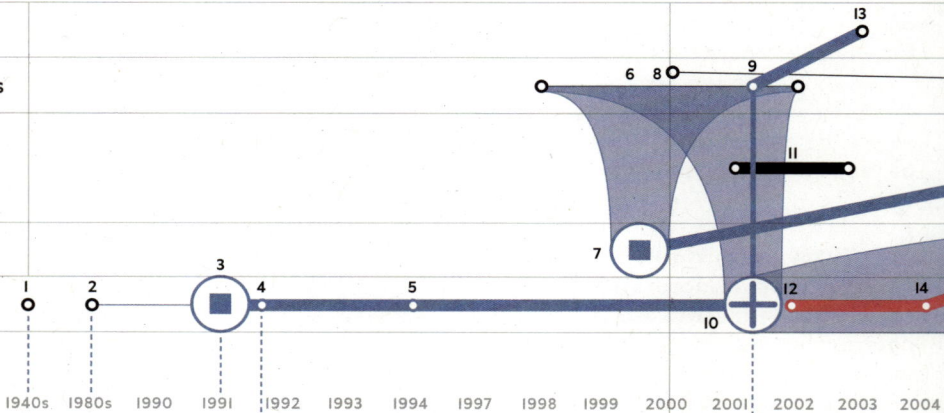

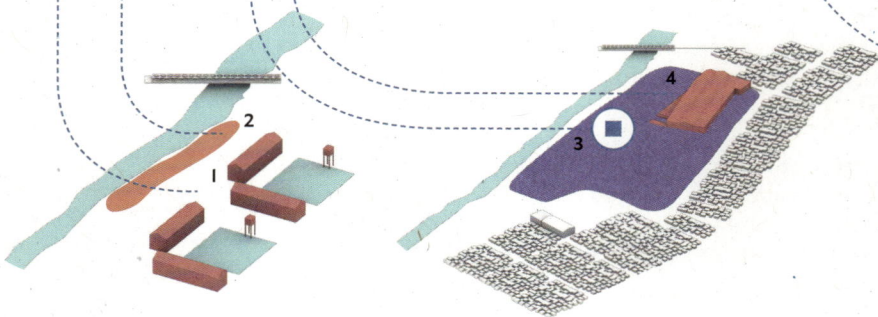

1940s 1980s 1990 1991 1992 1993 1994 1997 1998 1999 2000 2001 2002 2003 2004

13 Between 50,000 and 60,000 people from throughout the country pass through the fair every day. Between 400 and 500 buses arrive at La Salada daily.
14 Stalls added in 2001 are evicted in the midst of clashes resulting in one vendor's death.

2005–2010

15 A small logistics network connecting the fair is developed through the use of long-distance buses modified to carry passengers and cargo.
16 La Salada expands its business to the interior of the country through the 'Saladitas' – smaller fairs copying the La Salada model.

2010–2023

17 La Salada launches its own e-commerce platform, La Salada Online.
18 An analysis by *The Economist* magazine in 2012 finds out that in 2010 six of the world's ten fastest-growing economies were in sub-Saharan Africa. One of them was Angola.
19 Another eviction is carried out in the same sector, requested by the Matanza Riachuelo Basin Authority (ACUMAR).
20 MercadoPago, the digital payment platform, is developed by MercadoLibre.
21 Mauricio Macri takes office as president of Argentina, a benchmark for a coalition of traditional centre parties and new liberal-leaning parties. The attack on La Salada Fair promotes a change in attitude towards what academics call the 'popular economy'.

22 2015-2019 government attempts to shrink informal sector activities
23 Criminalisation of La Salada as a result of the change in government
24 More than 600 'Saladitas' in Buenos Aires
25 In a highly visible media-orchestrated operation that included fifty-five raids, Jorge Castillo is arrested in his mansion at an exclusive country club in an investigation concerning criminal association.
26 Beginning of a strict lockdown as a result of the COVID-19 pandemic
27 Avellaneda Avenue, another retail area located in the southwest of the city gains momentum because of the economic crisis and growing inflation left by the pandemic.

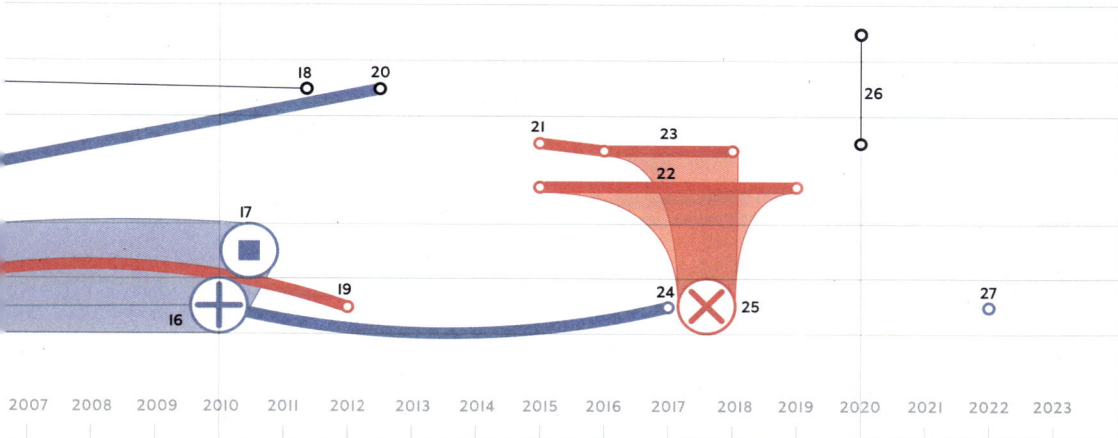

2007 2008 2009 2010 2011 2012 2013 2014 2015 2016 2017 2018 2019 2020 2021 2022 2023

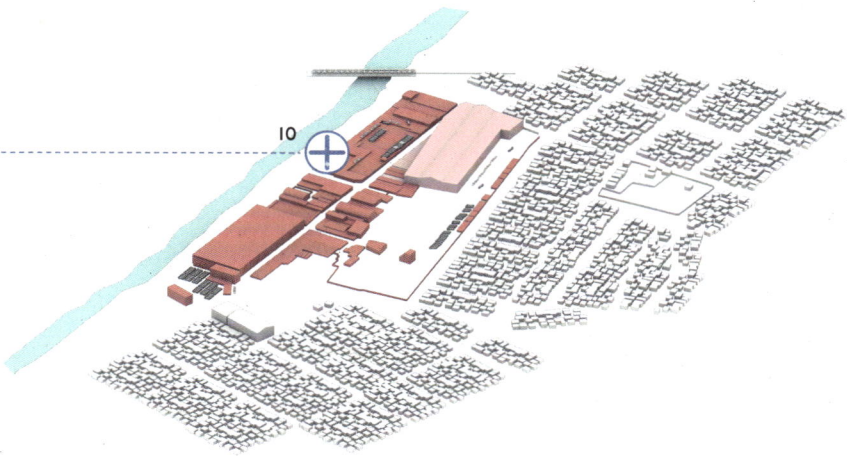

■ Spatial, social, economic and political interventions into in/formal markets
■ Informality as a survival method and means of adapting to changing socio-economic and political circumstances

Transatlantic export links between La Salada, Buenos Aires and Angola

Angola

Argentina

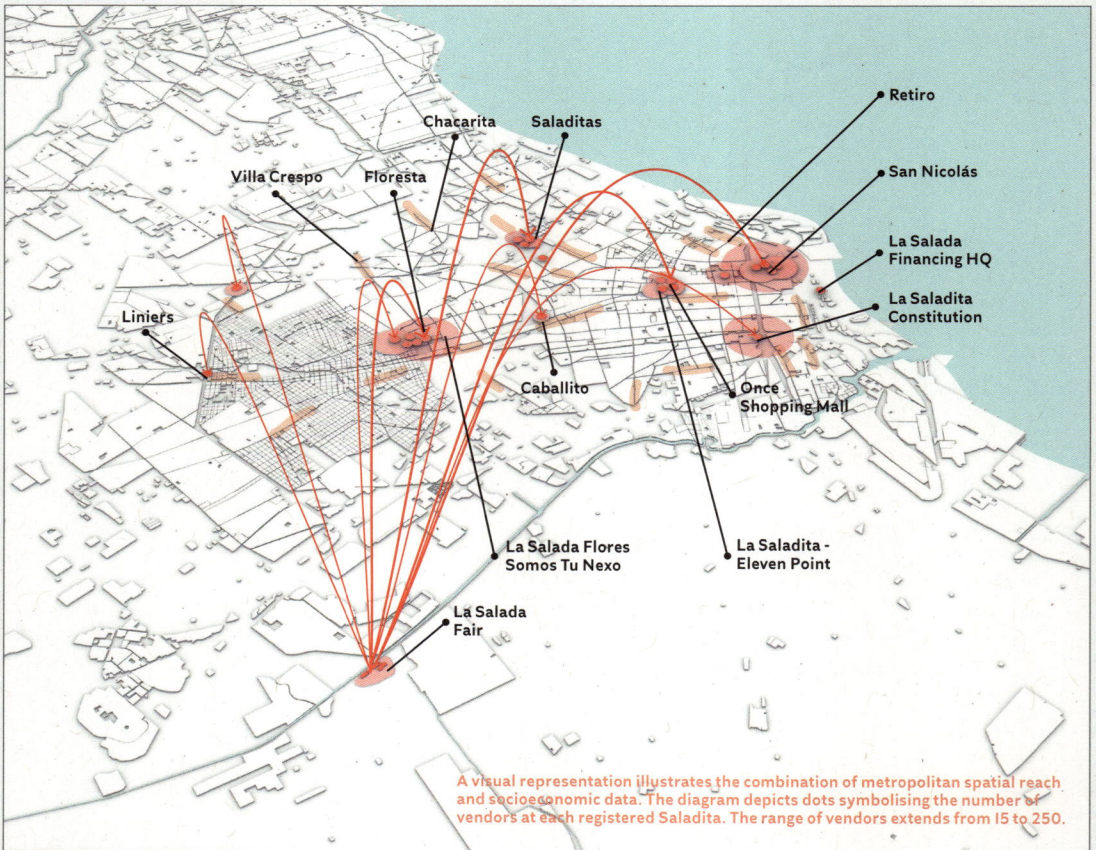

Retiro

San Nicolás

La Salada
Financing HQ

La Saladita
Constitution

Chacarita

Saladitas

Villa Crespo

Floresta

Liniers

Caballito

Once
Shopping Mall

La Salada Flores
Somos Tu Nexo

La Saladita -
Eleven Point

La Salada
Fair

A visual representation illustrates the combination of metropolitan spatial reach
and socioeconomic data. The diagram depicts dots symbolising the number of
vendors at each registered Saladita. The range of vendors extends from 15 to 250.

■ Commercial corridors   ■ Saladitas

Mushrooming of La Salada-style markets ('Saladitas') across the metropolitan area of Buenos Aires

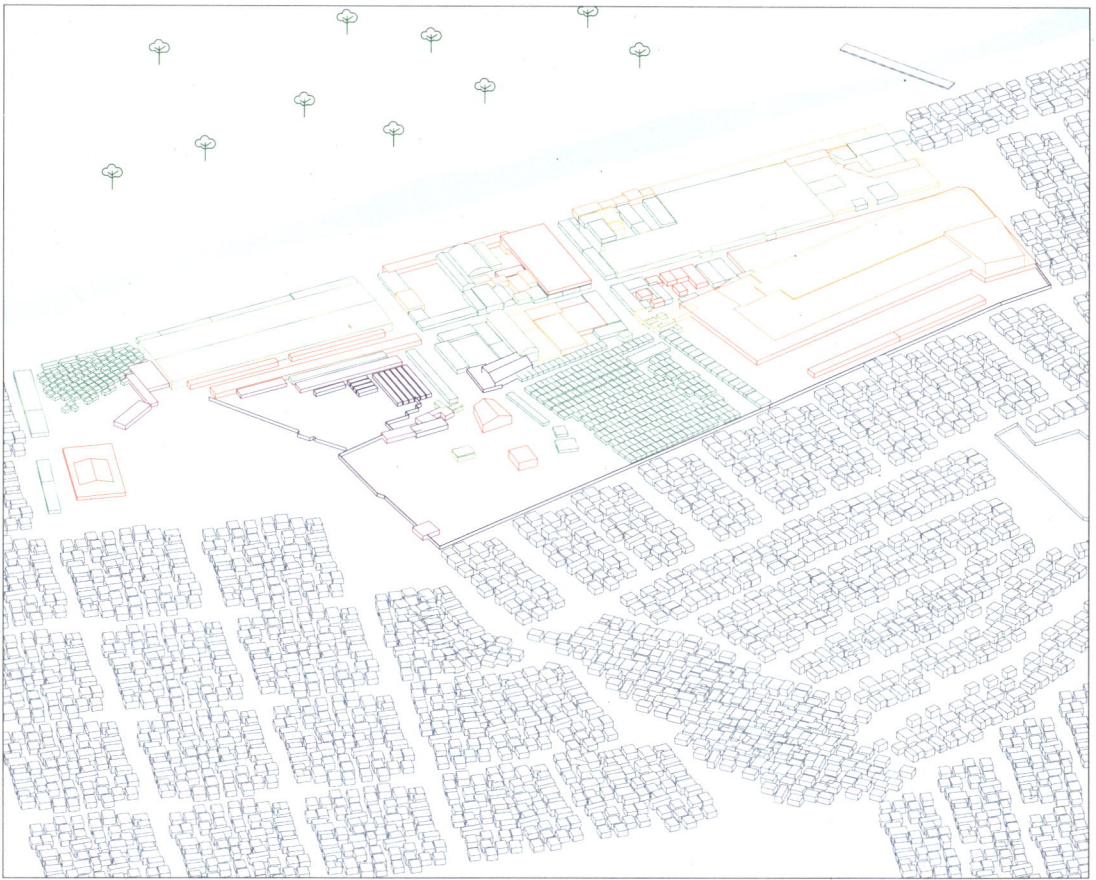

-2000 ■ 2000 ■ 2004 ■ 2005 ■ 2005 ■ 2010 ■ 2013 ■ 2017 ■ 2022

La Salada neighbourhood, Buenos Aires: key phases of spatial development

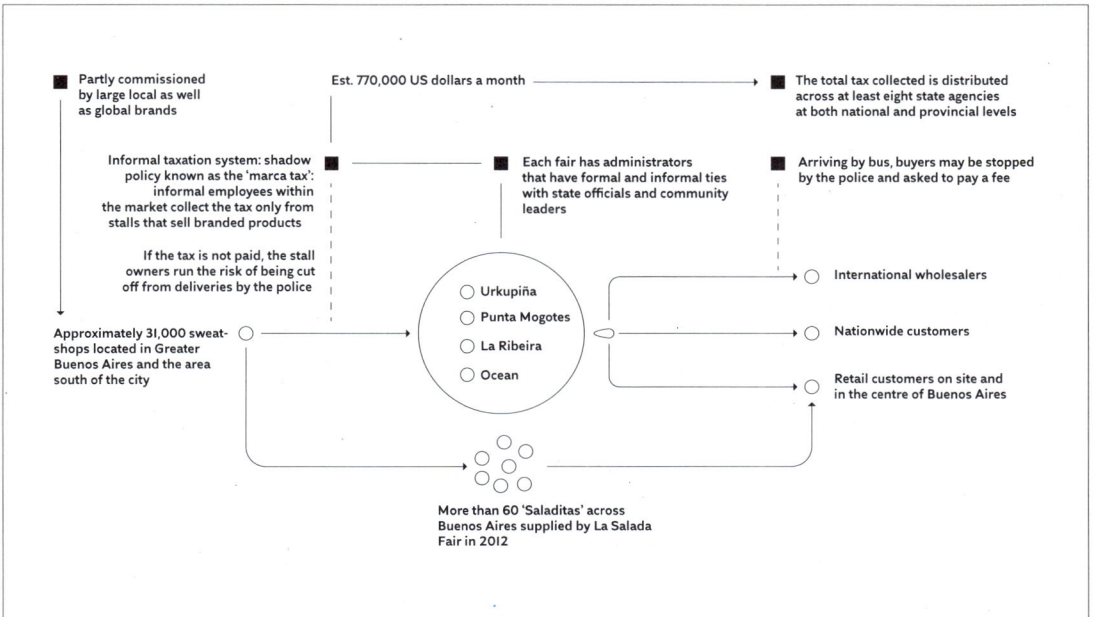

■ Partly commissioned
by large local as well
as global brands

Est. 770,000 US dollars a month

■ The total tax collected is distributed
across at least eight state agencies
at both national and provincial levels

Informal taxation system: shadow
policy known as the 'marca tax':
informal employees within
the market collect the tax only from
stalls that sell branded products

■

Each fair has administrators
that have formal and informal ties
with state officials and community
leaders

■ Arriving by bus, buyers may be stopped
by the police and asked to pay a fee

If the tax is not paid, the stall
owners run the risk of being cut
off from deliveries by the police

○ Urkupiña
○ Punta Mogotes
○ La Ribeira
○ Ocean

○ International wholesalers

○ Nationwide customers

Approximately 31,000 sweatshops located in Greater
Buenos Aires and the area
south of the city

○ Retail customers on site and
in the centre of Buenos Aires

More than 60 'Saladitas' across
Buenos Aires supplied by La Salada
Fair in 2012

Operational scheme of La Salada

■ Formal-informal linkages
○ Production and movement of goods and sale

Typical infrastructural components, La Salada, Buenos Aires

La Colada, Buenos Aires, 2022

BUS

Buses serve Argentine provinces and neighbouring countries such as Bolivia and Paraguay

KOMBI

Kombi buses serve as a practical means of transportation for visitors travelling from Buenos Aires and the metropolitan area to the La Salada Fair, which is situated on the outskirts of the city.

PLASTIC BAGS

Bulk shoppers at the market commonly employ large plastic bags as a practical means of transporting their purchases back to the buses and onwards to their home places.

CART

Carts are used for transporting goods inside the fair.

| 2000 | I5 | 0,5 | 0 |

Logistics by range
Distance in km

La Salada neighbourhood, Buenos Aires, 2022

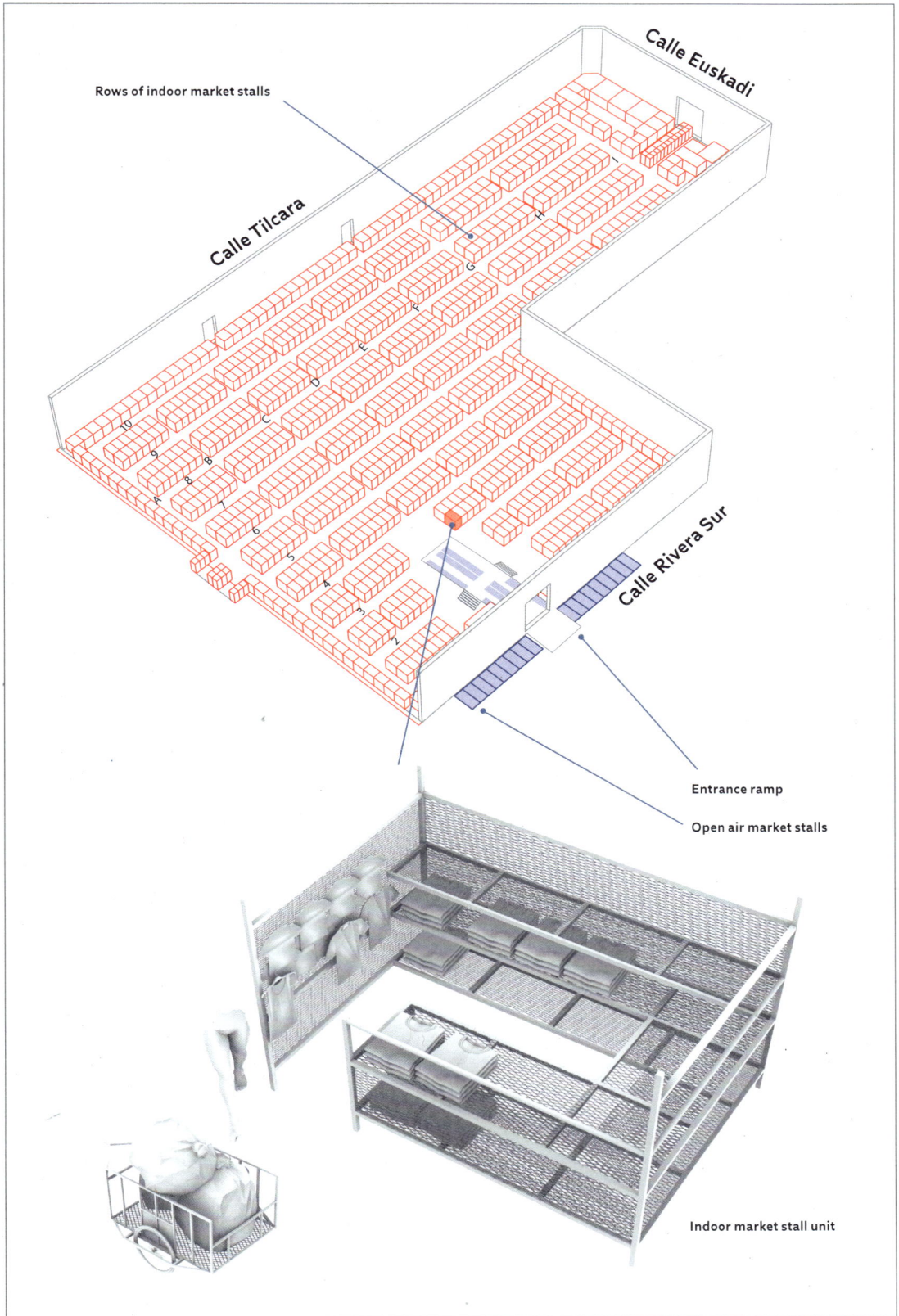

Rows of indoor market stalls

Calle Euskadi

Calle Tilcara

Calle Rivera Sur

Entrance ramp

Open air market stalls

Indoor market stall unit

Feria Punta Mogote, La Salada, market layout

La Salada, Buenos Aires, 2022

Relocation

Dajabón Binational Market, Dominican Republic, 2022

Melisa Vargas

Haitian-Dominican Markets as Places of Exception

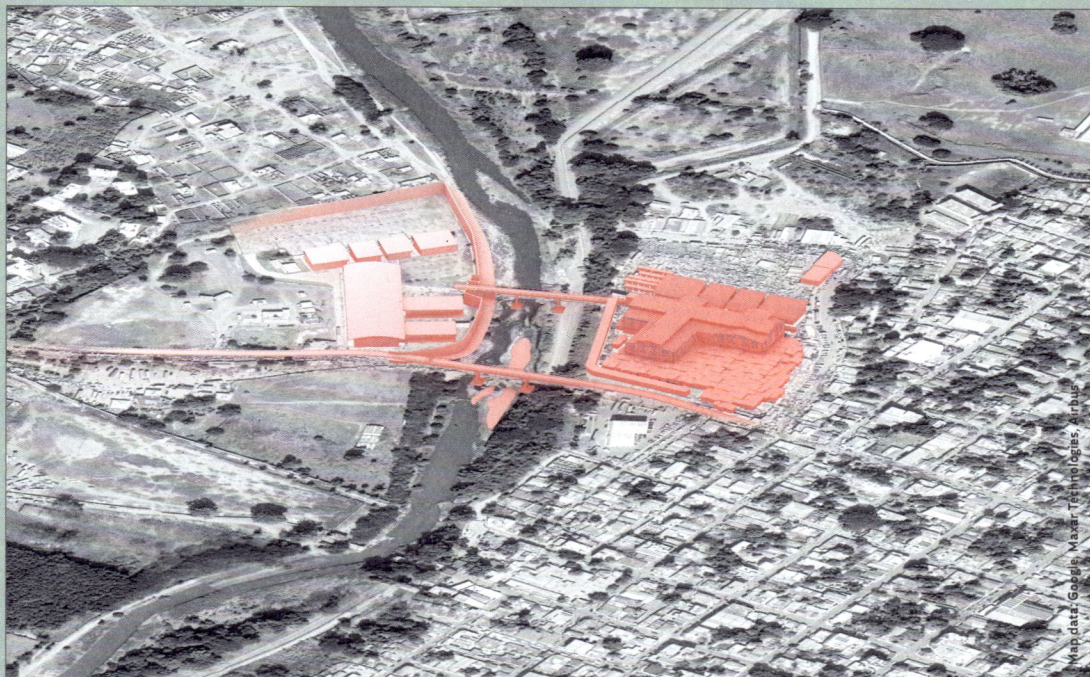

The current social, political, and economic context of cross-border trade relations between Haiti and the Dominican Republic is strongly influenced by the expansion of the existing border wall built in the past decade. This expansion has become an inevitable reality. This piece of infrastructure and its construction (deeply) impacts the environment and the communities surrounding it, and puts the markets (and the people involved) under tremendous pressure; these are challenges that will change the way the towns and commerce operate at the border. Even if informal movement and trade characterise the markets, their partial formality regarding spatial containment and military control on the Dominican side of the border contributes to corruption and reinforces existing power imbalances. The various ways in which the binational markets could potentially operate as places of exception, in combination with more structural and policy-related actions, can create new opportunities for economic cooperation and improvement of social and political relations between the two countries.

The border zone is shaped through bridges, timed crossing points, and buildings. New market halls funded by international aid have been erected on both sides of the border.

On the Dominican side these spaces are regulated by customs authorities and have fixed hours of operation, whereas on the Haitian side, more consolidated market activities have yet to develop.

Massacre River

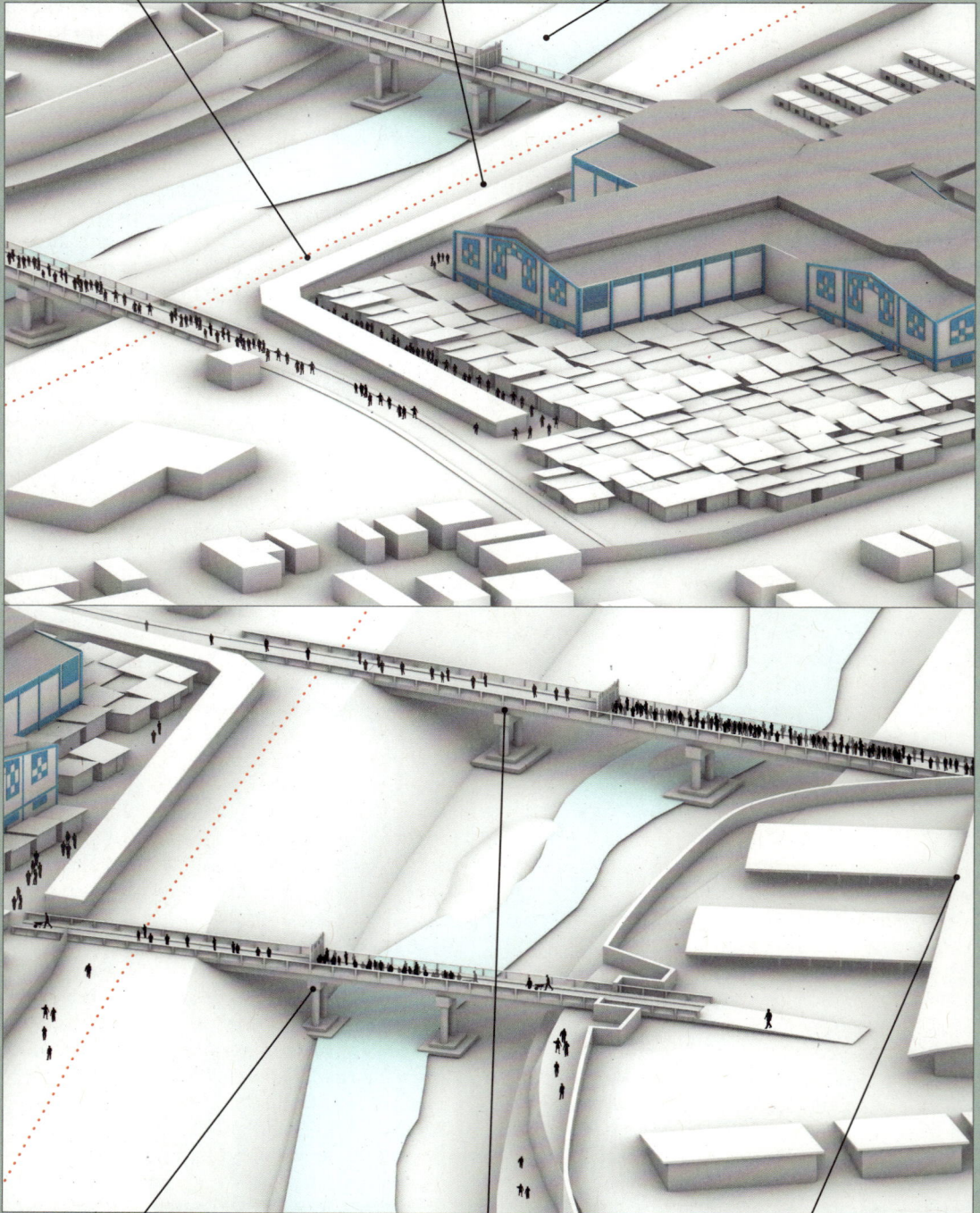

A new bridge offers a direct connection between the two markets for those on foot. Wheelbarrows are used to transport goods across the border.

When the market is open, thousands of pedestrians queue to cross the bridge. This is also the only bridge open for vehicles.

Following the opening of the market hall in Dajabón in March 2013, the new market of Ouanaminthe was initiated in 2015. Since its completion in 2019 it has remained unused.

Haiti and the Dominican Republic share a border that spans approximately 388 kilometres, and it features several international markets that facilitate cross-border trade between the two countries. The most well-known of these markets is the binational market of Dajabón, in the northern region of the Dominican Republic, which is one of the largest and busiest markets in the Caribbean. Cross-border trade with the Dominican Republic is an important source of income for many Haitians and a crucial supply system for various products, of which food is especially prevalent. However, it is difficult to quantify how much Haiti relies on these markets as there is limited data available on the volume and value of cross-border trade due to factors such as lack of customs regulations, corruption, and informal commerce. However, trade between both countries has been historically asymmetric.

Bilateral trade grew slowly in the 1990s, and by 2001 there was still a relatively small trade deficit – less than 100 million US dollars – in the Dominican Republic's favour. However, Haitian imports surged over the next twelve years – from 208 million dollars in 2002 to more than 1 billion dollars in 2013 – while exports barely budged. In 2015, the Dominican Republic officially exported about 1 billion dollars to Haiti but imported only 4 million dollars from it. The bilateral trade deficit remains. In 2017 the Dominican Republic's exports to Haiti came to about 853 million dollars, while its imports from Haiti totalled approximately 42 million dollars. Most of this bilateral trade (85 percent) moves overland, and much of it is never officially registered, making it hard to gauge the true dimensions of the Haiti/Dominican Republic trade imbalance. These unregistered imports include goods that are under-invoiced at the border and those that are simply unreported to Haitian authorities. A 2016 study estimated that about 259 million dollars in merchandise is registered as Dominican, still, not Haitian. Another 375 million dollars are not registered in either country, though the authors recognised that the 'exact values of informal trade are extremely difficult' to determine. This implies that Haitian authorities do not collect taxes on some 634 million dollars in imported

goods, many of which compete with domestically made products.[1]

Driven primarily by informal merchants who buy and sell goods at the markets, cross-border trade has always been important for Haiti's economy in the face of significant challenges in terms of poverty, unemployment, natural disasters, and political instability that have characterised its recent history. The markets, as they operate in the present, clearly reflect the difference between the commercial offer and the demand of each side. The existing structures and infrastructures, such as bridges, walls, fences, perimeters, customs offices, military posts and so on, clearly demarcate the spaces and passages for the Haitian population as the one that mobilises on mass towards the Dominican Republic. At the same time, Dominican vendors occupy most of the market buildings with new wholesale merchandise and locally grown agricultural produce; the Haitian offer is mainly of a small scale and consists of used clothes, donated items, some agricultural goods and canned items.

The binational market in the Dajabón-Ouanaminthe region has historically been the most important and largest of all the border markets. It represents a critical lifeline for Haiti during the many crises the country has faced in recent history and in the present. Though the need for doing business is mutual, certainly for Haiti, the possibility of obtaining basic products in Dajabón that are often scarce or inexistent in the main cities, especially the capital Port Au Prince, represents the difference between life and death.

The fragile condition of the country has worsened in the aftermath of Jovenel Moise's assassination, as two-thirds of Port au Prince is under the control of gangs. The insecurity has been made worse by the global economic crises generated by the invasion of Ukraine. In 2023, Haiti human rights observers documented a spike in serious abuses, such as sexual violence, alongside half of the population living without enough food and a recent surge of cholera, which has killed at least 594 people between October 2022 and March 2023.

1   Michael Matera et al, 'Cross-Border Trade and Corruption along the Haiti-Dominican Republic Border,' March 2019 (report, Center for Strategic and International Studies, Washington DC, March 2019), *https://www.csis.org/analysis/cross-border-trade-and-corruption-along-haiti-dominican-republic-border*

This crisis is placing enormous pressure on a practically non-existent hospital and medical system that depends almost entirely on international aid groups. As the gangs grow more powerful, they are terrorising humanitarian workers, who are on the front line responding to the crises.[2]

These binational markets are involved and affected by these extenuating conditions and tensions between Haiti and the Dominican Republic. Their spatial configurations are constantly pushed towards concealment and control on the Dominican side; the possibility of total closure consistently lurks as conflict and chaos takes hold of Haiti, but at the same time, the constant need to open keeps these spaces in cautious activity.

THE PARTIAL INFORMALITY OF THE BINATIONAL MARKETS

The Ministry of Defense claimed that a sign of 'tranquility' in the border region is the daily occasion of the binational markets, which 'even with the situation that prevails in the neighbouring country, take place without major setbacks, something that can only happen when there is an atmosphere of security, of which the Dominican Armed Forces are guarantors.'[3] Nevertheless, as the crossing points that are located towards the south of the border are closer to the Haitian capital, they have become more compromised by the threat from gangs; the Dajabón market is the only one that can reliably continue supplying Haiti with food and other essential goods.

The Dominican Republic has taken an approach strongly focused on domestic security when it comes to the border as the situation in Haiti becomes more severe. The militarisation of the Dominican border region has been a priority for the government as it has increased the salary of soldiers who opt to serve there and has made an unprecedented expenditure on vehicles, equipment, and defence infrastructure.[4] Its plans for the development of the border region have as its main intervention the construction of a wall

and/or fence, as it is widely referred to, that responds to the political pressure resulting from an imminent increase in Haitians trying to cross to the Dominican Republic and how the Dominican population perceives this as a significant threat to its currently exponential development.

The binational markets also persist in the face of this historical fear of Haitian immigration, even if they operate as hybrid informal-formal commercial hubs and as gateways for both legal and illegal traffic of goods and people. Paradoxically, the combination of highly informal commercial and human activity coming from the Haitian side with formal governmental and military structures on the Dominican side has created the conditions for corruption and unregulated transactions that disproportionally impact the most vulnerable participants.

Despite the fact that the markets offer a space for what can be considered a peaceful commercial exchange, the tensions of all the implicit forces that operate in and around them are felt and are ever-present. The need for their existence is exploited rather than potentiated. Its partial informality, rather than being recognised as the result of the historic organic interaction between border towns, is currently weaponised and perpetuated by those who profit from it in both countries, that is, organised crime networks, gangs, corrupt military personnel and customs officials, coyotes,[5] as well as drug, merchandise, and weapons smugglers.

Another factor that influences Haiti's criminal economy is its extensive dependency on imports. Indeed, every facet of the country's formal and informal economy is connected to goods imported from abroad. For example, approximately 80 percent of all rice and cooking oil and roughly 50 percent of all food products used by Haitians are imported. Another means by which firearms and ammunition are shipped to Haiti is via the Dominican Republic and to a lesser extent Jamaica. Media reports and interviews with

2   Luke Taylor, 'Warfare Is Encroaching: Aid Groups May Have to Cut Back Services in Haiti as Violence Grows,' *The Guardian*, 3 March 2023.
3   'Ministerio de Defensa dice cuidar la frontera es su prioridad; garantiza bandas de Haití no operan en RD - Diario Libre,' *Diario Libre*, 24 June 2022, *https://www.diariolibre.com/actualidad/nacional/2022/06/24/defensa-asegura-cuida-la-frontera-de-bandas-de-haiti/1909632*
4   Ramon Cruz Benzán, 'Tropas de frontera tendrán incentivos salariales. Tropas De Frontera Tendrán Incentivos Salariales,' *Listín Diario*, 10 October 2022, *https://listindiario.com/la-republica/2022/10/10/742755/tropas-de-frontera-tendran-incentivos-salariales*
5   Coyote is a term originally used in the context of the Mexico-United States border, that refers to those who organise, aid and make illegal migrants crossings happen. This term comes from Spanish, it is the common name for the North American wild dog (Canis latrans).

Dajabón Binational Market, Dominican Republic, 2022

Dajabón Binational Market, Dominican Republic, 2012

Haitian customs officials suggest that weapons may first transit through key ports in Santo Domingo such as Haina, before being transported across border crossings into Haiti, including from Jimaní, Comendador and Elias Piña. Officials at the Haina port alone reportedly seized over 112,000 'units of firearms and ammunition' in the first six months of 2022, most of them originating from the United States. Haitian customs officials also periodically intercept contraband at the border – including firearms – intermingled with food products such as beans, flour, and rice. Firearms and ammunition have been seized at border crossings including Pedernales and Dajabón in the Dominican Republic and Belladère, Malpasse, and the Codevi free trade factory in Ouanaminthe in Haiti. The extent of cross-border trafficking appears to be linked to the degree of police and customs presence as well as of gang control. For example, Malpasse recently registered a decline in the volume of cross-border transactions due to gang activity, resulting in a surge of illicit goods diverted through Belladère instead.[6]

THE BORDER WALL AND/OR FENCE

The Academy of Sciences of the Dominican Republic pointed out that the wall – as it is generally referred to – is being built in contravention of environmental regulations, especially in the segment that goes through Montecristi, putting the Saladilla Lagoon, an area defined by the Dominican Ministry of Environment as a conservation area for wildlife and protected by law, at risk and in danger. In a press release, the institution specified that, although the construction of the wall lends itself to many readings and evaluations, none of them justify violating laws 64-00 on the environment and 202-04 on protected areas, nor could they ever contravene the fact that protected areas are national assets, invulnerable, imprescriptible, and unseizable.[7] This statement omits the fact that this and many unique ecosystems along the border region do not simply end at the borderline and rely on the continuity of fauna movements and migrations, hydric systems, or mangroves to name a few, and that the construction affects these natural reserves in Haiti as well, a country

6   Angela Me, 'Haiti's Criminal Markets: Mapping Trends in Firearms and Drug Trafficking,' (United Nations Office on Drugs and Crime, 2023).
7   'Polvos y escombros en el mercado binacional,' Listin Diario, 4 Febuary 2023,
     https://listindiario.com/la-republica/2023/02/04/761168/polvos-y-escombros-en-el-mercado-binacional

already suffering from severe deforestation and other environmental issues.

In its construction process, this physical limit is already causing a transformation in the environmental, social, and commercial systems of the border region, partly due to the pressure to rapidly accelerate its execution and the lack of adequate technical assessment of exactly how or through which areas it should be built. The markets and the communities located around them are no exception in this regard. Commercial structures are being demolished to clear space for the wall without local owners having an appraisal of their value and without confirmation that they will receive compensation. The lack of planning for these demolition and construction operations has also left vendors surrounded by dust, debris, and poor accessibility to the areas where they sell their products in the market at Pedernales (southern Dominican province in the border region). This unsafe situation has resulted in a decrease in sales in combination with the lower demand that the crisis in Haiti had already generated.

Beyond the immediate repercussions of this infrastructural intervention on the communities and territories it is being built on, the long-term effects of the wall on the border region and its dynamics can be predicted based on what has happened in other borders that have been walled or fenced, especially in recent years. The most prominent example of a wall or fence being built on the premise of it being a form of defence against illegal immigration between two very unequal countries is the Mexico-United States barrier. The paper entitled 'Border Walls' co-authored by Stanford economist Melanie Morten, Stanford doctoral candidate Cauê Dobbin and Dartmouth economist Treb Allen, examines the effects of the Secure Fence Act of 2006, which added 548 miles of border fence between the two countries. At a cost of 2.3 billion dollars, the expansion increased total fencing to 658 miles, one-third of the entire U.S.-Mexico border. The wall did not significantly curtail migration, according to the research. Using data from Mexican consulates on the flow of adult Mexican citizens who migrated between 2006–2010, the researchers estimated that the wall expansion reduced the total number of Mexican-born workers coming into the United States by only 0.6 percent, roughly 83,000 people. Further analysis showed that the expansion of the wall largely harmed American workers. College-educated U.S. workers lost an equivalent of 4.35 dollars in annual income, while less-educated U.S. workers benefited on average by only 36 cents. Taken together, 'the costs far outweigh the benefits, even for low-skilled workers in the U.S.'[8] Wendy Brown considers that border walls are a response to the declining sovereignty of states, which in search of 'an endeavour to protect' citizens generate theatrical strategies that are, more than effective solutions, psychic containers that make the enclosed feel part of something defined. Thus, for Brown, the importance of border walls does not reside so much in their (doubtful) efficiency but rather in their ostentatious visibility.[9]

In February 2023 the outcomes of Operación Frontera (Operation Border) an operation carried out by the Ministerio Público de la República Dominicana (Dominican Republic Attorney General) exposed and prosecuted members of an organised crime network comprising fifteen people out of which five were part of Cuerpo Especializado en Seguridad Fronteriza Terrestre (CESFronT) of the Dominican National Army, a specialist unit deployed at the border region to guard and protect the area. Members of the criminal network moved along the banks of the Massacre River, on the Haitian side, made their way across a farm and then through a controlled gate. As detailed by the Attorney General, the farm belongs to a Dominican citizen. After being conveyed into the country, the Haitians were transferred along the Copey-Manzanillo highway towards the Copey municipality to be kept inside a chicken farm where the migrants slept. This place was referred to in code as 'the nursery' and functioned as a reception centre. They were then transferred by motorcycle to different parts of the Dominican Republic.

155

8   May Wong, 'Economists Find High Cost and Low Benefit to Border Wall for U.S. Workers,' *Stanford News Service*, *https://news.stanford.edu/press-releases/2018/11/15/border-wall-cameefit-u-s-workers*
9   Miguel Aguilar. 'Análisis dialéctico de los muros fronterizos,' in *Las ciencias sociales y la agenda nacional: Reflexiones y propuestas desde las Ciencias Sociales. Vol. VI: Migraciones y transmigraciones*, eds. Rodolfo Cruz, Ivy Rieger, Martha Judith Sánchez, (Mexico: COMESCO, 2018), 57–71.

E-044   E-045   E-046

Indoor market, Dajabón Binational Market, Dominican Republic, 2022

As this case illustrates, illegal migration often operates in a complex way that goes far beyond the mere act of individuals crossing a territorial limit. The participation of formal institutional and military systems that, as mentioned before, combine with informal and unregistered ones, generate a partial form of institutional control that enables individuals within those institutions to engage in criminal actions such as human trafficking. Therefore, despite there being a physical barrier, it lacks an institutional one. Seen from an optimistic perspective, border walls, although violent, seek security and allow the commingling of cosmopolitan citizens to take place in optimal conditions. Those who support this view generally assume that global processes weaken states and that national identity is necessary as long as it provides benefits. In terms of security, a pessimistic narrative, on the other hand, views border walls as a source of danger: these objects, far from granting protection, are obstacles that push different actors to generate strategies (crossing, sale, contact) that integrate violence and increase vulnerability. Although it seems easy to state these complementary narratives that speak of inclusion and exclusion, it is essential to say that these discourses will continue to modify temporally and spatially, changing with the years of existence of the walls and their effects on places and subjects they divide, cross and transform.[10]

THE BINATIONAL MARKETS AS PLACES OF EXCEPTION

Border communities have no other option but to coexist with the inevitable reality of the wall's construction. In this sense, the understanding of this limit includes the market enclaves as integral parts of its configuration, as defined by the Ministry of Economy and Development in their strategies for the border region: the markets become the spatial accidents in this linear limit and become the places of exception. Intense trading with neighbours reduces the duration as well as the intensity of the conflict. Trade reduces the incentives of contiguous countries to fuel civil conflict with their neighbours similarly

to the case of inter-state wars. These incentives may be particularly strong in areas, such as much of sub-Saharan Africa, where there are strong ethnic ties across borders. Trading with neighbours is also associated with a lower risk of conflict when such trade occurs under regional trade agreements. The strength of the effect of commodity exports on conflict varies across and within countries and depends on a number of local conditions. Changes in economic conditions have a much greater potential for generating conflict where there are deep-seated, historical grievances among groups, where economic inequality is high, and where government institutions are weak or corrupt.[11]

As stated in the report 'Trading Away from Conflict: Using Trade to Increase Resilience in Fragile States' published by the World Bank, the peaceful operation of markets highly depends on the creation of suitable conditions for it. Addressing the structural issues that have an impact on the level of safety and dignity at the border markets, as well as the more immediate ones, is crucial for these spaces to become places. Prior to the twentieth century, the border between the Dominican Republic and Haiti was highly porous and uncontrolled, but this began to change when United States troops invaded and occupied both the Dominican Republic (1916–1924) and Haiti (1915–1934); in like manner, they placed the expansion of the tax base of these regimes through better control of border trade at the top of their agenda. The first customs establishments date from that period, one of which was in Dajabón.[12]

We can consider this the beginning of the partial formalisation of cross-border trade. The history of the border immediately following this period is one of blockage, rejection, and massacre, as the Rafael Trujillo dictatorship (1931–1961) made the 'Dominicanisation of the border' an official government plan that ended in the dictator ordering the mass killing of Haitian and presumed Haitian people at Dajabón in 1937 in what is known as the Perejil Massacre. The killing of Haitians went on for months, continuing into 1938.

157

10   Aguilar, 2019.
11   Massimiliano Calì, 'Trading Away from Conflict: Using Trade to Increase Resilience in Fragile States,' (Washington DC: International Bank for Reconstruction and Development / The World Bank, 2015), https://www.worldbank.org/en/topic/trade/publication/trading-away-from-conflict
12   Haroldo Dilla and Sobeida de Jesús, 'De problemas y oportunidades: intermediación urbana fronteriza en República Dominicana,' Revista Mexicana De Sociología, 67, no. 1 (March 2005): 99–126.

Typical infrastructural components, Dajabón Binational Market, Dominican Republic

Top: Border bridge at the Binational Market, Dajabón, Dominican Republic, 2022
Bottom: Indoor market, Dajabón Binational Market, Dominican Republic, 2022

The decades between the 1930s and 1980s represented a period of political turmoil for both countries with significant influence and pressure from the United States. Democracy struggled to establish itself on the island. Border trade persisted throughout this period and began to grow consistently in the 1990s after a trade embargo imposed on Haiti in 1991 due to a coup d'état that deposed the first democratically elected president Jean-Bertrand Aristide, was lifted from the country in 1995. Haiti's economy suffered tremendously due to these sanctions imposed by the Organization of American States (OAS) and found in the binational markets a vital source of goods and the opportunity to conduct trade after a period of severe scarcity.

On various occasions since then, and usually due to major events, the border markets have temporarily stopped operating. The longest closures in recent times took place from March to November 2020 due to the COVID-19 pandemic, a measure taken by the Dominican authorities to control possible outbreaks. Even after the assassination of President Jovenel Moïse in 2021 and the high levels of unrest, gang violence and overall instability that exploded in Haiti, the longer border closure in that period was only for one week with intervals of one- or two-day closings.

The markets have been the only consistent form of civilian cooperation throughout the history of both countries and have become both a commercial and a cultural phenomenon that transcends the incredibly complex layers of politics, international relations, military conflict, civilian unrest, violence, socio-cultural tensions, and natural disasters that have characterised the existence of the two nations. If both countries did not benefit tremendously from the occurrence of the market fairs, they simply would not take place. That said, the imbalance in the profit margins between the countries is a red flag that points at the imperative need to rethink the binational markets as systems inserted in their national economies. The treatment of these spaces as enclaves devoid of articulation with public spaces and the disconnect between the level of development and formality of the cities on each side diminishes their dignity.

To evenly supply cities in the binational region, international entities such as the European Union have donated market buildings on both sides of the border at specific crossings, the most prominent example being the Dajabón–Ouanaminthe crossing point. This solution has made it obvious that Haiti doesn't possess the institutional or security capacities to host market fairs yet. The buildings on the Haitian side stand unused and empty as thousands cross the bridge to the Dominican side, where safety, regulation and a more functional customs authority provide the minimum conditions for commercial exchange. The offer Haitian vendors can provide is insufficient compared to their need for supplies. Due to the reality that illicit actions on a large to small scale prove to be more profitable and convenient than participation in legal exchanges, the eradication of the problematic activities that put the most vulnerable at risk will be very difficult.

Therefore, the following structural changes must take place: In the Dominican Republic, the priorities are abuse of military power, institutional corruption and the clandestine traffic of goods, drugs, weapons, and humans. In Haiti, the occurrence of democratic elections, institutional strengthening, the guaranteeing of food security, disease control and safety for its citizens, are primordial. Nevertheless, at the local level, improving the conditions of the markets in terms of their physical infrastructure can have a significant impact in the communities that benefit from them and motivate vendors, suppliers, and buyers to invest more in their efforts. The markets can improve by:

1.   More efficiently integrating the surrounding natural resources such as rivers and forests, thus avoiding their degradation and improving the quality of the spaces used for the markets.
2.   Integrating public spaces, facilities, and outdoor elements that allow for the type of display and shopping habits of vendors and buyers at the binational markets.
3.   Creating educational programmes for vendors that cover various topics related to the management of business, merchandise display as well as the logistics and operations of the markets.

4. Providing large scale sellers with adequate spaces for their merchandise, especially food products.

5. Facilitating large scale sellers and exporters with transparent mechanisms and incentive programmes, such as soft loans and tax exemptions, to trade and do business in a safe and legal way.

6. Creating trade agreements that benefit Haitian and Dominican small-scale producers, hand-made products, art, local fashion, and design that are sold at the binational markets.

According to the study 'Trading Away from Conflict: Using Trade to Increase Resilience in Fragile States' authored by Massimiliano Calì 2015 World Bank Study, trade policies have been shown to ease tensions in fragile countries and indicate general directions for the creation of such policies. These policy directions are summarised in the following way:

I. Trade policies in fragile countries must consider the implications for conflict. They should identify the changes in trade that would most benefit the country's stability. For example, this would identify the subset of traded goods (and services) that are most relevant for the economy and the types of economic changes (e.g. international price swings, changes in trade policies in the country concerned or its trading partners) that affect the domestic prices of these goods (and services). Also, they should assess the likely distribution of gains and losses across different groups within the country due to changes in trade. This assessment, along with a political economy analysis (PEA), could help policymakers understand to what extent the adversely affected may be willing and capable of destabilising the country (or areas of it) following an adverse change in trade flows.

2. Manage receipts from commodity exports in a conflict-sensitive way. An example of how this can be done is by transferring a percentage of the rents from extractive commodities to citizens. This option is perhaps best known as Direct Dividend Payments (DDPs).

3. Protect producers, consumers, and workers from adverse trade shocks. Examples of this are targeted transfers, public works programmes, price subsidies, and temporary trade protections.

4. Promote trade with neighbours. The basic principle behind this direction is that a high volume of trade between two neighbours A and B increases the costs to A of a conflict in B, thus reducing the likelihood that A would instigate or foment civil conflict in B (and vice versa). It is also in line with the idea that trade may raise the level of trust between the peoples of neighbouring countries.

5. Support labour-intensive exports. One approach to improving the efficiency of export production in fragile countries is to develop special economic zones. The idea behind this is that in conflict-affected countries, it should be easier and more effective to achieve international competitiveness for firms in a concentrated environment rather than dispersed throughout the country.

6. Build long-term conflict resilience. Reducing interpersonal economic inequality and tackling ethnic divisions are also priorities in building conflict resilience to trade-related changes. Conceive of accountable and honest government institutions to build resilience to changes in trade flows are key.

FINAL REMARKS

Binational markets at the border between the Dominican Republic and Haiti can improve the living conditions of communities surrounding them and the countries at large in several ways, including boosting economic activity as they can increase economic exchange in the border regions by providing a platform for cross-border trade. This can generate employment opportunities and increase income levels, which can have a positive impact on the living standards of communities in the region. The markets facilitate cultural exchange between the two countries, as traders and customers from both sides of the border interact and share ideas and experiences. This can help to build trust and understanding between the two communities, which can be a crucial foundation for peace and stability in the region.

These markets provide access to a broader range of goods and services for communities on both sides of the border. This can be particularly important for communities that are geographically isolated or have limited access to markets and necessities and even reach areas like Port au Prince, currently under severe pressure and affected by food, fuel, and water scarcity. By promoting cross-border trade and interaction, binational markets contribute to the process of regional integration between the Dominican Republic and Haiti and have the potential to be an attractive hub for the rest of the Caribbean region in the future. This can lead to the development of common infrastructure and institutions and help to create a more cohesive and prosperous region.

To maximise the potential benefits of binational markets, it is important to ensure that they are well-regulated and that the needs and interests of all stakeholders are considered. This may require serious cooperation between government agencies, civil society organisations, and private sector actors on both sides of the border. Additionally, efforts should be made to address any underlying issues that may be hindering cross-border trade, such as inadequate infrastructure or bureaucratic obstacles.

Trade is a human activity that historically has been a major motivation for change and adaptation. Trade promotes innovation and has been central in the formation of particular cultures and social systems, and it has been fundamental for the evolution process of entire civilisations. In that sense, the potential that is still dormant in these relatively young market systems is very significant. This represents, with poignancy, an opportunity for a country like Haiti that desperately needs to rebuild itself almost entirely after a collapse of its natural, institutional, and social systems through the provision of jobs, business and entrepreneurial opportunities, among many others.

There are clearly a plethora of obstacles challenging the border markets on Hispaniola Island currently. However, the sheer amount of human energy and resources that, despite these incipient conditions, pass through these markets, becomes a sign of hope for a more organised and dignified future for the growth of these commercial exchanges and movements, as well as better distribution of the vast wealth that these spaces transfer from one side to the other. These markets have proven to be resilient. If approached through a multi-levelled angle, policies, plans, strategies, and agreements can turn them into regional commercial hubs. If the Dominican Republic and Haiti have historically had a complicated relationship, the markets have proven to be an effective middle ground where the mutual interest for trade, even in the direst of circumstances, has prevailed and has made international cooperation possible. Fortunately, this does not seem to be something that will change in the future.

REFERENCES

Aguilar, M. 'Análisis dialéctico de los muros fronterizos.' In *Las ciencias sociales y la agenda nacional: Reflexiones y propuestas desde las Ciencias Sociales. Vol. VI: Migraciones y transmigraciones*, edited by R. Cruz, I. Rieger, M. J. Sánchez, 57–71. Mexico: COMESCO, 2018.

Allen, T., C. Dobbin, and M. Morten. 'Border Walls.' *Stanford Institute for Economic Policy Research*, November 2018.

Baez, O. 'Polvos y escombros en el mercado binacional.' *Listin Diario*, 4 February 2023. https://listindiario.com/la-republica/2023/02/04/761168/polvos-y-escombros-en-el-mercado-binacional

Bauer, J. 'For Peace in Haiti, First Win the War on Hunger.' *The Guardian*, 17 January 2023. https://www.theguardian.com/world/2023/jan/17/for-peace-in-haiti-first-win-the-war-on-hunger

Brown, W. *Estados amurallados, soberanía en declive*. Barcelona: Herder, 2015.

Calì, M. 'Trading Away from Conflict: Using Trade to Increase Resilience in Fragile States.' Washington, DC: International Bank for Reconstruction and Development / The World Bank, 2015. https://www.worldbank.org/en/topic/trade/publication/trading-away-from-conflict

Cruz Benzán, R. 'Tropas De Frontera Tendrán Incentivos Salariales.' *Listin Diario*, 10 October 2022. https://listindiario.com/la-republica/2022/10/10/742755/tropas-de-frontera-tendran-incentivos-salariales

Dilla, H., and S. de Jesús. 'De problemas y oportunidades: intermediación urbana fronteriza en República Dominicana.' *Revista Mexicana De Sociología*, 67(1), March 2005.

'Lamentan los daños por muro fronterizo.' *Listin Diario*, 4 March 2023. https://listindiario.com/la-republica/2023/03/04/765432/lamentan-los-danos-por-muro-fronterizo

Matera, M, et al. 'Cross-Border Trade and Corruption along the Haiti-Dominican Republic Border.' Report, Center for Strategic and International Studies, Washington DC, March 2019. https://www.csis.org/analysis/cross-border-trade-and-corruption-along-haiti-dominican-republic-border

Me, A. 'Haiti's Criminal Markets: Mapping Trends in Firearms and Drug Trafficking.' United Nations Office on Drugs and Crime, 2023.

'Ministerio de Defensa dice cuidar la frontera es su prioridad; garantiza bandas de Haití no operan en RD.' *Diario Libre*, 24 June 2022. https://www.diariolibre.com/actualidad/nacional/2022/06/24/defensa-asegura-cuida-la-frontera-de-bandas-de-haiti/1909632

'Operación Frontera: Militares dejaban entrar a haitianos hacia Rd por 300 pesos.' *Diario Libre*, 23 February 2023.

Taylor, L. '"Warfare is encroaching": Aid Groups May Have to Cut Back Services in Haiti as Violence Grows.' *The Guardian*, 3 March 2023. https://www.theguardian.com/global-development/2023/mar/03/gang-violence-aid-groups-consider-abandoning-haiti

Wong, M. 'Economists Find High Cost and Low Benefit to Border Wall for U.S. Workers.' *Stanford News Service*, 15 November 2018. https://news.stanford.edu/press-releases/2018/11/15/border-wall-cameefit-u-s-workers

1988-1994

1 Haiti suffers two coup d'états.
2 Opening of borders between Haiti and the Dominican Republic (DR) as part of efforts to promote cross-border trade
3 Military coup in Haiti
4 Trade embargos imposed on Haiti by the Organisation of American States (OAS)

1994-2005

5 UN-authorised and US-led military intervention 'Uphold Democracy' ends with the capitulation of the military regime.
6 Inception of the binational market in Dajabòn
7 Opening of the CODEVI industrial park in Ouanaminthe
8 Law 28-01: Special Border Development Zone Law passed to promote economic development and social integration in the border region
9 The International Finance Corporation (IFC), the private sector development arm of the World Bank Group, provides a first loan for the construction of the Codevi free zone in Dajabòn.

2005-2010

10 European Union agrees to financially support the building of a new market hall for the binational market in Dajabòn.
11 Haitian Hemispheric Opportunity through Partnership Encouragement Act of 2008 (HOPE II) affords preferential treatment for imports of apparel, textiles, and certain other goods from Haiti to the US.
12 New market hall in Dajabòn being built by the European Union.
13 Dajabòn Market closes in response to prohibition on sale of poultry products.

Socio-cultural events

Economic events

Political events

Trade interruptions

Spatial events

Relief programmes

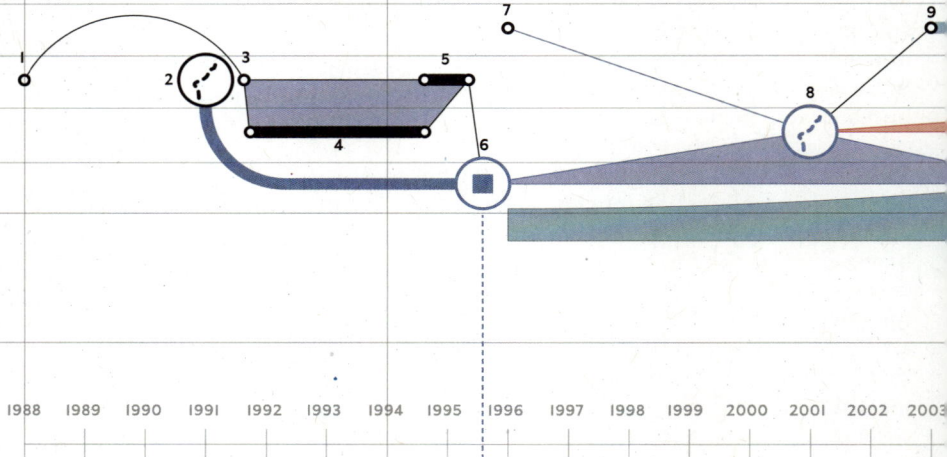

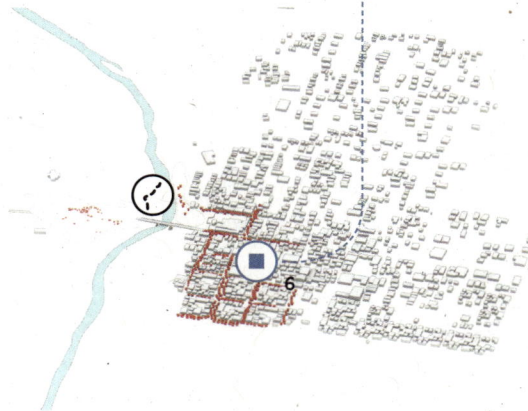

1988 1989 1990 1991 1992 1993 1994 1995 1996 1997 1998 1999 2000 2001 2002 2003

Timeline of key events shaping the transformation of Dajabón Binational Market

2010-2015

14 Following a devastating earthquake in Haiti, the market moves from the centre of Dajabòn to the site of the unfinished market building.
15 DR closes its border due to a cholera outbreak in Haiti.
16 After the 2010 earthquake, the IFC provides an additional 6 million US dollar financing package to the Codevi free zone; the International Monetary Fund (IMF) gives a loan of 102 million US dollars to Haiti.
17 Large-scale migration of Haitians into the DR
18 Haitian vendors block the border crossing demanding the release of an arrested co-national.
19 Opening of the new market building in Dajabòn

20 DR's Constitutional Court retroactively revokes citizenship of hundreds of thousands of people of Haitian descent.
21 DR closes the border as a result of a prison breakout in Haiti.

2015-2020

22 DR closes its borders in response to Haiti's general elections.
23 Protests at Pedernales Market
24 Another round of financing provided by the IFC to Grupo M for expansions related to Villas Codevi
25 Protests at Elías Piña Market
26 Opening of new border bridge
27 Murder at Pedernales Market
28 Planned opening of the new Ouanaminthe market building

2020-2023

29 DR and Haiti temporarily close the border because of the COVID-19 pandemic, severely impacting cross-border trade.
30 Assasination of Haitian president Jovenel Moïse
31 DR closes the border for several days in response to instability in Haiti.
32 Start of a 160 km 'intelligent' border fence project
33 Haitians protest at the border against mistreatment by the Dominican authorities.
34 Ouanaminthe market building still not opened

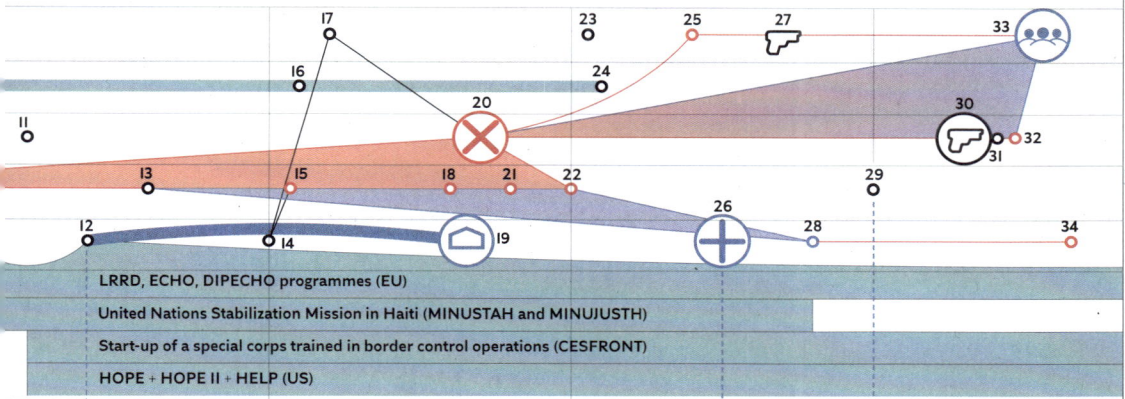

LRRD, ECHO, DIPECHO programmes (EU)

United Nations Stabilization Mission in Haiti (MINUSTAH and MINUJUSTH)

Start-up of a special corps trained in border control operations (CESFRONT)

HOPE + HOPE II + HELP (US)

2006 2007 2008 2009 2010 2011 2012 2013 2014 2015 2016 2017 2018 2019 2020 2021 2022 2023

10,12

26

29

Spatial, social, economic and political interventions into in/formal markets
Informality as a survival method and means of adapting to changing socio-economic and political circumstances

Despite the setting up of new market facilities on the Haitian side, binational trade is still concentrated on the Dominican Republican side of the border.

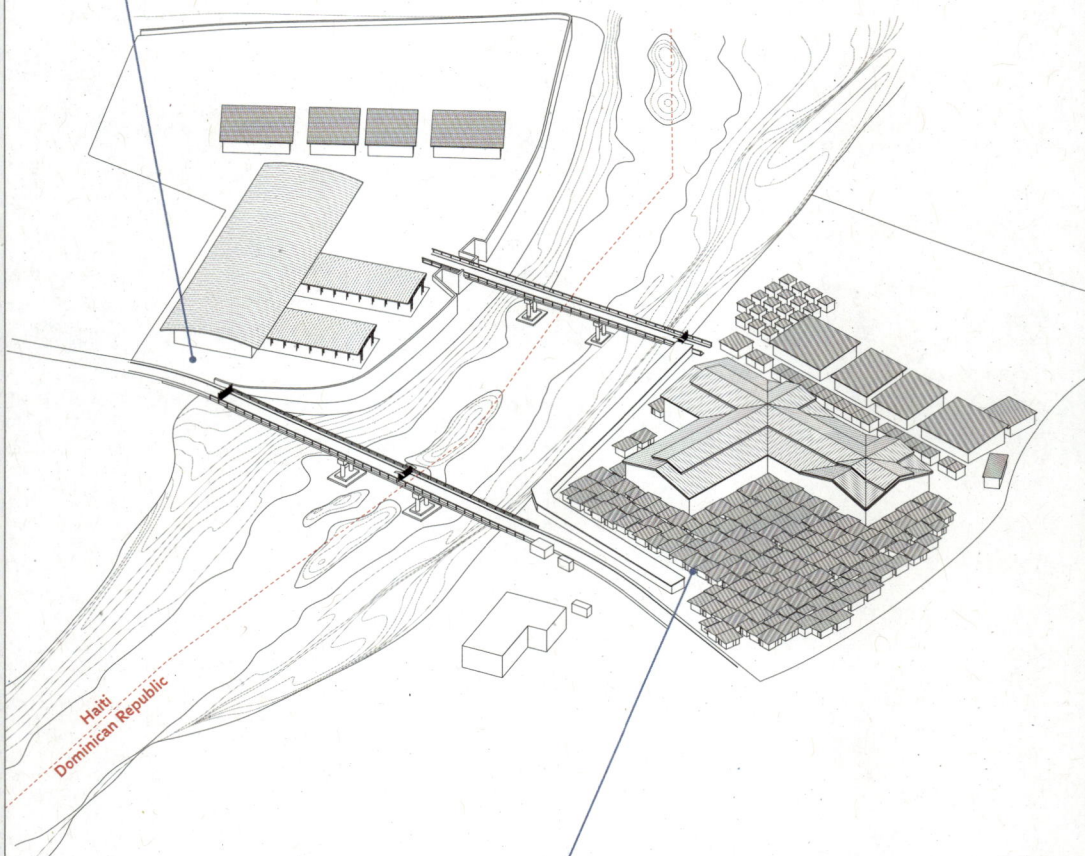

Haiti
Dominican Republic

The dense assemblage of stalls outside the market hall harks back to 2010, when the market was relocated from the streets of Dajabòn city centre to this new site further north along the border river: the new market hall had not yet been opened and vendors set up stall on the land around it. Many of these stalls have not been turned into solid structures.

Spatial context of the binational border markets in Ouanaminthe, Haiti and Dajabón, Dominican Republic (this page and opposite page top and bottom)

Haitians can cross into the Dominican Republic without a visa on market days. But as various tariffs are levied on goods they want to bring in or out, they face a structural disadvantage compared to Dominicans, who do not need to cross the border and hence do not have to pay such tariffs.

A flagship project of President Luis Abinader's government, the 'intelligent' border fence project involves a combination of several types of physical barriers with some segments made up of metal fences and others of solid walls, which become 'intelligent' through additional technical features such as surveillance towers and drones. This new infrastructure complements the management of the border through contained spaces such as binational markets and free trade zones.

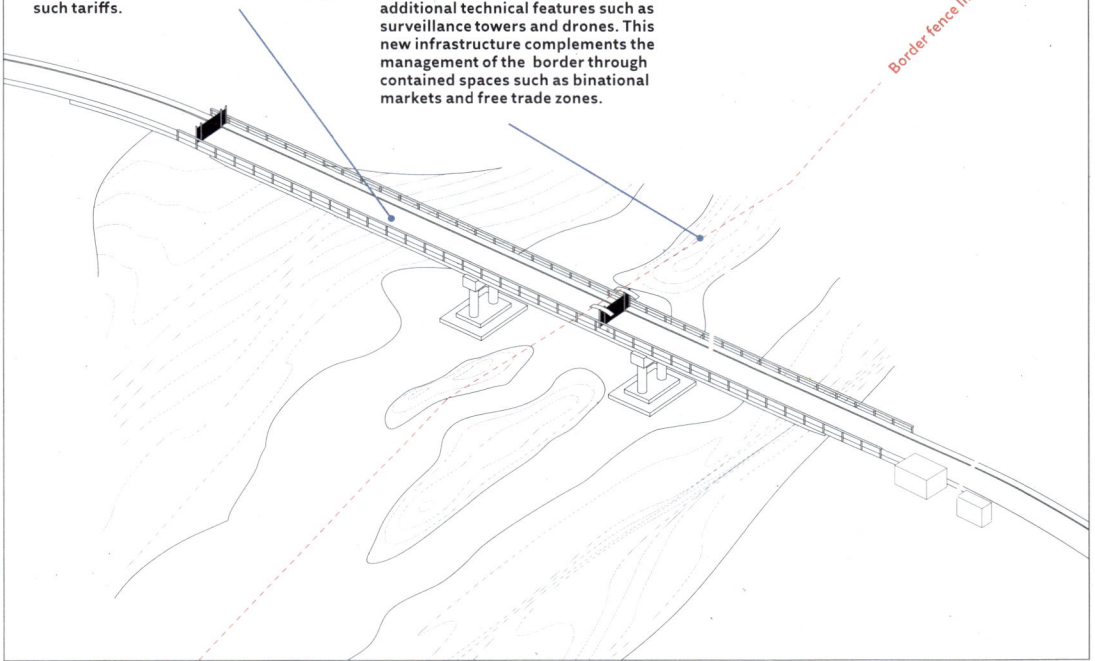

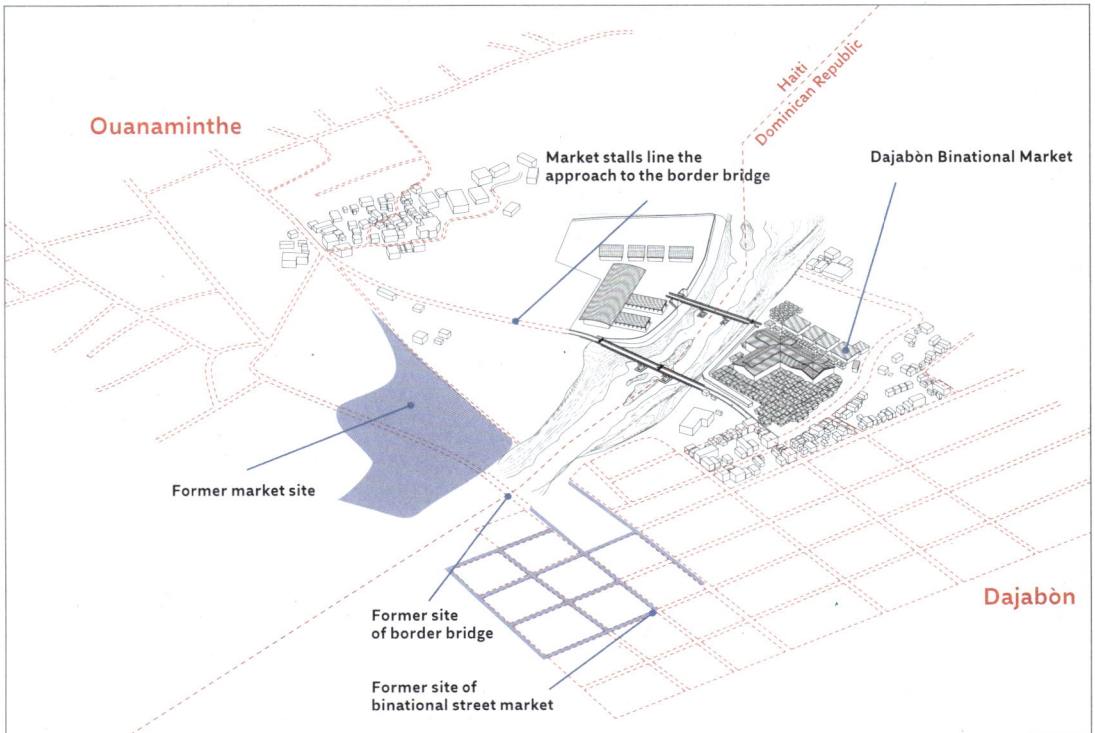

Border fence line

Ouanaminthe

Haiti
Dominican Republic

Market stalls line the approach to the border bridge

Dajabòn Binational Market

Former market site

Former site of border bridge

Former site of binational street market

Dajabòn

Ouanaminthe Binational Market

Border control point

Border gates

Dajabón Binational Market

Fences

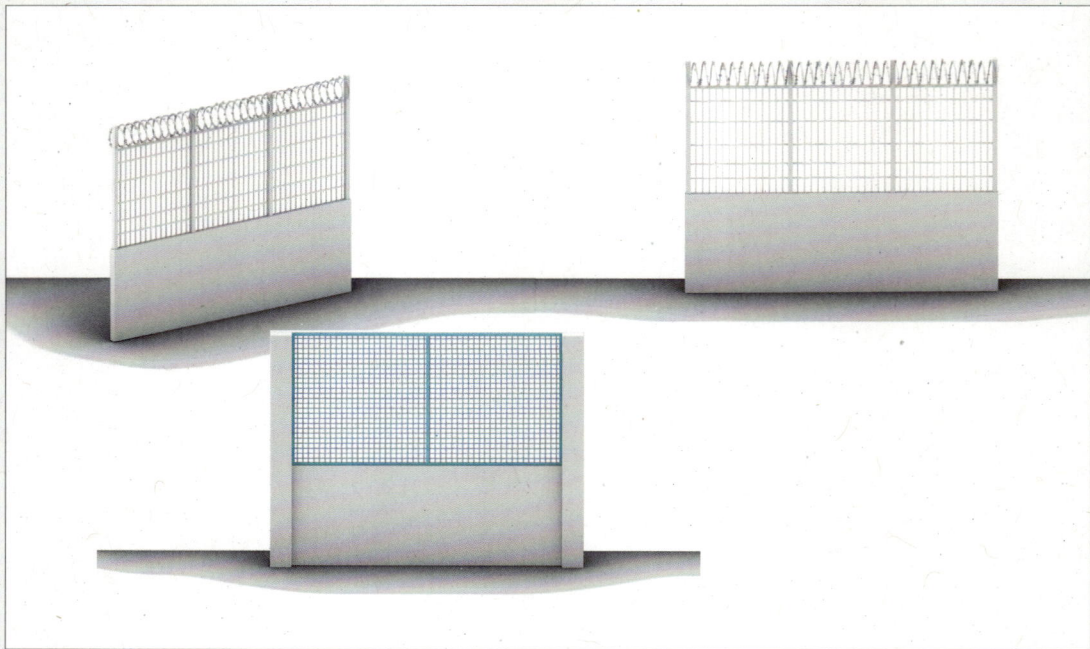

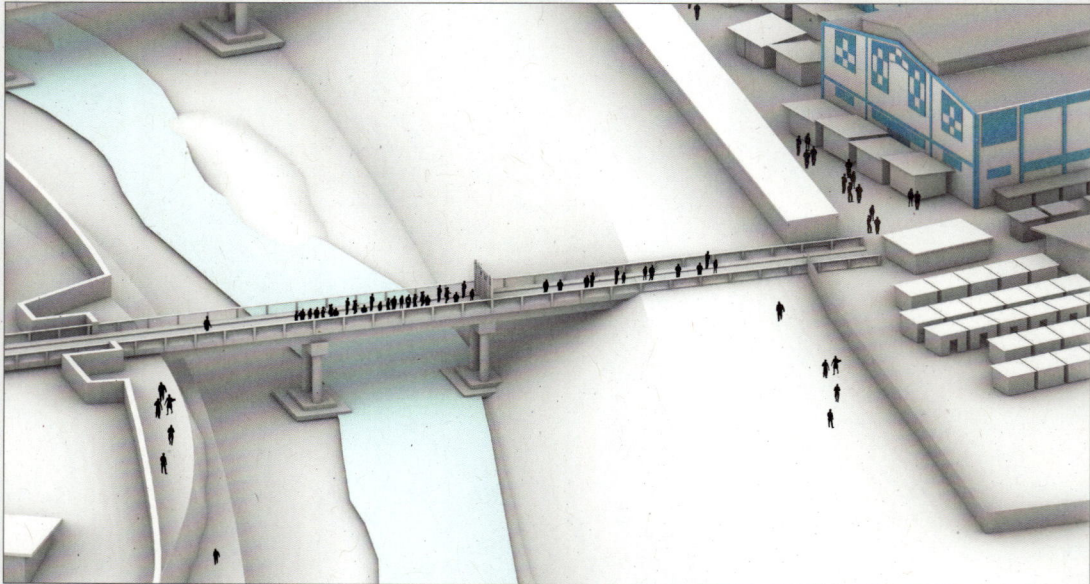

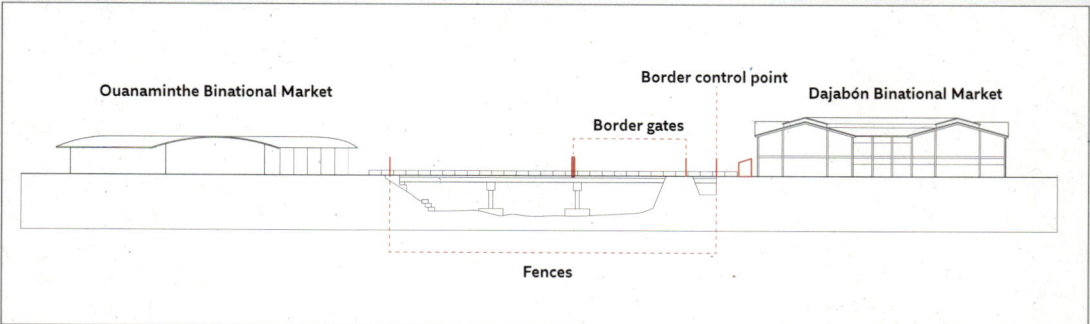

Fences, border gates and control points at and around Dajabón Binational Market (top, centre and bottom)

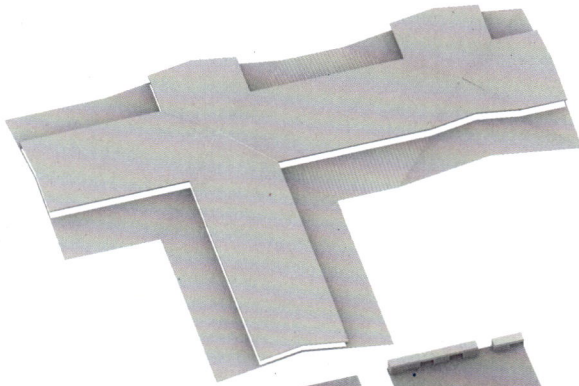

The market facility provides:

644 units of 4 m²
106 unites of 16 m²
18 units of 32 m²

It features a loading and unloading dock with a capacity for 28 trucks.

01

GF

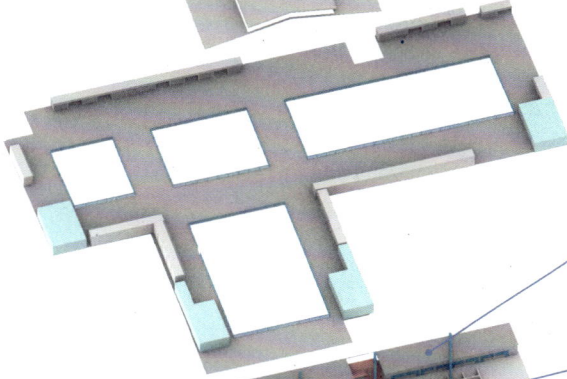

Larger walk-in units

Back-to-back market stands

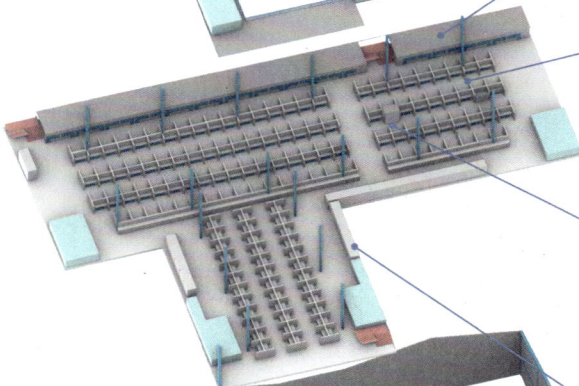

Informal transformations of open market stalls into storage closets

Market stands with rolling shutters

The closed façade has ventilation openings on all sides.

■ Staircases   ■ Sanitary stations

Spatial features of the indoor market at Dajabón Binational Market

Typical infrastructural components, Dajabón Binational Market, Dominican Republic

Dajabón Binational Market, Dominican Republic, 2022

Villas Codevi, an
eco-lodge resort
owned by Grupo M

Massacre River

Codevi Free Zone administered
by Grupo M; Grupo M manufactures
for US companies Calvin Klein, Polo,
Nordstrom, GAP, and others

Dominican Republic

Haïti

New vending area
(2020)

Ouanaminthe Binational Market
(completed in 2020)

Old border bridge damaged
by Hurricane Irma in 2017

Ouanaminthe (150,000 inhabitants)

Former Ouanaminthe market site

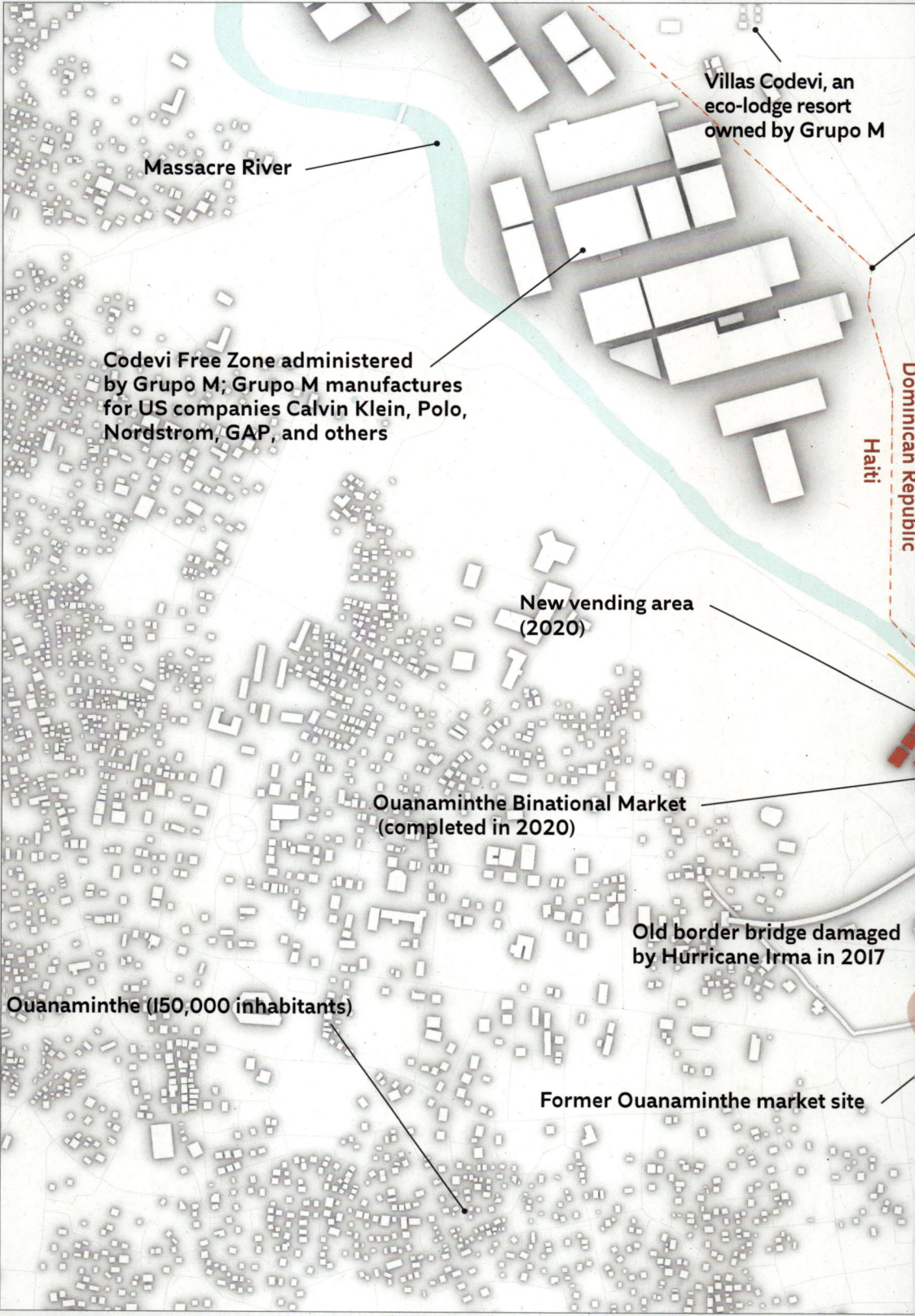

Spatial layout of the Dajabón-Ouanaminthe border area

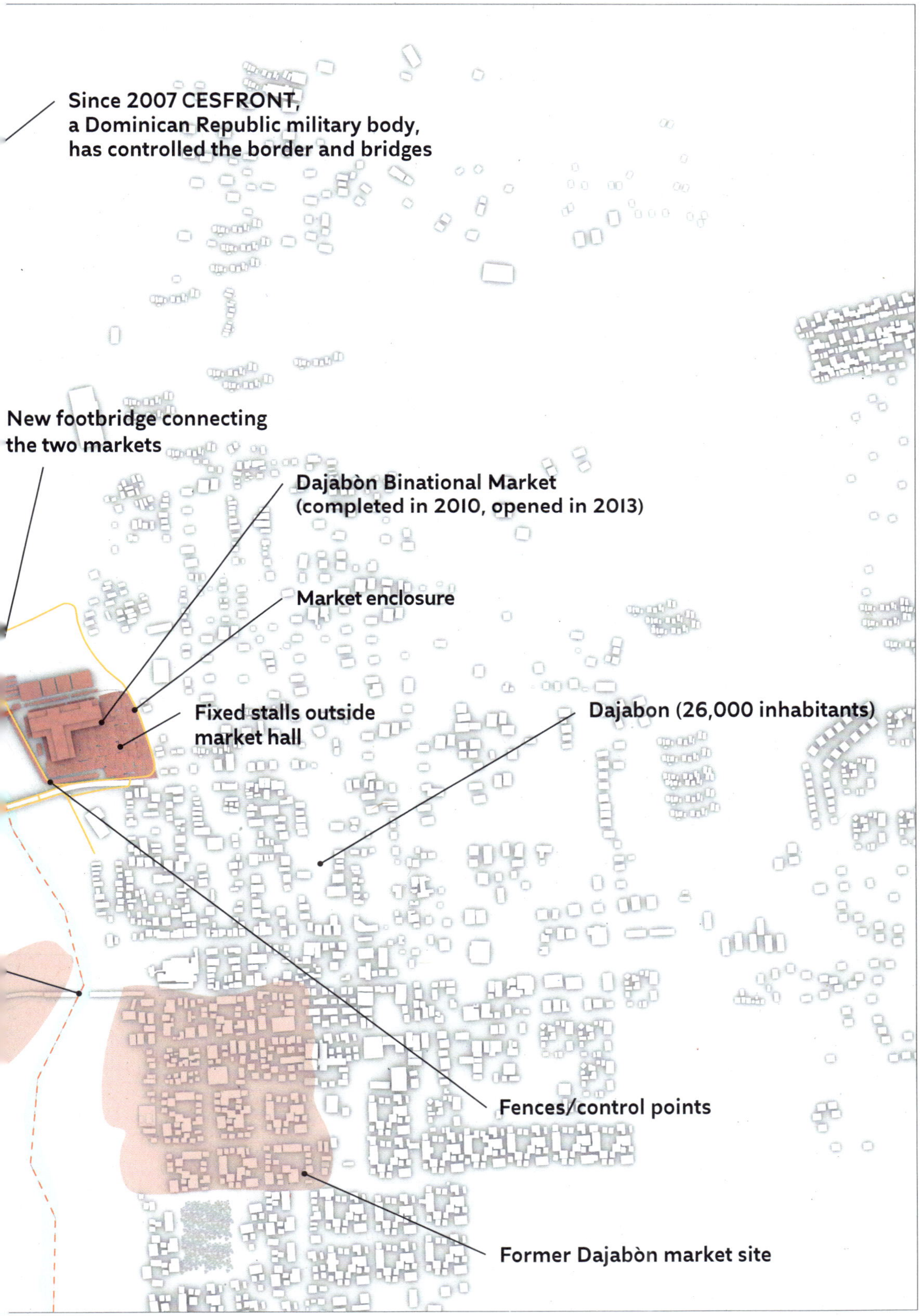

Since 2007 CESFRONT,
a Dominican Republic military body,
has controlled the border and bridges

New footbridge connecting
the two markets

Dajabòn Binational Market
(completed in 2010, opened in 2013)

Market enclosure

Fixed stalls outside
market hall

Dajabon (26,000 inhabitants)

Fences/control points

Former Dajabòn market site

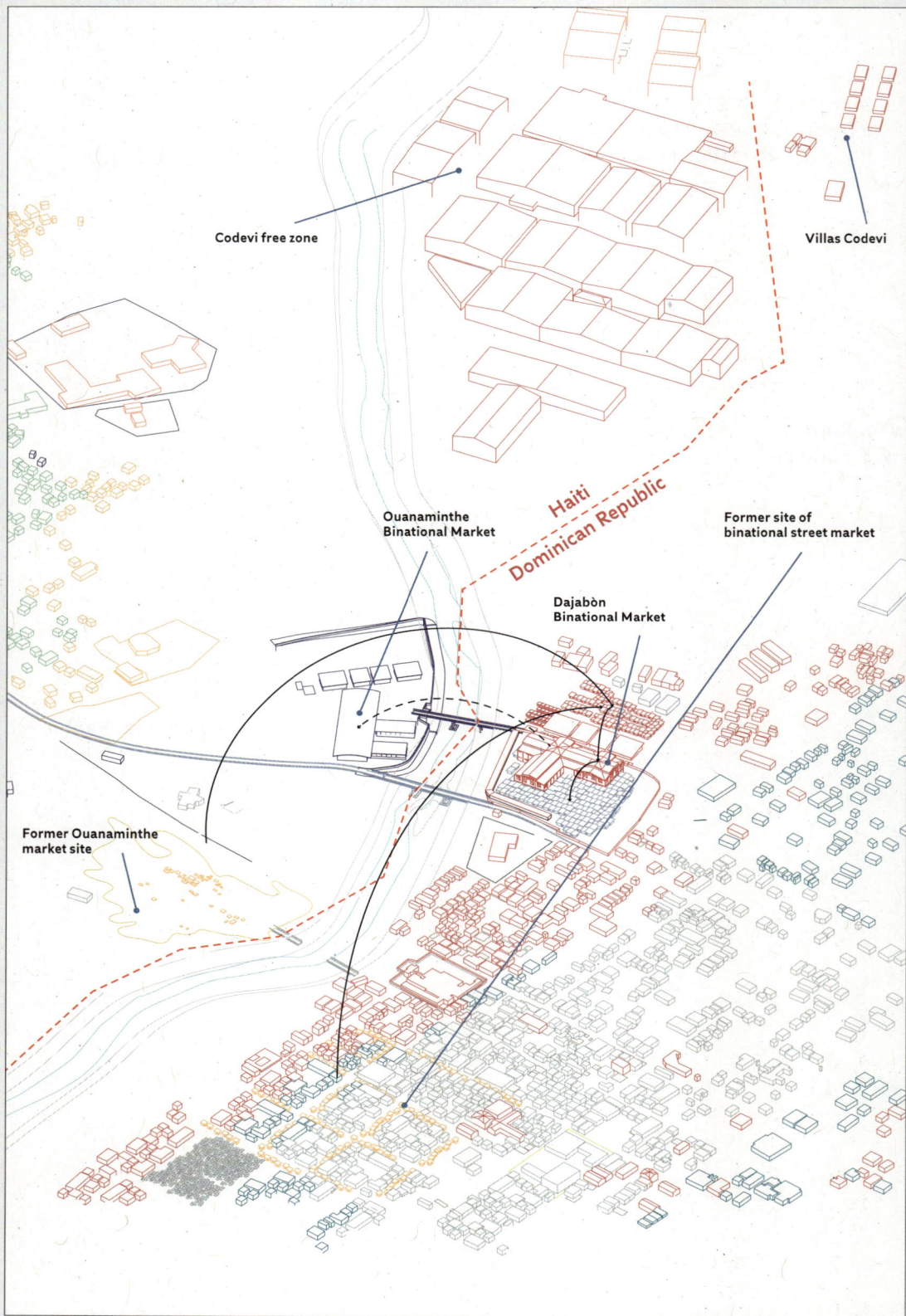

Codevi free zone

Villas Codevi

Ouanaminthe
Binational Market

Haiti
Dominican Republic

Former site of
binational street market

Dajabòn
Binational Market

Former Ouanaminthe
market site

■ Until 1980   ■ 1985   ■ 1990   ■ 1995   ■ 2000   ■ 2005   ■ 2010   ■ 2015

Dajabón Binational Market neighbourhood: key phases of spatial development

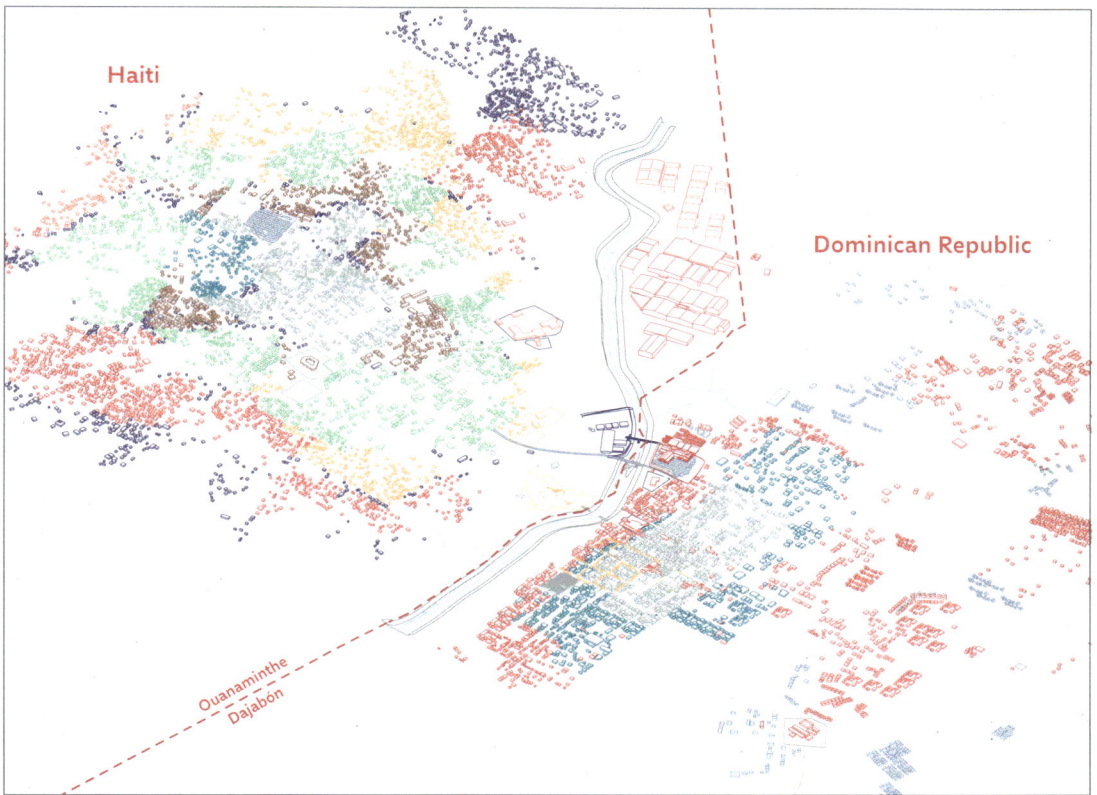

Haiti

Dominican Republic

Ouanaminthe
Dajabón

■ Until 1980 ■ 1985 ■ 1990 ■ 1995 ■ 2000 ■ 2005 ■ 2010 ■ 2015

Ouanaminthe-Dajabón border area: key phases of spatial development

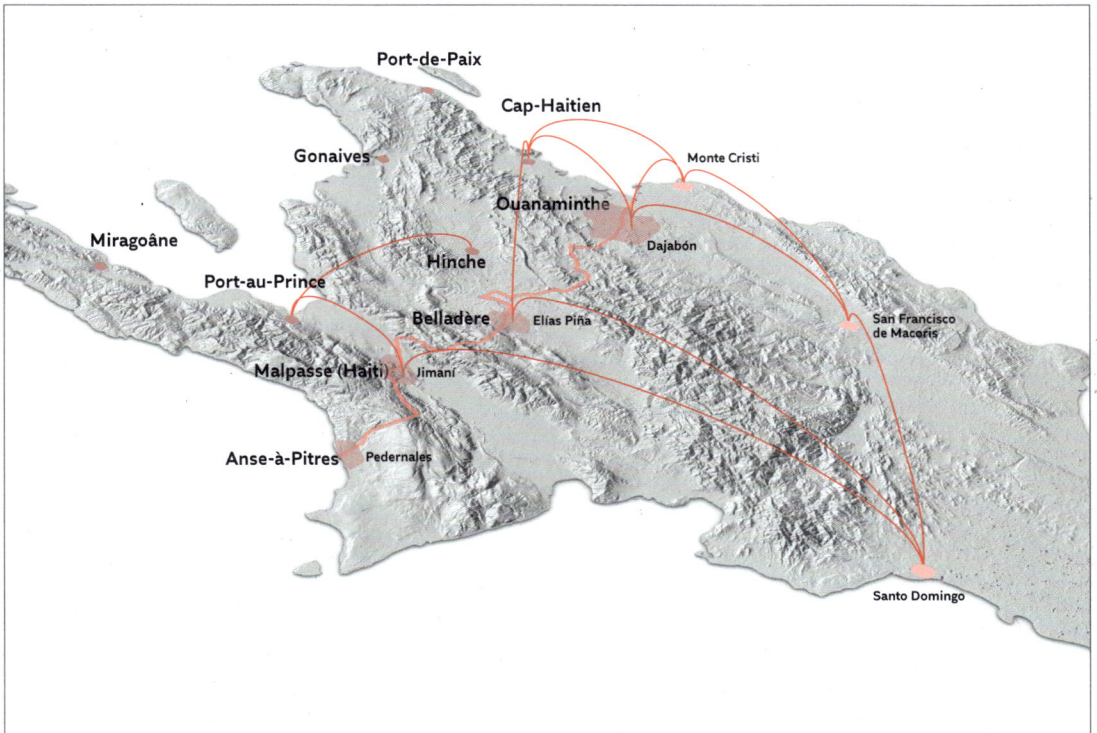

Port-de-Paix

Cap-Haitien

Gonaives

Monte Cristi

Miragoâne

Ouanaminthe

Dajabón

Port-au-Prince

Hinche

Belladère

Elías Piña

San Francisco
de Macorís

Malpasse (Haiti)

Jimaní

Anse-à-Pitres

Pedernales

Santo Domingo

Locations of binational markets and trade flows between Haiti and the Dominican Republic

Dajabón Binational Market, Dominican Republic, 2022.

178

What Ever Happened to the Roque?

Towards De-criminalising the Angolan Informal Market

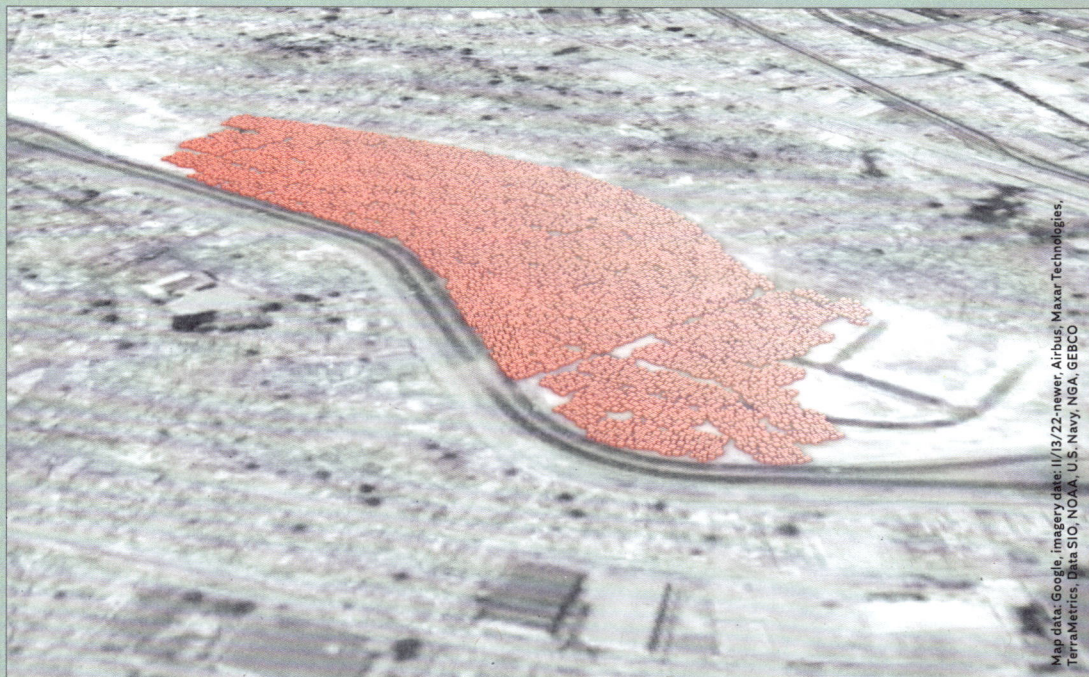

Map data: Google, imagery date: II/13/22-newer, Airbus, Maxar Technologies, TerraMetrics, Data SIO, NOAA, U.S. Navy, NGA, GEBCO

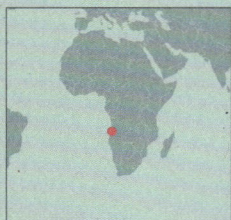

Roque Santeiro Market, the biggest and most important informal market in Angola and said to be the largest open-air market in Africa, was forcibly closed in 2010.[1] Angola's informal economy grew out of the indigenous African markets of the colonial era. After independence in 1975, it took on an increasingly important role in supplying goods, services, and employment as the state-managed economy eroded under Cold-War conflict and weak management. Roque Santeiro was born in the war years and permitted to flourish without oversight and little government intervention. The 'Roque,' known as the 'shopping centre for the poor,' became the centre of Luanda's economic life, functioning as a wholesale supplier to other district and neighbourhood informal markets.

179

---

1   Allan Cain, 'Roque Santeiro Market, Luanda,' in *Informal Market Worlds: The Architecture of Economic Pressure - Atlas*, eds. Peter Mörtenböck and Helge Mooshammer (Rotterdam: nai010 publishers, 2015), 103.

With the end of the Angolan Civil War in 2002, the municipal government announced a programme to transform informal commerce. The following year, the Provincial Directorate of Markets and Fairs launched a project to improve Luanda's 'image' by restructuring its urban network of markets to resemble how they functioned during colonial times, selling only fresh produce.

In 2010 the roque santeiro was forcibly closed and demolished. The last traders, who had not already abandoned the Market were obliged to find places in other markets or reverted to selling in the streets or from their homes.

The Roque occupied prime land which was attractive to real-estate developers due to its position overlooking the Bay of Luanda, but these ventures never materialised.

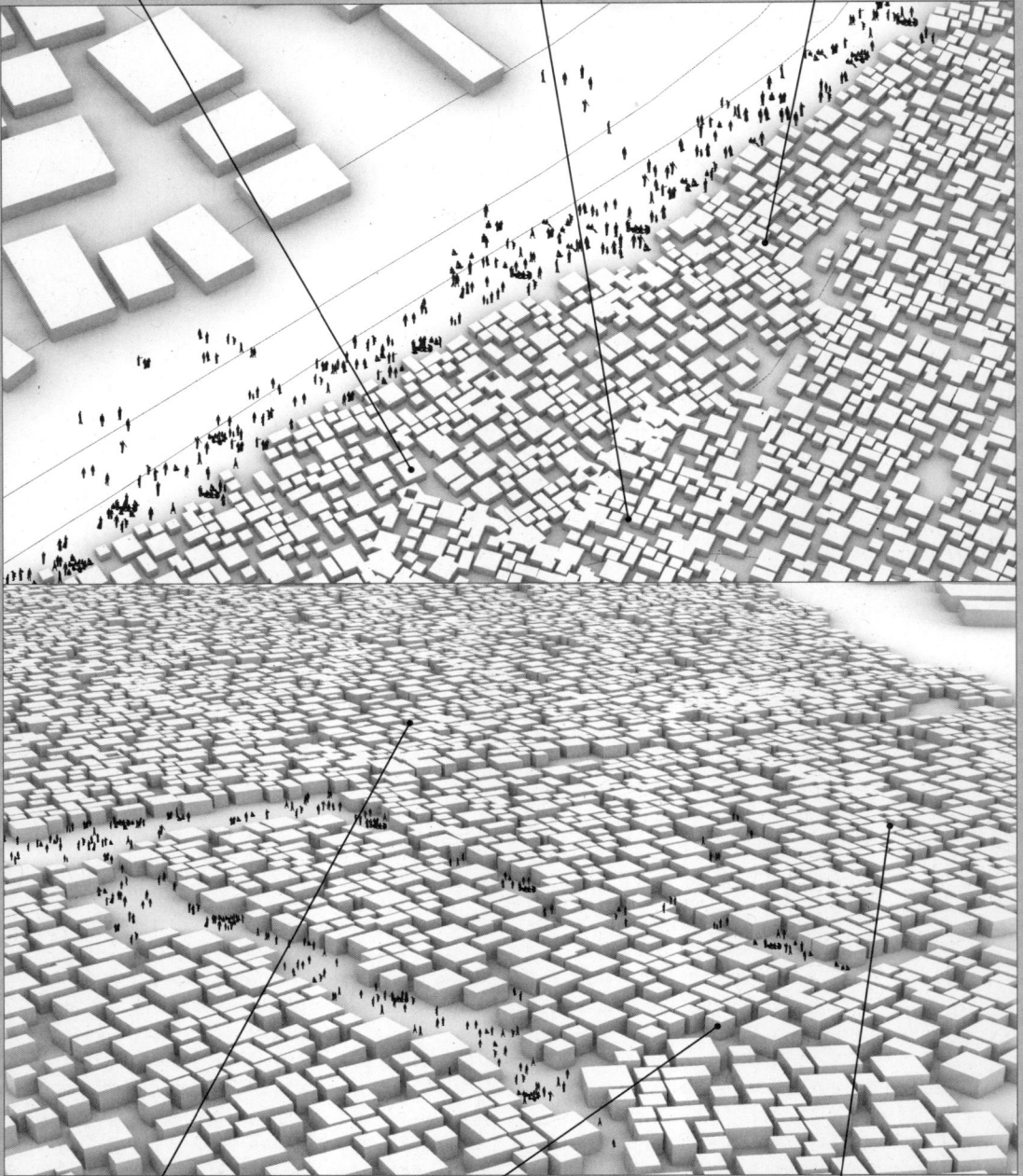

The market was organised in different sections according to varying products and services.

Covering an area of 50 hectares, Roque Santeiro accommodated over 20,000 traders serving 100,000 customers daily.

At Roque Qanteiro almost everything was sold: clothing, perfumes, modern and traditional medicines, all types of drinks, furniture, mattresses, building materials, tools, electrical appliances, televisions, hifi stereos, fish, fresh vegetables, weapons, currency, diamonds, ...

With the end of the civil war in 2002, the Angolan Government turned its attention to cleaning up Luanda and turning it into a modern world-class city. The chaotic and unsanitary informal markets and the surrounding slums were targeted for eradication. Informality had long been associated with criminality, and the state campaigned to restore 'order' to the post-war economy. The 'Roque' was the most famous victim. The market's closure displaced thousands of traders and support workers, who had to seek alternative livelihoods in the sprawling suburbs of Luanda. Despite the Government's campaign to formalise the economy, a decade after the closure of Roque Santeiro, the informal sector still provided 67 percent of urban employment. Angola has a higher rate of informal employment as a percentage of total employment (94.1 percent) than sub-Saharan Africa (89.2 percent) and Africa as a whole (85.8 percent).[2]

The current study tracks the evolution of government policy on dealing with informal markets. Public opinion and the attitudes of the state, as expressed in the media, have ranged over the two decades since the end of the war between the criminalisation and the formalisation of the informal economy. The research draws on Development Workshop's ongoing media-monitoring database of tens of thousands of articles dating from 2001. Day-by-day media-tracking of events and monitoring attitudes and policies as they evolve over the years are assessed. Using satellite imagery and aerial photography, remote sensing has permitted the mapping and spatial analysis of informal markets on the urban district and neighbourhood levels. Participatory urban diagnostic tools have allowed the research team to capture the memories, stories and perspectives of the informal market entrepreneurs and street traders. Oral histories were gathered from former traders from Roque Santeiro, who had been displaced before or during the 2010 closure.

A HISTORY OF LUANDA'S INFORMAL MARKETS

Unofficial markets in Luanda existed in the colonial era. Angola had been a Portuguese colony for almost four centuries. In colonial open-air markets or *musseque* markets, prepared goods and artisanal products such as traditional Angolan food and herbal medicines were traded. Customers were mainly African buyers/consumers with a minority of colonial settlers.[3] The Kinaxixe and São Paulo[4] Markets were the city's main covered markets, where most vendors were of European origin. Portuguese traders controlled most of the Angolan economy in colonial times, transporting and selling regionally produced commodities in the cities. Buyers/consumers in the urban markets were also mostly of European origin. Still, they were also frequented by some of the African population, mainly Europeanised *assimilados* and the families of salaried African workers.[5] The colonial administration's regulatory framework prohibited the sale of manufactured and industrial goods in the *musseque* markets when they represented a threat to the primacy of the official urban markets. However, the colonial administration demonstrated a degree of tolerance of indigenous/musseque markets for their picturesque side and function as a potential 'tourist attraction.'

Between 1974 and 1975, with the final tumultuous end to a fifteen-year war of liberation, the colonial organisation model of the economy, society and political system collapsed. With independence in 1975, the political-economic transformations profoundly altered the nature of markets. The relationship between musseque markets and the network of formal urban markets in Luanda changed when most sellers of European origin, and their administrative managers, abandoned the country. Urban markets progressively lost their supply-chain networks, and commodities became scarce. With the loss of their former managers, the control of hygiene and maintenance of market structures weakened.[6]

2   International Labour Office, 'Angola: Study on the Migration from Informal to Formal Economy,' ILO, 20 October 2021,
     https://www.ilo.org/wcmsp5/groups/public/---ed_dialogue/---act_emp/documents/publication/wcms_823469.pdf
3   Carlos Manuel Mira Godinho Fernandes Lopes, 'Elementos sobre o comportamento de compra em mercados informais: Estudo de caso no mercado Roque Santeiro (Luanda)' (PhD. diss., ISCTE - Instituto Universitário de Lisboa, 2008), 3.
4   São Paulo, Luanda's first public market, opened in 1948.
5   Daniel dos Santos, 'The Second Economy in Angola: Esquema and Candonga,' in *The Second Economy in Marxist States*, ed. Maria Łoś (London: Palgrave Macmillan, 1990).
6   Lopes, 'Elementos sobre o comportamento de compra,' 3.

Post-independence civil conflict, fuelled by Cold-War ideological allegiances and ethnic-regional divisions, resulted in massive population displacements in Angola's central highlands. With the spread and intensification of the civil war, the situation worsened with a rural exodus to the big cities on the coast in search of security and improved living conditions. Luanda was one of the leading destinations for internally displaced families.

As Luanda's population growth accelerated, so did the mass of buyers and consumers, despite increasingly scarce sources of income and high inflation levels. With the decline of the formal sector of the economy and the consequent reduction in public administration wages, a large part of the urban population depended on jobs and income in the informal sector.[7] From 1977 on, the centralised model of organisation and regulation of the economy prevailed within the framework of a one-party regime with aspirations to construct a socialist society. The attempt to build a centralised and administrative distribution system led to rationing access to goods and services.[8] During the decade after independence, there was significant growth in informal practices carried out in parallel markets, or within the framework of exchanges associated with illegal economy. The *candonga* and the *esquema* (schemes) were based on traditional trading practices and obligations of reciprocity, solidarity and access and were the only alternative available to secure goods and services essential to the survival of households.[9] Returning Angolan refugees were partly responsible for building the informal economy. The name *Regressados* was given to Angolans of Bakongo origin who had emigrated to Congo/Zaire during the War of Independence (mainly in 1961), to return to Angola following independence. Many had experience working with trading networks across various West African countries as well as Europe.[10]

THE STORY OF ROQUE SANTEIRO

The parallel economy developed through the 1980s and soon prevailed over the official one (with fixed and fictitious prices and reduced assortments of products). The popular imagination procured names for these open-air markets: Cala-a-Boca (keep your mouth shut), Ajuda-husband (where women go to sell to support the family budget traditionally earned by their husband), Tira-o-Bikini (because the prices left you completely naked), and Roque Santeiro (the name of a Brazilian soap opera where all the miracles happen).

In 1986, official approval was given to create a market in the municipality of Sambizanga, overlooking the bay in the Bairro da Lixeira (formerly a rubbish dump). Some markets that operated in the northeast region of Luanda were to be relocated to the site. The market's growth was spontaneous, beginning a few days after the installation of the first sellers when a sign with the name *Roque Santeiro* appeared. This name originated from the popular Brazilian telenovela Roque Santeiro, broadcast in 1985 by Televisão Popular de Angola. The television series was based on a banned play, *O Berço do Herói* by Dias Gomes, written in 1963. The Brazilian Military Government also banned the soap opera written in 1975. In Luanda, three markets: Roque Santeiro, Asa Branca and Beato Salú, were named after characters or locations in the soap opera.[11]

As a response to the post-independence failure of centralised economic management, a process of liberalisation began in 1987. With the approval of the Economic and Financial Sanitation Program (SEF), a policy of deregulation and privatisation of domestic trade was introduced.[12] The SEF semi-legalised the commerce carried out in markets and on the streets. By 1989, the network of informal trade in Luanda had evolved according to a format in which the Roque Santeiro Market was the main supplier of the other markets

7   Anthony Hodges, *Angola: do Afro-estalinismo ao capitalismo selvagem* (Cascais: Principia, Publicações Universitárias e Científicas, 2002), 54.
8   Law no. 2/82, 1982, on 'Centralised Socialist Planning of the Economy.'
9   dos Santos, 'The Second Economy in Angola.'
10   Luena Nascimento Nunes Pereira, 'Os regressados na cidade de Luanda: um estudo sobre identidade etnica e nacional em Angola' (Departamento de Antropologia, Faculdade de Filosofia, Letras e Ciencias Humanas, Sao Paulo: Universidade de Sao Paulo, Brazil), 161.
11   Henda Ducados, 'Women and Development: Women, Poverty and the Informal Sector in Luanda's Peri-urban Bairros' (unpublished report, Development Workshop (DW) Angola, 1998), 4.
12   The main inspiration for the SEF were the practices of economic reforms being carried out in the 1980s by socialist countries such as Hungary.
       See: Antonio Tomás, 'Refracted Governmentality Space, Politics, and Social Structure in Contemporary Luanda,' PhD dissertation (Columbia University, 2012), 168.

Top: Neighbourhood market square, Luanda, 2005
Bottom: Street market in urbanising Luanda, 2005

in the city, functioning as a wholesale supply centre for other markets and supporting many 'formal' commercial establishments, such as supermarkets, restaurants, pharmacies and clothing or furniture stores. The evolution of the market network reflected the tolerance of the authorities for the pace of advance of informal urbanisation and how migrants, in particular those displaced by war, were settling in the city.[13] By 1996, Roque Santeiro was a key component to a network of twenty-six informal markets, five of them with over 3,000 sellers each, and another 200 occasional *pracas* (markets in squares), scattered throughout *bairros* (neighbourhoods) of Luanda.[14]

The Angolan Civil War was finally concluded with a ceasefire only in 2002, ending more than four decades of conflict. The Cold War that had fuelled it ended over a decade before. The peace process grew from a countrywide civil society movement and a rejection of the illicit trade in weapons and blood diamonds.[15] Over four million people were displaced from their homes. Luanda had grown fivefold to a population of over three million in the period after independence.

At the war's end, there were thirty-two markets registered in Luanda. By 2005 there were fifty-five urban markets and six fairs, according to the Luanda Provincial Directorate of Community Services (DPMF). The Sindicato dos Trabalhadores do Comércio Informal (STCI) estimated that the number of sellers operating in Luanda's urban markets was 50,708. In addition, there were 2,600 *kinguilas* (money exchangers) and 55,499 informal business employees, constituting the 'parallel economy.' Roque Santeiro remained the focus point of the citywide network playing a significant role as a wholesaler supplier for all of the other major markets throughout peri-urban Luanda. At its peak, it covered 50 hectares, had over 20,000 traders (only 5,000 of them registered), and 100,000 consumers daily who spent over 2,000,000 US dollars.

Roque Santeiro had become a gigantic cash and carry store where almost everything was for sale: clothing, perfumes, modern and traditional medicines, drinks, furniture, mattresses, building materials, tools, electrical appliances, televisions, stereos, fish, fresh vegetables, weapons, currency, and diamonds. There were also houses of prostitution, and diamond traffickers. The Roque occupied prime land overlooking the Bay of Luanda, and sellers were organised by area according to product type. The location provoked competition with real-estate developers associated with the former president, who sought to acquire the site for high-end residential exploitation.[16]

With the war's end, the government announced a programme to restructure the trading system, which aimed to gradually transform informal commerce and bring it into the formal economy. Plans aimed to reduce the number of people permitted to trade in informal markets while preventing trading in the streets, especially near the city centre.[17] Luanda's provincial authorities argued that street trading negatively impacted the city's aesthetics.[18] The numerous regulations and legal decrees issued over the decades are summarised in the Annex.

In 2003 the Provincial Directorate of Markets and Fairs announced that a project was underway to improve Luanda's image by restructuring the urban network of markets to resemble how they functioned during colonial times, selling only fresh products, vegetables, etc. Some markets were to be closed, others to be rehabilitated and reorganised into official municipal markets, and some markets to be relocated, including Roque Santeiro, with a new market built in Panguila to replace it.[19] New lines of credit from China facilitated the replacement of informal markets with new ones managed by municipal authorities. The Ministry of Commerce's (DNIC) National Directorate of Internal Trade was mandated to formalise informal trade.

13   Lopes, 'Elementos sobre o comportamento de compra,' 148–51.
14   Carlos M. G. F. Lopes, 'A fixação de preços nos mercados informais de Luanda: estudo comparativo nos mercados Congoleses, Rocha Pinto e Shabba' (MA thesis, Economic and Social Development in Africa, ISCTE - University Institute of Lisbon, 1998), 115.
15   Development Workshop (DW) Angola, 'What to Do When the Fighting Stops: Challenges for Post-conflict Reconstruction in Angola' (Development Workshop Occasional Paper no. 7, 2006), 15.
16   Aguiar dos Santos, 'Roque Santeiro ameaçado pela FESA,' *AGORA*, 16 June 2001.
17   Presidential Decree no. 20/05, 2 June 2005, defined the responsibilities of the National Directorate for Internal Trade
18   Cain, 'Roque Santeiro Market, Luanda,' 105.
19   Lopes, 'Elementos sobre o comportamento de compra,' 161.

There were several policy initiatives to try to constrain its growth. DNIC claimed its goal was to break the connection between informal trade and the illegal trafficking of stolen merchandise in markets like Roque Santeiro, where goods were often pilfered from the port and state warehouses.[20]

Roque Santeiro Market also severely lacked sanitary facilities for operators, consumers and visitors. There were only two blocks of toilets serving the whole market.[21] The argument for closing Roque Santeiro thus emphasised the issue of public health, and the need to improve conditions for operators and consumers. Rather than upgrading the hygiene and infrastructure of the market, the master plan for the urban rehabilitation/renewal of the metropolitan region of Luanda envisioned the closure and removal of Roque and the other inner-city markets, and pushing the trade to new sites on the urban periphery.

DISPLACEMENT AND THE DISPERSION OF THE INFORMAL MARKET

In 2010 Roque Santeiro was forcibly closed and demolished. The last traders, who had not already abandoned the market, were obliged to find places in other markets or reverted to selling in the streets or from their homes. Many day workers, stevedores and casual labourers lost their source of income. This most likely contributed to increased levels of crime in Luanda in the years following the closure.[22] The municipal government's destruction of Roque Santeiro and the later closure of Estalagem and other large informal markets resulted in the dispersion of market sellers across the city. Few went to Panguila as provisioned by the authorities. Many migrated to other urban markets, setting up informal stalls outside the gates of the official municipal markets. Some began selling to their neighbours from their homes, street corners or public squares. Many were forced to become street sellers. Government attempts to take over the distribution of locally grown produce through a string of state-owned supermarkets resulted in the bankruptcy of

the Nossa Super chain in 2009. The government, however, renewed its determined effort to stamp out informal trade in early 2014 by announcing a punitive regime of fines for informal traders and their customers.[23] The informal trader was seen as an affront to those who wished to promote Luanda as a modern city.[24]

A new market in Panguila was built to re-house the Roque sellers. Promoted by the municipal government as 'a paradise' compared to Roque Santeiro,[25] the new market had space for only 8,376 traders (5,376 fixed stalls, 3,000 open air). While the new Panguila market offered more hygienic conditions than Roque Santeiro, access to the new market became a problem for most sellers. Located twenty-two kilometres from the city centre, it offered easy access to neither traders nor shoppers who must contend with spending hours stuck in traffic or having to pay two US dollars in taxi fare. Traders consequently could not sell their goods in sufficient volume to make a profit.[26]

With the closure of Roque Santeiro, its role as a wholesaling hub for secondary and municipal markets did not pass to Panguila, as provisioned in the General Metropolitan Master Plan (PDGML) for Luanda. Eventually, a new trading pole on the Catete road, thirty kilometres southeast of Luanda assumed that role. 'Km 30' started as a cluster of shipping containers and market stalls set up by traders displaced from Roque, Estalagem and other informal inner-city markets. By 2012, Km 30 had become the transit point for rural produce from the interior to be sold to urban traders; in 2015, with government-constructed pavilions, it had become the largest market in Luanda. By 2023 there were 120 informal food markets in the metropolitan area of Luanda. Many informal market sellers clustered outside the official municipal markets to avoid paying the obligatory fee required to rent a stall in the covered space. By 2022, the province of Luanda had a total of 208 registered markets spread across the nine municipalities of the capital, which generated,

20   National Directorate of Internal Trade, DNIC, 2000.
21   Lopes, 'Elementos sobre o comportamento de compra,' 203.
22   Cain, 'Roque Santeiro Market, Luanda,' 106.
23   'Fiscalização arrecada oito milhões de Kz de emolumentos,' *Jornal de Angola*, 9 January 2014.
24   Cain, 'Roque Santeiro Market, Luanda,' 106.
25   Semanário Factual. *Anarquia é posta ao fim*, 5–12 September 2010.
26   Cain, 'Roque Santeiro Market, Luanda,'106.

Roque Santeiro

Roque Santeiro after demolition, Luanda, 2010

in 2021, average monthly revenue from vendor fees of 132,000 US dollars.[27] The largest market at Km 30, located in the municipality of Viana, annually transacts 132.8 million US dollars,[28] at an average rate of over 400,000 dollars daily.

Some of the displaced sellers from Roque transformed their homes into places of business and started selling products or offering services to their neighbours. Semi-wholesalers and retailers sold various types of products in quantities stored in their homes in relatively small amounts. In some cases, the units used are not those used in formal trade (for example, sugar or beans are sold by the scoop, charcoal, fish, and vegetables are sold by the bunch); the level of specialisation is low, with home-based sellers often offering a diversity of products that can be stored in small quantities in their homes. For many former Roque Santeiro sellers, the last resort was street trading or itinerant vending, known in Angola as *zunga*, a word from the Kimbundu language that designates the act of 'rotating-moving.' The *zungueiras* are usually women who took informal marketing to the streets of Luanda. Some men also carry out the practice, though women make up the majority of the *zungueiras*. These itinerant informal operators sell diversified products in small enough quantities that they can carry as headloads—some work on commission for wholesalers, semi-wholesalers and large retailers, selling very small quantities by unit. The majority work on their own as resellers. However, in less frequent situations, some constitute a kind of freelance sales force for merchants established in a fixed location, to whom they sell goods on consignment. In other cases, the zungueiras work for traders installed in the markets, their income being the difference between the value merchants seek for the sale of their products, and the value at which zungueiras can mark up sales to their customers.

The day-to-day life of most of these operators begins at dawn and ends after dark. Most zungueiras leave their homes, some of them located several kilometres from the city centre and walk to the city, where they wander along routes chosen according to the expectations of sales of products or places of residence of regular customers, as is the case with those who resell food products. The return home is also invariably done on foot.[29] The 2010 regulation Licensing of Commercial Activities and Trade Service Providers[30] requires licenses to be issued by the municipal authorities to 'ambulant vendors,' which entitles them to trade only in the specific markets assigned to them. Most street vendors lack the documents to obtain a license to sell goods in a formal market. To obtain a license, an 'ambulant vendor' must present photocopies of their identity card, tax card, and health card and pay a small fee. The majority of street vendors do not even have an identity card.[31]

CRIMINALISATION OF INFORMALITY

Over almost five decades, Angola's political trajectory has evolved from a post-revolutionary one-party state in 1975 through democratic liberalisation after 1991. Civil war politics affected Angola until 2002, and post-conflict and post-socialist reconstruction had been the priorities of the state over the last two decades. The official post-independence policy on commerce was ambivalent, while public attitude regarded private business as antisocial. Informal commerce, *candonga*, was officially labelled a crime. Enforcement of punitive regulations accelerated in the post-war years, in line with the Angolan leadership's aspiration to project the country's image as having a modern, prosperous economy. Repression eased off in election years to mitigate bad publicity from journalists and cartoonists sympathetic to the plight of street sellers.

The author's NGO, Development Workshop, has tracked the evolution of public attitudes to the informal economy and official government policies as they have changed over almost two and a half decades by monitoring the daily and weekly published media. Since the 1980s, administrative authorities have

27   66 million Angolan Kwanzas.
28   70 billion Angolan Kwanzas.
29   Presidential Decree no. 288/10, 30 November 2010.
30   Presidential Decree no. 288/10.
31   Human Rights Watch, '"Take That Filth Away": Police Abuses Against Street Vendors in Angola' (HRW report, October 2013).

applied prohibitive and repressive measures to informal trade and, more specifically, to street trading. The 'economic police' (Política Economica), created during the one-party era after independence, enforced pricing by checking that no more than a 25 percent markup was being charged to the customer. At the time, private commerce was made prohibitive by a combination of monthly and annual taxes that produced an effective tax rate on profits of 47 percent.[32] The 'economic police' extracted surplus value from productive activities via bribes or other forms of corruption.[33] The severe repression in the first half of the 1980s resulted in the destruction of the Banga Sumo Market, in the Prenda area, which was burned down after the intervention of the police. Later in the early 2000s, the authorities destroyed the Cala-a-Boca and Tira Bikini Markets and closed the Estalagem, Kinaxixe and Rocha Pinto Markets.[34]

From 2006 onwards, a new government policy under the banner of PRESILD[35] aimed at the formalisation and restructuring of the commercial supply network. Under the programme, four new markets were built in Luanda with financing from China: the markets of Cazenga (formerly Asa Branca), Palanca (Kilamba Kiaxi), Kifica, in Benfica, and Vidrul, in Cacuaco were inaugurated. In addition to the construction of 163 municipal markets, PRESILD's objective in the formalisation of retail trade included public financing to build thirty-one commercial supermarkets in the Nosso Super network.

In the election year 2008 a new popular provincial governor of Luanda announced the reform of the economic police, reprimanding the commander. She promoted opening public squares three days per week for itinerant fairs as alternative neighbourhood spaces for street sellers. While Angola's first microfinance institution KixiCrédito, born earlier in Roque Santeiro, had already been approved, in the election year, several commercial banks launched microcredit products to attract small-scale entrepreneurs as clients. The municipality had second thoughts on closure due to the controversy and considered delaying it until after the next elections in 2012.[36] On 5 September 2010, Roque was finally closed.

The closure of Roque Santeiro resulted in increased crime and delinquency in several *bairros* of Luanda. New problems with criminality were reported in the bairros of Hoji-Ya-Henda and São Paulo, where petty criminals who previously operated in Roque Santeiro had relocated. Increased anxiety among local residents was compounded by a lack of response from the police, with local authorities complaining of being understaffed to address the issue properly. In some instances, police corruption was reported to be part of the problem.[37]

After the 2010 closure of Roque Santeiro, and between the periods of repression, the authorities limited themselves to remotely controlling the functioning of the markets. They focused on suppressing certain segments of informal commerce, namely medicines and pirated audio and video CDs and DVDs.[38] In 2012, the Provincial Government of Luanda returned to an aggressive interventionist strategy, reconstituting a new Polícia Economica unit to remove street vendors and to fine consumers who purchased products from zungueiras.[39] Confrontations between the economic police and zungueiras flared up when sellers resisted the confiscation of their goods and were arrested. In 2014, the President of the Administrative Commission of Luanda published penalty guidelines for street vendors. The effort to stamp out informal trading included a heavy regime of fines, not only for informal traders but also for their customers.[40]

32   United Nations Development Program, 'Angola Enterprise Program: Micro-finance Component' (UNDP, 2003), 8,
      https://www.findevgateway.org/sites/default/files/publications/files/mfg-en-paper-angola-enterprise-program-microfinance-component-2002.pdf
33   Steven Kyle, 'How Important Was Marxism for the Development of Mozambique and Angola?' (working paper, Cornell University, 2013), 6,
      http://kyle.dyson.cornell.edu/Working%20Paper%202013-18%20FINAL.pdf
34   Florita C. A. Telo, 'Mulheres e comércio (informal) em Luanda: um olhar para além da crise pandémica de Covid-19,' *Revista Espaco Academico* 21 (June 2021): 14.
35   PRESILD: Program for Restructuring the System of Logistics and Distribution of Essential Products to the Population – New Commercial Network.
36   Seminario Angolense. *O que impede a sua transferência*, 17 July 2010.
37   (no article title), *Novo Jornal*, 17 September 2010.
38   Lopes, 'A fixação de preços nos mercados informais de Luanda,' 8.
39   'Luanda cria unidade de Polícia Fiscal,' *Jornal de Angola*, 28 April 2012.
40   See: Edital Comição Administrativa da Cidade de Luanda no. 01-14 – de 8 de Abril – sobre venda ambulante em Luanda; See also: 'Fiscalização arrecada oito milhões
      de Kz de emolumentos,' *Jornal de Angola*, 9 January 2014.

Scrap metal dealers at Kikolo Market, Luanda, 2005

The ten years after the closure of Roque Santeiro was a period of increasing criminalisation of the informal economy and suppression, particularly of itinerant street sellers. During the election years of 2012 and 2017, market closures and arrests of zungueiras were paused but resumed with increasing repression during the intervening periods. Criminalisation culminated under the banner of Operation Resgate, launched in November 2017, aiming to 'recapture the economy.' Resgate was a national operation that arrested, heavily fined and imprisoned thousands of informal traders, closed hundreds of unregistered churches and mosques, and suppressed cross-border smuggling and illegal immigration. In early 2019, a law was passed to intensify Resgate.[41] Human rights advocates argued that 'the law prohibited practices but did not guarantee rights.' The debate entered parliament, where some opposition parties even argued to revive Roque Santeiro Market. The National Association of Street Vendors (ANVA) mounted a media campaign to defend their rights and sway public opinion.[42]

ATTEMPTS TO TRANSFORM AND FORMALISE THE INFORMAL ECONOMY

Despite attempts to eliminate the informal economy by force, the National Development Plan 2018–2022 admitted that the informal economy made up 40 percent of the national economy and formed an essential part of the survival strategies for 75 percent of the population.[43] 80.1 percent of all jobs were informal, and the informal sector provided 67 percent of urban employment. 73 percent of workers in the informal sector are women.[44] With the decline of Angola's petroleum-fuelled economy after 2016, informality became central for generating jobs and income, access to goods and services and, consequently, in the livelihood of families. Despite this contribution, informal work (commerce) is still precarious, it suffers from fragility in terms of labour guarantees and weaknesses in terms of work conditions and benefits.[45]

41   Law no. 15/19, 23 May 2019, on 'Market and Street Trade Activities.'
42   M. Manaça, 'Zungueiras criam programa televisivo para defender os seus direitos,' *Jornal OPAÍS*, 9 August 2019.
43   International Labour Organization, 'Angola: Study on the Migration from Informal to Formal Economy' (ILO, October 2021), 21.
44   UNDP, 'Angola Enterprise Program: Micro-finance Component.'
45   Telo, 'Mulheres e comércio (informal) em,' 6.

Electrical goods sellers at Roque Santeiro, Luanda, 2005

The first data available on the livelihoods of informal market vendors comes from the early 1990s research that Development Workshop conducted in Roque Santeiro Market and nearby neighbourhoods. The first citywide data collected in 1995 by the National Statistics Institute shows the educational status compared with contemporary data collected in 2020, that illiteracy rates have only been reduced from 23.3 percent to 10.9 percent over 25 years.

Informal economy workers have organised themselves to advocate for their protection from the police and supervisory agents of the provincial government who are threats to their physical safety, business and livelihoods. The principal organisations representing workers in Luanda operating in urban markets and street commerce are the Union of Workers of Informal Commerce (STCI) and the Association of Street Vendors of Luanda (AVAL), which is the representation structure of zungueiras. According to the STCI statutes, it is an autonomous and independent trade union organisation with a provincial scope, made up of manual and casual workers who labour on sites and in informal markets, intending to defend the rights and interests of its affiliates, namely '[...] to organise and support the struggle for better working conditions [...] to provide union and legal assistance to the affiliates [...] to ensure the effective representation of the affiliates in economic, private, state and state administration bodies [...].' There is an agreement between the STCI and the Ministry of Family and Women and INAPEM to offer training and retraining for the *kinguilas* (money changers).[46] AVAL became a vocal defender of zungueiras against their persecution after the launch of Operation Resgate in 2018.[47]

Decriminalisation of the informal market began only during the pandemic years, after 2020. Street sellers defied regulations/restrictions to provide food and essential commodities to Luanda's locked-down population. The zungueiras are seen by many as Angola's new public heroes, as their work was essential for the provision of services and food to thousands of families during the pandemic. Zungueiras carried out tasks that involved more risk because they work in conditions that oblige them to be in regular contact with their clients. In the opinion of the ILO – more than the virus itself – the measures taken by governments exacerbated the misery and vulnerability experienced by most of the population, especially those with a weak economic situation.[48] The measures to prevent contagion by COVID-19, such as social isolation and quarantine, the closure of markets, limitation on days and times for selling, and the ban on travel, significantly affected informal workers, especially women, who already live in a situation of increased vulnerability. With the emergence of COVID-19, there was a repressive attitude on the part of the authorities towards the practice of zunga, which, in this period, was expressly declared by the government as being a danger to the community.

This situation led to a drastic reduction in informal workers' income. Serious limitations on access to basic social services, such as water, energy, healthcare, and especially daily necessities such as food, soap and even bleach. Zungueiras are high-risk workers, for whom their 'business,' their subsistence, is always unpredictable, depending on trading encounters in the street. Despite the prohibitions, most zungueiras took preventive hygiene measures but, having no alternative, did not stop practicing their profession. These workers who earn a living daily, often risked disobeying the quarantine to feed their family. There was a substantial change in the types of products sold to adapt to the changing basic needs of the clientele for affordable food. Profits during the pandemic fell 50–85 percent, generating more monetary poverty. In many cases additional burdens fell on women who became the only financial providers in the home when their partners became unemployed due to the economic recession imposed by the COVID-19 prevention measures.[49] The urban unemployment rate by the beginning of 2022 had risen to 41.7 percent.[50]

46   Lopes, 'Elementos sobre o comportamento de compra,' 165.
47   Domingos Bento, 'Associação dos Vendedores Ambulantes alerta para os malefícios da Operação Resgate no seio da classe,' *Jornal OPAÍS*, 16 January 2019.
48   International Labour Organization. 'Informal Workers between Pandemic and Unemployment Risks.' *United Nations News*, 7 May 2020, *https://news.un.org/pt/story/2020/05/1712852*
49   Telo, 'Mulheres e comércio (informal) em,' 7–10.
50   Reis, J. J., 'Para cada quatro empregos criados, três eram informais,' *Jornal Expansão*, 20 May 2022.

The repressive actions of Resgate had not stopped the relentless growth of the informal market. It was estimated that informality, by 2020, generated 65 percent of gross domestic product (GDP).[51] The Angolan economy has been in recession since 2016, reflecting the decline in revenue from the petroleum sector. The state needed to seek alternative financing. Some economists proposed to capture untapped wealth beyond the reach of the tax authority, which they believed was tied up in the informal economy. The government saw formalisation as an opportunity to increase the tax base by registering entrepreneurs and providing them with taxation identity cards. It was envisioned that formalisation could initially 'recover 65 percent of wasted revenue tax that did not enter state coffers, estimated at USD 40 billion.'[52]

In early 2021, the government adopted a new 'transformative' approach under the banner of the Informal Economy Transition Programme (PREI), which reversed the aggressive strategy of Operation Resgate that had failed to 'stamp out' the informal economy. PREI's origin was in a presidential decree dating back to 2014.[53] The proposal for 'reducing the levels of informality in the Angolan economy and promoting the progressive formalisation of informal activities' was hidden as an item in the National Development Plan 2013–2017 but was allocated few resources. PREI, relaunched in November 2021, promoted a new way of looking at the economy and informal trade. PREI aimed to increase the security of informal businesses. The Minister of Economy and Planning declared that PREI 'conferred economic citizenship on informal entrepreneurs.'[54]

PREI proposed to seek solutions based on knowledge of the complex reality of the Angolan economy. The programme was built on a knowledge base of new studies on the informal economy. In 2020 the National Statistical Institute (INE) published research on poverty and employment[55] and the National Bank of Angola (BNA) a study of the informal economy. According to INE's 2020 'Survey on Employment in Angola,' of the 10,174,459 employed, 80.4 percent worked in the informal market, and only 19.6 percent had formal jobs. According to INE data[56], 92.5 percent of the younger age groups, between the ages of 15–24, and 88.5 percent of women worked in the informal market.[57] In the previous two years, the country had lost 719,000 formal jobs and 'gained' 1.2 million informal ones.[58]

The BNA study indicated that only 36.7 percent of informal entrepreneurs had access to banking services (women only 29.4 percent). 88.2 percent of transactions in the informal market were made in cash.[59] Several reasons were given by traders who resisted the formalisation of their businesses by opening bank accounts; 28 percent of them considered that they did not have the minimal capital required by banks to open an account; 12.6 percent said that they did not know how; 8.2 percent didn't have the appropriate documentation required; 17.3 percent stated that they were too busy; 2.8 percent that the nearest branch was too far away; and 10.6 percent said that they did not trust banks in any case.

In 2021, with financing from UNDP and the European Union, the Ministry of Economy and Planning set up a technical management unit to support PREI. A commitment was made to create better conditions for informal workers (especially women and young people), promoting their inclusion in social security programmes and improving access to credit, support services for business development and digital financial services. The proponents of PREI argued that 'street sellers must be treated with respect, dignity and consideration in dealings with other traders' and that they also have 'the right to make more convenient use of authorised locations within the limits imposed by law.'[60]

51   'O desafio de transformar a economia em formal,' *Jornal de Angola*, 18 November 2021,
      https://www.jornaldeangola.ao/ao/noticias/o-desafio-de-transformar-a-economia-em-formal/
52   Carlos Ferreira, 'PREI emperra na falta de BI e nas quebras de Sistema,' *Jornal Expansão*, 26 November 2021.
53   Decreto Presidencial no. 105/14, Política Comercial de Angola.
54   T. Marta, 'Programa confere mais cidadania a informais,' *Jornal de Angola*, 20 January 2022.
55   Instituto Nacional de Estatística, 'INE Poverty Report for Angola – Household Expenses and Income,' 2019.
56   *https://prei.ao/informalidade/*
57   Joel Costa, 'Dois em cada em três postos de trabalho criados este ano foram para a informalidade,' *Jornal Economia e Finanças*, 17 December 2021.
58   M. Chambassuco, '7.3 Angola perdeu 537 mil postos de trabalhos formais em 2020 e "ganhou" 786 mil informais,' *Jornal Expansão*, 9 July 2021.
59   Banco Nacional de Angola Relatório CNEF, 'Mercados Informais de Luanda' (2020), 31.
60   'Direitos e Devers Jornal Luanda,' *Jornal de Angola*, 15 November 2021.

Community-managed sanitary block at Roque Santeiro, Luanda, 2005

By the end of 2022, PREI indicated that almost a quarter-million entrepreneurs nationally had been formalised.[61] In Luanda, this corresponded to 43,748 registered, about half of whom had acquired taxation numbers, and 1,673 had subscribed to the optional contributory social security scheme that could provide assistance in sickness, disability, future retirement and maternity benefits for women. 4,240 had applied for microcredit loans, and 1,229 had received training through the programme.

An evaluation was carried out in 2022 on the perceptions of informal entrepreneurs of the PREI policy.[62] Regarding the impact of formalisation efforts, 56 percent of respondents indicated that they lacked adequate information about PREI, its objectives and potential benefits; other informal merchants (about 21 percent) indicated that they were not interested in formalising their businesses and/or did not believe in PREI. A further 64 percent of the entrepreneurs interviewed complained about the negative effect on their businesses of the currency depreciation

that had occurred since 2019. However, 54 percent of those interviewed recognised that formalisation generated greater security of their property rights. In comparison, 60 percent consider that they had improved their relationship with the market and tax administrations.

Informal traders were concerned about the effect of introducing sales tax (VAT) that they were now obliged to pay. They reported that it increased difficulty in purchasing goods (24 percent), reduced the number of customers (23 percent) and sales volume (16 percent). Most interviewed were indifferent to other taxation measures; 16 percent consider the 5 percent import tax on basic basket products unfavourable, while only 14 percent positively evaluate the VAT reduction on essential basic products.

The Observatory of the Informal Economy (OEI) was launched in mid-2022, as an independent consultative body to monitor and advise on public policy.[63] The OEI is composed of forty members, seventeen are public enti-

61   https://prei.ao/formalizacao-operadores-informais/
62   Banco Nacional de Angola and ISPTEC, 'Resultados do Estudo Sobre o Funcionamento do Mercado Informal,' 2020.
63   Decreto Executivo no. 222/22, 'do Ministério da Economia e Planeamento sobre o Observatório da Economia Informal.'

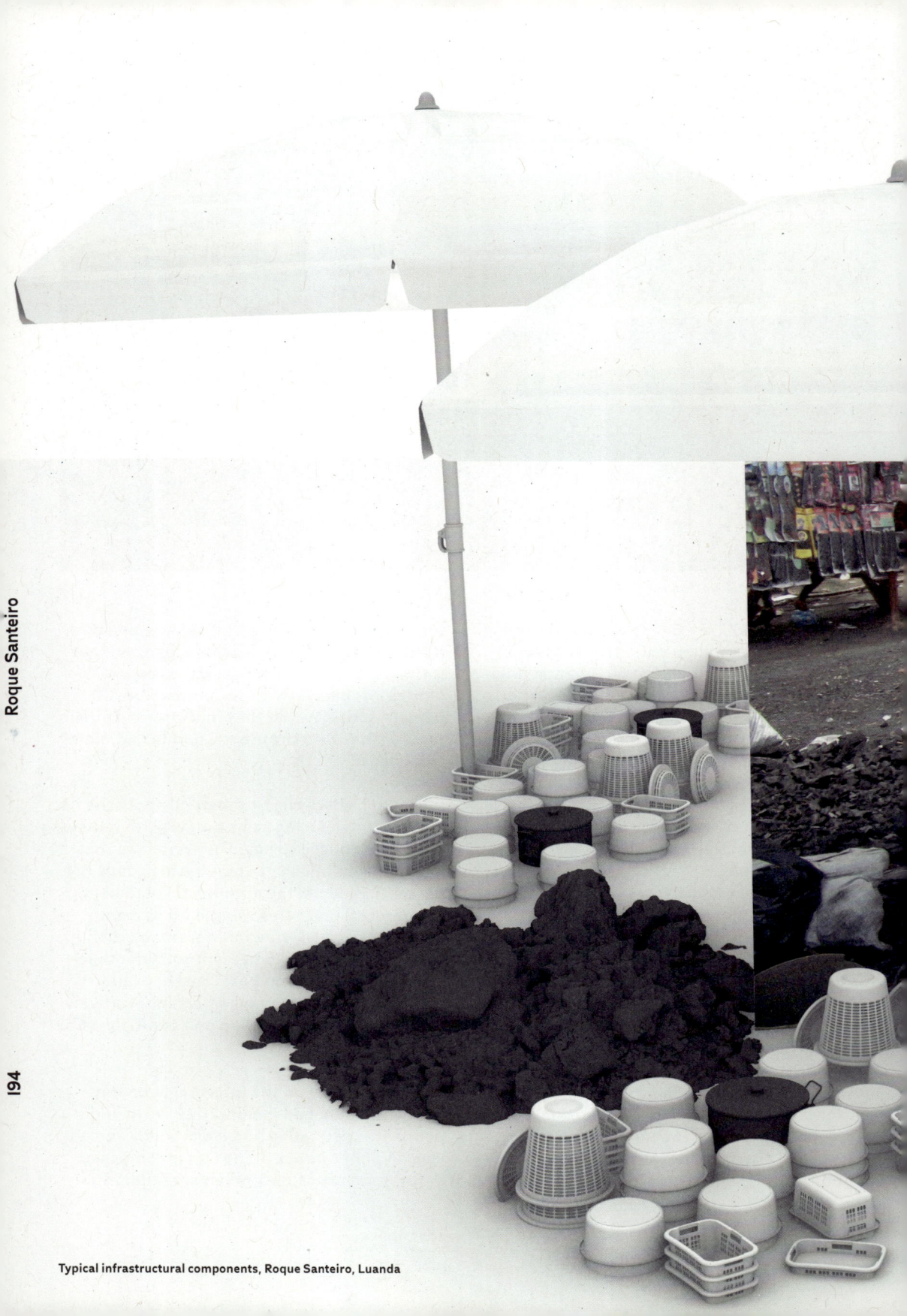

Typical infrastructural components, Roque Santeiro, Luanda

ties, and the remaining organisations represent the informal economy, trade unions, business associations, non-governmental organisations[64], academic institutions, and the development agency donors: the European Union (EU), the United Nations Development Programme (UNDP), the International Labour Organization (ILO) and the United Nations Children's Fund (UNICEF). The OEI aims to contribute to a better understanding of the actors in the sector and dynamics of the informal economy through research and monitoring. It is envisioned to use the evidence from ongoing observation to influence the policy on the formalisation of the economy.

The role of Angolan universities in the OEI is crucial. National universities have begun to be called upon to carry out studies, one of which being the National Bank of Angola's descriptive study on the dynamics of food selling in informal markets contracted to ISPTEC's Center for Research in Applied Social Sciences. Involving academia in policy-related research ensures that studies are not 'shelved' after they are delivered to government, and helps project data and findings into the public domain. The OEI provides a platform for academic institutions and civil society organisations to contribute to the evolution of public policy.[65]

RESEARCH FINDINGS – TIMELINE

Development Workshop's Documentation Centre in Luanda (CEDOC) has, since 2001, scanned, digitalised and archived all articles on the informal economy that have appeared in daily and weekly press (public, private and community media).[66] The diagram on page 208 used this archived media-data to analyse changing attitudes to the informal market, of the public and of state policy makers. The dataset was scanned for key words that indicate 'awareness' of the informal market phenomena, and words or phrases that could be qualified as 'negative' (such as criminal and illegal). A negativity index was produced based on the incidence of negative indicators per the number of articles each year. The graphic also shows the significant event that impacted the informal market that year and highlights 2002,

the year the war ended and the subsequent election years that appear to impact on policy. The negative index line indicates that aggressive attacks against the informal economy spiked in the non-election years and reached the highest point during the peak of the Resgate operation in 2018.

The increase in the awareness factor mirrors the decline in negative indicators, as the contribution of the informal economy has been acknowledged in public attitudes in the most recent years. During the electoral campaigns of the governing party, in attempts at capturing the votes of a large number of informal market workers and entrepreneurs, the graphic indicated an easing of the discourse in the years shown in grey. Finally, in the impact of the pandemic and the promotion of the pro-informal market regularisation programme PREI after 2020, the negativity index showed a steep reduction.

LUANDA'S INFORMAL MARKETS GO DIGITAL

In 2018 a young Angolan woman entrepreneur and some colleagues launched a company Roque Online which transformed informal commerce into a digital platform that allowed customers to 'go to the marketplace' without leaving home. Informal market vendors and small businesses could download the 'Roque' mobile app and start recording and advertising their inventory. With an investment of just 8,000 US dollars, in the first year, about 200 products were promoted, highlighting typical Angolan wares such as smoked catfish, *fuba de bombó* (manioc flour), baked items such as banana bread, and *gimboa* (sweet potato leaves). In the first year, the app had a turnover of only around 33,000 US dollars. The adoption of e-money in Angola has been very slow, and cash management challenges were encountered between informal market suppliers and the digital service provider.[67] Some informal sellers still encounter technological barriers, such as the need to own a cell phone and thereby pay the user charges and working from areas where network coverage is poor.

64   The Development Workshop is a founding member of the OEI along with the associations and unions representing informal sector workers.
65   Alexandre Lourenço, 'BNA contrata centro do ISPTEC para estudar mercado informal,' *Jornal Expansão*, 21 January 2022.
66   Angola Media Scan: *https://dw.angonet.org/pt-pt/cedoc*
67   Andre Samuel, 'Roque Santeiro agora está online para concorrer com negócios formais,' *Jornal Mercado*, 21 September 2019.

From March 2020, however, when Angola declared a pandemic emergency, restricting street trade and informal markets, online orders jumped five- or sixfold. By this point, there were more than a thousand items on offer on the app. Roque Online allowed sellers and buyers to comply with social-distancing rules while avoiding physical gatherings. During the state of emergency, sellers thus had a direct line to continue to market their products and make sales without being physically in the marketplaces. During the pandemic, Roque Online expanded nationally, providing services in Luanda, Lubango, Huambo and Cabinda, serving 18 informal markets with almost 100,000 sellers. The owners of Roque Online believe that the business will continue to grow through the increasing demand from both customers and sellers, bringing informal markets into the digital domain.[68]

CONCLUSIONS

This study has demonstrated that Luanda's informal economy has an extraordinary capacity for resilience. It provides the means through which the creativity and entrepreneurial spirit of most of the population has developed, despite the fact that these activities are carried out outside and often in opposition to policies imposed by the municipal government. This chapter tells the story of Luanda's informal marketplaces and follows the traders who, after the closure of Roque Santeiro, began to sell in the streets or from their homes. However, the informal market does more than just employ two thirds of Angola's urban families. The informal market provides Angolans with almost all of their basic needs, from housing, water, and transport, including getting to their informal jobs. Almost 90 percent of the land is occupied informally[69], leaving most families with precarious tenure, without land titles. Half of Luanda's population is supplied by informal truckers who transport water from the nearby river, meeting a demand for water that the state cannot provide.[70]

There are many reasons for the pervasive informality of the Angolan economy; the economic exclusion of the African population has roots in the colonial era's semi-fascist state policies; the chaotic transition to independence in 1975; the failure of the post-independence experiment in centralised socialist economics; the civil war that provoked massive internal displacement to Luanda's informal musseque settlements; the state monopoly of the petroleum-based formal sector economy, ensuring that the elites capture its benefits; the inequitable trickle-down of petroleum wealth[71]; the post-war attempt at rapid and brutal modernisation by removing signs of the informal market; and its criminalisation when it showed itself in the streets. All attempts of suppression over the years have failed. Recent evidence of the magnitude of this failure was made public by the state's statistic bureau[72] and studies commissioned by the National Bank.[73] New data revealed the enormous growth of the informal economy and its importance for sustaining most Angolan families.

With the decline of state revenue from extractive industries the government came to the potential of the wealth hidden in the informal market and how it might be tapped in some way.[74] The Informal Economy Transition Programme (PREI) and the launch of the Observatory on the Informal Economy (OEI) mark the beginnings of a public policy reform. The apparent change in attitudes to informal markets before the 2022 elections is illustrated by monitoring the public and social media. During that period, there was a decline in negative references in the press and government pronouncements. Angola appeared at that time to be on the way to de-criminalising informality. However, in January 2023, only a few months after the return of the governing party to power with a slim parliamentary majority, district authorities in Luanda reintroduced restrictions on informal trade in the urban centre. There had been a major shift of voters in Luanda, giving the opposition a strong majority but no executive power. In a renewed effort to remove informal traders from the city

68 Geraldine Gerardo, entrepreneur and owner of Roque Online interviewed in *VerAngola*, 4 May 2020.
69 Allan Cain, 'Luanda's Post-war Land Markets: Reducing Poverty by Promoting Inclusion,' *Urban Forum* 24 (2012): 12.
70 Allan Cain, 'Informal Water Markets and Community Management in Peri-urban Luanda, Angola,' *Water International* 43, no. 2 (2018): 2.
71 Paul Jenkins, Paul Robson and Allan Cain, 'Local Responses to Globalization and Peripheralization in Luanda, Angola,' *Environment and Urbanization* 14, no. 1 (2002), 199.
72 Instituto Nacional de Estatística, 2020.
73 Banco Nacional de Angola and ISPTEC, 'Resultados do Estudo Sobre o Funcionamento do Mercado Informal.'
74 Hernando De Soto, *The Mystery of Capital* (New York: Basic Books, 2000).

centre and assign them 'safe market places' in the periphery, the governor launched a new campaign against informality. The 'Strategy to Mitigate Uncontrolled Selling'[75] revived a Resgate-period 2014 bylaw that prohibited informal selling in urban centre districts, removed zungueiras from the street, and, since late May 2023, closed down 230 wholesaler warehouses that supplied the sellers.[76]

This chapter provides evidence of the resilience of the informal economy, despite decades of Angolan government attempts to eradicate it, then marginalise it to the periphery, or at least control it, or even profit from it. However, the pattern of cyclical repression and tolerance prevails. The research discussed in this chapter demonstrates a close link between electoral cycles and the promises of reform that are offered periodically to an electorate, the majority of whom earn their livelihoods in informal markets.

REFERENCES

'A lei vem proibir práticas, mas não garante direito.' *Jornal Expansão*, 31 May 2019.

Adauta de Sousa, M. *Informal Sector in Luanda: Contributions for a Better Understanding*. Luanda: Eurostat, 1998.

Banco Nacional de Angola and ISPTEC. 'Resultados do Estudo Sobre o Funcionamento do Mercado Informal.' 2020.

Bapolo, H. 'GPL proíbe comércio grossista instalado em zonas urbanas.' Expansão, 14 June 2023. https://expansao.co.ao/angola/interior/gpl-proibe-comercio-grossista-instalado-em-zonas-urbanas-113608.html

Bento, D. 'Associação dos Vendedores Ambulantes alerta para os malefícios da Operação Resgate no seio da classe.' *Jornal OPAÍS*, 16 January 2019.

Cain, A. 'Informal Water Markets and Community Management in Peri-urban Luanda, Angola.' *Water International* 43, no. 2 (2018): 205–16.

Cain, A. 'Luanda's Post-war Land Markets: Reducing Poverty by Promoting Inclusion.' *Urban Forum* 24 (2013): 11–31.

Cain, A. 'Roque Santeiro Market, Luanda.' In *Informal Market Worlds: The Architecture of Economic Pressure - Atlas*, edited by P. Mörtenböck and H. Mooshammer, 102–07. Rotterdam: nai010 publishers, 2015.

Calueto, F. 'Mercado do Panguila as mosca.' *Novo Jornal*, 20 February 2018.

Carmo, Y. 'Mais de 200 mercados movimentam comércio.' *Jornal de Angola*, 8 February 2022.

'Caso zungueira do Rocha: "Pode ser condenado até dois anos de prisão."' *Angola 24 Hours*, 17 March 2019.

Chambassuco, M. '7.3 Angola perdeu 537 mil postos de trabalhos formais em 2020 e "ganhou" 786 mil informais.' *Jornal Expansão*, 9 July 2021.

'Comércio Informal. Ambulantes com os dias contados,' *Jornal de Angola*, 17 January 2014.

Conselho Nacional de Estabilidade Financeira. *Inquéritos de Inclusão Financeira – Mercados Informais de Luanda*. 2020.

Costa, A. B. d., and C. Rodrigues. 'Estrategias de sobrevivencia e de reproducao social nas familias de bairros peri-urbanos de Luanda e Maputo – um olhar antropologico.' In *Urbanizacao acelerada em Luanda e Maputo: impacto da guerra e das transformacoes socio-economicas (decadas de '80 e '90)*, edited by J. Oppenheimer and I. Raposo. Centro de Estudos sobre Africa e do Desenvolvimento, Lisbon 2002.

Costa, J. 'Dois em cada em três postos de trabalho criados este ano foram para a informalidade.' *Jornal Economia e Finanças*, 17 December 2021.

Curreri, G. *Il Roque Santeiro: Wall Street dell'Angola - Una ricerca antropologica sul mercato informale di Luanda*. PhD diss., Università La Sapienza, Rome, 2008.

De Soto, H. *The Mystery of Capital*. New York: Basic Books, 2003.

Development Workshop (DW) Angola. 'Informal Trading in Luanda's Streets and Homes.' Report submitted to the International Development Research Centre (IDRC), May 2009.

Development Workshop (DW) Angola. 'Post-Conflict Transformation in Angola's Informal Economy.' Report submitted to the IDRC Eastern & Southern Africa Office - Nairobi, June 2009.

'Direitos e Devers Jornal Luanda.' *Jornal de Angola*, 15 November 2021.

Domingos, H. 'Alternativa a criacao de emprego.' *Jornal Economia e Mercado*, January 2014.

Domingues, J. *O Mercado Informal em Luanda*. Dissertation, University of Lisbon, 2019.

dos Santos, D. 'The Second Economy in Angola: Esquema and Candonga.' In *The Second Economy in Marxist States*, edited by M. Łoś. London: Palgrave Macmillan, 1990.

Ducados, H. L. 'Genero, raca e classe – a feminizacao da pobreza: a estratificacao do sector informal urbano de Luanda.' Paper presented at O desafio da diferenca: articulando genero, raca e classe Conference, Universidade Federal da Bahia, Brazil, 2000.

Ducados, H. L. 'Women and Development: Women, Poverty and the Informal Sector in Luanda's Peri-urban Bairros.' Unpublished report, Development Workshop (DW) Angola, 1994.

Ernesto, E. 'A Economia Informal em Angola: Caracterização do Trabalhador Informal.' Report, Open Society Institute for Southern Africa, 2018.

'Estudo de Mercado Provincia Luanda.' CESO, 2010.

Eugénio, A. 'Mercado do km 30 chega a movimentar mais de 70 mil milhões de kwanzas ao ano.' *Jornal Economia e Finanças*, 11 February 2022.

Ferraz, J.E. *O Poderda Econonia Informal: Characteristicas e Dimensoes*. Brazil: Editorial Reino, 2020.

Ferreira, C. 'PREI emperra na falta de BI e nas quebras de Sistema.' *Jornal Expansão*, 26 November 2021.

75   'Estratégia para Mitigação da Venda Desordenada,' 2023.
76   Horacio Bapolo, 'GPL proíbe comércio grossista instalado em zonas urbanas,' EXPANSAO, 14 June 2023, https://expansao.co.ao/angola/interior/gpl-proibe-comercio-grossista-instalado-em-zonas-urbanas-113608.html

'Fiscalização arrecada oito milhões de Kz de emolumentos.' *Jornal de Angola*, 9 January 2014.

Grassi, M. 'Genero e desenvolvimento em Angola: mulheres empresarias em Luanda e Benguela.' Paper presented at O desafio da diferenca: articulando genero, raca e classe Conference, Universidade Federal da Bahia, Brazil, 2000.

Hans Posthumus Consultancy. *Business Development Services Market Assessment*. Angola Enterprise Program, 2006.

Hodges, A. *Angola: do Afro-estalinismo ao capitalismo selvagem*. Cascais: Principia, Publicações Universitárias e Científicas, 2003.

Human Rights Watch. '"Take That Filth Away": Police Abuses Against Street Vendors in Angola.' HRW report, October 2013. *https://www.hrw.org/report/2013/09/30/take-filth-away/police-abuses-against-street-vendors-angola*

Instituto Nacional de Estatística. 'INE Poverty Report for Angola – Household expenses & income,' 2019.

International Labour Organization. 'Angola: Study on the Migration from Informal to Formal Economy.' ILO, 20 October 2021. *https://www.ilo.org/wcmsp5/groups/public/---ed_dialogue/---act_emp/documents/publication/wcms_823469.pdf*

International Labour Organization. 'Informal Workers between Pandemic and Unemployment Risks.' *United Nations News*, 7 May 2020. *https:// news.un.org/pt/story/2020/05/1712852*

International Labour Organization. *Men and Women in the Informal Economy: A Statistical Picture*. Geneva: International Labour Office, 2002.

Jenkins, P., Robson, P., & Cain, A. 'Local Responses to Globalization and Peripheralization in Luanda, Angola.' *Environment and Urbanization* 14, no. 1 (2002): 115–27.

Kyle, S. 'How Important Was Marxism for the Development of Mozambique and Angola?' Working paper, Cornell University, 2013. *http://kyle.dyson.cornell.edu/Working%20Paper%202013-18%20FINAL.pdf*

Lopes, C. 'Elementos sobre o comportamento de compra em mercados informais: estudo de caso no mercado Roque Santeiro (Luanda).' PhD diss., Instituto Superior de Ciencias do Trabalho e Rmpresa, Lisbon, 2008.

Lopes, C. 'A economia de Luanda e Maputo: olhares cruzados.' In *Urbanizacao acelerada em Luanda e Maputo: impacto da guerra e das transformacoes socio-economicas (decadas de '80 e '90)*, edited by J. Oppenheimer and I. Raposo. Centro de Estudos sobre Africa e do Desenvolvimento, Lisbon 2002.

Lopes, C. 'A economia informal em Angola breve panorâmica.' *Revista Angolana de Sociologia* 14 (2014): 61–75.

Lopes, C. 'A fixação de preços nos mercados informais de Luanda: estudo comparativo nos mercados Congolenses, Rocha Pinto e Shabba.' MA thesis, Economics and Social Development in Africa, ISCTE - University Institute of Lisbon, 1998.

Lopes, C. 'Angola, a OIT e a Economia Informal.' Polytechnic Institute of Technology and Science, Luanda, 2018.

Lourenço, A. 'BNA contrata centro do ISPTEC para estudar mercado informal.' *Jornal Expansão*, 21 January 2022.

'Luanda cria unidade de Polícia Fiscal.' *Jornal de Angola*, 28 April 2012.

Manaça, M. 'Zungueiras criam programa televisivo para defender os seus direitos.' *Jornal OPAÍS*, 9 August 2019.

Marta, T. 'Programa confere mais cidadania a informais.' *Jornal de Angola*, 20 January 2022.

'Mercados Informais de Luanda.' Banco Nacional de Angola Relatório CNEF, 2020.

Monteiro, D., and N. Andre. 'Estudo sobre a situação da mulher zungueira.' ASSOGE, Luanda, 2018.

Morice, A. 'Commerce parallele et troc a Luanda.' *Politique Africaine* 17 (1985): 105–20.

'O desafio de transformar a economia em formal.' *Jornal de Angola*, 18 November 2021. *https://www.jornaldeangola.ao/ao/noticias/o-desafio-de-transformar-a-economia-em-formal/*

Oppenheimer J., and I. Raposo, eds. *Lisbon, Centro de Estudos sobre Africa e do Desenvolvimento* (n.d.).

Pereira, L. N. N. 'Os regressados na cidade de Luanda: um estudo sobre identidade etnica e nacional em Angola.' Departamento de Antropologia, Faculdade de Filosofia, Letras e Ciencias Humanas, Universidade de Sao Paulo, 2004.

Queiroz, F. *Economia Informal, o caso de Angola*. Coimbra: Almedina, 2016.

Reis, J. J. 'Para cada quatro empregos criados, três eram informais.' *Jornal Expansão*, 20 May 2022.

Robson, P., ed. 'What to Do When the Fighting Stops: Challenges for Post-conflict Reconstruction in Angola.' Occasional Paper no. 7, Development Workshop (DW) Angola, 2006.

Rocha, A. 'Estudo sobre o Empreendedorismo em Angola.' Universidade Católica de Angola (UCAN), Centro de Estudos e Investigação Científica, 2012.

'"Roque Online" trouxe experiência de ir ao mercado sem sair de casa.' *VerAngola*, 4 May 2020.

Samuel, A. 'Roque Santeiro agora está on-line para concorrer com negócios formais.' *Jornal Mercado*, 21 September 2019.

Sela, E. 'Reordenamento do Comercio Estabelecimentos encerrados perdem mais de 2 milhoes de Kz/dia.' *Novo Jornal*, 2 June 2023.

Shea, P., and H. L. Ducados. 'Participatory Sub-sector Study on the Marketing of Fish.' Report, Development Workshop (DW) Angola, 1996.

Telo, F. C. A. 'Mulheres e comércio (informal) em Luanda: um olhar para além da crise pandémica de Covid19.' *Revista Espaco Academico* (June 2021).

Tomás, Antonio. 'Refracted Governmentality Space, Politics, and Social Structure in Contemporary Luanda.' PhD dissertation. Columbia University, 2012.

'Transformation of the Informal Economy in Post-war Angola Luanda.' Development Workshop (DW) Angola, 2004.

'Transição da economia informal para a formal mais célere,' *Jornal de Angola*, 9 October 2021.

United Nations Development Programme. 'Angola Enterprise Program: Micro-finance Component.' UNDP, 2003. *https://www.findevgateway.org/sites/default/files/publications/files/mfg-en-paper-angola-enterprise-program-microfinance-component-2002.pdf*

'Volume I: Angolan Micro-finance Sector Review: Baseline Study.' Banco Nacional de Angola, 2006.

Yngstrom, I. 'Vulnerability, Poverty and Social Exclusion in Post-Conflict Angola: Opportunities and Constraints for Social Capital Building.' Third Social Action Fund (FAS III), World Bank, 2004.

Zamora, P. 'Roque Santeiro: el fútbol se vive en el mercado de África.' *Diario AS*, 14 January 2010.

ANNEX: LEGISLATION

1980–2000

LAW NO. 2/82, 8 FEBRUARY 1982 – on Centralised Socialist Planning of the Economy. The National Plan governs economic and social activity, which should guarantee proportional development and economic independence, a constant increase in productivity, and promote better living conditions for workers. Drafted by the Ministry of Planning when it was the senior ministry within the Council of Ministers.

DECREE NO. 92/82, 18 OCTOBER 1982 – all enterprises established in Angola must register their statistical data with the INE (National Statistical Institute) by completing a questionnaire to enable the INE to collect relevant information to accurately measure business activity in the country.

LAW NO. 10/87, 26 SEPTEMBER 1987 – on administrative transgressions.

LAW NO. 6/99, 3 SEPTEMBER 1999 – on Offenses Against the Economy, the legal regime of offenses against the economy and establishes the actions and omissions considered against the economy.

EXECUTIVE DECREE NO. 33/00, 5 MAY 2000 – regulation on the setting of prices in commercial establishments and at all points of sale.

DECREE LAW NO. 5/00, 2 JUNE 2000 – organisational structure of the Ministry of Commerce is defined and the attributions that correspond to the different levels of responsibility, including the National Directorate of Internal Commerce, provincial delegations and the National Institute of Consumer Defence.

DECREE NO. 29/00, 2 JUNE 2000 – regulates the licensing of commercial activities and the conditions for providing commercial services to obtain a license to carry out said activities. This license applies to certifying commercial activities of wholesale, retail, mixed trade, general trade, import and export, provision of commercial services, and other activities not regulated by other specific legislation.

EXECUTIVE DECREE NO. 43/00, 2 JUNE 2000 – on precarious trade regulations. Precarious commerce under the terms of this decree is conceived as the exercise of commercial activity in non-conventionally constructed establishments in rural or suburban areas.

EXECUTIVE DECREE NO. 44/00, 2 JUNE 2000 – regulation on rural markets. Rural markets are considered to be concentrations of agricultural, livestock and handicraft products, unprocessed or manufactured, coming from rural areas with a view to their commercialisation.

EXECUTIVE DECREE NO. 45/00, 2 JUNE 2000 – regulation on urban markets. Urban markets are the fixed or temporary locations where where the buying and selling of retails products takes place.

EXECUTIVE DECREE NO. 47/00, 2 JUNE 2000 – regulation on marketplaces in non-fixed premises, carried out in a non-sedentary manner in open-air markets or in installations not stably fixed to the ground in covered markets.

EXECUTIVE DECREE NO. 48/00, 2 JUNE 2000 – regulation on street vending carried out in a non-sedentary way by individuals who transport goods, either manually or by animal-drawn vehicles for sale during their transit, outside urban and/or municipal markets and in places fixed by the municipal administrations.

EXECUTIVE DECREE NO. 55/00, 14 JULY 2000 – regulation on the commercial register that regulates the definition and classification of the commercial network and the organisation of the commercial register, defines eleven different categories of activities and establishes the legal regime for all other purposes.

ORDER NO. 142/00, 30 JUNE 2000 – authorisation of provincial governments to license trade, large commercial areas for wholesale, retail, trade agencies, shopping centres and commercial service activities of a relevant size in accordance with the classification of the commercial network.

2000–2010

ORDER NO. 15/04, 27 JANUARY 2004 – delimitation of jurisdiction between the Ministry of Commerce and the Government of the Province of Luanda (DPL).

DECREE LAW NO. 20/05, 2 JUNE 2005 – The Ministry of Commerce defined the organic structure and the attributions corresponding to the different levels of responsibility; the National Directorate for Internal Trade (DNCI) and the National Directorate for Foreign Trade, provincial delegations, National Institute for Consumer Protection, Quality Control Laboratory. The objective of the DNCI is 'to formalise informal trade […] there are several initiatives to try to control its growth […] there is a lot of connection between informal trade and illegal trade […] see the case of Roque Santeiro […].'

EXECUTIVE DECREE NO. 98/05, 24 OCTOBER 2005 – concerning the National Institute of Consumer Defence (INADEC). Establishes the function and norms of the provincial nuclei of the National Institute of Consumer Defence.

LAW NO. 1/07, 14 MAY 2007 – to regulate and control commercial activity and contribute to the ordering and modernisation of commercial infrastructures to protect free and fair competition between traders and to safeguard the rights of consumers established by law. This law applies to the exercise of commercial activities and services carried out in national territory by merchants or by those who act on their behalf and aims at promotion, preparation and cooperation in carrying out commercial operations.

PRESIDENTIAL DECREE NO. 263/10 – a retail trade regulation to establish the general legal regime for the organisation, exercise, control and operation of retail trade activities and the regulation of commercial practices in sales promotion, sales and special sales. This regulation applies to natural and legal persons who engage in retail trade.

PRESIDENTIAL DECREE NO. 288/10, 30 NOVEMBER 2010 – regulation on the licensing of commercial activities and providers of commercial services.

PRESIDENTIAL DECREE NO. 69/10, 19 MAY 2010 – the statute of the Ministry of Commerce to conduct, execute, evaluate and manage the Executive's policy in the field of commerce and the provision of mercantile services.

2010–2023

LAW NO. 12/11, 16 FEBRUARY 2011 – establishes the general basis applicable to administrative transgressions committed by public and private natural or legal persons.

EXECUTIVE DECREE NO. 87/11, 6 JUNE 2011 – regulation defining the National Directorate of Internal Trade as the central executive service of the Ministry of Commerce, which is responsible for registering and licensing commercial activity and monitoring production, mercantile distribution and logistics.

LAW NO. 30/11, 13 SEPTEMBER 2011 – on micro, small and medium enterprises. According to the legislation: Micro-enterprises are companies that employ up to ten workers and/or have a gross annual turnover below 250,000 US dollars (or the equivalent in Angolan kwanza); small businesses are companies that employ between 10–100 workers and/or have a gross annual turnover between 250,000 US dollars and 3 million US dollars (or the equivalent in Angolan kwanza); medium-sized businesses are companies that employ between 100–200 workers and/or have a gross annual turnover between 3 million US dollars and 10 million US dollars (or the equivalent in Angolan kwanza).

EXECUTIVE DECREE NO. 135/11 – regulation of commercial activity carried out in urban and suburban markets to regulate the commercial activity of selling products in premises, as a general rule, covered or semi-covered, closed or delimited, formally designated by the respective municipal administration as markets. Establishes the legal framework for this type of commercial activity and regulates every act of commerce carried out in connection with this activity.

PRESIDENTIAL DECREE NO. 41/12 – support programme for micro, small, and medium enterprises; general guidelines for promoting fiscal and financial incentives, organisation and reinforcement of competitiveness and technological innovation of MSMEs.

PRESIDENTIAL DECREE NO. 43/12 – regulation of micro, small and medium-scale enterprises establishes the legal regime for the constitution, organisation and operation of micro, small and medium-sized companies, and the forms of qualification for the benefit of differentiated and priority treatment provided for in law no. 30/11.

JOINT EXECUTIVE DECREE NO. 103/12 – regulation of micro-credit entitled Meu Negócios Minha Vida, created within the scope of the Small Business Support Programme (PROAPEN), approved by Presidential Decree no. 42/12. This programme aims to promote the development and consolidation of small businesses by facilitating credit for micro-entrepreneurs.

PRESIDENTIAL DECREE NO. 48/12 – approves the Rural Commerce and Entrepreneurship Plan for the Development of Rural Commerce and Entrepreneurship (PLAINDECOR). PLAINDECOR aims to drive sustainable economic growth, reduce poverty, increase production and foster entrepreneurship and employment.

PRESIDENTIAL DECREE NO. 84/14 – approves the Informal Economy Reconversion Programme (PREI), which aims to promote, consolidate, and formalise small businesses, facilitating access to credit for micro-entrepreneurs, micro-companies and cooperatives, as well as entrepreneurial training, the increase in the supply of goods and services and the creation of jobs.

PRESIDENTIAL DECREE NO. 105/14 – Angola's new commercial policy, which is an integral part of the National Development Plan (PND) of 2013–2017, as the commercial policy outlines the guiding principles, the short, medium and long-term objectives for the development of commercial activity in Angola. This actively involves the private sector, taking into account the laws governing the market, public-private partnerships and the regulatory and facilitating role of the state, to achieve three goals; macroeconomic stabilisation; growth and employment; and recovery of domestic production.

PUBLIC NOTICE BY THE ADMINISTRATIVE COMMITTEE OF THE CITY OF LUANDA (CACL) NO. 01/14, 8 APRIL – on street vending in Luanda.

DISPATCH NO. 04/15 – delimitation of the responsibilities between the Ministry of Commerce and the Provincial Government of Luanda. This temporarily awards to the Province of Luanda, from the National Directorate of Internal Trade, the authority to issue licenses for commercial activity that was delegated through Dispatch no. 142/00, of 30 June.

JOINT EXECUTIVE DECREE NO. 326/16 – regulation of the Informal Economy Reconversion Programme of the National Development Plan 2013–2017, establishing the requirements for access to credit, the responsibilities of the participating parties, the financial conditions, the operational procedure and the accountability mechanisms of the PREI.

LAW NO. 15/19, 23 MAY 2019 – to establish rules on the organisation, exercise and operation of street commerce, street vendors and market stalls, without prejudice to usage and customs, under the terms of the Constitution and the law. The law controls street market and commercial activities under Operation Resgate. There is a clear intention to suppress street vendors, imposing 'a discipline and operating logic,' starting with the demarcation of locations, subject to obtaining formal authorisation for access and, consequently, for the use of these spaces. This political intention to order is grounded in the official discourse that sees street commerce as a phenomenon: disorderly, a garbage generator, obstructive and detrimental to human health, one of the activities that contributes to the 'total chaos' of informal commerce.

EXECUTIVE DECREE NO. 143/20 OF 9 APRIL 2020 – on merchants and service providers, for the duration of the COVID-19 state of emergency. This decree urges merchants to strictly observe the procedures stipulated in paragraph 7 of article 22 of Law no. 01/07 (on Commercial Activity), and the provisions of articles 39 and 42 of Law no. 6/99 (on Infringements Against the Economy), while the state of emergency is in force.

DISPATCH NO. 1/21 OF 11 JANUARY 2021 – regulation of the Law of Administrative Transgressions.

EXECUTIVE DECREE NO. 222/22 – issued by the Ministry of Economy and Planning on the Informal Economy Observatory as a consultative body for assessing and supporting the process of formalising the (informal) economy for the purposes of consultation and social dialogue. The OEI is an autonomous body that does not form part of the public administration and has its attributions and competencies within the scope of its activity.

PRESIDENTIAL DECREE NO. 123/22 – moto-taxi legal regime applicable to the carrying out of individual or collective paid transport of passengers and goods in moped, motorcycle, tricycle and quadracycle vehicles.

LAW NO. 19/22 – general legal regime of administrative offenses and the respective procedures. The administrative offense is defined as any unlawful act that can be legally sanctioned, which is combined with a fine.

1975-1991

1 Civil war breaks out with the proclamation of the People's Republic of Angola by the People's Movement for the Liberation of Angola (MPLA).
2 Angola faces macro-economic difficulties and a significant rise in public debt.
3 Inception of Roque Santeiro Market
4 Roque Santeiro becomes the main supplier of other formal and informal markets in Luanda.

1991-2000

5 The privatisation of public services contributes to a decline in the living conditions within the *musseques* (informal settlements).
6 Dramatic increase in the level of unemployment
7 The first land law (Lei de Terras) confers the state with authority over agricultural land and paves the path for the involvement of private investors.
8 1975-2002 – duration of civil war; from 1992 onwards the ruling MPLA adopts principles of the market economy.
9 Roque Santeiro becomes a key component in a network of 26 informal markets, five of which host over 3,000 vendors.

2000-2005

10 The endorsement of the 'Plan for Land Use and Growth Management of Luanda,' formulated in the 1990s is abandoned in the face of Luanda's rapid expansion.
11 End of the Angolan Civil War
12 New credit lines from China are used as an opportunity to replace informal markets with markets managed by municipal authorities.
13 A new land law (Law no. 09/04) mandates landowners to undergo an official registration process for their land before the designated deadline in 2010. Failure to comply would result in the transfer of ownership of any unregistered land in Angola to the state.
14 The government implements a strategy aimed at regaining control over urban space and eradicating the *musseques*.

Roque Santeiro

202

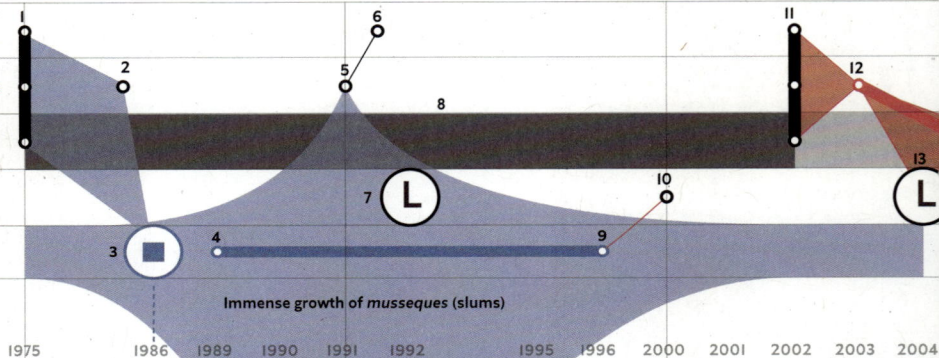

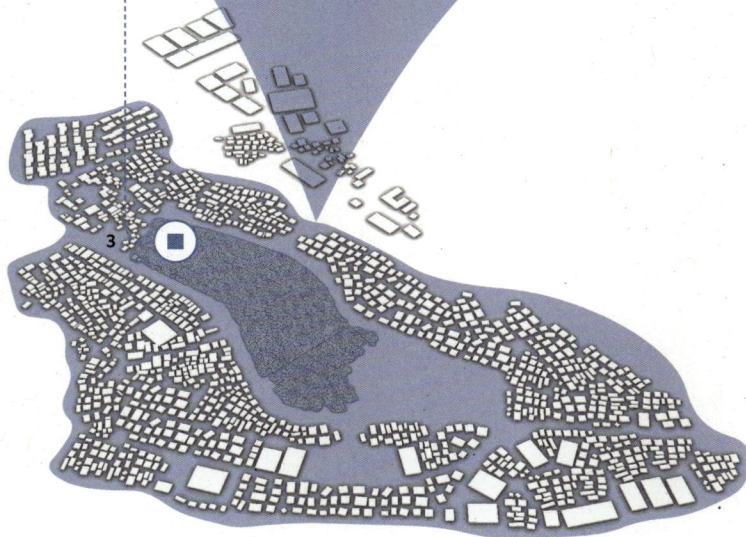

Timeline of key events shaping the transformation of Roque Santeiro, Luanda

2005-2010

15 The Angolan government initiates PRESILD (Programme of Structuring the System of Logistics and Distribution of Essential Products to the Population) which seeks to formalise and restructure the commercial supply network.
16 The implementation of the Law of Housing Development introduces a provision enabling the state to demolish constructions deemed 'inappropriate'.
17 Panguila Market Complex is constructed with the aim of absorbing vendors after the closure of Roque Santeiro.
18 The National Programme for Urban Development and Housing, commonly known as the 'My Dream, My Home' programme, is introduced.

2010-2015

19 Roque Santeiro is demolished and vendors are evicted.
20 Since 2002 – post-war period; further economic liberalisation and free market policies
21 The government announces a regime of heavy fines, targeting not only informal vendors but also their customers.

2015-2020

22 Introduction of a masterplan for the municipal districts Sambizanga (which includes the area of Roque Santeiro) and Cazenga
23 Km 30 becomes the largest market in Luanda.
24 Measures against informality culminate in 'Operation Resgate,' with arrests and heavy fines against informal vendors.
25 Launch of Roque Online

2015-2020

26 Markets in Luanda are closed during the COVID-19 pandemic, but many informal vendors continue to sell.
27 The government embraces a transformative approach, known as the Informal Economy Transition Programme (PREI), which marks a departure from the 'Resgate Operation' strategy, which aimed to eliminate the informal economy but proved ineffective.
28 There are 208 registered markets spread across the province of Luanda.

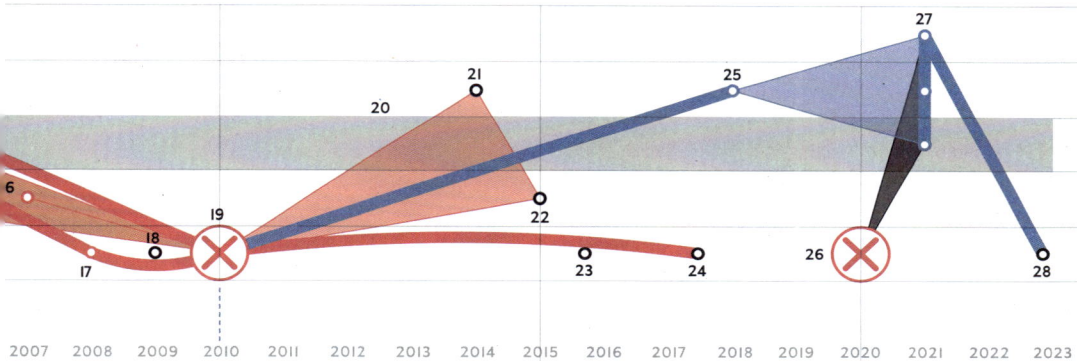

Spatial, social, economic and political interventions into in/formal markets
Informality as a survival method and means of adapting to changing socio-economic and political circumstances

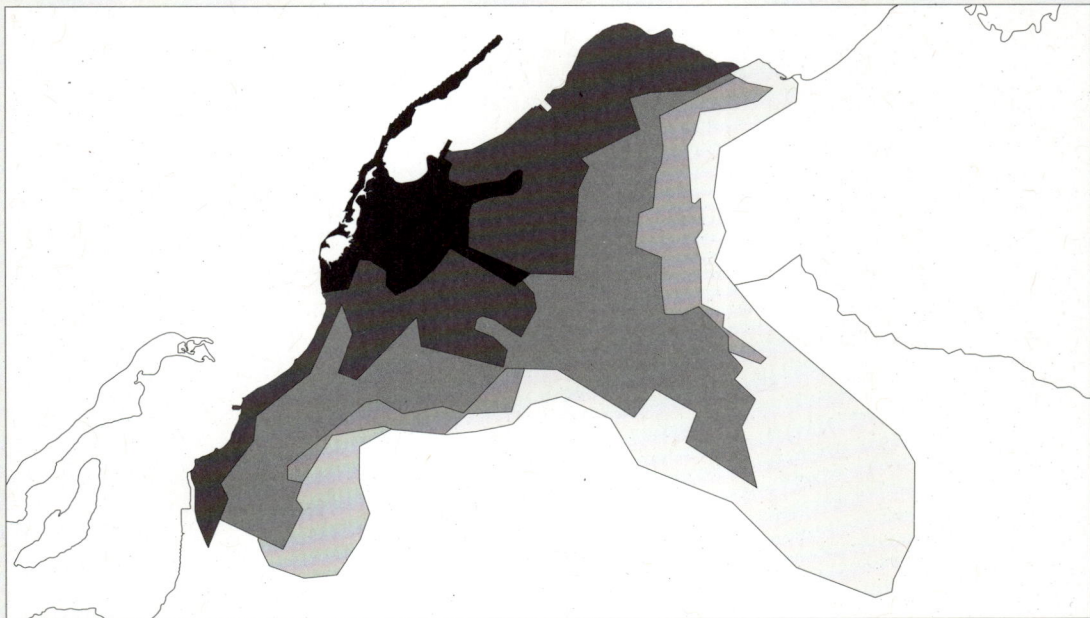

■ 1980: 20km² ■ 1989: 100km² ■ 1998: 250km² ■ 2002: 270km² □ 2015: 350km²

Luanda's spatial expansion from 1980 to 2015

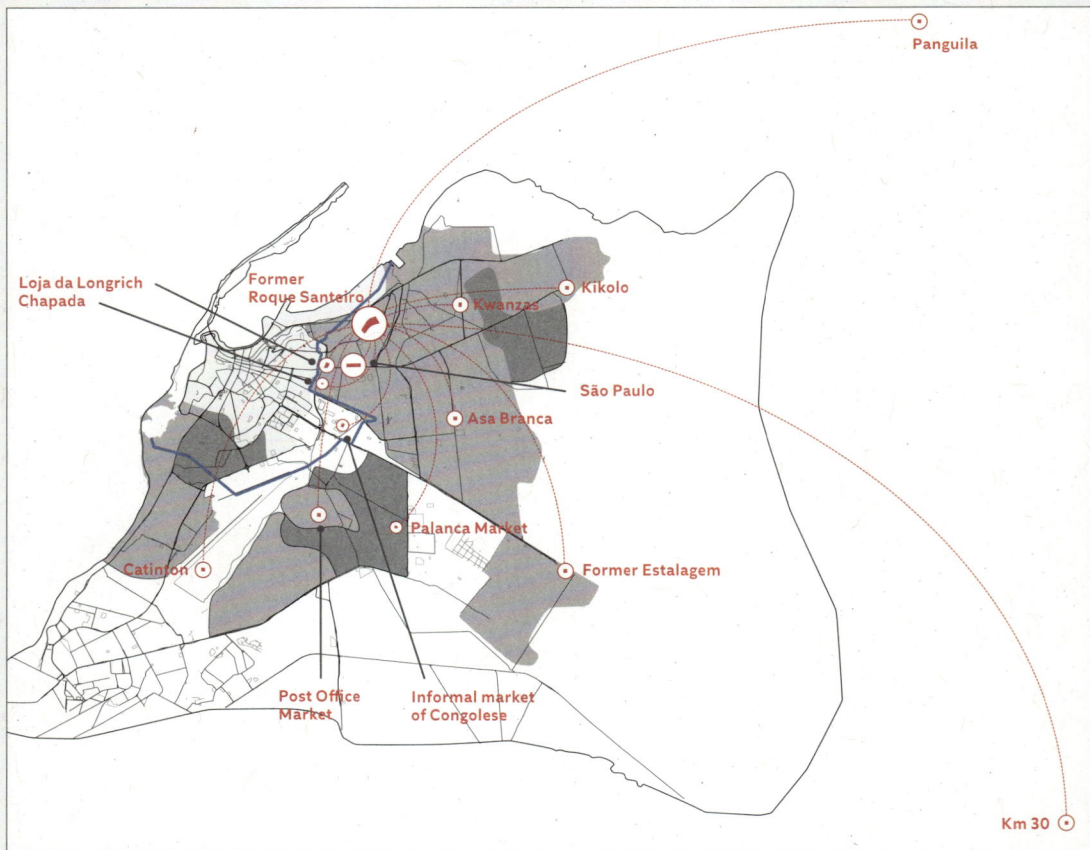

Panguila

Loja da Longrich
Chapada

Former
Roque Santeiro

Kwanzas

Kikolo

São Paulo

Asa Branca

Palanca Market

Former Estalagem

Catinton

Post Office
Market

Informal market
of Congolese

Km 30

□ Historic urban centre   ■ Old *musseques* – under-developed areas   ■ Organised *musseques*

■ Zone of the city of Luanda where informal street trading is prohibited

Supply flows from Roque Santeiro to smaller markets across Luanda

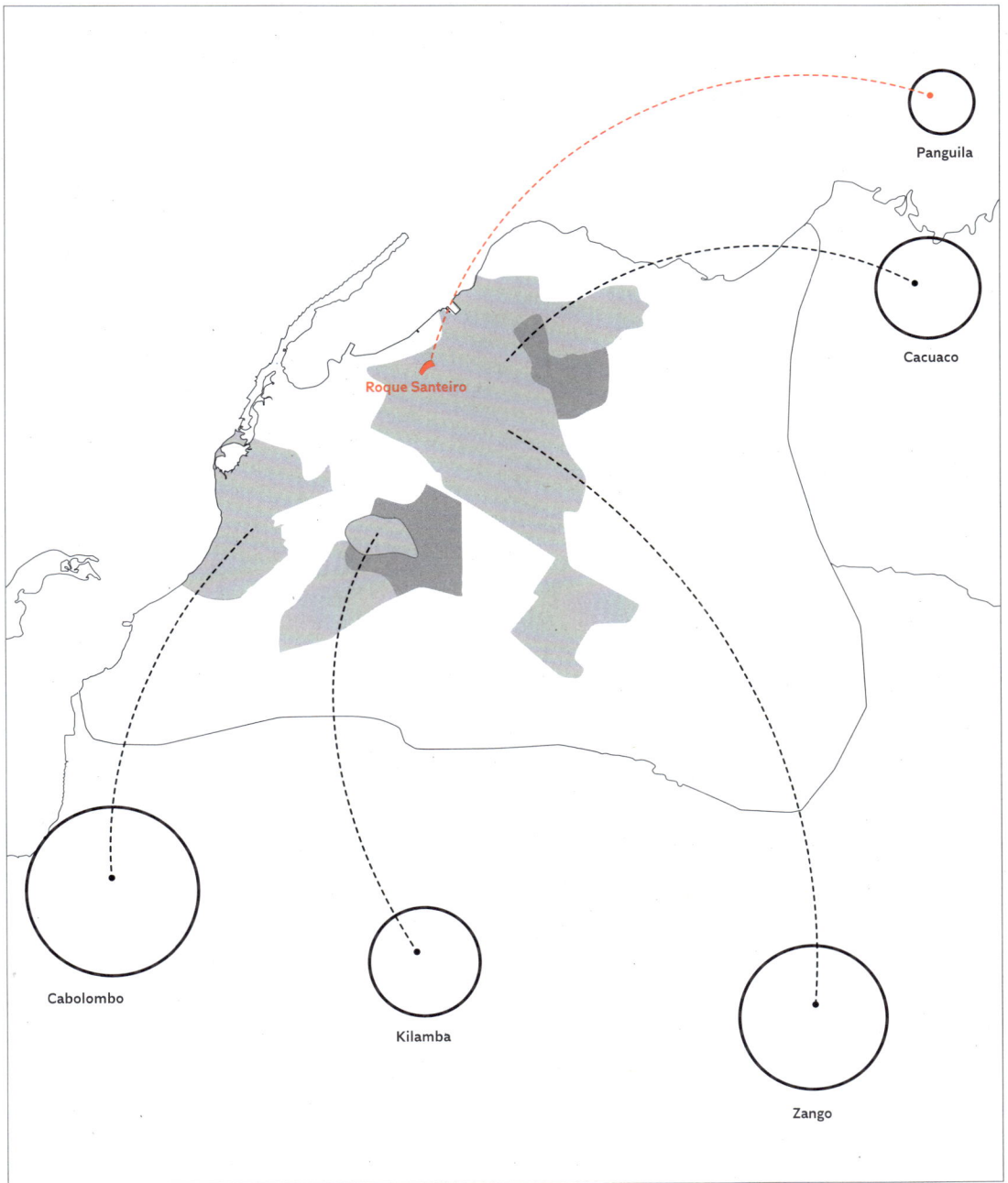

Panguila

Cacuaco

Roque Santeiro

Cabolombo

Kilamba

Zango

■ Historic urban centre   ■ Old *musseques* – under-developed areas   ■ Organised *musseques*
○ Developing peri-urban areas

Relocation of Roque Santeiro's vendors to the peri-urban development Panguila

Typical infrastructural components, Roque Santeiro, Luanda

1576 **1975** **1980** **2000** **2007** **2011** **2013** **2019** **2022**

Roque Santeiro neighbourhood: key phases of spatial development

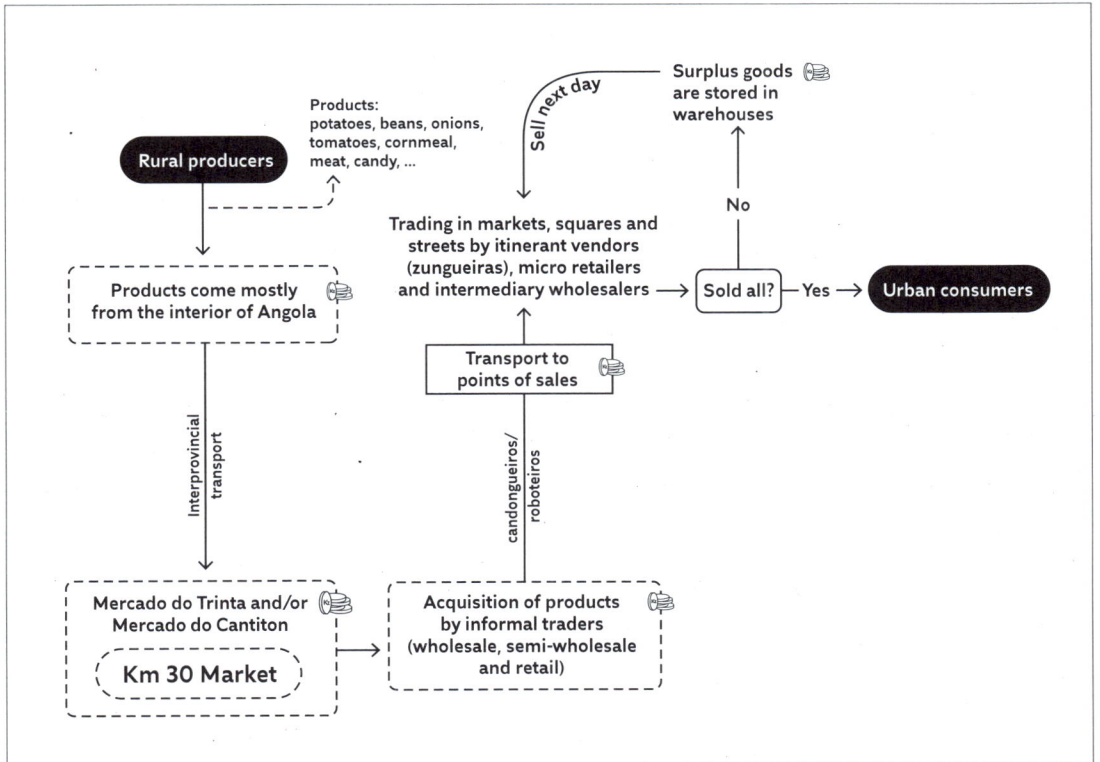

Products:
potatoes, beans, onions,
tomatoes, cornmeal,
meat, candy, ...

Rural producers

Products come mostly
from the interior of Angola

Interprovincial transport

Mercado do Trinta and/or
Mercado do Cantiton

Km 30 Market

Acquisition of products
by informal traders
(wholesale, semi-wholesale
and retail)

candongueiros/
roboteiros

Transport to
points of sales

Sell next day

Trading in markets, squares and
streets by itinerant vendors
(zungueiras), micro retailers
and intermediary wholesalers

Sold all? — Yes → **Urban consumers**

No

Surplus goods
are stored in
warehouses

Operational matrix of Luanda's informal markets

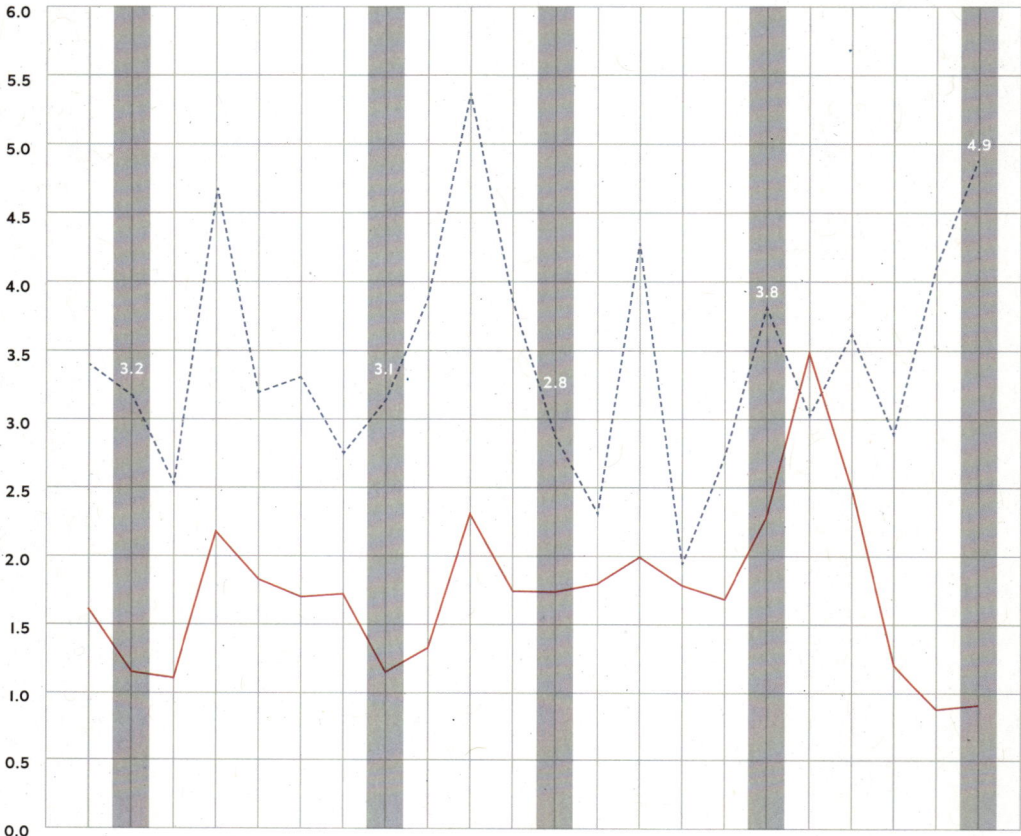

'01	Real-estate study of Roque site	'10	Closure of Roque Santeiro
'02	War ends, rural-urban commerce	'11	Inspectors become more tolerant while parallel markets multiply
'03	Providence plans municipal markets	'12	Election year, programme to reduce informality in the economy (PROAPEN)
'04	Protest over Estalagem Market closure		
'05	Privatisation of Kinaxixi Market, launch of fiscal police	'13	Warehouses and wholesalers removed from the city
'06	Chinese credit for civil construction and new markets	'14	Criminalisation of street vendors and their customers
'07	Law on market regularisation	'15	Rural markets open, Mercado Km 30
'08	Election year, new markets open, reform of economic police, micro credits	'16	Economic crisis and closure of Kinguila currency exchanges
'09	Transfer of wholesale warehouses to Cacao and Viana	'17	Election year, privatisation of markets

'18	Operation 'Resgate' to regain government control over the economy
'19	Protests and political resistance to Resgate grow
'20	COVID-19 restrictions partially close all markets
'21	Programme for the revonversion of the informal economy
'22	Election year, Observatory of the Informal Economy launches

■ Awareness factor   ■ Negativity index

Changing attitudes to informal markets: negativity index versus awareness factor

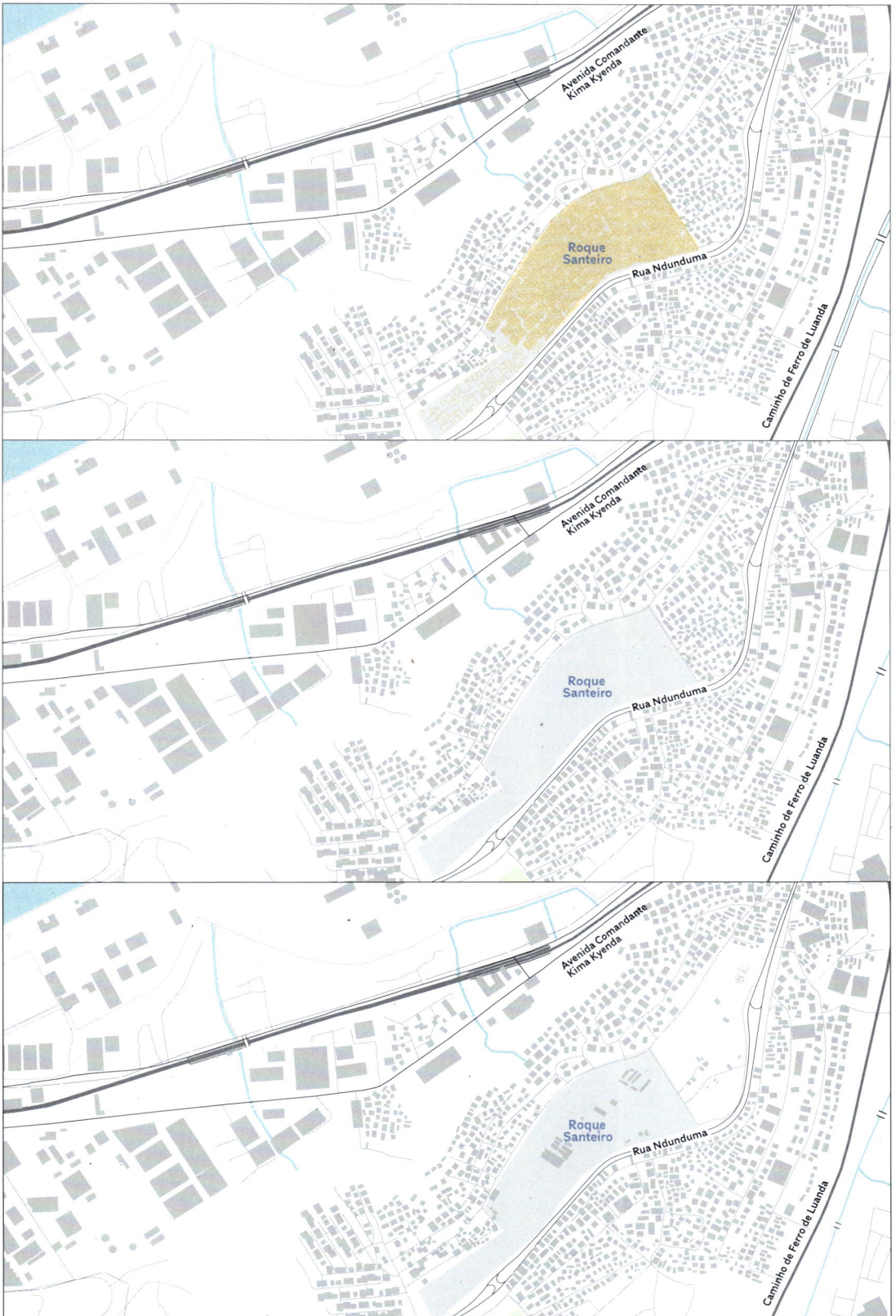

Satellite image of Roque Santeiro market in 2001, 2011 and 2019.

Stevadore making bairro delivery, Luanda, 2005

Gujari Bazaar, Ahmedabad, 2022

Vyjayanthi V. Rao and Simpreet Singh

Ahmedabad's Riverfront Market – Form, De-form, In-form

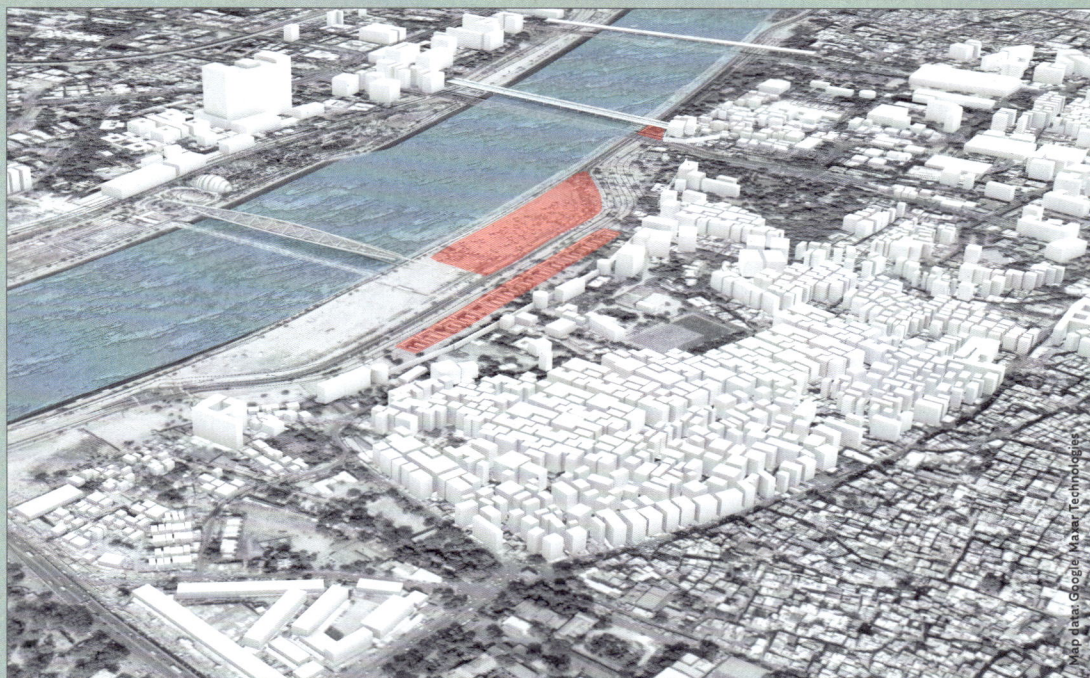

© Map data: Google, Maxar Technologies

Amongst the most iconic images of Ahmedabad are scenes composing life along the Sabarmati River, which winds its way through the heart of the city, much like the Thames River does in London, twisting and bending, dividing the city into two contentious halves. Throughout the city's six-hundred-year existence, the river has provided a backdrop for its economy and entertainment for politics and play. Since its inception in 1414 CE, three years after the foundation of Ahmedabad by decree of Sultan Ahmed Shah, a Sunday market (*Ravivari* in Gujarati), also known popularly as Gujari Bazaar, occupied various sites close to the river, eventually being located along the banks of the river, spilling over onto the dry riverbed beneath one of the city's essential bridges: Ellis Bridge, which connects the eastern and western halves of the city. Initially an artisans' market, after India's independence in 1947, this riverfront market began serving the city's low-income populations with a variety of inexpensive goods, ranging from cookware to furniture, tools, books, clothes, appliances and electronics.

New market site with raised platforms

Throughout its history, Gujari Bazaar vendors were scattered across different parts of the Sabarmati River. In 1947 the market was shifted to the riverbank near Ellis Bridge.

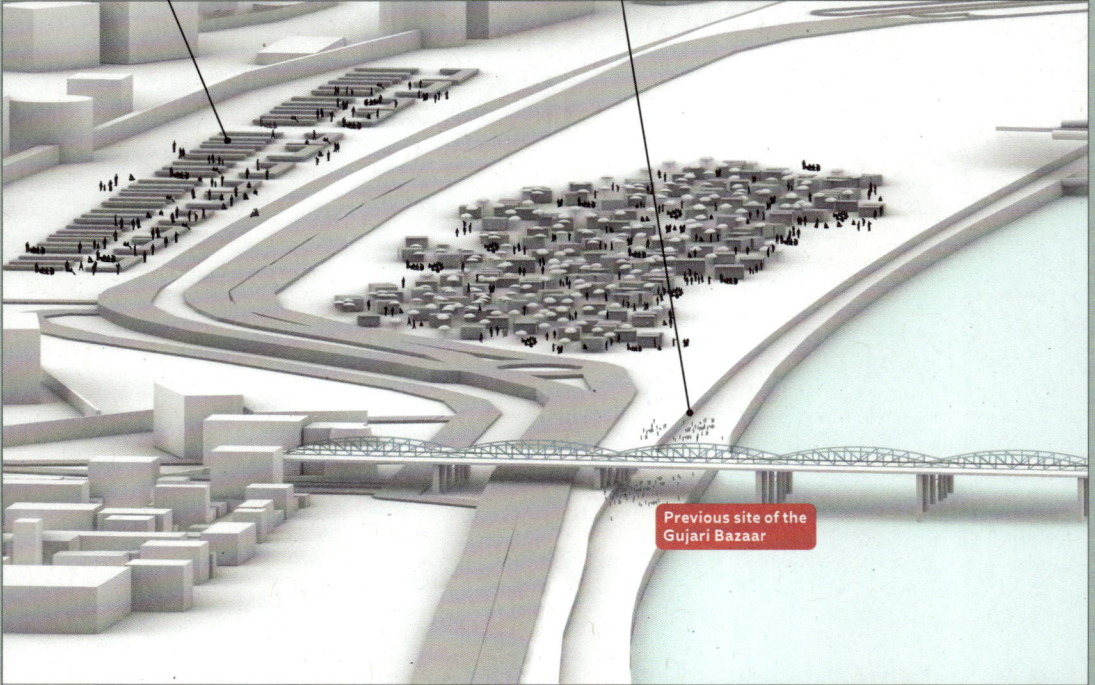

Previous site of the Gujari Bazaar

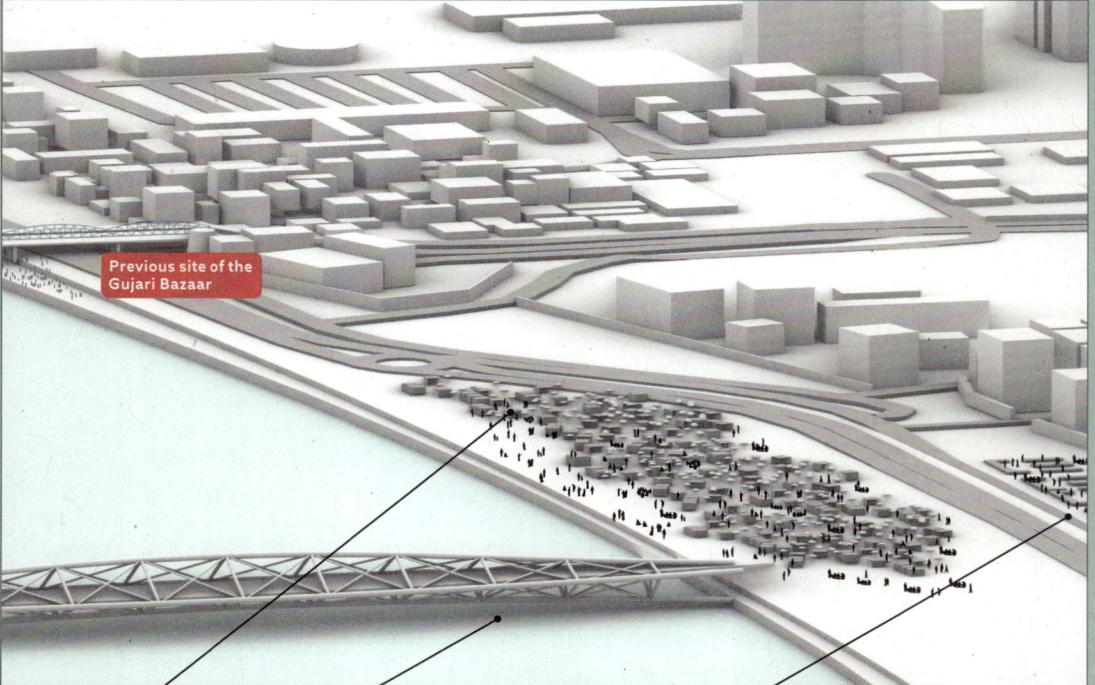

Previous site of the Gujari Bazaar

Intermittent site of Gujari Bazaar

Previously a monsoon-fed river with a dry riverbed for most of the year, the dammed waterway is now permanently filled with water at a constant level.

This new site is spread over 70,000 square metres and provides space for 1600 vendors on 778 raised platforms and 783 pitches. Parking is available for 280 two-wheelers, 425 four-wheelers and eight heavy vehicles. More than eight hundred trees have been planted to offer shade. Lights, toilets, food courts, drinking water and seated areas are also provided.

The market was renowned for its capacity to furnish an entire lower-income family's home in just one visit.

Vendors and their customers occupied the river's banks and beds along with many other actors and activities vital to the city's everyday life. Amongst these activities, farming, carpentry, the dyeing and block printing of cloth, laundry, carpentry, manufacturing and small-scale trading turned the riverbed into a de facto commons and infrastructure upon which the city functioned. By 1947, when the market site was shifted to the riverbank near Ellis Bridge from its previous location near the old city's walls, the self-organised Gujari Bazaar grew to accommodate over 1000 vendors, supplying goods to an estimated 75 percent of the city's population. Although it only took place once a week, the bazaar's geographic network was vast, with a supply chain extending north and south of Ahmedabad. Residents of the city of Mumbai of a certain age may recall the itinerant vendors who exchanged new utensils of stainless steel for old clothes, which frequently ended up in Ahmedabad's Gujari Bazaar and whose name evocatively suggests a market for goods departed (in many Indic languages, *gujari* invokes times and things that have parted, passed through or been left behind) from their previous owners. The physical site itself is, therefore, a threshold or node where this network is performed on a regular basis.

As a symbolic site, Gujari Bazaar's significance is immense in relation to Ahmedabad. Over the course of its six-hundred-year history, the bazaar developed into a self-governed space for the weekly exchange of essential goods, serving different social classes and groups over decades and centuries. At present, it primarily serves low-income communities. Still, its clientele continues to evolve in the era of virtual commerce with the greater visibility of the market on social media platforms. More than the other activities along the riverbank, the market is a visible indicator of changes in the city's culture and communities. Much like other markets explored in this volume, Gujari Bazaar brings together social drama in physical space with economic exchange and the goods themselves serving performatively as communicative media. The market's weekly experience represents the city to its residents and serves as a portal through which the world encounters the city.

Although Ahmedabad has been an important economic and political centre throughout its history, its significance and prestige as an industrial and modern metropolis was especially visible during the colonial period and after independence. With the establishment of Gandhi's ashram on the banks of the Sabarmati River, Ahmedabad was firmly positioned at the vanguard of the anti-colonial nationalist movement. Following independence, the city's business and cultural elites invited renowned international architects, including Le Corbusier and Louis Kahn, to help shape the city's identity as a centre of modernism within South Asia. However, with the decline in the city's industrial base during the 1970s and the 1980s, the city experienced a reduction of formal employment avenues, resulting in casualisation of labour and an increase in street vending, as well as augmented tensions between the major religious communities that had shared the city from its inception in the fifteenth century. These growing factors, exacerbated by the uncertainties of economic liberalisation, led to concerted efforts from civic and business leaders to search for means of urban renewal and to position the city on the list of notable cities within the nation, to finance its rebirth. The transformation of the Sabarmati riverfront was a critical project in this quest for renewal, and specifically, as we shall see, the relocation of the Gujari Bazaar turned out to be a key site for understanding the transformations within Ahmedabad's urban culture and its ethos of conviviality. We situate the market in the city and the city in the market through our spatial and ethnographic observations of the interactions on-site and through our visualisations of the market's shifting dynamics over time to draw out the significance of the bazaar as a site of urban politics and culture.

CITY IN THE MARKET

In the late 1990s and early 2000s, the nine-kilometre stretch of the Sabarmati River that runs through Ahmedabad city was dammed and flooded to create a perennial water body for the first time in the city's history. Before this re-engineering, the Sabarmati was a monsoon-fed river, and its bank and dry bed could accommodate a larger or smaller number of activities and actors, depending on the season. This significant modification of the urban landscape by design was symbolic of other changes within the urban fabric, brought on by new forms of capital and investment that began circulating through India's globalising economy. In common with many Indian cities, industrial urbanisation with formal employment was never the dominant mode of urbanisation. Indian cities, whether colonial or pre-colonial, were places with many competing cultures of 'city-ness.' Yet the standards by which these cities were judged and deemed inadequate – not yet modern or not quite modern – were deeply informed by the dominant post-Second World War standards of urbanism.

The emergence of discourses concerning world-class cities in the early 2000s added another layer to urbanisation processes by enabling the further demonisation of the pluralistic practices of the urban majority. As many scholars have argued, 'world-class' city discourses circulate idealised images of contemporary cities such as Dubai or Shanghai. Urban development then becomes beholden to practices of mimicry and mirroring, trying to approximate these images. In practice, however, attempts to reconstruct the Indian city in the image of the successful, post-globalisation Asian city remained confined to brochures and billboards. At the same time, construction on the ground was dedicated to maximising profits, resulting in haphazard and hasty developments of luxury housing and commercial spaces, which remained unaffordable for most urban residents. The casualties of these processes were popular urban neighbourhoods and markets like Gujari Bazaar, which had to be displaced to make way for the realisation of new urban visions.[1] How might these transformations, enabled by discourses of efficiency and improvement, appear when we look at them from the bottom-up?

During the period after the liberalisation of India's economy in 1990, the closure of the city's sixty-four textile mills had already led to layoffs for the majority of Ahmedabad's formally employed workforce. According to Navdeep Mathur, a Professor at Ahmedabad's renowned Indian Institute of Management (IIM), an estimated 75–80 percent of the city's working population, many of them women, depended on open markets and street vending as significant sources of their livelihood and sustenance by the early years of the twenty-first century.[2] The economic circuit of the market focuses not only on the production of commodities but on the cultivation of supply chains, consumption practices, and the social lives of *things*. Analysis of markets as social, cultural, economic and political spaces thus connects Marx's analysis of commodity fetishism and the circulation of interest-bearing capital in addition to his writings on the labour theory of value, and the production of surplus value in the process of manufacture.[3]

The commodities sold in markets like the Gujari Bazaar are simultaneously bearers of surplus value from the process of their manufacture and bearers of superfluous value or a form of value that constantly empties and reformulates 'any exchange or use value that labour might have.'[4] Furthermore, Achille Mbembe, the African political philosopher argues in his paper on Johannesburg, 'The Western imagination defines the metropolis as the general form assumed by the rationalisation of relations of production (the increasing prevalence of the commodity system) and the rationalisation of the social sphere (human relations) that follows it. A defining moment of metropolitan modernity is realised when the two spheres rely upon purely functional relations among people and things, and subjectivity takes the form of calculation and abstraction.' His reading of the metropolitan ideal suggests that we could posit the bazaar as not merely a site of the exchange of things but also of *ideas* and the introduction of new forms of socialisation.

1   There is a substantial academic literature on the ideologies of the 'world-class' city (see Asher Ghertner, Aihwa Ong and Ananya Roy) and on speculative urbanism (Michael Goldman) which exposes the nexus between construction and the circulation of capital, building on the insights of Marxist philosophers like Henri Lefebvre and David Harvey.
2   Navdeep Mathur, 'On the Sabarmati Riverfront: Urban Planning as Totalitarian Governance in Ahmedabad,' *Economic and Political Weekly* 47, no. 47/48 (2012): 65.
3   See: Arjun Appadurai, 'Introduction,' *The Social Life of Things: Commodities in Cultural Perspective* (Cambridge: Cambridge University Press, 1989).
4   As Achille Mbembe explains: 'Superfluity does not refer only to the aesthetics of surfaces and quantities, and to how such an aesthetics is premised on the capacity of things to hypnotize, overexcite, or paralyze the senses. To my mind, superfluity refers also to the dialectics of indispensability and expendability of both labor and life, people and things. It refers to the obfuscation of any exchange or use value that labor might have, and to the emptying of any meaning that might be attached to the act of measurement or quantification itself, insofar as numerical representation is as much a fact as it is a form of fantasy.' See: Achille Mbembe, 'Aesthetics of Superfluity,' *Public Culture* 16, no. 3 (2004): 373–405.

Gujari Bazaar, Ahmedabad, 2010

Following the social life of the market and the kinds of relations that are established between things and people in the market provides valuable clues to cultural differences within this framework of metropolitan modernity, as sites where the global circulation of mass-produced and artisanal commodities meets local norms of socialisation. As such, markets are also important sites to study ruptures and continuities within the urban transformation.

To return specifically to Ahmedabad once again, we observe that even as the urban economy transitioned from the manufacture of tangible goods to an intangible, service and finance-based one, its effects were nevertheless felt physically upon the urban landscape through the tremendous rise in construction of commercial and residential real estate and in the expansion of the 'urban popular economy' of street vending, which supported and was supported by the same group of disenfranchised workers. This concept of the urban popular economy, elaborated on recently by a

collective of scholars, connects these manifestations of economic activity in space to the expansion of a politically disenfranchised and economically marginalised urban majority.[5] Evicted from gentrifying popular neighbourhoods, the urban majority finds space and sustenance precariously on the streets of the physically changing city, thus registering their presence and visibility as promise and threat. Moreover, in the deeply hierarchical social context of India, where class, caste and religious affiliation often converge to marginalise specific groups, Gujari Bazaar's vendors and customers are mainly from Muslim and Dalit communities. An estimated 40 percent of the vendors are also women.[6]

MARKET SPACE

By the early 2010s, as the Sabarmati Riverfront Development Project took concrete shape, the vendors and their customers were forced to contend with the reality of their imminent eviction from the site the market had occupied continuously since 1954. This move

5   See: The Urban Popular Economy Collective et al., 'Urban Popular Economies: Territories of Operation for Lives Deemed Worth Living,' *Public Culture* 34, no. 3 (2022).
6   For key empirical research that informed this chapter, see Vineet Diwadkar's 2012–2014 study 'Ahmedabad Gujari Bazaar: An Alternative Rehabilitation Plan': *https://www.diwadkar.net/gujaribazaar*

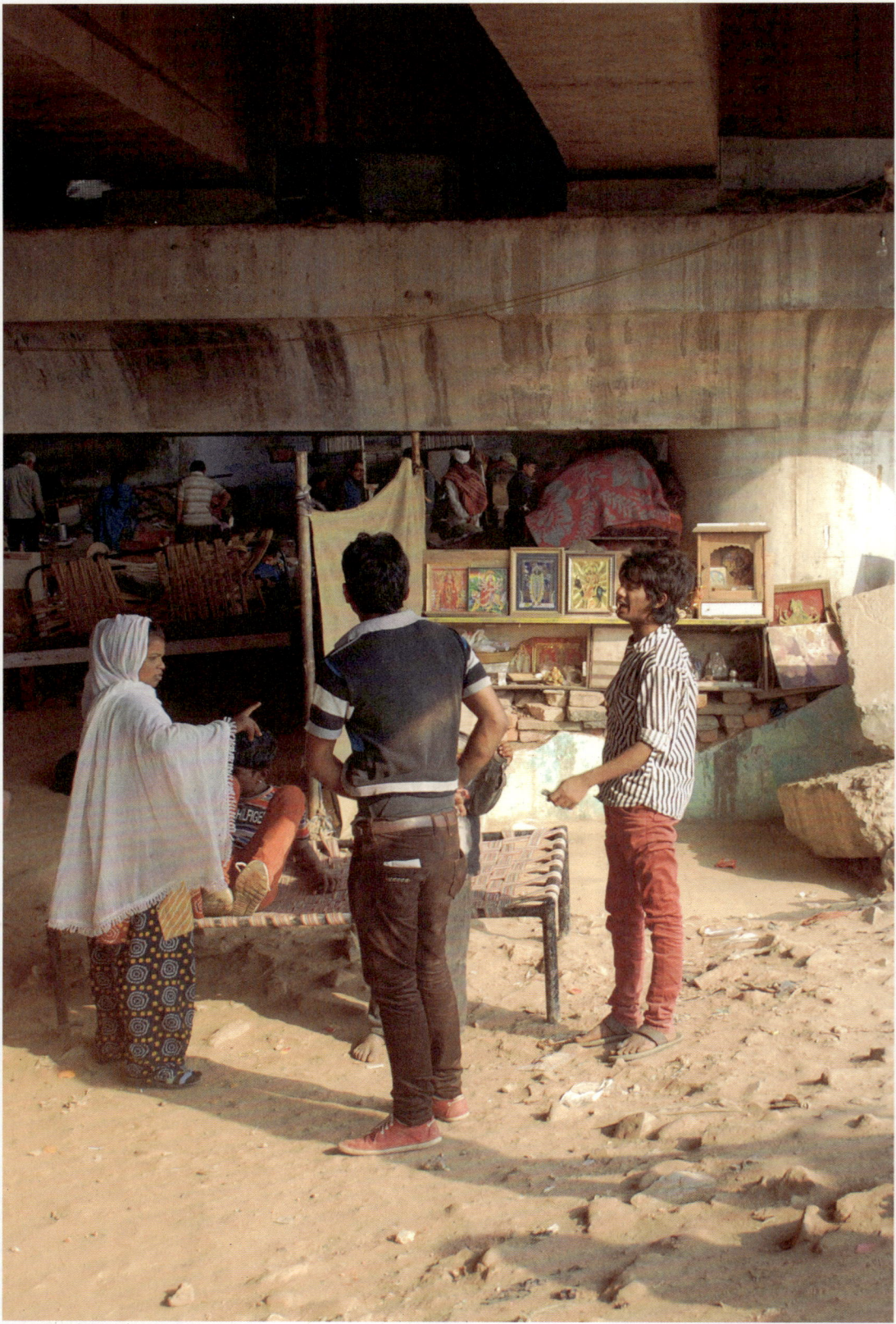

Gujari Bazaar, Ahmedabad, 2013

was not only a displacement of activities but also a de-formation of certain practices and relationships that had formed and sedimented over time. Before the traders were moved to a new site further south and behind the walled riverside promenade, the spread of the market would depend on the number of vendors who came on any given Sunday. Since there were no clear geographical or physical markers, it was possible to accommodate larger numbers of customers and vendors who came together to buy, sell and exchange goods and animals.[7] The vendors would usually set up at the same location with minor variations that were micro-managed amongst themselves. If a particular vendor was absent from the market, their usual neighbour might extend their stall and spread their products, enabling them more visibility. Upon the return of their neighbour, they would withdraw to their designated space. This tacit understanding of norms enabled the smooth operation and governance of what appeared from the outside as a vast and haphazard spread of people and things in a dusty and chaotic arrangement.

Although there appeared to be no clear demarcations or pathways for customers, market space was nevertheless organised in rows grouped by the types of goods sold, the craft that was being practised or the services offered. Spatial arrangements were flexible and negotiated, and despite the fact that many vendors offered similar items for sale, there were enough customers to keep businesses going, sometimes over multiple generations of the same family. The public square, or *chowk*, was the one empty space within the market which served as a visible landmark and acted as a node for the circulation of shoppers in and out of the various sections of the market. Vendors would generally sit on the dusty ground and place goods either directly in front of them or on rope cots and wooden platforms for greater visibility. Much of the trade was in second-hand goods like pots and pans, clothes, scrap iron, tools, antique furniture and decorative items. Unlike European flea markets, which would attract customers in search of items with provenance and vintage value, few of the second-hand

and refurbished goods sold at the Gujari Bazaar were sought for their provenance. Rather, they were valued for their cost and for the skill invested in their repair since many of the customers were not in search of authentic antiques or vintage goods representing pure surplus value.

A series of conducted interviews revealed how vendors at the market have gradually moved away from the second-hand goods trade to new items, which are purchased in wholesale markets in Ahmedabad and Mumbai. These goods have become more affordable as manufacturing processes improve efficiency, and supply chains have expanded with inexpensive goods from China flooding Indian markets in recent years. Rekha Behn, one of the women vendors, described how her family used to make and sell coal-fired stoves, but with the increasing use of electric stoves and LPG gas, this business lost customers. They therefore transitioned to selling new utensils made of steel and aluminium, which they continue to buy directly from local manufacturers. The family accepts cash only and they have a feel for when the economy is buoyant. As Rekha put it, 'these days there is not much money in the market and that is why our business is low. From the sales at our stall, I can tell that these days the market is down. Also, these days people prefer buying from online platforms – even utensils; there they get good discounts, which we are not able to provide.'[8] In one sense, market activity is a symptom through which one could monitor changes in the urban atmosphere.

Nafis Bhai, a third-generation vendor at the bazaar, spoke about the changes that he had personally seen since he was a child, hanging around his grandfather's stall. His grandfather started his stall around the time of India's independence (1947) and had initially sold second-hand or used brass utensils. But as aluminium and steel became popular, procuring brass vessels which had been used for cooking and storage became difficult. His father shifted the business to selling hardware tools which he sourced from the wholesale market in Ahmedabad. When Nafis in turn took over from his father, he shifted over

7   Although the Ahmed Shah Gujari Association has an official membership of 1400 trader members, they were joined by approximately 1000 ad hoc traders on a regular basis.
8   Rekha Behn in conversation with the authors, 18 December 2022.

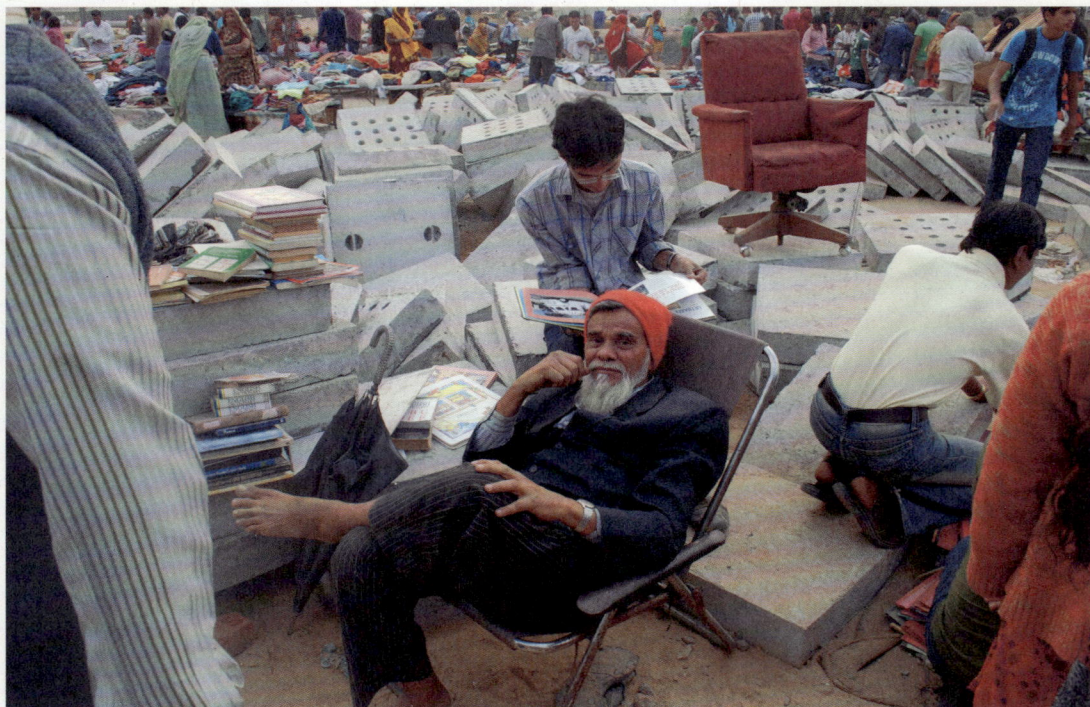

Gujari Bazaar, Ahmedabad, 2013

to selling imitation jewellery and added a juice stand.

Nafis observed: 'Over the years, there has been a great change in the way the market functions, its layout, the products that are sold and even the customers who visit the market ... earlier it used to be dusty, vendors would sit on the ground with dust all around. Things sold were mostly old and used, like utensils, clothes, iron products and scrap. Women from the Vagri samaj (a tribal community) used to go door to door to exchange old clothes for utensils and women from the Marwari samaj (a caste group from Rajasthan) used to collect brass items.'[9]

As alluded to before, the women traders mentioned by Nafis played an important part of Gujari Bazaar's imaginary, because they were the suppliers of goods parted from their previous owners. Another story relayed by Ashok Kahar illustrates this point poignantly.[10] Ashok began his life in the market when he was eight years old when he would go with his father to sell clothes. Soon after, he took

a loan of a single rupee from his father and started his own business selling *papads* (dried wafers). Later he began selling clothes collected by the women traders, which he would wash, repair and iron to make them appear new. In the course of his long career at the market, he would also travel to Mumbai's red-light district Kamathipura to buy things that sex workers pawned to moneylenders, which many of them could not afford to redeem. If one takes these itinerant suppliers and their tales of acquisition into account, one could argue that the market's footprint extended well beyond its Sunday manifestation on the riverbank. What we think of as market space should also be physically expansive.

Another way in which market space extends beyond the physical site of the market was underlined in an interview with Bura Bhai, one of Gujari Bazaar's most famous vendors.[11] Like Nafis Bhai, Bura Bhai also comes from a family that has a multigenerational presence in the market. His grandfather was selling at the market even before independence. For Bura Bhai, the market was distinct because

9   Nafis Ahmad Mohammad Ishaq in conversation with the authors, 16 December 2022.
10   Ashok Kahar in conversation with the authors, 16 December 2022.
11   Bura Bhai in conversation with the authors, 18 December 2022.

the vendors must sell in one day what others can sell in seven days, requiring unique skills so that they can sell at a much greater speed. His grandfather was skilled at repairing bicycles and especially the torchlights that were fitted on bicycles during the colonial period. People would come to him from far-off places and his father then also supplemented the bicycle repair business by sourcing parts for bicycles and other used items like umbrellas, lighters, torches and so on. Bura Bhai used to accompany him to the market and developed an interest in antique things and began to source them from different parts of western India, from Rajasthan to Punjab and Delhi. He would visit old homes in villages asking around for belongings that families were looking to sell and would market them as antiques in Gujari Bazaar.

Through the years, he has seen an increasing interest in antiques, especially from younger clients who desire owning things that have the aura of being passed on from an older generation, even if they did not come from their own families. These pieces of furniture and older technologies like telephone handsets and gramophone record players command higher prices, allowing people to signify heritage through décor. Bura Bhai's observations cast a specific cultural lens on the taste for antiques in a social world that is not always comfortable with acquiring objects from people who are socially distant or not known to them. In other words, although the antique trade is historical, there was a continued unease with the uncertain provenance of these objects, which is slowly changing, allowing the market's activities to expand to include objects not only from distant geographic locations but also other time periods.

More recently, the extension of the market's footprint has taken place through its connection with the internet. Jeetu Bhai, another third-generation vendor, explains that his grandfather started selling porcelain teacups and saucers and would only sell that single item. His father continued the business, and they would buy their goods from a factory in Narodia, a suburb of Ahmedabad. Jeetu started accompanying his father as a child to the bazaar. He picked up the skills of vending

from his father, learning how to interact with customers and distinguish those who were going to buy from those who were just passing the time. He learned to gauge the changing preferences of his customers, and realised they were no longer interested only in white cups and saucers. He now uses social media regularly to understand the trends and interests of customers and tailors his offerings according to these trends, sourcing his glassware and bone china products from Chinese imports because they are cheaper compared to locally manufactured products.[12] Jeetu's interview reminds us of the increasing influence of social media and of global supply chains in the changing offerings of the market and the increasing intersection of market space across global and virtual space.

Nafis Bhai also observed that as the market space changed dramatically as it became incorporated into the Sabarmati Riverfront Development Corporation's plan, the profile of customers changed. He explains: 'Earlier, it used to be mostly poorer customers and those who wanted to buy something very specific that they knew would be available in Gujari Bazaar. Now, after the riverfront development, the "gentry" also visits the market. Many people have made YouTube videos, and reels on Instagram. Customers take photographs and post them on social media, because of which the market has become more famous across the world. Even international tourists who have read about the market online come and visit and tell us about this phenomenon.'

With each of the interviews presented here, we begin to see the temporal and spatial expansion of the market and the transformation of the circuits and sentiments of practices of exchange. From multigenerational vendors to the changing profiles and preferences of customers, Gujari Bazaar is a fascinating case for studying the market as an experience and performance of social life across time and space. The spread of the market as an extensive network existed and exists in dialogue with practices of regularisation and routinisation, which imagine the market in terms of physical sites marked by regular temporal rhythms. This tension is particularly exacerbated after

12   Jeetu Bhai in conversation with the authors, Gujari Bazaar, 18 December 2022.

globalisation, which has brought the world to the city and the city to the world in new ways. The regulation and governance of the spatial and social experience of the market are particularly affected by the acceleration of changes in political economy, and in urban life.

GOVERNANCE IN PRACTICE

The boundaries between the formal and the informal are concretised through the ordering of space, becoming notoriously difficult to pin down. Certain features of the Gujari Bazaar lend the market a complexity that is difficult for outsiders and casual observers to interpret. For example, a very important feature of the market is the lack of fixed prices, which in turn creates a culture in which bargaining and negotiations between buyer and seller are extremely performative. Both sides must participate in the rituals leading to an agreement on the price of the goods being bought and sold. These practices persisted even as the market transformed over time from a place where artisans and craftspeople, like the stove makers from Rekha Behn's family, sold goods that they had directly manufactured and were thus entitled to assign personal value to a place where vendors were mainly sellers rather than makers who sold.

Another important aspect of the market is its independent and self-governing structure which operates at different scales. From the example cited earlier of vendors who expand and contract their spatial spread depending on what is happening in their vicinity to the organisation and grouping of vendors, most matters were settled interpersonally. All these activities occurred under the umbrella of the Ahmad Shah Gujari Association (AGA), the market's governing body. While Sultan Ahmad Shah, the city's founder, originally organised the market to operate in accordance with the weekly call to prayer at the Jama Masjid, the traders' decision in 1944 to regulate through the AGA prioritised economic over community affiliations. The association registered the vendors, collected a membership fee, issued membership cards, and regulated the market space by hiring security and arranging for water and other infrastructure.

The AGA also signed the lease with the District Collectorate and later the Ahmedabad Municipal Corporation (AMC) for the riverside land, which the market occupied until approximately 2010, and paid land use taxes to those city governance bodies. There were no market-wide democratic elections for the officers of the AGA, nor for the AGA president. Instead, a council of representatives from each trade selects the AGA president for a five-year term. Many of the vendors seem to agree that there was a tacit agreement to alternately appoint Muslim and Hindu representatives to the association's presidency, maintaining a balance of power between the communities. The AGA traders' co-dependence and culture of governance, in turn, have provided a measure of stability throughout the city's history of violent clashes between religious communities. The market's operation and its governance thus provide an insight into the crucial issues at stake for the city. At a more mundane level, Imran Bhai, one of the vendors interviewed, reiterated that markets like Gujari Bazaar only functioned on the principle of trust because even when vendors did not have a fixed place or a shop number, people came to the market due to the implicit belief they had in the vendors which enhanced confidence in the market as a whole.[13]

This modern history of trader solidarity, cooperative dependence on customers and weekly access to the Sabarmati riverbed highlight the efficacy of this socio-spatial structure and its ability to signal crucial aspects of the city's culture. These cultural aspects include relations of solidarity based on mutual trust through material exchange and the availability of urban commons to be shared between the city and the market. The transformation of the Sabarmati riverfront, through the activities of the Sabarmati Riverfront Development Corporation (SRFDC) has gradually fractured these solidarities as this common resource became privatised and material relations of solidarity were consequently transformed.

13   Imran Bhai in conversation with the authors, Gujari Bazaar, 18 December 2022.

Gujari Bazaar, Ahmedabad, 2013

SRFDC AND THE FORMALISATION OF GUJARI BAZAAR

The physical relocation of the bazaar began to take shape with the formation of the AGA in 1944 since the association was an identifiable bargaining partner for various city agencies. As mentioned, the AGA signed leases with the District Collectorate for the land near the Ellis Bridge when the market first shifted to the riverfront. In 1976, a voluntary group of planners, architects and decision-makers formed the River Front Development Group (RFDG) and produced the first technical survey following a 1961 proposal for the riverfront development by French architect and planner, Bernard Kohn. Soon after the survey, in 1978, the Ahmedabad Municipal Corporation (AMC) issued an eviction notice to the Gujari Bazaar vendors after the land was transferred to the city from the district. The AGA successfully challenged the order, and in 2004 the association signed a lease with the AMC paying a nominal monthly rent to the corporation.

However, in 2006 the Sabarmati River Front Development Corporation (SRFDC), which had been formed in 1997 by the government, began construction on the project.

The work was contracted to the Environmental Planning Collaborative (EPC), a local firm headed by architect Bimal Patel. EPC developed earlier proposals and added a four to six-lane road parallel to the river. This meant that all the activities located on the river and its bed would have to be moved behind this road, causing general insecurity amongst the occupants of the riverfront. By the early twenty-first century, the closure of the textile mills and other economic changes has increased the precarity in the city. In addition to the Gujari Bazaar and other places, the riverfront also saw the growth of a slum population. In 2011, the evictions of slum-dwellers and the demolition of slums led the vendors to file a public interest litigation (PIL) against the SRFDC, with support from Navdeep Mathur from the Indian Institute of Management (IIM) as co-petitioner. As a result of the PIL, an MoU (memorandum of understanding) was signed between the AGA and the SRFDC and a new market site was included in the development proposal.

This new site is spread over 70,000 square metres within the riverfront development plan and provides space for 1600 vendors on 778 raised platforms and 783 pitches.

223

Parking is available for 280 two-wheelers, 425 four-wheelers and eight heavy vehicles. Lights, toilets, food courts, drinking water and seated areas are also provided, and more than eight hundred trees have been planted around the raised platforms to give shade to the vendors and their customers. These raised platforms, with their orderly arrangements and the enclosure of the new market area, are the physical devices of formalisation. Symbolically, the enclosure signifies the complete transformation of the riverfront from an infrastructural commons to a privatised zone. Although theoretically open to all citizens, these forms of enclosure and walling communicate a sense of exclusion to certain groups. The formalisation of the governance structure is the intangible transformation that has, in turn, produced some unintended consequences.

Following the move to the new site, the AGA has developed greater regulating and policing functions to ensure that the new market is not overrun and disorderly in appearance and in substance. The AGA has a list of nineteen rules that govern the business. These include prohibition of the auction and bidding on the products inside the market, selling or trading of animals/birds that are prohibited under Indian law, subletting of vending space, and the sale of anything that is in contravention of the rules and laws of the land. The AGA has a total of thirty-five staff members, including security guards and the committee. They regulate an area of 35,000 square metres, including public amenities like toilet blocks and parking areas. Issuing of identity cards was started in the 1970s and has continued until now.

Early every Sunday morning, starting from 5 am, vendors begin setting up their stalls. Around 7 pm, they start winding up and closing their stalls. Committee members take on the responsibility of arriving before the vendors in the morning to see to it that everyone takes their own designated space and to ensure that no non-member vendor sets up inside the bazaar. Committee members leave the market at night only after the market is empty. They come back the following morning to ensure that there was no one left. During the course of the market day (Sunday), they collect the weekly fees from members.

Members are issued an identity card by the association that becomes the verifying document in the event of any dispute. Annual elections are supposed to be held, but most of the same committee members have been 'elected' year after year.

These new governance structures appear to have created a distance between the vendors and the administration, one that did not seem to exist in the former market, in which the representatives of the AGA were also themselves vendors. Although some of the AGA representatives, like Nafis Ahmed, who is the current president of the AGA, are from multi-generational vendor families, the deployment of a paid labour force to police the market has contributed to the transformation of the market's self-governing culture and spirit. Since the completion of the new enclosed market and its inauguration, many observers suggest that power within the traders' association has been consolidated and that the organisation of the market is also being shaped by the presence of several wholesale traders operating from within the new market site.

Subramaniam Iyer, who is the lawyer representing vendors excluded from the formal Gujari market now arguing for the formalisation of their street vending rights under the National Street Vendors Act (2014), noted when the case [AGA vs. SRFDC] was filed, 'maybe there was an oversight, or someone overlooked the fact that it was put on record that only 1200 vendors were registered with the AGA while there were many more vendors who were putting up their stalls in and around the area.' Thus, he said, 'those who could not be accommodated in the formalised market began sitting on the Swami Vivekanand Road, starting from Victoria Garden to the Khamasa Gate.' These vendors ended up starting a separate trust, called the Victoria Garden Gujari Seva Trust, which has around 600 members who were not included in the formalised Gujari market. Under the protection of this trust, these vendors carry out their businesses every Sunday outside the areas of the formalised Gujari Bazaar. Because they were not included in the MoU signed between the AGA and the AMC, they have been subject to harassment by the municipal and police authorities and, at times, prevented from vending.

Gujari Bazaar, Ahmedabad, 2013

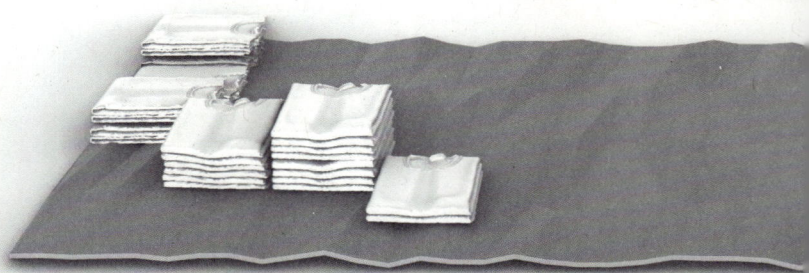

Typical infrastructural components, Gujari Bazaar, Ahmedabad

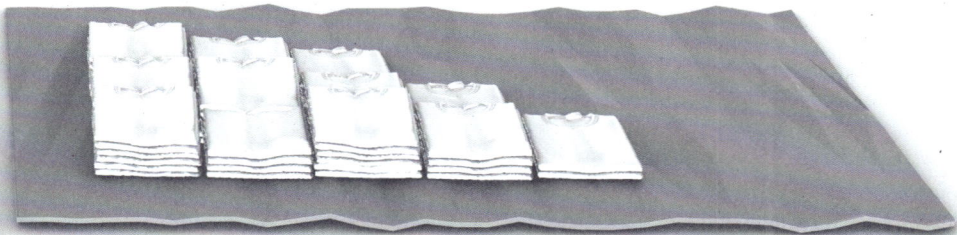

Gujari Bazaar, Ahmedabad, 2022

The SRFDC has taken the position that since they are not part of their project, they are under no obligation to them, and the AMC has taken the position that they never evicted them from the Sabarmati riverbed, so they are not their responsibility. Iyer's opinion is that the recent push from the state authorities to evict them has come as they are now considered a cause of traffic jams. A few years ago, there was no objection from anyone towards them doing business on the Swami Vivekananda Road. Still, as the traffic has increased, the vendors are seen as the cause of congestion around the area. The solution to the traffic jams that are offered involves removing these particular street vendors, those who were cut out of the original MoU. Also, the Swami Vivekananda Road now has a BRTS lane, and this has reduced the width of the road that is available for vehicular traffic.

Eventually, these disenfranchised vendors had to file a public interest litigation at the Ahmedabad High Court, requesting the court to order municipal authorities to allow them to carry on vending. In 2014, the court granted them an interim order, directing the authorities and the police to allow the vendors to continue their business outside the formalised market. However, the vendors complain tacitly that they are being asked to pay dues to the AGA even though they are not part of the formalised market.

MARKET AS THRESHOLD

Markets are frontier zones where the metropolitan logic of abstraction and calculation are constantly being subverted and reconfigured, thus allowing for the formation of distinct languages of urbanisation with their site-specific practices and other forms of cultural improvisation to take root. In this sense, they are threshold conditions, where the line between inside and outside is constantly being negotiated. The physical space of the market is a like a lamp placed on a threshold, which is capable of simultaneously illuminating both sides of the threshold. These broader processes impact and bring change at the urban scale and the micro-behaviours in which these changes are registered and sedimented. Thus, markets are both physical manifestations of exchange and experiences and activities that signal the thresholds between abstract formalisation and everyday practice. In the context of spaces like Gujari Bazaar and its enclosure within the SRFDC plan, everyday practices that depend on common resources, as the previous iteration of the bazaar did, are interpreted as transgressive of the totalising authority of Ahmedabad's administrators. But the question remains whether it is useful to continue to use the informal label to identify transgressive practices.

The concept of informality itself is deeply relational, as we already know from numerous attempts to define informal environments. A vibrant debate about informality now suggests that practices of urban occupation that do not conform to planned norms are made legible through the label of informality. On its own, the term informality is an empty signifier, a concept whose meaning is deeply dependent on time and place. Modernist urban planners, whose practices were being applied vigorously to cities in newly decolonised countries identified local, culturally inflected practices as informal. The pre-colonial bazaar or the souk within modernising cities in the postcolonial world could be represented as the seat of informal practices, always with the implication that they must be rooted out or transformed through modernisation into rational, calculative, transactional relations. Yet, given the slow pace of urban transformation, not only did these old forms of exchange and transaction persist, but new versions also spawned in due course as urban growth outpaced planners' abilities to *keep up*.

The liberalisation of India's economic policies beginning in 1990 involved the homogenisation of urban form by projecting efficiency and competence to attract investment. As with many other cities across the globe, economic liberalisation was accompanied by a shift to entrepreneurial urban governance with a key emphasis on city imagineering practices, including city branding, the staging of mega-events and the construction of flagship urban projects such as the SRFDC's riverfront revitalisation plan. This package of branding, staging and construction steers the spotlight away from the violence and rhetoric of xenophobic and exclusionary political practices of the state. The spatial products[14] associated with entrepreneurial governance, therefore, perform the dual functions of pro-

jecting a mirage of efficiency and using that mirage to root out improvisation and adaptive urban tactics that continue to inform the lives of urban majorities. This account of Gujari Bazaar's multiple spatial iterations, which is developed through observation and in conversation with the market's many actors, takes us on a journey through a landscape that continues to evolve, transgress and resist its homogenisation. Reflecting on the question of how space maintains its cultural distinctiveness, despite these attempts to redirect its experience, we find that it is ultimately the openness of markets as sites of exchange to new and unfamiliar experiences that enable the bazaar to remain distinctive as it changes and to reflect its function as a symptom of the interests that shape urban life.

REFERENCES

Appadurai, A. *The Social Life of Things: Commodities in Cultural Perspective*. Cambridge: Cambridge University Press, 1986.

Easterling, K. *Enduring Innocence: Global Architecture and Its Political Masquerades*. Cambridge, MA: MIT Press, 2005.

Ghertner, A. *Rule by Aesthetics: World Class City Making in Delhi*. Oxford: Oxford University Press, 2015.

Mathur, N. 'On the Sabarmati Riverfront: Urban Planning as a Totalitarian Governance in Ahmedabad.' *Economic and Political Weekly* 47, no. 47/48 (I December 2012): 64–75.

Mbembe, A. 'Aesthetics of Superfluity.' *Public Culture* 16, no. 3 (2014): 373–405.

Rao, V., and A. Simone. 'Securing the Majority: Living through Uncertainty in Jakarta.' *International Journal of Urban and Regional Research* 36, no. 2 (2012): 315–35.

Roy, A., and A. Ong. *Worlding Cities: Asian Experiments and the Art of Being Global*. London: Wiley Blackwell, 2011.

The Urban Popular Economy Collective, et. al. 'Urban Popular Economies: Territories of Operation for Lives Deemed Worth Living.' *Public Culture* 34, no. 3 (2022): 333–57.

14   For an elaboration of the concept of 'spatial product,' see Keller Easterling, *Enduring Innocence: Global Architecture and Its Political Masquerades* (Cambridge, MA: MIT Press, 2005).

1414-1973

1 Gujari Bazaar opens following a royal decree by Sultan Ahmed Shah.
2 The market relocates from Royal Maidan to Sidi Sayyed Masjid and Lal Darwaza.
3 Gujari Bazaar moves to the riverside underneath the Ellis Bridge.
4 Proposal by French architect Bernhard Kohn for the redevelopment of Sabarmati riverfront

1973-1997

5 Ahmedabad Municipal Corporation (AMC) issues an eviction notice to the Gujari Bazaar vendors which is later challenged in court.
6 The River Front Development Group produces the first technical survey for the riverfront development.
7 AMC issues another eviction notice to the Gujari Bazaar vendors.

1997-2002

8 Sabarmati Riverfront Development Corporation is set up and funded by the Government of India.
9 The proposal for the Sabarmati Riverfront Development Project is published.
10 Ahmedabad witnesses the rise of information technology and IT-enabled service sectors, which attract new companies contributing to the city's economic diversification.

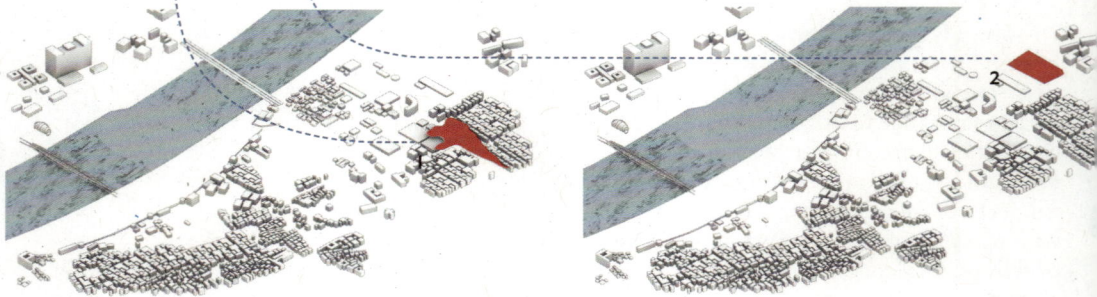

Timeline of key events shaping the transformation of Gujari Bazaar, Ahmedabad

2002-2007

11 AMC launches the Sabarmati Riverfront Development Project, envisioning the transformation of the riverfront as an opportunity to attract global investment.

12 A Public Interest Litigation is filed in the Gujarat High Court, articulating the rights of the informal dwellers. The court ruling issues a stay order, requesting the government authorities not to evict any families until further orders are issued by the court.

13 Ahmedabad is included in the Government of India's list of 'Mega Cities' earmarked for focused urban development and infrastructure improvements.

2007-2012

14 Despite the stay order, AMC tries to evict residents from the informal riverfront settlements.

15 Construction starts on the Sabarmati River Front Development Project (SRFDP).

16 Sabarmati Riverfront Development Corporation demolishes most of the informal settlements along the riverbanks.

17 An eviction notice is served to the Gujari Bazaar vendors.

18 The Gujarat Government introduces the Gujarat Industrial Policy to promote industrial growth and attract investment.

19 Sabarmati Riverfront Development Corporation relocates the remaining informal settlements, raising the number of displaced persons to 10,500.

2012-2015

20 Public Interest Litigation filed by Navdeep Mathur, a professor at Ahmedabad's Indian Institute of Management, argues for the inclusion of Gujari Bazaar in the SRFDP.

21 Ahmedabad High Court issues an interim order directing the authorities not to evict vendors from outside the Victoria Gardens until further orders.

22 Gujari Bazaar officially relocates to its new premises within the Sabarmati riverfront redevelopment.

23 From 2003, Ahmedabad hosts the bi-annual Vibrant Gujarat

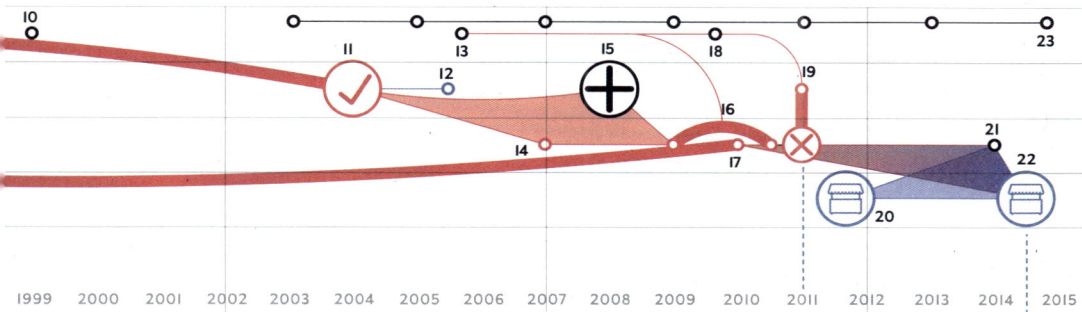

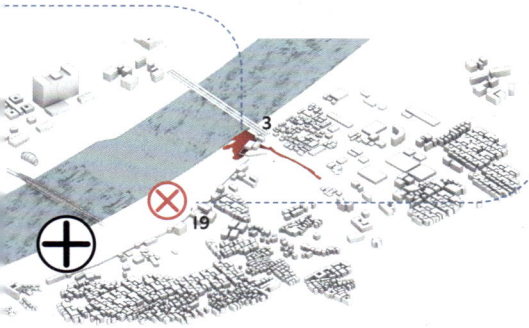

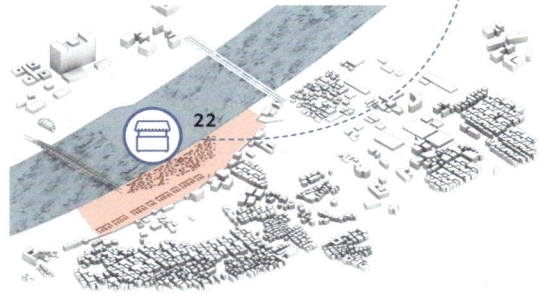

1999 2000 2001 2002 2003 2004 2005 2006 2007 2008 2009 2010 2011 2012 2013 2014 2015

Spatial, social, economic and political interventions into in/formal markets
Informality as a survival method and means of adapting to changing socio-economic and political circumstances

Typical infrastructural components, Gujari Bazaar, Ahmedabad

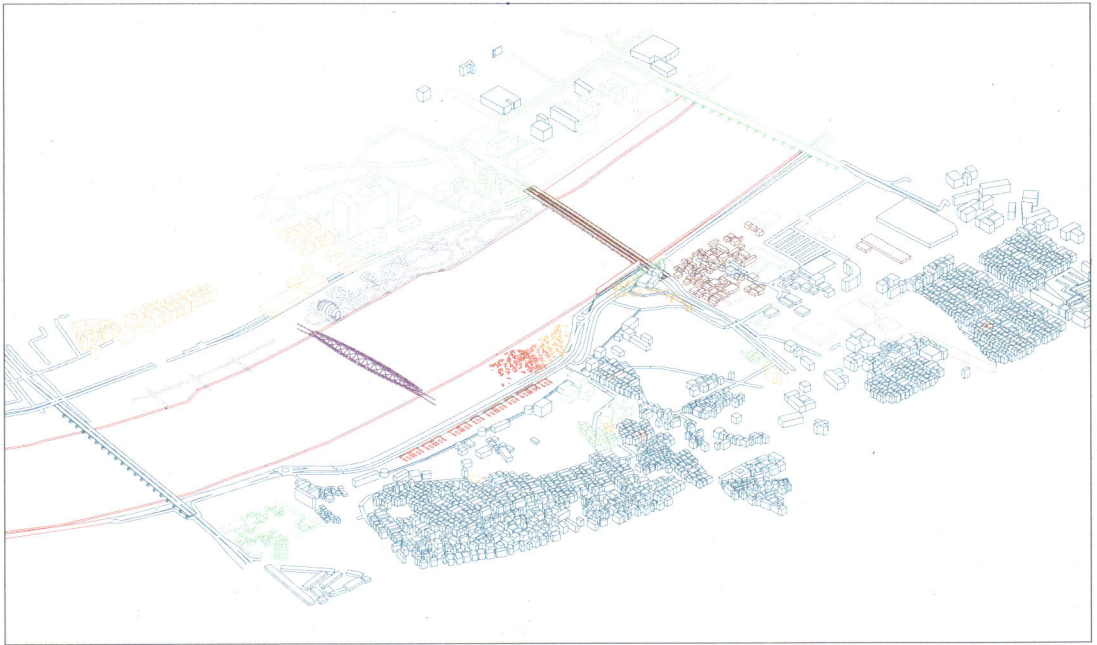

Legend: ▪ 1414 ▪ 1892 ▪ 1941 ▪ 1954 ▪ 2012 ▪ 2013 ▪ 2014 ▪ 2018 ▪ 2022

Gujari Bazaar neighbourhood: key phases of spatial development

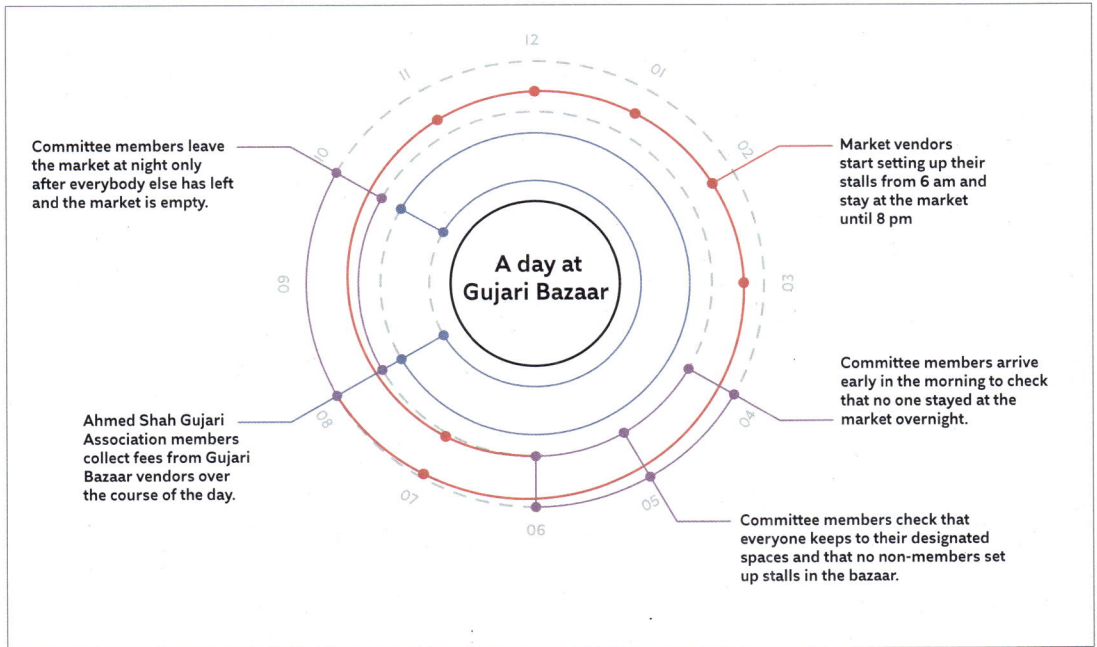

Committee members leave the market at night only after everybody else has left and the market is empty.

Market vendors start setting up their stalls from 6 am and stay at the market until 8 pm

A day at Gujari Bazaar

Committee members arrive early in the morning to check that no one stayed at the market overnight.

Ahmed Shah Gujari Association members collect fees from Gujari Bazaar vendors over the course of the day.

Committee members check that everyone keeps to their designated spaces and that no non-members set up stalls in the bazaar.

24-hour operational scheme of Gujari Bazaar, Ahmedabad

Gujari Bazaar, 2022

Old clothes

Gym equipment

Sewing machine

Books

Sound systems & speakers

Bird cages

Shoes

Pots & pans

Toys

TVs & DVD players

Furniture

Antiques

Used tyres

Chickens

Sheep

Goats

Typical merchandise at Gujari Bazaar, Ahmedabad

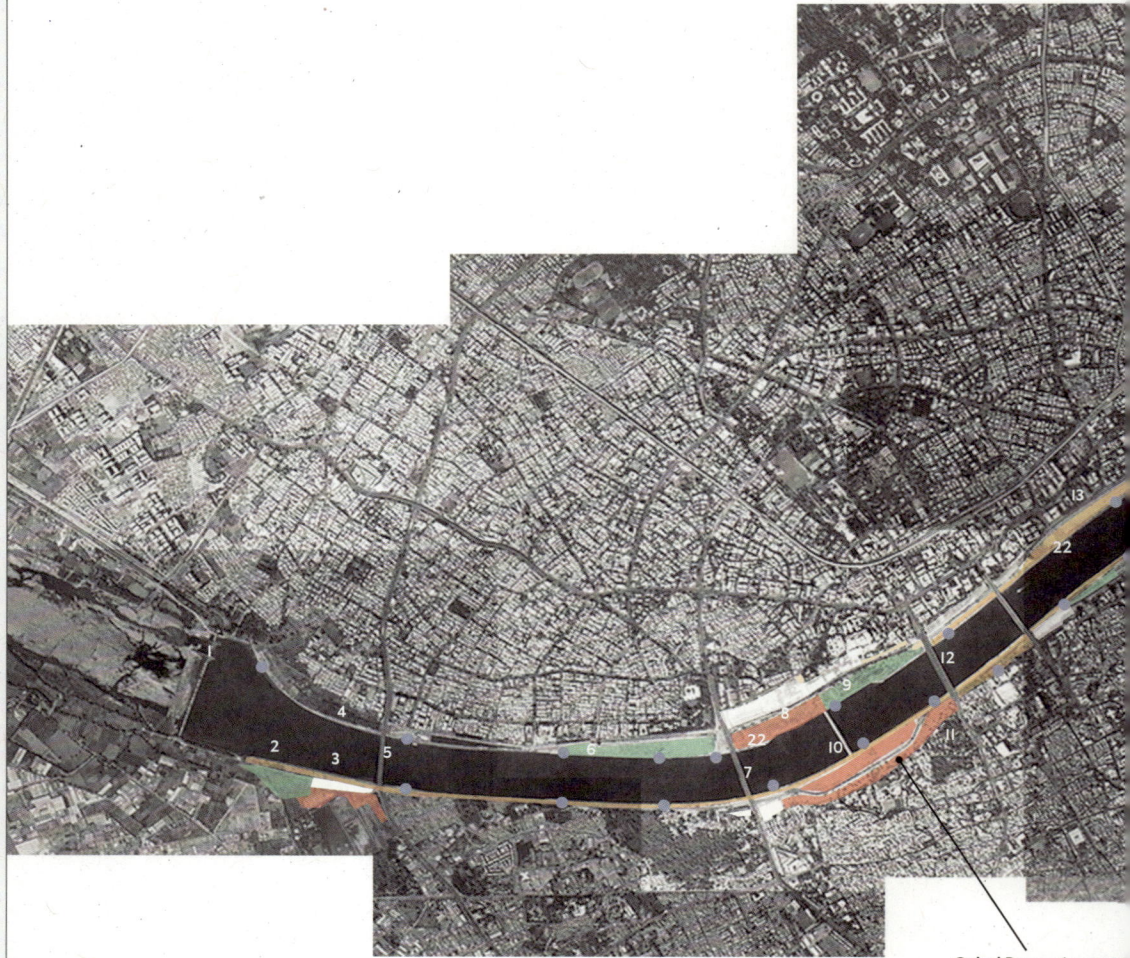

1   Vasna Barrage
2   Pirana Sports Ground
3   Laundry Campus
    (completed)
4   Paldi Urban Forest

5   Ambedkar Bridge
6   Paldi Sports Complex
7   Sardar Bridge
8   Events Ground
9   Flower Garden

10 Exhibition Centre
11 Gujari Bazaar (present)
12 Ellis Bridge
13 Vallabhsadan Plaza
14 Khanpur Riverfront Sports Park

Gujari Bazaar (present

Redevelopment of the Sabarmati Riverfront, Ahmedabad; map data: Google, Maxar Technologies

15 Gandhi Bridge
16 Usmanpura Riverfront Park
17 Shahpur Sports Park
18 Amusement Park
19 Dadhichi-Rushi Bridge

20 Subhash Bridge Riverfront Park
    (completed)
21 Gandhi Ashram Plaza
22 Riverfront Boating Stations
23 Ghats

24 River Promenade East
25 River Promenade West

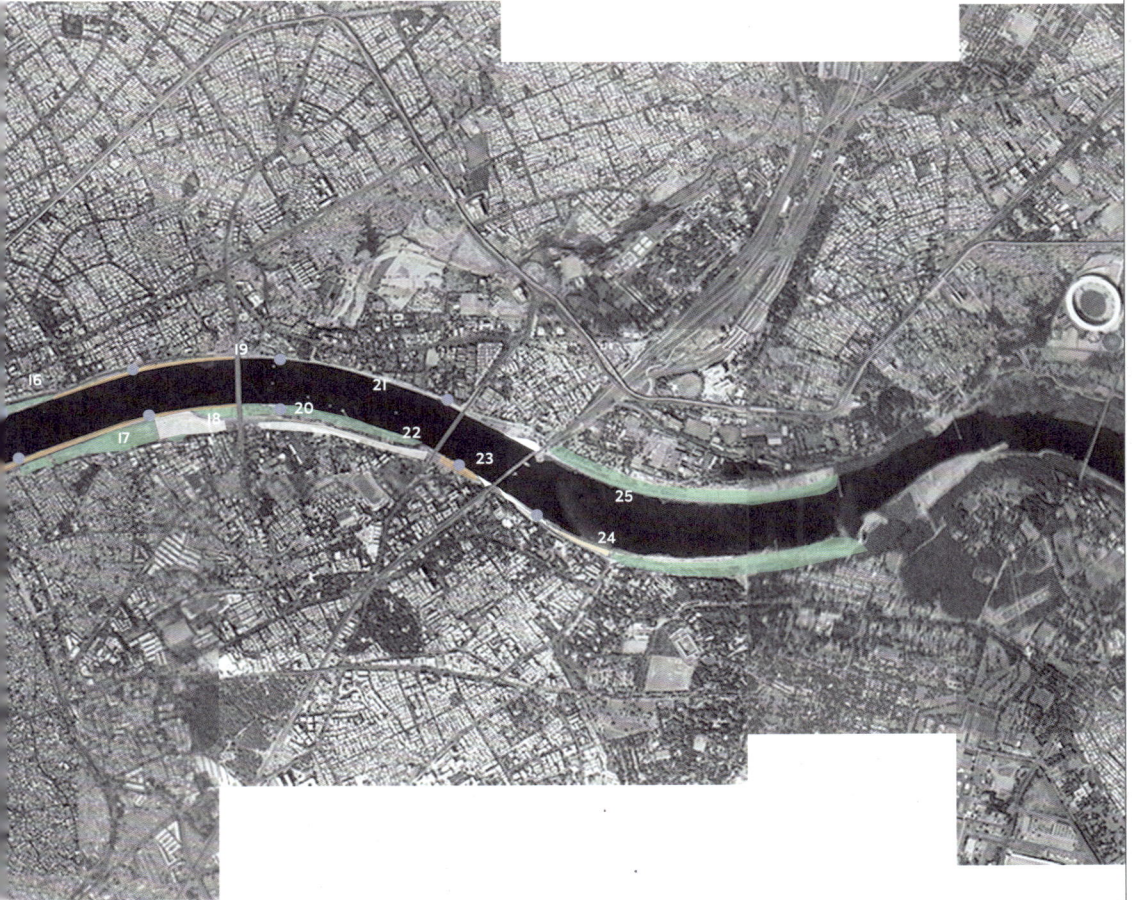

☐ Services/Infrastructure   🟩 Parks/Recreation   🟥 Events   🟧 Public Space   🟦 Ghats

Sale of coal-fired stoves, Gujari Bazaar, Ahmedabad

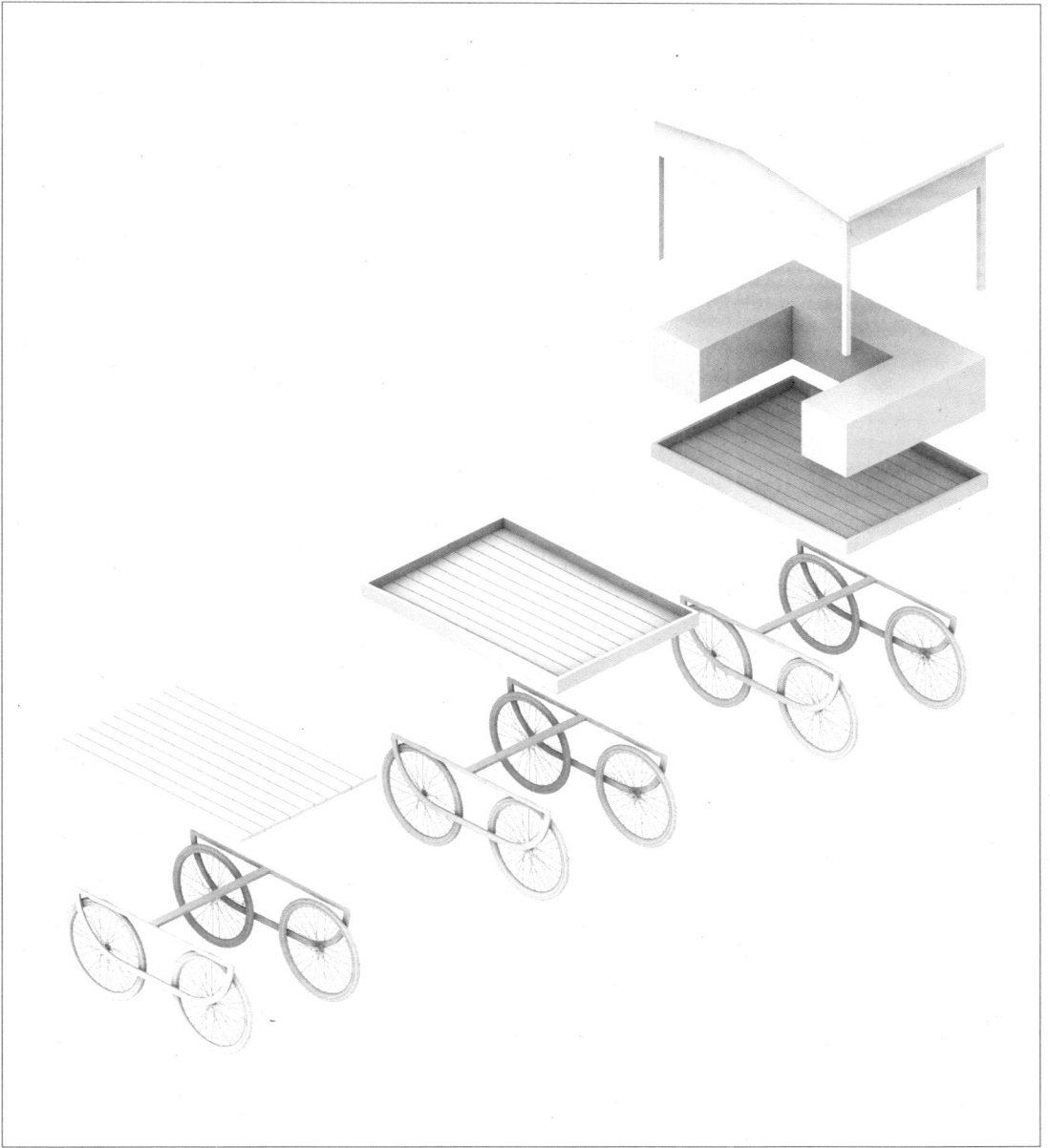

Mobile stall, Gujari Bazaar, Ahmedabad

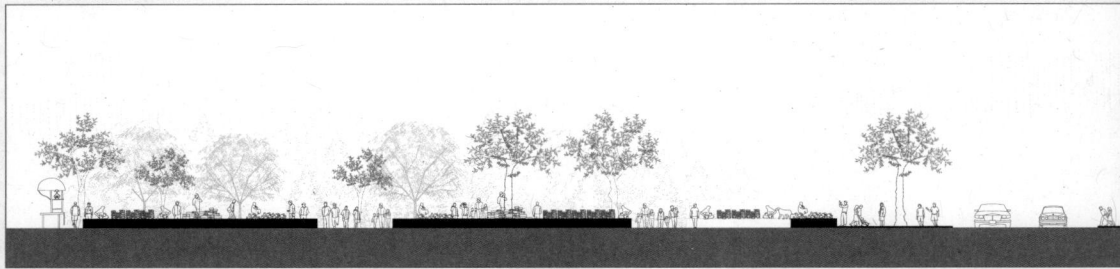

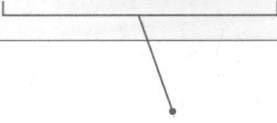

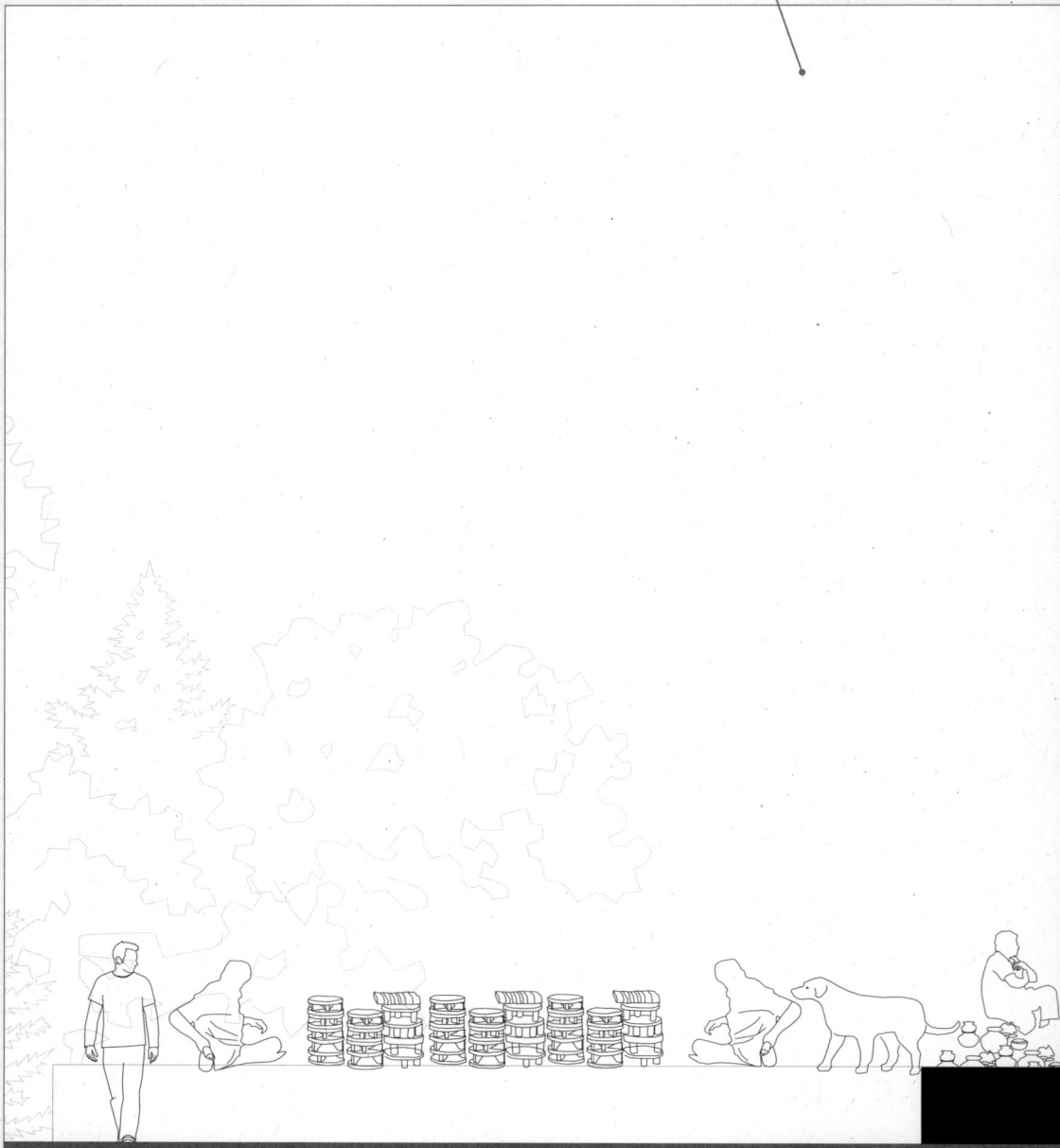

Section of the redeveloped Sabarmati riverfront showing the fragmented locations of Gujari Bazaar

242

Gujari Bazaar, Ahmedabad, 2013

Improvement

Karama Market, Dubai, 2018

Samar Halloum

I — Karama Market

Urban Regeneration in Dubai – Informality Out of Sight

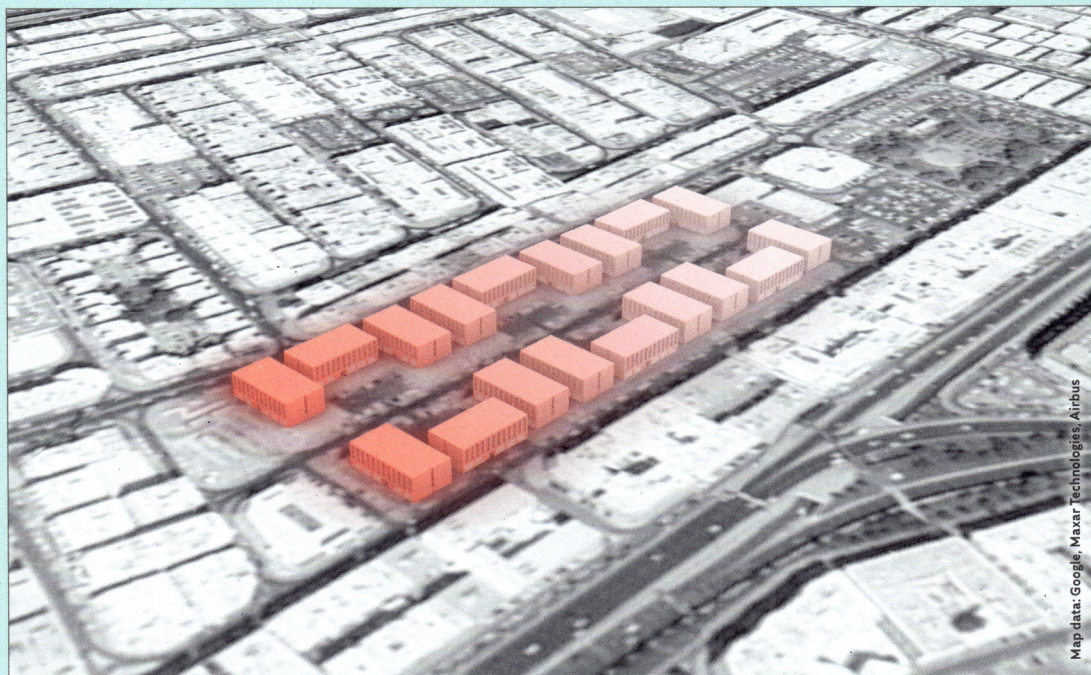

Map data: Google, Maxar Technologies, Airbus

Long before Dubai transformed into a giant metropolis attracting foreign investment from all over the world, the modest economy of its coastal settlements largely depended on trade and commerce enabled by its geographical location at an intersection of a global network of trade relations. The history of the city's urban development between the beginning of the nineteenth century until the discovery of oil in the 1960s surrounded its creek (known as Khor Dubai) and responded to its geographical location, which allowed it to function as a vital artery of commerce and an ideal stop en route for trading ships sailing between Africa, Europe and South Asia. With strategic investment from the ruling tribe in the infrastructure of the creek that supported trading activities and handled high volumes of cargo, the neighbourhoods adjacent to the creek attracted immigrant merchants who settled in the city, taking it as a base for their businesses and trading activities and capitalising on its location at the intersection of major trade routes. The neighbourhoods around the creek continue to be shaped by their history as the core from which the city's

Al Karama district has long been dominated by state-funded low-income housing. Increasingly, these housing blocks from the 1970s are being demolished and replaced by more expensive condominiums.

The primary building typology of Karama Market consists of four-storey buildings with three floors of apartments above a retail ground floor. Arranged around three open squares, the shops are lined up along arcades that criss-cross the complex.

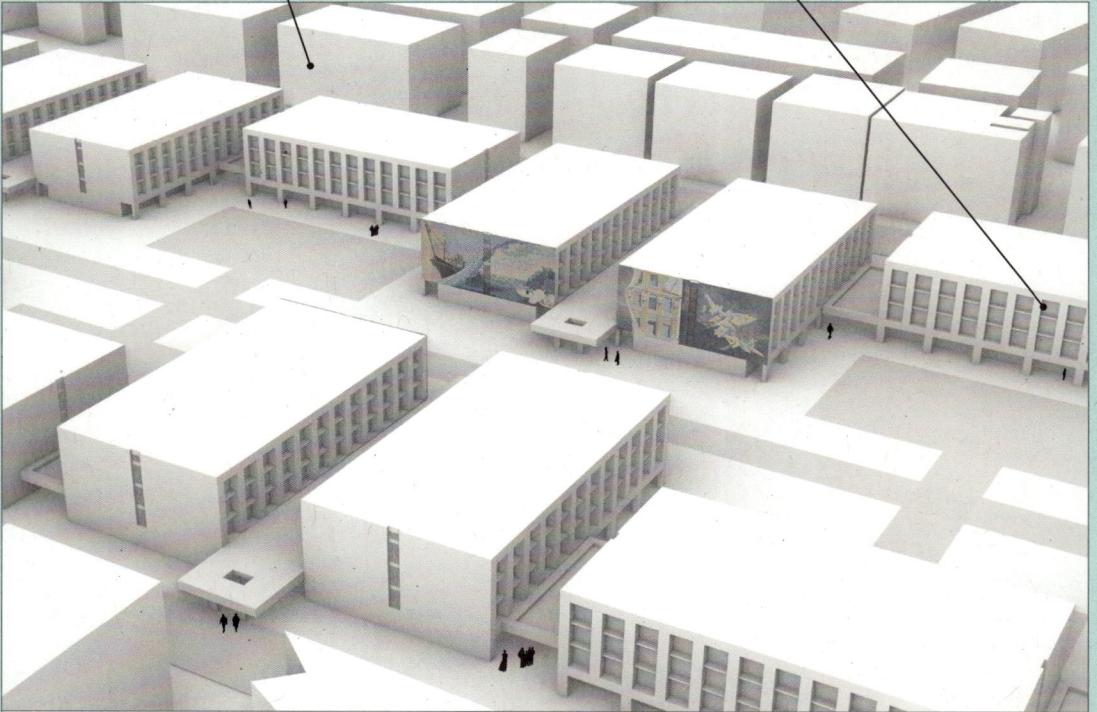

In a concerted campaign to boost Karama Market's appeal as a shopping destination, large-scale murals and hanging baskets were introduced along both sides of the market's main axis in 2016.

Despite efforts undertaken by the UAE government, intellectual property interest groups continue to report Karama Market as a major hub for the trade in counterfeit goods.

trade and commerce developed over the past century.

With the discovery of oil followed by the formation of the United Arab Emirates,[1] investments in the city's urban development flourished, making Dubai an opulent city that is recognised as a world-class hub for commerce and tourism. The government's ambitions to push forward the city's economic momentum fuelled an expansion in its infrastructural development, leading its urban fabric to sprawl and it to become home to high-end luxury brands from all over the world. With the rapidly growing tourism industry, its tax-free markets, and a geographic location that allows easy access to trade routes connecting to regions with low labour costs, lax intellectual property laws, and alongside increasing demand for luxury products, a counterfeit economy emerged across the city.

The Karama Market, which is the focus of this essay, is one of the most locally known markets offering counterfeit goods to fashion enthusiasts wanting to associate with certain luxury brands without having to pay their prices. The Karama Market Complex is located at the heart of what is designated today as Old Dubai, a district that combines Dubai's oldest residential and commercial neighbourhoods. The Karama Market's location within the city strongly impacts its cultural, economic, and political development. This research unpacks and investigates the multiple scales at which global, international, and national cultural, economic, and political dynamics continue to shape the evolution of informal economic activities within this market. Despite efforts from the government to clamp down on counterfeit goods and protect intellectual property, the counterfeit market in Dubai continues to persist, albeit more confidentially and discreetly. The research suggests that the efforts to regulate the counterfeit trade are driving a redirection of energy towards clandestine exchange points and online platforms growing out of sight.

THE SEEDS OF INFORMAL TRADE IN KARAMA MARKET

Highlighting certain aspects of the history of trade in Dubai is crucial to understanding how the market's location within the city shapes how informal exchanges started to operate. As the first coastal settlements in Dubai occupied the areas directly surrounding the creek, its water course became the divider, splitting Dubai into two parts during the nineteenth and twentieth centuries. It was first described in written archives in a report dating back to 1822 by a British Royal Navy officer[2] as it served as a commercial hub forming the basis for the existence of its first settlements (currently known as Old Dubai). While the creek was also a site for pearling and fishing industries, its importance in the second half of the twentieth century largely centred on commerce, enabled by its first documented engineering mega-project that facilitated accessibility to larger vessels.[3] Finished by the early 1960s, the development project led to a surge in commercial activities at the creek. In 1972, a year after the formation of the United Arab Emirates, Mina Rashid – Dubai's new port – opened just a short distance from the creek, setting the emirate on course as a global centre of trade and commerce. With that, the neighbourhoods surrounding the creek – including the Karama neighbourhood – flourished, and their populations increased with significant numbers of South Asian merchants settling in the city to capitalise on the creek's location.

The Karama neighbourhood drew its strong transnational identity from its South Asian inhabitants, who infused it with the cultural interactions and customs that they brought and shared from their countries of origin. Despite living in the neighbourhood for decades, people continued to use the space in ways that activate their multiple heritages, characterised by complex intertwined webs of social and cultural interactions that later continued to support their informal trade relations. Remittances sent by immigrant merchants settling in Dubai back to their families

1 Dubai is one of the seven sheikhdoms that united into a modern state in 1971 forming the United Arab Emirates (UAE).
2 National Council of Tourism and Antiquities, 'UNESCO Tentative Lists: Khor Dubai,' submission to UNESCO, 30 January 2012, https://whc.unesco.org/en/tentativelists/5662/
3 John Dennehy, 'Dubai Creek: the Making of Sheikh Rashid's First Mega Project,' *The National News*, 26 September 2019; Sketch Map of Dubai Creek (1941), Qatar Digital Library: IOR/L/PS/12/1978, f 48 [the original is held by the British Library: India Office Records and Private Papers], https://www.qdl.qa/archive/81055/vdc_100061345823.0x00005f

Karama neighbourhood, Dubai, 2018

contributed to engaging the immigrants in relations within their communities in their countries of origin. On the other hand, living within an immigrant community in Dubai gave the merchants access to resources, mutual support, and commercial information that would have otherwise been difficult to navigate. Through the strong trade connections with South Asia, merchants established networks that facilitated the supply of goods (e.g. garments, perfumes, and spices) shipped from South Asia and sold in the souks[4] in Dubai's old neighbourhoods. Clearly identified by the city's residents as an immigrant neighbourhood, the retailers focused on offering daily necessities and affordable accommodation for the immigrant communities in Dubai.

In 1975, only four years after the establishment of the United Arab Emirates, the government constructed the Karama Complex covering 45,000 square metres.[5] The complex was planned as a mixed-use development offering retail and residential rental spaces. It consists of six identical U-shaped buildings,

each offering street-level retail spaces topped with three floors of apartments. Surrounding the Karama Market, other low-rise residential developments and commercial buildings populate the neighbourhood, many of which are currently owned and managed by the same development entity that runs the market. Other markets in the neighbourhood include the fish market and the gold market. Three years later, the government established the Sheikh Rashid Colony in 1978 in the Karama neighbourhood as the first publicly planned housing development that recognises the need for affordable accommodation. The seventeen blocks offered mostly Asian and South Asian-expatriate families domestic apartments for a low fixed rent.[6] The colony was not the only affordable offering of the neighbourhood as its markets were known for providing daily essentials at low prices. Those realities started shifting with the continuous growth that drove the city's urban development.

As the importance of trade increased, the state's recognition of the value of improved

4   A souk is an open-air street market.
5   Sharmila Dhal, 'Karama Shopping Complex: Old District, New Kaleidoscope,' Gulf News, 3 August 2016, https://gulfnews.com/uae/karama-shopping-complex-old-district-new-kaleidoscope-1.1873337
6   Preeti Kannan, 'Dubai's Sheikh Rashid Colony Slowly Being Reduced to Rubble,' The National News, 22 March 2013, https://www.thenationalnews.com/uae/dubai-s-sheikh-rashid-colony-slowly-being-reduced-to-rubble-1.295573

Karama neighbourhood, Dubai, 2018

infrastructure supporting the trade activities happening along the creek crystallised. In April 1982, the *Khaleej Times* newspaper reported on the completion of yet another development project improving trade infrastructure in the city;

'Dubai Creek has received a facelift with the successful completion of work on the 800-metre customs wharf extension project in front of the British Embassy. The project started two years ago at the initiative of His Highness Shaikh Rashid bin Saeed Al Maktoum, Vice-President and Prime Minister of the UAE and Ruler of Dubai, has been completed recently. As a result, the Bur Dubai side of the creek is also ready to contribute its share in the Emirate's flourishing sea.'[7]

The continuous investment in trade infrastructure kept attracting merchants that aimed to connect goods imported from the Indian subcontinent and other eastern regions to the rest of the world. Dubai's efforts to capitalise on its geographical location

enabled it to climb the ladder to becoming one of the world's most-known destinations for high-end fashion brands at the end of the twentieth century. Simultaneously, the Al Karama neighbourhood, where Karama Market is located less than four kilometres away from the mouth of the creek, continued to be home to immigrant communities who put down their roots in the country, promising prosperous commercial development decades ago.

The sprawling urban development along an axis parallel to Dubai's coastline and the increased cost of living were forces that pushed retailers to shift their merchandise from affordable products targeting the neighbourhood's residents toward products that attracted tourists. The trade in counterfeit products enables reaching prices per product that a product of similar quality and material, but a different brand, does not achieve. Goods appealing to tourists included a wide range of counterfeit products that later faced heightened restrictions and criminal fines.

251

7   Defense Attache's annual report on the Armed Forces of the United Arab Emirates (UAE) for 1981,' Arabian Gulf Digital Archives: FCO 8/4385 (1 January 1982 - 31 December 1982), 72, UAE, *https://www.agda.ae/en/catalogue/tna/fco/8/4385/n/72*

Unlike informal markets that materialise as street markets or informal bazaars occupying parts of public city space, the research reveals that the informal trade within the Karama Market spills into the private sphere of residential apartments and, more recently, into a virtual network that is largely controlled and run by individuals living outside the country, but have networks to secure a delivery process within it. At this market, although some of the shops sell souvenirs, most sell fashion products that include shoes, handbags, sunglasses, and clothes. Wandering through the shops, one notices the emphasis on products that attempt to imitate luxury fashion brands with minor changes or intentional misspellings in the brand names, that maintain the appearance of goods that mirror luxury products. Other products could bear the trademark of a legitimate and well-known luxury brand but are illictly produced by another party that is not legally connected to the trademark owner.

SPACE AS AN INSTRUMENT OF INFORMALITY

Studying the Karama Market reveals multiple layers of in/formalities. Under its current management developer, all vendors are formal in their rental agreements, licensing and holding valid permits. Informalities within the market are, however evident in the processes taking place in the economic exchanges. Informality in procuring the goods, their storage, and in the spatial alterations that enable informal exchanges away from the public eye. Spatially, the informal trade interactions within Karama Market are interconnected with multiple spatial scales where a customer's request or exchange has implications on informal labour processes occurring at the borders, inter-state, and outside the country. At the scale of the market, one walks through an arcade extending in front of the storefronts. On the side walls of the arcade, metal signage is attached stating regulations for using the market spaces. The regulations reflect modern planning strategies that seek the sanitisation of public spaces. Part of the sign reads: 'Please be informed that the following activities are forbidden: Salesmen promoting outside shops, and storing items in the shopfront area.'

These tightly moderated regulations put limitations on the use of spaces outside the rented interior of the retail shops and attempt to create a clear division between public space and the interior where commercial exchanges are to happen. However, as visitors walk between the shops in the Karama Market, vendors attempt to attract them inside by listing the variety and the quality of products they offer. Inside the store, high-end display units showcase fashion goods that mimic the overall appearance of luxury brands. Once the shopper shows an interest in the products displayed, some vendors then reveal the availability of what are referred to as 'master copies' of designer brands. The copies are shown through a phone-recorded video of products displayed in showrooms off-site. The vendors offer to bring the goods that the shopper is interested in from apartments in the same complex. Unable to store or directly sell counterfeit goods from their shops, vendors use rented residential apartments for that purpose.

When entering one of the apartments of the Karama Complex in 2022, what seems to have been built as a two-bedroom apartment on the second floor of a four-storey block, is refurbished as an informal extension to a shop located on the ground floor. Upon entering the apartment, no windows are visible. The interior is fitted with commercial display units. Walls are covered with rows of shelves fitted with concealed lights, room spaces are laid out into a grid with clear aisles and accessories are displayed on stands covered with glass cases. The look and feel of the outfitted apartment spaces mimic the thematic approach that luxury brands follow in the design of their retail spaces. From the street level, windows rarely reveal what is happening behind them; thick curtains often conceal the interior of residential apartments. The sellers in the apartment are not the same salesmen working in the shops, indicating a wider labour network that facilitates the process of securing, delivering and selling counterfeit goods.

The informal process disconnects the productivity of the labourer from the capitalist models that feed the economic hierarchies. While the economic activities and exchanges happening at the Karama Market are based on formal market existence, the sellers

Housing earmarked for demolition, Karama neighbourhood, Dubai, 2023

Karama Market, Dubai, 2013 (top and bottom)

formally rent shops and sign leases; they are also registered and pay taxes for the goods they sell and issue receipts for. However, this base is the enabler for extending their activities into the informal sector. The apartments where they store their goods are also officially rented, despite them being for residential use.

THE ON-GOING FIGHT AGAINST COUNTERFEIT GOODS

The government of Dubai has undertaken varying steps and strategies over the years to crack down on the counterfeit market, including implementing stricter laws and penalties, conducting raids on counterfeit sellers, and collaborating with international brands to combat counterfeiting. The first official law addressing the trade of counterfeit goods was the UAE's Civil Transactions Law (Federal Law No. 5, 1985) which allows trademark owners to pursue civil remedies against those who infringe on their trademarks by selling or distributing counterfeit goods. This includes seeking damages and injunctions to prevent further infringement. This law indicated that the copyright holder is entitled to initiate (legal) procedures towards addressing informality.

Decades later, the regulations expanded in their areas of enforcement and became more severe in their punishments. Border control measures that allow efforts of fighting counterfeit trade to extend beyond the physical parameters of the market were put in place in 2002; The UAE's Federal Law No. 7 of 2002 on Copyrights and Related Rights provides for border control measures to prevent the importation of counterfeit goods into the country. Customs officials have the authority to seize and destroy counterfeit goods at the border. The government has also implemented several laws and regulations to further combat the sale and distribution of counterfeit goods in the country. The UAE's Federal Law No. 19 of 2016 on combating commercial fraud criminalises the sale and distribution of counterfeit goods. The law imposes fines and prison sentences on those who sell, offer for sale, possess, or distribute counterfeit goods.

According to the law, individuals who commit commercial fraud can face fines of up to 1 million AED (approximately 272,000 US dollars) and imprisonment for up to two years, excluding the cost of seizure and destruction processes of the counterfeit goods that the perpetrator also bears.

A news article from *Al Khaleej* reported on the seizing of 353,000 counterfeit products from residential units over the span of four months in 2015.[8] These raids are recurrent and are often announced in national news. The Department of Economic Development (DED), recorded by a national news agency, carried out a raid on six different shops in the Karama Market in 2018. The raid resulted in the seizure of more than seven thousand items from various apartments within the complex and the shop owners were prosecuted according to the laws.[9] The publicity from the raids that reach online platforms and local newspapers forms a threatening deterrent for other shop owners and sellers in the market. In the same news article, testimonies of shop owners bear witness to the difficulty of the financial situation and the high rate at which shops are closing down, and sellers who are unable to pay their rents.

In December 2019, national news in the UAE reported a joint operation by police in China and the UAE that resulted in a seizing of counterfeit goods estimated at a value of 257 million US dollars.[10] The operation included raids in Dubai and the arrest of several suspects in China who provided forged customs documents. This operation followed several attempts to eliminate the city's reputation for the sale of counterfeit goods to both its residents and tourists alike. The international joint effort reflects an awareness of the global supply chain networks that are essential for counterfeit products to exist in the local market.

The Review of Notorious Markets for Counterfeiting and Piracy is an annual report issued by the Office of the United States Trade Representative (USTR) that identifies markets around the world engaging in or

255

8   Zainab Suleiman, 'The Confiscation of 353,000 Counterfeit Items in Dubai from 157 Apartments,' *Alkhaleej News*, 4 November 2015.
9   Nilanjan Gupta, 'There's No Point in Selling Counterfeits: "It's a Losing Business,"' *Khaleej Times*, 17 June 2019,
     https://www.khaleejtimes.com/uae/theres-no-point-in-selling-counterfeits-its-a-losing-business.
10   'Joint UAE and China Raids Seize $257 Million in Counterfeit Goods,' *The National News*, 3 December 2019,
     https://www.thenationalnews.com/uae/government/joint-uae-and-china-raids-seize-257-million-in-counterfeit-goods-1.946069

Typical infrastructural components, Karama Market, Dubai

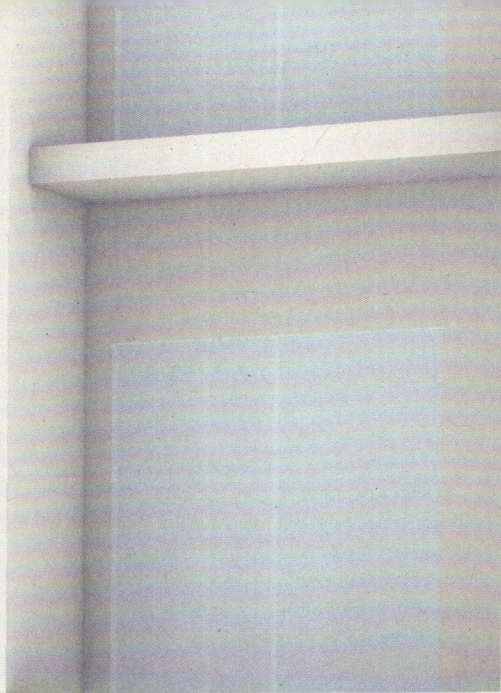

Karama Market

258

facilitating intellectual property theft and piracy. The report includes a list of physical and online markets where counterfeit and pirated goods are sold, including luxury brands. Several markets in Old Dubai were listed in the 2022 review.[11] The report states that 'these markets are well known among tourists and locals alike for selling infringing goods. Right holders report that the Dubai police and the Dubai Department of Economic Development conduct frequent raids against sellers of infringing products at these markets. However, while authorities will fine sellers for IP violations, the sellers are typically not assessed deterrent-level fines or forced to close their shops, even if they are repeat violators.'[12] The impact of this review for luxury brands is significant, as it highlights the scope and scale of the problem of counterfeiting and piracy, which is a major threat to the profitability and reputation of those chains.

The pressure from the USTR list and the increased visibility that the selling of counterfeit goods received aligns with the timeline of the updated and tightened laws and regulations targeting copyright fraud. To protect the city's prestigious reputation as a fashion hub and a touristic destination for luxury-brand enthusiasts, the laws get repeatedly updated and tightened, restating and emphasising a commitment to punish and eliminate informal economic activities. The UAE's Ministry of Economy works closely with trademark owners to identify and seize counterfeit goods. The ministry continues to conduct raids on markets and shops to confiscate counterfeit goods and prosecutes those who sell them.[13] In recent years, with the shift to counterfeit trade exchanges happening in discrete locations, governmental enforcement efforts have been focused on managing and controlling points of entry to the country, given that the majority of the counterfeit products are imported from abroad. Emirates News Agency announced at the beginning of 2023 the Dubai Customs figures stating that 14.5 million counterfeit items with a street value of 29 million US dollars had been confiscated in 2022.[14]

REDIRECTED URBAN SPOTLIGHTS

Understanding the timeline of the development of trade, commerce, and investment overlapped with the urban development of the city reveals how intertwined the informal economy is with urban development plans within the city. The research maps the impact of the geographical proximity of the market to surrounding touristic, cultural, and infrastructural developments within the city. These developments resulted in increasing the visibility of the market and hence, put pressure on authorities to enforce anti-informal policies and tighten restrictions on the trade dynamics within the market. Drawing connections between the urban development of the city and dynamics happening within the Karama neighbourhood highlights the impact of the city's evolving urban fabric on the informal trade within the market.

Over time, and while maintaining its status as the main centre of trade relations in the Middle East, the city's ambition to establish a strong foundation in tourism fuelled exceptional urban development that continues to shape refurbishment and modernisation efforts in the old side of the city. With the expansion of the giant metropolis that started away from Dubai Creek, its newer developments – the man-made islands, The Dubai Downtown development, Burj al Arab, Jebel Ali Port, all contributed to redrawing a map of Dubai that foregrounds its luxurious, upper-class areas. Simultaneously, several government-led development projects taking place in/around Old Dubai at the turn of the twenty-first century brought pressure on the aesthetic, reputational and legal aspects of the Karama Market's commercial activities. The area previously at the periphery of development started to undergo several redevelopment projects that included the demolition of older domestic buildings to make space for new structures. Today, the neighbourhood lies a mere twelve-minute car ride from the world's tallest building, the Burj Khalifa, and a metro ride away from the majority of Dubai's

11   Office of the United States Trade Representative, '2022 Review of Notorious Markets for Counterfeiting and Piracy,' (Washington DC: USTR, 2023), *https://ustr.gov/sites/default/files/2023-01/2022%20Notorious%20Markets%20List%20(final).pdf*
12   Office of the United States Trade Representative, '2022 Review of Notorious Markets for Counterfeiting and Piracy.'
13   'Ministry of Economy Presents Details of New Legislation on Commercial Companies, Commercial Registry and Trademarks' (Ministry of Economy, UAE, 21 December 2021).
14   Ahlam Almazrooi and Saleh Amjad, 'Dubai Customs Completes 25.7 Million Transactions, 2,147 Seizures in 2022,' *Emirates News Agency*, 22 January 2023, *https://www.wam.ae/en/details/1395303121214*

Room advertisements, Karama neighbourhood, Dubai, 2018

most luxurious developments. Demolition of buildings built in the 1970s continues, clearing space for developments aimed at the middle-classes and the continuing gentrification/beautification of the neighbourhood.

Al Fahidi District is another one of the major developments that contributed to bringing the Al Karama neighbourhood and its markets into the spotlight. The area located at the mouth of the creek, Al Fahidi District (previously Al Bastakiya neighbourhood), was officially recognised for its historical value in showcasing vernacular residential architecture built in the mid-nineteenth century. The neighbourhood was scheduled for demolition in the 1980s before the decision was terminated after Prince Charles's visit to Dubai and the neighbourhood at the time. In early 2000, rumours about plans to demolish the distinctive historic core of Dubai generated discussion and arguments that emphasised the value of the old neighbourhoods in preserving and celebrating the city's history and legacy. The rumours were denied when the Fahidi District was announced as a major cultural destination repositioning it on the map of tourist destinations. For the following years, the district became home to cultural and

creative events that were hosted regularly between the houses and inside their courtyards. The location of the development meant that its visitors would drive through the Karama neighbourhood to reach it, emphasising the immigrant neighbourhood as an integral part of their journey through the old part of the city. A few years after the opening of the Fahidi, the Al Seef commercial development that extends from Al Fahidi along the creek was announced, increasing the traffic across the Karama neighbourhood.

In 2010, the mega development of The Dubai Downtown and Burj Khalifa redirected global attention toward the high-class shopping and leisure destination. Centred by Dubai Mall, a shopping centre populated by hundreds of designer retail stores, and dissected by its boulevard, connecting various retail destinations to their surroundings. Dubai Mall re-emphasised the city's commitment to offering an attractive, luxurious environment for prestigious fashion brands from all over the world. In the same year, and as the government continued to improve the infrastructure within the city, a metro station opened at the edge of the Karama neighbourhood (only a four-minute walk from Al Karama Shopping Complex),

Karama neighbourhood, Dubai, 2018

Karama Market, Dubai, 2018

Karama Market and Dubai Frame, 2023

connecting it to the city's most luxurious, and dynamic destinations.

The Dubai Frame landmark is a major addition to Dubai's skyline that has as its main vision the recognition and celebration of two identified faces of the city; the historical and the new. In 2012, the 120 million AED (around 32 million dollars) Dubai Frame launch added another layer of visibility pressure on the Karama Market. Consisting of a 150-metre-high platform that gives its visitors a framed view of Old Dubai, highlighting and emphasising the urban fabric and the aerial view of these districts. The Dubai Frame, having been developed less than 400 metres away from the complex, bestows on it an unprecedented status of touristic visibility. Its proximity to the Karama Market increased attention on the visual and contextual content of the market. Following the announcement of the Frame, the Karama Complex received a refurbishment that covered its façades and what is appearing to the public. Graffiti artists were commissioned by the property development company that manages the complex. The eight commissioned artists painted twenty-four murals.[15] When discussing the murals with the vendors in the market, they recognise the graffiti as a visual beautification project that does little to improve trade or attract more shoppers to the market.

With the shift in urban developments happening near the Karama neighbourhood, pressure on land in Old Dubai grew, and the visibility of older structures associated with low-income inhabitants increased. The fate of the Sheikh Rashid Colony, Dubai's first affordable housing development, was decided following the announcement of Dubai Frame; it was set for demolition to clear its land for newer residential units.[16] In their place, newly built units cater to higher-class residents and offer standardised modern façades.

While the field research reveals varying strategies that respond to spatial interventions, the legal and enforcement practices that target informal activities within the market suggest that energies are funnelling into remote, virtual platforms that conceal their visibility.

15   Melanie Swan, 'Street Art Turns Karama Turned into a Gallery on a Giant Scale,' *The National News*, 4 August 2016.
16   Swan, 'Street Art Turned into a Gallery.'

The rise of digital channels facilitating the sale and purchase of consumer goods has fuelled a rapid increase in the trade of counterfeit products worldwide. Powered by attempts to find hidden spaces for selling counterfeit products, social media platforms became virtual spaces that offer and exchange 'master copies.' When expressing an interest in newer collections, vendors revealed to me an even more exclusive service of creating a master copy of a specific product (often a handbag) on request. In these cases, communication through WhatsApp or social media accounts is the preferred method to share a link to the original handbag. The vendors expressed confidence in their ability to secure a master copy of any desired handbag as long as they have sufficient photos of it. Depending on the shopper's bargaining skills, these were usually offered at one-tenth of the price of the original.

Social media platforms like Instagram, WhatsApp, and Facebook allow informal networks to exist transnationally. Accounts are run by individuals and groups who aren't necessarily city residents. These virtual platforms also allow informal economies to intersect with networks aimed at ther gulf countries. Many of the accounts explicitly state that they extend to operate or deliver goods in Saudi Arabia, Kuwait, Qatar, Bahrain, and UAE to advertise their ability to provide counterfeit products across borders. While global networks are embedded in these exchanges, sellers mainly mention China and South Asian countries.

At the local scale, the evolving intensity and complexity of spatial relations triggered by urban developments, global markets, technological advancements, and changing customer habits reshape the form and location where informal exchanges occur. The process of importing, storing, displaying, and selling counterfeit goods demonstrates how informal governance, informal labour, informal exchanges, and informal use and its ramification on space largely depend on complex international relations that connect sellers in the market to suppliers elsewhere. Despite attempting to operate discretely or virtually, the informal counterfeit trade relations within the Karama Market face a cul-de-sac as they no longer lie at the periphery of the city; they interact with and respond to the multiple complex layers that are largely impacted by global capitalist networks and legislative efforts to protect the city's commercial reputation.

REFERENCES

Almazrooi, A., and S. Amjad. 'Dubai Customs Completes 25.7 Million Transactions, 2,147 Seizures in 2022.' *Emirates News Agency*, 22 January 2023. *https://www.wam.ae/en/details/1395303121214.*

'Defense Attache's annual report on the Armed Forces of the United Arab Emirates (UAE) for 1981.' Arabian Gulf Digital Archives: FCO 8/4385 (1 January 1982 - 31 December 1982). *https://www.agda.ae/en/catalogue/tna/fco/8/4385*

Dennehy, J. 'Dubai Creek: The Making of Sheikh Rashid's First Mega Project.' *The National News*, 26 September 2019.

Dhal, S. 'Karama Shopping Complex: Old District, New Kaleidoscope.' *Gulf News*, 2016. *https://gulfnews.com/uae/karama-shopping-complex-old-district-new-kaleidoscope-1.1873337*

Gupta, N. 'There's No Point in Selling Counterfeits: "It's a Losing Business."' *Khaleej Times*, 17 June 2019. *https://www.khaleejtimes.com/uae/theres-no-point-in-selling-counterfeits-its-a-losing-business*

'Joint UAE and China Raids Seize $257 Million in Counterfeit Goods.' *The National News*, 3 December 2019. *https://www.thenationalnews.com/uae/government/joint-uae-and-china-raids-seize-257-million-in-counterfeit-goods-1.946069*

Kannan, P. "Dubai's Sheikh Rashid Colony Slowly Being Reduced to Rubble." *The National News*, 22 March 2013. *https://www.thenationalnews.com/uae/dubai-s-sheikh-rashid-colony-slowly-being-reduced-to-rubble-1.295573*

'Ministry of Economy Presents Details of New Legislation on Commercial Companies, Commercial Registry and Trademarks.' UAE Ministry of Economy, media briefing, 21 December 2021.

National Council of Tourism and Antiquities. 'UNESCO Tentative Lists: Khor Dubai.' Submission to UNESCO, 30 January 2012. *https://whc.unesco.org/en/tentativelists/5662/*

Office of the United States Trade Representative. '2022 Review of Notorious Markets for Counterfeiting and Piracy.' Washington, DC: USTR, 2023. *https://ustr.gov/sites/default/files/2023-01/2022 %20Notorious%20Markets%20List%20(final).pdf*

Suleiman, Z. 'The Confiscation of 353,000 Counterfeit Items in Dubai from 157 Apartments.' *Alkhaleej News*, 4 November 2015.

Karama Market

1975-2000

1 Inception of the Karama Market
2 Construction of the Hamdan Colony, the largest and most affordable housing complex in Karama district
3 About 8,000 displaced Omani nationals move into the Hamdan Colony.
4 The Dubai government establishes the Dubai Economic Department (DED) as the regulatory body responsible for enforcing intellectual property rights and combating counterfeit trade.
5 Introduction of the first federal trademark law (Law no. 37/1992) in UAE
6 The UAE becomes a member of the World Trade Organisation.

2000-2005

7 DED announces that shops in Karama Market have two weeks to sell any remaining illicit stock before the imposition of heavy fines and unannounced raids.
8 Amendment of the federal trademark law to meet international standards and criteria

2005-2010

9 The annual rent for a typical one-bedroom flat in Karama district is 11,500 US dollars.
10 Sheikh Mohammed bin Rashid Al Maktoum issues Law no. 25/2008 giving the DED the responsibility to plan and regulate the overall economic performance of Dubai, supervise its functions and enhance its economic development.
11 Karama Market vendors start to use apartments as hidden boutiques to sell counterfeit items in order to avoid raids, thereby gradually expanding commercial activities into the residential floors above the shops.

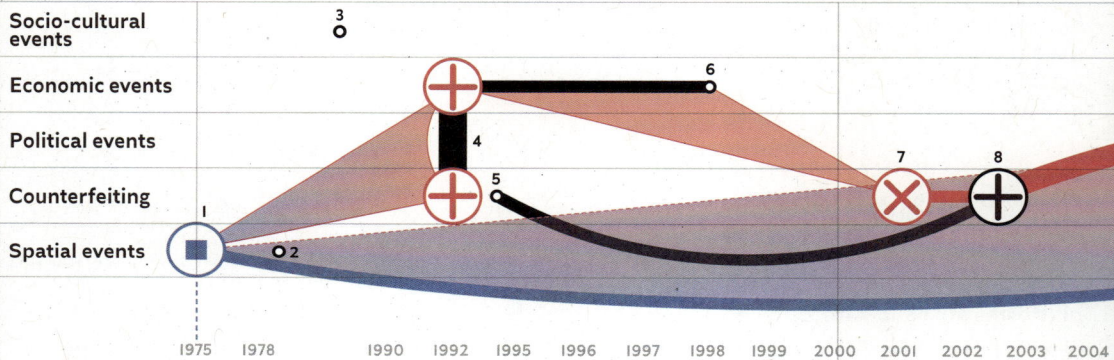

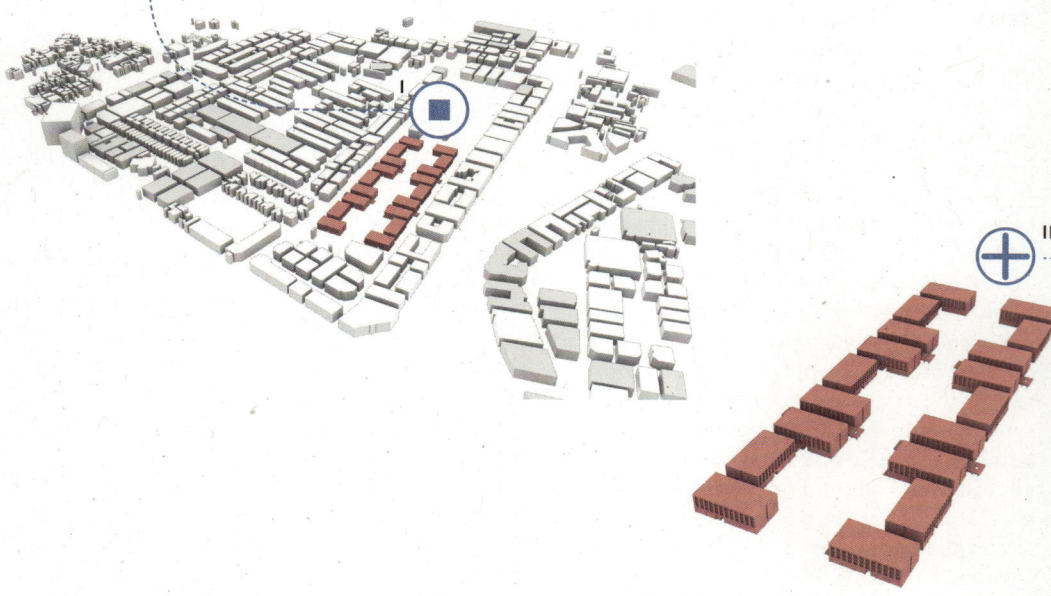

Timeline of key events shaping the transformation of Karama Market, Dubai

2010-2015

12 The Hamdan Colony gets demolished to make way for mixed-use residential buildings constructed and managed by Al Wasl Properties, a real estate assets management and development company created following the merger of two government organisations: Dubai Development Board and Real Estate Department.

2015-2020

13 Introduction of the Anti-Commercial Fraud Law (Law no. 19/2016) increases the fines for counterfeiting and introduces prison sentences.

14 Wasl Properties commissions the addition of colourful murals on 24 walls across all 12 buildings at Karama Market.

15 DED introduces measures against online counterfeiting.

16 26 million pieces of seized counterfeit goods with an estimated net value of 324 million US dollars are destroyed in Dubai.

17 The annual rent for a typical one-bedroom flat in Al Karama has risen to 16,335 US dollars.

18 7,000 counterfeit items seized in shops and hidden boutiques / apartments in the Karama Market during a one-day raid

19 Counterfeit goods worth 257 million US dollars seized in a joint operation by police in China and the UAE

2020-2023

20 The COVID-19 pandemic leads to a dramatic increase in the online sale of counterfeit items.

21 During the first nine months of the year, the authorities stop 2,699 attempts to introduce counterfeit products into the country, representing a sharp increase in comparison with previous years.

22 Since 2016, DED has closed over 8,000 pages and accounts on social media websites.

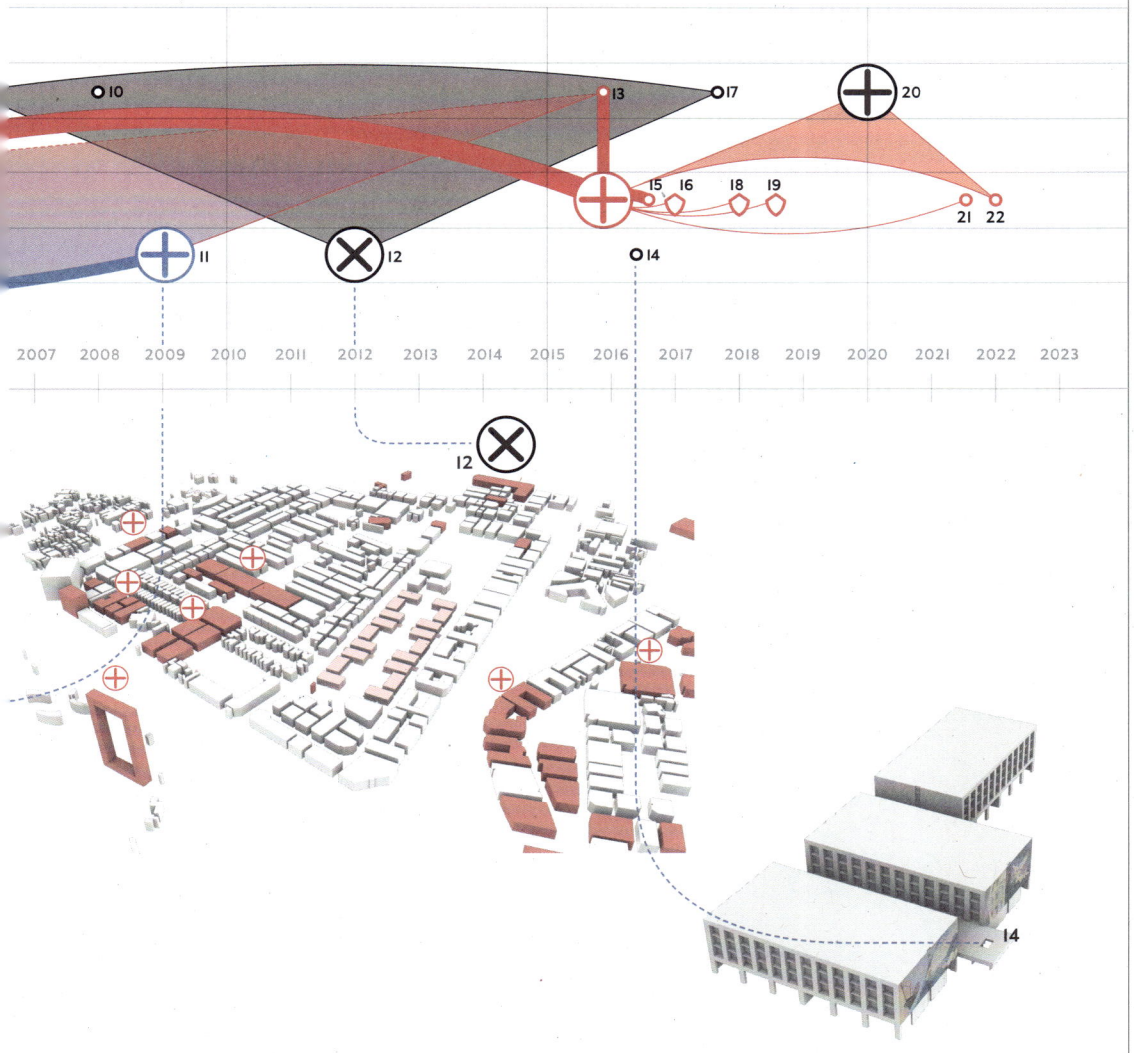

■ Spatial, social, economic and political interventions into in/formal markets
■ Informality as a survival method and means of adapting to changing socio-economic and political circumstances

Karama Market, Dubai, 2023

Typical infrastructural components, Karama Market, Dubai

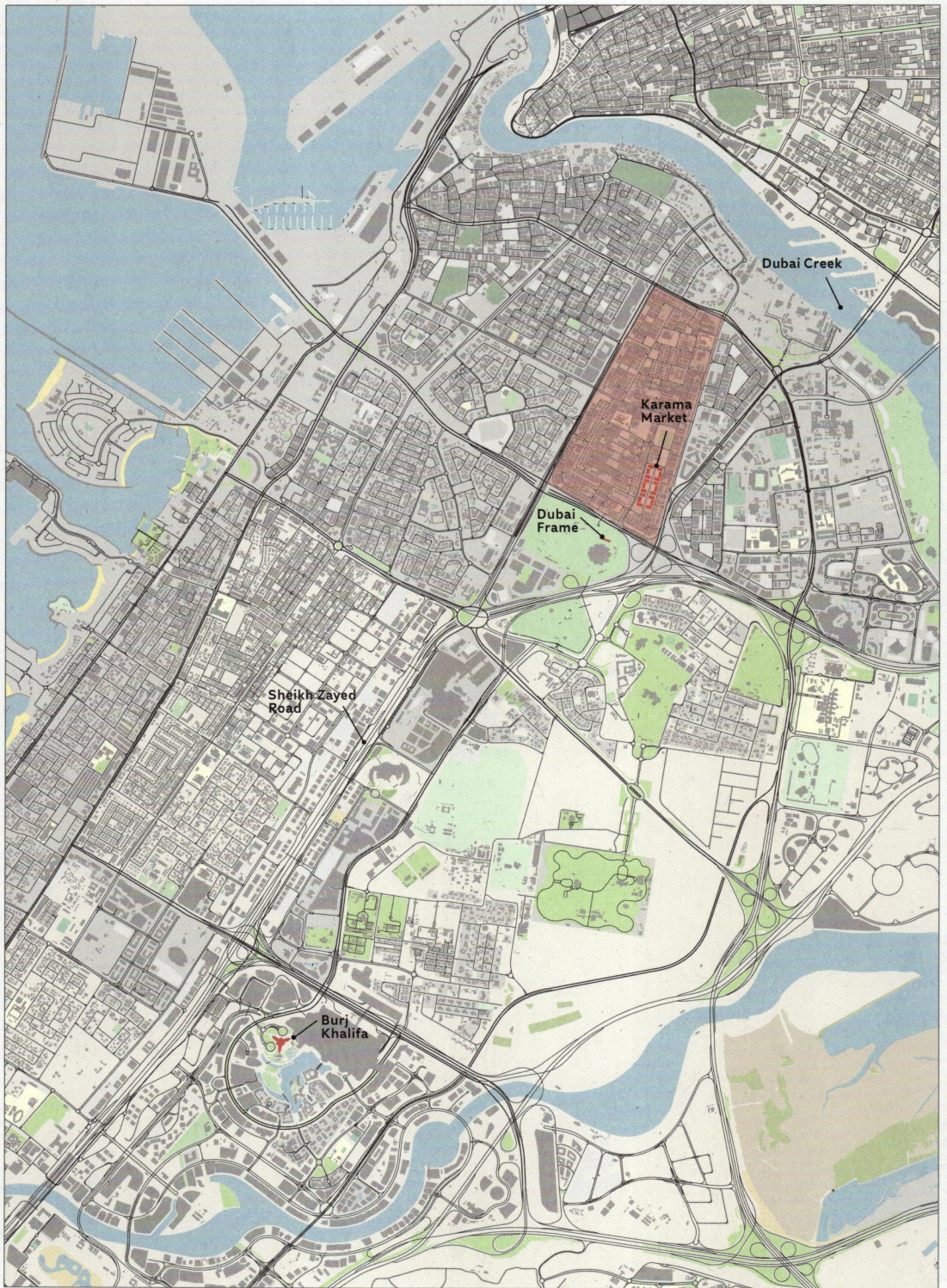

Dubai Creek

Karama
Market

Dubai
Frame

Sheikh Zayed
Road

Burj
Khalifa

Location of Al Karama district (red) in Dubai

Second Master plan of Dubai
by John Harris

| | 1820 | | 1966 | | 1971 | | 1980 | | 2001 | | 2004 | | 2009 | | 2016 | | 2022 |

↓ Discovery of oil in Dubai

Al Karama neighbourhood: key phases of spatial development

Residential

Commercial

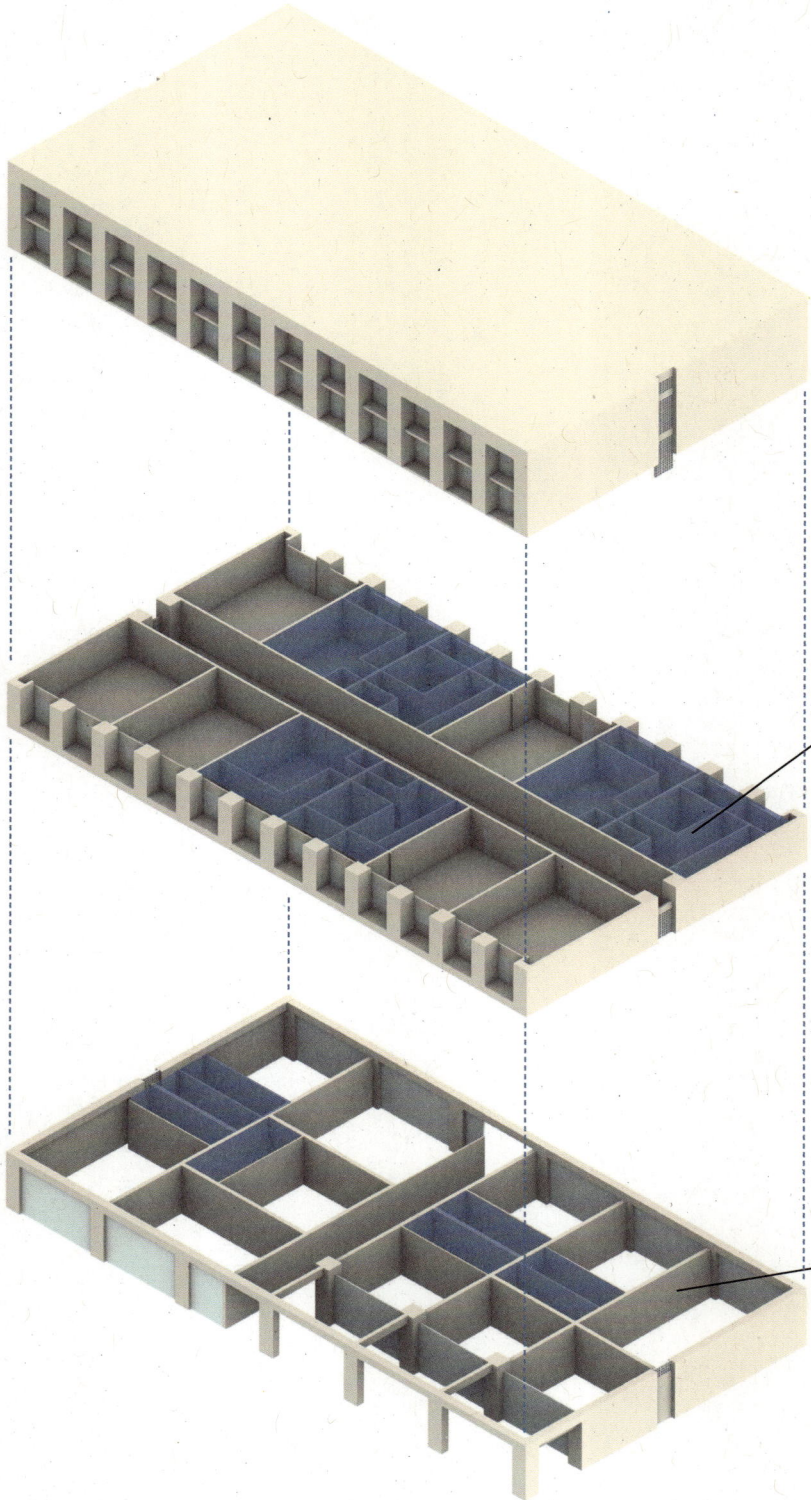

Expansion of trade activities into residential floors of the Karama Market complex

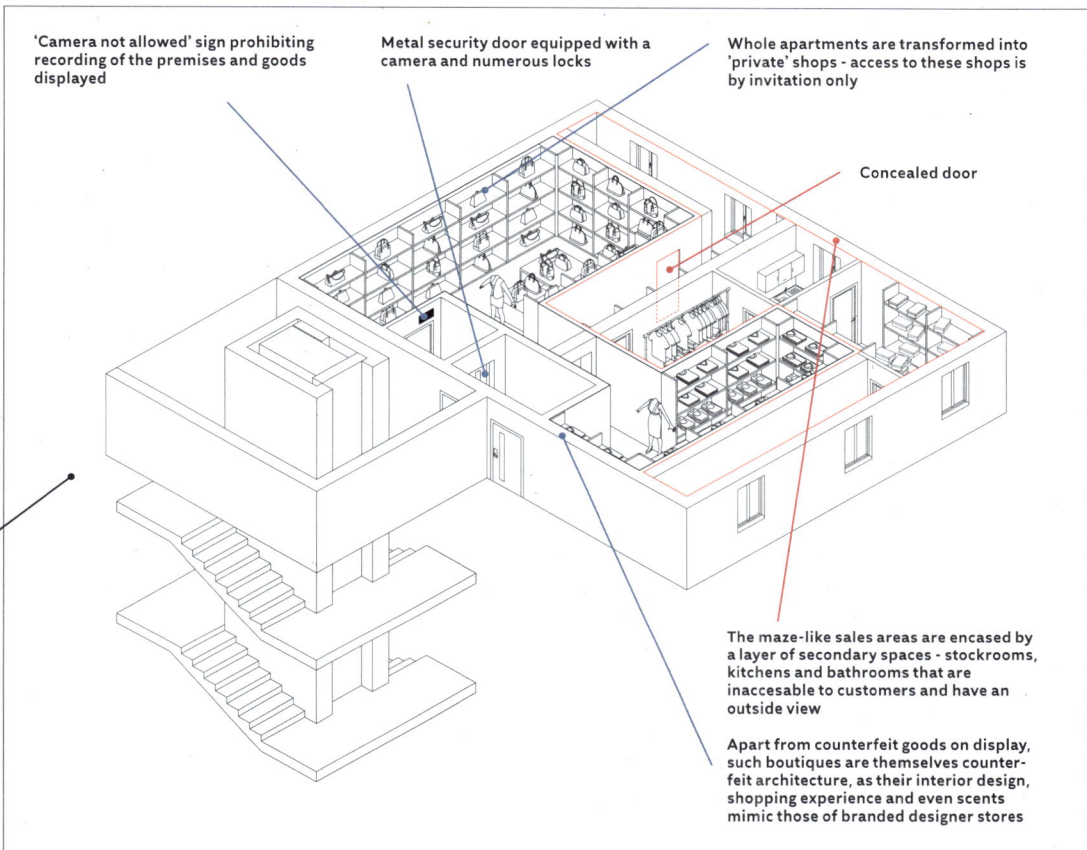

'Camera not allowed' sign prohibiting recording of the premises and goods displayed

Metal security door equipped with a camera and numerous locks

Whole apartments are transformed into 'private' shops - access to these shops is by invitation only

Concealed door

The maze-like sales areas are encased by a layer of secondary spaces - stockrooms, kitchens and bathrooms that are inaccesable to customers and have an outside view

Apart from counterfeit goods on display, such boutiques are themselves counterfeit architecture, as their interior design, shopping experience and even scents mimic those of branded designer stores

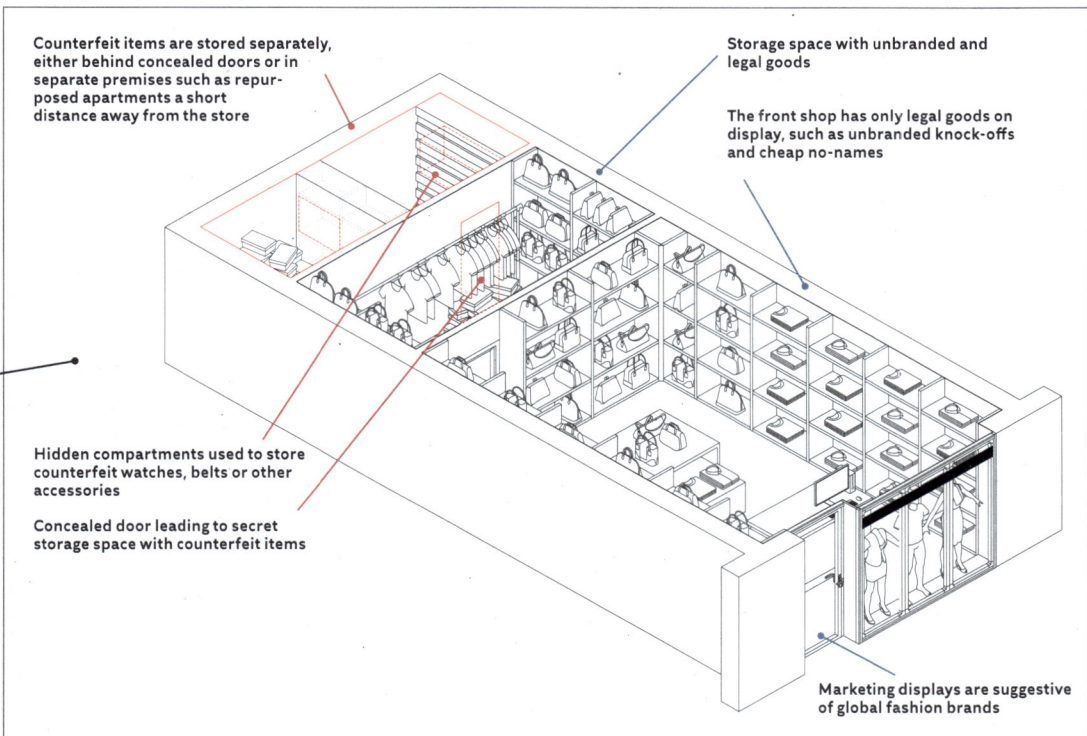

Counterfeit items are stored separately, either behind concealed doors or in separate premises such as repurposed apartments a short distance away from the store

Storage space with unbranded and legal goods

The front shop has only legal goods on display, such as unbranded knock-offs and cheap no-names

Hidden compartments used to store counterfeit watches, belts or other accessories

Concealed door leading to secret storage space with counterfeit items

Marketing displays are suggestive of global fashion brands

Karama Market, Dubai, 2018

274

SLOW 慢駛

Tin Shui Wai dawn market, Hong Kong, 2022

Paul Chu Hoi Shan

Informal Markets in One of Hong Kong's Planned Satellite Towns

Map data: Google, imagery date: 10/7/22-newer, Maxar Technologies

Tin Shui Wai (TSW) is a satellite town developed by the Hong Kong Government in the 1980s. Planned to be self-sufficient, the 4.3 square kilometres 'new town' is situated on a relatively flat piece of land in the northernmost part of the *New Territories* in Hong Kong, where agricultural and fishery production existed. Apart from the traditional farming by indigenous villagers, starting from the 1930s, villagers around Shan Pui Tsuen in Yuen Long began to construct fishponds and raise a variety of fish. Along the shore of Deep Bay, fishponds of different sizes emerged in TSW, Ha Tsuen, San Tin, Lok Ma Chau, Shap Pat Heung and Nam Sang Wai. Both fishpond area and freshwater fish production peaked in the period of the 1980s, after which both fishpond area and production began to decline.[1]

275

1 Due to the wave of immigration after the end of the second phase of the Chinese Civil War (1949–1952), the number and area of fishponds started to increase. This rapid increase in population led to shortages in food supply. With rising demand for freshwater fish, both the number and total area of fishponds increased and peaked in the 1980s. See: Census and Statistics Department Hong Kong, '漁翁移山: 香港本土漁業民俗誌, 張展鴻; 米埔自然保護區的經營管理; 林務局 [Fishermen Moving Mountains: A Folklore Journal of the Local Fishing Industry in Hong Kong]' (1983); Agriculture, Fisheries and Conservation Department, 'Fish Pond Culture,' The Government of the Hong Kong Special Administrative Region, https://www.afcd.gov.hk/english/index.html

The dawn market in Tin Shui Wai, a satellite town of Hong Kong bordering Shenzhen, moves location as dawn breaks. The market starts on and around a footbridge at 5:00 am and ends by 7:00 am ...

Drainage channel

Tin Shui Path

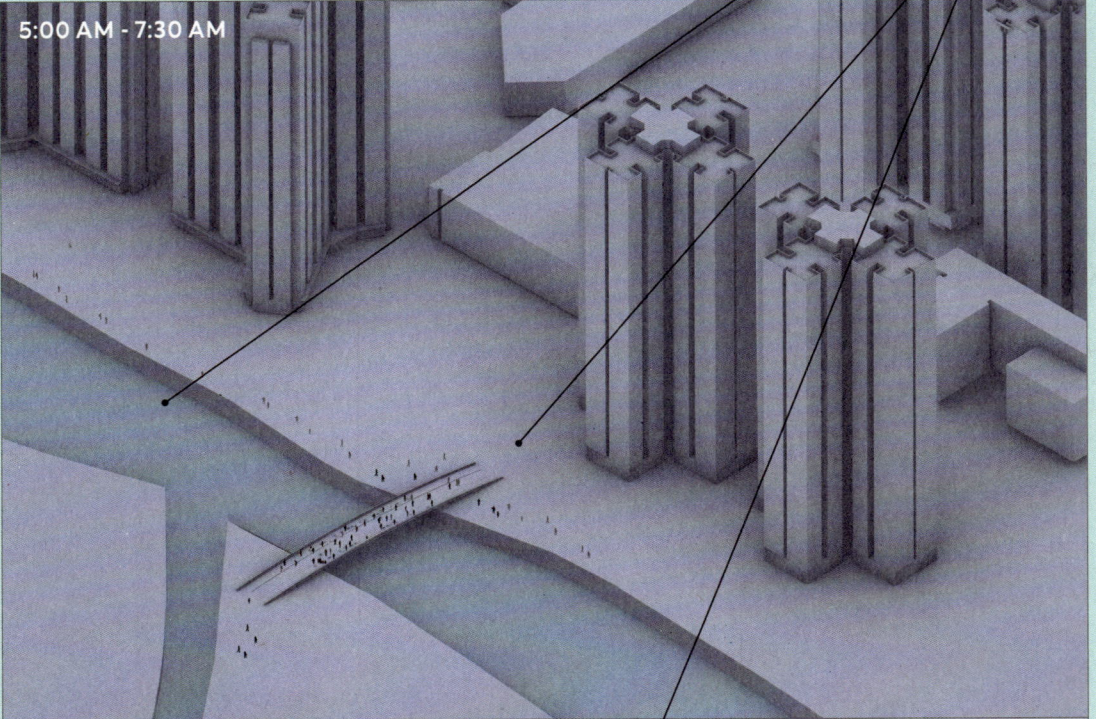

5:00 AM - 7:30 AM

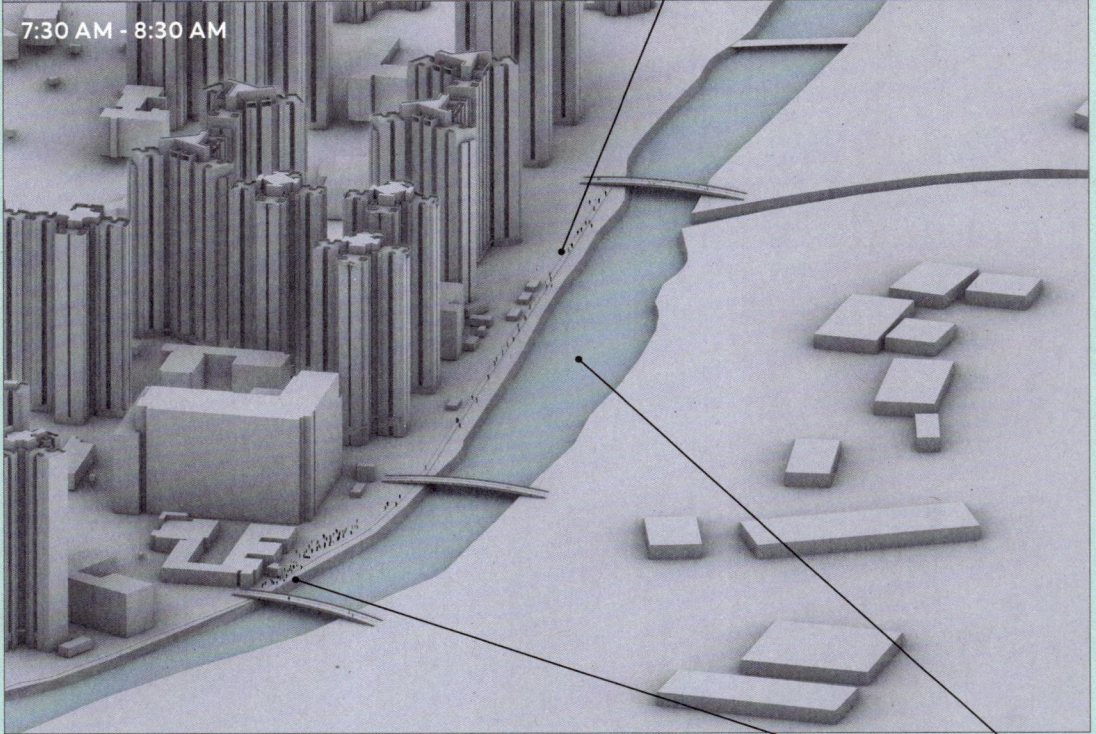

7:30 AM - 8:30 AM

... and then moves to the footpath along the canal between 7:30 am and 8:30 am. Thereafter, the market dissolves to avoid confrontation with the city's Hawker Control Teams.

Market moves location

Drainage channel

TSW was the eighth 'new town,' considered a 'third generation' of such and was conceived to be a 'self-contained and balanced community' for a planned population of 299,000.[2] Unlike other 'new towns' where the government mainly initiated development, TSW was developed with participation from the private sector even before the site had been surveyed. However, the government of Hong Kong subsequently decided on housing plans that completely altered the mix of the community, resulting in 'a large number of people from a relatively low-income group moved to this remote area in a relatively short period of time.'[3]

The first batch of the 'new town' residents started to move into the standardised public-housing blocks in 1992 as part of the relocation plan for the Sau Mou Ping and Ching Lok Estates in Kowloon. The emergence of informal markets, or so-called 'dawn markets,' selling different kinds of agricultural produce in the streets, was welcomed by the community newly moved there, partly because traffic to and from TSW was very limited and also the relatively low-income level of the residents. Today, TSW has become a middle-class residential area of 300,000 people with a mature transportation system and good facilities, including a public hospital, local and international schools, a district library, community centres, commercial malls, hotels, and a wetland park and conservation area. While new types of markets ranging from bazaar-type local markets, medium-sized modern markets selling quality food, to contemporary high-end hypermarkets exist, it is interesting to note that informal markets selling a wider range of products than the 1990s model still prevail and serve the residents today. This analysis aims to document and examine the persistent, though morphing, informal markets along the morphology of TSW, which evolved from 'a planned community in the rural area' in the 1990s to 'a middle-class residential district situated midway between

prosperous Hong Kong and Shenzhen city centre at present.'[4]

TSW DEVELOPMENT AT A GLANCE

Since the 1960s, the Hong Kong Government carried out new town development to cope with 'the increase in population and to improve the living environment by decentralising the population from the overcrowded urban districts to the rural area.' Following the development of Tsuen Wan, the first self-contained new town away from the Central Business District established in the 1960s, TSW, a relatively 'young' new town located in the almost northernmost part of the New Territories in Hong Kong, was developed from fishponds and greenery area to a planned, self-contained community in the late 1980s.

It was the third version of the new town model, and as noted by the Civil Engineering Development Department (CEDD), developing a new town is 'to provide a balanced and self-contained community as far as possible in terms of the provision of infrastructure and community facilities, […] to tackle population growth, to decant the existing population and to provide or upgrade facilities. The functional, environmental and aesthetic aspects of the developments are given priority consideration.'

The southern part of TSW was the first development section, with Tin Yiu Estate being the first public housing estate completed, among other new developments. Its first batch of residents, some being moved there as a result of the relocation package of the redevelopment plan of the Sau Mou Ping and Ching Lok estates in Kowloon, arrived from 1992 onwards. With the completion of other public housing estates, Tin Wah Estate and Tin Shui Estate, and the private homeownership schemes Tin Chung Court, Tin Oi Court, etc., an expanding population of residents progressively

2   Civil Engineering and Development Department, 'Hong Kong: Facts – New Towns, New Development Areas and Urban Developments' (GovHK, 2021).
3   TSW was planned with 'half public rental housing and half public sale flats or private housing with industry, community facilities, shopping centres, open spaces and a park for leisure activities. However, the Hong Kong Government's later decision to transfer 13,200 sale flats to rental use in 1998–2001, the cessation of the production and sales of Home Ownership Scheme (HOS) flats and the termination of Private Sector Participation Scheme (PSPS) in 2003 changed the planned district demographics in TSW completely. See: Chi-kwong Law, et al., 'A Study on Tin Shui Wai New Town Final Report' (University of Hong Kong, Department of Social Work and Social Administration, 2009).
4   Hong Kong is planning 'to consolidate and enhance her status as an international financial, transportation, and trade centre as well as an international aviation hub, strengthen its status as a global offshore Renminbi (RMB) business hub and its role as an international asset management centre and a risk management centre,' while Shenzhen is 'to leverage its leading role as a special economic zone, a national economic core city and a national innovation city, expedite its transformation into a modern and international city, and strive to become a capital of innovation and creativity with global influence.' See: Central Government People's Republic of China, 'Outline Development Plan for the Guangdong-Hong Kong-Macao Greater Bay Area' (2019), https://www.bayarea.gov.hk/filemanager/en/share/pdf/Outline_Development_Plan.pdf

occupied the originally natural landscape on the east side of TSW River. Further to the east, the newly completed higher-end private developments Locwood Court and Kenwood Court also started to receive residents. The population in TSW grew continuously from 1992 to 1995.

The infrastructure and provision of social services, however, was criticised for being 'not in place' and 'not ready' for the new population. Commercial developments were restricted by the agreement signed between the government and the then developer, Mighty City Company.[5] This, plus the lack of transportation channels to and from TSW, made the daily necessities sold there unaffordable. It also made TSW lack job opportunities, pushing up the unemployment rate with the welfare centres still unfinished. Therefore, with social workers, counsellors and psychologists not yet in place, people newly moved there suffered from a lot of pressure. After a couple of suicides and serious criminal cases were reported, TSW became known as the 'city of sadness' in Hong Kong.

Today, TSW has a population of around 300,000 residents. It has fifteen light railway stops (started operation from 1993 to 2003) and one MTR station connecting to different parts of Hong Kong (started operation in 2003). With the rapid development of Shenzhen, a city considered to be a global centre in technology, business and economics, finance, tourism and transportation in the Guangdong province of China over the last three decades, TSW greatly benefits from close proximity – literally twenty-five minutes by car to the border. This favours commuters and businessmen who choose to live in TSW for the ease of travel within the Greater Bay Area (GBA) under the 'Twin Cities, Three Circles' concept.[6]

INFORMAL 'DAWN MARKET' THAT EXERTS TEMPORALITY, SPONTANEITY AND ORGANICITY

Geographically, the TSW River divides and defines rural areas to the west and new development to the east. Since the arrival of the first batch of residents, it was found that informal, provisional buying and selling activities occurred around the TSW River. The vendors were mostly farmers residing in indigenous villages like Lo Uk Tsuen, Hong Mei Tsuen and Tung Tau Tsuen, who sold vegetables, fruit and poultry grown and kept by them. Fisherman living nearby also occasionally sold fish.

Street traders started daily business before 5:00 am and ceased and cleared out by 7:00 am, in order to avoid being otherwise caught and fined by officers of the Food and Environmental Hygiene Department (FEHD).[7] Most of the activity was concentrated on the footbridges and extended to the paths along the river. The market was called the 'dawn market' by the locals due to its operating time and has numbered over a hundred traders in the past. Most of the farm produce was transported manually by bamboo on the traders' shoulders, or by bicycle. Goods were placed on a vinyl sheet on the ground, and the sellers allowed a certain degree of bargaining. The buying and selling at the dawn market have mutually helped the lives of the people living on both sides of the river.

According to some traders there, the dawn activities dated to a time even before the new residential development came to TSW. The dawn market, literally pronounced 'Tin Kwong Hui' in Cantonese, depicts the features of traditional Hui (墟) and Shi (市), which denote 'larger and smaller periodic markets consisting of temporary structures,' (verandah, 廊) and 'can occur anywhere on the ground respectively in Guangdong, China.'[8] Dawn markets have appeared not just in TSW but

278

5 To the poor people of TSW, more shops, markets and commercial developments would have meant more jobs close to home. This could have been the difference between survival and desperation in the 'city of sadness,' a place with a long history of family tragedies and abuse. 'Colonial Deal Built "City of Sadness",' *South China Morning Post*, 6 December 2010, *https://www.scmp.com/article/732536/colonial-deal-built-city-sadness*
6 'Twin Cities' stands for 'Hong Kong and Shenzhen,' and the 'Three Circles' means 'the Shenzhen Bay Quality Development Circle, the Hong Kong-Shenzhen Close Interaction Circle and the Mirs Bay/Yan Chau Tong Eco-recreation/tourism Circle.' It facilitates 'close collaboration between Hong Kong and Shenzhen in various areas such as economy, infrastructure, people's livelihood and ecological environment, so as to leverage complementary advantages and promote development integration between both cities.' 'Northern Metropolis Development Strategy Report' (Hong Kong Special Administrative Region Government, 6 October 2021).
7 During the interview the street traders and buyers expressed that the 'dawn activities' mostly took place before FEHD officers began work. Street traders would normally earn 20–30 HK dollars per day, and they would be fined a couple of hundred dollars and have their goods confiscated should they be caught. *The Sun*, 26 October 2007.
8 Long Denggao, 中國傳統市場發展史 [*The History of Chinese Traditional Markets*] (Beijing: Renmin chubanshe, 1997).

Tin Shui Wai dawn market, Hong Kong, 2022

also in many other residential areas of Hong Kong such as the more centrally located Sham Shui Po.

In 2011, the goods sold at the TSW dawn market had a greater variety than that reported in 2007. Apart from produce, grocery products, clothes, and other items were sold on the street.[9] Social workers made proposals to the government requesting time to formalise and legalise the activity but in vain. The relevant authorities had stopped issuing new licenses to 'itinerant hawkers' since the 1970s, other than a batch of new licenses given out between July 2009 and April 2012 following a review of the licensing policy. Currently, there are 430 'itinerant hawker' licenses remaining valid in Hong Kong. Under this regulatory system, it is illegal for anyone to sell goods and food on the street without obtaining a license in advance. The FEHD officers have the right to arrest, and also to confiscate and destroy the relevant goods.

In 2022, on-site observation and documentation at the TSW dawn market was conducted by the author and the research team, including interviews. Unlike the practice previously reported, it was found that the number of street traders had decreased. There was a moving pattern that reflected the operation of the traders – from near the footbridge to along the river path (6:00–7:30 am) and concluding inside Tin Shui Park (7:30–8:30 am). The sellers did so in order to avoid being charged by the authorities, and the business operating time could be extended slightly (to 8:30 am) as the park was managed by another government department, the Leisure and Cultural Services Department, whose main duty was not to catch and fine street traders. After 8:30 am, opportunities for business are less promising, and this marks the end of daily business.

In terms of transportation devices employed, many traders use trolleys, some use bicycles, and a few carry goods by hand or on shoulder at this time. In order to be able to exit as fast as possible, a trader stays under the footbridge and prepares the poultry which is sold on the bridge. After the buyer has confirmed the order with the trader's partner and paid, a basket containing the fresh poultry in a plastic

9   The TSW 'dawn market' was filmed and reported on by TVB News which revealed the diversity of goods being traded. It departed from the conventional farm produce and food to daily necessities and groceries. Buyers expressed that the goods were cheaper than those sold in shopping malls and supermarkets and helped their lives. *TVB News*, 29 May 2011.

bag is hoisted up from the river and passed to the buyer – this reflects the wisdom of the business operator under conditions of strict law enforcement.

In 2012, the Tung Wah Group of Hospitals (TWGH), a local NGO (non-governmental organisation), lobbied the government and received support to set up a market providing low-rent stalls for street traders and TSW residents to earn a living through selling everyday necessities. The idea was to provide the community with more shopping options, create employment opportunities for the disadvantaged groups, allow the street traders to have a proper place to do business, and thereby replace the informal and illegal dawn market with a regulated, domestic market, 'Tin Sau Hui.'

To ensure the market would sell an attractive and diverse selection of goods, twenty-seven 'distinctive businesses' that were claimed to 'meet the needs of the community' were identified by an advisory panel of TWGH and the corresponding goods were approved for sale in the market.[10] This list became one of the eligibility criteria to rent a stall in the market. The 'dry goods' category allowed the sale of clothes, footwear and accessories; the 'service' category included haircuts, repair services for clothing, etc. For the rest of the stalls, a points system was introduced to select the stallholders, using such criteria as 'recommended by social workers,' 'recommended by social workers and has been a street trader in the dawn market, 'low income' and 'having relevant operating experience.' For the former, each category contained a quota. For the latter, those with the highest score would be selected. In both categories, a lottery would take place should the quota be exceeded.

The 3,800-square-metre market named 'Tin Sau Hui' began operation in February 2013. It consisted of 182 cubicle-like stalls ranging from two-by-two-metres to two-by-four-metres standard footprints. Water and electricity were provided, so the conditions for trading were supposed to be better than that of the

dawn market. Sixty-seven street traders, which was about half of the overall number at the dawn market, successfully obtained a stall in the market.

Though the name contained the word Hui, which means 'can occur anywhere on the ground,' the market was regulated not only in terms of area but also in the mode of operation. For ease of management, the TWGH requested stallholders to report each type of item they were selling and any undeclared goods were prohibited from being sold. This not only eradicated the stallholders' flexibility and ability to respond to the changing needs of customers and made the type of goods sold relatively monotonous but also reduced the buyers' desire to visit the market and shop. Moreover, due to insufficient supporting facilities, the market was unable to obtain a license to sell fresh fish and meat. This caused inconvenience to those who would like or need to buy all things in one stop due to their busy daily schedule of childcare and work.

Each stall was required to be open for at least twenty days a month and four hours a day. It was reported that the terms stipulated in the rental contract were unfavourable to farmers' work schedule to grow, harvest and then sell vegetables and other farmed produce. To ensure a certain number of stalls were open, TWGH required the stallholders to sign in every two hours. Those who wanted to leave the market early had to make a request and justify this at the management office. Some stallholders reported that they refrained from going to the bathroom in order not to miss the regular check-in times. All this made businesses and lives more difficult to manage than selling things on the street in the early mornings had otherwise been.

The above, plus the market's relatively remote location, lack of appropriate indicators, lack of protection against the elements, and the absence of activities and events to attract customers caused stallholder disappointment. Realising the decline and/or absence of business opportunities, some stallholders chose to return to the dawn market while

10 The twenty-seven district businesses listed by TWGH covered vegetables, fruits, dry foods, household necessities, stationaries, computer wares, clothes, shoes, etc. See: TWGH, 'Tin Sau Hui Stalls Application Guidelines' (2012).

Sham Shui Po dawn market, Hong Kong, 2011

Tin Sau Bazaar, Hong Kong, 2022 (top and bottom)

others did both to make enough to pay rent.[11] The regulating framework was imposed on 'Tin Sau Hui' to manage the originally organic, spontaneous business modes performed by the street traders. There was obviously a discrepancy between the nature of the (trading) business and governance. After the market was changed to an open-bid format to determine the stallholders, and with more flexibility being handed over to the stall operators, it became more lively a few years later. The research team visited and studied the market a couple of times during 2022. It was found that frequent communal activities and events were organised, and with more artistic inputs (like paintings on the floor) and a flexible use of public space implemented (like extending the café area to the common corridor with sun shades), the situation was improving.[12]

CUSTOMER-ORIENTED, MONOPOLISING CHAIN-MARKET TYPOLOGY FOR CHANGING DEMOGRAPHICS

Today, TSW benefits from the fruition of public transportation infrastructure development, such as the MTR system, light railways, buses, minibuses, etc. and decent allocations of public facilities. With the addition of new high-end residential developments in recent years, TSW is progressively moving away from the title of 'city of sadness' and has characterised itself as 'a self-sufficient town with close proximity to Shenzhen.' It is now attracting increasingly more middle-class families. The demographics have changed from the first batch of older, relocated public-housing residents in the 1990s to the current ones who are more educated, younger and relatively prosperous.

In 2020 a temporary market, namely Skylight Market, was built next to Tin Sau Hui (which was once criticised for being remote) as 'a transitional arrangement to meet the local demand for additional choices in fresh food

provisions.' It would remain until the completion of the new public market planned for the section of Tin Fuk Road outside TSW MTR Station. Relatively small in scale, the Skylight Market was constructed with eighteen large and eighteen small stands with different combinations of containers where meat and produce are sold. It also adopted an open and vibrant design approach which allows for natural ventilation.

The existence and operation of the Skylight Market symbolise a new era of TSW and reflect the living style of the new generation of TSW residents. During the fieldwork in 2022, it was observed that very commonly, buyers drove their vehicles and parked temporarily along the laybys outside the market. Due to the small number of stalls and, therefore limited choices of food, buyers tended not to spend much time in wandering around the market stalls but rather performed pragmatically to buy the things they needed. With this mode of 'pragmatic shopping,' one could spend as little as ten minutes to make all purchases, put them in the trunk, and drive back home. The bargaining, exchanges and social processes, which had occurred between the buyers and sellers in the dawn market or Tin Sau Hui did not appear in this scenario. Nevertheless, the products sold there were not cheap in price – most of them were fruit, organic vegetables and quality meat imported from overseas. Locally grown produce was not found.

On the other hand, new markets operated and managed by market investors and operators such as the Links and Hong Kong Markets emerge in the vicinity. These markets would normally feature specific design themes to make them appealing and attractive. These markets are fully air-conditioned, spacious and clean, offering a variety of food, including cooked meals and pre-cut fruit to suit the customers' needs after work. They are highly regulated, usually operating in a chain market manner in different parts of the city. In order

11   This reflected that business was not good at Tin Sau Hui at all: as in the cases of Ping Tse and Mr Lui (reported in *NOW News*, 15 February 2013), though they rented stalls in Tin Sau Hui, they still had to take the goods to sell in the 'dawn market' in order to earn enough to pay the stall rent.

12   '[...] TWGH now arranges the weekly Tin Sau Weekend Market featuring arts performances and street stalls. In May 2023 TWGH organised the Music Viva Day where performances by the Hong Kong Community Philharmonic Orchestra were staged in Tin Sau Bazaar. In addition, TWGH organises pre/post-festival fairs and carnivals of different themes at Tin Sau Bazaar, and makes space available there for district organisations to stage their events. Since April 2016, for example, other large-scale events held at Tin Sau Bazaar include the South Asian Culture Experience Day, Tin Sau Hui Mother's Day Fair, Tin Sau Farmers' Market, Tin Sau Retro Flea Market, Tin Sau Magic Experience Day, Tin Sau Mid-Autumn Fair, etc. The Working Group on Building a Safe Community in Yuen Long of the Yuen Long District Council (YLDC) plans to organise the Yuen Long Health and Safety Carnival at Tin Sau Bazaar in January 2018. See: 'LCQ19: Operation and management of Tin Sau Bazaar,' (press release, HKSAR Government, 18 October 2017).

Typical infrastructural components, Tin Sau Bazaar, Hong Kong

Top: T Market, Tin Shui Wai, Hong Kong, 2022
Bottom: Skylight Market, Tin Shui Wai, Hong Kong, 2022

to impress customers, the markets usually have different themes in decoration. The grandly opened T Market in Chung Fu, TSW, features modernised Japanese-style design. The timber decorations, Japanese cooking utensils as well as the paper lanterns in T Market create a stylish, comfortable and spacious shopping ambience. The nearly seventy stands offer a diversified mix of food stalls that sell different kinds of fresh ingredients, dry goods, grocery items and cooked food. Customers enjoy the one-stop shopping experience inside the new themed market. On the other hand, Tin Shui Market was renovated in 2014 to provide an upgraded space, improved facilities and modernised services, making a synergy with Tin Shui Shopping Centre upstairs.

Despite the recent emergence of the Skylight Market and chain markets, dawn markets still prevail and operate in TSW today. The elderly enjoy buying things on the street as part of their morning exercise; some buyers like and prefer the freshness of farm produce grown in the fields nearby or the fresh chicken kept in the farms next door to frozen ones from the supermarket. The street trading business persists over time, not because of the 'artistic input' nor 'specific management style,' but the adaptive urbanism strategies, that is, the social capital that responds to the socio-economic and authoritative context. The cross-examination of the evolution of the markets' development over time in TSW informs decisions in contemporary urban governance and trade formalisation processes. The value of social capital outweighs street trading's economic capital and leads us to think of a way to achieve a symbiotic status for sustainable growth of the urbanisation process. As such, the study of market evolution leaves traces for the design of the upcoming district-wide public market at Tin Fuk Road to follow. It is with hope that the new one could be truly 'public.'

REFERENCES

Agriculture, Fisheries and Conservation Department. 'Fish Pond Culture.' The Government of the Hong Kong Special Administrative Region. https://www.afcd.gov.hk/english/index.html

Census and Statistics Department. '漁翁移山：香港本土漁業民俗誌, 張展鴻; 米埔自然保護區的經營管理; 林務局 [Fishermen Moving Mountains: A Folklore Journal of the Local Fishing Industry in Hong Kong].' Hong Kong, 1983.

Central Government People's Republic of China. 'Outline Development Plan for the Guangdong-Hong Kong-Macao Greater Bay Area.' 2019. https://www.bayarea.gov.hk/filemanager/en/share/pdf/Outline_Development_Plan.pdf

Civil Engineering and Development Department, 'Hong Kong: Facts – New Towns, New Development Areas and Urban Developments.' GovHK, 2021.

'Colonial Deal Built "City of Sadness".' South China Morning Post, 6 December 2010. https://www.scmp.com/article/732536/colonial-deal-built-city-sadness

HKSAR Government. 'LCQ19: Operation and management of Tin Sau Bazaar.' Press release, 18 October 2017.

Law, Ch., et al. 'A Study on Tin Shui Wai New Town Final Report.' University of Hong Kong, Department of Social Work and Social Administration, 2009.

Long, D. 中國傳統市場發展史 [The History of Chinese Traditional Markets]. Beijing: Renmin chubanshe, 1997.

Typical infrastructural components, Tin Shui Wai dawn market

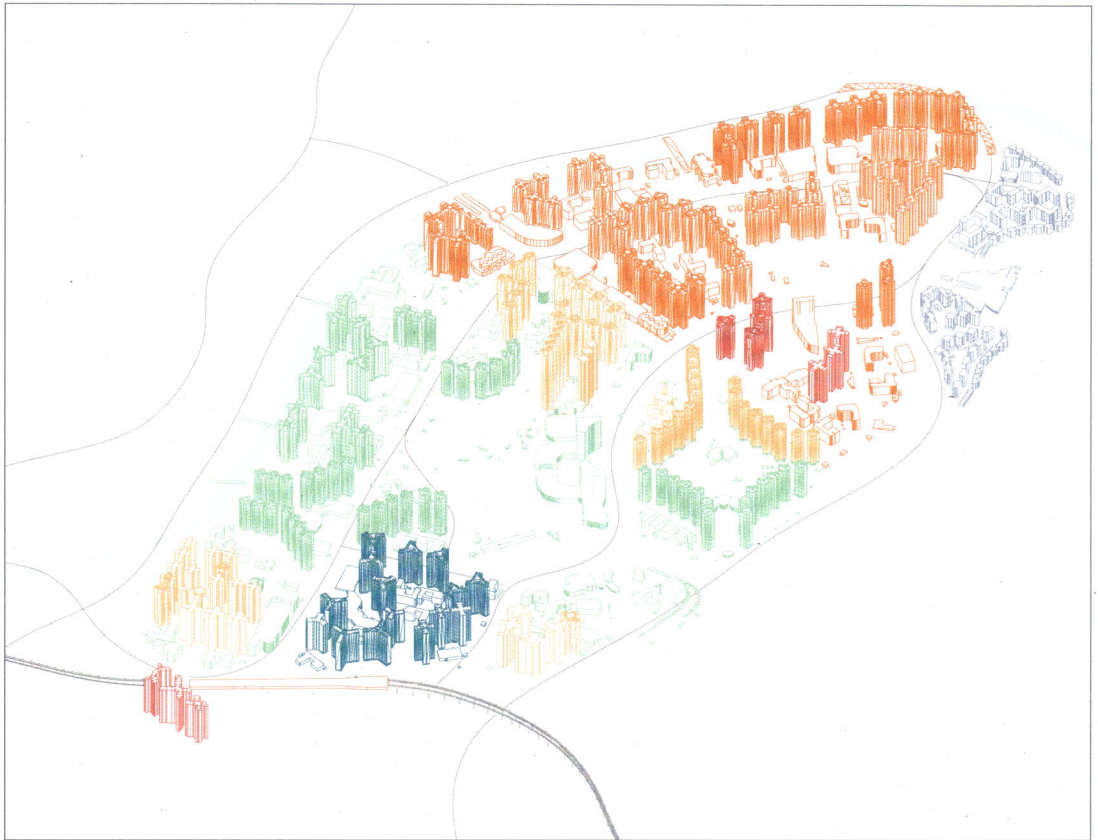

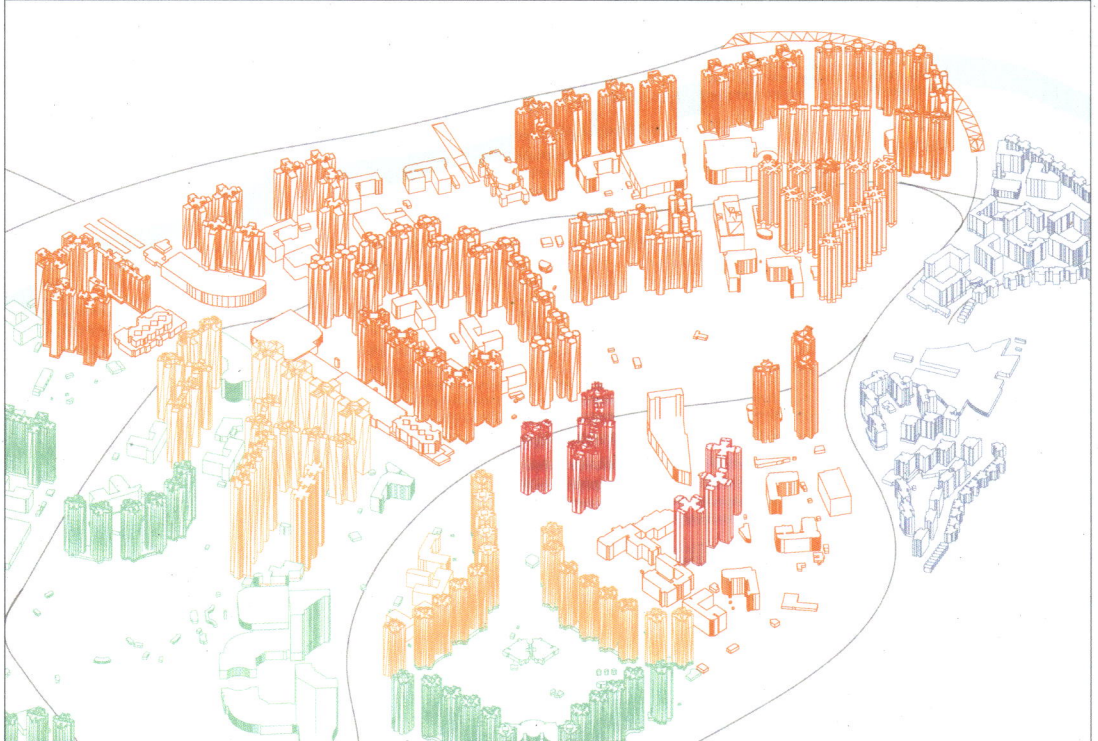

Before 1980 ■ 1985 ■ 1991 ■ 1996 ■ 2001 ■ 2006 ■ 2011 ■ 2016 ■ 2022

Tin Shui Wai neighbourhood: key phases of spatial development

1970-1990

1 1973-1974 stock market crash
2 Global energy crisis
3 50,000 licensed and as many unlicensed hawkers in Hong Kong.
4 Hong Kong's Food and Environmental Hygiene Department (FEHD) stops issuing new licenses to itinerant hawkers.
5 Closure of factories and a severe decline in the manufacturing sector in Hong Kong
6 The Hong Kong Government begins development of Tin Shui Wai (TSW), a 4.3 square kilometre satellite town in the northwestern New Territories of Hong Kong.

1990-2002

7 Informal 'dawn markets' selling different kinds of farm produce in the streets are welcomed by the TSW community, especially due to the limited transportation opportunities to and from TSW and relatively low income levels of the residents.
8 Boost in the population of Tin Shui Wai due to the rapid construction of large housing estates.
9 A programme lasting for five years is introduced, urging itinerant hawkers to willingly give up their licenses. In return, they are offered various incentives, including a single, one-time ex gratia payment, the option to rent an empty stall in public markets under favourable terms, or the opportunity to become a fixed pitch hawker selling non-cooked food. As a result of this initiative, there is a significant reduction in the number of licensed hawkers.

2002-2012

10 Sharp decrease in the number of hawkers – 4,000 unlicensed hawkers and about 6,000 licensed hawkers in Hong Kong
11 The number of unlicensed hawkers in Hong Kong drops to 2,000.
12 A batch of new licenses is issued after a review of the hawker licensing policy is implemented.

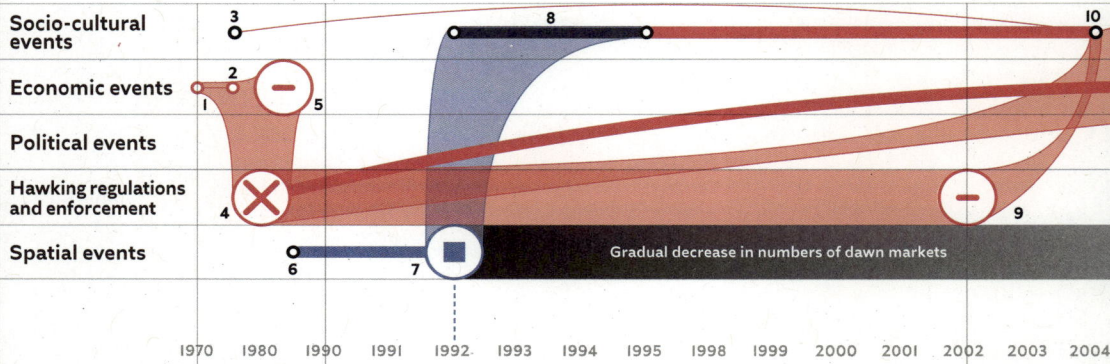

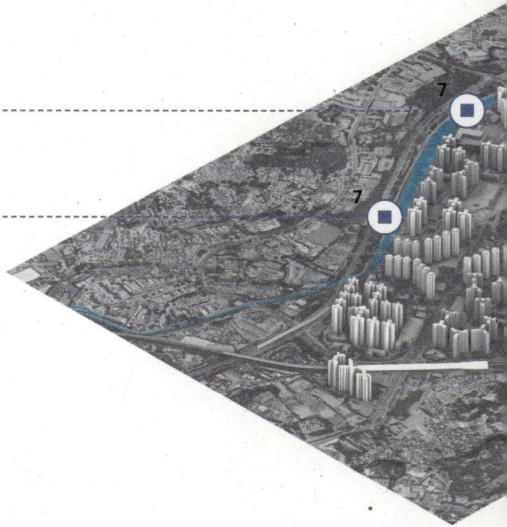

Socio-cultural events

Economic events

Political events

Hawking regulations and enforcement

Spatial events

Gradual decrease in numbers of dawn markets

1970 1980 1990 1991 1992 1993 1994 1995 1998 1999 2000 2001 2002 2003 2004

Timeline of key events shaping the transformation of Tin Shui Wai dawn market, Hong Kong; map data: Google, imagery date: 10/7/22-newer, Maxar Technologies

2012-2015

13 The Tung Wah Group of Hospitals (TWGH), a non-profit local Non-Government Organization (NGO), puts forward a proposal to the government to establish a market that would offer affordable rental stalls for street traders and TSW residents. This initiative would enable them to earn a livelihood by selling daily food, groceries, and other goods. The primary goals of this plan are described as to increase shopping options for the community, to generate employment opportunities for disadvantaged groups, to provide street traders with legitimate and proper stalls for conducting business, and ultimately to replace the informal 'dawn' markets.

14 The Hong Kong government offers lump sums of 120,000 HK dollars to hawkers who are willing to surrender their licenses. More than 310 licenses are forfeited in one year.

15 The 'Tin Sau Hui' market, occupying an area of 3,800 square metres, commences its operations. It comprises 182 cubicle-like stalls with varying standard footprints ranging from 2m x 2m to 2m x 4m. The market is equipped with water and electricity and aims to provide better business conditions compared to the 'dawn markets'. Notably, 67 street traders, approximately half of the total number present in the TSW's dawn markets, are able to secure a stall in the newly established Tin Sau Hui Market.

16 The Hong Kong Government implements an assistance scheme in 43 fixed-pitch hawker areas starting June 2013 to reduce the fire risks and enhance the operating environment of the hawker areas.

17 Start of temporary district-led bazaars

2015-2023

18 5,911 hawkers hold fixed-pitch or itinerant hawker licenses as of the end of December 2016; the number of unlicensed hawkers continues to decrease.

19 The Hong Kong Government announces its intention to build sizable public markets in new development areas and initially identifies suitable sites in the Tung Chung New Town Extension Area and Hung Shui Kiu New Development Area.

20 A temporary market, called Skylight Market, is built next to 'Tin Shau Hui' (once criticised as being too remote) as a transitional arrangement to meet the local demand for additional choices of fresh food.

21 There are 4,168 convictions of unlicensed hawker or hawker-related offenses in 2021.

22 About 1,200 unlicensed hawkers in Hong Kong

2007 2008 2009 2010 2011 2012 2013 2014 2015 2016 2017 2018 2019 2020 2021 2022 2023

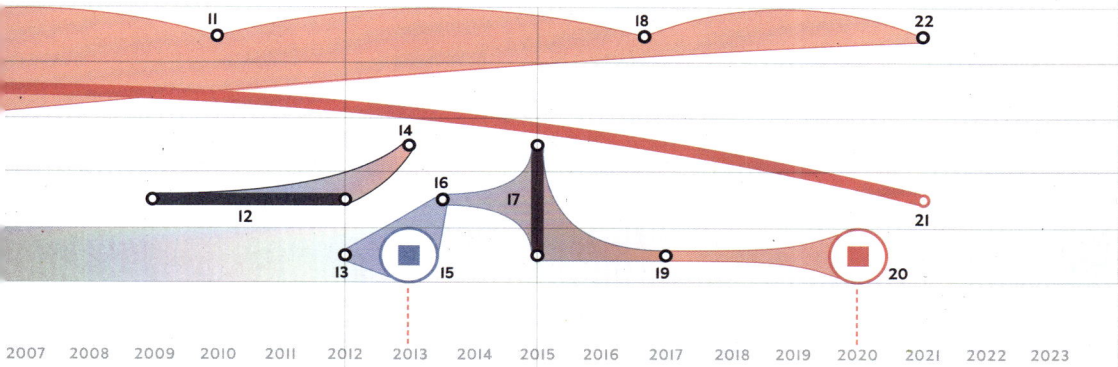

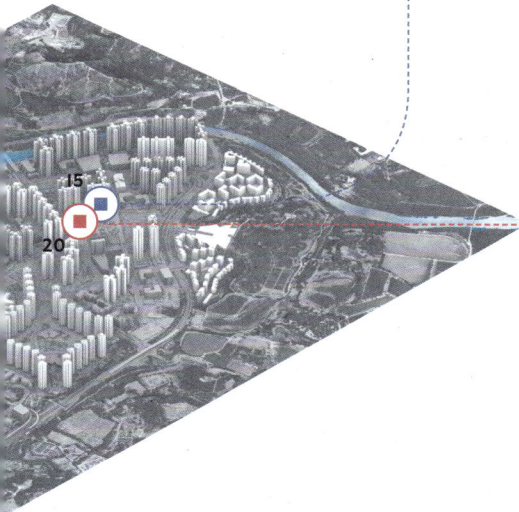

■ Spatial, social, economic and political interventions into in/formal markets
■ Informality as a survival method and means of adapting to changing socio-economic and political circumstances

6.00 am:
setting up

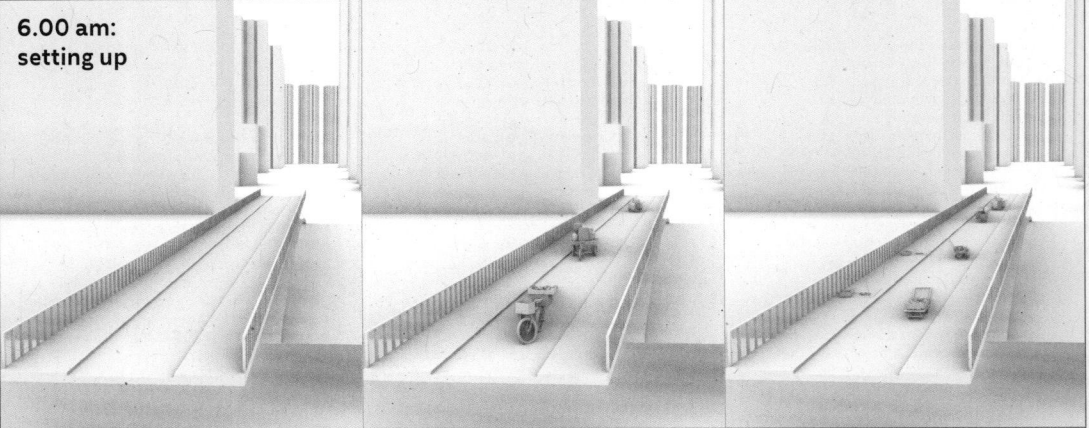

6.30 am - 8.00 am:
vending

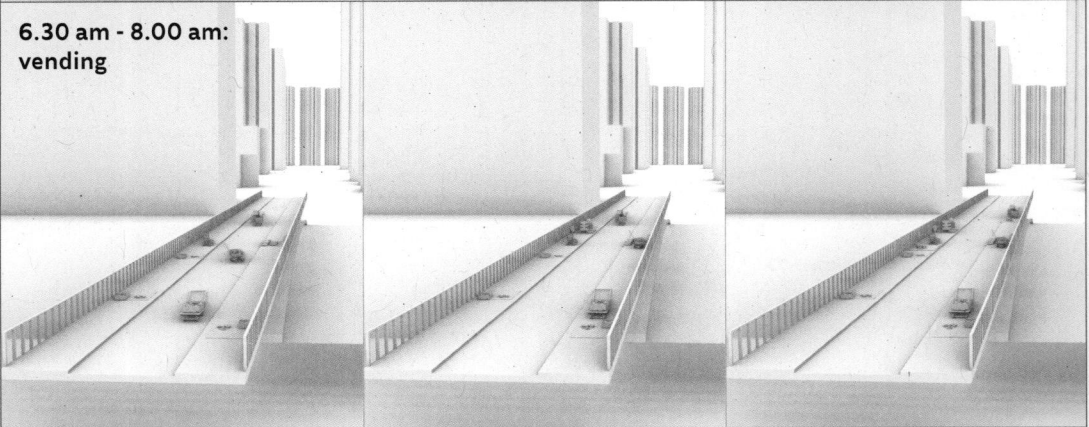

8.00 am:
relocating

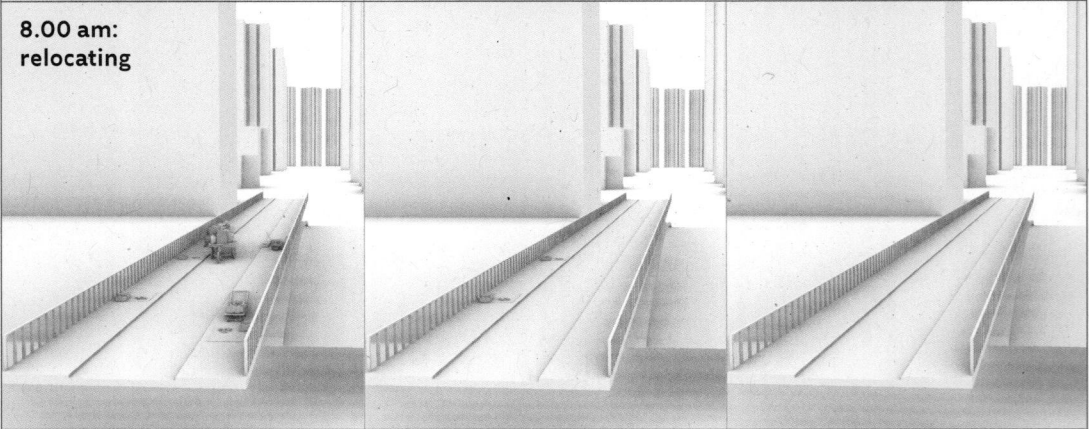

Time-based relocation

Blankets

Crates and bags

Trolleys

Transport vehicles

Trading devices, Tin Shui Wai dawn market, Hong Kong

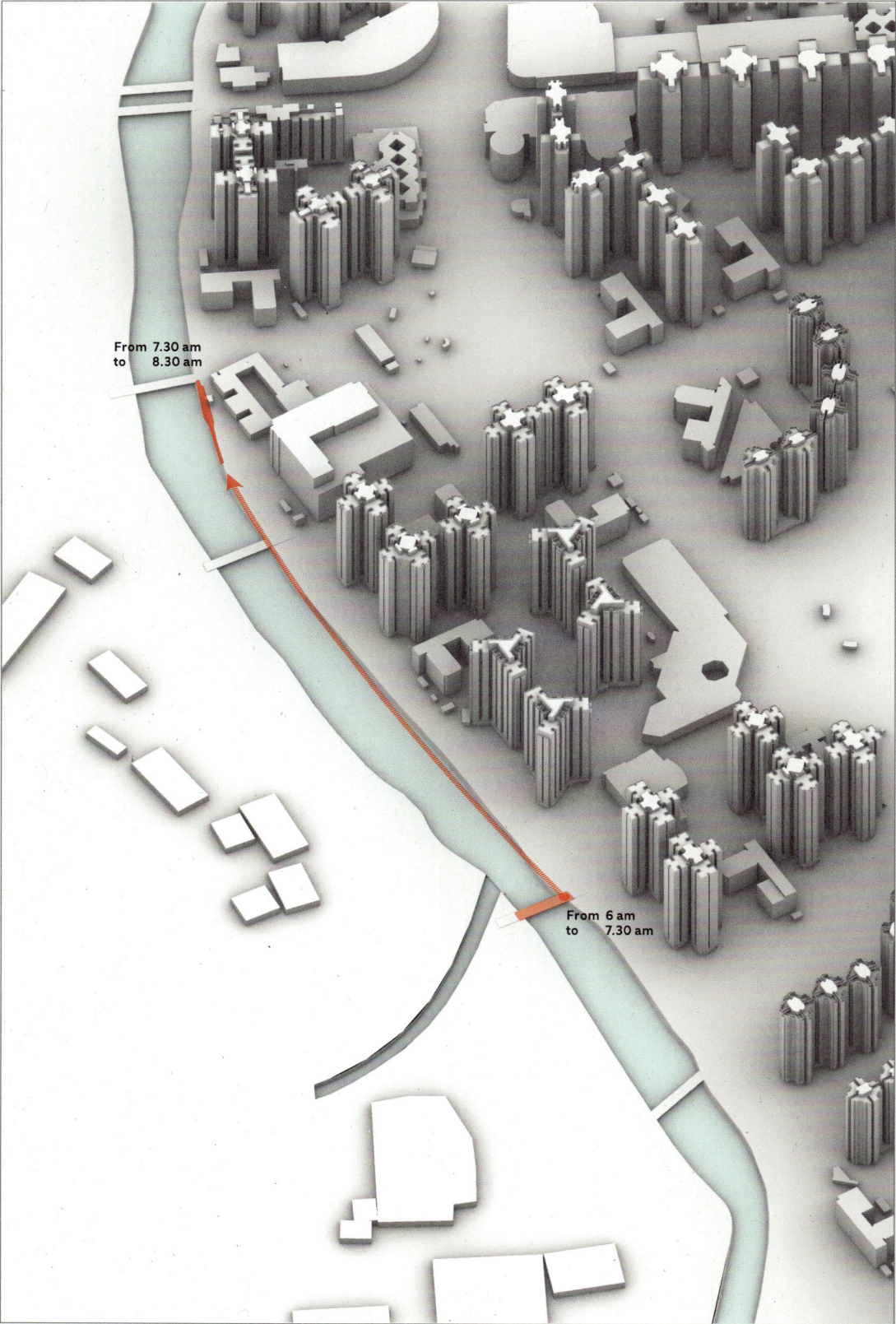

From 7.30 am
to 8.30 am

From 6 am
to 7.30 am

Vendors at Tin Shui Wai dawn market relocate as dawn breaks

Tin Heng Stop
Wetland Park Stop
Tin Sau Stop
Tin Yat Stop
Tin Sau Bazaar
Skylight Market
Tin Fu Stop
Tin Yuet Stop
T Market
Chung Fu Stop
Chestwood Stop
Tin Wing Stop
Ginza Stop
Tin Shui Market
Tin Shui Stop
Tin Wu Stop
Locwood Stop
Tin Tsz Stop
Tin Yiu Stop
Tin Shui Wai Market
Tin Shui Wai MTR Station

Sha Kong Wai

Dawn Market

Lo Uk Tsuen

Ha Tsuen Shi

295

Villages   Informal market   Regulated market   Semi-controlled market   Light Rail Station

Urban layout of Tin Shui Wai and locations of markets

Tin Shui Wai Nullah

Tin Shui Path

Car park

Tin Chak Market

Tin Shui Road

Car park

Tin Yat

Wetland Park

Light Rail

Wetland Park Rd

Tin Sau Bazaar

Tin Sau

Tin Sau Road

Tin Fu

Tin Yuet

Shopping mall T Town North

T Town South

Tin Sau Bazaar surrounded by major traffic arteries

Floor marking for retractable marquee holiday stalls

■ Dry Goods Zone
Prefabricated cabins
■ Services/Gifts Zone
Prefabricated cabins
■ Wet Goods Zone
Prefabricated cabins
■ Refreshment/Special Stalls Zone

Tung Wah Group of Hospitals Management Principles:

1. Non-profit-making
2. Set up a social enterprise which will lease the stalls in the bazaar at lower rents to small businesses for selling daily necessities
3. Encourage the self-reliance of the underprivileged
4. 30 stalls to be allocated to organisation applicants and about 160 stalls to be allocated to individual applicants

Spatial layout of Tin Sau Bazaar, Tin Shui Wai, Hong Kong

Tin Sau Bazaar, Hong Kong, 2022

Encants Vells, Barcelona, 2023

Carmen Lael Hines

The Urbanisation of 'Exchange' in Barcelona

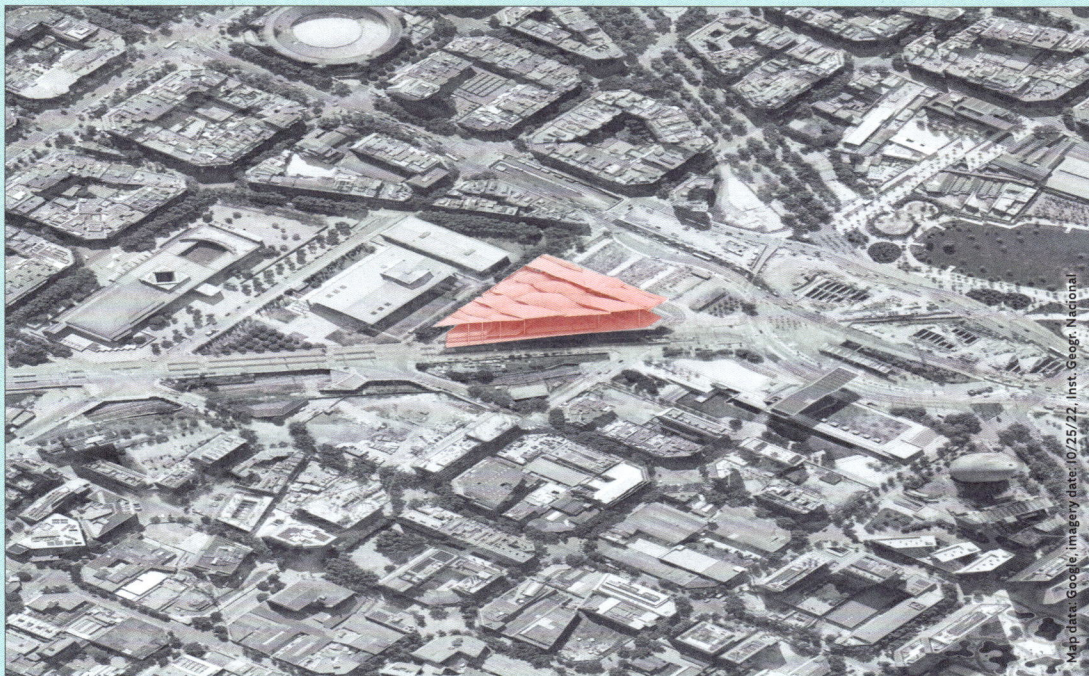

Map data: Google, imagery date: 10/25/22, Inst. Geogr. Nacional

Barcelona's Encants Vells (meaning 'old shouting' or 'singing'), officially named Mercat Fira de Bellcaire, is one of the longest-running markets on the European continent. Evidence indicates that as early as the mid-thirteenth century, vendors congregated at the gates of Barcelona's Roman city walls: bartering, exchanging goods, and conversing with one another, hence the name Encants Vells, 'old shouting.'[1] It is possible that from these activities emerged the word used for auction in Spanish: *subhasta*. This is because goods were placed on the ground under a flagpole flying a banner, literally 'under the flagpole' (*sub asta*), thus forming the word for auction in the Spanish language.[2] Indeed, mutually informing linkages between space, exchange and communication continue to define Encants to the present day.

1   Rosa Martell et al., *Encants I La Fira De Bellcaire – Imatge I Història De Barcelona* (Barcelona: Ajuntament de Barcelona, 2014), 9.
2   'History,' Mercat dels Encants, *https://encantsbarcelona.com/en/history/*

The new Encants Vells market structure is part of a series of spectacular architectures embodying the transformation of Plaça de les Glòries Catalanes from industrial periphery to a new cultural, economic and touristic axis of Barcelona.

A key feature of the new indoor/outdoor hybrid market opened in 2013 is its floating roof structure. The ensuing protection from sun and rain was a major selling point in the relocation campaign.

Fixed market stalls line ramps that wrap like a Moebius strip around a sunken atrium. This open area is used for morning auctions that hark back to the origins of Encants Vells in the Middle Ages.

The market stall design ranges from roll-top closets fronted by fixed tables to walk-in shops.

Even though its location has changed on numerous occasions over the past seven centuries, certain defining features remain, such as the placing of second-hand goods directly on the ground. More than a specific structure, Encants is often described as an *emotional landscape* maintained through close personal dialogue, ties, and trust between vendors and participants.[3] Over the course of several interviews with Encants patrons and vendors, there was a recurring consensus that the core community of *Encantistas* is small and insular. *Encantistas* are those who regularly participate in the exchange of objects from the tri-weekly influx of surplus commodities, usually originating from the home of someone recently deceased or surplus stock from a factory or warehouse.[4] Nacho Abad, for instance, is a human-rights lawyer and one of the Encants regulars who attend the auction early Monday, Wednesday, or Friday mornings to source vintage technological objects, like radios, watches, or electric instruments.

On the one hand, Encants acts as a symbol or spectacle for the culture of Barcelona, suggested to international visitors in guidebooks and 'must-do' lists since the 1990s.[5] At the same time, the market's operations remain localised, obscured, and built through the shared bonds of those who have participated for decades, if not generations. It is a market that, emerging from its urban fabric, becomes a concrete manifestation of the local, global, and 'glocal' economic circuits shaping that fabric. As a transhistorical organism mediating various scales, Encants has extraordinary significance in how we understand the many interests shaping the urbanisation of Barcelona from the thirteenth century to the present day. The market's characteristic linking of exchange, space, and communicative media make it a nodal point for analysis of the urbanisation of 'exchange,' or the spatialisation of economy, and importantly – how these processes are *communicated* to align with broader intentions of city-planning in Barcelona.

A BRIEF HISTORY OF ENCANTS AS ORGANISM

It is important to note that Encants as an activity has had a series of parts with diverging locations and temporal logics, causing some confusion about how we define it and trace its movement. A seemingly synonymous term for Encants is the Fira del Bellcaire. In a private diary on 24 January 1816, referring to the Fira del Bellcaire, the governor of the city of Barcelona wrote: 'It is truly a fair or market that, introduced during the occupation of this city by the enemy armies, has continued afterwards without any authority.' This statement refers to the foreign character of the market, which in the governor's opinion, was a product of the plundering by the invading French army of 1808, Napoleon's army.[6] The market's association with foreign cultures, with many vendors originating from areas beyond Spain, such as North Africa, continues today.

From the arrival of the French in 1808–1816, evidence shows that the Fira del Bellcaire was located on las Ramblas de Barcelona, extending from Palacio Moja to the barracks of Estudis. After several prohibitions by the Barcelona authorities, in 1822, what was described as 'the exchange of old clothes and other items' was moved to the Paseo de la Explanada, located between El Born and the convent of Sant Agustí Vell. Finally, in 1835 a *part* of the Fira del Bellcaire was moved to the so-called Voltas dels Encants, next to the Carrer del Consolat del Mar. This relocation is credited with causing the confusion between Els Encants and Fira del Bellcaire that persists until today.[7] What distinguished these markets from one another were the days they occurred and certain prejudices attached to the quality of the goods sold. The Fira de Bellcaire was held only on Sundays, while Els Encants had three days of operation: Monday, Wednesday, and Friday. The Fira de Bellcaire, was described as 'traperos de carretón' (rag-and-bone), while Encants claimed a 'higher' quality selection of goods. In 1888 both

3   Rosa Cerarols Ramirez, 'Els Encants, Barcelona,' in *Informal Market Worlds: The Architecture of Economic Pressure - Atlas*, eds. Peter Mörtenböck and Helge Moosshammer (Rotterdam: naiO10 publishers, 2015), 466.
4   Nacho Abad, human rights lawyer and regular Encants participant in conversation with the author, February 2023; Jaume Benavent Bosch, architect and Encants participant in conversation with the author, March 2023.
5   Guidebooks found in Archivo Histórico de la Ciudad de Barcelona; *Barcelona Sales Guide 1989/1990* (Barcelona: Ajuntament de Barcelona, 1989).
6   Manuel Guardia, 'Els Encants i La Fira de Bellcaire: una mirada des de la historia urbana,' in *Encants I La Fira De Bellcaire – Imatge I Història De Barcelona* (Barcelona: Ajuntament de Barcelona, 2014).
7   Guardia, 'Els Encants i La Fira de Bellcaire,' 8–23.

Encants Vells, Barcelona, at its former site, 2011

markets were brought together in one place. The result was the merging of these market activities into one organism – which explains the dual nature of the market.

The market, now a mix of Fira de Bellcaire and Els Encants, was forcibly moved to make space for the Universal Exposition of 1888, with its new location on the Avinguda de Mistral, where the Sant Antoni market stands today. In anticipation of the 1929 International Exposition, it was once again transplanted outside the city centre to Plaça de les Glòries Catalanes, an industrial area on the periphery of Barcelona. This movement was another effort to extradite the 'traperos de carretón,' and its association with ruggedness, informality and chaotic relations away from the urban centre. At this time, Encants was a controversial force, an object of both prejudice and pride. In a satirical novel published in 1844, titled *Encyclopaedia of Vulgar Costumes and Types of Barcelona* (my translation) Encants was satirised for the randomness and quantity of objects sold and

the yelling of the vendors. The author lists the objects sold for an entire page, including items such as 'trips,' 'tickets,' 'syringes,' 'pulleys,' 'pigs,' and 'hats of human hair.'[8] Encants emerges as a product of various kinds of negotiation relating to what *is* or *is not* the 'actual' Encants and whether these defining features can occur in decided locations.

Encants' new peripheral location after 1929 was between Plaça de les Glòries Catalanes and Camp del Sidral del Clot (on the mountainside, between Castillejos and Dos de Maig).[9] It remained there for over eighty years. In 2013, it was transferred to a new location next door, also in les Glòries, at the square on the Avinguda Meridiana. In the past, the forced relocations of Encants were motivated by the need to 'make way' for something else, to displace the 'undesirable' activities of Encants to the edges of the city. But the recent movement of Encants takes on a different character. Les Glòries has transformed over the past eighty years from an industrial area on the periphery

8   Book found in the Archivo Histórico de la Ciudad de Barcelona; Don Jose Maria de Freixas, *Enciplopedia de tipos vulgares y costumbres de Barcelona* (Barcelona: Joaquin Bosch, 1844).
9   Guardia, 'Els Encants i La Fira de Bellcaire,' 9.

Former site of Encants Vells, Barcelona, after demolition, 2013

to a 'new cultural, social and touristic axis of Barcelona.'[10] In 2013, Encants was thus moved into a slick, new location at the centre of Glòries. This centralisation of Encants into a monumental market site at the most nodal point Glòries raises questions about the role of market activities in the changing landscape of Barcelona's (relatively) peripheral zones. Reflecting upon this centralisation, a crucial point is that this was in combination with the systemic dislocation of *some* vendors, described in local media as 'misery markets' or unlicensed vendors selling 'low-quality' goods.[11] In incorporating Encants into the evolving urban fabric of Glòries and its specific political economy, some facets and fissures of Encants were given priority over others.

However, the recent spectacularisation and consolidation of Encants as market activity has not been total but a curated selection of some of its preferred parts. Like its recently designed kaleidoscopic roof, Encants can be understood in different ways depending on your perspective. From the inside, Encants does not feel like a building, but an infrastructure, oriented towards the act of looking. From the outside, it looks like a monument.

ENCANTS AND THE PLATFORM CITY

Encants indicates the many ways that the city of Barcelona approaches its own urban identity through the kaleidoscope of the mobile. In many ways, Encants exists in relation to multiple circuits of the mobile. Its history indicates an ongoing relationship to the major expository platforms occurring within the city fabric, such as the Expositions of 1888 and 1929. As has been described, in the past, these instances of international networking expropriated Encants because its features did not align with the circuits afforded by these platforms.[12] Today, *certain* aspects of Encants are placed at the centre of these efforts towards international networking. Parts or fragments of Encants as activity and experi-

10   Ramirez, 'Els Encants, Barcelona,' 466.
11   Carlos Rufas, 'el mercado de la miseria de las glories crece sin parar,' *Metropolia Abierta*, 9 March 2019, *https://metropoliabierta.elespanol.com/distritos/sant-marti/el-mercado-de-la-miseria-de-las-glories-crece-sin-parar_14775_102.html*
12   M. Pirretas, *Inconveniencias y perjuicios que los Encantes y el Rastro causan al Comercio al detall en particular y a Barcelona en general, Conferencia en la Liga de Defensa Industrial y Comercial de Barcelona* (Barcelona, 1895). Quoted in: Manuel Guàrdia and José Luis Oyón, *Making Cities through Market Halls: Europe, 19th and 20th Centuries* (Ajuntament de Barcelona: Museu D'Historia de Barcelona, 2015).

ence may no longer be perceived as interrupting architectures of international exchange, but useful to them.

To explain this, it is important to briefly mention the city of Barcelona's relationship to platformisation. Throughout its history, Barcelona was an industrial port city. The hosting of the 1992 summer olympics became a critical turning point to a touristic axis on the international stage. Indeed, Barcelona became what can be referred to as a 'platform city,' a city that in creating conditions for the hosting of platforms is rendered into a kind of platform itself.[13] As explained in an interview with urban historian and theorist Eduardo Gonzalez De Molina, the tourist-ification of Barcelona after the 1992 Olympics certainly brought Barcelona onto the international stage as a 'destination,' furthered by the construction of a beach. However, this tourist-oriented economy led to the creation of precarious, low-paid, and seasonal jobs. In response to the economic crises of the early 2000s, the city of Barcelona developed multiple strategies to address this economic precarity, one of them being a movement toward a 'digital economy' of 'digital humanism' to attempt to create 'higher-paid' employment opportunities in keeping with the identity Barcelona's administration had formed for the city, as a 'destination' for international visitors. This has led to the growing platform urbanisation of Barcelona, epitomised, amongst other examples, by the city hosting of the Mobile World Congress each year.[14]

Sant Martí, and Plaça de les Glòries Catalanes in particular, is an area of Barcelona that profoundly indicates the spatial implications of the movements towards a digital economy. In 2008, the BIMSA announced the demolition and regeneration of the les Glòries square.[15] As part of this, the city council announced a European-wide competition for the construction of a new market complex for Encants in the area of Glòries, which could be permanent. The proposal by Barcelona-based b720 Fermin Vasquez Architects was chosen as the winning design, and in 2013, the market was moved to its new location, also in Glòries at the recently redeveloped square on the Avinguda Meridiana, one of Barcelona's main entrance roads.[16] Once again, this newly constructed market complex was part and parcel of the urban programme to redevelop the entirety of Poblenou, the area which includes les Glòries, from an area oriented around a primarily industrial to a post-industrial economy, epitomised through programmes such as 22@, one of the first 'smart urbanism' initiatives in Europe. The construction of the market complex for Encants was one of many architectural programmes designed to 'transform' Poblenou into a nodal point for the 'new' urban economy of Barcelona, predicated on platform urbanisation.[17] Platform urbanism, or the spatialisation of the digital economy, is the process by which a city orients itself around Web 4.0 by creating the conditions necessary for the residence of platform-related economies, such as tech companies, and in turn, is rendered into a kind of platform in itself (or perhaps vice versa).[18] As of 2018, Barcelona was estimated to be the third highest city for Airbnb rentals, behind London and Paris. With a population of around 1.8 million, Barcelona is less than a quarter the size of London.[19]

As described by urban theorist Manuel Castells, the wider area of Poblenou (which includes Glòries), meaning 'new town,' is the area of Barcelona that most poignantly expresses the city-wide platformisation programme, enacted through investment in infrastructure, public housing, *shared* cultural space, and *smart urbanism*, which intends to build upon the area's industrial heritage while, in most cases, simply replacing it. Importantly, these platform initiatives have not been party specific. They have transferred and floated across the political leanings of parties with diverging policy perspectives.

13   See: Peter Mörtenböck and Helge Mooshammer, 'Platform Urbanism and Its Discontents,' in *Platform Urbanism and Its Discontents*, eds. Peter Mörtenböck and Helge Mooshammer (Rotterdam: nai010 publishers, 2021).
14   Eduardo Gonzalez de Molina in conversation with the author 27 February 2023. See also: Manuel Castells, 'Prologo,' in *Luces y Sombras del Urbanismo de Barcelona*, 2nd edition, ed. Jordi Borja (Barcelona: Editorial UOC, 2010).
15   'Inici de la Desconstrucció del Tambor de la Plaça de les glories,' *BIM/SA*, 10 July 2008, *https://www.bimsa.cat/noticia/inici-de-la-deconstrucciodel-tambor-de-la-placa-de-les-glories/*
16   'Encants Market Barcelona,' *Arquitectura Viva*, *https://arquitecturaviva.com/works/encants-market*
17   Borja, ed., *Luces y Sombras del Urbanismo de Barcelona*, 101–105.
18   See: Niccolo Cuppini, 'On Platforming. Notes for Navigating Contemporary Hyper-Urbanscapes,' *Platform Austria* (blog), February 2021, *https://www.platform-austria.org/en/blog/on-platforming-notes-for-navigating-contemporary-hyper-urbanscapes*
19   Harel Richavia, 'Statistical Overview of Barcelona's Airbnb Market,' *Medium*, 14 August 2018, *https://towardsdatascience.com/statistical-overview-of-barcelonas-airbnb-market-83dc7d6be648*

Top: Encants Vells, Barcelona, at its former site, 2011
Bottom: Former site of Encants Vells, Barcelona, 2022

As described by Gonzalez de Molina, some of these parties have been more capital-oriented. In contrast, others have been more labour-oriented, making urban initiatives something that fluctuates on the hinge of this moving, ideological axis.

The current city government, Barcelona en Comú (Barcelona in Common), led by Ada Colau, has adopted more labour-oriented planning without radically shifting from the initiatives of its more capital-oriented past. 'It is the adoption of the best parts of the past and their incorporation into new frameworks based on new phenomena,' explains Gonzalez de Molina. The urban economy of Barcelona is one of continuation – programmes float across the boundaries of ideological intention, re-purposed or re-packaged depending upon their framing.

Examining the area immediately around Els Encants becomes a spatial essay on the various negotiations, transitions, and practices of framing that define the Barcelona city economy. A thirty-minute stroll around the market proper indicates its positioning between these folded, framed economies. Indeed, like other urban practices and initiatives, the transformation of Encants was not conceived by Colau's government but incorporated into it after the plans had already been drawn. Again, the area of Les Glories reads almost like a diary on urban-economic transition and transference.

As of May 2023, the Avenida Diagonal, connecting the neighbourhoods of Sant Marti to les Glòries, shows signs of the speculative *Superblock Barcelona*, an initiative which intends to create a network of green hubs and squares across the central axis points of Barcelona with the 'aim of reclaiming for citizens part of the space currently occupied by private vehicles.'[20] This superblock will cross through 22@, an initiative indicative of the more capital oriented politics of the parties proceeding Barcelona en Comú. The 22@ district results from an ambitious government initiative first introduced in 2000 with the intention of making Barcelona a hub for innovative technology companies. Designed to 'create new employment, housing and live-work spaces through a series of knowledge-intensive clusters: Information and Computer Technology, Media, Bio-Medical, Energy, and Design,' the 22@ district is the urbanisation of the 'glocal' – the bringing together of international and local economies through both formal and informal networks.[21] 22@ has crystallised spatially in Sant Marti and Poblenou, where the superblock continues to be under construction. Nestled between these framings, the city government has invested in the re-development of historical, local markets in both of these areas, the food market of Sant Antoni and the market of Encants Vells.

Directly aligning with the intentions behind the transformation of Poblenou, b720 Fermin Vasquez Architects' market complex was built with the intention to both 'preserve' the century-old character and feeling of Encants while adapting to the changes in the surrounding area, actively becoming 'a *mediating device* between the revived square (of Plaça de les Glòries Catalanes), its built-up environs and Avinguda Meridiana.'[22] As a nodal point in the platform urbanisation of 'glocality,' the design of this market complex shows that intentions oriented around serving local inhabitants and that of the global platform economy are enmeshed into a hybrid structure. The localised sociality of Encants is directed to serve both ends. Encants functions as a kind of *boundary object*, which can traverse and appeal to multiple interests and economies simultaneously through specific positionings. Encants, as a market organism, compiles components that can carry different meanings and serve contradictory functions depending upon their framing and filters. This fluidity is not isolated within Encants as *a device* but speaks to the broader urban political economy of Barcelona, which is conceived in and through a process of transfer, framing, and boundary objects – which mediate state, society, and private interests into a planned, multi-faceted assemblage with overlapping trajectories.

20 'Superilles,' Ajuntament de Barcelona, *https://ajuntament.barcelona.cat/superilles/en/*
21 ECPA Urban Planning, 'Case Study: 22@ Barcelona Innovation District,' Smart Cities Dive, *https://www.smartcitiesdive.com/ex/sustainablecitiescollective/case-study-22-barcelona-innovation-district/276011/*
22 'Encants Market,' b720 Fermín Vázquez Arquitectos, *https://b720.com/*

In their 1989 publication, Susan Leigh Star and James R. Griesemer coined the term boundary object. Boundary objects are 'elements that embody a stable core meaning, but can be appropriated by different groups for different ends.'[23] Coming from the fields of sociology, technology, and science studies, a boundary object is described as 'any object that is part of multiple social worlds and facilitates communication between them; it has a different identity in each social world that it inhabits. As a result, a boundary object must be simultaneously concrete and abstract, simultaneously fluid and well-defined.'[24] In broad terms, boundary objects are liminal zones where the concrete becomes plastic. They may carry a consistent set of associations and aesthetics, which can be transported between different social contexts. In these contexts, the implications of these associations may change while 'appearing' the same. As a concept, it traces how *something*, whether an object, architecture, or set of characteristics, can be instrumentalised for interests detached from those in which they are conceived. Comparable to Laclau's idea of the floating signifier, boundary objects allow for the 'contact and transmission between otherwise incompatible spheres.'[25] While a floating signifier is a linguistic sign that points to no actual object, thus enabling it to have different meanings in different contexts, boundary objects instead are so concrete in their meanings that they can be appropriated, instrumentalised, and applied to different contexts.[26] Like a floating signifier, they interrogate how we consider framing, orientation, and transference as dictators of how space is produced. The crucial question becomes under what conditions these mobilities are configured. Or rather, what interests are dictating what *things* float from one context to another.

The architecture of Encants, historically and today, indicates the role of informal or spontaneous markets in the complex transmissions between social worlds. Indeed,

Encants carries a set of consistent, concrete characteristics that can be utilised (or instrumentalised) in different scenarios, contexts, and interests for various means, including its predication on exchange, sociality, transference of second-hand objects, and elusive operational logistics. As a kind of boundary object in itself – Encants is indicative of how the cultures of informality are deployable tools in the complex linkages between state, society, and private interests.

In the first essay of the *Informal Market Worlds* reader, Helge Mooshammer crucially establishes the connection between informal markets and boundary objects. In his essay, Mooshammer argues that labelling something as informal is a matter of projection. 'The parameters of informality are not a given but a matter of definition, that the value systems attached to the informal are thus an issue of framing and perspective, of interest and intention.'[27] His analysis shows that the very fact of an *informal* or *spontaneous* market is a product of framing. The informal market mechanism emerges in and from the economic, territorial, and ideological frameworks that procure its status of 'informal' as such. As organisms founded in and through interests, informal markets become, to use the Foucauldian term, 'heterotopias' where different interests and value systems collide, conflict, and take on varied forms.[28] 'The very fact of informality is the establishing of referential frameworks attuned to the ideologies of competing interests; in essence, what Mooshammer shows is that a market is formed in and through a reverberation of many different forms of exchange and value production which may be informed by divergent ideologies. He writes: 'An essential characteristic of market protocols is their capacity to enable contact and transmission between otherwise often incompatible spheres, either through regimes of externalisation, or he employment of boundary objects that can move between different realms of meaning.'[29]

23   This definition is provided by Helge Mooshammer, as a footnote in the chapter 'Other Markets: Sites and Processes of Economic Pressure,' in *Informal Market Worlds: The Architecture of Economic Pressure - Reader*, eds. Peter Mörtenböck and Helge Mooshammer (Rotterdam: nai010 publishers, 2015), 30.
24   Susan Star and James Griesemer, 'Institutional Ecology, "Translations" and Boundary Objects: Amateurs and Professionals in Berkeley's Museum of Vertebrate Zoology, 1907–39,' *Social Studies of Science, 19, no. 3 (1989)*: 387–420.
25   Mooshammer, 'Other Markets,' 18.
26   For more detailed description of the floating signifier and its relevance to political thinking, see: Ernesto Laclau, *On Populist Reason* (New York: Verso, 2005).
27   Mörtenböck and Mooshammer, 'Introduction,' *Informal Market Worlds Reader*, 9.
28   Mooshammer, 'Other Markets,' 17.
29   Mooshammer, 'Other Markets,' 18.

Encants, and its comprising features, can have different meanings and serve conflicting interests, depending on their framing. Aligning with Mooshammer's seminal analysis, Encants is not detached from the boundary objects it 'employs' but becomes a kind of boundary object itself. Through this, Encants connects to economies beyond just the direct exchange of second-hand goods on the market floor, but the economies of platformisation, speculation, and policy-shape-shifting that circumvent the market space.

Boundary objects can be approached not as a fact but as a methodology or 'epistemic viewpoint.' This takes cues from Sandro Mezzadra and Brett Neilson's 2013 text: *Border as Method*. In this text, the authors propose a new methodology for making sense of globalisation and the multiplicity of labour on different geographical scales. Using metaphors of 'flow' and 'hop,' Mezzadra and Neilson propose 'border thinking' as an epistemic viewpoint for describing 'the very *production* of the deep heterogeneity of global space and time.' In their words, the border is not fact, but instead: 'Abstract methodology that can be detached from its material contexts and generally applied across any number of empirical situations.'[30] The notion of the 'boundary object' as proposed by Leigh and Greseimer, becomes a methodology for looking at the ways that Encants is imbricated in several conflicting, socio-economic formations.

ENCANTS FOR HIRE

A defining feature of Encants is that it does not occur daily but every Monday, Wednesday, Friday, and Saturday (excluding public holidays). On Sunday, 25 September 2022, during the citywide celebrations of La Mercè, the patron saint of Barcelona, there was activity in the Encants market complex on Avenida Meridiana. The market was closed the previous day (Saturday) because of the public holiday. Though Sunday was also an official holiday, market activities occurred inside the site of Encants – not despite, but because of these celebrations.

The century-old festivals for La Mercè are citywide days of celebration, where spaces throughout the city are transformed into sites for live music, drinks, and gastronomy. The festivals of La Mercè create a different kind of rhythm and temporality in the city. Most offices and businesses are closed as Barcelona residents devote the days to public gatherings and free celebrations – which, are in some cases sponsored by the city itself. On Sunday, 25 September – as part of this wave of celebrations, Encants became the host of El Flea, an open-air market organised by Flea Market Barcelona. Founded in 2007, Flea Market Barcelona is an organiser of flea market experiences, operating a platform for selling vintage clothes, sustainable goods, and artisanal products. El Flea usually occurs in Plaça de Blanquerna in El Raval – but like other markets operated by Flea Market Barcelona – 'it' can be transported to different locations, as was the case on 25 September when it took place at Encants. Of course, 'it' does not necessarily refer to a consistent set of vendors or a fixed market architecture, but instead – the transplanting of the market as a 'brand' – with typical banners and general aesthetic strategies such as a live DJ set, food trucks, and communal eating tables. Potential vendors buy spots online for one of the market's transient locations. In the case of the rendition in Encants, the most expensive booths are situated centrally under the reflective roof. Those stalls on the second level of the subtly elevating platform, which are neither as central nor as visible in the reflection of the canopy, pay slightly less. Space that is more central and situated within the 'market spectacle' (as produced by the mirrored roof) becomes more 'valuable.' This is a core feature of platform capitalism – where centrality and intermediation drive economic relations.

For a market activity that occurs at the site of another market activity, El Flea and the 'normal' Encants feel, look, and sound entirely different from one another. During El Flea, techno reverberates from a DJ booth, whereas during Encants, music is played on individual radios from different shops – creating a sonorous cacophony. When entering El Flea, visitors are welcomed by typographical banners and an information booth with signs

---

30   Sandro Mezzadra and Brett Neilson, *Border as Method, or, The Multiplication of Labor* (Durham: Duke University Press, 2013).

warning against pickpockets. Depending on the entrance, a visitor entering *typical* Encants may be unsure if the threshold they are passing through is an entrance at all, were it not for the logistical fact of it being a large open gate directly in front of the bike lane, tram stop, and direct line to the metro exit. To be blunt, during a designated *normal* Encants day, entering feels like stumbling upon activities not oriented towards a presentation of itself as *experience*. The entrance becomes a means to an end, open enough to make way for a trolley, a bike, or whatever you may need to navigate the activities ensuing beyond the market barrier.

Encants (when it occurs as Encants) is not just *a market experience* but a series of activities that may serve to maintain the livelihoods of participants. As an economic constellation, it makes sense that the market would then be closed for the public holiday of La Mercè. The fact that Encants can be rented when it is not in session speaks to how the building allows for another use-function of the market when 'it' is not occurring in its traditional form. The architecture fosters a hybrid terrain for floating activities and divergent economies. In the marketing and communication of El Flea, the hosting at Encants was not presented as a passive arena or container. Instead, Encants was integrated as part and parcel of El Flea as market experience 'El Flea en Els Encants.' This wording was displayed in unified typography on posters at the market site days prior and plastered throughout the market and different areas of Barcelona.

This is significant, as it indicates a marketable potential in El Flea's placement within Encants. Encants did not just become a physical host through its architecture but also as an activity that adds value to a new market constellation through association. It adds value because of its historical notoriety, cultural importance and long-standing legacy. The use-value of Encants for El Flea is not just physical but symbolic. Beyond being a convenient architecture for market functions and cultural platforms, it is the notoriety of Encants as an activity that makes it all the more appealing for 'external' platforms and networking activities. It is important to note that the 'typical' vendors in Encants are not present during such activities.

Encants as a regular market activity, with the same vendors in the same designated locations – coincides with Encants as a symbolic host of market experiences. During El Flea, vendors placed their goods on tables in front of the Encants' market shops. A crucial detail, this would be because Encants vendors' merchandise was not forced to make way for El Flea, as the market would ensue in the proceeding days. The market building is designed to enact this latent value in Encants as something with potential value, brought from the symbolic capital.

El Flea is not the only platform that has taken residence in the Encants market building. Indeed, it is a regular occurrence, another example being hosting the launch of the second edition of the Model Barcelona Architectures festival in April 2023. Much like El Flea, the promotional material emphasised its being hosted at Encants: 'From 6 pm to 10 pm on Thursday, 20 April, Mercat dels Encants will be transformed into a party space.' The word 'transformed' indicates that Encants is not a container – but a terrain from which value can be extracted and transferred. The new market site, with its layers of stainless steel – becomes the carrier – the device for these transferences. The architecture of the new market site allows the sociality at the core of Encants to float between different kinds of economies and circuits of capital relations. A hybrid architecture of code-switching and transition, it becomes the boundary object for varied driving forces of capital.

FORMALISING EXCHANGE

Formalising has a dual connotation. It can mean giving form to, FORM-alising. It can also suggest the antithesis of informal. Following Mörtenböck and Mooshammer's analysis of informality as a result of projection, formalising in this context suggests the contrary of whatever is deemed informal by certain interests or structures. In this case, formal may relate to logistical seamlessness and order, in contrast to what is construed as disordered. The Encants market structure formalises exchange relations in both senses of the word. It gives an aesthetic *form* to economic activity and *formalises* activities by making them navigable, organised, controlled, and monitored. The act of exchange becomes a

312

floating signifier – a terrain for intervention by interests that align with diverging but interconnected circuits of economic relations.

The large canopy above the market is open on all sides. Nearly twenty-five metres high, it is comprised of stainless-steel panels that appear as either gold or silver depending on the angle and the light. The canopy protects the market from rain while maintaining its open-air character. The b720 Fermin Vasquez Architects' website describes this canopy as a feature 'resembling a huge gold mirror, it cantilevers out to the edges of the surrounding pavements, sheltering the market stalls, announcing the presence of the market to the city and multiplying the daily hustle and bustle in its kaleidoscopic reflections.' The canopy primarily reflects the second-hand part of the market – the portion of Encants where goods are placed directly on the ground. Once again, there are three available spaces in Encants: stands, shops, and 'squares' on the auction floor. Stands consist of metal cabinets with goods placed in front on tables or boards. Shops are fixed spaces that cannot be disassembled. The auction square (the market's ground floor) as described on the Encants website, is available in rentable portions: 'The square is divided into thirty-nine spaces that are the property of the auctioneers who sell their lots every Monday, Wednesday, and Friday from 7:45–9:30 a.m. The rest of the day, the buyer of the lot can sell the items at the retail price until their withdrawal when the market closes.'

The Encants website estimates 300 shops in total within the market. The auction square, which is characterised by porous ownership – where auctioneers barter access to space for a maximum period of forty-eight hours – is the section of the market that is captured by the reflective ceiling. Is there more aesthetic value in this porosity? Might the reflective ceiling suggest a degree of vigilance regarding activities that are less formalised than the traditional stands and shops that circumvent it? The act of fluid and spontaneous exchange characterising the auction's unique century-old features make it something *capturable* by the monumental, reflective canopy.

The canopy announces the actions of exchange through reflection – and enhances or multiplies these activities through geometry. It becomes a filter that augments the performance of exchange. Gazing above, figures and bodies dart back and forth in concentric unison, a spiral dance of commodity cultures. In the first volume of *Capital*, Karl Marx writes that 'we shall find, in general, that the characters who appear on the economic stage are but the personifications of the economic relations that exist between them.'[31] In his descriptive analysis, written in the wake of industrialisation, the capitalist system is performed through the social relations that it engenders on a curated stage of interaction. In this context, the roles performed on the economic stage are those of capitalists and landowners in a world divided between those who own the means of production, and those who sell their labour. The intrinsic linkage between performativity and exchange – between the personification or actualisation of economic relations, is played out in the Encants' visual multiplication of 'the daily hustle and bustle.' The kaleidoscope ceiling becomes the monumental spectacle of capital.

Baroque architecture of the thirteenth and fourteenth centuries used reflection, monumentality, grandeur, and a direct connection to viewers as a way of attracting converts to a rapidly declining Catholic Church in the wake of the Protestant Reformation. The canopy of Encants feels akin to this typology of the spatial simulation of salvation. The golden grandeur, direct engagement with viewers, and monumentality render the space a kind of altar, not to God – but to capital. One witnesses oneself as part of this spectacularised, collective performance – enhanced and designed via the ceiling's geometry to appear more *multiplicitous*.

Architecture theorist Douglas Spencer, in his essay 'Bearing Capital: Platforms, Performance, and Personification,' argues that platforms, and specifically platform urbanism – are the architectures onto which the performance of capital as a 'character mask' is played out. Quoting Marx directly, he argues that in the platform economy, the performers are neoliberal subjects engaged

313

Typical infrastructural components, Encants Vells, Barcelona

on the 'economic stage' of 'capital relations.'[32] The reflective ceiling of Encants, in its sacralisation of exchange, can serve as an emblem of subjective entrepreneurialism. It renders the market a self-reflective vision of itself, a destination, a reproducible spectacle in a platform economy driven by aesthetics and visual reproductions of sociality. Using the 'discover' feature on Instagram as a research method, hashtag Encants leads to a feed of photos that predominantly depict the roof and its kaleidoscopic movement. The act of exchange creates value from aesthetics in an economic circuit driven by platforms. A monument of networking – the canopy is the spatial pipe dream of platform capitalism, which reverberates through the fibres of the smart-urban models that contain Els Encants as activity. Exchange is FORM-ed.

While processes of exchange are, on the one hand, monumentalised, the logistics of the market are regulated and relatively hidden from immediate view. The logistics area of the market is two floors below the main ground floor. It is not open to the public and is impossible to access via the elevator without a specific keycard, exclusively given to vendors and Encants personnel. There are two adjacent elevators, one designated for vendors, and the other for visitors. The logistics behind commodity circulation are regulated in a way that obscures their presence. All goods in the stands, which circle the second-hand market on the ground floor, are held in metal cabinets with retractable blinds, opened via a key. In the early hours of the morning, around the same time as the auction, stand vendors usually move goods via trolleys. The gradually elevating platform creates an effective means to move these trolleys across the market platform, as a 'continual platform of gradual elevation,' comprised of several *carrers* (streets). The effect is that of a seamless, folded, and gated collection of roads. The streets are united through *bend* as the boundaries and barriers between floors are blurred as much as they are designated. The feeling is an architecture of precise simultaneity – a detailed and material consideration of the architectural 'betweens' of exchange.

In the case of the canopy, this 'between' becomes spectacle. In terms of the market's logistical architecture, 'between' is arranged and organised for directed functionality and spatial division. The market certainly provides an impressively precise structure for facilitating the logistics of exchange, from what is visible to a non-vendor. Well-equipped with easily navigable entrances and exits, the structure becomes a seamless plane for different sized vehicles such as trolleys or small forklifts. The market activities are formalised, or given a directive order and arrangement. The directive signs and precisely designed infrastructure, with categorised sections and clearly marked emergency exits – exist alongside the kaleidoscopic spectacle of chaotic movement simulated by the reflective panels of the canopy. Indeed, considering these two forms(ing)s of exchange alongside one another speaks to the varied way that exchange processes are intervened into or projected upon. On the one hand, the spectacle of commodity exchange created by the canopy adds aesthetic value in an economy directed toward tourists, shoppers, or stakeholders. The architecture's enactment of the act of exchange appeals to the economic circularity of the vendors. These interconnected economic circuit function simultaneously – allowing the process of exchange to transfer across registers. The logistical, aesthetic, performative, and obscured coalesce into a mutually informing assemblage of relations. Such is the architecture of boundary objects.

COMMODITY FETISHISM AND THE RECYCLED OBJECT

The most notorious portion of Encants is the second-hand dealers' market occurring on the ground floor, despite it only consisting of thirty-nine 'squares' amidst the stated 300 total shops at Encants. The stands and shops that circumvent the market, which are more traditional in character, do not seem to receive the same degree of cultural attention when considering visual reproductions or references in local and international media.[33] Walking across the ground floor on a Friday morning in September, I take note of a red

32   Douglas Spencer, 'Bearing Capital: Platforms, Performance and Personification,' in *Platform Urbanism and Its Discontents*, eds. Peter Mörtenböck and Helge Mooshammer (Rotterdam: nai010 publishers, 2021), 377.
33   These conclusions come from reflections after two sessions of on-site fieldwork in Barcelona, the first being during September 2022 and the second in February 2023. For more indications on the particular cultural notoriety of the second-hand portion of the Els Encants Market, see: Rafael Vargas et al., *Encants i miralls de Barcelona* (Barcelona: Ajuntament de Barcelona, 2021).

plastic race car, a miniature piano, a marble Dalmatian and framed family photos clustered together in a neat triangular formation. Adjacent to this, there are vintage watches, silver crucifixes, lighters, and pendants as a rectangle. A few feet ahead, still-life oil paintings, framed prints, and ornate vases form a precise and unwavering triangle on the ground. Looking upwards at the reflective roof, the train passes by these rectangular and triangular arrangements and the bodies that move between them. These objects and figures become specks that coalesce into an arranged mirage of 'things' – spots of colour united through the roof's gold-tinted gradient. The clustering of geometric forms, colour filtering, and spaces designed to stop and observe make the experience very photographable. There is a certain allure or fluid form of value attached to second-hand market wares.

Analysing images of Encants on social media and print/digital media campaigns (some of which are city-sponsored), there is an indication that piles of used objects are a recurring motif. These objects have a certain appeal or aesthetic value when presented in digital and print media. As surplus commodities flowing from the homes of the recently deceased or from a factory or shop recently closed, the objects indicate the excesses of commodity culture. It is, to quote Jaume Benavent Bosch, a market for recycled goods. The 'squares,' designed so auctioneers can exchange the commodities easily, simultaneously function as 'showrooms' for shoppers and camera lenses. This fascination with perusing and capturing the aura of an old object is a state described by Walter Benjamin as commodity fetishism. Concerning the objects exchanged in the Paris arcades after Haussmann's reconstruction, Benjamin writes of commodity fetishism as 'the process by which we perceive value as innate, pre-social, almost divine – the commodity's theological niceties;' a configuration, where 'the course of the world is a whole series of facts congealed in things.'[34] This congelation of time, history, and space in the boundaries of the object as such are communicated as much as the object's charming mysteriousness obscures them.

Where was this object before? What is its meaning? Could it be valuable? This becomes the driving question that, as suggested by Benjamin, drives the fetish of the once-owned and free-floating commodity.

The fetishism attached to these objects, which drives the urge to photograph, if we follow Barthes' analysis of the photograph as the result of the 'punctum,' or affective 'sting' – differs from an adjacent circuit of interests attached to these objects.[35] Albeit connected, these interests are those of detecting specific value in the items. Many auction participants are not necessarily Encants vendors but antique specialists, collectors of potentially high-value items, and curators. As described by Nacho Abad and Jaume Benavent Bosch, who both participate in Encants as antique specialists, the objects circulated in Encants have inherent 'value' far exceeding the price they may be sold for. In some cases, this produces a rather emotionally charged exchange between the vendors and bidders. During the auction, prospective bidders inspect the objects (sometimes with magnifying glasses), handle them, and converse or speculate on potential inherent values. Visiting the market around 7:30 am at the beginning of the auction, the atmosphere feels competitive, comprised almost entirely of men, and very verbal and gestural. The auction crier recounts the rising prices of a lot via a microphone – once the lot is bought, cash is handed to one of his two bodyguards, and the buyer of the square is given an official receipt. Looking through a series of drawings and prints, a vendor points to a pencil signature on a charcoal drawing – and tells me it could very well be a masterpiece (bid: 250 euros).

The objects become specimens for projections of value – or *potential* value points. This could be argued as a kind of 'speculative' value – a potential of profit attached to futurity. How could this object create 'profit?' This is driven by emotion, gesture, and negotiation. The mechanisms of how objects are sourced remain obscure.

In Marxist economics, surplus value is broadly defined as the difference between the

34   Walter Benjamin, 'Paris, the Capital of the Nineteenth Century (1935),' in *The Arcades Project* (London: The Belknap Press, 1999), 7.
35   Roland Barthes, *Camera Lucida: Reflections on Photography* (New York: Hill and Wang, 1982).

amount raised through a sale of a product and the amount it costs to manufacture, including labour and material costs. The key issue at stake in considering surplus value, as articulated by Marx, is that workers do not own the means of production, which means that surplus value is accumulated and retained by the managerial class.[36] Over the course of fieldwork, it proved to be extremely difficult to fully grasp the extent to which the vendors own and control the means of production in the Encants organism or whether external managers, or the market administration itself retain the surplus value generated through the sale of commodities. The stalls and shops are almost entirely owned or rented by individuals who do not work in the market itself.[37] The case of the squares on the ground floor is even less clear. Visiting the auction on 3 March 2023, the most expensive square sold for 5,550 euros, paid in cash. Anecdotally, some squares can be sold for up to 20,000 euros. This could suggest the existence of investors, managers, or certain logistical circuits that support the transfer of large sums of capital. Is there a deep network and organisational mechanism behind the capital flows of the auction which are not immediately visible? Interviewing vendors and participants, it is apparent that deep-rooted organisational mechanisms inform how these recycled commodities arrive and are auctioned. The question of where the value generated from the sale of these objects ends up and how surplus value is generated warrants deeper analysis. What is clear is that these commodities are enmeshed in an intricate circuit of labour and value production that is obscured from *immediate* view.

The recycled object of Encants is one traversing the enmeshed interests of aesthetic, speculative, and surplus value systems. Like the market architecture and market site, the recycled object becomes a mechanism that floats between interests and spheres, depending on its framing. Within the logics of the market structure, a vintage record player, a statue of the Virgin Mary, and a stack of prints – are simultaneously appealing to an Instagrammer, an antique specialist, and a vendor. This simultaneity speaks to *the architecture of the floating signifier.*

BARCELONA AND URBANISATION AS BOUNDARY OBJECT

Barcelona is a primary example of a city whose urban design is predicated on the changes brought by capitalism. During industrialisation and the beginnings of capitalism in the mid-nineteenth century, the City Council of Barcelona and the Ministry of Public Works saw the need to renovate the 'old' city and plan the expansion of the city to meet the needs of industrialisation. In 1860, the civil engineer Ildefons Cerdà was commissioned to re-design Barcelona, which he did, carefully considering the necessities, changes, and dangers brought by capitalism. As quoted by Pier Vittorio Aureli, Cerdà saw capitalism as 'an unprecedented "vast swirling ocean of persons, of things, of interests of every sort, a thousand diverse elements" that work in permanent reciprocity and thus form a totality that cannot be contained by any previous finite territorial formation such as the city.'[38] His plan thus redefined how borders and boundaries are formed in Barcelona.

Cerdà's plan proposed a design that 'avoided class conflict by imagining class differences.'[39] In broad terms, it expanded the city beyond its medieval walls into the 'modern' format of a regular orthogonal grid. This allowed surrounding rural villages and towns to be incorporated into the parameters of the city, to, in literal terms, provide a working force for the 'swirling ocean' of capital relations. Addressing the issues of class conflict, Cerdà's plan facilitated mobility as well as spaces of rest. He saw the key to this being the incorporation of the suburbs into the definition of the city through planned mobility mechanisms – 'To ruralise the city and to urbanise the countryside' was for Cerdà the double agenda of urbanisation,' writes Aureli.[40] Cerdà's plan would become the district of Eixample, with les Glòries at its periphery. Indeed, the word for 'urbanisation'

36   See: Marx, *Capital: A Critique of Political Economy.*
37   These conclusions were made as a result of on-site interviews with Encants vendors held in September 2022.
38   Ildefonso Cerda, *The Five Bases of the General Theory of Urbanization* (Berkeley: Ginko Press, 1999), 79. Quoted in Pier Vittorio Aureli,
      The Possibility of an Absolute Architecture (Cambridge: MIT Press, 2011), 9.
39   Aureli, *The Possibility of An Absolute Architecture*, 10.
40   Aureli, *The Possibility of An Absolute Architecture*, 10.

Encants Vells, Barcelona, auction day, 2022

originates with Ildefons Cerdà, which he outlines in his seminar text 'The Five Bases of the General Theory of Urbanization' and which summarises and defends his invention of the term. Cerdà can be considered the first urban planner through his concern with not just engineering cities but conceptualising a *device* which serves not a representative or iconic function but 'for the reproduction of the labour force,' in a space shaped in and for capitalist relations.[41]

Though Cerdà's plan was not fully realised, compromised by speculation and property accumulation – it is a crucial point of consideration in any spatial analyses of Barcelona because it speaks to a dilemma at the heart of urban planning as a means of social reproduction. Urbanisation is a kind of spatial managerialism designed to encourage 'self-sufficiency on the social level.'[42] Indeed, as described by Aureli, Cerdà's plan functions to suppress the city's political character through a 'managerial paradigm,' which proposes that there is no political power governing the city, but rather, the city becomes a 'managerial processes based on the economy.'[43] In essence, the city is produced through the mediation of relation – and the architecture of exchange.

Within the managerial paradigm of urbanisation, varied interests dissolve into the bleeding edge at the centre of social reproduction, an edge which can be described as consisting of actions that support well-being and mutual support in an exploitative system, or simply reproduce the social norms of that exploitative system by normalising them through fluidity and comfort. The phrase 'self-sufficiency on the social level' used by Harney and Moten to describe social reproduction through the lens of planning, aptly describes this bleeding edge at the centre of spatialised, economic planning. On the one hand, it forms a context in which ideologies of 'self-sufficiency' are sustained. But this maintenance is socialised into a reproducible terrain. It makes the forming of capital relations possible. There is a plethora of critical debate on whether planning and social reproduction can, in essence, challenge the system. The answer to this might not be black-and-white, nor either/

or. Indeed, a nuanced analysis would indicate the tensions at the centre of social reproduction as an issue of perspective and framing. Returning to boundary objects as a methodology for detecting the transference between interests and economies – one could argue that Cerdà's plan suggests that Barcelona is a city built in and through collisions, conflicts, and cohesions between varied interests that materialise and function through boundary objects. What urban features in Barcelona, from public spaces to slick train lines, to city-sponsored public art, function for public benefit or private interest? These are all examples of the boundary object as framing – as they each traverse and float across the interests shaping social reproduction on the urban scale.

The formalisation of Encants is a case study for detecting, tracing and analysing the architecture of floating signifiers and boundary objects. Its bringing together of transforming, amorphous characteristics speak to an urban-economic paradigm predicated on negotiations of interest – materialising as urbanism claiming to serve the interests of multiple structures and social worlds simultaneously. Encants as boundary object emerges through this context's specificities, an urban fabric navigating complex registers of formality, informality, spontaneity, planning, platformisation and local protections. It can be a space for mutual support, as much as it is a touristic emblem for Barcelona's endeavours towards spatialisation of the industrial revolution 4.0. These tensions exist in an amalgamated assemblage and are a source of contention, debate, and continual reconsideration. The first step to questioning said activities is a detailed analysis of their concrete forms – to detect patterns and recurrences for furthering critical debate.

41   Aureli, *The Possibility of An Absolute Architecture*, II.
42   Stefao Harney and Fred Moten, *The Undercommons: Fugitive Planning & Black Study* (New York: Minor Compositions, 2013), 76.
43   Aureli, *The Possibility of An Absolute Architecture*, II.

REFERENCES

Ajuntament de Barcelona. *Barcelona Sales Guide 1989/1990*. Barcelona: Ajuntament de Barcelona, 1989.

Aureli, P. *The Possibility of an Absolute Architecture*. Cambridge: MIT Press, 2011.

Barthes, R. *Camera Lucida: Reflections on Photography*. New York: Hill and Wang, 1982.

Benjamin, W. 'Paris, the Capital of the Nineteenth Century.' In *The Arcades Project*. London: The Belknap Press, 1999.

Castells, M. 'Prologo.' In *Luces y Sombras del Urbanismo de Barcelona*, 2nd edition, edited by J. Borja. Barcelona: Editorial UOC, 2010.

Cerdà, I. *The Five Bases of the General Theory of Urbanization*. Berkeley: Gingko Press, 1999.

Cuppini, N. 'On Platforming. Notes for Navigating Contemporary Hyper-Urbanscapes.' Platform Austria (blog), February 2021. *https://www.platform-austria.org/en/blog/on-platforming-notes-for-navigating-contemporary-hyper-urbanscapes*

de Freixas, D. *Enciplopedia de tipos vulgares y costumbres de Barcelona*. Barcelona: Joaquin Bosch, 1844.

ECPA Urban Planning, 'Case Study: 22@ Barcelona Innovation District,' Smart Cities Dive. *https://www.smartcitiesdive.com/ex/sustainablecitiescollective/case-study-22-barcelona-innovation-district/27601/*

'Encants Market.' b720 Fermín Vázquez Arquitectos. *https://b720.com/*

'Encants Market Barcelona.' *Arquitectura Viva*. 18 May 2023. *https://arquitecturaviva.com/works/encants-market*

Guàrdia, M., and J. Oyón. *Making Cities through Market Halls: Europe, 19th and 20th Centuries*. Ajuntament de Barcelona: Museu D'Historia de Barcelona.

Guàrdia, M. 'Els Encants i La Fira de Bellcaire: una mirada des de la historia urbana.' *Encants I La Fira De Bellcaire – Imatge I Història De Barcelona*. Barcelona: Ajuntament de Barcelona, 2014.

Harney, S., and F. Moten. *The Undercommons: Fugitive Planning & Black Study*. New York: Minor Compositions, 2013.

'History.' Mercat dels Encants. *https://encantsbarcelona.com/en/history/*

'Inici de la Desconstrucció del Tambor de la Plaça de les glories.' *BIM/SA*, 10 July 2008. *https://www.bimsa.cat/noticia/inici-de-la-deconstruccio-del-tambor-de-la-placa-de-les-glories/*

Laclau, E. *On Populist Reason*. New York: Verso, 2005.

Marx, K. *Capital: A Critique of Political Economy*, vol. I, translated by B. Fowkes. London: Penguin, 1990.

Mezzadra, S., and B. Neilson. *The Border as Method, or, The Multiplication of Labour*. Durham: Duke University Press, 2013.

Mooshammer, H. 'Other Markets: Sites and Processes of Economic Pressure.' In *Informal Market Worlds: The Architecture of Economic Pressure - Reader*, edited by P. Mörtenböck and H. Mooshammer Rotterdam: nai010 publishers, 2015.

Mörtenböck, P., and H. Mooshammer, eds. *Platform Urbanism and Its Discontents*. Rotterdam: nai010 publishers, 2021.

Morell, J. et al. *Encants I La Fira De Bellcaire – Imatge I Història De Barcelona*. Barcelona: Ajuntament de Barcelona, 2014.

Pirretas, M. 'Inconveniencias y perjuicios que los Encantes y el Rastro causan al Comercio al detall en particular y a Barcelona en general.' Conferencia en la Liga de Defensa Industrial y Comercial de Barcelona, Barcelona (speech given 1895).

Ramirez, R. 'Els Encants, Barcelona.' In *Informal Market Worlds: The Architecture of Economic Pressure - Atlas*, edited by P. Mörtenböck and H. Mooshammer, 466–71. Rotterdam: nai010 publishers, 2015.

Richavia, H. 'Statistical Overview of Barcelona's Airbnb Market.' *Medium*, 14 August 2018. *https://towardsdatascience.com/statistical-overview-of-barcelonas-airbnb-market-83dc7d6be648*

Rufas, C. 'el mercado de la miseria de las glories crece sin parar.' *Metropolia Abierta*, 9 March 2019. *https://metropoliabierta.elespanol.com/distritos/sant-marti/el-mercado-de-la-miseria-de-las-glories-crece-sin-parar_14775_102.html*

Spencer, D. 'Bearing Capital: Platforms, Performance and Personification.' In *Platform Urbanism and Its Discontents*, edited by P. Mörtenböck and H. Mooshammer, 311–20. Rotterdam: nai010 publishers, 2021.

Star, S., and J. Griesemer. 'Institutional Ecology, "Translations" and Boundary Objects: Amateurs and Professionals in Berkeley's Museum of Vertebrate Zoology, 1907-39.' *Social Studies of Science*, 19, no. 3 (1989): 387–420.

Vargas, R. et al. *Encants i miralls de Barcelona*. Barcelona: Ajuntament de Barcelona, 2021.

1251-1822

1 First documented evidence of the Encants Market in Barcelona on the porches of the Church of Saint Jaume
2 The Encants Market relocates to Plaça Nova.
3 The Encants Market moves to Llotja.
4 Fira del Bellcaire appears on Las Ramblas de Barcelona, extending from Palacio Moja to the Estudis barracks.

1822-1931

5 Fira del Bellcaire moves to the Paseo de la Explanada, located between the Born and the convent of Sant Agustí Vell.
6 A part of the Fira del Bellcaire is moved to the so-called Voltas dels Encants, next to the Carrer del Consolat del Mar, a transfer which is credited with causing the confusion between Els Encants and Fira del Bellcaire that still persists today.

7 Ildefons Cerdà is commissioned by the Ministry of Public Works to re-design the city of Barcelona.
8 To make room for the Universal Exposition 1888, the Encants and the Fira del Bellcaire move to the area of the Sant Antoni market.
9 In the lead-up to the International Exposition of 1929, both markets relocate to the Sidral area in 1928, a peripheral junction of roads and railways that will eventually transform into Plaça les Glòries.
10 Plaça les Glòries is intended to become a city centre in Cerdà's plan but remains underdeveloped. The peripheral area becomes a large road and railway junction.

1931-2005

11 Encants Nous (New Encants), an indoor market, is opened by a group of traders in response to the controversy surrounding the noise coming from Encants.
12 The hosting of the 1992 Summer Olympics marks a critical turning point for Plaça les Glòries and the redevelopment of the Avenida Diagonal into one of the city's major cultural axes.

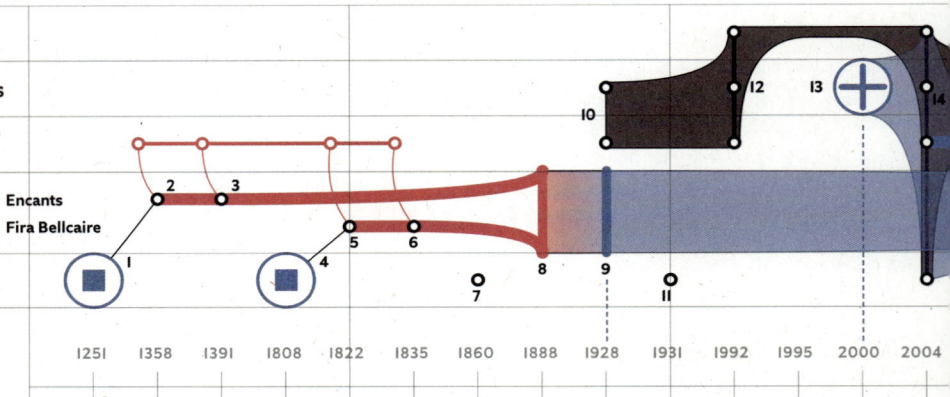

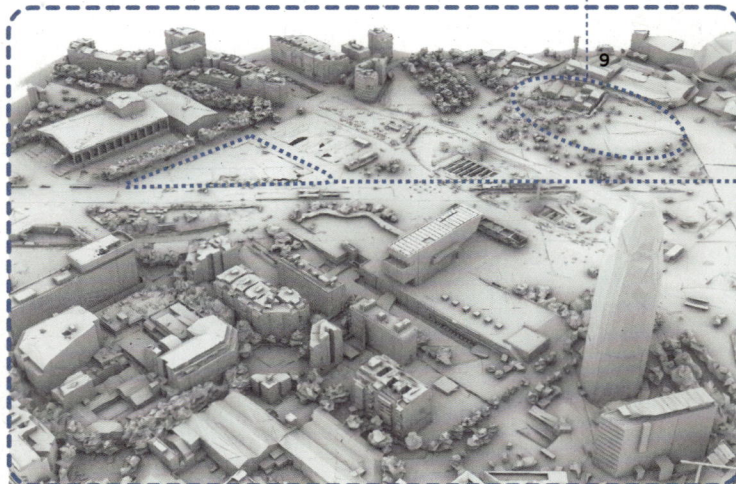

Timeline of key events shaping the transformation of Encants Vells, Barcelona

13 Inception of 22@ – a smart city government initiative introduced with the intention of making Barcelona a hub for innovative technology companies; 22@ uses the adjacent neighbourhood of Poblenou as a testbed for design-led economic growth.

14 The first Universal Forum of Cultures takes place and is hosted in buildings that started a wave of high-profile architectures along Avenida Diagonal, such as the Forum Building by Herzog & de Meuron, the Parc dels Auditoris by Foreign Office Architects (FOA) and the Torre Agbar by Jean Nouvel.

2005-2010

15 Founding of 'El Flea,' an open-air market organised by Flea Market Barcelona – offering a platform for the sale of vintage clothes, sustainable goods, and artisanal products; El Flea is usually held in Plaça de Blanquerna in El Raval but – like other markets operated by Flea Market Barcelona – it is also held as a pop-up market at different locations.

16 Announcement of the demolition and of changes to the Plaça les Glòries area

17 Barcelona City Council announces a European competition for the construction of a market complex that is to become the new permanent home of Encants Vells.

18 80 percent of the vendors at the Encants Market vote to approve the project and agree to relocate to the new premises.

2010-2015

19 Encants Vells/Fira del Bellcaire relocates to the new market hall on the opposite side of Plaça les Glòries.

20 Plaça les Glòries undergoes another major redevelopment, with a new tunnel replacing the roundabout of elevated highways; the Barcelona Design Museum opens; the old site of the Encants Market is transformed into grassland.

2015-2023

21 Encants Market becomes the host of El Flea.

22 The second edition of the MODEL Barcelona Architectures Festival is inaugurated at the Encants Market.

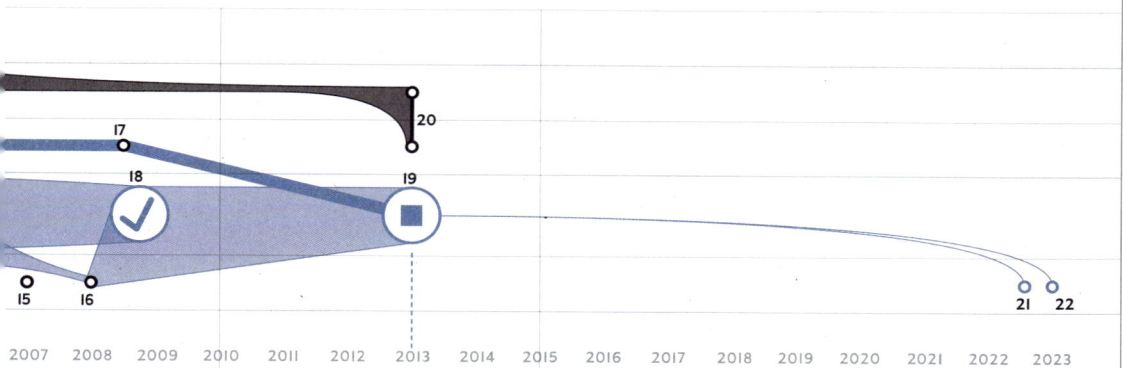

2007 2008 2009 2010 2011 2012 2013 2014 2015 2016 2017 2018 2019 2020 2021 2022 2023

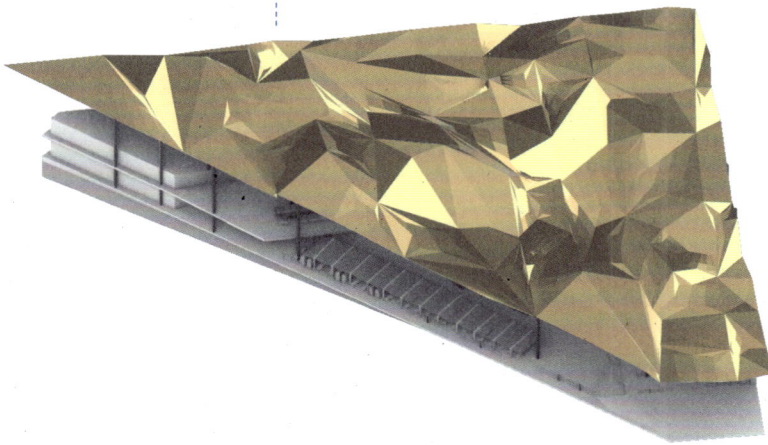

323

■ Spatial, social, economic and political interventions into in/formal markets
■ Informality as a survival method and means of adapting to changing socio-economic and political circumstances

The facility provides approximately 500 to 600 market stalls in total, spread across an area of around 15,000 square metres. It features an underground parking and logistics area.

Large mirrored canopy covering the entire market that reflects the surroundings and creates a unique visual effect

Fixed tables with storage closets

Small walk-in shops

Auction space located in the lower level atrium

Parking

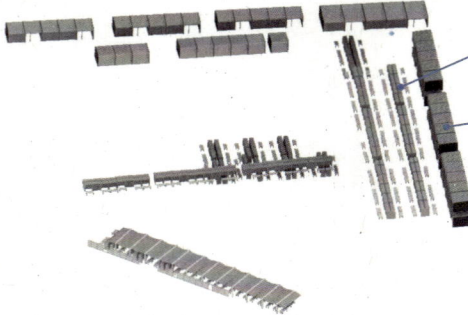

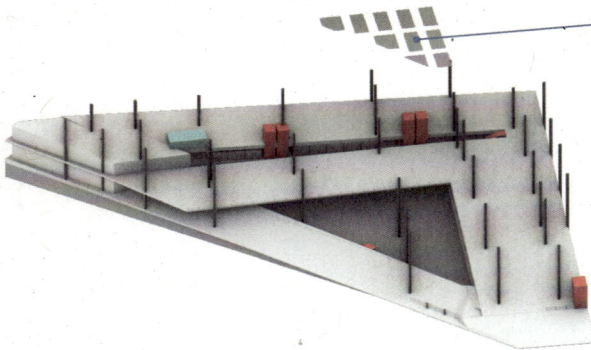

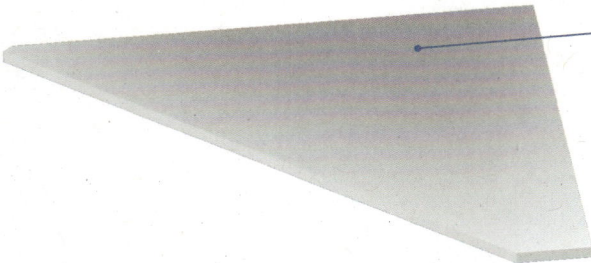

■ Staircases / Elevators   ■ Sanitary stations

Spatial features of the new market structure of Encants Vells, Barcelona

Encants Vells, Barcelona, 2022

Typical infrastructural components, Encants Vells, Barcelona

Sant Antoni market

Plaça Nova

Plaça de Sant Jaume

Plaça del Palau / Llotja

Plaça les Glòries / informal street trade

Plaça les Glòries / incorporated into the formal urban plan

Sant Antoni market

Plaça Nova   Plaça de Sant Jaume   Plaça del Palau / Llotja

Plaça les Glòries / new permanent location of Encants Vells
Plaça les Glòries / informal street trade

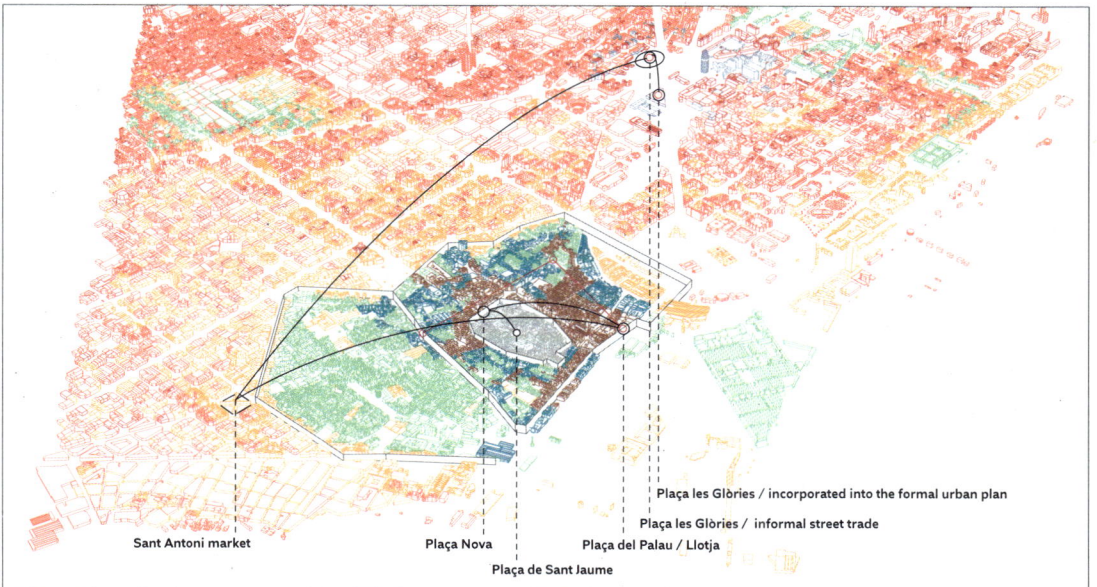

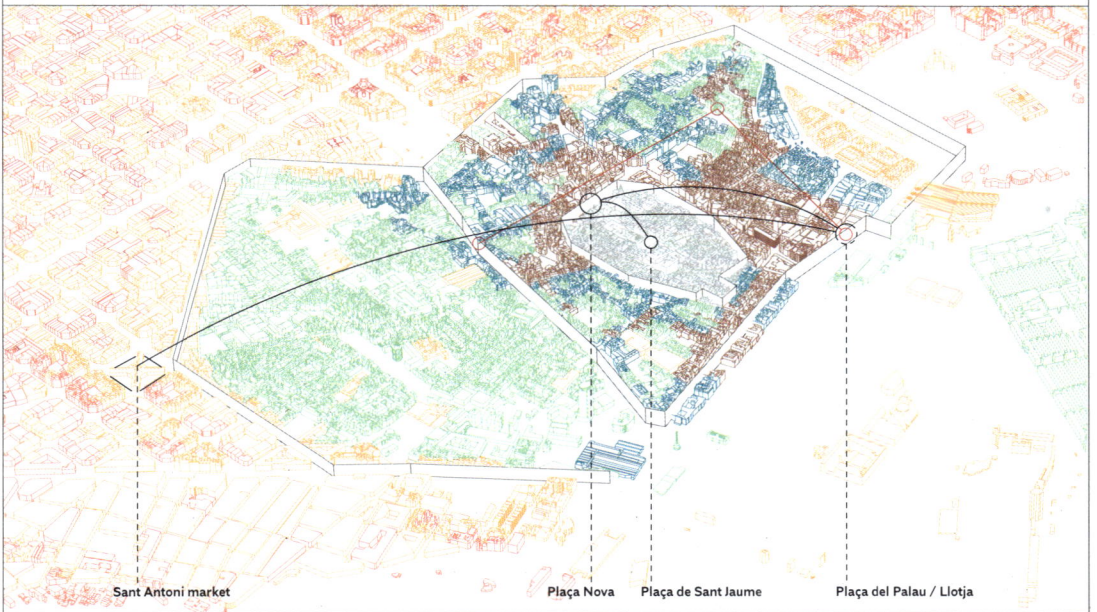

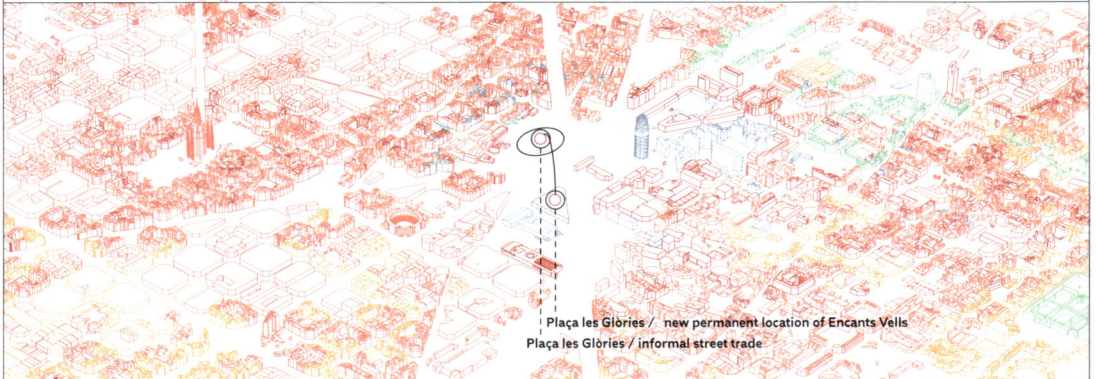

| | 1000 | | 1250 | | 1500 | | 1860 | | 1890 | | 1980 | | 1990 | | 2004 | | 2022 |

Encants Vells neighbourhood: key phases of spatial development

Encants Vells

Encants Vells, Barcelona, 2022

Appropriation

Arizona Market, Brčko, Bosnia and Herzegovina, 2006

Lovro Koncar-Gamulin

Navigating Change in Brčko's Post-conflict Landscape

Map data: Google, CNES/Airbus

Arizona Market, one of the largest and most well-known markets in Eastern Europe, is situated in Brčko, a self-governing district under the sovereignty of Bosnia and Herzegovina (BiH), located in the northeast of the country. Spanning 45 hectares, the market consists of 2,500 units comprising shops, boutiques, workshops, restaurants and enter- tainment venues. During its most successful period, it received up to 3 million visitors each year and directly or indirectly employed up to 100,000 people.[1] The market was initially praised for its capacity to kickstart and facil- itate inter-ethnic collaboration following the Bosnian War (1992–1995). But soon after, it became notorious for illegal practices on the premises. The infamous Arizona Market thus reflects the complexities of post-war recon- struction and the human cost of uncontrolled growth. Some perceived the market as an ab-

1 Peter Mörtenböck and Helge Mooshammer, 'Arizona Market: Inter-ethnic collaboration in Brčko,' in *Informal Market Worlds: The Architecture of Economic Pressure - Atlas*, eds. Peter Mörtenböck and Helge Mooshammer (Rotterdam: nai010 publishers, 2015), 125.

Site of the never-finished
Trade City of China

Main market halls erected in 2004 to
accommodate relocated vendors

Traffic islands and irregular spaces in the
primary street layout are occupied
by smaller kiosks.

Cafés populate the
pedestrianised cross-axis.

Parking

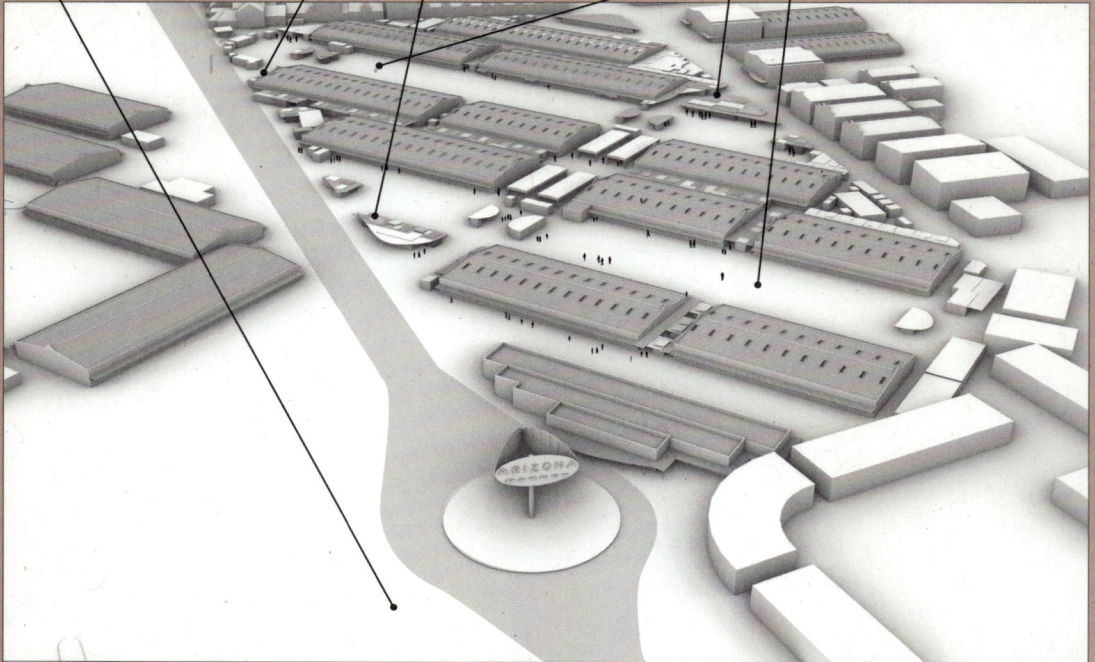

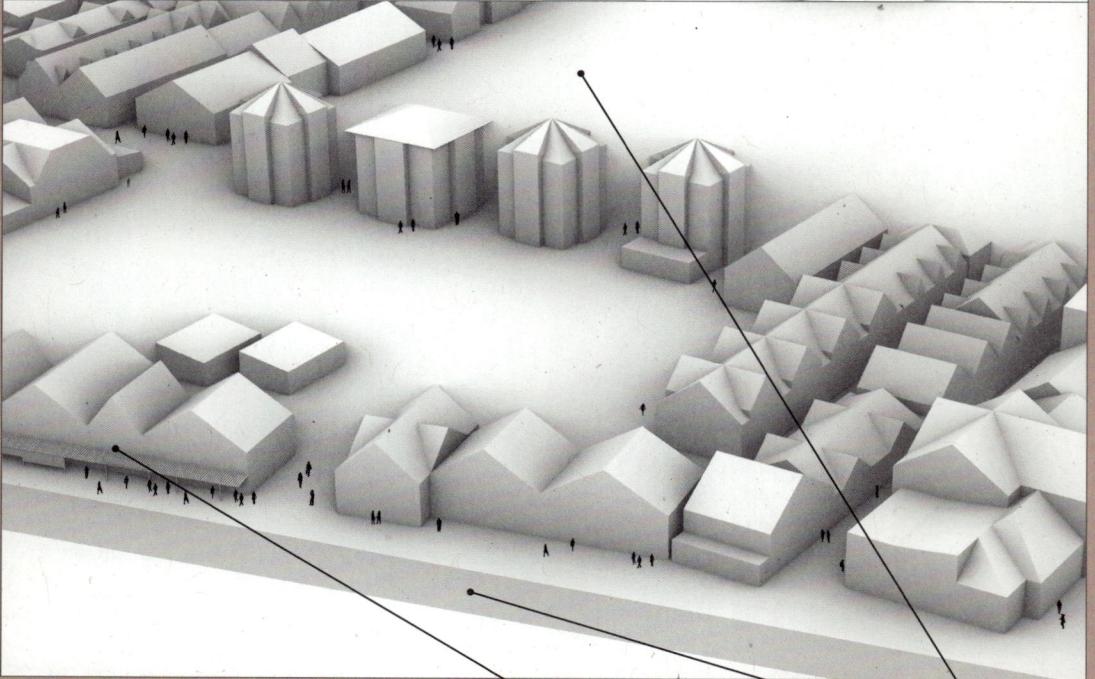

Despite ambitious plans to turn Arizona
Market into a key trading centre for the
Western Balkans, the market's spatial
infrastructure has not seen significant
development since 2004.

In the early consolidation phase of Arizona
Market around 2000, successful vendors
built residential-type houses whose ground
and first floors were adapted for trade.

Arizona Corridor   Parking

solute necessity for daily survival, while others saw it as an opportunity for making swift monetary gains by any means necessary. Others experienced it as an unbearable and torturous place, enmeshed in crime involving the drug trade and human trafficking. These varied perspectives testify to a plethora of 'layers' of Arizona Market's transformation since its emergence, embodying BiH's changes over the past twenty-five years. Drawing upon archival documents and the fieldwork conducted in 2022, this case study presents an analysis of the Arizona Market during its unregulated period (1995–2001), its transformation into a privately-operated shopping mall, Arizona 2 (2004–today), as well as plans for Arizona 3, which were never realised. This multidimensional analysis addresses the layers of Arizona Market's spatial and operational transformations since its emergence to detect their causes and consequences on the local, regional and international scales.

THE INFORMAL MARKETPLACE AS A MECHANISM OF PEACEKEEPING

Arizona Market emerged in Brčko after the Bosnian War in 1995 as the country struggled to rebuild its economy and political institutions. In 1990, the estimated GDP of BiH was approximately 11 billion US dollars, with a per capita income of 2,400 US dollars.[2] By the time of the ceasefire in 1995, the country's GDP had plummeted to 1.87 billion dollars and per capita income dropped to 500 dollars. When the war ended, most of the population faced unemployment, with figures ranging between 70 and 80 percent.[3] Wartime destruction and the economic consequences of the conflict amounted to 90 billion dollars.[4] This alarming statistic is a stark reflection of the war's profound impact on local communities. The war devastated the economy, leaving most of the population dependent on international aid. With reliance on the international community for employment, the labour market became highly polarised and dependent on international presence.[5] It was in this

environment of economic, political, and legal uncertainty that the Arizona Market sprang to life. Just as the Dayton Peace Accords[6] were going into effect, the sprawling marketplace emerged along the 'Arizona Route' – a demilitarised zone controlled by NATO's Stabilization Force (SFOR) in the northeast of BiH that connected the towns of Doboj in the Republika Srpska (the Serb entity) and Tuzla in the Federation (the Bosnian-Croat entity), where US forces were headquartered. In this volatile and conflict-riven region, the interests and territories of Bosnians, Bosnian Croats, and Serbs intersected. A US Army checkpoint along the Arizona Route ensured a safe and secure space for trade within this conflict zone. Hence, the market earned the name 'Arizona,' derived from the code name used by the SFOR troops patrolling the area, signifying the direct engagement of the international community in shaping the market since its inception.

Like many post-socialist marketplaces such as the Cherkizovsky in Moscow, 7th Kilometer in Odessa or Jarmark Europa in Warsaw, the Arizona Market emerged in response to severe economic difficulties. By the late 1990s, Arizona Market grew into a crucial transregional and cross-border logistical node of the post-war period, embodying Victor I. Diatlov's characterisation of a post-Soviet ethnic market as '[...] a key element of the supply mechanism in the complete collapse of the socialist distribution system, having become a vitally important institution for the low-income strata of the society.'[7] Despite the significant tensions among ethnic groups in post-war BiH, the emergence of Arizona Market showcased the remarkable resilience and adaptability of informal markets amid conflict-stricken environments. As argued by Peter Mörtenböck and Helge Mooshammer: 'During armed conflicts and in post-war contexts, informal trade helps to meet the basic needs of large segments of affected populations, at least for a short time. Apart from the immediate task of providing for livelihoods on

2   Dina Francesca Haynes, 'Lessons from Bosnia's Arizona Market: Harm to Women in a Neoliberalized Postconflict Reconstruction Process,' *University of Pennsylvania Law Review* 158, no. 6 (2010): 1779–1829.
3   Data on the BiH's unemployment statistics from 1994 onwards can be found at the World Bank's Open Data platform, *https://data.worldbank.org/indicator/SL.UEM.TOTL.NE.ZS?end=2021&locations=BA&start=1991&view=chart*
4   Meho Bašic, 'Osnove ratne ekonomije: s osvrtom na rat u BiH 1992.-95. godine,' *Ekonomski Pregled* 57 (February 2006): 139.
5   Haynes, 'Lessons from Bosnia's Arizona Market,' 1783.
6   The General Framework Agreement for Peace in Bosnia and Herzegovina also known as the Dayton Peace Accords or the Dayton Peace Agreement is the peace agreement reached at Wright-Patterson Air Force Base near Dayton, Ohio in November 1995.
7   Victor I. Diatlov, 'Ethnic Markets in Post-Soviet Transitional Space: Their Role in Society and the Research Area,' *Žurnal Sibirskogo Federal'nogo Universiteta* 9, no. 4 (2016): 796.

both sides of the conflict, informal markets also act as connectors across conflict divides. Bringing together members of different communities despite mutual enmity and dislike, they create a common ground for exchange in war-torn environments and play a vital role in peace-building processes.'[8]

Therefore, during its early stages, Arizona Market could be described as an influential network of opportunities for local communities, operating as a result of the non-functioning formal economy. By not conforming to legal rules and regulations, this meant more flexibility and agility in creating a common space for exchange. These features were visible in the market's operational structure and area – the market initially appeared as a bazaar-like formation of ramshackle stalls along the route. The market had a characteristic 'temporary' appearance due to these rudimentary structures constructed from basic materials such as wood, metal, and tarpaulins. The stalls varied in size and shape, ranging from small, compact setups to larger, more complex, but equally flimsy structures. Some vendors had permanent stalls, while others set up temporary stands or spread their goods out directly on the ground. The layout of the market was fluid and ever-changing. Stalls were positioned in a seemingly haphazard manner, with little organisational structure – such informal arrangements allowed for swift and frequent alterations and expansions of the market. As word travelled fast, the market thrived – stalls proliferated, incorporating more and more vendors and customers by the day. However, the chaotic and provisional appearance of Arizona Market also signalled uncertainties regarding its future, which was not determined by those who sold in the market – but rather by representatives of the international community responsible for the administration of Brčko District during the post-war period.

'International attention to conflict zones can take a variety of forms, ranging from humanitarian aid and emergency response efforts to self-interested engagement in the peace process of a region as a means of controlling the structure of emerging markets.'[9] In the context of post-war BiH, the international community saw the market as an opportunity to demonstrate the capabilities of free trade over a centrally planned economy in the wake of post-war reconciliation. Praised as a model for harmonious inter-ethnic collaboration between the conflicted parties, the market was seen as an embodiment of peace under a common denominator: profit.[10] As the market grew rapidly, the peaceful coexistence of Croatian, Serbian and Bosniak vendors and visitors was evident – Arizona thereby did indeed become a tool for peace-building at the hands of the international community, at least on the surface. Beneath that surface, Arizona Market soon became a hub for various illicit activities. The absence of effective regulation facilitated the proliferation of these illegal activities, revealing the market's dark underbelly of exploitation, criminality, and human rights abuses.

CONTESTING NARRATIVES OF SUCCESS AND MISERY AS AGENTS OF MARKET TRANSFORMATION

Since its inception, Arizona Market has been surrounded by layered threats and hazards, illustrating the root causes of its transformations over time. The most imminent threat at the market's inception in 1995 took place at the spatial dimension – the vicinity of the tri-border area where the IFOR checkpoint was initially set up represented a significant territory for all sides of the conflict, leading to the immediate surroundings of the market together with its supply and trade routes being lined with landmines.[11] These issues challenged the safety and security of the market vendors and visitors not only during the 1990s but also during the market's spatial transformation into a privately owned shopping mall in the early 2000s. Other types of hazards occurred on the socioeconomic layer, which had to do with the suffering caused by the lucrative but illicit activities such as human trafficking and the drug trade. These activities were driven by the economic vacuum and

8   Peter Mörtenböck and Helge Mooshammer, 'Post-conflict Markets' in *Informal Market Worlds: The Architecture of Economic Pressure - Atlas*, eds. Peter Mörtenböck and Helge Mooshammer (Rotterdam: nai010 publishers, 2015), 92.

9   Mörtenböck and Mooshammer, 'Post-conflict Markets', 93.

10   Adam D. Moore, 'Localizing Peacebuilding: The Arizona Market and the Evolution of US Military Peacebuilding Priorities in Bosnia,' *Journal of Intervention and Statebuilding* 13, no. 3 (2019), 12.

11   Information on minefields has been extracted from the EUFORBIH (European Union Force in BiH) website, *https://www.euforbih.org/index.php/bih-minefield-maps*

Initial site of Arizona Market, Brčko, Bosnia and Herzegovina, 2001 (top) and 2022 (bottom)

Arizona Market, Brčko, Bosnia and Herzegovina, 2001

political uncertainties of the post-war era and further facilitated by the poor organisation and regulation of the market during its early days.

The final threat to the communities affected by Arizona Market occurred on the political layer, consisting of the local, regional, and international regulatory entities who were often pursuing different agendas. Local regulatory bodies comprise the Brčko District Assembly, which is the legislative body responsible for local laws and regulations, and the Brčko District Government, which is the executive body responsible for implementing policies and managing the day-to-day affairs of the district. International decision-making bodies such as the Office of the High Representative (OHR) appointed by the international community, which had significant powers to make binding decisions and ensure compliance with the Dayton Peace Accords, and the Brčko Arbitral Tribunal appointed by the United Nations Security Council, were tasked with resolving the dispute over the Brčko District.

Decision-making bodies had a significant role in the market's transformations over time and, in that sense, contributed to the uncertainties and consequences that followed. The toleration of the completely unregulated Arizona Market from 1995 to 2001 opened the door for the violent events and crime that followed. It normalised human trafficking and prostitution – turning the market into a significant trafficking node on a global scale.[12] Arizona Market thrived on the remnants of the black market solidified during the war, with traders engaging in smuggling, distribution of stolen goods, narcotics and other criminal activities. The absence of effective regulation and oversight facilitated the proliferation of such activities, exposing those most vulnerable to unspeakable abuse, causing irrevocable damage and suffering to many that have set foot in Arizona. For instance, private military contractors, such as DynCorp, established to provide recruitment for the International Police Task Force (IPTF), were reportedly involved in setting up the human trafficking network during the post-war period.

Some of their 'contractors' actively participated in the trafficking chain, allegedly engaging in sexual exploitation and committing multiple instances of sexual assault and rape outside the confines of that network.[13] The involvement of peacekeeping forces and humanitarian NGOs is further demonstrated by a deeply disturbing incident that took place in Brčko, where the bodies of two murdered women involved in a prostitution ring were discovered in the vicinity of Arizona Market. Particularly shocking was the presence of tape with the OSCE's (Organisation for Security and Co-operation in Europe) stamp and symbol over one victim's mouth, suggesting the possible complicity of their personnel in human trafficking and murder.[14]

These reports have contributed significantly to the shift from an attitude of toleration to a more restrictive one – resulting in concrete policy measures against the 'old' Arizona and toward a more regulated one. In October 2000, after these events became the market's dominant feature and were no longer possible to ignore, the international community's OHR publicly acknowledged the steep rise in illicit activities, including: '[...] prostitution; trafficking in women; abetting and exploiting the flow of illegal immigrants; trafficking in drugs; trafficking in stolen and illegal goods.'[15] It was decided that the market would be formalised and relocated to a new, neighbouring site where all needed infrastructure and facilities would be provided. Such an arrangement has allowed for the financial gain, fuelled by human misery at the market, to be incorporated into the formal regulatory framework.

The market was closed on 17 February 2001, when the Brčko District Government passed a land use motion restoring the government's control over the land in the area of the Arizona Market. From that moment on, the land was to be used exclusively for agricultural purposes – meaning that all commercial activity on the premises was forced to cease operation immediately. On 2 August 2001, referring to Arizona Market as a true trading town, the district supervisor Henry L. Clarke announced plans to appropriate the market.

12   Moore, 'Localizing Peacebuilding,' 5.
13   Bernard Markušić, 'Teorija Geneze Trgovanja Ljudima Na Području Jugoistočne Europe Kroz Analizu Utjecaja Militarizacije, Političkih Procesa i Globalne Ekonomije,' *Pravnik: Časopis Za Pravna I Društvena Pitanja*, 48, no. 97 (July 2015): 119–43.
14   Haynes, 'Lessons from Bosnia's Arizona Market,' 1796.
15   The full OHR press release can be viewed on their website, *https://www.ohr.int/international-community-to-clean-up-trade-at-the-arizona-market-brcko-2/*

Arizona Market, Brčko, Bosnia and Herzegovina, 2006

He invited private enterprises and businesses to join the Brčko District Government in constructing the new market – Arizona 2. In December 2001, the Italo-Bosnian-Serbian consortium Italproject d.o.o. won the tender to build and operate the new market. The consortium entered into a leasing agreement with the district administration, granting them the exclusive rights to collect all rental income from the market for seventeen years. In exchange for developing the market's infrastructure, the consortium invested 120 million euros. The project, overseen by the European Union Force in BiH (EUFOR), aimed to create a modern trading infrastructure spanning an initial area of 60,000 square metres. What stood out in this approach to reclaim control over Arizona Market was the collaboration between the international community, exercising political and territorial power, and a global investor privatising the market's public domain. Additionally, Arizona 2's new market location was not under the jurisdiction of the district, but rather in the hands of the farmers and individuals whose livelihoods depended on it. Therefore, simultaneous to the unveiling of the plans for the market's future, Brčko District Government announced the expropriation of private property in the area of Arizona 2 – pushing the farmers and landowners off of their land to make space for private enterprise. Italproject d.o.o. now had the rights to control the future market's area in any way they saw fit. The market's formalisation thereby became itself a threat to the very community that it was created to cater for.

Even though the construction of Arizona 2 was eventually halted due to uncleared landmines in the area, most of the new market was already constructed by 2004. Italproject d.o.o. proposed that vendors could purchase stalls in module-like arrangements in newly erected large halls. Many of the vendors quickly accepted the opportunity, and bought one or more spaces at the new market, convinced that Arizona 2 would be as successful as its predecessor. However, the 2008 global economic crisis, steep increases in prices at the market, and the construction of neighbouring shopping malls all contributed to Arizona's decline. In 2010, the Brčko District Assembly accused Italproject d.o.o. of negligence in the running and development of the market and awarded exclusive management rights to another enterprise, Santovac d.o.o., that operates Arizona 2 to this day.

Arizona Market, Brčko, Bosnia and Herzegovina, 2006

According to the market's owners, the reasoning behind the decision was connected with the failure of Italproject d.o.o. to repay loans to Hypo Alpe Adria Bank d.d. that had lent the funds for the Arizona 2 complex to be built. This led to many vendors and business owners who had already bought retail and commercial spaces being exposed to having their premises seized by the bank. From the illegal Arizona Market to its formalised iteration, the market was a victim of different spheres of influence and appetite for financial gain, no matter the cost.

COMMUNITY-BUILDING AT THE INTERSECTION OF ETHNIC FRONTLINES

Because informal markets do not comply with most formal rules and regulations, in the event of wars and severe crises, they are resilient and able to adapt or 'bounce back' faster than any other formal economies. In these instances, informal markets tend to meet communities' needs when formal channels halt or when trust in these channels is lost. Their informality can result in agility, which is how they adapt to changing circumstances on the local, regional and global scales to cater to local communities' most basic needs. In the context of Brčko District, the critical challenge was integrating all the different ethnicities and communities peacefully. According to the official census, in 1991, the population of Bosniaks in the Brčko District was 22,994, with 8,253 Serbs, 2,894 Croats and 7,265 others, while in 2013, there were 17,489 Bosniaks, 19,420 Serbs, 1,457 Croats and 1,527 others.[16] The steep rise of Serbian nationals from 19.9 percent in 1991 to 48.7 percent in 2013, together with a significant drop in Bosniak, Croat and other nationalities in the same timeframe, signalled the complex relations and apparent tensions between these groups in the post-war period when the initial Arizona Market emerged. Being an international market located only twenty kilometres away from the tri-border area, Arizona Market had to become a space where ethnic differences were put aside. The absence of effective regulation and the protection the market enjoyed during the post-war period of the 1990s initially allowed all communities to make ends meet by taking part in the market, whether in the role

16   Official census data has been extracted from the BiH Agency for Statistics, *https://www.popis.gov.ba/popis2013/mapa/?lang=bos*

of vendors who could sell their goods without having to pay taxes, or customers who had access to cheaper goods at Arizona than anywhere else. However, as the unregulated market grew and expanded, protection from the international community, which was once inclusive towards all communities participating in trade, very quickly became exclusive.

The subsequent transformation of the market into a privately operated shopping mall represented a dramatic change for both the business owners and visitors. Unlike the former bazaar-like market, the privately-operated Arizona 2 was in sync with the aspirations and ambitions of both the international community and the Brčko District Government. After the new market was constructed in 2004, most of the retail spaces were soon formally sold – marking the official birth of the community of vendors and entrepreneurs who took part in the market. Today, after a series of layered crises it is evident that Arizona has managed to stay active largely due to the persistence of that very community. They have managed to survive by switching to wholesale trade, as well as through the introduction of on-site manufacturing, transforming the market into a significant production node in northeast BiH. The market's continued development and operation therefore demonstrate the resilience of the Arizona community in adapting to changing circumstances and capitalising on new economic opportunities. However, its continuing informal and unregulated nature also underscores the challenges of achieving sustainable and equitable economic development in post-conflict settings.

The Arizona Market serves as a stark illustration of the complex interplay between economics, politics, and social dynamics in post-conflict societies. It demonstrates how the pursuit of economic prosperity and the ideals of a free market can inadvertently perpetuate inequalities, human rights violations, and structural violence. The market's existence and the IC's involvement raise critical questions about power dynamics, accountability, and the long-term implications of neoliberal policies on communities recovering from conflict.

FROM A SPACE OF BARE SURVIVAL TO A PLACE OF UBIQUITOUS CONSUMPTION

A new era of privatisation was ushered in for the Brčko District in 2001, promising a transformative approach unlike the national entity programmes that came before. The new model, introduced by Brčko District Supervisor Henry L. Clarke, aimed to encourage new investment and the preservation of existing jobs. By 2003, four 'strategic enterprises' had already changed ownership, marking a significant milestone in the unfolding narrative of privatisation during the transition from a centrally planned economy to a market-oriented one.[17] This process generated debates around property rights, economic restructuring, and the role of foreign investors in the context of shaping the economic landscape of the district. Arizona Market's privatisation was therefore not an isolated phenomenon, but rather part of the broader privatisation initiatives in Brčko District. What initially started as a few stalls along the Arizona Route eventually expanded into a substantial private commercial venture, reflecting the shifting dynamics of market relations in the post-war society.

While the first iteration of Arizona Market was in the public domain, Arizona 2 was conceived as a public-private partnership, resulting in the new market being built and maintained exclusively by private enterprise. With the involvement of Italproject d.o.o, Arizona Market in Brčko underwent a significant transformation, both in its physical appearance and operational dynamics. 'In only ten years, the market was transformed from a space of bare survival into a centre of ubiquitous consumption,'[18] making it difficult for many local vendors to continue their trade. The market, once an informal and bustling open-air space, evolved into a structured and privatised shopping mall as Arizona 2, with mandatory permits, licences, taxes and compliance to certain standards. At that point the market's illegal activities dropped significantly, but the 'victimless' informal activities seem to have persisted, with many stores still offering counterfeit and illegally produced

17   International Crisis Group, 'Bosnia's Brčko: Getting In, Getting On and Getting Out,' *Balkans Report* 144 (2 June 2003).
18   Mörtenböck and Mooshammer, 'Arizona Market,' 127.

Arizona Market, Brčko, Bosnia and Herzegovina, 2006

goods exclusively – mostly knock-offs of designer garments and counterfeit electronics, but also toys, appliances, tools, car parts and many other items. The sale of such items at Arizona 2 persisted thanks to the formal-informal linkage via the managing enterprise's (Italproject d.o.o. and later Santovac d.o.o.) accommodating attitude towards the informal sector business-owners.

For the first time with a clear regulatory policy, roads, housing, a police station and formalised parking spaces organised around the newly built retail halls, Arizona 2 was not merely a market anymore but rather an aspiring trading city. Architectural changes reshaped the landscape of the market, and the post-war makeshift stalls gave way to permanent structures and modern facilities. Arizona 2 was and still is organised into distinct sections positioned both indoors and outdoors, each catering to specific types of goods and services. The market appears as a labyrinth of interconnected corridors and alleys, lined with retail spaces, workshops and entertainment venues. In spite of the formalisation of the market's layout and improvement of necessary facilities and infrastructure, the new Arizona Market became a victim of short-sighted and profit-oriented design. Many of the retail spaces resemble enclosed cages thanks to the metal bars and grill panels often used as storefronts, dominating the market's aesthetic. All of the spaces outside of individual retail units are lined with merchandise, placed provisionally throughout the length of the hallways to attract and stop visitors – a sight that could be described as a visual materialisation of informality. The absence of any design features that address comfort or visual appeal are responsible for Arizona 2's purely functional, almost warehouse-like aesthetic. This is especially evident when the market is closed for visitors – with security guards patrolling the premises and barriers placed in front of the parking areas to block unauthorised entrance. The spatial disparities between Arizona 2 and its predecessor raise questions about the conflicting dynamics of self-organisation and top-down control, and the resulting impacts on trade.

Although commercialised and privately operated, the market remained a hub for informal commerce – however, in a much more subtle manner compared to the initial market. Most of the appalling illegal activities that dominated the original market became completely absent in Arizona 2. Besides the improved regulation in comparison to its predecessor, the reason for this lies in the significant change in the spatial typologies – since privatisation, the market was no longer configured as a space solely for commerce, but rather as a hybrid space comprising retail and housing. The introduction of living space to the market's area seems to have significantly raised the stakes for those participating in serious criminal acts. Since it began operating, Arizona 2 has been responsible for the livelihoods of all the entrepreneurs who bought land and built their homes in Arizona's designated residential area, and none were willing to risk involvement in such illicit activities.

As the mid-2000s marked the successful beginning and steady growth of Arizona 2, the market's management intended to expand the commercial area further. The plans for Arizona 3 were soon unveiled, consisting of the mall's significant expansion as well as the addition of hotels, casinos and leisure facilities. The appetite for profit grew, but tax rates and the construction of rival markets and malls along with a series of layered economic crises have slowed down trade over the years.

What the vendors and the market's management did not realise at the time was that with formal sector businesses and suppliers taking a more dominant role in the market, the prices could not be kept as low as before. As steep price rises coincided with the 2008 economic crisis, the number of visitors shrunk significantly, resulting in many entrepreneurs having to close their businesses for good in the following years. Due to this, the plans for Arizona 3 were never realised. However, after change in the market's ownership, Arizona has managed to stay in business despite the negative forecasts. Furthermore, the shift of focus from a solely profit-oriented approach to a more adaptive approach that takes into account the varied forms of market relations in market management and design proved to be positive for businesses at Arizona Market. According to management, Arizona is now entering another phase of expansion similar to Arizona 3, in which additional retail spaces

Arizona Market, Brčko, Bosnia and Herzegovina, 2022

as well as new retail structures will be built. Nevertheless, the number of empty commercial spaces on the premises is still rising and the fate of the market remains unclear.

THE MARKET AS A SITE WHERE FORMAL-INFORMAL LINKAGES MATERIALISE

Since its inception, Arizona Market's operation relies on a broad range of formal-informal linkages, which have played a crucial role in the market's transformations since the 1990s. A key formal-informal linkage that appeared within the frame of the initial Arizona Market was the legal recognition it received during its completely unregulated period in the 1990s. The international community's protection acknowledged the importance of the informal market as a vital economic and social space in the Brčko District. The validation of the informal market's role in the post-war reconstruction constituted a formal-informal linkage that provided a level of legitimacy to the informal and illegal activities taking place within it.

However, most of the current formal-informal linkages have to do with the relationships between the various actors involved in the commerce. With around 2,000 businesses currently active, Arizona 2 serves as a significant source of employment for many individuals, particularly those in the informal sector. Stall owners and service providers within the market often hire local residents, including those who may have limited access to formal employment opportunities. This creates a labour market linkage between the formal businesses and informal workers that provides income and livelihoods for the local population. Moreover, not only are there formal-informal linkages between the employers and employees operating at Arizona, but also between all stakeholders participating in the supply chain. The Arizona Market acts as a hub for manufacturing, trade and commerce, connecting informal sector entrepreneurs with formal sector businesses and customers. Formal retailers in the region may source goods from informal sector producers and suppliers within the market. This enables them to access a diverse range of products and meet consumer demand while providing a market for informal sector entrepreneurs to sell their goods. These examples illustrate the complex web of interactions and relationships between formal and informal actors within

Typical infrastructural components, Arizona Market, Brčko, Bosnia and Herzegovina

Arizona Market, Brčko, Bosnia and Herzegovina, 2022

and outside of Arizona Market. However, it is important to acknowledge the potential pitfalls and drawbacks of these formal-informal linkages. While they have contributed to the market's growth and longevity, they have also perpetuated inequalities and exploitation, particularly affecting vulnerable groups within the market in its early stages. Therefore, the narratives of business owners' success must be observed alongside the hardships faced by marginalised individuals who have been impacted by the market's transformations.

Finally, how do formal-informal linkages manifest in space? While observing Arizona 2, the experimental cacophony of contrasting architectural typologies cannot be missed. The sterile design of the retail halls and warehouses enmeshed with the chaotic and vibrant merchandise laying within and around the boutiques with no clear order give the impression of a market rather than that of a shopping mall. Additionally, increasingly bizarre structures can be found at the margins of the retail complex: these include totally unfinished and improvised-appearing commercial objects with differing design elements, materials and construction types which can

be seen to represent the materialisation of informality itself. These are placed next to the hybrid housing-retail structures where many entrepreneurs and business owners live with their families. Most of these structures comprise three storeys, which are used for retail and domestic life. While stores and workshops in these structures are situated on ground floors, additional goods are often kept on the first floor, leaving only the second floor for family living space . If for example their business slows down, the space needed for storing the goods shrinks, and the space for the family expands (and the other way around). Apart from these spatial features, there are architectural devices that also signal the informal nature of the complex. These can be found in many areas where there is ongoing construction within the complex and most often include wooden or metal planks as improvised barriers and fences, as well as concrete slabs as roadblocks. All of the described formal-informal linkages in space most often appear as indicators or consequences of operational inadequacies. The market's transformation has been marked by a complex web of formal and informal connections, representing a dynamic interplay between formalised regulations and informal practices.

TROUBLED PAST,
AN UNCERTAIN FUTURE

The Arizona Market in Brčko has undergone significant transformations, serving as a complex site of economic, social, and spatial change. The market's transformation from a space of basic survival into an experimental architectural typology signifying purely profit-driven intentions, reflects the broader shifts in BiH's socioeconomic landscape. It has evolved from an informal, ad-hoc market to a more formalised-appearing, privately owned and profit-driven business venture. This transformation has brought both opportunities and challenges, as the market's expansion and integration into the global economy have led to increased prosperity for some while marginalising others. The Arizona Market in Brčko encapsulates the complexities of urban development, peace-building, and market dynamics. It symbolises the tensions between economic progress and social justice, highlighting the need for inclusive and sustainable approaches that address the diverse needs and aspirations of all market participants.

Looking ahead, the future of the Arizona Market remains uncertain. The market's trajectory is influenced by various factors, including shifting economic conditions, changing consumer preferences, and BiH's steadily evolving regulatory frameworks. Additionally, the challenges of globalisation and digitalisation pose new threats and uncertainties that will shape the market's viability and sustainability. To ensure a more equitable and inclusive future for Arizona Market, it is crucial to address the underlying structural issues that have hindered its progress. Efforts should be directed towards fostering a supportive environment that promotes entrepreneurship, protects the rights of all market participants, and provides opportunities for economic mobility. Finally, Arizona Market in Brčko represents a microcosm of the challenges and opportunities faced by post-conflict societies in their quest for economic revitalisation and social cohesion. Its troubled past and uncertain future underscore the need for comprehensive and holistic approaches that address the complexities of market dynamics, social inclusion, and peace-building efforts. Only through sustained efforts and collective action can Arizona Market become a catalyst for sustainable development, shared prosperity, and lasting peace.

REFERENCES

Bašić, M. 'Osnove ratne ekonomije: s osvrtom na rat u BiH 1992.-95. godine.' Ekonomski Pregled 57 (February 2006): 130–45.

Diatlov, Victor I. 'Ethnic Markets in Post-Soviet Transitional Space: Their Role in Society and the Research Area.' Žurnal Sibirskogo Federal'nogo Universiteta 9, no. 4 (2016): 795–814.

Haynes, D. F. 'Lessons from Bosnia's Arizona Market: Harm to Women in a Neoliberalized Postconflict Reconstruction Process.' University of Pennsylvania Law Review 158, no. 6 (2010): 1779–1829.

International Crisis Group, 'Bosnia's Brčko: Getting In, Getting On and Getting Out,' Balkans Report 144 (2 June 2003).

Markušić, B. 'Teorija Geneze Trgovanja Ljudima Na Području Jugoistočne Europe Kroz Analizu Utjecaja Militarizacije, Političkih Procesa i Globalne Ekonomije.' Pravnik: Časopis Za Pravna I Društvena Pitanja 48, no. 97 (July 2015): 119–43.

Mörtenböck, P. and H. Mooshammer. 'Arizona Market: Inter-ethnic collaboration in Brčko.' In Informal Market Worlds: The Architecture of Economic Pressure - Atlas, edited by P. Mörtenböck and H. Mooshammer, 124–131. Rotterdam: nai010 publishers, 2015.

Mörtenböck, P. and H. Mooshammer. 'Post-conflict Markets.' In Informal Market Worlds: The Architecture of Economic Pressure - Atlas, edited by P. Mörtenböck and H. Mooshammer, 92–95. Rotterdam: nai010 publishers, 2015.

Moore, A. 'Localizing Peacebuilding: The Arizona Market and the Evolution of US Military Peacebuilding Priorities in Bosnia.' Journal of Intervention and Statebuilding 13, no. 3 (2019): 263–80.

OHR. 'Brčko Supervisor Issues an Order on the Arizona Market.' Office of the High Representative, Brčko, 17 November 2000. https://www.ohr.int/brcko-supervisor-issues-an-order-on-the-arizona-market/

OHR. 'Ohr Bih Media Round-up (5/8/2002).' Office of the High Representative, Brčko, 5 August 2002. https://www.ohr.int/ohr_archive/ohr-bih-media-round-up-582002-2/

OHR. 'Supervisor of Brčko, Henry L. Clarke, Halts Privatization in Brčko District.' Office of the High Representative, Brčko, 14 August 2001. https://www.ohr.int/supervisor-of-brcko-henry-l-clarke-halts-privatization-in-brcko-district/

OHR. 'Supervisor of Brčko Issues Second Order on the Arizona Market.' Office of the High Representative, Brčko, 17 February 2001. https://www.ohr.int/supervisor-of-brcko-issues-second-order-on-the-arizona-market-2/

OHR. 'The Arizona Market Contract Is Clear, Binding and Just.' Office of the High Representative, Brčko, 10 May 2002. https://www.ohr.int/the-arizona-market-contract-is-clear-binding-and-just/

OHR. 'The New Arizona Market, Remarks by Supervisor of Brčko, Henry L. Clarke.' Office of the High Representative, Brčko, 2 August 2001. https://www.ohr.int/the-new-arizona-market-remarks-by-supervisor-of-brcko-henry-l-clarke/

OHR, OSCE, UNMBIH, SFOR. 'International Community to Clean up Trade at the Arizona Market, Brčko.' Office of the High Representative, Brčko, 26 October 2000. https://www.ohr.int/international-community-to-clean-up-trade-at-the-arizona-market-brcko-2/

1990-1995

1 Bosnia and Herzegovina has a GDP of 11 billion US dollars and per capita income of 2,400 US dollars.
2 Bosnia and Herzegovina is a constituent republic within the Socialist Federative Republic of Yugoslavia.
3 Breakup of Yugoslavia prompted by the declarations of independence signed by Croatia and Slovenia.
4 According to the official census, in 1991 the population of Bosniaks in the Brčko District is 22,994, alongside 8,253 Serbs, 2,894 Croats and 7,265 other ethnicities.
5 Black markets emerge during the Bosnian War.

1995-2000

6 Clearing of the 'Arizona Route' and the market's future site of landmines
7 Brčko District has 17,489 Bosniaks, 19,420 Serbs, 1,457 Croats and 1,527 others; the steep rise in Serbs from 19,9% in 1991 to 48,7% in 2013, together with a significant drop in Bosniak, Croat and other ethnicities in the same period, indicates the upheaval of relations between the different ethnic groups as a consequence of the war.
8 Bosnia and Herzegovina's GDP plummets to 1.87 billion US dollars and per capita income drops to 500 US dollars.
9 Inception of Arizona Market
10 Informal roadside vendors cluster next to a checkpoint on Arizona Route; tolerated by the international community (OHR, OSCE, UNMIBH, SFOR) this trade soon expands into adjacent fields, with fixed stalls forming the first Arizona Market.

11 Arizona Market grows into a crucial trans-regional and cross-border trade node in Bosnia and Herzegovina's postwar period.

2000-2005

12 Arizona market becomes a major hub for drug and human trafficking in Eastern Europe.
13 The international community's Office of the High Representative raises concerns about the steep rise in illicit activities and commits to ridding the market of these problems.
14 Temporary closure of the Arizona Market
15 Plans for reorganising Arizona Market as a privately operated market are announced.

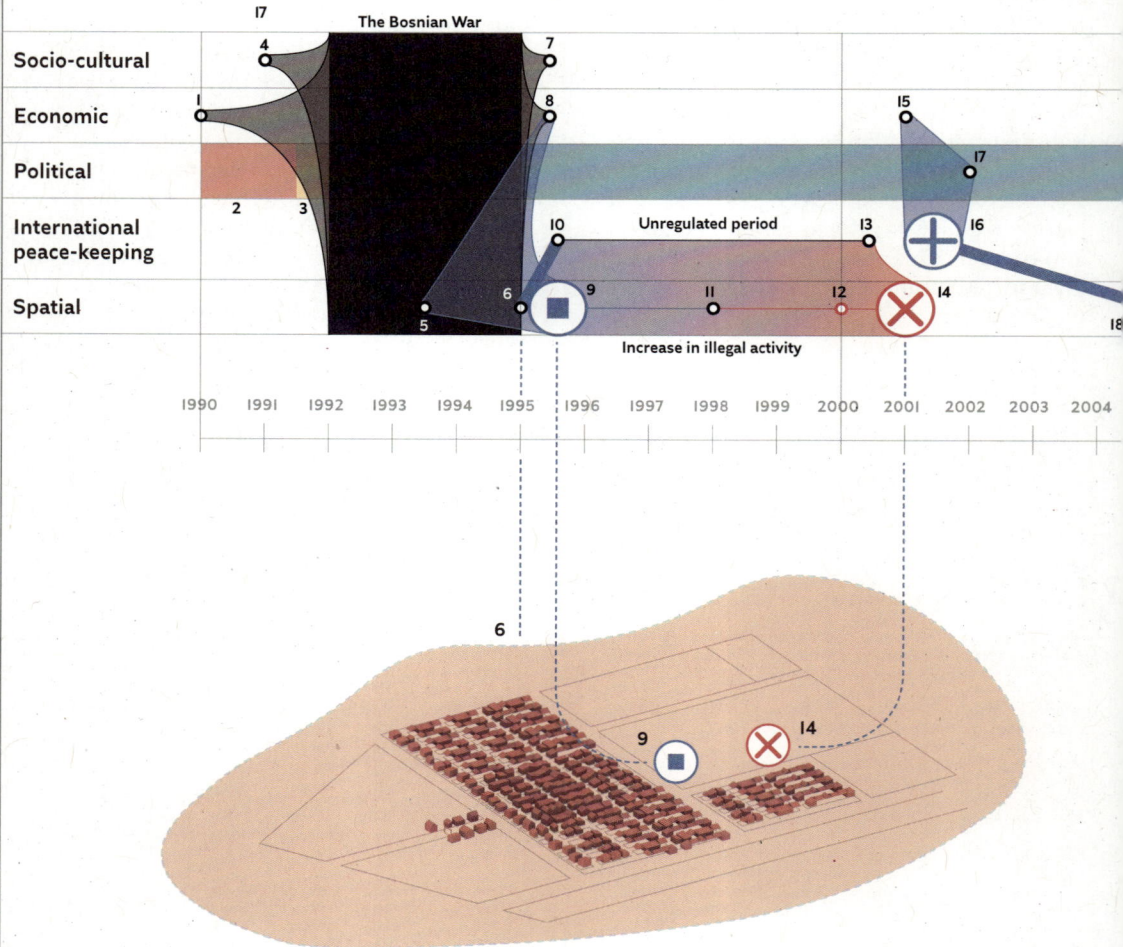

Timeline of key events shaping the transformation of Arizona Market, Brčko, Bosnia and Herzegovina

16   The Supvervisor of the Brčko District invites tenders from private enterprise to build and operate a new and improved Arizona Market.
17   The Italian-Bosnian-Serbian consortium Italproject wins the tender and enters into a leasing agreement with the district administration, granting them the exclusive rights to collect all rental income from the market for seventeen years; in the agreement, the consortium commits itself to investing 120 million euros in the development of the market infrastructure.

2005-2010
18   Opening of the new market in November 2004
19   Most of the retail spaces at the new market are quickly taken up by individual businesses.
20   Beginning of the decline of business at Arizona Market
21   Introduction of tax rates for the Brčko District and the Arizona Market in accordance with the rest of BiH (prior to this, the district was granted favourable taxation)
22   Construction of further shopping malls and commercial premises nearby
23   Beginning of the global financial crisis
24   Brčko District added to the BiH constitution

2010-2015
25   Steep increases in prices at the Arizona Market
26   The Brčko District Assembly claims negligence in the running and development of the market by Italproject and awards its sole management to another enterprise, Santovac.
27   Brčko District supervisor Roderick Moore suspends his functions and the district's authorities assume full responsibility for governance in the district.

2015-2020
28   Poor infrastructure and lax safety conditions cause a fire in a section of the Arizona Market.
29   An estimated 2,500 workers remain at the Arizona Market.
30   Initially planned beginning of the expansion of Arizona Market

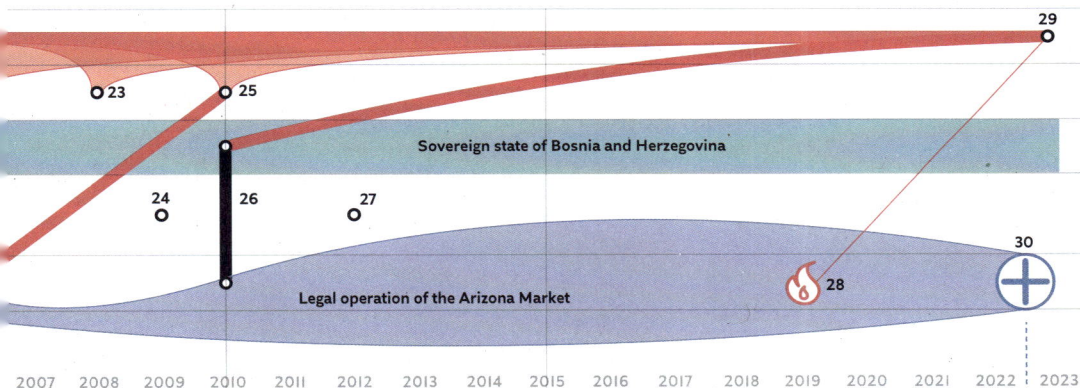

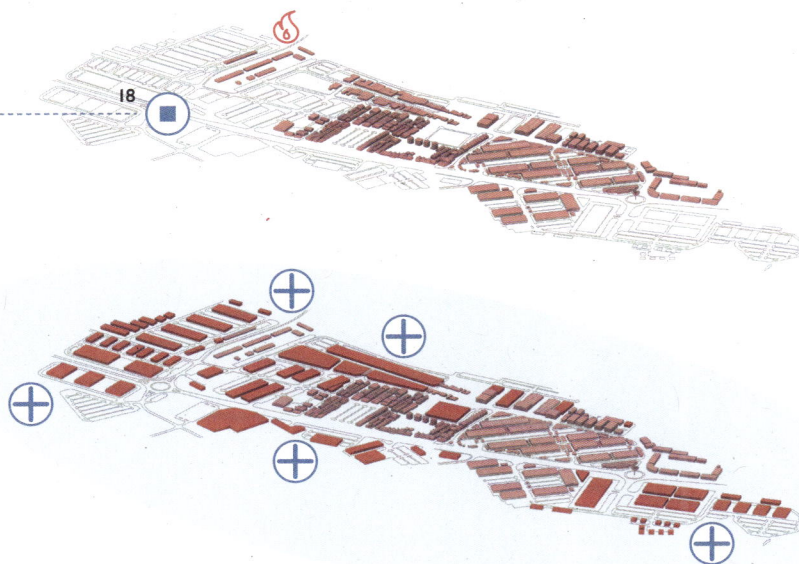

29

23   25

Sovereign state of Bosnia and Herzegovina

24   26   27

30

28

Legal operation of the Arizona Market

2007 2008 2009 2010 2011 2012 2013 2014 2015 2016 2017 2018 2019 2020 2021 2022 2023

18

30

■ Spatial, social, economic and political interventions into in/formal markets
■ Informality as a survival method and means of adapting to changing socio-economic and political circumstances

Typical infrastructural components, Arizona Market, Brčko, Bosnia and Herzegovina

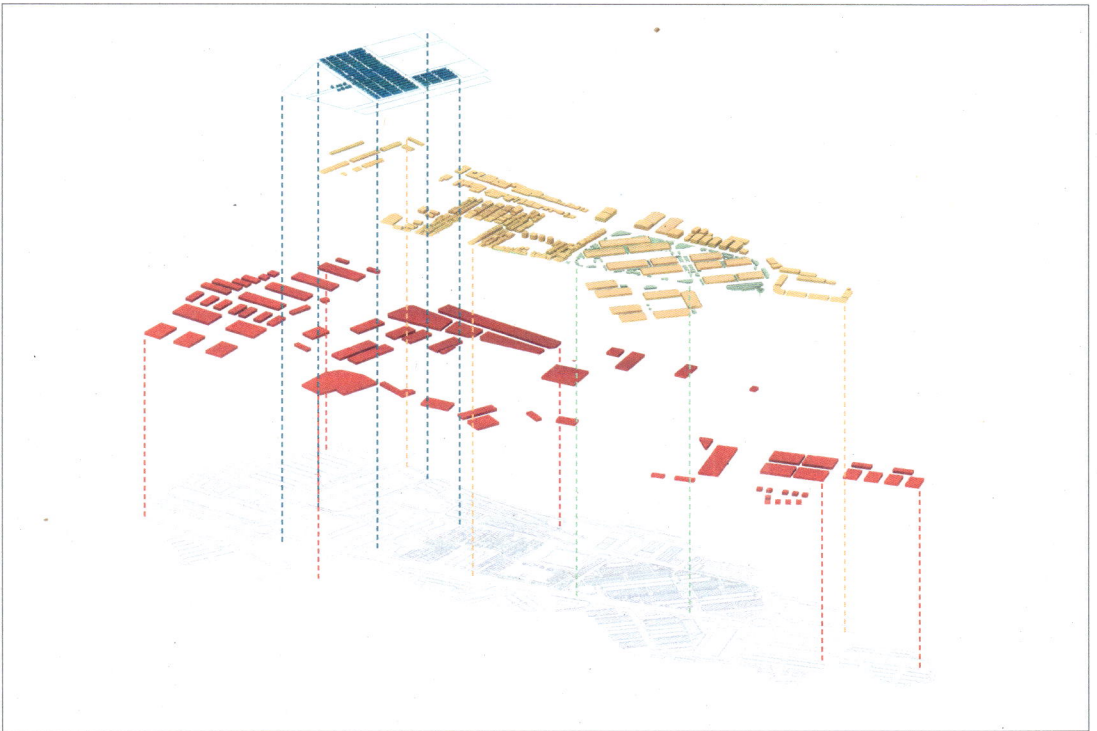

■ Post-war unregulated market, 1995-2001　　■ Privately operated shopping mall, 2004 onwards　　■ Future expansion plans

Transformation of Arizona Market, Brčko, Bosnia and Herzegovina

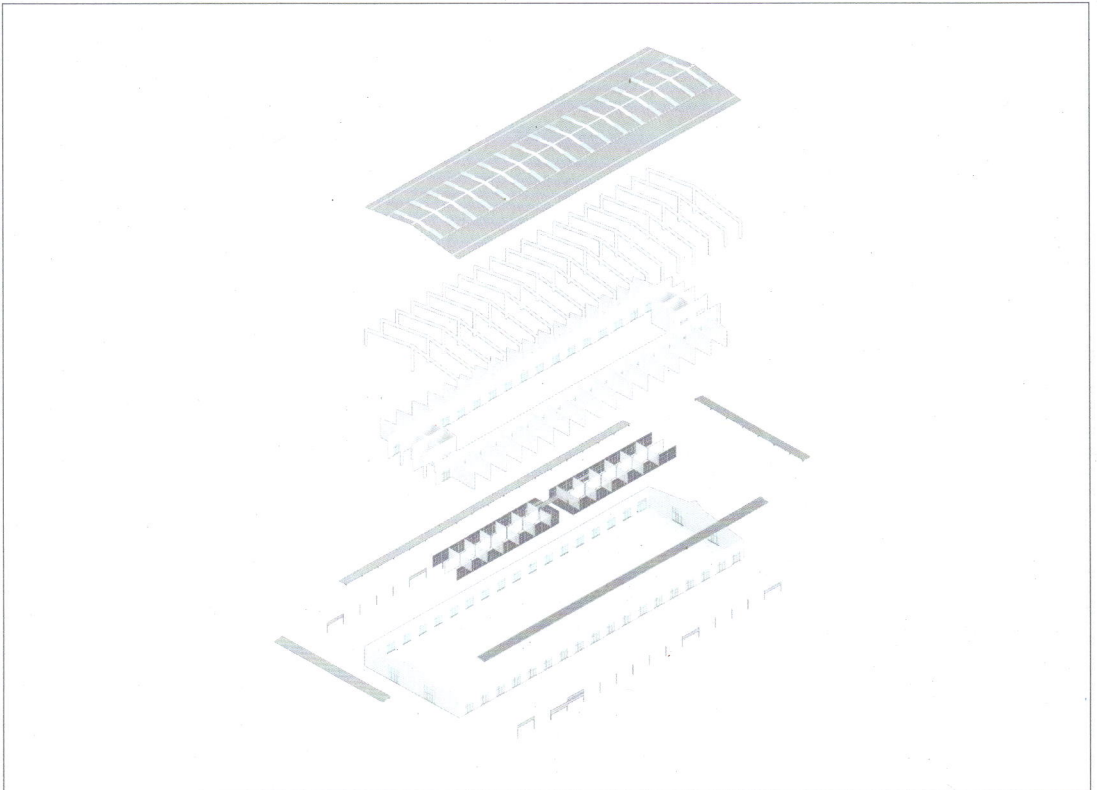

Spatial features of the indoor markets at Arizona Market, Brčko, Bosnia and Herzegovina

Map 1 (top)

Brčko

Border BiH - CRO

Cleared areas

No obvious risk   Risk areas

Dayton Peace Accord   Founding of BiH Mine Action Center

Bosnian War   Mine action ongoing

1992   1995   1997

Map 2 (middle)

Brčko

Border BiH - CRO

US military checkpoint

Cleared areas

No obvious risk   Risk areas

Dayton Peace Accord

4km

Inter-Entity Border Line   Zone of separation

1992   1995

Map 3 (bottom)

Orasje

Zagreb   Novi Sad
Belgrade

Border BiH - CRO
Brčko

Arizona Market

Zenica

Tuzla   Sarajevo

Cleared areas

No obvious risk   Risk areas

Dayton Peace Accord   Emergence of Arizona Market

1992   1995   1996

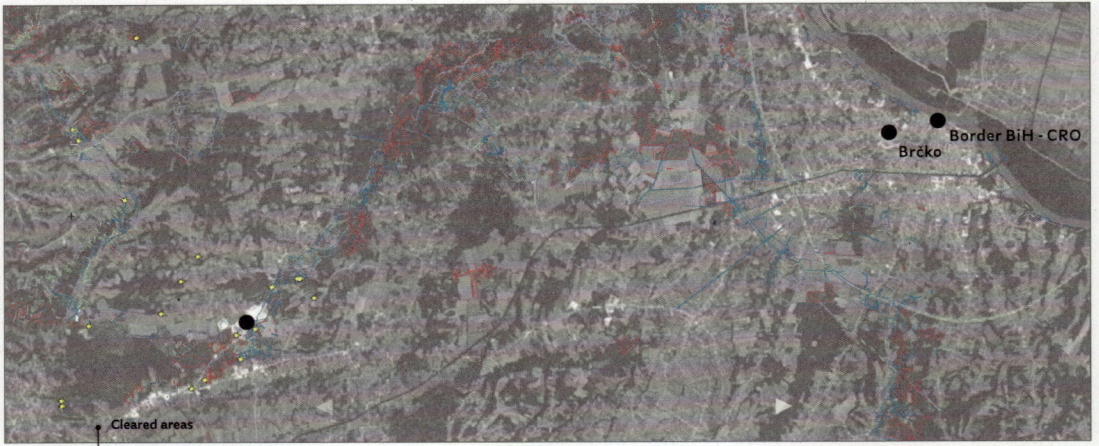

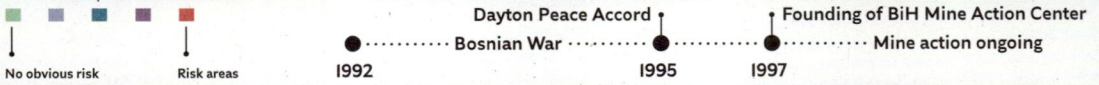

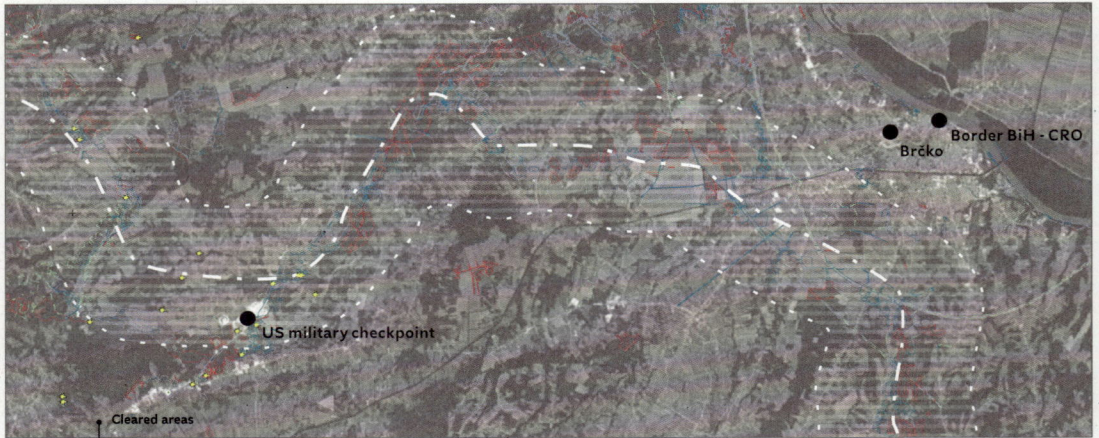

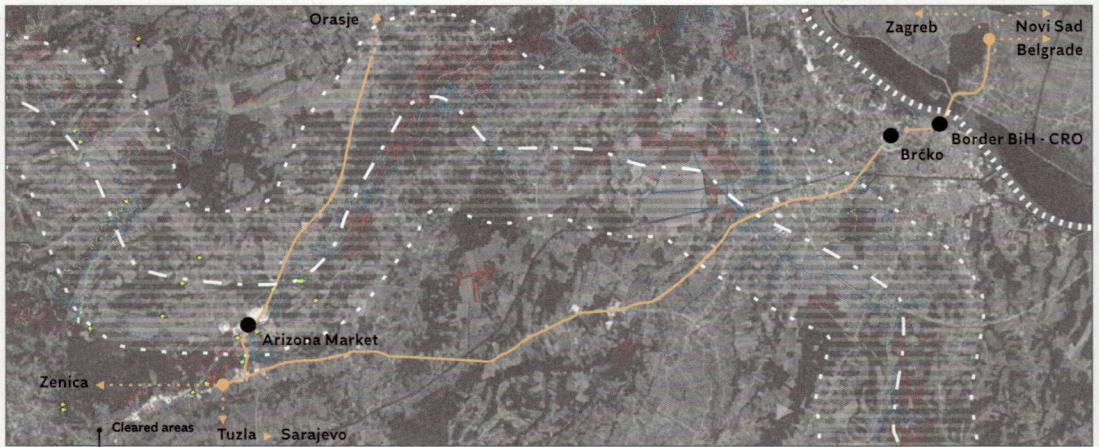

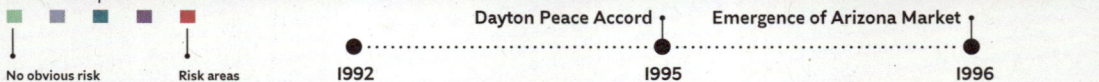

Mine fields, borders and supply routes, Brčko District, Bosnia and Herzegovina; Map data: Google, CNES/Airbus

Arizona Market, Brčko, Bosnia and Herzegovina, 2006

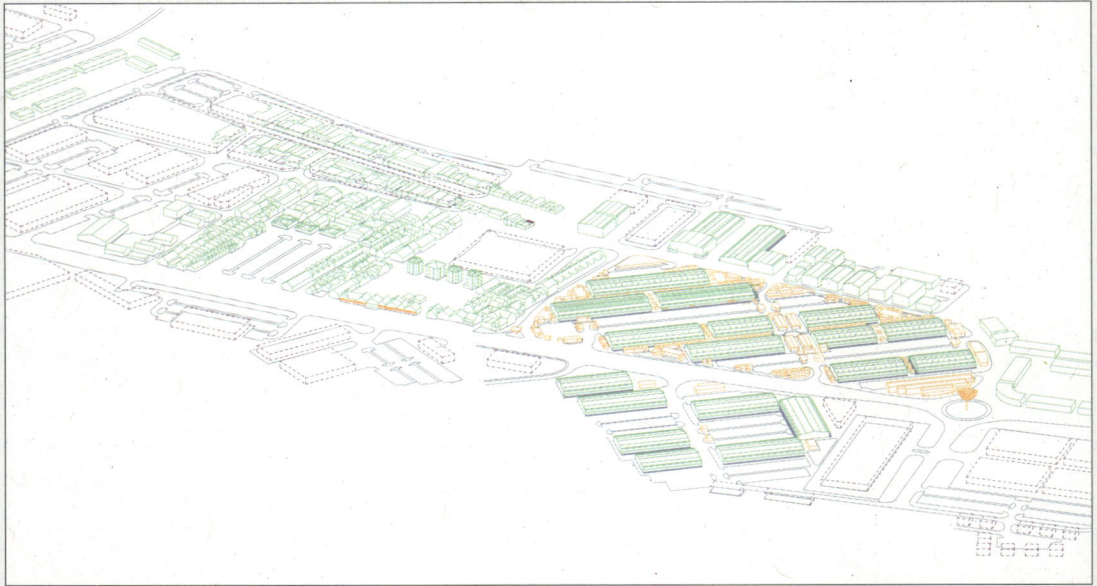

Timeline of key events shaping the transformation of Arizona Market, Brčko, Bosnia and Herzegovina

Arizona Market

356

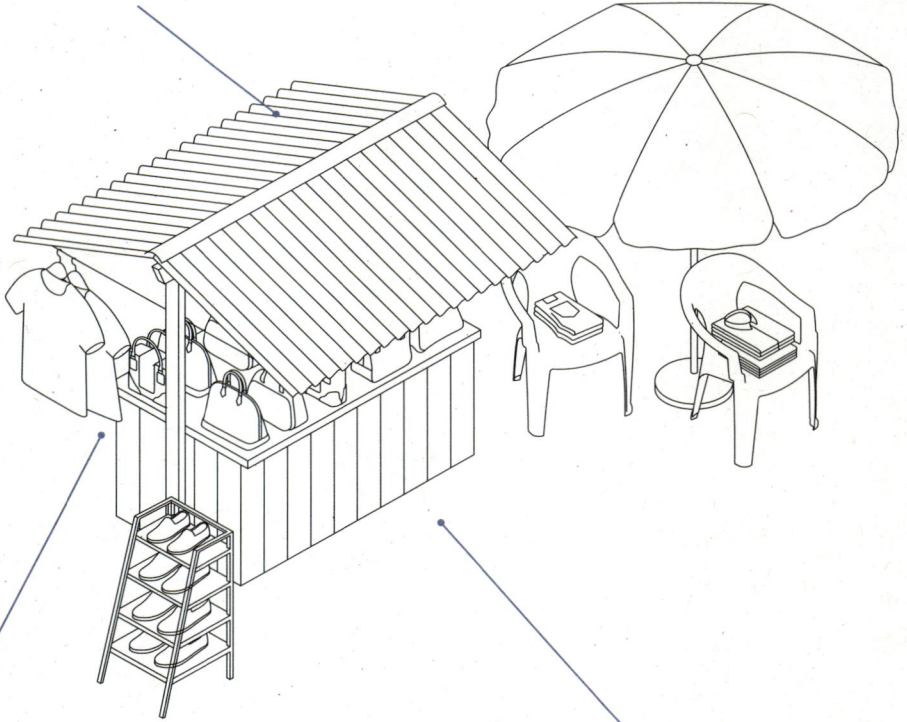

The destruction wrought by the Bosnian War, in combination with the systemic transition from a socialist regime to a market economy throughout the 1990s, created economic havoc that people sought to overcome by establishing an informal market environment

Initially catering to the remaining local population and members of the international peace-keeping troops, Arizona Market soon transformed into a trans-regional shopping destination

In its first formation, Arizona Market consisted mostly of wooden stalls and temporary structures

Spatial features of the initial Arizona Market (1995-2001)

Top: Initial Arizona Market, Brčko, Bosnia and Herzegovina, 2001
Bottom: Arizona Market, Brčko, Bosnia and Herzegovina, 2022

Arizona Market, Brčko, Bosnia and Herzegovina, 2006 (top) and 2022 (bottom)

During the early phase of consolidation of
the Arizona Market, rows of individually-
styled buildings combining residential
and commercial spaces under one
roof are erected

One or two storeys of sales floors and
storage spaces are supplemented with a
residential storey on top boasting typical
features of contemporary residential
estates: balconies, flower arrangements,
garden furniture, awnings, loft
conversions, balustrades and miniature
turrets in different styles and colours

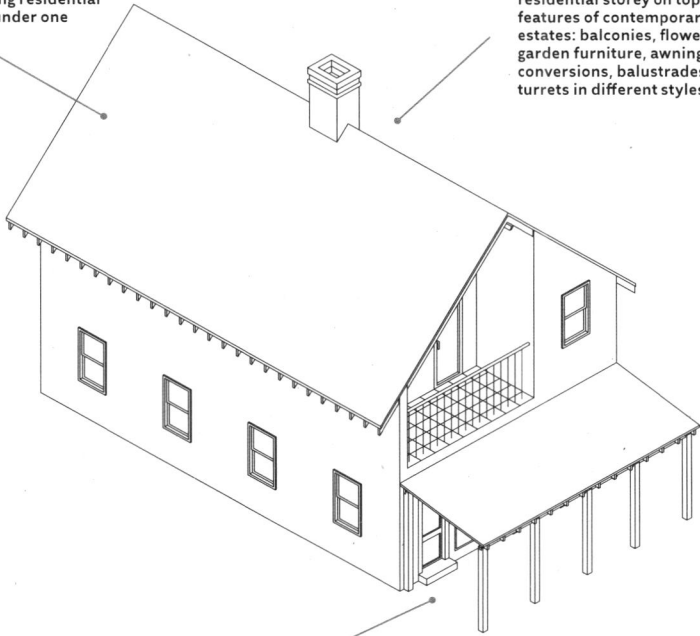

Front porches form an essential component of these houses:
they are used to display goods to passers-by on Arizona Road

Spatial features of the consolidation period of Arizona Market (2001-2004)

The privatisation of the market triggers a signicant change in
architectural typology and scale: large, identical warehouses are
set up in a grid, their interiors divided into small retail units which
the market operators let to individual traders

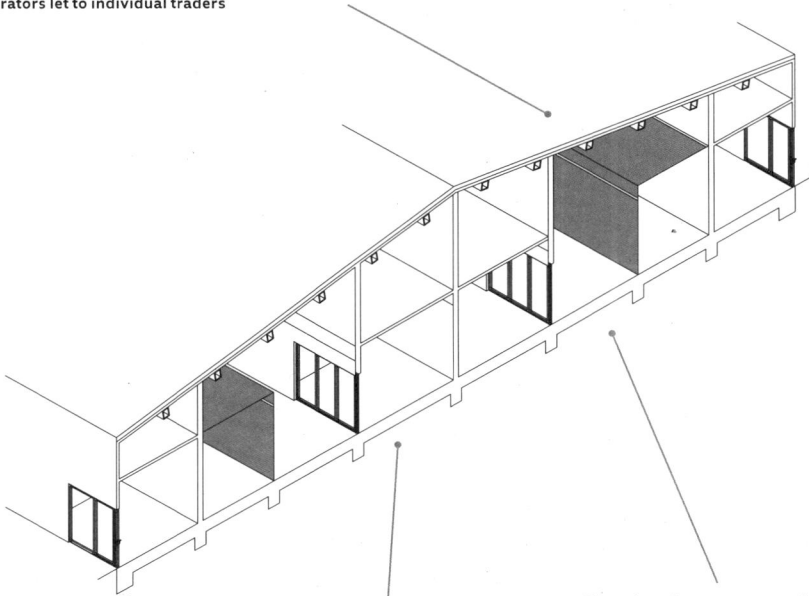

An increasing number of shops in the
warehouses are oriented to wholesale

Shops have begun to encroach on the
hallways with improvised additions for
storage and display

Spatial features of the privately operated indoor markets at Arizona Market (2004 onwards)

Arizona Market, Brčko, Bosnia and Herzegovina, 2022

Brooklyn Flea, Dumbo, New York, 2023

Carmen Lael Hines

The 'Between' of Urban Financialisation in New York

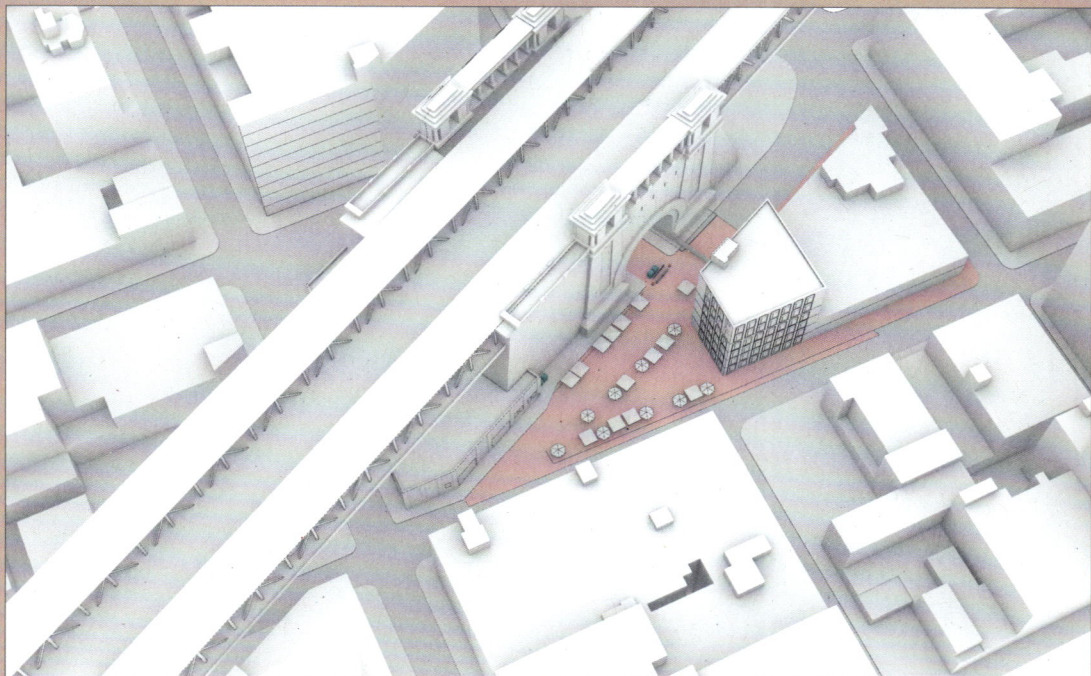

'We want to create the effect of (Brooklyn Flea) being stumbled upon,' explains Brooklyn Flea CEO Eric Demby at a coffee shop in Dumbo, Brooklyn.[1] The coffee shop feels like a homage to urban industrialism, with exposed brick, cardboard boxes, and iron scaffolding. My coffee, served in a glass, sits upon a long communal wooden table surrounded by bulbous lamps and enough plants to second as a botanical garden. The americano costs seven dollars, and the arrangement of the chairs is such that I am shoulder to shoulder with the person next to me, which makes it difficult to hear. He expands, explaining that the intention is to curate a feeling, or semblance, of the market having always been there. In this instance, he refers to one of the most prominent and attended iterations of the Brooklyn Flea Company, the Brooklyn Flea (of the same name), which occurs every Saturday and Sunday from April to December under the Manhattan Bridge Archway in Dumbo.

1   Eric Demby, in conversation with the author, 14 October 2022.

Open gates on market days allow the marketplace to function as a connective corridor between streets.

Chelsea Flea

Unified white canopies homogenise the appearance of the market.

Temporary barriers set up to separate the market from the public realm of the street

Parking attendant kiosk indicating the site's primary use as a parking lot

Shipping containers used as storage space and administrative office

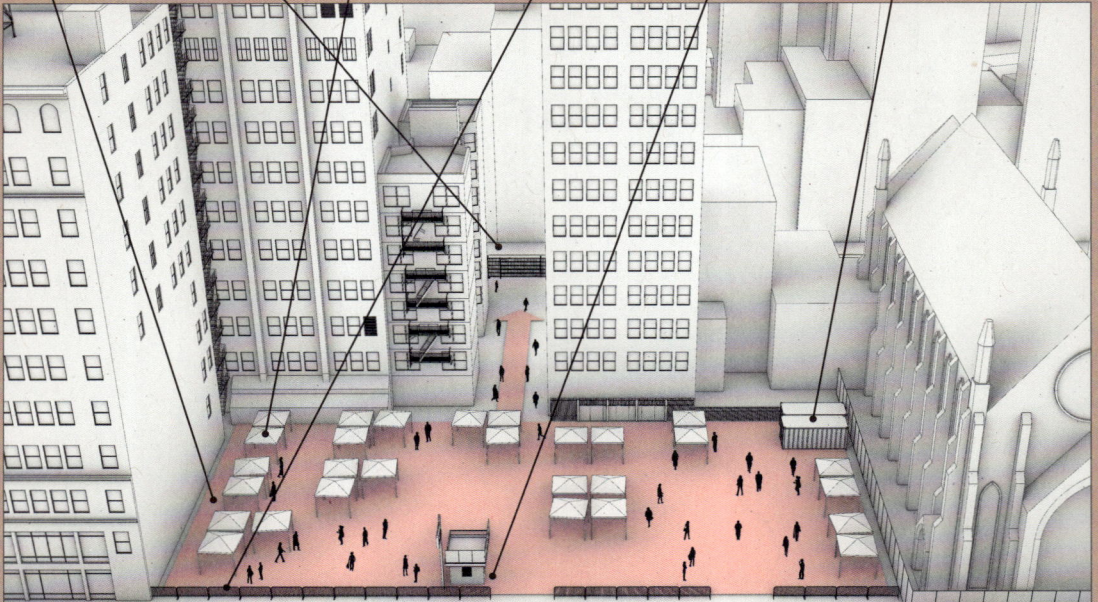

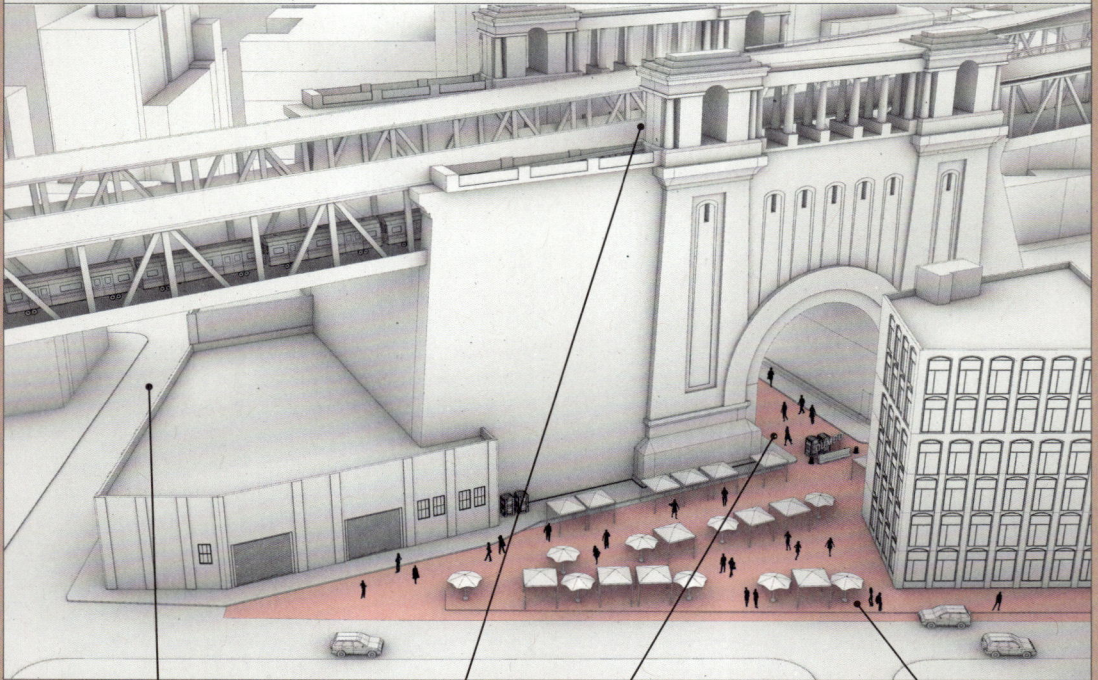

Manhattan Bridge

The cavernous space of the Manhattan Bridge Anchorage forms the heart of Brooklyn Flea Dumbo.

Dumbo (Down Under the Manhattan Bridge Overpass) was once an area zoned exclusively for manufacturing. It is now the centre of Brooklyn's tech triangle and one of Brooklyn's most visited neighbourhoods.

Brooklyn Flea Dumbo spills out onto what is designed to become Pearl Triangle Plaza.

In this anecdote, Demby suggests that Brooklyn Flea is built to feel like something that is not contained by the city, but is the city itself. Appearing as an organism growing from its environment, Brooklyn Flea indicates what can be referred to as the marketisation of the urban, or the urbanisation of the market, into a mutually informing dialectic. What becomes clear throughout our discussion, and over several weeks of fieldwork, is that Brooklyn Flea is formed through the material architecture and symbolic value of *Brooklyn*. As a case study, it offers crucial insights into contemporary productions of the city not only as a place where economic exchange takes place, but as a terrain where economic exchange and cultural activity merge to turn the city into a 'stage set' for new kinds of market relations.[2] To analyse Brooklyn Flea is to examine how *Brooklyn*, as a borough, became a kind of theme park for cultural capitalism and the policy formations that paved the way to this.

Since its inception in 2008, Brooklyn Flea has grown to be one of the largest market operators on the east coast of the United States, coordinating markets across the New York City boroughs as well as in Jersey City, Philadelphia, Los Angeles, Miami, Toronto, Osaka, Japan and Sao Paolo, Brazil.[3] Taking home an estimated revenue of 2.3 million US dollars each year,[4] it defines itself as an 'incubator' for 'participatory, entrepreneurial capitalism.'[5] Brooklyn Flea currently operates multiple outdoor markets, including Smorgasburg (a food market), Chelsea Flea, and Brooklyn Flea (both non-edible commodities).

Each iteration of Brooklyn Flea is different, but shares some fundamental similarities: They are curated and selective, they are designed to appear as spontaneously arising from the urban fabric, and the 'value' they generate is related to forms of symbolic and cultural capital generated by the neighbourhoods in which they are nestled. Brooklyn Flea prides itself on providing authentic goods. Vendors are advertised as local and

independent, selling items ranging from vintage t-shirts and artisanal soaps, to analogue cameras. Smorgasburg offers local, 'authentic' cuisines, with branded typographies, banners and scannable QR codes for each vendor's website or Instagram page. Each market location provides a theatrical, aestheticised experience for consumption, not only of foods or curated goods, but consumption of the city as an *experience*. Attending Brooklyn Flea is advertised on top-things-to-do-in-Brooklyn lists on multiple media sites, aimed at tourists, influencers and other media figures.[6] Each location has an ephemeral architecture that functions between a historic site, contemporary art space, live-music venue, public plaza and theme park.[7] Vendors pay 150 US dollars a day (depending on the location); During our interview, Demby refers to vendors as both 'clients' and 'family.'

Eric Demby and Jonathan Butler started the market in 2008. Neither of them had professional backgrounds in flea market organisation. Both were from divergent but interconnecting threads of the spatial politics of New York City. Eric Demby was an architectural journalist and speech writer for Marty Markowitz, the Brooklyn Borough President. This political connection helped him secure access to spaces and contracts necessary to build a flea market. Jonathan Butler launched an online platform for exchange of information about the real estate market in Brooklyn, and subsequently the popular real estate magazine, *Brownstoner*. Their idea to open a flea market started in the wake of one of the biggest financial crises in history, which supposedly 'helped' them (to a certain degree) in the same way that it aided the real estate market in the long term. The reasons for this are multi-faceted, but to quote David Harvey: 'It is in the course of crises that the instabilities of capitalism are confronted, reshaped and re-engineered to create a new version of what capitalism is about.'[8] The financial crash produced territory ripe for new configurations of capital 'between' collapsing pillars of

2   Kari Conte and Hakan Topal, 'Blueprint for a New Marketplace: The Transformation of Williamsburg, Brooklyn,' in *Informal Market Worlds Atlas*, eds. Peter Mörtenböck and Helge Mooshammer (Rotterdam: nai010 publishers, 2015), 477–481.
3   'About,' Smorgasburg, *https://www.smorgasburg.com/about*; 'About,' Brooklyn Flea, *https://brooklynflea.com/about*.
4   'Brooklyn Flea LLC,' Buzzfile: Company Information Database, updated 2022.
5   'Brooklyn Flea Co-Founder Eric Demby,' *Storytellers* (podcast), 15 May 2013, *https://podcasts.apple.com/us/podcast/brooklyn-flea-co-founder-eric-demby/id584061763?i=1000333467745*
6   Shaye Weaver, 'The Best Things to do in New York City,' *Time Out*, 24 April 2023.
7   Conte and Topal, 'Blueprint for a New Marketplace,' 481.
8   David Harvey, *Seventeen Contradictions and the End of Capitalism* (London: Profile Books, 2014), ix.

the economy. The city became the terrain onto which these new configurations were exercised. Thus, productive architectures of the between emerged; spaces of enmeshment, where the volatility of capital could be hosted and reproduced through spatial hybridities, which allow value to be extracted in many shapes and forms. Following Harvey's analysis of the marketisation of the urban as 'a fictitious form of capital that derives from expectations of future rents,' the financial crisis engendered more theatrical sets for these fictions – the performativity of speculation solidified into form.[9]

In 2008, Brooklyn Flea began as one market in one location; the schoolyard of Bishop Loughlin High School in Fort Greene, Brooklyn.[10] A schoolyard was an ideal site for the specificities of a weekend market, as it is, by definition, temporarily vacant on weekends. The booth dimensions for each vendor were marked out by Demby and Butler themselves using eight-foot lengths of timber bought from Home Depot, as they were not permitted to use paint on the schoolyard.[11] Since then, Brooklyn Flea has taken residence in over eighteen locations in Brooklyn alone.[12] It has also evolved from the specificities of the Brooklyn Flea market into a platform for other markets or market experiences, operating or taking over Smorgasburg, Chelsea Flea, and the vendors of Central Park Summer Stage. Smorgasburg occurs in cities across the US and beyond – carrying a Brooklyn branding and tailored operational strategy across state and national lines. In our Dumbo interview, I asked Eric Demby how locations are selected. He responds, that many locations, such as the current configurations in Dumbo, at the World Trade Centre, and in Jersey City, are usually chosen through invitation. A real-estate developer or local-private partnership (such as the Dumbo Improvement District or Port Authority) usually extends these invitations directly to Brooklyn Flea. In essence, Brooklyn Flea is

invited because it serves an *interest*. It creates conditions that serve the intentions behind the transformations of a neighbourhood. What shapes these interests and how they are enacted become vital points when addressing the city as a terrain rendered malleable for the speculation of future profits.

Brooklyn Flea is an example of what can be referred to as *hipster markets*, open-air shopping malls which add value to land for speculative investment. Indeed, Brooklyn Flea is not a spontaneously organised market. It is a market operator, linking the *informality* associated with flea-market activities to the private interests surrounding those activities and alienating working-class consumers through inflated prices. Brooklyn Flea is part and parcel of the economic policy models accelerated by the Bloomberg Administration in the first decade of the 2000s – which solidified neoliberal models of the 'city as enterprise.'[13] Aligning itself with entrepreneurial 'empowerment,' Demby describes markets as 'organisms.' Expanding, he explains: 'It is our job to create a petri dish for these markets to exist.'[14] In its translucency and finitude, Brooklyn Flea is a petri dish, a formal-informal linkage between the circuits of small-scale cultural production – and the structures that rely on these 'productive activities' to speculate future profits from space.

In 2013, real-estate mogul Jared Kushner, the son-in-law of Donald Trump, invited Brooklyn Flea to take residence at the Piazza at Schmidt in Philadelphia the year he purchased it from Bart Blatstein Tower Investments.[15] The Piazza at Schmidt is located in Northern Liberties, an area of Philadelphia that, until around 2000, was described as a working-class, blue-collar enclave.[16] Kushner speculated value from the site by 'rebranding' it into a live-work-play space, enacted through the construction of 500 luxury apartment units, a name-change to *Schmidt's Commons*, Philly's first-ever

9   David Harvey, *Rebel Cities: From the Right to the City to the Urban Revolution* (London: Verso, 2012), 29.
10   'Introducing "The Brooklyn Flea," The Largest Outdoor Market in New York!' *City Guide New York*, 10 April 2008,
      https://www.cityguideny.com/article/Introducing-The-Brooklyn-Flea-The-Largest-Outdoor-Market-in-New-York
11   Demby, Storytellers (podcast), 04:55–05:10.
12   Information provided by Eric Demby in email exchange with the author, 30 November 2022.
13   Conte and Topal, 'Blueprint for a New Marketplace,' 479.
14   Demby, *Storytellers*, 15:30.
15   Valerie Russ, 'Blatstein Sells Controlling Interest in Piazza at Schmidt,' *Philadelphia Inquirer*, 8 February 2013; Liz Spikol, 'Brownstoner Founder Brings Successful
      Brooklyn Flea Market to the Piazza,' *Philly Magazine*, 15 April 2013,
      https://www.phillymag.com/property/2013/04/15/brownstoner-founder-brings-brooklyn-flea-to-northern-liberties-piazza/
16   Emily Dowdall, 'Philadelphia's Changing Neighborhoods,' (report, The Pew Charitable Trusts' Philadelphia Research Initiative, May 2016), 37.

Smorgasburg, Brooklyn Pier Park, New York, 2014

WeWork, a series of platform start-ups, and finally: Brooklyn Flea.[17] Local journalists reported that this invitation would make Northern Liberties the Brooklyn of Philadelphia.[18] As proven by the PEW think tank in a study of Philadelphia's urban gentrification between 2000–2014, Northern Liberties is one of the most drastic examples of rapid gentrification in Philadelphia.[19] Despite being in Philadelphia, Demby and Butler decided to retain the name Brooklyn Flea.[20] The reasons for this, as discussed in the *Storytellers* podcast, were two-fold. The name Brooklyn was the company's brand, and by maintaining brand recognisability, it became the beginnings of a flea market 'franchise.' As explained by the podcast host, this would make Brooklyn Flea the Subway of hipster markets. Retaining the name Brooklyn Flea imbued the Plaza at Schmidt with the value brought from Brooklyn as signifier. The signified of 'Brooklyn' floats, but links

to particular models of cultural capitalism. Indeed, bringing Brooklyn (as signifier) outside of Brooklyn (as area), reproduces the spatial dynamics which allowed for Brooklyn to become a signifier for speculation and cultural capitalism in the first place. After four months, Brooklyn Flea in the Piazza at Schmidt was shut down due to a lack of customers. Local journalists speculated this was due to the name.[21]

As explained by documentary filmmaker Kelly Anderson – it was in the latest stages of Brooklyn's gentrification that it became a consumable product in itself down to the scale of the hand-held commodity: branded onto t-shirts, trinkets, or 'experiences'; Brooklyn as franchise.[22] Peter Mörtenböck and Helge Mooshammer argue in their analysis of the urbanisation of capital, specifically technology capital, that the city itself becomes something which can be 'ordered on demand' via paid

367

17   Michael Tanenbaum, 'Kushner Companies Sells Stake in Northern Liberties' Schmidt's Commons to Post Brothers,' *Philly Voice*, 25 May 2018, https://www.phillyvoice.com/kushner-companies-northern-liberties-schmidts-commons-post-brothers-philadelphia/
18   Lauren Thomas, 'Brooklyn Flea Philly,' *The Triangle*, 12 July 2013: https://www.thetriangle.org/entertainment/going/
19   Dowdall, 'Philadelphia's Changing Neighborhoods,' 36–37.
20   Joe Coscarelli, 'Brooklyn Flea Will Still Be Called Brooklyn Flea in Philly,' *NY Magazine*, 15 April 2013, https://nymag.com/intelligencer/2013/04/brooklyn-flea-expanding-to-philadelphia.html
21   John McDevitt, 'Brooklyn Flea Market Pulls Out of Philadelphia Because of Lack of Customers,' *CBS News*, 1 November 2013.
22   *My Brooklyn*, directed by Kelly Anderson (New Day Films, 2012).

Brooklyn Flea, Dumbo, New York, 2023

subscriptions and experiences.[23] Building upon this analysis, the case of Brooklyn Flea indicates what can be described as *the city brand on demand*. The value of Brooklyn can be used, as signifier, to extract similar forms of value from other cities. The city, as a brand, becomes a device. Brooklyn Flea is the spatial glue bringing together different architectures of capital. As a transferable transnational brand, it shows how this glue seeps beyond the specific, localised markets themselves and into a way of applying this strategy to analogous spatial scenarios. Hipster market as a tool. The critical contextual question to address, in turn, is under what policy formations did 'Brooklyn' become brand?

CITY BRAND ON-DEMAND – CONTEXTUALISING BROOKLYN FLEA

Brooklyn as a borough has experienced what some critics refer to as *super-gentrification*, an accelerated marketisation of the area which has resulted in an augmentation of rents and demographic changes so drastic that many neighbourhoods have become unrecognisable in the short span of ten years, or less. Data accrued and collated by the NYU Furman Center shows drastic changes in demographics over the past twenty years. In a data profile updated in 2023, the research centre reported that in 2000, the population of the BK02 district of Brooklyn, which includes Dumbo, was 61.1 percent Black and Latino. By 2019, this demographic percentage had dropped to 32.6 percent. In 2006, the median household income in BK02 for home-owners and renters was 72,020 US dollars per year; in 2021, it was estimated to be 127,910 US dollars.[24]

In their analysis of Brooklyn Flea for *Informal Market Worlds*, Kari Conte and Hakan Topal claim that the neoliberalisation of New York City, starting sometime in the mid-1990s, re-positioned the city into a 'hybrid marketplace for the cosmopolitan, global elite.'[25]

The CEO of Bloomberg Companies, Michael Bloomberg, who held the position of Mayor from 2002–2013, was the prime instigator of this hyper marketisation of New York City, rendering 'the city as enterprise, where development equals income and progress.' In Conte and Topal's words: 'The Bloomberg administration took a patchwork approach to city planning and development. On the one hand, New York City's public space was re-imagined; new public squares emerged from leftover intersections, waterfronts and old subway high-lines were renovated and opened to the public, and bike lanes were built to promote alternative transportation. On the other hand, the administration took a bluntly neoliberal approach by relaxing zoning rules and changing building codes to allow new high-rises to grow in the midst of small neighbourhoods all over the city.'[26]

Zoning are laws that organise how land can be used.[27] Mass changes to zoning regulations and a movement towards private-public partnerships were two essential policy changes that have characterised spatial politics in New York City since the Bloomberg administration.[28] Following its inception in 1916, municipal zoning has become one of the most widespread institutions of urban governance in the United States,[29] and is a product of the surrounding economic forces, which consistently lobby for these changes to land-use regulations. During the Bloomberg administration, 11,000 blocks, one third of the city's landmass, or forty-nine out of the city's fifty-nine community districts, were re-zoned.[30] The economic and governmental interests that lurk behind these mass re-zonings is the neoliberal marketisation of space into zones for hybrid forms of production and consumption.

In 1997, five years before Bloomberg became Mayor of New York City, a new form of zoning was introduced: special mixed-use district zoning.[31] Special mixed-use zoning

23   Peter Mörtenböck and Helge Mooshammer, 'Platform Urbanism and Its Discontents,' in *Platform Urbanism and Its Discontents*, eds. Peter Mörtenböck and Helge Mooshammer (Rotterdam: nai010 publishers, 2021), 17.
24   NYU Furman Center, 'Neighborhood Indicators: Fort Greene/Brooklyn Heights BK02,' Neighborhood Profiles as part of Core Data NYC, *https://furmancenter.org/neighborhoods/view/fort-greene-brooklyn-heights*, updated 2023.
25   Conte and Topal, 'Blueprint for a New Marketplace,' 477.
26   Conte and Topal, 'Blueprint for a New Marketplace,' 477.
27   NYC Department of City Planning, 'What is Zoning?,' *https://www.nyc.gov/site/planning/zoning/about-zoning.page*
28   See: Samuel Stein, *Capital City: Gentrification and the Real Estate State* (New York: Verso, 2019)
29   Christopher Berry, 'Land Use Regulation and Residential Segregation: Does Zoning Matter?' *American Law and Economics Review* 3, no. 2 (Fall 2011): 251–74.
30   Stein, *Capital City*, 101.
31   NYC Department of City Planning, 'Special Purpose Districts: Brooklyn – Special Mixed Use District,' *https://www.nyc.gov/site/planning/zoning/districts-tools/special-purpose-districts-brooklyn.page*

relaxes how space can be used. Inspired in many ways by the *artist-loft-studio* paradigm, Special Mixed Use Districts grant legal permission for commercial, residential or industrial uses simultaneously. According to the Bloomberg website, special mixed-use zoning is ideal for 'smart growth' or areas near 'mass transit.'[32] Housing activist Sam Stein explains that this zoning ordinance asserts the creation of 'live-work-play-zones'; the pop-up concept shop meets a start-up next door to an artisanal coffee roastery. [33] Two examples of the transition to mixed-use districts in New York City include Dumbo and Williamsburg, Brooklyn. Both were re-zoned from exclusively manufacturing to mixed-use in 2009 and 2005 (respectively).[34] This resulted in what Conte and Topal refer to as a 'neoliberal urban renaissance' where Williamsburg and Dumbo rapidly transformed into hubs for high concentrations of speculative capital.[35] These are also two areas where Brooklyn Flea has or continues to operate.

The Bloomberg Administration expedited public-private partnerships throughout the city, one example being the creation and proliferation of BIDs (Business Improvement Districts), or private entities recognised by the state. In the space of a decade, the Bloomberg administration created twenty new BIDs.[36] BIDs, or business and property owners' coalitions, are defined as a geographical area where local stakeholders oversee and fund their commercial district's maintenance, improvement, and promotion.[37] BIDs often *brand* their districts and create aesthetic and architectural landscapes to support certain forms of economic activity. They have been proven to raise property values of a particular area by over 15 percent.[38] As public-private partnerships, BIDs render public spaces as privatised performances of publicness rather than actual facilitators of diverse uses of space. Public-private partnership plazas, such as the Pearl Street Triangle in Dumbo, are only appropriate for a curated clientele,

epitomised by seating which is hostile to public sleeping. Brooklyn Flea was invited to take residence under the archway and in this extended Pearl Street Triangle by the Dumbo Improvement District, Dumbo's BID.

The marketisation of the city is visible in multiple layers of urban life, from physical streets to how 'urban experience' is produced, performed, communicated and consumed. These policy formations shape and continually construct what Conte and Topal call New York's transformation into an 'open-air shopping mall.' These policy formations are formed through architecture and aesthetics, a visual culture fostering negotiations on *authenticity*, and the strategies used to ensure this cultural selectivity.[39] These aesthetic and architectural processes have resulted in the packaging of Brooklyn into an amalgamation of branded, consumable experiences for the urban flaneur, one example being the presence and proliferation of curated markets – of which Brooklyn Flea is a prime example.

Analysing the marketisation of the urban, indicates that the aesthetic of the 'old' helps build for the 'new.' Taking cues from sociologists such as Sharon Zukin, processes of marketisation exist through the overlapping or transmedial layering, between politics, economics, architecture, media, and design.[40] At its core, this rapid marketisation of space is a process of tactical displacement, 'where poor areas of a city experience an influx of middle-class or wealthy people who renovate and rebuild homes and businesses and which often leads to an increase in property values and the displacement of previous, usually poorer residents.'[41] This displacement is the outcome of claiming ownership of what is culturally deemed *authentic*. An area decided as *authentic*, usually due to localised efforts of producing culture in that specific context, is extracted and transformed to speculate future profits through neoliberal policy formations. However, the essential value at the

32   Benjamin Schneider, 'CityLab University: Zoning Codes,' *Bloomberg*, 6 August 2019,
      https://www.bloomberg.com/news/articles/2019-08-06/how-to-understand-municipal-zoning-codes
33   Samuel Stein, in conversation with the author, 27 January 2023.
34   Data accessed via 'ZoLa - New York City's Zoning & Land Use Map,' NYC Planning, *https://zola.planning.nyc.gov*
35   Conte and Topal, 'Blueprint for a New Marketplace,' 479.
36   Laura Kusisto, 'New York's Shadow Mayors: The BIDs That Ate New York,' *The Observer*, 4 May 2011.
37   NYC Small Business Service, 'Business Improvement Districts,' *https://www.nyc.gov/site/sbs/neighborhoods/bids.page*
38   'Bloomberg Touts Findings of Furman's BID Study,' *NYU Law News*, 2007.
39   For more on gentrification and authenticity, see: Sharon Zukin, *Naked Cities* (Oxford: Oxford University Press, 2011).
40   Transmedia refers to the interaction between different forms of media leading to convergence and the transfer of the contents of one form of media to another.
      In other words, transmedia refers to the relationship between different forms of media.
41   'Gentrification' (definition), *Oxford Languages*.

Top: Smorgasburg Williamsburg, New York, 2023
Bottom: Brooklyn Flea, Dumbo, New York, 2023

heart of *authenticity* must remain intact for the area to retain its speculative value. The results of this, as is evident in a city such as New York, are a new kind of urbanity, where the 'city is no longer a sight where economic exchange takes place, but rather [as] a theatrical set where new cultural and economic activity seamlessly merge [...] a perceived authenticity and exclusiveness implemented throughout the whole neighbourhood.'[42] In Zukin's words, citing Walter Benjamin and Jean Baudrillard, 'a city is authentic if it can create the experience of origins. This is done by preserving historic buildings and the development of small boutiques and cafés, and branding neighbourhoods in terms of distinctive cultural identities.'[43] In other words, returning to Demby's description of Brooklyn Flea, the feeling of something having 'always been there.'

Brooklyn Flea is not a local flea market. It is a facilitator of local flea market experiences. It is a brand, a platform producing market value through façades of the locale in an economy increasingly predicated by the performative presentation of what is *locale* and for whom. The networks of value creation circulating in and around Brooklyn Flea are not just physical objects. Brooklyn Flea itself produces spatial value in a speculative real estate market.

The proceeding sections will explore the significance of the fact that market features themselves indicate the structural contexts from which they emerge, and consider the importance of the comprising features of hipster markets as devices for the marketisation of the urban. Indeed, Brooklyn Flea's market features, from its architecture, operational logics, aesthetics and typologies, indicate the varied ways value is produced in an urban-political economy predominantly oriented by the interests of real-estate speculation. These indicators exist because Brooklyn Flea and its comprising features are not only representations of, but foundational to, these processes of speculation. The significance of feature as an indicator illustrates how market design and architecture, from the large scale to the

small, become the building blocks onto which urban financialisation is produced and maintained. The many components of Brooklyn Flea amalgamate to perform, form and produce an urban fabric of mass individuation, speculation, and digitisation. These components can be charted as indicators of the processes behind real-estate speculation in New York City over the past few years. Lenses of policy in New York City, all of which link to real estate speculation: zoning changes, BIDS, brandification, and capitalisation of culture, which are enacted through architecture and aesthetics, crystallise through particular market dimensions, from the architecture of the market themselves, their communicative and logistical fabrics, their linkage with the digital, and finally, their aesthetics and merchandise.

DOWN UNDER THE MANHATTAN BRIDGE OVERPASS: MONUMENTS OF INFRASTRUCTURE AND ARCHITECTURE OF HYBRIDITY

Through the nineteenth and twentieth centuries, Dumbo was an area zoned exclusively for manufacturing. In 1980, the now billionaire and founder of Two Trees Developers, David Walentas, paid developer Harry Helmsley 12 million US dollars for ten turn-of-the-century industrial buildings – 2 million square feet of space – in what was then called Fulton Landing in Brooklyn.[44] This comprised what is essentially the entirety of the neighbourhood we now call Dumbo. Dumbo is now called 'the centre of the Brooklyn tech triangle' because it has the highest concentration of tech firms by neighbourhood, with 500 headquartered within a ten-block radius of the Brooklyn Flea market.[45] It is estimated to be the second most expensive neighbourhood in Brooklyn, with a median sales price of 1,767,500 US dollars.[46] In 2021, *The New York Times* named it the sixth most expensive neighbourhood in New York City overall.

The rapid rise of pricing in Dumbo occurred for many reasons, the most instrumental being the policy shift from manufacturing to mixed-use, which allowed Two Trees to

42   Conte and Topal, 'Blueprint for a New Marketplace,' 479.
43   Zukin, *Naked Cities*, 3.
44   Caleb Welby, 'Brooklyn Billionaire: How One Man Made A Fortune Rebuilding Dumbo,' *Forbes*, 9 February 2014.
45   Jefferson Graham, 'It's Hip to Be Tech in Brooklyn's Dumbo,' *USA TODAY*, 7 May 2013.
46   'Dumbo Real Estate Market Trends,' *Property Shark*, Market Overview for Quarter I - 2023,
        https://www.propertyshark.com/mason/market-trends/residential/nyc/brooklyn/dumbo

build residential and commercial buildings with fashionable industrial aesthetics. In 2016, seven years after Dumbo was re-zoned, Brooklyn Flea was invited to take residence below the Manhattan Bridge overpass by the Dumbo Improvement District. Jed Walentas, the now CEO of Two Trees Developers, is a primary board member, and David Lombino, also from Two Trees Developers, is secretary of the entire BID.[47]

Walentas' purchase did not include ten towers of public housing projects adjacent to these industrial buildings, 0.3 miles from Brooklyn Flea and the Two Trees headquarters. One of the largest public housing estates in Brooklyn, the Farragut Houses has over 3,272 residents where the average household income is approximately 21,000 US dollars per year, a margin below the official poverty line in New York City (27,740 US dollars for a four-person household).[48]

According to Wikipedia, the population of 'Dumbo' is 1,139. This statistic does not include the street adjacent to the Two Trees headquarters, where the towers stand. The area is not zoned for special mixed use, not considered part of Dumbo, but described as 'next to the Brooklyn Navy Yard.' It is also not included in the jurisdiction of the Dumbo Improvement District. The boundaries of what is called 'Dumbo' are designated by what is owned by Two Trees and what forms the tech triangle. Walking passed the Farragut Houses, I am surprised by the immediate and drastic change in design, architecture and aesthetics – aside from posters advertising speculative luxury condominiums currently under construction. This indicates that the architectural and aesthetic outputs of mixed-use zoning and public-private partnerships are only accessible to high-income residents and consumers. The working-class person is alienated from these marketised universes.

Spatially, Brooklyn Flea in Dumbo indicates the hybrid foundations of special mixed-use zoning, and the economic incentives behind them, are designed and oriented for middle- and upper-class consumers and with

some curated working-class aesthetics. The market site is hybrid in character to align with mixed economic assemblages. As explained by Pedro Cruz, a New York-based architect, activist and expert on urban market activities: 'These architectures of hybridity are all around Brooklyn. Brooklyn is known for having new retrofit structures built into its industrial character precisely because of the different typologies and varying space scales originally designed to fit manufacturing. The flexibility of building aligns with the shift to a mixed-use zone. The bridge anchorage is not an exception.'[49]

The initial impression is that of a monument of infrastructure or homage to industrialism. The market, as discussed, is nestled directly below the Manhattan Bridge overpass. The Pearl Street Triangle extends the market around 4,000 square feet, making the market site, which can be described as infrastructure-as-platform, even more hospitable to flea market activities.

The market frames and is framed by development. The borders of the market are created by the archway as infrastructure. Planter boxes, which have solidified as part of the plaza, demarcate the Pearl Street Triangle from the area subject to extension and a Dante-esque circle of construction. The architecture of construction scaffolding, with posters covering them north, south, and east of the market proper, suggests the market's presence before it is immediately encountered. Carrying an aesthetic somewhere between the 1950s/1850s *circus Americana* kitsch with promotional phrases such as 'walk to Jay & Pearl Street and take a detour under the Manhattan Bridge overpass, the best in indie shopping': the posters announce not only where the market is, but what the market has, and perhaps what the market means.

The retro quality of the posters, merchandise and overall communication certainly make Brooklyn Flea seem like something 'historical,' supplanted by the Manhattan Bridge overpass functioning as a kind of monumentalising of urban infrastructure – a gesture to

373

47   'Finances/Leadership,' Dumbo Improvement District, *https://www.dumboannualreport.com/#financesleadership*
48   NYC Housing Authority, 'My NYCHA Developments,' *https://my.nycha.info/DevPortal/Portal/DevelopmentData*; 'Farragut Neighborhood Brooklyn,' CityData, *https://www.city-data.com/neighborhood/Farragut-Brooklyn-NY.html*
49   These quotes are the result of an ongoing communication and collaboration with Pedro J Cruz, as an invited on-site collaborator who supported with the analysis of the market. The quotes are taken from exchanges between December 2020–April 2023.

Top: Smorgasborg WTC, New York, 2022
Bottom: Smorgasburg Prospect Park, New York, 2023

'vintage' New York as the rugged urbanisation of exchange, on various scales. However, to anyone familiar with this area before Brooklyn Flea was first installed in 2016, or perhaps with the aesthetics which emerged through Dumbo's transformation in the early 2000s, this market may feel anything but local to the area. Perhaps encountering this market would feel profoundly new, under a curated sense of the historical.

The peculiarity of the market site in Dumbo, as well as Brooklyn Flea's many other locations, are essential to market activities which warrant specific spatial configurations. Locations are typically liminal and sparse in character to host what is in essence, a hybrid assemblage of logistics, moving bodies, vehicles and transactions, while also being attractive, appealing and extremely urban. In other words, the location must allow for the complexity of a pop-up market of over fifty vendors to be staged, whilst being very Instagram-able in the process. The physical space that hosts each vendor is fluid enough to adapt to what are a series of hybrid and mixed activities, while being substantive enough to form a functioning platform onto which these activities can be hosted. This hybridity is precisely what special mixed-use zoning is designed to produce.

The market site's features facilitate a mixing of seemingly dichotomous characteristics. One of these elements is size and density. In New York City, Brooklyn Flea's market locations must host a sprawling, horizontal activity (in a spatial sense), in one of the densest cities in America. These markets are not hosted in buildings of multiple floors. They are on and of the street or in architectures which function as street-like replicas. Analysing thirteen separate market layouts, the quantity of vendors averages around fifty, with as many as eighty-four in the Prospect Park Smorgasborg and sixty-one at Chelsea Flea. Booths range from: ten by ten, ten by twenty, twelve by six, twelve by eight, eight by six, or seven by seven feet, depending on location.

To host these vendors, fulfil fire safety regulations, bathroom compliance rules, cope with extensive pedestrian traffic (in some cases, upwards of 10,000 visitors in one day), consumer loitering, and the passing of vehicles, these locations must be large and sparse enough to become adaptable to the hybrid activities that come with markets and their logistical maintenance and functionality. Building upon this analysis, Pedro Cruz adds: 'The streets are precisely what gives the vendor its livelihood and allows them to become part of the essence of the public while keeping Jane Jacobs famous phrase of "eyes on the streets" very applicable. It allows them to become a character within the urban fabric and giving flexibility to not just sell food. That's why vending activities work well on the horizontal plane. Indoor buying experiences are left to malls, food courts, and big chain stores.'

As sprawling activities occupying substantial space, the market sites cannot be situated remotely. They need to be at the centre of urban density, well connected, easily accessible, and close to structures or infrastructures that bring circuits of consumers. This becomes a somewhat awkward or specific spatial configuration in a city as dense as New York City. The market must emerge in the *cracks* of industrial and post-industrial urbanity. Some examples of past market sites include parking lots, schoolyards, a former tobacco factory, cemented lots in public parks and spacious 'under-zones,' as is the case with Dumbo Brooklyn Flea, nestled under the Manhattan Bridge Archway, and Smorgasburg at the World Trade Centre, situated under the wings of Santiago Calatrava's Oculus Building, built on Ground Zero. Commenting on Brooklyn Flea's use of parking lots, Cruz adds: 'we can see some of the benefits of allowing for flexibility in the public realm, especially when considering the transformation of an old parking lot into a plaza. Chelsea Flea also gives up the parking space managed by Manhattan Parking Garage Company (MPG) on the weekends, allowing for a complete space transformation. In these instances, the streetscape is liberated from cars, allowing street life to occur on the temporary pedestrianised thoroughfares. But when these spaces are heavily tailored by defining who gets to use them for profit, whose streets are we talking about?'

The Brooklyn Flea locations indicate how the live-work-matrix, produced and procured via special mixed-use zoning, capitalises on all the niches, crannies, and *betweens* of space. It accumulates and amalgamates all that spatially has potential for value. In analysing the four instalments of Brooklyn Flea at the time of fieldwork (October 2022), each location is either directly next to, or extremely close to monument-like buildings or structures, another expression of hybrid architectures. The monument paves the way for spectacle, facilitates photographability of the market site, consumer presence, and in the case of Dumbo, convenient coverage. Indeed, these buildings allow the experience of the space to adapt to different forms. An influencer may linger in Brooklyn Flea not only to buy a vintage t-shirt, but to see and photograph the overall site as a spectacle.

In the case of Dumbo, the positioning of the market under the archway allows for the use of infrastructure as architecture. The archway creates a 'natural' architecture, which differentiates the market from its surroundings while facilitating fluid barriers for market extension. The public plaza extending beyond the archway, which is set to be expanded further, encourages the growth of the market, vis-à-vis the potential for more vendors, more space for booths, and more space for visitors to linger. Its position at the foot of the Manhattan and Brooklyn Bridges makes it an ideal site for commodity transport from other parts of New York City. Indeed, it is a public plaza meets infrastructural niche, an urban spatial configuration that in its peculiarity, becomes ideal for the hybridity of Brooklyn Flea.

The area under the Manhattan Bridge overpass is appropriately sparse to become whatever it is required to, the adaptable commons of consumption for the economic exchanges surrounding it. Furthermore, the Dumbo Brooklyn Flea is surrounded and buttressed by networks of capital. This spatial character is coupled by the assurance of consumers, brought from established, dense circuits of capitalist relations which surround the market site and offer two mutually informing circuits of potential consumers: tourists and employees of one of the 500 tech companies within a ten-block radius.

CHELSEA FLEA AND FORMALISING INFORMALITY

As explained by Cruz: 'For years informal street trade has been one of the main practices that have been moulded by penalising policies tied to social injustices like discriminatory criminalisation, racism, and displacement practices. As a neoliberal city, New York City has not been kind to spontaneous street vending practices despite its deep roots in the vending and market culture brought on by each new wave of immigrant populations. The politics of space in New York plays out as a looping street performance – where private and public interests contest on the uses of the public realm as to who has the right to use and benefit economically and socially from its temporary or permanent appropriation. While some in the private sector denounce vending issues like sidewalk congestion, sanitation and undesirable aesthetics, that same sector also partakes in the form of formalised informality that sets the stage for the extraction of the production of places and spaces which vendors and markets can create for themselves as a set of mutually benefiting economic networks, and for others as wonderful spaces of leisure, urban ambulation, discovery, and sociability.'

Chelsea Flea is one of the oldest and most iconic markets for antique exchange in New York City. Originally housed in a two-storey garage of over one hundred vendors on West 25th Street, it was famous for drawing celebrities like Andy Warhol and Michael Jackson throughout the 1970s and 1980s. From these activities, this section of Manhattan became a hub of spontaneously organised markets in open-air parking lots. Today, the parking garage where this market once stood is a luxury condominium with a Walgreens at the base Walking through Chelsea is a solemn realisation of what occurs when space is marketed to its limits, becoming a collection of chain stores, condominiums, and not one but three dog grooming facilities. Chelsea Flea is renowned for selling high quality, luxury antiques and *relatively* affordable 'treasures.'

By the early 2000s, Chelsea Flea was effectively obsolete because the owners were abusive to their vendors. According to Demby, Brooklyn Flea 'saved' Chelsea Flea by finding

Brooklyn Flea

376

a way to secure rental of a parking lot next to the Cathedral of St. Sava, also under construction. The only reason they were able to secure the contract, as explained by Demby, it is because the owners of the parking lots were no longer on speaking terms and, due to this, have not been able to organise to sell the lot to developers, as seems to have been done on every other square foot of the neighbourhood.[50]

Brooklyn Flea chose to retain the name for this location because of the symbolic value of the Chelsea Flea as intrinsic to the culture of New York City in the 1970s. Chelsea Flea feels like a curated experience of New York's *authentic*, quirky history, nestled inside the developments that eradicated the possibility for the kind of diverse spontaneity which formed these market constellations decades prior. Cruz adds to this, reflecting that this market feels like a 'counter-hegemonising anomaly,' sitting right next to the glaring developments on 6th Avenue and Broadway. However, there are non-member vendors scattered around the boundaries of the Chelsea Flea who were not 'accepted' by the Chelsea Flea to sell in the market proper. I ask Eric Demby about his attitude towards them, 'well, it's annoying, but you're not going to call the police, are you.' He expands, 'no one wants to send anyone to Riker's Island,' but in some cases, the local BID can aid in a kind of 'alternative' form of policing. Demby does not specify what this kind of policing entails.

During Chelsea Flea, tents do not designate the booth areas in a regimented fashion – long tables extend beyond the covered areas, as some objects are scattered around what appear to be spontaneous, ownerless showrooms, un-sellable still lifes crystallised in space. Museum-like, this fluid sense of a showroom of one-of-a-kind antique commodities relates to the unique history and cultural value of the Chelsea Flea. In a sense, as a pop-up activity with deep roots of cultural value, it is situated 'between' the urbanisation of capital.

In *All Incomplete*, Stefano Harney and Fred Moten describe how the architectures of contemporary capitalism are epitomised by two interconnected concepts: access and movement. In broad terms, access involves curating spaces of belonging mediated through mobility structures. Access 'to' implicates directionality, openings, closings and a notion of the barrier on various terms. Who can or cannot participate and what designates participation exactly are continually emerging as the key strategies behind contemporary capitalist urbanisation. In a platform economy where access functions as capital, cities' look, feel, and construction emerge as re-enforcing and symptomatic features of these economic models. In the proceeding section, I will explore a phenomenon I describe as 'brandscaping,' the branding of space, environment, and network. Brandscaping, a phenomenon which tangles together aesthetics, architecture and language – functions through the production of asymmetrical plains of access – the curation of whom or what is invited or involved in the barriers of brand. This becomes one of the foundational creases in the overlapping that is the marketisation of the urban.

BRANDSCAPING: AESTHETICS OF MARKETISATION AND CULTURE AS COMMODITY

On the Dumbo Improvement District website, images of Brooklyn Flea are everywhere. The physical and digital branding of Brooklyn Flea and the Dumbo Improvement District are aesthetically synonymous. As one enters the archway, the sign reading 'Dumbo' (announcing the market) is the same design strategy on the banners that span Dumbo, designed and produced by the Dumbo Improvement District.

This policy formation, broadly defined as 'brandification,' is part and parcel of the policy formation of public-private partnerships. Signage and general typographies indicate these aesthetic and economic assemblages; the brand designates space. Throughout the Brooklyn Flea locations, the vendor's brand is what spatially distinguishes one vendor from the other, based on boundaries formed by the aesthetics of their specific stall or demarcated zone. Branding becomes a strategy of differentiation through presenting an aesthetic universe that demarcates itself from

377

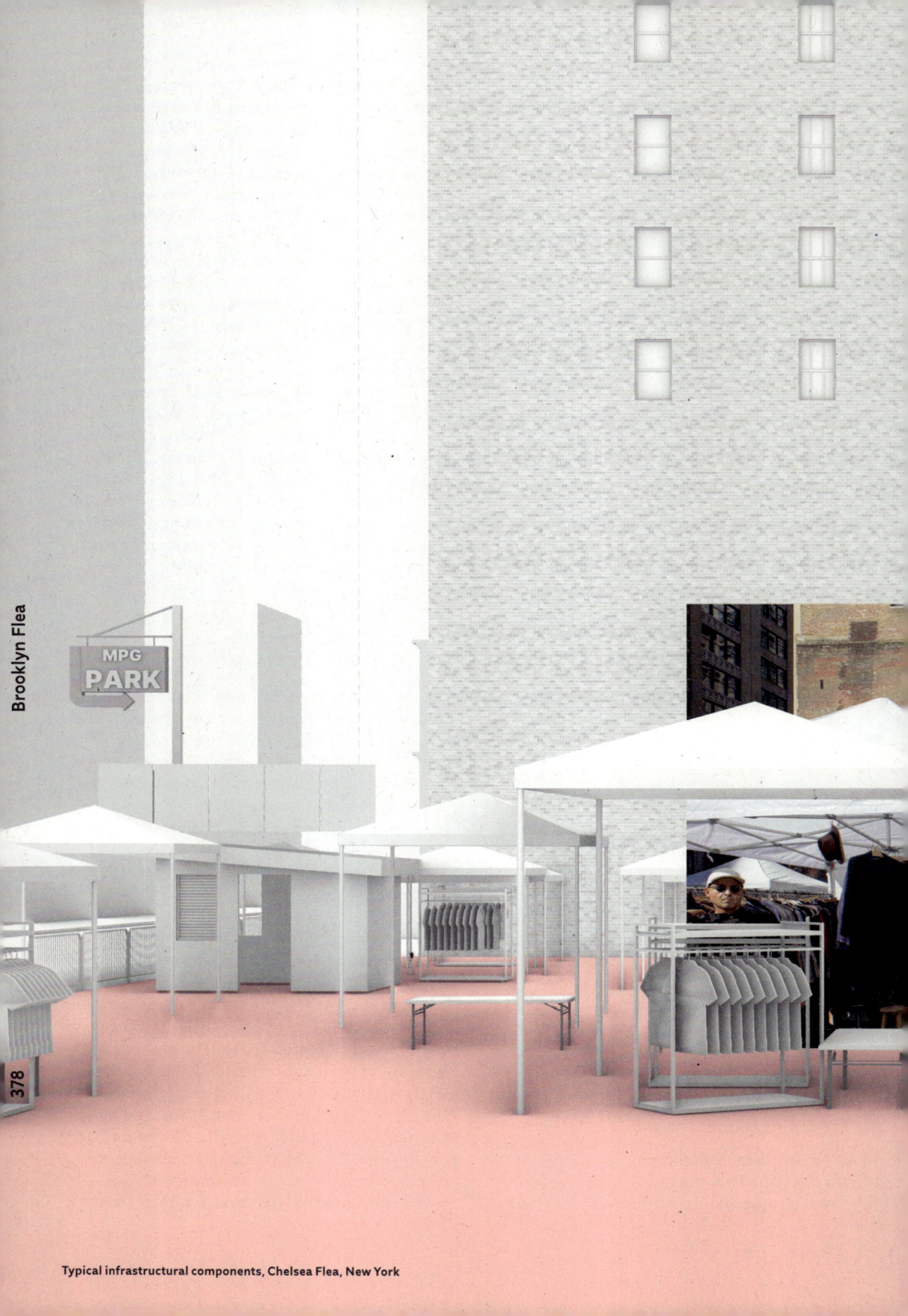

Brooklyn Flea

Typical infrastructural components, Chelsea Flea, New York

adjacent universes. This can be connected to how the Dumbo Improvement District uses branding to separate Dumbo from its surrounding areas, such as the Farragut Estate. This indication shows how brandification is a tool, a spatial indicator, for the public-private partnership as a policy formation.

Smorgasburg is a very clear indicator of these processes of brandification. Once again, the food market is nestled under the wings of Calatrava's Oculus building. The vendor stalls are all in front of a series of concrete planter boxes or roadblocks decorated with murals. These planter boxes show how the market has materialised into the public architecture of the city, which differs profoundly from the eight-foot lengths bought from Home Depot, used as demarcation borders, only fifteen years ago. Each of these murals has a street art aesthetic with a positive slogan atop, such as 'never give up' or 'stay positive.'

In the corner of each, there is the Instagram handle of the particular artist behind each mural. These concrete roadblocks form the boundaries of the market. They are organisational mechanisms, serving the logistical use function of blocking the generators used by the Smorgasburg vendors (the vendors have to pay the market platform (Brooklyn Flea) to use the generators). Though they are blocked, they certainly make large sounds. Each food vendor also presents a different cuisine, aesthetic and brand. No two renditions of the same cuisine exist alongside one another. They each offer a distinct culinary experience, in some cases, with music aligning with the cuisine's culture via large speakers, maybe just a few metres apart. Once again, most stalls do not indeed have physical restaurants but instead function as culinary platforms moving between markets around New York City, illustrated by the fact that the same stalls appear at different locations.

The architecture of the Smorgasburg vendor follows the spatialisation of the brand. In researching each of the vendors, it becomes clear that most stalls do not exist as restaurants or physical food businesses but as online platforms which become physical when the market occurs. Therefore, the vendor's brand, communicated online and off, defines it in space. The materialisation of this

aesthetically and spatially shows how 'brand' is not just a passive repercussion but a spatial and aesthetic component used to organise architecture and space. An orienting device, the brand is material – and in this case, physical.

Brandification, as a device, is also apparent when spatially analysing the Brooklyn Flea in Dumbo. Each of the stalls, again, functions as a kind of showroom with a very tailored aesthetic presentation complete with curated fonts, business cards, and in some cases, clothes or products from one particular time in history or focusing on one particular object (carpets, moccasins, denim jackets, vintage concert shirts). From someone selling vintage postcards and New York magazine covers, to a person selling paintings of hipster bicycles as house décor, adjacent to a terrarium vendor, next to a couple selling accessories from sourced metals used during times of war – indeed, it is the curation of independence structured to form the circular whole. Walking through the Dumbo Brooklyn Flea feels like moving through a three-dimensionalised Instagram or Pinterest feed. Each section of space is another sensorial 'experience' of the vendor as brand – which amalgamates to form the circuit of Brooklyn Flea, an experience of the bringing-together of 'indie' consumerism. In the words of Pedro Cruz, 'Brooklyn Flea is where the brick-and-mortar business becomes mobile.' The 'brandification' is the structure, or architecture, which allows for this mobility, because it is the feature that distinguishes the vendors from one another. This indicating feature is further amplified by the fact that in front of each stall, there is a sign which links to the social media channels of each vendor – the 'doorway' to their shop, which, again, is structured through brand.

DISPLACEMENT IN RESOLUTION: THE REPERCUSSIONS OF ARCHITECTURE AS ASSET

Housing policy activist Sam Stein, author of *Capital City*, explains, in reference to the marketisation of urbanity, that land and space are essentially valueless. Certain forms of labour, whether 'physical,' such as the making and maintaining of architecture and infrastructure, or 'cultural,' like cultural production (the creation of 'cool') – can bring potential 'value' to land. Marketisation, or *gentrification*, is the

Smorgasburg Los Angeles, 2023

process by which these labours are captured by private interests to generate profit inaccessible to those who have done the labour of creating 'capturable' value to the land. As he explains, hipster markets form the spatial and 'economic glue between new, high-price real estate developments […] a real estate amenity where owners of the nearby buildings can say: come here, you can go shopping at Brooklyn Flea on the weekends.'[51] 'Hipster market' is the space where the energies of 'informal' market activities are curated in a way oriented towards the interests of those who produce the market's cultural vibrancy and maintenance through consistent presence. Curated markets produce surplus value in the circuits of real estate speculation that buttress and surround them.

During the course of the fieldwork, Sam Stein invites me to a demonstration outside of City Hall, just a five-minute walk from Smorgasburg at the World Trade Center. This demonstration, led by elected officials, immigration and housing advocates and tenants, criticises New York Mayor Eric Adam's plan to house over 500 asylum seekers in a tent encampment on Randall's Island, most of whom have come from Central and South America since the spring of 2022. It has been estimated that 18,670 asylum seekers have arrived in New York City since the Spring of 2022.[52]

Stein explains the driving force of the protests: 'New York City is exaggerated in the way that capitalists strike.' He expands, describing how despite the housing crisis, in the year 2021, over 61,000 rent-stabilised or affordably priced flats were rendered vacant or 'warehoused' by their landlords, citing erroneous claims that the price of maintenance for tenants overruled the 'stabilised monthly rent.' This, as explained by Stein, is because these landlords 'strike' against limitations on them to increase the rents.

The marketisation of space exceeds a disturbing mirage of homogenised, 'soulless' urbanscapes. The prioritisation of housing on a mass scale diverts what housing and architecture mean, as structures decided for and by its inhabitants, and instead, as a commodity in a finalised housing market. In a homelessness crisis, the financialisation of space creates a configuration of architecture as an asset, an abstract entity for speculative profits – rather than something decided in and for the materiality of its uses.

I ask Stein about his impressions of Brooklyn Flea and similar hipster markets and whether it is relevant to analysing and thinking about gentrification through an urban, theoretical lens. He points me to a piece of writing by Gryphon Hanson. A psychoanalyst, Hanson analyses the processes behind urban marketisation: 'people really want New York to be like the shopping mall they grew up in the suburbs, but transplanted here. It is re-creating suburban alienation into the city and imposing it on a place not designed for that kind of sociality.'[53]

What Brooklyn Flea indicated, following Hanson's psychoanalytical provocation, is a formation where the aesthetics of 'informality' can be curated to generate value in a speculative real estate economy. This urban political economy, within which Brooklyn Flea is nestled, and emerges, produces and reproduces a conception of architecture as an asset. This financialisation of space turns the city and its activities into a playground for the speculation of future increased rents. The repercussions of these policy frameworks are significant for some, but not all, as those who do not fit the curated remit are pushed further into the periphery. However, as discussed, two fundamental spatial indicators of these policy frameworks become the architecture of hybridity and brand as a structuring device. The outstanding question becomes whether these tools or indicators could be re-appropriated to challenge the policy frameworks from which they emerge: frameworks built in and through displacement and mediated access. How could these counter-tools be designed, proliferated, and instrumentalised? Importantly, whose interests would they serve?

51   Samuel Stein, in conversation with the author.
52   Chau Laum, 'NYC Officials Rally Outside City Hall, Call on Mayor to Ditch Migrant Tent Plan,' *Gothamist*, 13 October 2020,
        https://gothamist.com/news/nyc-officials-rally-outside-city-hall-call-on-mayor-to-ditch-migrant-tent-plan
53   Stein, in conversation with the author.

REFERENCES

Anderson, K., dir. *My Brooklyn*. New Day Film, 2012.

Berry, C. 'Land Use Regulation and Residential Segregation: Does Zoning Matter?' *American Law and Economics Review* 3, no. 2 (Fall 2011).

'Bloomberg Touts Findings of Furman's BID Study.' *NYU Law News*, 2007.

'Brooklyn Flea Co-Founder Eric Demby.' *Storytellers* (podcast), 15 May 2013. *https://podcasts.apple.com/us/podcast/brooklyn-flea-co-founder-eric-demby/id584061763?i=1000333467745*

Conte, K., and H. Topal. 'Blueprint for a New Marketplace: The Transformation of Williamsburg, Brooklyn.' In *Informal Market Worlds: The Architecture of Economic Pressure - Atlas* edited by P. Mörtenböck and H. Mooshammer. Rotterdam: nai010, 2015.

Coscarelli, J. 'Brooklyn Flea Will Still Be Called Brooklyn Flea in Philly.' *NY Magazine*. 15 April 2013. *https://nymag.com/intelligencer/2013/04/brooklyn-flea-expanding-to-philadelphia.html*

Department of City Planning. 'What is Zoning?' NYC Planning. *https://www.nyc.gov/site/planning/zoning/about-zoning.page*

Dowdall, E. 'Philadelphia's Changing Neighborhoods.' Report, The Pew Charitable Trusts' Philadelphia Research Initiative, May 2016. *https://www.pewtrusts.org/~/media/assets/2016/05/philadelphias_changing_neighborhoods.pdf*

'Dumbo Real Estate Market Trends,' Property Shark, Market Overview for Quarter I, 2023. *https://www.propertyshark.com/mason/market-trends/residential/nyc/brooklyn/dumbo*

'Farragut Neighborhood Brooklyn,' CityData. *https://www.city-data.com/neighborhood/Farragut-Brooklyn-NY.html*

Graham, J. 'It's Hip to Be Tech in Brooklyn's Dumbo.' *USA Today*, 7 May 2013.

Harvey, D. *Rebel Cities: From the Right to the City to the Urban Revolution*. London: Verso, 2012.

Harvey, D. *Seventeen Contradictions and the End of Capitalism*. London: Profile Books, 2014.

'Introducing "The Brooklyn Flea", The Largest Outdoor Market in New York!' *City Guide New York*, 10 April 2008. *https://www.cityguideny.com/article/Introducing--The-Brooklyn-Flea-The-Largest-Outdoor-Market-in-New-York--*

Kusisto, L. 'New York's Shadow Mayors: The BIDs That Ate New York.' *The Observer*, 4 May 2011.

Laum, C. 'NYC Officials Rally Outside City Hall, Call on Mayor to Ditch Migrant Tent Plan.' *Gothamist*, 13 October 2020. *https://gothamist.com/news/nyc-officials-rally-outside-city-hall-call-on-mayor-to-ditch-migrant-tent-plan*

McDevitt, J. 'Brooklyn Flea Market Pulls Out of Philadelphia Because of Lack of Customers.' *CBS News*, 1 November 2013.

Mörtenböck, P., and H. Mooshammer. 'Platform Urbanism and Its Discontents.' In *Platform Urbanism and Its Discontents*, edited by P. Mörtenböck and H. Mooshammer. Rotterdam: nai010 publishers, 2021.

NYC Department of City Planning. 'Special Purpose Districts: Brooklyn – Special Mixed Use District.' *https://www.nyc.gov/site/planning/zoning/districts-tools/special-purpose-districts-brooklyn.page*

NYC Housing Authority. 'My NYCHA Developments.' *https://my.nycha.info/DevPortal/Portal/DevelopmentData;*

NYC Planning. 'ZoLa - New York City's Zoning & Land Use Map.' *https://zola.planning.nyc.gov*

NYC Small Business Service. 'Business Improvement Districts.' *https://www.nyc.gov/site/sbs/neighborhoods/bids.page*

NYU Furman Center. 'Neighborhood Indicators: Fort Greene/Brooklyn Heights BK02,' Neighborhood profiles as part of Core Data NYC, updated 2023. *https://furmancenter.org/neighborhoods/view/fort-greene-brooklyn-heights*

Russ, V. 'Blatstein Sells Controlling Interest in Piazza at Schmidt's.' *Philadelphia Inquirer*, 8 February 2013.

Schneider, B. 'CityLab University: Zoning Codes.' *Bloomberg*, 6 August 2019. *https://www.bloomberg.com/news/articles/2019-08-06/how-to-understand-municipal-zoning-codes*

Spikol, L. 'Brownstoner Founder Brings Successful Brooklyn Flea Market to the Piazza.' *Philly Magazine*, 15 April 2013. *https://www.phillymag.com/property/2013/04/15/brownstoner-founder-brings-brooklyn-flea-to-northern-liberties-piazza/*

Stein, S, *Capital City: Gentrification and the Real Estate State*. New York: Verso, 2019

Tanenbaum, M. 'Kushner Companies Sells Stake in Northern Liberties' Schmidt's Commons to Post Brothers.' *Philly Voice*, 25 May 2018. *https://www.phillyvoice.com/kushner-companies-northern-liberties-schmidts-commons-post-brothers-philadelphia/*

Thomas, L. 'Brooklyn Flea Philly.' *The Triangle*, 12 July 2013. *https://www.thetriangle.org/entertainment/going/*

Weaver, S. 'The Best Things to Do in New York City.' *Time Out*, 24 April 2023.

Welby, C. 'Brooklyn Billionaire: How One Man Made A Fortune Rebuilding Dumbo.' *Forbes*, 9 February 2014.

Zukin, S. *Naked Cities*. Oxford: Oxford University Press, 2011.

1961-1990

1   New York's entire zoning code is overhauled, resulting in a spell of new high-rise construction and privately owned public spaces.

1990-2000

2   By the 1990s, the line between planners and real estate developers blurs – public/private partnerships flourish, as planners increasingly seek profit-oriented entities to do the work of urban design, construction and maintenance.

3   Special zoning type titled 'Mixed-use District Zoning' is introduced to attract investments and enhance the vitality of existing neighbourhoods in NYC.

2000-2005

4   The Bloomberg Administration introduces a major zoning initiative known as the New York City Zoning Resolution of 2002.

2005-2010

5   Rezoning: Williamsburg transitions to mixed-use district zoning.

6   Northern Liberties is one of the most drastic examples of rapid gentrification in Philadelphia.

7   Before 2007, the Pearl Street Triangle is a parking lot for twelve vehicles; in August 2007, the New York City Department of Transportation and the local business group Dumbo Improvement District invest 20,000 US dollars and 25,000 US dollars respectively in the creation of a new public space.

8   Inception of Brooklyn Flea with an initial location in Fort Greene

9   Rezoning: Dumbo transitions to mixed-use district zoning.

10   Brooklyn Flea expands to DUMBO.

Political events

Gentrification

Zoning changes

Spatial events

1961   1990   1997   1998   1999   2000   2001   2002   2003   2004

Brooklyn Flea locations in New York City in 2023

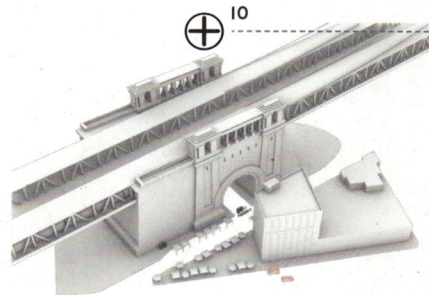

Brooklyn Flea (Dumbo, Brooklyn)

Global expansion of Smorgasburg

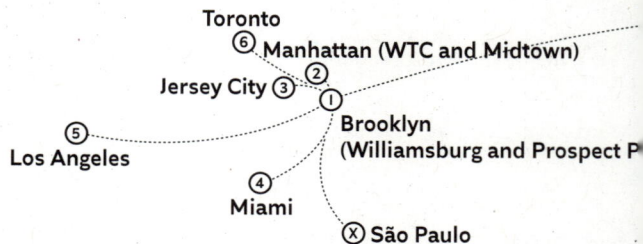

Toronto
⑥ Manhattan (WTC and Midtown)
Jersey City ③ ②
                ①
⑤   Brooklyn
Los Angeles   (Williamsburg and Prospect P

④
Miami

Ⓧ São Paulo

Timeline of key events shaping the transformation of Brooklyn Flea and Smorgasburg, New York

2010-2015

11 In 2010, the population of the BKO2 district of Brooklyn, which includes Dumbo, is 61.1% Black and Latino, with a median household income of 67,870 US dollars; by 2019, this percentage drops to 32.6% and the median household income rises to 117,200 US dollars.
12 Brooklyn Flea appears in Williamsburg and Smorgasburg is launched.
13 Brooklyn Flea is invited by Jared Kushner to take up residence at Piazza at Schmidt's, Northern Liberties in Philadelphia.

2015-2020

14 Smorgasburg opens in Miami.
15 Smorgasburg makes its international debut with a pop-up in Osaka, Japan.
16 Brooklyn Flea takes up residence in Dumbo, the Manhattan Bridge underpass.
17 Brooklyn Flea opens in Chelsea, Manhattan.

2020-2023

18 Temporary suspension of all Brooklyn Flea activities due to the COVID-19 pandemic
19 NY Times names Dumbo the 6th most expensive neighbourhood in NYC overall with a median sales price of 1,767,500 US dollars.
20 Brooklyn Flea resumes its operations.
21 More than 100,000 asylum seekers arrive in New York City between spring 2022 and August 2023.

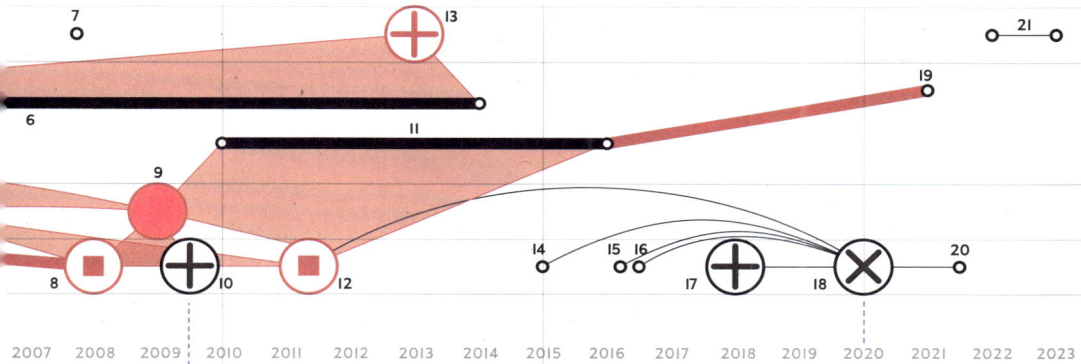

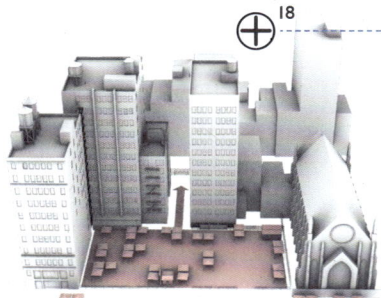

2007 2008 2009 2010 2011 2012 2013 2014 2015 2016 2017 2018 2019 2020 2021 2022 2023

Chelsea Flea (Manhattan)

Osaka

■ Spatial, social, economic and political interventions into in/formal markets

■ Intermediate risk of displacement   ■ High risk of displacement   ■ Highest risk of displacement

Displacement risk map. Source: (Equitable Development Data Explorer) Department of City Planning, Housing Preservation & Development

■ Super gentrification   ■ Ongoing exclusion   ■ Stable exclusion   ■ Advanced gentrification   ■ Risk of gentrification

Gentrification and displacement map of Brooklyn. Source: urbandisplacement.org; map data: Google, imagery date: 6/20/22

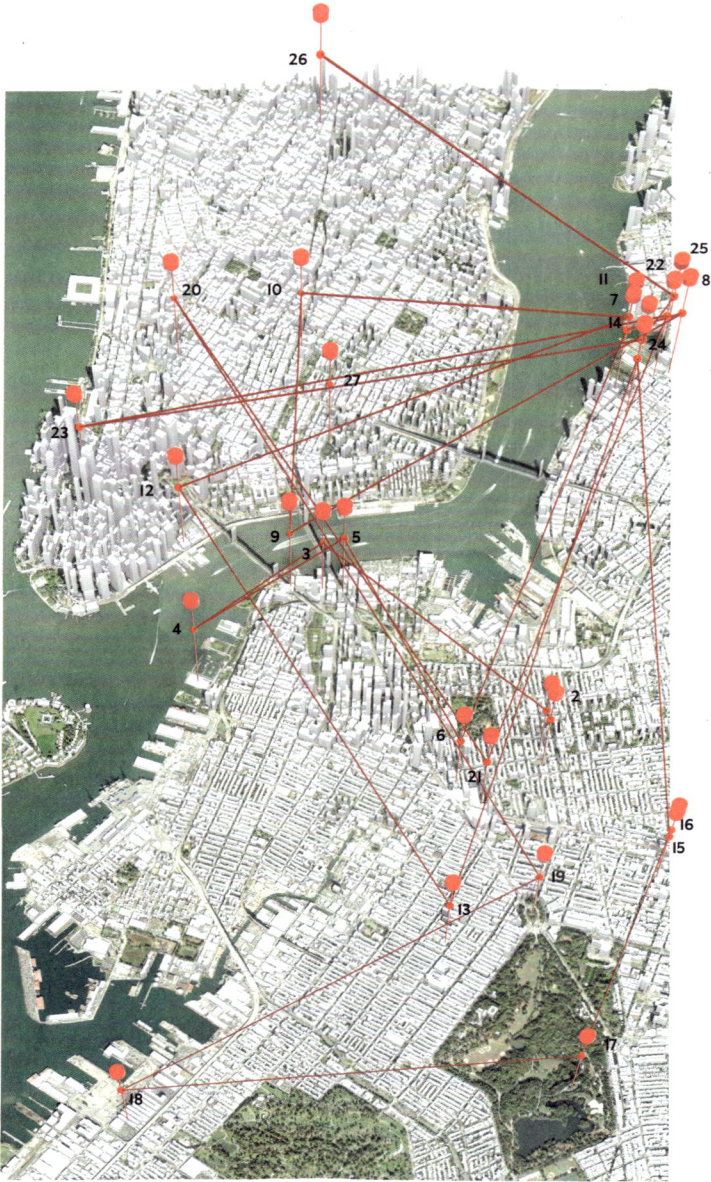

Trajectory of the expansion of Brooklyn Flea and Smorgasburg across New York; map data: Google, imagery date: 6/20/22

387

Typical infrastructural components of Brooklyn Flea, Dumbo

Smorgasburg WTC, New York, 2023

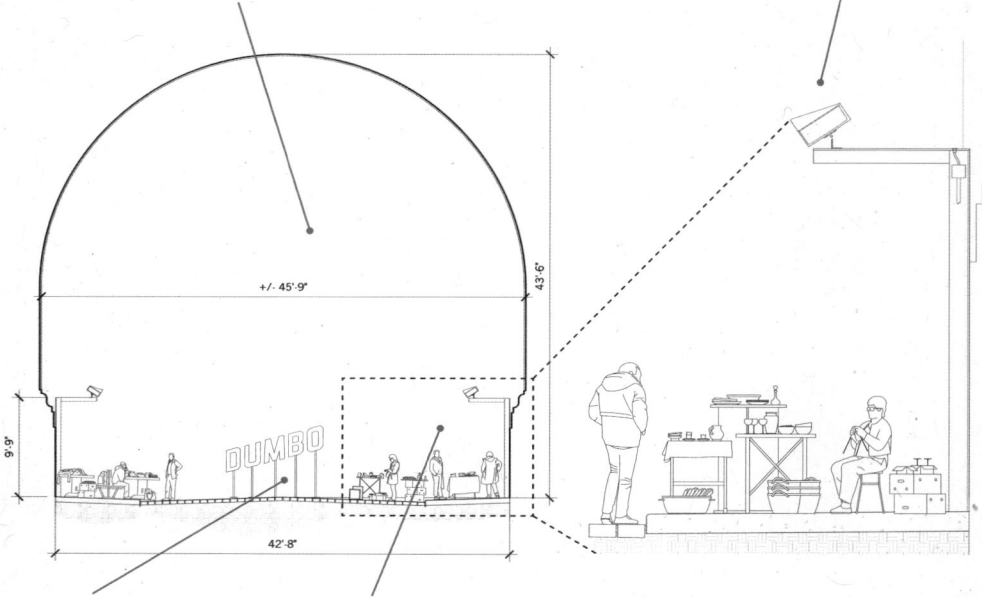

The archway appears simultaneously as an interior and exterior space whose monumentality provokes a heightened sense of place; effects like this are indicative of Chelsea Flea/Smorgasburg's tactic of creating 'destinations' by blending the appeal of both location and the shopping on offer

Temporary infrastructure such as lighting and power outlets has been installed inside the landmarked anchorage

The instagramable DUMBO sign placed at the entrance to the arch examplifies 'brandscaping' efforts

According to its own description, Brooklyn Flea features 'top vendors of antiques, furniture, vintage clothing, collectibles, and more, as well as a tightly curated selection of jewellery, art, and crafts by local artisans and designers, plus delicious fresh food'

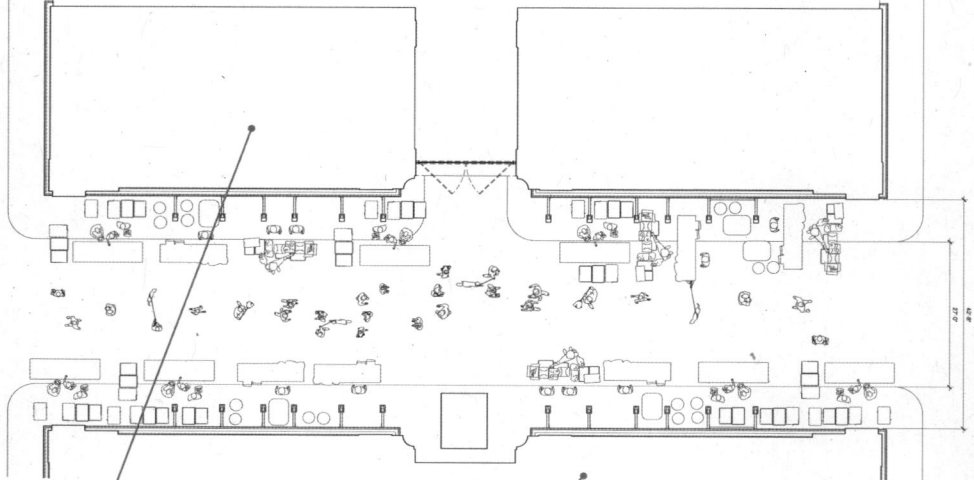

Stalls, vendors and visitors densely populate the underpass on market days; their presence transforms the throughway into a gathering place

Food and drink stalls play an important role in making people stay (and shop) for longer; for many markets the placement of food outlets has become a decisive factor in their design and organisation – a trend reflected in the rising popularity of street food markets such as Smorgasburg, the sibling of Brooklyn Flea

Spatial features of Brooklyn Flea (top: Dumbo; bottom: Chelsea)

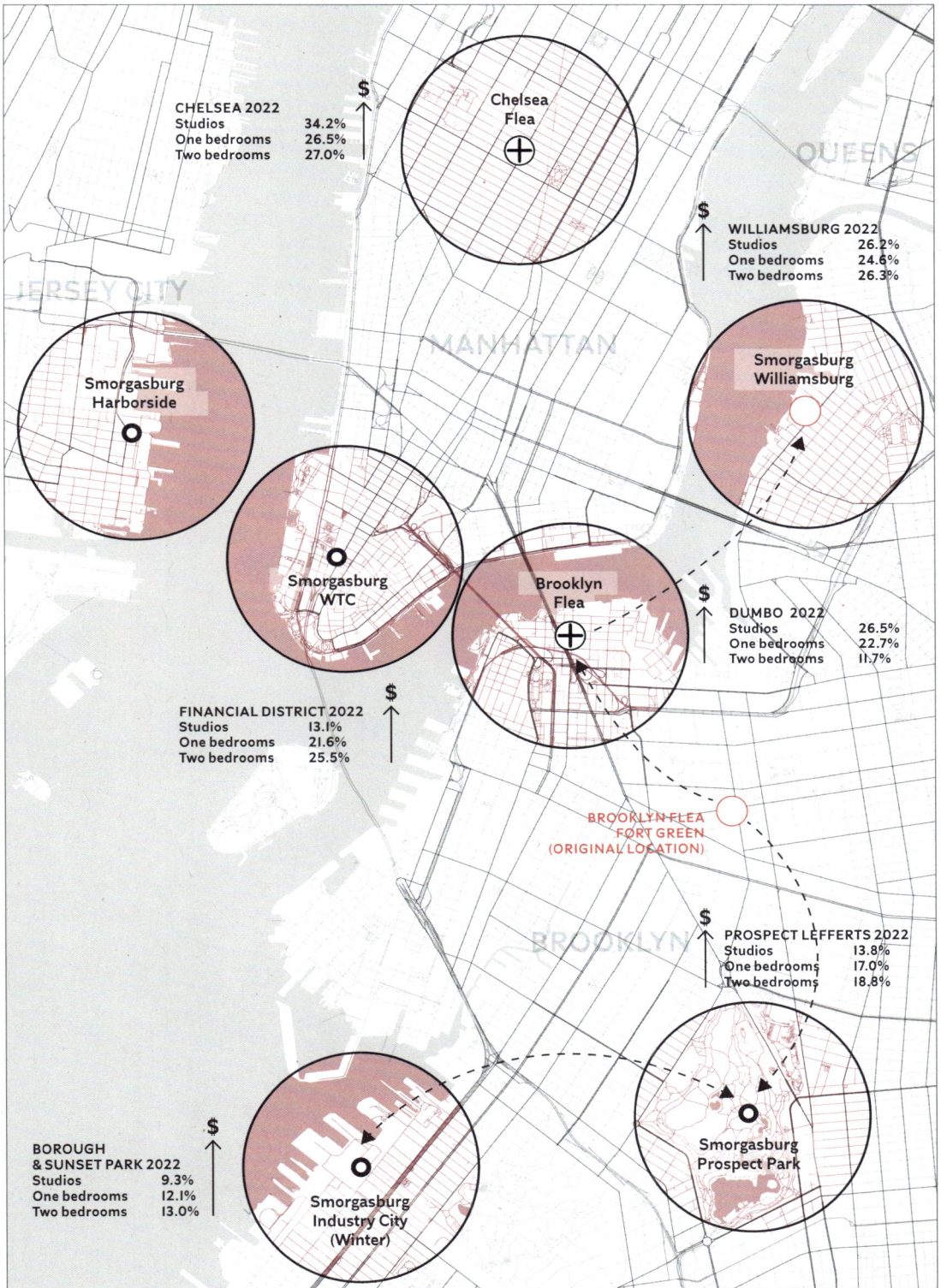

CHELSEA 2022 $
Studios   34.2%
One bedrooms   26.5%
Two bedrooms   27.0%

Chelsea
Flea

QUEENS

WILLIAMSBURG 2022 $
Studios   26.2%
One bedrooms   24.6%
Two bedrooms   26.3%

JERSEY CITY

Smorgasburg
Williamsburg

MANHATTAN

Smorgasburg
Harborside

Smorgasburg
WTC

Brooklyn
Flea

DUMBO 2022 $
Studios   26.5%
One bedrooms   22.7%
Two bedrooms   11.7%

FINANCIAL DISTRICT 2022 $
Studios   13.1%
One bedrooms   21.6%
Two bedrooms   25.5%

BROOKLYN FLEA
FORT GREEN
(ORIGINAL LOCATION)

BROOKLYN

PROSPECT LEFFERTS 2022 $
Studios   13.8%
One bedrooms   17.0%
Two bedrooms   18.8%

Smorgasburg
Prospect Park

**BOROUGH
& SUNSET PARK 2022** $
Studios   9.3%
One bedrooms   12.1%
Two bedrooms   13.0%

Smorgasburg
Industry City
(Winter)

391

Housing market data for locations of Brooklyn Flea and Smorgasburg, New York

Brooklyn Flea

Chelsea Flea, New York, 2022

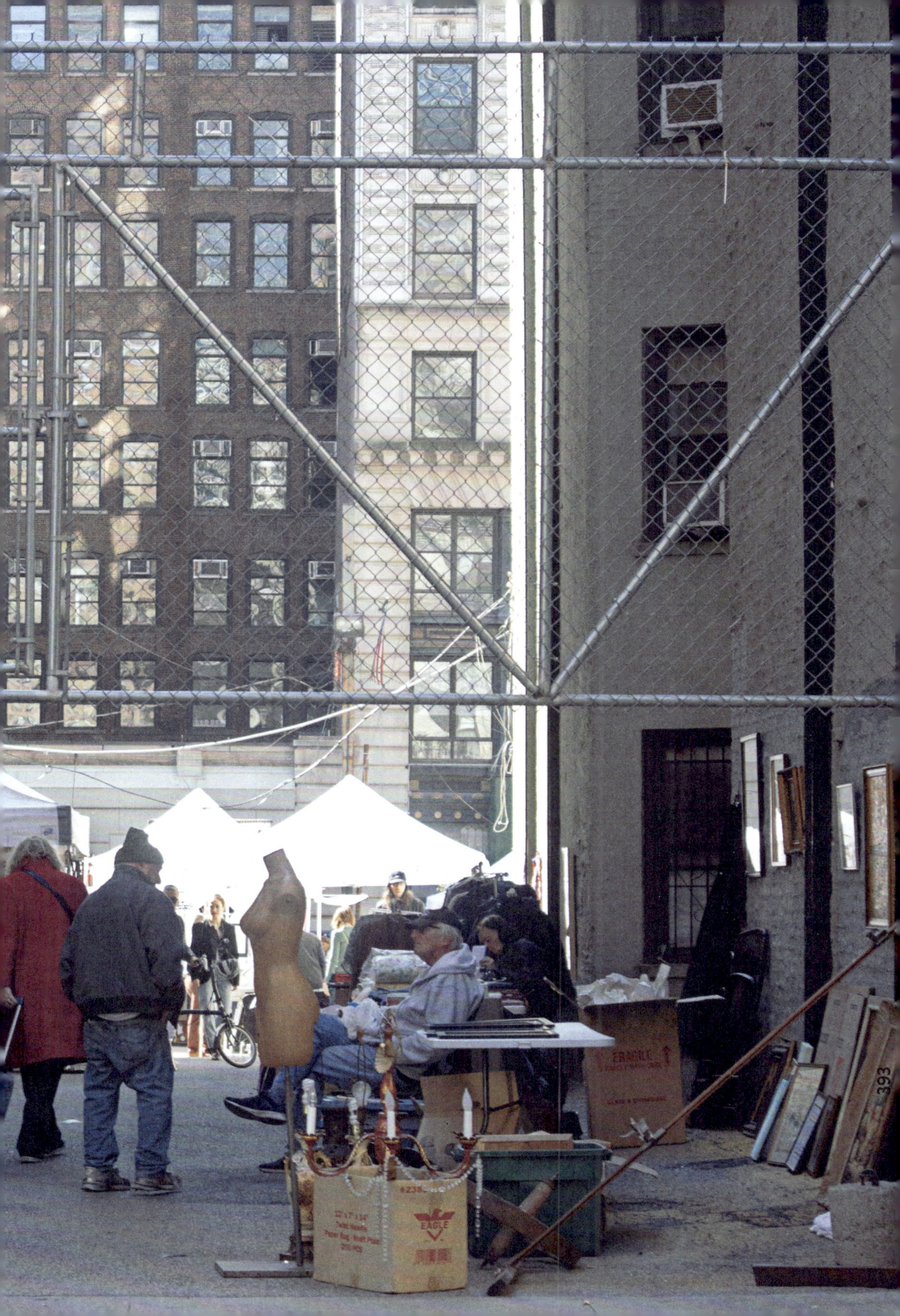
EAGLE
EAGLE

Talad Rot Fai, Srinagarinda, Bangkok, 2023

Trude Laura Renwick

Precedent or Problem: An Ecology of Thailand's Private Markets

Map data: Google, Maxar Technologies

Bangkok is distinct from cities like Singapore and Hong Kong where the majority of street vendors were incorporated into public markets in the twentieth century. Centralised market spaces in Bangkok take a multitude of forms. They are not only run by district officials on public lands and waterways but also by private developers in the city's malls and office towers. Although there have been policies by municipal and national leaders to support street vending through permits and centralised markets since the 1940s, they have been inconsistently upheld. Instead, street vendors are often not consulted by these heads of government and consistently face discrimination and eviction.[1]

After the 2014 coup and accession of Thailand's military government led by Prime Minister Prayut Chan-O-Cha, intensified street vending restrictions swept across Bangkok. Hitting its peak between 2015 and

1   See table in: Gisèle Yasmeen and Narumol Nirathron, 'Vending in Public Space: The Case of Bangkok,' *WIEGO Policy Brief (Urban Policies)*, no. 16 (May 2014): 8.

Main entrance building with indoor shops

Rod's Antiques

Smaller open-air stalls arranged in a grid

Covered food court

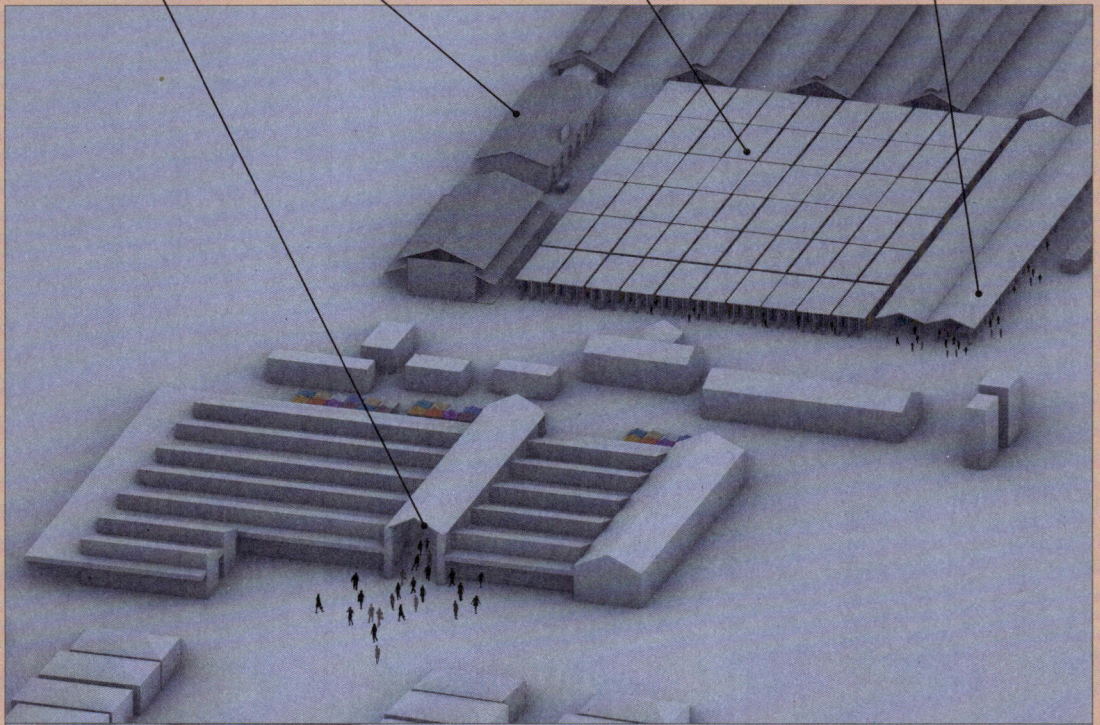

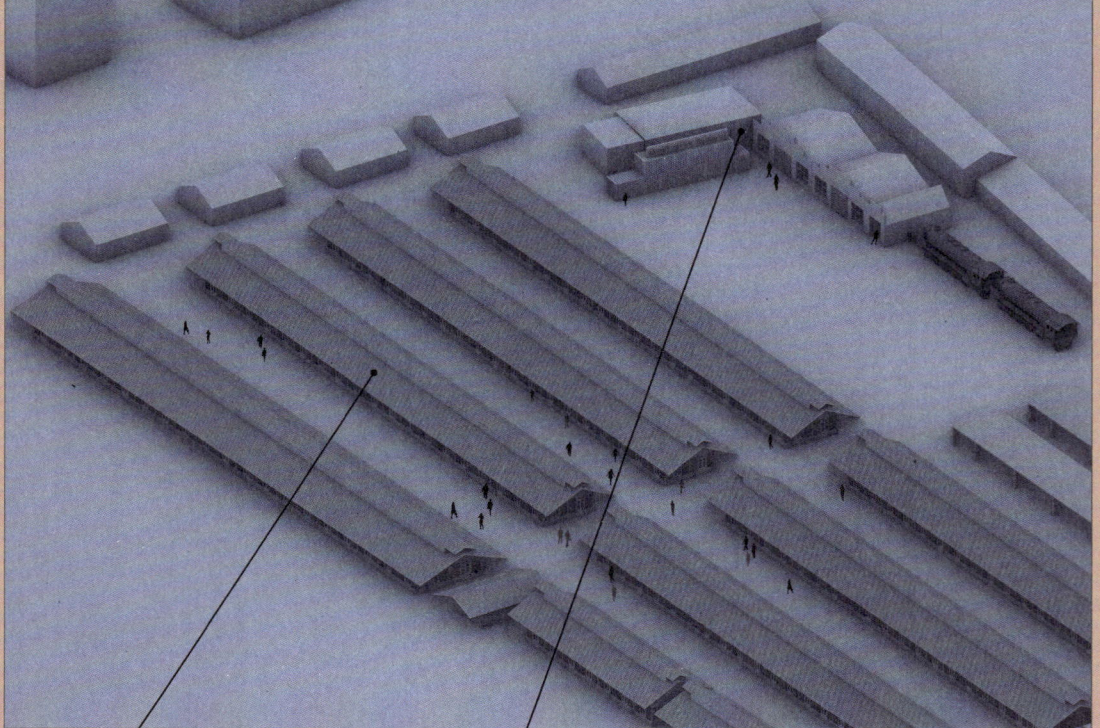

Rows of shops housed in purpose-built mock rail yard buildings

'Rod's Motor Garage' and other fake vintage façades lining open area used for car shows and concerts

2018, this policy was known as 'Returning the Pavement to Pedestrians'.[2] After evicting street vendors throughout the city, private markets were encouraged by municipal officials and presented as 'creative' alternatives to 'illegal' markets along the city's pavements. Facing little or no government oversight, mall and other private developers neglected to make rent in these new commercial spaces tenable for nearby vendors facing eviction at the hands of the government. No longer competing with 'informal' markets and spurred by government investment in the creative industries, private markets boomed across the city.

Talad Rot Fai or the Train Market is a private market themed around antiques that was established prior to these restrictions on street vending.[3] Opened in 2010 by Pairod Roikaew and initially located on a plot of land adjacent to one of the largest public markets in the world, Chatuchak Market, the Train Market was closed and moved in 2013. Under the careful direction of its founder, the market has migrated to several other locations in the city and expanded as a brand over the past decade. Pairod Roikaew graduated from college with a degree in management after initially studying engineering. After twenty years working as a propman for a production company, he decided to start selling antiques. His initial inspiration for Talad Rot Fai came from a market that sold donated second-hand goods from the US in the beach town of Hat Yai, located southwest of Bangkok on the Gulf of Thailand. From selling on Ayutthaya's streets, he would eventually set up an antique store in Bangkok with the help of his family.[4] An early example of entrepreneurial appropriation in Bangkok, Roikaew has created a rare, private, yet affordable space for vendors in Bangkok, with a range of shop-types available for rent. This market's survival, success, and expansion is a product of its founder's ability to establish a flexible yet stable space for its vendors from a variety of economic and social backgrounds.

Roikaew's growing brand is part of a larger ecology of private markets in Thailand that, drawing from the role of street vending in nation-building campaigns over the past century, appropriate this simultaneously everyday and symbolic commercial practice.[5] This chapter describes the history of public markets in Bangkok and how the policies of municipal and national political figures have influenced the emergence of a range of private markets including Talad Rot Fai over the past decade. Although markets like Talad Rot Fai provide some insight as to how a more inclusive approach to street vending could be achieved in Bangkok, Bangkok's private markets are not producing the 'solution' to street vending that many of the city's administrators have tried to sell to the public and tourists over the past decade.

SHAPING THE MODEL MARKET

Bangkok's markets are everyday, minority, commercial spaces that have been appropriated into Thai nationalism over the past century by national and municipal policy. Since 2014 municipal and national government leaders shifted away from a centralised, government-led approach in the mid-twentieth century that established public markets throughout the country. Instead, government alternatives to 'informal' street markets are often sponsored and driven by private actors.

Originally a Chinese trading village, in Bangkok's earliest years as the nation's capital the Chinese community played a central role in market activities that were located along the city's canals and eventually its streets. Chinese minorities in Bangkok were able to maintain businesses throughout the nineteenth century as they did not have to spend extended periods as corvée labour to the king. It was through restrictions on this community and the establishment of centralised market spaces by governmental policy that street vending was incorporated into the national identity and sold to a global audience.

2   'Giving the Pavement Back to Pedestrians,' *The Nation*, 26 November 2014, *https://www.nationthailand.com/perspective/30248642*
3   Talad Rot Fai is translated as Train Market. It gained this name when its original location was on Thai railway land adjacent to the Weekend Market or JJ Market located in Chatuchak on the north side of the city. After its eviction, the company kept this name, making it its brand.
4   Kanin Srimaneekulroj, 'Rod Fai Market Founder Pairod Roikaew: "Honesty Can't Be Bought",' *BK Magazine*, 22 February 2015, *https://bk.asia-city.com/city-living/news/rod-fai-market-founder-pairod-roikaew*
5   The notion of 'everyday' draws on Margaret Crawford's concept of 'everday urbanism'. It is 'an approach to urbanism that finds its meanings in everyday life' and the everyday spaces that constitute it are often considered banal and repetitive. John Chase, Margaret Crawford, and John Kaliski, *Everyday Urbanism* (New York: Monacelli Press, 1999).

In 1941 the Thai government first attempted to monitor street vending, when the Bangkok municipal government enacted separate regulations monitoring fixed and mobile vending.[6] A few years later, authoritarian leader Plaek Phibunsongkram decreed that every city and village in Thailand establish a central market in 1948. As a result, at the heart of most villages is a large market space in addition to a temple, the religious and educational centre of the community. In Bangkok, the weekend market was established at Sanam Luang.[7] Sanam Luang is an open grassy field where the king and the public would interact through religious holidays and funeral rituals for the royal family.[8] Establishing the weekend market in Sanam Luang was a way of reclaiming this traditionally royal space as public after the abolition of the absolute monarchy.[9]

Not only did the concentration of vending activities in politically potent spaces like Sanam Luang fuel the agenda of Phibunsongkram, but the restrictions he placed on the Chinese community and appropriation of this minority commercial practice that involved the banning of noodle stalls within a certain radius of schools played a key role in his approach to nation-building.[10] By 1983 the market would be moved from Bangkok's heart to Chatuchak, a district north of the city where it remains until today. The impetus for this move was partially the heritagisation of Bangkok's historic core or Rattanakosin.[11] Spread over thirty-five acres of land, the weekend market now consists of over 15,000 stalls that are organised into twenty-seven sections.[12]

In contrast to the large-scale establishment of public markets in the mid-twentieth century, the municipal and national governments have used a public-private hybrid approach to establishing new markets since the coming to power of the military-led government in 2014.

After the military government appointed Asawan Kwanmuang as governor in 2016, the national and municipal governments worked together to put widespread restrictions on street vending activities in place. It was rumoured amongst vendors and street-vending advocates during this period that the severe restrictions were driven by private interests, especially given that some of the biggest crackdowns were in central districts with some of the highest land values. However, it was in the government's vision for the future of street vending that the central role of the private sphere in these policies became clear. One alternative presented by government authorities to street markets was the incentivisation of the development of food courts by allowing developers to build additional floors. In one interview I conducted with Vallop Suwandee in 2018, the chairman of advisers to the Governor of Bangkok and a key figure spearheading vendor evictions, he celebrated this developer-oriented solution to the street vending 'problem.' When probed as to how this process would be regulated, including who could sell and how much rent would cost in these spaces, he stated that regulation and oversight of developers was not part of the government's plan for this incentivisation programme.[13]

After experiencing a backlash for the 'Returning the Pavement to Pedestrians' initiative from international media outlets like CNN, academics, and food critics, government agencies ran a number of temporary markets that celebrated street food. Many of these events did little to silence critics as they were tourist-oriented and co-sponsored by corporations. In June 2017, I attended the Amazing Thai Taste Festival that was located adjacent to the city's airport-rail link. Banners for this market featured the logos of sixty sponsors including food corporations,

6   See: Yasmeen and Nirathron, 'Vending in Public Space.'
7   Although it was moved outside of the city for a few years, in 1958 Bangkok's weekend market was reestablished in Sanam Luang or the Royal Field.
8   Trude Renwick and Bronwyn Isaacs, 'Power and Ritual in the City: Mourning and Political Juncture at Bangkok's Sanam Luang,' Journal of Southeast Asian Studies (forthcoming).
9   Lawrence Chua, 'A Tale of Two Crematoria: Funeral Architecture and the Politics of Representation in Mid-Twentieth-Century Bangkok,' Journal of the Society of Architectural Historians 77, no. 3 (September 2018): 319–38; Lawrence Chua, Bangkok Utopia: Modern Architecture and Buddhist Felicities, 1910–1973 (Honolulu: University of Hawaii Press, 2021).
10 Trude Renwick, 'Jay Fai and the Anomaly of the "Good" Street Vendor,' Food, Culture & Society 24, no. 1 (January 2021): 127–41.
11 In Noobanjong's chapter, 'The Royal Field: Bangkok's Polysemic Urban Palimpsest,' he describes how the field has transformed from a unifying space in which a new national identity after the fall of the absolute monarchy was formed, to a contentious public space where some of Thailand's deadliest protests played out in the 1976. The park was shut down in 1993, 2003, and 2010 for renovations as well as to eliminate unwanted activities including prostitution. The largest renovation project occurred in 2010 when the park was shut down for nine months and its grounds and hours of public access became tightly controlled by the Department of Parks and Recreation. Koompong Noobanjong, 'The Royal Field (Sanam Luang): Bangkok's Polysemic Urban Palimpsest,' in Messy Urbanism: Understanding the "Other" Cities of Asia, ed. Manish Chalana (Hong Kong: Hong Kong University Press, 2016), 97.
12 Peter Mörtenböck and Helge Mooshammer, 'Market Fashion - Talad Rot Fai,' in Informal Market Worlds: The Architecture of Economic Pressure - Atlas, eds. Peter Mörtenböck and Helge Mooshammer (Rotterdam: nai010 publishers, 2015), 495.
13 Vallop Suwandee in conversation with the author, 31 May 2018.

Talad Rot Fai, at its former site near Chatuchak, Bangkok, 2012

mall developers, and telecommunication companies that were working in tandem with the Tourism Authority of Thailand (TAT) as well as several other departments within the national government. The 'Bangkok street food' stalls that made up the majority of this market sold food from restaurants as well as products from these same brands including Popeye's, Dunkin Donuts, and CP.

This carnivalesque atmosphere was reproduced in some of the markets constructed for evicted street vendors in popular tourist areas by public-private partnerships like Yodpiman River Walk. This 'Thai heritage mall' was opened in 2016 along the Chao Praya River and now houses Pak Khlong Talad, one of the city's oldest produce markets known for its flowers. Of the three main markets that exist on this site, one belongs to the Market Organisation, a department of the Interior Ministry. The other two markets, Yodpiman Market and Song Serm Kaset Thai Market, are run by private operators.[14] The riverside mall, designed in a neoclassical style, houses a range of chain stores in addition to the vegetable and flower market.

More recently, in 2022 Governor Chadchart Sittipunt announced that the municipal government would establish a Singaporean model for Bangkok's street vending. Singapore's 'hawker centres' were established in the 1950s and 1960s as part of public housing and sanitation projects spurred by the city-state's growth and a strong centralised government.[15] Through the census, licensing, and collaboration with the Housing and Development Board (HBD), the state was able to relocate almost 18,000 vendors in 1968.[16] These culinary centres consist of large halls holding individual stalls and dining areas and are often tied to residential estates. Protected by UNESCO as an example of intangible world heritage since 2019, they are celebrated for their Michelin-rated vendors, range of dishes, and cheap prices.

Governor Chadchart Sittipunt's announcement that the establishment of 'hawker centres' in Bangkok would clear footpaths and provide 'clean' market spaces for tourists was not a surprise.[17] In fact, municipal government officials had been sent to Singapore under Asawin Kwanmuang to visit the centres. However, Chadchart's vision was certainly more developed than his predecessor's. His plan included designating thirty-one sites for vendors throughout the city where pavements would be expanded to two metres with one metre set aside for stalls.[18]

In February 2023, a walking street (pedestrian precinct) was opened as a public-private initiative between the municipal government and a mixed-use shopping complex, Samyan Mitrtown. Governor Chadchart attended the opening of the 'Hello Hab-Re' (Hello 'Hawker') project, which was meant to launch his Singapore-style approach to street vending in the city. Rent in the market is free for vendors who are permitted to sell from 8 am–2 pm and 3 pm–8 pm Monday through Friday.[19] After thanking Samyan Mitrtown for the space, Chadchart expressed his hope that more private real-estate owners would follow in their footsteps, stating: 'the project does not require the city to invest in building more space for street vendors but instead promotes the use of existing space to the fullest.'[20]

Public-private markets like Hello Hab-Re, Yodpiman Riverwalk, and Amazing Thai Taste Festival are not anywhere near the large-scale and government-led approach to formalising street vending used in Singapore. However, they do demonstrate how the appropriation of these practices has evolved from a government-led nation-building campaign meant to absorb a minority commercial practice into a public-private enterprise. The emphasis on creativity, history, and art found in many of the government-run markets celebrating street vending is partially spurred by the growth of the creative industries in Thailand.

14   Wanant Kerdchuen, 'Uneasy Neighbours,' *Bangkok Post*, *https://www.bangkokpost.com/thailand/special-reports/492088/uneasy-neighbours*; See also: *https://mgronline.com/stockmarket/detail/9590000012746*

15   Hong Kong underwent a similar process when the British colonial government established centralised market spaces in the late 1960s and early 1970s.

16   Andrew Tam, 'Singapore Hawker Centers: Origins, Identity, Authenticity, and Distinction,' *Gastronomica* 17, no. 1 (2017): 45.

17   Mark Footer, 'Bangkok's Street Food Vendors Are Disappearing – Those Who Survive May Soon Be inside Singapore-Style Hawker Centres,' *South China Morning Post*, *https://www.scmp.com/magazines/post-magazine/travel/article/3189209/bangkoks-street-food-vendors-are-disappearing-those*

18   Supoj Wancharoen, 'BMA Eyes Hawker Centres to Resolve Street Stall Free-for-All,' *Bangkok Post*, 13 July 2022, *https://www.bangkokpost.com/thailand/general/2344903/bma-eyes-hawker-centres-to-resolve-street-stall-free-for-all*

19   'Bangkok Opens First Free Space for Street Hawkers in Project to Tidy City,' *The Nation*, 2 February 2023, *https://www.nationthailand.com/thailand/general/40024548*

20   As a result, Bangkok has established its first creative district and the Creative Economy Agency is expanding its vision for creative urban interventions to include peripheral cities.

Chatuchak, Bangkok, 2012

Investment in the creative economy began in the early 2000s under Prime Minister Thaksin Shinawatra and has continued under Prayut Chan-O-Cha's Thailand 4.0 development plan.[21] Thailand 4.0 seeks to move Thailand 'forward,' away from an agricultural economy and towards the creative industries. This course of national development in tandem with street vending restrictions echoes Phibunsongkram's nationalist agenda in the mid-twentieth century, yet is distinct in its emphasis on the private sector.

In the following sections, I begin to describe Bangkok's many private market spaces that have emerged over the past decade. Documenting the establishment and expansion of Talad Rot Fai and other private markets sheds light on both the range of improvisational commercial forms that have emerged in Bangkok over the past decade, as well as the problematic policies of the municipal and national government that favour the private sector over the needs of street vendors facing eviction. The aesthetics of these private markets are ultimately meant to attract well-educated and wealthy Bangkok hipsters as clientele and vendors who are feeding the creative economy.[22]

TALAD ROT FAI: FROM CHATUCHAK TO SRINGARINDRA

Pairod Roikaew and several other antique dealers in the city opened the Chatuchak location of Talad Rot Fai in 2010. Located only 500 metres from the weekend market, its original location consisted of large warehouses atop a nine-acre site owned by the State Railway of Thailand. When the lease for the JJ Train Market location ended in June 2013 due to the construction of a new train line, the market had to either be closed completely or moved to another site. In a 2015 interview with BK magazine, Roikaew describes the sense of duty he felt towards the vendors selling in Talad Rot Fai in 2013 as well as his broader business philosophy: 'Business owners need to find a balance between profits and goodwill. It's better for your business if the people paying you are happy to do so.

21   This is notable as Thaksin Shinawatra's sister Yingluck Shinawatra was ousted from office as prime minister by a military coup that installed Prayut Chan-O-Cha as prime minister.
22   Richard Florida, *Rise of the Creative Class*, New York: Basic Books, 2002.

Talad Rot Fai, Srinagarinda, Bangkok, 2023 (top and bottom)

While other markets tend to charge 400 to 500 baht for a single night's stall rental, I only charge 200 baht. I still get my profits, and the merchants get an affordable location to peddle their wares.'[23]

Not only does this quote note Roikaew's commitment to keeping rent affordable to vendors, but it reflects his business philosophy based on responsible, sufficiency-oriented patronage.[24] Two Talad Rot Fai markets were opened after the closure of the Chatuchak location: Srinagaindra and Ratchada. The name Train Market no longer described the location of the market, but became a theme and brand. The Ratchada location became popular as it was located next to an MTR stop (subway station) and a number of large malls including Esplanade and The Street Ratchada.[25] Shoppers would move seamlessly in between the mall and market. This element of promenade made the market a beneficial commercial development for the adjacent mall developers. Iron scaffolding soared above the entry to the market displaying a large sign featuring the market's train logo. In addition to multiple rows of tents, a large portion of the site was dedicated to bars featuring live music and food. Corrugated metal, roughly hewn wood tables, and shipping containers were all used to craft the vintage industrial aesthetic of this lively section of the market.

Because of the reasonable rent and central location, many street vendors relocated to Talad Rot Fai Ratchada after facing eviction in 2016. One street vendor that I had previously interviewed, traded and protested alongside in Bangkok's central commercial district was able to re-open their stall in this popular night market. Consisting of food vendors, restaurants, and bars in addition to clothing and other goods for sale, Talad Rot Fai Ratchada was a great alternative for vendors who previously sold in Bangkok's highly congested and centrally located commercial areas like Siam Square, Silom, and the Ratchaprasong intersection. However, this market was closed during the COVID-19 pandemic, leaving only the Srinagarindra Train Market location open on the far eastern side of the city. The site has

since been transformed into another privately run market.

The longest-running location of the Train Market is its Srinagarindra location. Opened in 2013, the Srinagarindra Talad Rot Fai draws its name from the main road running in front of the site named after the late king's mother Princess Srinagarindra. Located in Prawet District near the Suvarnabhumi Airport, this area was planned to be part of a special economic zone around the airport that was cancelled in 2006 after the coup d'état that overthrew Prime Minister Taksin Shinawatra. Situated on the outskirts of the city and only accessible by car or multiple transfers on public transportation, this market is a far cry from the Ratchada and Chatuchak locations.

Set back from Srinagarindra Road, as one approaches the site, soaring overhead is an extension of the MRT that was opened in 2023. Adjacent to the market is the Seacon Square Srinagarindra Mall, a driving range, and an extensive parking lot. Like the Ratchada location, marking the entrance to the market from the road is a large billboard hung on rough iron scaffolding. However, unlike the Ratchada location where patrons flowed seamlessly between the mall and market, pedestrians arriving here are kept separate from the mall. Those arriving by public transport walk down a narrow lane of covered shops and restaurants that leads to the market site.

There are a range of commercial spaces available for rent within the market from large warehouses holding antique shops to small tented enclosure holding a variety of products including sneakers, t-shirts, and watches. One woman I spoke with runs a shop selling umbrellas and previously sold at the Chatuchak location. After trading at the Train Market for a total of ten years, she is grateful that she and other vendors were invited to move with the market in 2013. She explained to me that rent is 300 baht for two square metres per day, and for larger restaurants and shops, the rent is monthly. She guessed that the restaurant across from her was about 20,000 baht per month, which is approximately 1,250 baht per

23   Srimaneekulroj, 'Rod Fai Market Founder Pairod Roikaew.'
24   This language focused on good will and responsibility and the rhetoric of economic sufficiency I discuss in the chapter on the Saphan Lek Market. See: Daena Funahashi, 'Rule by Good People: Health Governance and the Violence of Moral Authority in Thailand,' *Cultural Anthropology* 31, no. 1 (February 2016): 107–130.
25   This mall was rebranded and renovated in 2016 by Architectkidd. The architecture of the mall's new skin was meant to reflect the boundary between public and private space.

Typical infrastructural components, Talad Rot Fai, Bangkok, 2023

day if they are able to sell about sixteen days or four weekends a month. The consistent customer base and reasonably priced rent is what keeps her and many other vendors selling in this space even though the market runs only four days a week.

Young people walking through the market stop and pose in front of vintage cars and antique petrol-station signs. These design elements broaden the theming of the Srinagarindra Train Night Market to include transportation more broadly. Like the Ratchada location, large portions of the market are dedicated to activities other than shopping. Beyond the market's large number of restaurants and bars featuring live music, a small skatepark is located on a large plot on the eastern side of the site. Corrugated metal structures featuring graffiti and housing a number of vehicles, including a train car and airstream trailer, mark the edge of the site just beyond the skate park. Bright red signage announces the building as 'Rod's Motor Garage.' Promotional materials for the market also feature the car shows and concerts that are run in this quieter section of the market.

Although the Srinagarindra and Ratchada Markets were closed for much of the COVID-19 pandemic, Pairod Roikaew's vision has expanded over the past two years. Jodd Fairs is at the heart of this and has been widely advertised on social media. With the first location just steps away from the Ratchada Train Night Market (which was closed in 2021), Jodd Fairs Rama 9 is a mall-market hybrid. Roikaew has dedicated the front plot of land to a tented market and has plans to develop a four-floor mall modelled after Chelsea Flea on the same site.[26] One Instagram post attempting to attract vendors to the Rama 9 location includes a rendering of a mall, half glass and half brick, with extensive tents, a vintage muscle car, and a red telephone booth placed in the foreground. At one marketing event in 2022, Jodd Fairs was described by Roikaew as on a par with the most popular locations for tourists in the city, including Khaowsan Road, Icon Siam, Siam Paragon, and Central World Malls. As the newest evolution of Roikaew's interpretation of the public market model, the upscale theming of Jodd Fairs is distinct from the Srinagarindra location that serves a growing middle class living on the outskirts of Bangkok. Although events run at Jodd Fair locations still feature classic cars, its theming has moved towards a fantasy, Euro-American playground aesthetic. In fact, the front of its newest Lad Prao location near Chatuchak Market takes the European theme a step further by including a large three-to-four storey castle.[27]

THE HIPSTER MARKET PLAYBOOK

Talad Rot Fai and Jodd Fairs fit into a growing group of themed markets in the city. While ranging in degrees of permanence, these markets are often themed around topics of history, art, and creativity. Chang Chui is one market that is similar to Talad Rot Fai in theming and social media presence. Opened in 2017, Chang Chui meaning 'sloppy artisan' was started by Somchai Songwattana, the CEO and art director of the Thai brand FlyNow. Chang Chui was featured in *Time* magazine's World's 100 Greatest Places list in 2018. Both Chang Chui and Talad Rot Fai feature life-size planes set at the centre of the markets in combination with numerous food stalls and temporary event spaces. Unlike Rot Fai, the theming of Chang Chui is driven by designer-oriented tenets rather than antiques. It is also open every day from 11 am–11 pm and advertises rent at as little as 100 baht per day. Set up as a boutique market, the architecture of Chang Chui includes surreal fusions of modernist and derelict aesthetics. While the Train Market's buildings consist of subdivided long warehouses, Chang Chui's eighteen buildings are a modern, sculptural potpourri of reused materials, including glass and steel, corrugated metal and wood. Some shops even play with the form of rural Thai homes, distinguishing the more open bottom floor consisting of a mixture of used and new materials from the upper, private level made primarily of a single material like corrugated metal. Pathways and gardens have been formed throughout the area, creating a photogenic environment for visitors seeking Instagrammable backdrops.

---

26   This new project was in partnership with Property Perfect, a residential property developer.
27   In one article, Roikaew states that his favourite antiques are typically over a century old, and from the Victorian era and the Baltic region.

Talad Rot Fai, Srinagarinda, Bangkok, 2023

Talad Rot Fai, Srinagarinda, Bangkok, 2023

An even smaller-scale private market is the Knack Market, located at the Jam Factory along the Chao Praya River. It is the brainchild of architect Duangrit Bunnag, a key figure in the Creative District Foundation. This architecture firm and its small complex, including a Michelin-rated restaurant, coffee shop, and art gallery, is located along Bangkok's Chao Praya River. Up until 2021, Knack Market attracted young people to the complex to shop, listen to music, and eat. In an interview I conducted with Bunnag, he stated that he wanted to provide a space for young creative entrepreneurs to sell their products.[28] Like Talad Rot Fai and Chang Chui, rent is affordable at approximately 200 baht per day and its hippie theming created a similar nostalgic, retro aesthetic; however, since 2021, there have been very few markets or events held there.

Perhaps one of the most compelling private market projects, distinct from the themed markets discussed throughout this chapter, was developed in 2012, not far from the Srinagaindra Train Market. In 2012,

Ratchaporn Choochuey and her architecture firm Allzone were hired to design an outdoor market space by Dhanapa Asset Development. This market flourished in the early 2000s, serving the large number of construction workers who were housed in this area as they built Suvarnabhumi Airport. After the airport opened in 2006, the market remained in the area, with custom coming from a growing suburban population in the area. The developers decided that rather than evict vendors and then redevelop the land, they would build a flexible structure to hold the market. The Airport Market design has been recognised internationally for its flexible tent typology and is an example of how vendors, developers, and architects can actually work together.

Beyond these semi-outdoor private market complexes, Bangkok's developers have long seen the benefits of incorporating markets into the city's malls and office towers. Between 1985 and 1996, when Thailand had one of the fastest-growing economies in the world, Bangkok's mall developers sought to broaden their customer base to include a rapidly growing middle class.[29] Incorporating food courts into malls was one method of increasing profits from lower-middle-class clientele that spent time in malls but were unable to afford the international luxury brands hosted by these new commercial spaces. The developers of Bangkok's most popular malls, including Central World, Siam Paragon, Terminal 21 and Iconsiam, are still using this approach to draw in middle-class customers, tourists, and to expand their clientele to include well-educated hipsters. Inaugurated in 2018 as one of the largest malls in Southeast Asia, the ground floor of Iconsiam was designed as a floating market. Structures throughout the ground floor of this mall incorporated architectural elements from each of Thailand's four major regions. Temporary events themed around the city's history, holidays, and the Thailand 4.0 development plan promoting the creative industries also fill the open plazas and hallways of these malls.

Beyond individuals designing and running malls, larger land developers in central Bangkok have encouraged the opening of private markets just steps away from illegal markets that were dismantled in 2016. Only weeks after the eviction of the Siam night Market vendors, who operated stalls in one of the most notorious markets in Bangkok's Pathumwan commercial district, Chulalongkorn University Property Management held a temporary market under the same name in one of its narrow streets: 'Siam Night Market 2.' This same developer tore down an entire alleyway of vendor stalls after the municipal government declared the space unfit for commercial activity. Months later, the land management company permitted another business to redevelop the alleyway, repainting and renovating the row of stalls that had been deemed illegal by municipal officers. When I asked one of the partners involved in this project about whether they would allow vendors who previously sold in the market to return, he stated that they would not. He argued that they did not offer the quality of goods he felt necessary to attract their desired clientele as they 'sold only fake products from China.'[30] Rent prices

for these more permanent stands constructed by malls and these types of small market developers in Bangkok's busiest districts are high. In 2016, the cost of a small stall from Chulalongkorn Property Management was around 2,000 baht per night, whereas vendors selling in the adjacent market feet away rented their spaces for 200 baht per night. In fact, the business of establishing temporary events and markets in Bangkok's malls has become so profitable that malls are hiring specialised marketing teams and event management companies to run these spaces.

The success of private markets is so far-reaching that some of these businesses are expanding throughout the region. Art Box is another market that started in 2015 and has managed to expand to other countries, including Singapore and Malaysia. This market was started by an event management company and was set up for short periods at different locations within Bangkok. Event coordinators are often hired by malls to develop temporary events to fill their empty spaces. Art Box stands out, as much of its profit is generated via transient locations. Before lockdown they were in possession of a concrete location which was then closed. Through special events, they sell the image of the Thai Market globally. This model of the market is part of a larger trend of night markets that is visible in other parts of the world, including the United States. 626 Night Market and FoodieLand are two such examples that are advertised as Asian night markets. Established respectively in 2012 and 2019 in California, these markets have hosted up to 750,000 attendees annually in the case of FoodieLand and hundreds of vendors. 626 Market even advertises itself as 'inspired by the famous open-air nighttime bazaars of Asia.'

BANGKOK'S IMPROVISATIONAL URBANISM

This private appropriation of markets in Bangkok and the range of forms it takes is a product of what Jonathan Anjaria calls 'improvisational urbanism.' For Anjaria, improvisational urbanism aligns with trends in architecture and urban planning, and new

29   Chris Baker and Pasuk Phongpaichit, *Thailand's Boom and Bust: Revised Edition* (Chiang Mai: Silkworm Books, 1998).
30   Interview with the author, 28 September 2018.

Talad Rot Fai, Srinagarinda, Bangkok, 2023

attention is being brought to the 'ordinary ways people in megacities of the Global South use and produce city spaces.'[31] This way of reading urban landscapes has the potential to make visible the poor and their everyday spatial practices; however, Anjaria emphasises that proponents of improvisational urbanism do not always critically engage with the social and economic injustices that have led to the production of such spaces.

The Train Market and many of the above examples of market appropriation, whether by government or private actors, reflect precisely what Anjaria describes. Ratchaporn's open-air market, as well as developers who have kept rent tenable for evicted vendors, illustrates the potential of Bangkok's growing sector of private markets. However, even though markets like Talad Rot Fai can provide affordable rent and a stable location for many of Bangkok's street vendors currently being pushed/forced out of existing spaces, they are not a solution to the underlying tensions surrounding street vending in Thailand. Their focus remains on profit and brand development, and the boom in Bangkok's privately run markets is ultimately a product of Thai policies on street vending that seek to privatise the public market and lack government oversight in this process.

It is easy to see the appropriation of Bangkok's markets as a new problem and a product of gentrification brought about by the creative industries, however, the larger history of the centralisation and appropriation of street markets as a commercial practice by the national government demonstrates that it is not entirely new.[32] I see private markets as neither the source of 'problems' nor the 'solution' to tensions around street vending in Thailand. Mapping out this larger ecosystem and history of market appropriation in Thailand is instead meant to unpack the range of forms these spaces take and mark their potential to influence the future of improvisational urbanism in Thailand. Only time will tell if the new government will build on the methods and tools presented by these private markets, which have emerged amidst a tumultuous moment in history for Thailand's street markets.

REFERENCES

Anjaria, J. 'The Slow Boil: Street Food, Rights and Public Space in Mumbai' In *South Asia in Motion*. Stanford: Stanford University Press, 2016.

Baker, C., and P. Phongpaichit. *Thailand's Boom and Bust: Revised Edition*. Chiang Mai: Silkworm Books, 1998.

Chase, J., M. Crawford, and J. Kaliski. *Everyday Urbanism*. New York: Monacelli Press, 2008.

Chua, L. 'A Tale of Two Crematoria: Funeral Architecture and the Politics of Representation in Mid-Twentieth Century Bangkok.' *Journal of the Society of Architectural Historians* 77, no. 3 (September 2018): 319–38.

Chua, L. *Bangkok Utopia: Modern Architecture and Buddhist Felicities, 1910–1973*. Honolulu: University of Hawaii Press, 2021.

Florida, R. *The Rise of the Creative Class*. New York, Basic Books, 2002.

Footer, M. 'Bangkok's Street Food Vendors Are Disappearing – Those Who Survive May Soon Be inside Singapore-Style Hawker Centres.' *South China Morning Post*. https://www.scmp.com/magazines/post-magazine/travel/article/3189209/bangkoks-street-food-vendors-are-disappearing-those

Funahashi, D. 'Rule by Good People: Health Governance and the Violence of Moral Authority in Thailand.' *Cultural Anthropology* 31, no. 1 (February 2016): 107–130.

Kerdchuen, W. 'Uneasy Neighbours.' *Bangkok Post*, 9 May 2015. https://www.bangkokpost.com/thailand/special-reports/492088/uneasy-neighbours

Mörtenböck, P., and H. Mooshammer. 'Market Fashion - Talad Rot Fai, Bangkok.' In *Informal Market Worlds: The Architecture of Economic Pressure - Atlas*, 494–99. Rotterdam: nai010 Publishers, 2015.

Noobanjong, K. 'The Royal Field (Sanam Luang): Bangkok's Polysemic Urban Palimpsest.' In *Messy Urbanism: Understanding the "Other" Cities of Asia*, edited by M. Chalana. Hong Kong: Hong Kong University Press, 2016.

Renwick, T. 'Jay Fai and the Anomaly of the "Good" Street Vendor.' *Food, Culture & Society* 24, no. 1 (January 2021): 127–141.

Renwick. T., and B. Isaacs. 'Power and Ritual in the City: Mourning and Political Juncture at Bangkok's Sanam Luang.' *Journal of Southeast Asian Studies* (forthcoming).

Srimaneekulroj, K. 'Rod Fai Market Founder Pairod Roikaew: "Honesty Can't Be Bought."' *BK Magazine*, 22 February 2015. https://bk.asia-city.com/city-living/news/rod-fai-market-founder-pairod-roikaew

Tam, A. 'Singapore Hawker Centers: Origins, Identity, Authenticity, and Distinction.' *Gastronomica* 17, no. 1 (2017): 44–55.

Wancharoen, S. 'BMA Eyes Hawker Centres to Resolve Street Stall Free-for-All.' *Bangkok Post*, 13 July 2022. https://www.bangkokpost.com/thailand/general/2344903/bma-eyes-hawker-centres-to-resolve-street-stall-free-for-all

Wetherell, S. 'Richard Florida Is Sorry.' *Jacobin*, blog. https://jacobin.com/2017/08/new-urban-crisis-review-richard-florida

Yasmeen, G. and Nirathron, N. 'Vending in Public Space: The Case of Bangkok.' *WIEGO Urban Policies*, no. 16 (May 2014).

31 Jonathan Shapiro Anjaria, *The Slow Boil: Street Food, Rights and Public Space in Mumbai*, South Asia in Motion series (Stanford: Stanford University Press, 2016), 162.
32 Sam Whetherell, 'Richard Florida Is Sorry,' *Jacobin*, blog, https://jacobin.com/2017/08/new-urban-crisis-review-richard-florida

1976-2000

1 Governor Rattakul implements strict measures to regulate street vending.
2 The Thai baht is devalued after the removal of its peg to the US dollar, triggering the Asian financial crisis.
3 Thailand's economy experiences a severe recession, with GDP contracting by approximately 10% alongside a sharp increase in unemployment.

2000-2005

4 Governor Sundaravej removes restrictions on no-vending days and authorises the establishment of 353 new designated vending areas.
5 Governor Kasayodhin initiates a comprehensive city-wide clean-up campaign targeting street vendors.

2005-2010

6 Srinagarindra area is planned to become a special economic zone around the airport, an idea that is abandoned after the coup d'état.
7 Thai coup d'état

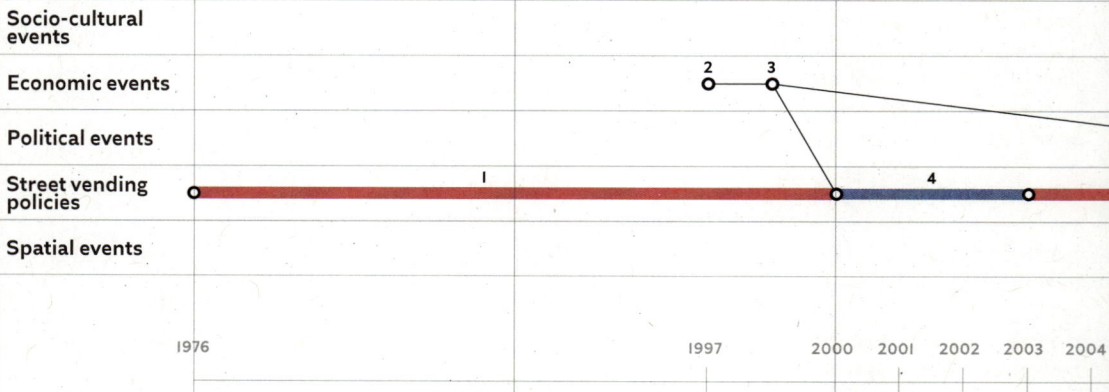

Socio-cultural events

Economic events

Political events

Street vending policies

Spatial events

1976   1997   2000   2001   2002   2003   2004

Liab Duan Night Market

Hua Mum Night Market

Airport Market

JJ Green 2

Owl Night Market

9   Ratchada

Jodd Fairs

18

Knack Market

Indy Market

Timeline of key events shaping the transformation of Talad Rot Fai, Bangkok

2010-2015

8 Major political protests and demonstrations in Bangkok

9 Talad Rot Fai (Train Market) opens on a plot of land adjacent to Chatuchak Market.

10 Governor Paribatra introduces a series of policies that demonstrate a strong support for street vendors.

11 A reported six million illegal and counterfeit products are seized in Bangkok's illegal markets.

12 Under the administration of Governor Sukhumbhand a shift towards more stringent regulation on street vending occurs.

13 Talad Rot Fai next to Chatuchak closes and reopens at a new site in Srinagarinda in East Bangkok.

14 Thai coup d'état

2015-2020

15 A public spaces clean-up programme led by the Bangkok Metropolitan Administration (BMA) comes into effect following the military coup.

16 A further site of Talad Rot Fai is opened in Ratchada.

17 The eviction of street vendors from Bangkok's city centre contributes to making private and temporary market ventures more popular.

18 Chang Chui Market (dubbed 'Plane Market'), which has many similarities with the Train Market, opens in West Bangkok.

19 More and more private markets expand into other countries, e.g. Singapore and Malaysia.

2020-2023

20 Public and privately operated markets are closed due to the COVID-19 pandemic.

21 Following the relaxation of COVID-19 related restrictions, a number of large private night markets comparable to Talad Rot Fai open across Bangkok, including Jodd Fairs, the Indy Market, One Ratchada, etc., which attract thousands of customers.

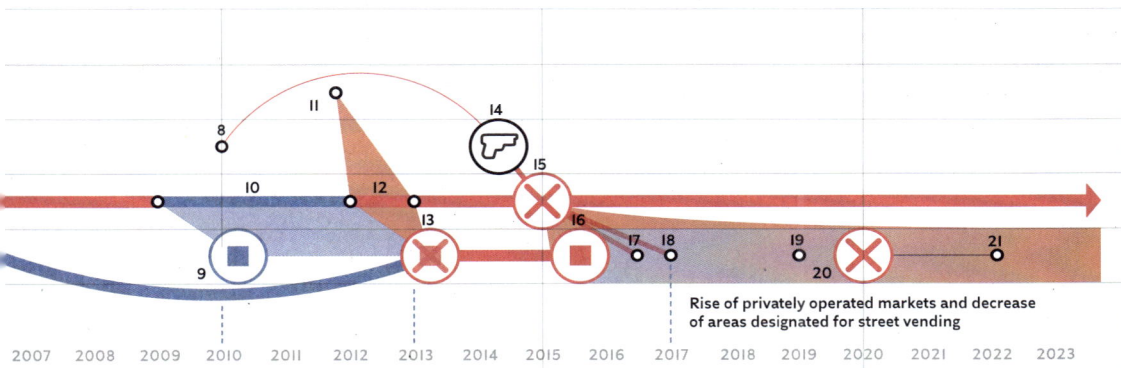

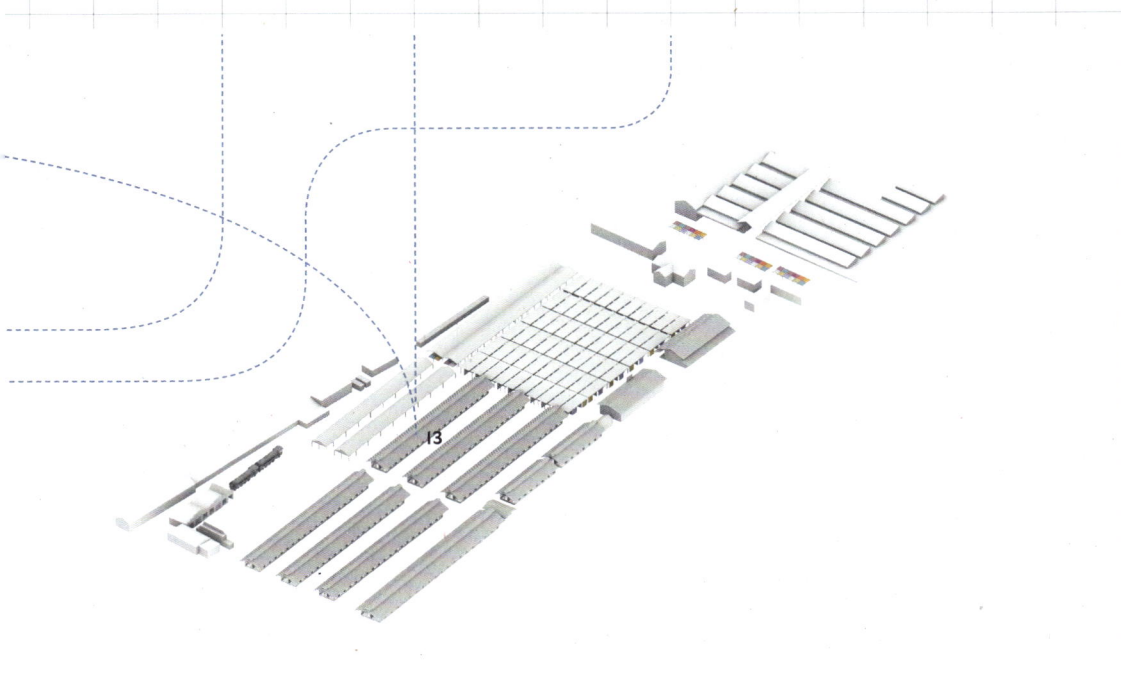

Rise of privately operated markets and decrease of areas designated for street vending

2007   2008   2009   2010   2011   2012   2013   2014   2015   2016   2017   2018   2019   2020   2021   2022   2023

■ Spatial, social, economic and political interventions into in/formal markets
■ Informality as a survival method and means of adapting to changing socio-economic and political circumstances

413

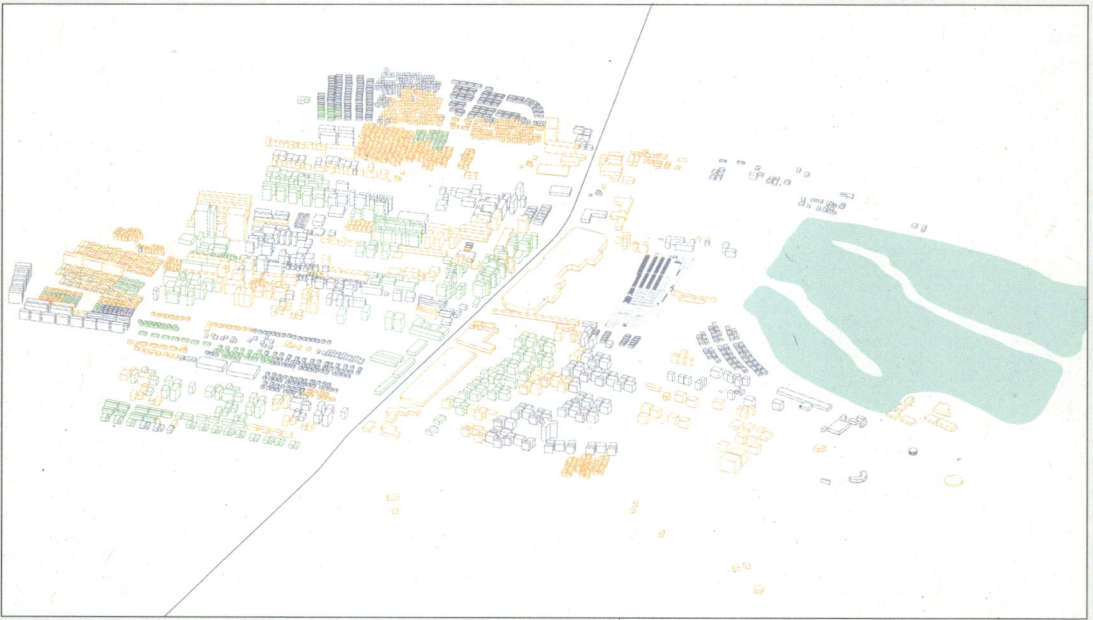

■ 1414   ■ 1892   ■ 1941   ■ 1980   ■ 1990   ■ 2000   ■ 2004   ■ 2010   ■ 2022

Talad Rot Fai, Srinagarinda neighbourhood: key phases of spatial development

Typical infrastructural components, Talad Rot Fai, Bangkok (bottom and opposite page)

Talad Rot Fai, Srinagarinda, Bangkok, 2023 (top and bottom)

Talad Rot Fai, Srinagarinda, Bangkok, 2023

Talad Rot Fai, Srinagarinda, Bangkok, 2023

41

EDITORS

Peter Mörtenböck is Professor of Visual Culture at the TU Wien, founding Co-Director of the Centre for Global Architecture, and Research Fellow at Goldsmiths College, University of London. His current research is focused on the architecture of the political community and the economisation of the city, as well as the global use of raw materials, urban infrastructures and new data publics.

Helge Mooshammer is an architect, author and curator. He conducts urban and cultural research in the Department of Visual Culture at the TU Wien, is founding Co-Director of the Centre for Global Architecture, and Research Fellow at Goldsmiths College, University of London. He has initiated and directed numerous international research projects focusing on issues relating to (post) capitalist urban economics and urban informality.

Mörtenböck und Mooshammer curated the Austrian Pavilion at the Venice Architecture Biennale 2021, which explored the phenomenon of platform urbanism. Their most recent book publications include *Informal Market Worlds: The Architecture of Economic Pressure – ATLAS & READER* (ed. with Teddy Cruz and Fonna Forman, nai010 publishers, 2015), *Visual Cultures as Opportunity* (Sternberg/MIT Press, 2016), *Data Publics: Public Plurality in an Era of Data Determinacy* (Routledge, 2020) and *Platform Urbanism and Its Discontents* (nai010 publishers, 2021). They are currently working on the forthcoming monograph *Building Capital: Urban Speculation and the Architecture of Finance*.

Allan Cain O.C. is a founding director of Development Workshop and has lived and worked in Africa since 1980. He is an architect specialising in project management, participatory planning, sustainable urban development and water & sanitation. He has a degree in Environmental Studies and completed his professional studies at the Architectural Association (London, UK) and further specialist studies at Harvard University and Boulder, Colorado and in 2022 received an Honorary Doctorate in recognition of his practice. He has been a Visiting Professor at the School for International Development and Global Studies at the University of Ottawa, an Adjunct Research Professor at Carleton University and has lectured at universities in Angola, China, Norway, USA, South Africa, Portugal and UK. Allan Cain was awarded an Order of Canada in 2004 for his work in international development and social housing and his contribution to peacebuilding in Angola. He has worked as a consultant and led research projects for the World Bank, the African Development Bank, UN-Habitat and other international organisations. He is on the boards of several development institutions. His articles and papers have been published widely in international journals.

Paul H.S. CHU is Dean of the Faculty of Science and Engineering cum Head of Architecture Department of Hong Kong Chu Hai College. Professor Chu studied architecture and urban design at the University of Hong Kong and Columbia University, and is a Fellow at the Hong Kong Institute of Architects and a Registered Architect of Hong Kong and China (Class 1). He has been the recipient of a Rotary International Ambassadorial Scholarship and has received a number of awards, including Contemporary Construction Expert of China, Hong Kong Young Architect Award, 20 for 21st Century Emerging Hong Kong Architect, and Hong Kong Ten Outstanding Designers. His research interest in social aspects of informal architecture and urbanism is reflected in co-edited books such as *Villages in the City: A Guide to South China's Urban Informality* and *Factory Towns of South China: An Illustrated Guidebook*. His exhibitions include *Sectional Urbanism* and *Urban Living Room* at the Venice Architecture Biennale 2018, *Bi-City Biennale of Urbanism/Architecture of Shenzhen and Hong Kong* and *HK International Artists Workshop – Creativity Exchange x Community Experiment*. He is currently the curator of the 2023 Kuala Lumpur/Nanjing/Hong Kong Architecture and Urbanism Exhibition, which has the theme of *In-between Urbanism*.

Samar Halloum is an architect and researcher and holds a post-professional Masters Degree in Architecture (M.Arch II) from Yale University. Upon graduation, Samar was awarded the William Wirt Winchester Travel Fellowship, the Yale School of Architecture's most prestigious award, for her independent research project *Negotiations within Refugee Camps*. Before earning her Masters degree, Samar graduated with honours from the American University of Sharjah and worked for seven years in the United Arab Emirates on culturally and environmentally driven projects. Samar was the Design and Research Lead for the National Pavilion UAE at the 18th International Architecture Exhibition at La Biennale di Venezia. She was also the Lead Editorial Researcher for *In Plain Sight: Scenes from Aridly Abundant Landscapes*. Samar's research investigates the role of spatial communal practices in shaping built environments rooted in their environmental and social contexts.

Carmen Lael Hines is a writer, researcher and curator particularly interested in tech, bodies, and the implications of their entanglements. She is based in the Department of Visual Culture at the TU Wien, where she teaches courses on new media theory and social reproduction. She is currently co-editing the book *Dissident Practices: Posthumanist Approaches to Critique of Political Economy*, to be published by Bloomsbury. She has curated exhibitions/programmes at e-flux screening room NY, Austrian Cultural Forum NY, Architekturzentrum Wien (as part of the Claiming*Space Collective), Galerie Kandlhofer and Parallel Vienna, amongst others. She was curatorial assistant for *Platform Austria*, Austria's contribution to the Venice Architecture Biennale 2021, where she supported the production of two publications and multiple displays. She has lectured in teaching programmes at the Royal Institute of Art, University of Bologna, TU Graz and the Academy of Fine Arts Vienna. In 2023 she co-curated the exhibition *Bordering Plants* in the Exhibit Galerie at the Academy of Fine Arts Vienna.

Lovro Koncar-Gamulin is an architect and researcher at the Centre for Global Architecture, TU Wien, with relevant experience in participatory urban design, as well as a longstanding engagement in projects dealing with the spatial effects of various economic, political, social and cultural phenomena. His innovative framework for mapping and planning in urban environments has been selected for the OeAD Citizen Science Award 2023. He has contributed to numerous architecture and urban projects. Koncar-Gamulin's engagement in the field of 'platform urbanism' led to his creation of over 40 video clips for the exhibition *Platform Austria* presented at the Venice Architecture Biennale 2021 and the MAK – Museum of Applied Arts Vienna.

m7red is an independent research group co-founded by **Mauricio Corbalan** and **Pio Torroja** in Buenos Aires in 2005. In 2020, m7red was awarded the Prince Claus Laureate in the architecture and urbanism category. m7red have presented works in Argentina, Korea, Sweden, USA, Turkey, Netherlands, Brazil, Ghana, and the United Kingdom. Some of their key projects are *Paraformal*, *Mil Cuencas* and *Que Pasa, Riachuelo?*, two research project books, and a public monitoring platform for the Matanzas-Riachuelo basin. m7red also worked on the creation of an information system for the Tecnopolis Sanitary Park during the COVID-19 pandemic.

Anton Nikolotov is an independent researcher, multimodal anthropologist and art maker. His research is located at the intersection of the anthropology of popular cosmo-economies, the study of improvisational informality, and the sociology of outer space in post-Soviet Eurasia. Nikolotov has a PhD from the Institute of Asian and African Studies at Humboldt University in Berlin, and a BA from Central Saint Martins College of Art and Design in London. Through ethnographic fieldwork and experiments with drawing, sound, and animation, Nikolotov seeks to narrate alternative imaginaries of borders, technoscientific futures and wealth.

Vyjayanthi V. Rao is an anthropologist, writer, and curator focussing on displacement, memory, the built environment, and imaginaries of the future and has a particular interest in speculative practices in contemporary social life. Her work explores the connections between violence, ruination, uncertainty, and speculation in contemporary culture and has been published widely in journals, edited volumes, catalogue texts, and magazines. Vyjayanthi received her PhD in Socio-Cultural Anthropology from the University of Chicago. She has taught at The New School for Social Research and at the Spitzer School of Architecture, City University of New York. Currently, she is a Visiting Professor at the Yale School of Architecture and the Co-Editor-in-Chief of the journal *Public Culture* (Duke University Press). Her curatorial work is related to her academic research interests. In 2016, she curated an installation at the Kochi-Muziris Biennale, collaborating with a group of housing-rights activists and architects. In 2022, she was part of the curatorial team of the Lisbon Architecture Triennale's 6th edition, co-curating the exhibition *Multiplicity* with Tau Tavengwa. Her current projects include an installation based on her dissertation, *Ruins and Recollections*, for the Chicago Architecture Biennale and curating a show for the Center for Architecture in New York titled *CFA Lab: Seeking Refuge and Making Home in NYC*.

Trude Laura Renwick, PhD, uses ethnographic methods to examine issues of inequality, aesthetics and labour that surround the development of commercial and infrastructural space in Thailand and Southeast Asia. Her current book project examines the uneasy symbiosis of spiritual and commercial space in Bangkok, Thailand. She is currently a Postdoctoral Fellow in the Society of Fellows in the Humanities at the University of Hong Kong affiliated with the Department of Art History, and served as a fellow at the International Institute for Asian Studies in Leiden, Netherlands. Prior to receiving a PhD in Architecture from the University of California, Berkeley, she received a Masters in Design Studies from the Graduate School of Design at Harvard University.

Simpreet Singh is an Indian activist who, since quitting his career as a successful engineer, has worked relentlessly on exposing housing scams and corruption in the city of Mumbai, where slum-dwellers are being evicted, in many cases unfairly, to make way for upmarket developments. Simpreet is fighting to stop these land grabs by using India's Right to Information laws. As part of his work with the Ghar Bachao Ghar Banao (GBGB) Movement, he persistently investigates alleged scams involving public land and environment violations. Simpreet is employed at the Tata Institute of Social Sciences (TISS) and is a member of the National Alliance of the Peoples Movement (NAPM). He is also currently pursuing a PhD on Mumbai's slums.

Melisa Vargas is a Dominican architect, urban planner and teacher. She has worked as an analyst, contractor and consultant for the United Nations, the Inter-American Development Bank (IDB), the ERASMUS+ European Union, the University of Pennsylvania, Columbia University, and the Technical University of Vienna. She has led editorial projects for the Venice Architecture Biennale, and has collaborated in publications such as *MONU Magazine on Urbanism* and *Informal Market Worlds*. Her research on the Haitian-Dominican border and informal settlements in Santo Domingo was recognised by the Caribbean Architecture Biennale as well as by the Vice President of the Dominican Republic. She was manager of the Research Division of the Institute of Higher Education of the Ministry of Foreign Affairs of the Dominican Republic, where she developed research on the fragility and resilience of the Haitian-Dominican border, and is currently a consultant for IDB on the renovation of El Conde Street and Columbus Park in Santo Domingo.

INDEX

IMAGE CREDITS

COLOPHON

Editors: Peter Mörtenböck and Helge Mooshammer

Copy editing: Joe O'Donnell (Incorporating Informality), Mark Hamilton (case studies A1 to D3)

Translation: Bruno Borgna (case study A3)

Graphic design: Koehorst in 't Veld, Bureau Sporken

Printing: Drukkerij Wilco

Paper: Rebello 110, 100 grams

Publisher: Eelco van Welie, nai010 publishers, Rotterdam

This publication was made possible through support provided by the Austrian Science Fund (P 22809, P 30232).

nai010 publishers is an internationally orientated publisher specialized in developing, producing and distributing books in the fields of architecture, urbanism, art and design.
www.nai010.com

nai010 books are available internationally at selected bookstores and from the following distribution partners:

North, Central and South America - Artbook | D.A.P., New York, USA, dap@dapinc.com

Rest of the world - Idea Books, Amsterdam, the Netherlands, idea@ideabooks.nl

For general questions, please contact nai010 publishers directly at sales@nai010.com or visit our website www.nai010.com for further information.

Printed and bound in the Netherlands

ISBN 978-94-6208-809-2
NUR 648
BISAC ARC001000, ARC010000

IN/FORMAL Marketplaces is also available as e-book:
ISBN 978-94-6208-823-8 (e-book)